NORTH FLORIDA & THE PANHANDLE

EXPLORER'S GUIDE

NORTH FLORIDA & THE PANHANDLE

THIRD EDITION

SANDRA FRIEND & JOHN KEATLEY

THE COUNTRYMAN PRESS
A division of W. W. Norton & Company
Independent Publishers Since 1923

To the fellow globetrotters in our family, Jim Keatley and Sally White
—keep sharing the memories, and keep making more!

"Wherever you go becomes a part of you somehow." —Anita Desai

EXPLORE WITH US!

Welcome to the third edition of *Explorer's Guide North & the Panhandle*, the original comprehensive travel guide to this diverse region. No paid advertisers are included in this guide. All attractions, accommodations, restaurants, and shopping have been included by your authors on the basis of merit and personal experience. The following points will help you understand how the guide is organized.

WHAT'S WHERE The book starts out with a thumbnail sketch of the most important things to know about traveling in Florida, from where the waterfalls are (yes, water-falls!) to which beaches you should head to first. We've included important contact information for state agencies and advice on what to do when you're on the road.

LODGING All selections for accommodations in this guide are based on merit. Most of them were inspected personally or by a reliable source known to us. No businesses were charged for inclusion in this guide. Many bed and breakfasts do not accept pets or children, so if there is not a specific mention in their entry, ask about their policy before you book a room. Some places have a minimum-stay requirement, especially on weekends. Vacation rentals are mentioned where relevant (see *Vacation Rentals*).

RATES Rates quoted for lodgings are for double occupancy, one night, before taxes, and only include resort fees when noted. When a range of rates is given, it runs the gamut from the lowest of the low season (which varies around the region) to the highest of the high season. Rates for hotels and motels are subject to further discount, with programs offered through organizations such as AAA and AARP, and may be negotiable depending on occupancy. Most private campgrounds offer discounts to members of certain affiliate clubs, like Good Sam or Thousand Trails. Local, state, and federal campgrounds may offer active military, senior, resident, and veteran's discounts as well.

ONE OF TWO SUSPENSION BRIDGES ACROSS THE RAVINE AT RAVINE GARDENS STATE PARK, PALATKA

DINING Restaurants in Florida are more casual than anywhere else in the United States—you'll find folks in T-shirts and shorts walking into the dressiest of steak houses. If a restaurant has a dress code, it's noted. Destinations farther from the beach tend to have dressier clientele, especially in city centers. Smoking is not permitted within restaurants in Florida if the bulk of the business's transactions are in food rather than drink. Many restaurants now provide an outdoor patio for smokers.

Your feedback is appreciated for subsequent editions of this guide. Feel free to write us via Countryman Press, 500 Fifth Avenue, New York, NY 10110 or reach us online at trailsandtravel.com.

KEY TO SYMBOLS

🐿 **Special value.** The special-value symbol appears next to lodgings and restaurants that offer quality not usually enjoyed at the price charged.

🐾 **Pets.** The pet symbol appears next to places that accept pets, from B&Bs to bookstores. All lodgings require that you let them know you're bringing your pet; many will charge an additional fee.

✐ **Child-friendly.** The crayon symbol appears next to places or activities that accept children or appeal to families.

& **Handicapped access.** The wheelchair symbol appears next to lodgings, restaurants, and attractions that provide handicapped access, or at least offer assistance when needed.

⌾ **Weddings.** The wedding-rings symbol appears beside facilities that frequently serve as venues for weddings.

((p)) **Wi-Fi.** Locations that offer wireless Internet.

✎ **Ecofriendly.** In the case of lodgings, this symbol denotes certified participants in the Florida Green Lodging Program. In the case of other businesses and non-certified lodgings, these properties have been noted by the authors as establishments that take special initiatives to reduce, reuse, and recycle.

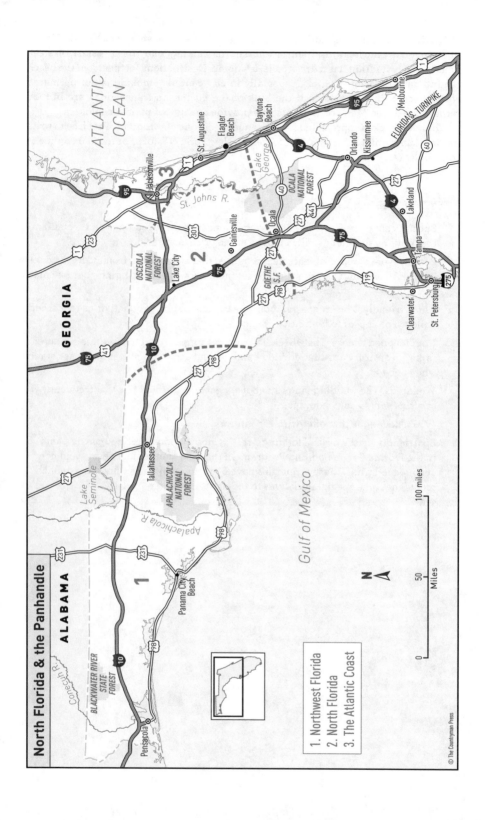

North Florida & the Panhandle

ATLANTIC OCEAN

Gulf of Mexico

ALABAMA

GEORGIA

FLORIDA'S TURNPIKE

BLACKWATER RIVER STATE FOREST

APALACHICOLA NATIONAL FOREST

OSCEOLA NATIONAL FOREST

OCALA NATIONAL FOREST

GOETHE S.F.

Lake Seminole

Lake George

St. Johns R.

Apalachicola R.

Conecuh R.

Pensacola

Panama City Beach

Tallahassee

Lake City

Gainesville

Ocala

Jacksonville

St. Augustine

Flagler Beach

Daytona Beach

Melbourne

Orlando

Kissimmee

Lakeland

Tampa

Clearwater

St. Petersburg

1. Northwest Florida
2. North Florida
3. The Atlantic Coast

N

0   50   100 miles

Miles

© The Countryman Press

CONTENTS

MAPS

ACKNOWLEDGMENTS

For assisting with our research on this edition, we'd like to thank Kaitlin Harris, Hayworth PR; Barbara Golden, Florida's Historic Coast; John Pricher, Visit Gainesville; Laurie Rowe and Ruth Sykes Birch, Laurie Rowe Communications; Dan Rowe, Jayna Leach, and Catie Feeney, Visit Panama City Beach; and members of Riverway South, including Program Manager Betty Webb, Christy Andreasen with Jackson County, Ashley Pettis with Holmes County, Heather Lopez of Visit Washington County, and Janice McClean with Walton County. We've been fortunate to attend two recent Florida Outdoor Writers Association conferences in this region, with thanks to Florida's Suwannee River Valley/Columbia County and Flagler County for granting attendees special access to attractions and tours worth writing about.

We couldn't have explored such a large region—seven hours' driving end to end—without help, so many thanks to friends who pitched in with extended lodgings, personal recommendations, research, and/or good meals, including Linda and Jerry Benton, Dawn Brown, Don and Kathy Ford, Laura Hallem and Robert Seidler, Debi Lander, Linda Patton, Mary McKinley, and Sally and Randal White. Thanks, too, to our friends Tim and Ami Seener for coming to the rescue when the car battery died during a research trip.

Lodging assistance also came from Riverway South, including The Hinson House in Marianna; Skip and Kathy Frink at The Old Carrabelle Hotel; Best Western Gateway Inn in DeFuniak Springs; and Comfort Inn in Chipley. We'd also like to thank Cornelia Holbrook for providing accommodations at Sweetwater Branch Inn, Gainesville, and Dan Rowe and Catie Feeney for arranging our stay at the Sheraton Bay Point Resort.

We appreciate the time of many museum docents, shopkeepers, restaurateurs, outfitters, and other folks we met and interviewed while revisiting old favorite spots and learning about new places, especially Devoe Moore at the Tallahassee Automobile and Collectibles Museum, Ricky Quick at Seacrest Wolf Preserve, and Dana Phillips at Old Cypress Canoe Rentals.

INTRODUCTION

Welcome to the quiet side of Florida, the oldest part of Florida, the region where life goes on at a mostly unhurried pace. In North Florida and the Florida Panhandle—known better within our state as Northwest Florida—you can still swim in a wild spring and cup giant tadpoles in your hands, search for waterfalls along rugged tributaries, glide down a crystalline stream on an inner tube, and in general have a great time. North Florida feels like the Old South, and it's never more evident than in towns like White Springs, Madison, Marianna, and Milton, places that retain vital historic downtowns where people still go to work and sip a cup of coffee. Genteel culture remains intact: You'll hear a lot of "yes, ma'am" and "no, sir" up here, where live oaks and magnolias thrive and rolling acres of cotton and wheat dance off into the distance. In the early-morning sun, Spanish moss casts shadows on centuries-old antebellum mansions, and a light mist rises from the cotton fields. And that's why—from a Florida resident since childhood and a Florida native—we both like it up here.

It is across this swath that Florida's history runs deepest. Spanish missionaries traced trails west from St. Augustine to found missions among the Apalachee in the 1600s. The French, British, and Spanish fought for control of the deepwater port at Pensacola. Florida's capital, Tallahassee, was founded in 1824 as a halfway meeting point between the state's only truly populous cities, St. Augustine and Pensacola.

THE AUTHORS IN DEFUNIAK SPRINGS

Jacksonville, a modern metropolis both vibrant and historic, anchors the eastern corner of this canvas along with Amelia Island, where the city of Fernandina Beach still shows its colonial character, and St. Augustine, Florida's oldest European settlement and one of our favorite places to get in touch with art and history. Our coverage follows the languid flow of the St. Johns River upstream to the historic centers of Green Cove Springs and Palatka, and swings across the state to encompass the university city of Gainesville and the laid-back coastal communities of Cedar Key and Steinhatchee.

As you move west, you step back in time—literally. The Central Time Zone begins at the Apalachicola River and extends west to Pensacola. Vacationers have the seashores buzzing as they soak up the sun along the powdery quartz beaches that extend west from Panama City through Seaside, Grayton Beach, Destin, Fort Walton, Navarre Beach, and Pensacola. But along the Gulf of Mexico, shrimpers still come in at dawn after a hard night's work harvesting the sea, and in hilly rural areas, farming is still king. This is a region of natural wonders, where rugged clay cliffs rise high above clear, sand-bottomed rivers; rhododendron, azalea, and mountain laurel bloom in profusion along streams that seem straight out of the Appalachians; and vast savannas of pitcher plants shake their draping lemon-yellow blooms in an April breeze.

Welcome to the best that Florida has to offer. Slow down and savor the views.

—Sandra Friend and John Keatley

WHAT'S WHERE IN NORTH FLORIDA & THE PANHANDLE

ADMISSION FEES If an admission fee is $8 or less, it's simply listed as "fee." Those fees greater than $8 are spelled out. Although fees were accurate when this book went to press, keep in mind that yearly increases are likely, especially for the larger attractions and the more popular Florida State Parks.

AIR SERVICE Major international airports in the region covered by this book include **Jacksonville International Airport (JAX)** (904-741-4902; flyjacksonville.com), 2400 Yankee Clipper Drive, Jacksonville, and **Northwest Florida Beaches International Airport (ECP)** (850-763-6751; iflybeaches.com), 6300 West Bay Parkway, Panama City Beach. Smaller regional airports served by commuter flights are listed in their respective chapters.

ALLIGATORS The American alligator is a ubiquitous resident of Florida's lakes, rivers, streams, and retention ponds. Most alligators will turn tail and hit the water with a splash when they hear you coming, unless they've been fed or otherwise desensitized to human presence. Do not approach a sunning alligator, and never, ever feed an alligator (a felony, and downright dangerous to boot) in the

PANHANDLE PIONEER SETTLEMENT, BLOUNTSTOWN

wild. Nuisance alligators should be reported to the **Florida Fish and Wildlife Conservation Commission Alligator Hotline** (866-FWC-GATOR; myfwc.com).

AMTRAK Two daily Amtrak (800-USA-RAIL; amtrak.com) trains make their way from New York and Washington, DC, to Florida: the **Silver Service/Palmetto**, ending in either Tampa or Miami, and the **AutoTrain**, bringing visitors (and their cars) to Sanford. Since Hurricane Katrina, rail service through Northwest Florida has been suspended, although there are signs it may resume soon. Stops in North Florida are noted in *Getting There*.

ANTIQUES While **Micanopy** is a favorite North Florida destination for antiques, you won't want to miss the great finds in **Havana, High Springs, Lake City**, and **Fort Walton Beach**, each worth an afternoon for antiques browsing. St. Augustine boasts a don't-miss antiques row on San Marcos Avenue. Since 1985, the free magazine *Antiques & Art Around Florida* (352-475-1336; aarf.com) has kept up with the trends throughout the Sunshine State; pick up a copy at one of the antique stores you visit, or browse the publication's website to do a little pretrip planning. No matter what you're collecting, it's out there somewhere!

ARCHAEOLOGICAL SITES Florida's archaeological treasures date back more than 10,000 years, including temple mound complexes such as those found near Tallahassee at **Leitchworth Mounds** and **Lake Jackson Mounds** and thousands of middens (prehistoric garbage dumps) of oyster shells found along the state's rivers, streams, and estuaries. Of the middens, the most impressive in size and area are those at **Timucuan Preserve** in Jacksonville, **Mount Royal** in Welaka, and **Shell Mound** near Cedar Key. More recent archaeological finds focus on the many **shipwrecks** found along Florida's

coasts and in its rivers, protected by underwater preserves. The discovery of a flake tool knife matching the marks on a tusk carved off a mastodon skull carbon-dates the **Aucilla River** as being the first area of human settlement in the southeastern United States, where pre-Clovis peoples lived more than 14,000 years ago. For information about archaeological digs and shipwrecks, contact the Florida Division of Historical Resources, Bureau of Archaeological Research (dos.myflorida.com/historical/archaeology).

ARCHITECTURE From Edward Beadel to Frank Lloyd Wright, architects—particularly those from Chicago and New York—have influenced the look and feel of residential areas and city centers in historic districts. Some have built grand homes now open to the public. This category calls your attention to walk-up and drive-by sites as well as to historic home museums. See *Churches* for more examples of fine architecture.

ART GALLERIES Florida is blessed with many creative souls who draw their inspiration from our dramatic landscapes, working in media that range from copper sculpture and driftwood to fine black-and-white photography, giclee, and watercolor. Many artists gravitate into communities, so you'll find clusters of art galleries in places like **Apalachicola**, **Cedar Key**, and **St. Augustine**, with unique works worth taking home.

ARTS COUNCILS The **Florida Division of Cultural Affairs** (dos.myflorida.com/cultural) offers resources, grants, and programs to support the arts throughout Florida; its Florida Artists Hall of Fame recognizes great achievements in the arts.

BEACHES Florida's 2,000-mile coastline means beaches for every taste, from the busy social scene at **Atlantic Beach** to the remote serenity of **St. Vincent**

SUNRISE AT ALLIGATOR POINT

Island. In the Panhandle, resorts and condos cluster around the beaches at **Fort Walton–Destin, Pensacola Beach**, and **Panama City Beach**; if you want a quieter experience on the same brilliant white sands, seek out **Mexico Beach, Cape San Blas**, and **St. George Island**. On the peninsula, **Fernandina Beach** offers beautiful strands. Public lands are your best places to enjoy pristine dunes and uncluttered beachfronts. Our personal favorites in this region include **Topsail Hill State Park, St. Joseph Peninsula State Park, St. George Island State Park, Little Talbot Island State Park**, and **Anastasia State Park**, as well as the **Gulf Islands National Seashore**. We call out the Best Beaches in each area for those that have coastal beaches.

BED & BREAKFASTS Given the sheer number of B&Bs throughout Florida, we do not list each one, but we offer information about the ones we feel are the best we've encountered. Some of them are members of associations such as **Superior Small Lodging** (superiorsmall lodging.com) or the **Florida Bed & Breakfast Inns** (877-303-FBBI; florida-inns .com), both of which conduct independent inspections of properties.

BIKING Bicycle tourism has taken off throughout this region, as a growing network of established paved bicycle paths are connected by the Florida Department of Transportation in a program called **Sun Trails** (fdot.gov/planning/systems/ SUNTrail/maps.shtm). Two major projects underway are the St. Johns River-to-Sea Loop between St. Augustine and Titusville, and the Coast to Coast Trail across central Florida. Two nonprofit organizations, **Bike Florida** (bikeflorida .org) and the **Florida Bicycle Association** (floridabicycle.org), advocate for bike paths and lead bike tours. Other regional clubs and nonprofit organizations have done a great job of establishing and maintaining both on-road bike routes and off-road trails suitable for mountain biking. Information on these routes and trails is listed in the text. Check with the **Office of Greenways and Trails** (see *Greenways*) for details on dedicated bike trails throughout the state.

BIRDING As home to millions of winter migratory birds, Florida is a prime destination for bird-watching. The **Great Florida Birding Trail** (floridabirdingtrail .com), supported by the Florida Fish and Wildlife Conservation Commission, provides guidance to birders on the best overlooks, hiking trails, and waterfront parks to visit and which species you'll find at each location. Sites listed in the regional Great Florida Birding Trail brochures are designated with brown road signs displaying a stylized swallow-tailed kite. Certain sites are designated "Gateways" to the Great Florida Birding Trail, where you can pick up detailed information and speak with a naturalist. In the region covered by this guidebook, these sites include **Fort Clinch State Park** for the East Section, **Paynes Prairie Preserve State Park** for the West Section, and **Big Lagoon State Park** for the Panhandle.

BOATING AND SAILING EXCURSIONS Exploring our watery state by water is part of the fun of visiting, from the blasting speed of an airboat skipping across the marshes to the gentle toss of a schooner as it sails across Matanzas Bay. Many ecotours rely on quiet, electric-motor pontoon boats to guide you down Florida's rivers and up to its first-magnitude springs. We greatly recommend a sail on the **Schooner *Freedom*** in St. Augustine and on the **narrated cruises at Wakulla Springs**, but you'll find that almost any boat tour you take will be a delight.

BOOKS To understand Florida, you need to read its authors, and none is more important than **Patrick Smith**, whose *A Land Remembered* is a landmark piece of fiction tracing Florida's history from settlement to development. A good capsule history of Florida's nearly 500 years of European settlement is *A Short History of Florida*, the abbreviated version of the original masterwork by **Michael Gannon**. To see through the eyes of settlers who tried to scratch a living from a harsh land, read the award-winning books of **Marjorie Kinnan Rawlings**, including *The Yearling, Cross Creek*, and *South Moon Under*. For insights into the history of African American culture in Florida, seek out novelist **Zora Neale Hurston**; her works *Their Eyes Were Watching God* and *Jonah's Gourd Vine* will touch the soul. For the feel of life in North Florida, **Connie May Fowler** sets powerful characters against these landscapes in her novels *How Clarissa Burden Learned to Fly, The Trouble with Murmur Lee, Remembering Blue*, and *River of Hidden Dreams*.

The nonfiction classic *Palmetto Leaves* from **Harriett Beecher Stowe** captures life during Reconstruction along the St. Johns River; to understand Florida culture, read *Palmetto Country* by **Stetson Kennedy**, a Florida icon who worked to compile Florida's folklore with the 1940s WPA project and went on to fight for civil rights throughout the South. For a glimpse of Florida's frenetic development over the past century, read *Some Kind of Paradise: A Chronicle of Man and the Land in Florida* by **Mark Derr** and *I Lost It All to Sprawl: How Progress Ate My Cracker Landscape* by **Bill Belleville**. All visitors to Florida who love the outdoors should read *Travels* by **William Bartram**, a botanist who recorded his adventures along the St. Johns River during the 1700s, as well as *A Thousand-Mile Walk to the Gulf* by **John Muir** and *A Naturalist in Florida: A Celebration of Eden* by **Archie Carr**. *River of Lakes: A Journey on Florida's St. Johns River* by **Bill Belleville** is a celebration of our state's mightiest river. When planning your outdoor activities, don't forget that Florida has more than 5,000 miles of trails—which we personally explore to share with readers in our many outdoors books, including *50 Hikes in North Florida*. We also cover the history and beauty of our longest trail in Florida, celebrating its 50th anniversary, in *The Florida Trail: Florida's National Scenic Trail*.

BUS SERVICE **Greyhound** (800-229-9424; greyhound.com) services an extensive list of Florida cities; see their website for details and the full schedule. Stops are noted in the text under *Getting There*.

CAMPING AND CAMPGROUNDS We list places to camp under two different categories. *Parks, Preserves, and Camping* includes campgrounds found in natural settings in our Florida state parks and county parks and on Federal lands. Under Lodging, *Campgrounds* lists privately owned campgrounds. In both places, rates are quoted for single-night, double-occupancy stays. If pets are permitted, keep them leashed. All Florida state parks, state forests, and federal lands use **Reserve America** (800-326-3521; floridastateparks.reserveamerica.com) for campground reservations, but sometimes a handful of sites are kept open for drop-ins or remain unreserved. Ask at the gate. Depending on the public land, Reserve America may add a reservation fee above the listed price and will definitely charge a cancellation fee. Many Florida campgrounds belong to the **Florida Association of RV Parks & Campgrounds** (campflorida.com), which you can join to receive discounts to campgrounds statewide. Generally, campgrounds offer discounts for club membership as well as for weekly, monthly, and resident (six months or more) stays, and they often charge more for extra adults.

CHILDREN, ESPECIALLY FOR The crayon symbol ✐ identifies activities and places of special interest to children and families.

CHURCHES Under the *Churches* category, you'll find architectural marvels, notable historic sites, and churches that hold unique musical events, such as the Mother's Day Sing at the New Effort Congregational Church in the small town of Bonifay.

FARMERS' MARKETS AND U-PICK We list both weekly/monthly farmers' markets and roadside stands (some permanent, some not) in the Farmers' Markets category under *Shopping*. This includes stands and stores at a few citrus groves; citrus no longer grows well in North Florida and has not been a crop in the Panhandle in our lifetimes. Listed under *To Do*, U-pick is seasonal. Florida's growing seasons run year-round: citrus in winter and spring, strawberries in early spring, blueberries in late spring, and cherries in early summer. For a full listing of farmers' markets around the state, visit the **Fresh From Florida** (freshfromflorida.com) website, maintained by the Florida Department of Agriculture.

CIVIL WAR As the third state to secede from the Union, Florida has a great deal of Civil War history to explore, particularly in the region covered by this book. Civil War buffs shouldn't miss **Olustee Battlefield**, the site of Florida's largest engagement, and they should also check out **Florida Reenactors Online** (floridareenactorsonline.com) for a calendar of reenactments held throughout the state.

CRABS Florida's seafood restaurants can lay claim to some of the freshest crabs anywhere; blue crabs and stone crabs are caught along the Gulf Coast. October is Crab Festival time in **St. Marks,** and you'll find them celebrating the seafood harvest down at **Cedar Key** that month, too. Eat your crab legs with melted butter for optimum effect.

DINING Florida is a very casual state when it comes to dining, although shoes

REENACTORS AT THE ANNUAL BATTLE OF NATURAL BRIDGE REENACTMENT NEAR WOODVILLE

and shirt are pretty much required—except at pool or beachfront bars. Locations listed under *Elegant and Romantic* may require a bit of dressing up. Seafood is bountiful here, so you'll find some seafood restaurants under *Seafood* and others under *Waterfront* or *Oceanfront,* depending on location.

DIVE RESORTS Dive resorts cater to both open-water and cave divers, and feature on-site dive shops. They tend toward utilitarian but worn accommodations—wet gear can trash a room! Lodgings categorized under this header will appeal to divers because of their locations, and they may not meet the room quality expected of other accommodations in this guide.

DIVING Certification for open-water diving is required for diving in Florida's rivers, lakes, and streams; certification in cave diving is required if you plan to enter the outflow of a spring. Expertise in open-water diving does not translate into expertise in cave diving; many experienced open-water divers have died attempting to explore Florida's springs. Play it safe and stick with what you know.

A DIVER DOWN flag is required when diving. Designed and popularized by diver Denzel James Dockery and his wife Ruth in the 1950s, the highly recognizable flag calls attention both to divers in the water and dive shops along the highway. Denzel established dive training at Vortex Springs in 1972. Open-water diving is popular offshore in the Gulf between Panama City and Pensacola, as there are many wrecks. Go with a knowledgeable outfitter.

THE DIXIE HIGHWAY Conceptualized in the 1910s by Carl Graham Fisher and the Dixie Highway Association as a grand route for auto touring, the Dixie Highway had two legs that ran along the East Coast of the United States into Florida, both ending in Miami. Because it ran along both coasts of Florida, you'll find Old Dixie Highway signs on both US 1 and US 17 on the East Coast and along US 19, 27, and 41 on the West Coast, and even US 441 in the middle—the highway ran through places as far apart as **Jacksonville**, **Tallahassee**, and **Micanopy**.

EMERGENCIES The locations of hospitals with emergency rooms are noted at the beginning of each chapter. Dial 911 to connect to emergency service anywhere in the state. For highway accidents or emergencies, contact the Florida Highway Patrol at *FHP on your cell phone or dial 911.

FERRIES Florida has only a few remaining ferryboats. In the region covered by this book, you'll find FL A1A crossing the St. Johns River on the **Mayport Ferry**, and the **Fort Gates Ferry** crossing from the Ocala National Forest to Welaka.

FISH CAMPS Rustic in nature, fish camps are quiet retreats that allow anglers and their families to settle down along a lake or river and put in some quality time fishing. Accommodations listed under this category tend to be older cabins, mobile homes, or concrete-block structures, often a little rough around the edges. If the cabins or motel rooms at a fish camp are of superior quality, we mention it in our description.

FISHING The **Florida Fish and Wildlife Conservation Commission** (myfwc.com) regulates all fishing in Florida, offering both freshwater and saltwater licenses. To obtain a license, visit any sporting goods store or call 888-FISH-FLORIDA for an instant license; or apply online at gooutdoorsflorida.com, choosing among short-term, annual, five-year, and lifetime options. No fishing license is required if you are on a guided fishing trip, are fishing with a cane pole, are bank fishing along the ocean (varies by county), or are 65 years or older.

FLORIDA GREEN LODGING PROGRAM Established in 2004 by the Florida Department of Environmental Protection, this innovative program recognizes lodgings that go the extra mile to protect Florida's natural resources by lessening their environmental impact. **Designated Green Lodgings** are marked with a ❧ symbol in this guide. To learn more

about the program, visit the Florida Green Lodging website (dep.state.fl.us/greenlodging).

FLORIDA TRAIL The **Florida Trail** is a 1,400-mile National Scenic Trail running from the Big Cypress National Preserve north of Everglades National Park to Fort Pickens at Gulf Islands National Seashore in Pensacola. Recently celebrating its 50th year, the Florida Trail is the best place to backpack in the winter months in the United States. The USDA Forest Service manages it, and it is maintained by volunteer members of the nonprofit Florida Trail Association (877-HIKE-FLA; floridatrail.org), 5415 SW 13th Street, Gainesville 32608, your primary source for maps for the trail. We wrote a comprehensive guidebook to the trail, *The Florida Trail Guide*, in addition to a related smartphone app, to share details about hiking logistics and the trail's best hikes, as part of our website FloridaHikes.com (floridahikes.com/floridatrail).

FORESTS, NATIONAL There are three national forests in Florida (Apalachicola, Ocala, and Osceola), all of which lie in the regions covered by this book. These forests are administered by the **USDA Forest Service, National Forests in Florida** (850-523-8500; www.fs.usda.gov/florida) offices in Tallahassee. Established in 1908 by President Theodore Roosevelt, the Ocala National Forest is the second-oldest national forest east of the Mississippi River. A little-known fact is that Choctawhatchee National Forest was established at the same time in Florida's Panhandle. But in the 1940s, it was turned over to the Air Force to become Eglin Air Force Base.

FORESTS, STATE The **Florida Division of Forestry** (freshfromflorida.com/Divisions-Offices/Florida-Forest-Service/Our-Forests/State-Forests) administers Florida state forests, encompassing thousands of acres of public lands throughout

North Florida. Each offers an array of outdoor activities from hiking, biking, horseback riding, and camping to fishing, hunting, and even motocross and ATV use. Most (but not all) developed state forest trailheads charge a per-person fee of $3 for recreational use. For $30, you can purchase an annual day-use pass good for the driver and up to eight passengers—a real bargain for families! If you're a hiker, get involved with the **Trailwalker** program, in which you tally up miles on hiking trails and receive patches and certificates; a similar program, **Trailtrotter**, is in place for equestrians. Information on both programs can be found at trailhead kiosks or on the Florida State Forests website.

GAS STATIONS Gas prices fluctuate wildly around the state—and not in proportion to distance from major highways, as you might think. Part of the variation arises from county transportation taxes that add to per-gallon costs, with the Gainesville area being one of the highest.

GENEALOGICAL RESEARCH In addition to the excellent resources found at the **Florida State Archives** (dos.myflorida .com) in Tallahassee and local genealogical libraries, check the **Florida GenWeb project** (flgenweb.org) for census data, vital records, pioneer families, and links to the state's many historical societies.

GOLF Golfing is a favorite pastime for many Florida retirees, and there are hundreds of courses across the state. These are impossible for us to list in any detail, as we aren't golfers. We mention some of historic interest and others with top-notch facilities. **GolfNow** (floridagolf .com) offers a comprehensive look at golf courses statewide, with a built-in booking engine. The Florida **Historic Golf Trail** (floridahistoricgolftrail.com) is a state website showcasing courses built before the 1940s. Florida is home to both the PGA and LPGA headquarters; Ponte

Vedra Beach is the base of the acclaimed TPC Sawgrass, home of **The Players Championship** (pgatour.com/tournaments/the-players-championship.html).

GPS COORDINATES Since the first edition of this book, GPS units have become popular additions to vehicles. Some readers have written in, saying they needed more complete directions to certain locations, especially listings in *Birding*, *Hiking*, and other outdoor pursuits. For destinations that aren't especially easy to find, we've added GPS coordinates in decimal degrees, designated in brackets [ ].

HANDICAPPED ACCESS The wheelchair symbol ♿ identifies lodgings, restaurants, and activities that are, at the least, accessible with minor assistance. Many locations and attractions provide or will make modifications for people with disabilities, so call beforehand to see if they can make the necessary accommodations.

HERITAGE SITES If you're in search of history, watch for the brown signs with columns and palm trees that mark official Florida Heritage Sites—everything from historic churches and graveyards to entire historic districts. According to the **Florida Division of Historical Resources** (dos.myflorida.com/historical), to qualify as a Florida Heritage Site, a building, structure, or site must be at least 30 years old and have significance in the areas of architecture, archaeology, Florida history, or traditional culture. Alternatively, it should be associated with a significant event that took place at least 30 years ago.

HIKING We note the best hiking experiences in each region in the *Hiking* section—from our own personal experience—and you can find additional walks in places mentioned under *Parks, Preserves, and Camping*. The most comprehensive hiking guides for this portion of

Florida include our *50 Hikes in North Florida; Florida Trail Hikes; The Florida Trail Guide; Five Star Trails Gainesville & Ocala; The Hiking Trails of Florida's National Forests, Parks, and Preserves;* and *Hiker's Guide to the Sunshine State.* Our website **Florida Hikes** (floridahikes .com) provides in-depth information on trails, parks, and other outdoor activities across the state.

HORSEBACK RIDING Bringing your own horses? You'll find working ranches and B&Bs with boarding stables listed in this guide, and believe it or not, some hotels will put up your horse. Remember, under state law, riders utilizing trails on state land must have proof with them of a negative Coggins test for their horses. If you're interested in riding, hook up with one of the many stables listed in the text. Under state law, equine operators are not responsible for your injuries if you decide to go on a trail ride.

HUNTING The **Florida Fish and Wildlife Conservation Commission** (myfwc .com) regulates hunting; general gun season falls between October and February in various parts of the state. Check the website for specific dates, the wildlife management areas (WMAs) open to hunting, and hunting license regulations. If you're planning to visit sites listed under *Parks, Preserves, and Camping,* cross-check against the FWC website to see if it's hunting season there; if you hunt, you must wear a bright orange vest or shirt when hunts are permitted, which can fall on dates anywhere between October 1 and May 1.

HURRICANES Hurricane season runs June through November, and when the big winds from Africa start moving across the Atlantic, it pays to pay attention. Follow public announcements on what to do in the event of a tropical storm or hurricane.

CAVERNS HIKING TRAIL ABOVE THE CHIPOLA RIVER FLOODPLAIN, FLORIDA CAVERNS STATE PARK

INFORMATION Roadside billboards will tempt you to come in to information centers for vacation deals. Most of these centers are tied to time-shares or are operating in their own interest. True visitors centers offer information without trying to sell you something. At the beginning of each chapter under *Guidance,* we have listed the visitors bureaus and chambers with no commercial affiliation.

INSECTS Florida's irritating insects are legion, especially at dawn and dusk during summer months. We love it when our winters get chilly enough to kill the little buggers off for a few months. Flying annoyances include the **mosquito** (which comes in hundreds of varieties), **gnat**, and **no-see-um**; troublesome crawling bugs are the **chigger** and the **tick**, which you'll find in deeply wooded areas, and **red ants**, invaders that swarm over your feet, leaving painful bites if you dare step in their nest. Florida has had confirmed cases of both Lyme disease and malaria, as well as several other tropical mosquito–borne diseases. Bottom line: use insect repellent when you're outdoors, and carry an antihistamine with you to counter any reaction you have to communing with these native residents.

JELLYFISH At almost any time of the year, you will find jellyfish in the ocean and washed up on the shore. Take particular care with the blue man o' war jellyfish; the sting from this marine creature is excruciatingly painful. Do not touch the dead jellyfish on the beach, as their venom is still potent. Contrary to popular belief, jellyfish won't chase you down, but in case you get stung, consider carrying a small bottle of white vinegar in your beach bag; this seems to help alleviate some of the pain. After applying vinegar, seek medical attention. Just as with bee stings, reactions vary.

THE KINGS HIGHWAY Established between 1763 and 1819 to connect coastal communities south from Brunswick through Cow Ford (Jacksonville) and St. Augustine to New Smyrna, this military trail is now approximated by the route of US 1; you will see KINGS HIGHWAY signs on historic sections of the road that are not part of US 1, most notably from Dupont Center south.

LODGINGS With more than 400,000 hotel rooms statewide, Florida is a destination with no lack of places to stay. Subheads in the *Lodgings* section categorize accommodations by type; the *Tried and True* are primarily chains. Since chain hotels are everywhere—and all travelers have their favorite loyalty programs—we only list those we've personally stayed in or inspected.

MARITIME HERITAGE In a state where many still pull their living from the sea, it's only appropriate that we have a **Florida Maritime Heritage Trail** (info .flheritage.com/maritime-trail) that ties together the elements of our maritime heritage: working fishing villages such as Cedar Key, Steinhatchee, and Apalachicola; coastal fortresses built to defend Florida from invasion; lighthouses; historic shipwrecks; and our endangered coastal communities, such as the coastal pine flatwoods and coastal scrub.

MUSEUMS AND HISTORIC SITES Explore our centuries of history: The **Florida Association of Museums** (850-222-6028; flamuseums.org) provides a portal to more than 340 museums throughout the state, from the small Heritage Museum of Northwest Florida in Valparaiso to the high-tech Florida Museum of Natural History in Gainesville. Their website also provides a calendar of exhibits in museums around the state.

With nearly five centuries of European settlement in Florida, historic sites are numerous, so this book's coverage of Florida history is limited to sites of particular interest. For the full details on designated historic sites in Florida, visit the **Florida Division of Historical Resources** (dos.myflorida.com/historical/preservation), especially for its **Florida Heritage Trails** (dos.myflorida.com/historical/preservation/heritage-trails) guides for thematic road trips. The **Florida Trust for Historic Preservation** (850-224-8128; floridatrust.org), 906 East Park Avenue, Tallahassee 32302, advocates for preserving historic sites and presents an annual list of endangered historic sites. Their Florida's Historic Passport program enables you to visit multiple sites statewide for a single fee; contact them for details.

OYSTERS Nowhere in the United States can compare to **Apalachicola** and its oysters, pulled fresh from the Gulf estuary. Eat them locally; as the steamed or fried oysters melt like butter in your mouth, you'll be hooked for life. Oyster farming is now supplementing traditional oyster tonging, as fewer oysters now grow in Apalachicola Bay, after years in which Georgia held back the natural flow of the Apalachicola River to the Gulf of Mexico.

PADDLING Canoeing and kayaking are extraordinarily popular activities in Florida, especially during the summer months. Most state parks have canoe livery concessions, and private outfitters are mentioned throughout this guide. The **Florida Saltwater Circumnavigational Paddling Trail** (dep.state.fl.us/gwt/paddling/saltwater.htm) is one of the longest such trails in the nation, sticking close to the coast and covering over 1,500 miles. Local segments, overseen by the nonprofit **Florida Paddling Trails Association** (floridapaddlingtrails.com) may also be part of shorter coastal blueways. Some Florida counties boast their own blueway systems on lakes, streams, and rivers as well. See a full list of **Florida's Designated Paddling Trails** (dep.state.fl.us/gwt/guide/paddle.htm) on the DEP website.

PETS The dog-paw symbol ☙ identifies lodgings and activities that accept pets. Always inform the front desk that you are traveling with a pet and expect to pay a surcharge. Some establishments may limit acceptance of pets to small dogs and cats only.

POPULATION According to the 2015 federal census, Florida's population is **20.3 million people.** What's scary to those of us who live here is that our governor's office reports a net gain of 1,000 people moving into Florida every day—which means an increasingly serious strain on our already fragile water resources.

RAILROADIANA Florida's railroad history dates back to 1836 with the **St. Joe & Lake Wimico Canal & Railroad Company,** followed shortly by the 1837 opening of the mule-driven **Tallahassee & St. Marks Railroad,** bringing supplies from the Gulf of Mexico to the state capital. Railroad commerce shaped many Florida towns, especially along David Yulee's **Florida Railroad** (circa 1850), which connected Fernandina and Cedar Key, and the later grandiose efforts of Henry Plant and the **Plant System** (later the Seaboard Air Line) on the West Coast and Henry Flagler's **Atlantic Coast Line** on the East Coast. Sites of interest to railroad history buffs are noted throughout the guide under this heading; this region is especially rich in railroad heritage.

RATES When a range of rates is provided, it spans the lowest of low season to the highest of high season (which varies from place to place) and does not include taxes or discounts such as those enjoyed by AARP, AAA, and camping club members. In most cases, we list the lowest rate for low season; expect that to be the minimum you might pay. Expect to pay a premium on weekends, during holidays, and during special events.

RAILROAD MURAL IN DOWNTOWN CHIPLEY

RIVERS For recreation on the Suwannee River and its tributaries, contact the **Suwannee River Water Management District** (386-362-1001; srwmd.state .fl.us), 9225 CR 49, Live Oak 32060, for a map that indicates boat ramps; you can also download their recreational guide from their website. The **St. Johns Water Management District** (386-329-4500; sjrwmd.com), 4049 Reid Street, Palatka 32177, can provide similar information for the St. Johns River and its tributaries, and it has an excellent free guidebook to recreation on their public lands. The **North Florida Water Management District** (850-539-5999; nwfwater.com), 81 Water Management Drive, Havana 32333-4712, oversees major rivers in the Panhandle, such as the Apalachicola and Blackwater.

SCENIC HIGHWAYS The Florida Department of Transportation has designated scenic highways throughout the state, some of which are also federally designated Scenic Byways. Both are numerous in this region. Along the Atlantic Coast, the **A1A Scenic and Historic Coastal Byway** (scenica1a.org) stretches from Fernandina Beach to Flagler Beach and beyond. The **William Bartram Scenic & Historic Highway** (bartramscenichighway.com), FL 13, follows the eastern shore of the St. Johns River south from Mandarin to Hastings, and the **Florida Black Bear Scenic Byway** (floridablackbearscenicbyway.org) crosses the St. Johns River on the Fort Gates Ferry. The **Old Florida Heritage Highway** (scenicus441.com), includes 48 miles of back roads around Gainesville. In Northwest Florida, the **Big Bend Scenic Byway** (floridabigbendscenicbyway .com) is the biggie, looping over 250 miles between Apalachicola and Tallahassee. **Scenic 30A** (30a.com/map) is a seaside county road in Walton County, and the **Pensacola Scenic Bluffs Highway** (floridascenichighways.com/our-byways /panhandle-region/pensacola-scenic -bluffs) provides some excellent and unusual views for Florida. You'll also find local designations, such as the **Apalachee Savannahs Scenic Byway,** and county-designated **canopy roads** in places like Tallahassee and Alachua

County, where the dense live oak canopy overhead makes for a beautiful drive.

SEASHORES, NATIONAL Encompassing large portions of Santa Rosa Island and Perdido Key, **Gulf Islands National Seashore** (nps.gov/guis) provides vast unbroken stretches of white quartz beaches near Pensacola, perfect for sunning and swimming.

SEASONS Florida's temperate winter weather makes it ideal for vacationers, but we do have a very strong tropical delineation of wet and dry seasons, which strengthens as you venture farther south. Winter is generally dry and crisp, with nighttime temperatures falling as low as the 20s in the Panhandle and the 30s in North Florida. For travelers, high season begins after **Easter** in North Florida, peaks in the summer, and slows after kids start school in mid-August to early September, winding down after **Labor Day**. Bargain prices can be had along the beaches during the winter months.

SHARKS Yes, they are in the water. At any given time, there are a dozen or more just offshore, but for the most part, they will leave you alone. To avoid being bitten, stay out of the water if there is a strong scent of fish oil in the air. The smell indicates that fish are already being eaten, and you may be bitten by mistake. You will also want to avoid swimming near piers and jetties, which are active feeding zones. Save metallic-colored and sparkly swimsuits for pool use only, as they make you look like a fish from a shark's view underwater.

SHRIMP You'll find different types of shrimp fried, broiled, sautéed, and blackened up and down the coast, from Pensacola to Flagler Beach. The most sought-after are red, white, pink, rock, "brownies," and "hoppers." When you dine, ask for fresh Gulf shrimp and support Florida shrimpers!

STATE PARKS One of the United States' best and most extensive state park systems, **Florida State Parks** (850-245-2157; floridastateparks.org) encompasses more than 160 parks and paved trails. All Florida State Parks are open 8 AM–sunset daily. If you want to watch the sunrise from a state park beach, you'll have to camp overnight. Camping reservations are centralized through **Reserve America** (800-326-3521; floridastateparks .reserveamerica.com) and can be booked through the Florida State Parks website (floridastateparks.org). One caveat for bookings through Reserve America: you pay a reservation fee equal to more than a third of your first night's stay, and the cancellation fee is almost equal to your first night's stay. Choose your dates wisely. Walk-in campers are welcome on a first-come, first-served basis, based on availability. An annual pass is a real deal if you plan to do much in-state traveling: Individual passes are $60 plus tax, and family passes are $120 plus tax, per year. The family pass is good for up to eight people in one vehicle. These passes are honored at all state parks except the Sunshine Skyway Fishing Pier, where they are good for a 33 percent discount. Pick up a pass at any state park ranger station, or order through the website.

THE SUNSHINE STATE *Sunshine State* was an effective 1960s advertising slogan that was also required on motor vehicle tags; it became the state's official nickname in 1970 by a legislative act.

TAXES Florida's base sales tax is 6 percent, with counties adding up to 2 percent of discretionary sales tax. In addition, a tourist development tax of up to 12 percent, may be levied on hotel accommodations in some cities and counties. Keep this differential in mind when your hotel bill ends up higher than you expected it to be.

THEME PARKS You could say Florida is the birthplace of the theme park, starting with glass-bottom boats drawing tourists to enjoy **Silver Springs** in 1878 and to gawk at alligators in the **St. Augustine Alligator Farm** in 1893. But the real heyday came with Dick Pope's water-ski and botanical garden wonder called **Cypress Gardens**, circa 1932, soon followed by **Weeki Wachee Springs**, the "Spring of Living Mermaids," in 1947. The 1960s saw an explosion in roadside attractions and zoos like **Gatorland**, while fancier parks like **Rainbow Springs** and **Homosassa Springs** showed off Florida's natural wonders. But when Walt Disney started buying up Osceola County in the 1950s, Florida changed forever. After **Walt Disney World** opened in 1971, most of the old roadside attractions that made Florida so much fun in the 1960s folded. Many, thankfully, have become state parks, like Wakulla Springs. But the St. Augustine Alligator Farm is still going strong!

VACATION RENTALS If you're bringing a large family on vacation, it pays to look into renting a home for the duration. Booking sites such as airbnb.com, homeaway.com, and VRBO.com act both as search engines and intermediaries with homeowners. Florida also has an excess of condomium rentals that are often managed by local real estate agencies that post listings online. When looking into a home or condo rental, find out if any sort of cleaning service is provided (it often isn't, so ask whether a washer and dryer are on-site) and if the rental price includes all taxes (Florida charges a "bed tax" of up to 12 percent on top of sales tax of 6–8 percent on rentals of less than six months). Some sites also charge a cleaning fee of $100 or more on top of your rental fee. It's also smart to check reviews of the property before you book sight unseen. Some rental homes are in lovely places, others aren't. Similarly, even two condos in the same complex can be as different as night and day in quality. We've dropped condo hotels (a trend that started around the time we launched this series in Florida) from this

guide; not only are there inconsistencies in quality from unit to unit, but booking an overnight stay often requires signing a multipage lease agreement. This can also be the case with vacation rentals through major booking sites, so be sure to read the fine print before you sign an agreement.

VISIT FLORIDA The state's official tourism marketing bureau, **Visit Florida** (visitflorida.com) is a clearinghouse for every tourism question you might have. The bureau's partners cover the full range of destinations, from the sleepy hamlets of the Big Bend to snazzy new hotels along the beach at Destin. Utilize their website resources to plan your trip, from the interactive map that lets you explore destination possibilities, to the vast amount of editorial content that tells the story of each experience.

WATERFALLS Yes, Florida has natural waterfalls! They may flow into deep sinkholes (such as the ones at **Falling Waters State Park** and **Devils Millhopper Geologic State Park**) or drop over limestone ledges along creeks and rivers (**Steinhatchee Falls**, **Falling Creek**, and others). Florida's highest concentration of waterfalls lies along the Suwannee River and its tributaries; you can see many of these along the Florida Trail.

WEATHER Florida's weather is perhaps its greatest attraction. Balmy winters are the norm, with temperatures dropping into the 50s during the daytime and into the 30s at night. When it snows (which is rare), it doesn't stick for long. Our summers are predictably hot and wet, with thunderstorms guaranteed on a daily basis and temperatures soaring up into the high 80s in North Florida and the Panhandle. Florida thunderstorms come up fast and carry with them some of the world's most violent and dangerous lightning. Should you see one coming, it's best to get indoors and out of or off the water.

FALLING CREEK FALLS, NORTH OF LAKE CITY

WINERIES Florida's wineries run the gamut from small family operations to large production facilities. Some provide a storefront in a high-traffic region while doing the growing, fermenting, and bottling in an area more favorable for agriculture. Native muscadine grapes are the cornerstones of the state's wines. For an overview of Florida wineries, contact the **Florida Grape Growers Association** (941-678-0523; fgga.org), 343 W Central Avenue, #1, Lake Wales 33853.

NORTHWEST FLORIDA

■

PENSACOLA

DESTIN–FORT WALTON

PANAMA CITY BEACH, PANAMA CITY & REGION

APALACHICOLA RIVER

TALLAHASSEE & THE BIG BEND

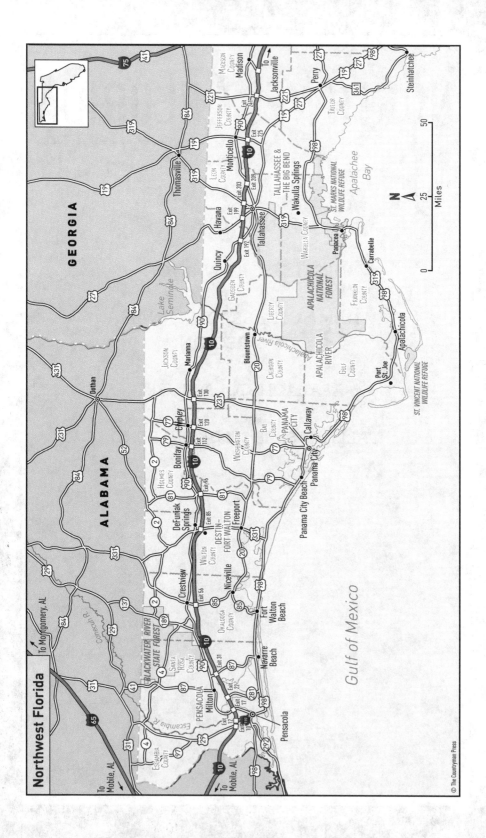

Northwest Florida

GEORGIA

ALABAMA

Gulf of Mexico

© The Countryman Press

PENSACOLA

Pensacola Bay Area (Perdido Key, Pensacola, Pensacola Beach) and Santa Rosa County (Milton, Navarre, Navarre Beach)

With powdery white beaches, lush pine forests, broad open prairies, rugged riverside bluffs, and clear sandy-bottom rivers to attract outdoors enthusiasts, the region around **Pensacola** has a deep and rich history. While this unusually deep bay first attracted Spanish explorer Juan Ponce de León, it was Don Tristán de Luna y Arellano who settled on its shores in 1559, founding the first European settlement in what is now the continental United States. A devastating hurricane struck soon after, and within two years, the 1,400 colonists were scattered far and wide. The second Spanish settlement, in 1686, persisted. Over the next two centuries, five flags flew over Pensacola. Spain had three reigning periods: 1698–1719, 1722–1763, and 1781–1819. France took control of the region in 1719, only to be driven out by a hurricane in 1722. At the end of the French and Indian War in 1763, England held the city until 1781, when the United States became the governing body. In January 1861, Florida became the third state to secede from the Union. Shots were fired by Confederate militia at the federal encampment in Fort Barrancas hours before the cannonade opened on Fort Sumter in South Carolina. In 1868, Florida was readmitted to the United States.

Because of its strategic military importance as a deepwater port, Pensacola has always had a significant military presence, with three major forts flanking the entrance to the bay. Two are now significant historic sites. A vibrant military presence continues today, with **Pensacola Naval Air Station** as the home of the Blue Angels flight demonstration squadron and **Whiting Naval Air Station** as an important helicopter training facility.

To the east of Pensacola, **Milton** began as an early-1800s trading post along the Blackwater, a river deep enough to navigate up from the Gulf of Mexico for trade with the indigenous peoples. The bluffs made it tough to get from the ships to the land, resulting in the town's early names of "Scratch Ankle" and "Hard Scrabble." Thanks to its lush canopy of live oaks and vast longleaf pine forests, Milton

COLDWATER CREEK

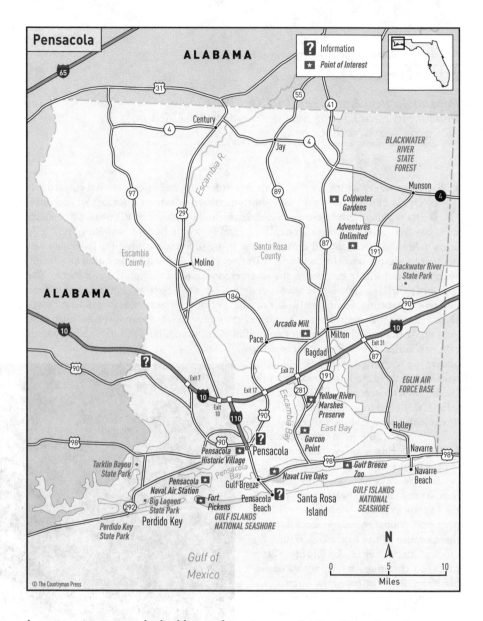

became an important shipbuilding and repair center. In 1842 Santa Rosa County was created from parts of Escambia and Walton counties. Milton became the county seat and applied to be an official port of entry. Adjacent **Bagdad** developed as a company town for a new lumber mill in 1840 and grew as the size of the enterprise increased. As you drive north from Milton on FL 87, you can see a series of ridges off in the distance, giving the sense of ascent into mountains, something only experienced in this corner of Northwest Florida.

GUIDANCE **Pensacola Bay Area Convention & Visitors Bureau** (800-874-1234 or 850-434-1234; visitpensacola.com), 1401 E Gregory Street, Pensacola 32502. For activities east of the Escambia River, contact the **Santa Rosa County Tourism**

Development Office (850-981-8900; floridasplayground.com), which has a visitor information center at 8543 Navarre Parkway, Navarre 32566. Not to confuse Santa Rosa County with the beach of the same name, you'll find Santa Rosa Beach located in Walton County, west of Destin (see the *Destin–Fort Walton* chapter), and Santa Rosa Island, shared by Navarre Beach and Pensacola Beach. In Milton, stop at the **Santa Rosa County Chamber of Commerce** (850-623-2339; www.srcchamber.com), 5247 Stewart Street, for brochures and information on local attractions.

GETTING THERE *By air:* **Pensacola Gulf Coast Regional Airport** (850-436-5000; flypensacola.com), 2430 Airport Boulevard, Pensacola 32504, is served by a broad range of top-name carriers, from American to Southwest, with commuter flights.

By bus: **Greyhound** (850-476-4800; greyhound.com), 505 W Burgess Road, Pensacola 32503.

By car: **I-10**, **US 90**, and **US 98** run east–west through the Panhandle. **US 90** stays north of I-10 through Milton. As it heads west to Pensacola, it dips south of I-10 into the city and continues west into Alabama. **US 98** is the east–west coastal route and will take you along the coast from Navarre to downtown Pensacola and to Alabama. From I-10 follow **FL 87** south to Navarre Beach or north to Pace; and follow **FL 191** north to Bagdad and Milton or south to Navarre Beach (toll bridge). **FL 292** heads west from downtown Pensacola to Perdido Key.

GETTING AROUND Escambia County's public transportation system, **ECAT** (850-595-3228; goecat.com), runs 285 miles throughout the Pensacola area ($1.75 adults, 85¢ seniors and disabled; children shorter than the fare box ride free), with 1- and 7-day passes available. The seasonal **Beach Trolley**, operating Friday–Sunday from early March to Labor Day along Santa Rosa Island, is free for everyone.

PARKING Pensacola has two-hour metered slots throughout downtown, free on weekends. Milton has free two-hour parking throughout downtown. Ample free beach parking is available at Pensacola Beach and Navarre Beach along CR 399 and Fort Pickens Road.

MEDICAL EMERGENCIES In Pensacola, **Baptist Hospital** (850-434-4011; ebaptisthealthcare.org), 1000 W Moreno Street, West Pensacola; **Sacred Heart Hospital** (850-416-7000; sacred-heart.org), 5151 N 9th Avenue, Pensacola; and **West Florida Hospital** (850-494-3212; westfloridahospital.com), 8383 N Davis Highway, Pensacola. For the eastern beaches, there is **Gulf Breeze Hospital** (850-934-2000; ebaptisthealthcare.org/GulfBreezeHospital), 1110 Gulf Breeze Parkway, and **Baptist Medical Park** (850-939-4888; ebaptisthealthcare.org/BMPNavarre), 8888 Navarre Parkway, with a walk-in clinic Monday–Saturday in Navarre. In Milton visit **Santa Rosa Medical Center** (850-626-7762; srmcfl.com), 6002 Berryhill Road. Always call 911 for life-threatening emergencies.

✳ To See

ARCHAEOLOGICAL SITE ♦ ♿ The **Arcadia Mill Archaeological Site** (850-628-4438; historicpensacola.org/explore-arcadia-mill), 5709 Mill Pond Lane, Milton, interprets the first and largest industrial complex built in Northwest Florida, circa 1830. Excavation of the site began in 1990 under the auspices of the University of West Florida. It included a silk cocoonery, along with a water-powered sawmill, gristmill, cotton mill, and textile mill, all of which turned local resources into trade goods. Stop in the new Visitor Center and museum before exploring the site along an interpretive boardwalk above the digs. Hiking trails meander upstream over swinging bridges. Open Tuesday–Saturday 10 AM–4 PM, with guided tours. Free.

ARCHITECTURE In **Bagdad**, a walking tour brochure from the local museum will lead you to the **1867 post office** and **New Providence Missionary Baptist Church**, as well as an original shotgun cottage. Just up the street, the imposing **Thompson House**, 4620 Forsyth Street, is a Greek revival home built in 1847 for timber baron Benjamin Thompson; Union troops camped on the front lawn in October 1864. It's a private residence.

Milton boasts 117 buildings of historic significance, from 1850s Victorians to Spanish Mission–style homes erected during the 1920s boom. The 1872 **St. Mary's Episcopal Church and Rectory**, 300–301 Oak Street—built in Greek and Gothic revival styles, respectively—is also known as the **McDougall House**. Dr. Charles E. McDougall was both the rector and the town physician. The **Santa Rosa County Courthouse**, 6865 Caroline Street, was dedicated on July 4, 1927, and the Gothic **Ollinger-Cobb-Tilghman House**, 6829 Pine Street, is a large Gulf Coast cottage dating from 1871. A simple cottage, the **Ollinger-Cobb House** (circa 1870), 302 Pine Street, includes Gothic elements. The home was built by Joseph Ollinger, a ship's carpenter and immigrant from Luxembourg.

ART GALLERIES **Dragonfly Gallery** (850-981-1100; sracf.org), 6815 Carolina Street, Milton, showcases the creativity of local artists in stained glass, photography, folk art, natural wood sculptures with stone accents, and fine paintings in acrylics and oils. It's a co-op staffed by the artists of the Santa Rosa Arts & Culture Foundation, who also put on the annual Riverwalk Art Festival (see *Special Events*).

Quayside Art Gallery (850-438-2363; quaysidegallery.com), 17 E Zaragoza Street, is the artists' co-op downtown. Founded in 1973 and serving more than 60 member artists, it's one of the largest co-ops in the Southeast. Housed in the historic Germania Steam Fire Engine and Hose Company Building, it has both expansive spaces and small niches to showcase everything from large acrylics and fiber arts to delicate art glass and turned wood. Open Monday–Saturday 10 AM–5 PM, Sunday 1–5 PM.

Pensacola Museum of Art (850-432-6247; pensacolamuseum.org), 407 S. Jefferson Street, Pensacola. The museum's permanent collection is of nineteenth-, twentieth-, and twenty-first-century artists, including John Marin and Salvador Dalí, with rotating exhibits by world-renowned artists such as George Rodriguez. The museum also has a superb collection of European and American glass and African tribal art. From 1910 to the mid-1940s, the building was used as a jail. Note original fixtures and hardware on many of the doors and windows. Open Tuesday–Friday 10 AM–5 PM, Saturday 10 AM–4 PM, and Sunday 2–4 PM. Fee.

CONCERTS Inside a Masonic Lodge more than a century old, the hip **Vinyl Music Hall** (877-435-9849; vinylmusichall.com), 2 S. Palafox Street, is the hot place for music in downtown Pensacola, featuring both major acts on tour and top local artists.

LIGHTHOUSE First lit in 1859, the **Pensacola Lighthouse** (850-393-1561; pensacola lighthouse.org), 2081 Radford Boulevard, stands on a 40-foot hill above Fort Barrancas at the Pensacola Naval Station. Climb to the top of the 177-step ascent to see the first-order Fresnel lens, which was removed during the Civil War for safekeeping. In the restored lighthouse keeper's quarters, the Richard C. Callaway Museum provides an overview of the region's earliest settlements. For a different take on history, try the

BLUE ANGELS AND NAVAL AVIATION

As World War II drew to a close in 1946, Admiral Chester Nimitz wanted to keep the public interested in naval aviation, the better to draw future recruits. Forming a flight demonstration team at Jacksonville Naval Air Station at Mayport, the **Blue Angels** (blueangelsassociation.org) were born. After serving in Korea, the squadron was permanently moved to Pensacola NAS, which served as their home base. Flying some of the fastest and most modern aircraft, they perform spins, rolls, and dives in synchronous patterns, wowing spectators below. As they train regularly for air shows around the country, you can catch them in flight over Pensacola during your visit from March to November, most Tuesdays and Wednesdays at 11:30 AM. Visitors are welcome at the Naval Air Aviation Museum during the practices overhead, and they may be able to meet the aviators afterward for autographs. As we accidently discovered, the top of Fort Pickens (see *Museums, Exhibits, and Historic Sites*) is also a popular spot from which you can watch the practice.

WATCHING THE BLUE ANGELS OVER FORT PICKENS

✏ ♿ Here at the Blue Angels home, exhibits of the navy's role in the nation's defense are at the **National Naval Aviation Museum** (850-452-3604; navalaviationmuseum.org), 1750 Radford Boulevard, Pensacola NAS. The museum has more than 140 beautifully restored aircraft from US Navy, Marine Corps, and Coast Guard aviation. You'll see wood-and-fabric biplanes, an NC-4 flying boat, and a Douglas "Dauntless" bomber in Hangar Bay. Then you can fly an FA-18 flight simulator on a mission in Desert Storm. Immerse in the *Blue Angels 4D Experience* in Hanger Bay One, where you feel like you're in the middle of the show. Open daily 9 AM–5 PM; free general admission, fee for 4-D show and simulators.

"Light of the Moon Tour" offered monthly on full-moon nights to learn the legends of "one of America's most haunted lighthouses." Daily 10:30 AM–5:30 PM; fee.

MEMORIALS The **Florida Vietnam Veterans Memorial** on Bayfront Parkway near Ninth Avenue, Pensacola, is the nation's only full-name, permanent replica of the Vietnam Veterans Memorial in Washington, DC. The historic **St. Michael's Cemetery** (stmichaelscemetery.org), at the corner of Alcaniz and Chase streets in Pensacola, dates back to 1822, with 3,200 marked burials. Open daily. ♿ At the **Veterans Memorial** along the shores of the Blackwater River at the Milton Riverwalk, reflective slabs of black granite hold relief images of warfare, with a roll call of all American wars and their key dates, each with a sidebar showing the population of the United States at that time, the commander in chief, number of service members, combat deaths, and casualties. The Milton Riverwalk extends for a quarter-mile through downtown Milton.

MUSEUMS AND HISTORIC SITES At one time, everything you needed to build a house was created in Bagdad, so it's no surprise that so many fine homes remain. Stop in at the **Bagdad Village Museum** (850-983-3005), 4512 Church Street, Bagdad, to see artifacts of the early logging and shipping history that shaped this riverside town; call ahead for hours.

Paralleling US 90 between Harold and CR 87, the Old Pensacola Highway is a stretch of historic roadway. Completed in 1921, this early brick highway known as **Florida Highway 1** connected Pensacola with Jacksonville, enabling Model Ts to putter across the state. Walkers and cyclists now utilize the stretch closest to Milton.

🌶 ♂ One of the largest outdoor history museums in Florida, **Historic Pensacola Village** (850-595-5993; historicpensacola.org) spans several blocks between downtown and Seville Square and includes 27 properties on the National Register of Historic Places inside the **Pensacola Historic District**. You are welcome to roam the village any time. The furnished period homes span in age from the earliest Spanish settlements to the Florida real estate boom of the 1920s. You'll see the most significant ones on the walking tour. One of the oldest buildings in the complex is the **Charles Lavalle House**, built in 1805. Inside, you can see the starkness of the era; a rope bed occupies a simple bedroom next to a kitchen room, complete with a fireplace and clever devices to ward off insects and vermin from food storage. The adjoining **Julee Cottage** is a simple saltbox of the same vintage, home later to an African American family during the difficult

BEHIND THE LAVALLE HOUSE, PENSACOLA VILLAGE

PENSACOLA'S FORTS

After Pensacola was selected to be a federal naval yard in the early 1800s, four forts were built (or shored up) to protect it. Originally built by the British Royal Navy as a log redoubt in 1763, **Fort Barrancas** sits on a hill above the western shore of Pensacola Bay. The Spanish added their touches in 1797, and the fort went through another update between 1839 and 1844, supervised by Major William H. Chase. The nearby **Advanced Redoubt of Fort Barrancas** was built between 1845 and 1859 to protect the Pensacola Naval Yard but was never used. **Fort McRee** on Perdido Key dated back to 1834, with 128 cannons trained on the entrance to Pensacola Bay. It succumbed to erosion by wind and waves over the decades; only a single battery built in 1942 remains. Of the four forts, **Fort Pickens** on Santa Rosa Island has the most storied history. Chase supervised construction between 1829 and 1834. Construction materials came from all over the world, including copper from Switzerland for the drains and granite from Sing-Sing; the fortress contains 21.5 million locally made bricks. The night before Florida seceded from the Union (January 10, 1860), Federal commander Lieutenant Adam J. Slemmer moved his men from the mainland to Fort Pickens to hold what President Lincoln considered a key position in coastal defenses. Confederate troops attempted to rout the entrenched Federals on September 2, 1861, during the Battle of Santa Rosa Island, but they failed and subsequently turned the city over to the Union forces. In 1886 the Apache chief Geronimo was imprisoned at the fort as a tourist attraction. Fort Pickens came into play during World War I, with new defensive batteries constructed to protect Pensacola, but no shots were fired. All of Pensacola's forts are part of Gulf Islands National Seashore; fee.

period of Reconstruction. If there isn't a wedding going on, you'll walk through the **1832 Christ Church** overlooking Seville Square, which is filled with ancient live oaks and interesting pieces of art. At the **Dorr House**, circa 1871, see the spaces upstairs that their daughters shared and Victorian furnishings downstairs. The tour ends at the grand Victorian **Lear-Rocheblave House**. Built in the 1890s, it is filled with the finery you would expect in a captain's residence of the era, including a china cabinet, a vanity, a canopied bed, and a thicket of furniture that fills the broad hallway. Historic Pensacola Village is open Tuesday–Saturday 10 AM–4 PM, with docent-led tours at 11 AM and 1 PM; fee.

✐ ♿ Flanking Zaragoza Street, two historic warehouses have been converted into stand-alone museums (tickets required) to visit after the formal walking tour at Historic Pensacola Village. The **Museum of Commerce** feels like a movie set, complete with a full-size retired streetcar amid storefronts of classic Pensacola businesses that are no longer found downtown. A museum-within-a-museum sponsored by the local newspaper showcases printing presses of yesteryear and explains to Internet-age kids what fonts are all about. Inside the **Museum of Industry**, massive displays and larger-than-life dioramas evoke the sounds and smells of the past. Discover the many different types of bricks that were created in the region, learn the ongoing importance of fishing as a regional industry, and find out how many items came from the great forests that once surrounded Pensacola. Fee.

✐ ♿ Built as Pensacola's city hall in 1907, the **T. T. Wentworth Jr. Florida State Museum** (850-595-5990; historicpensacola.org), 330 S. Jefferson Street, holds the vast collection of Florida-related artifacts that Theodore Thomas Wentworth Jr. (1898–1989) amassed over his lifetime, more than 100,000 items—and that was before eBay! To showcase his collection a bit at a time, there are changing exhibit galleries, plus two permanent exhibitions, one on the history of Pensacola and the other on local culture as seen through the eyes of "Trader Jon," a beloved bar owner who collected photos and memorabilia from the pilots, astronauts, and movie stars who came through his doors. Open daily; fee.

PERFORMING ARTS Between Pensacola and Milton, **Panhandle Community Theatre** (850-221-7599; panhandlecommunitytheatre.com), 4636 Woodbine Road, Pace, showcases local talent with live performances, dinner shows, and special community events.

Pensacola Little Theatre (850-432-2042; pensacolalittletheatre.com), 400 Jefferson Street, Pensacola, puts on main-stage and children's shows throughout the year. Note the remnants of the old county jail in the courtyard. The 1936 building is also home to the Pensacola Cultural Center and **Ballet Pensacola** (850-432-9546; balletpensacola.com).

Saenger Theatre (850-595-3880; pensacolasaenger.com), 118 S. Palafox Street, Pensacola, hosts top acts like *Rent* as well as classic musicals in a grandly renovated and expanded Spanish baroque/rococo theater that debuted in 1925. It's the place to see and be seen during its busy slate of comedy, drama, and symphony performances.

RAILROADIANA ✍ In the historic Milton Depot, the **West Florida Railroad Museum** (850-623-3645; wfrm.org), 5003 Henry Street, focuses on the railroad history of the historic logging districts of Northwest Florida and Southern Alabama, particularly the L&N Railroad. Volunteers continue active restoration of rolling stock, some of which dates back to 1911. See the live coal-burning miniature steam engine, walk through the Museum of Railroading History, and come for the annual open house, their big event, in October. Open Friday and Saturday 10 AM–3 PM, or by appointment.

ZOO ✍ ♿ Ride the Safari Line train through 50 acres of free-ranging wild animals at **Gulf Breeze Zoo** (850-932-2229; gulfbreezezoo.org), 5701 Gulf Breeze Parkway, Gulf Breeze, where you'll see wildebeests, pygmy hippos, capybaras, and more—over 900 species in all. Then walk along the perimeter enclosures and boardwalk to get an up-close look at lions, tigers, and bears. Oh my! Daily 9 AM–4 PM; Adventure Pass $20 adult, $19 seniors, $16 ages 2–12.

✱ To Do

BIKING Breathe in the salt air—and carry lots of water—while pedaling along the coast. Linking two segments of Gulf Islands National Seashore (see *Parks, Preserves, and Camping*), the paved **Pensacola Beach Trail** extends 9 miles through the commercial district of the beach. At the east end of the national seashore on Santa Rosa Island, the paved **Navarre Bicycle Path** picks up and leads you through that beachfront community, up and over the bridge, to a park at US 98, just shy of 5 miles. Both rides parallel CR 399, without many views of the beach. In the gap between, CR 399 has 25–35 MPH traffic and a marked bicycle lane.

♿ 🐾 A paved rail-trail conversion following the old Whiting Naval Railway, the **Blackwater Heritage State Trail** (850-983-5338; floridastateparks.org/trail/Blackwater), 5533 Alabama Street, Milton, is the region's premier forested cycling venue, stretching 8.5 miles north from downtown Milton to Whiting Field NAS.

BIRDING **Big Lagoon State Park** is the western portal for the statewide Great Florida Birding Trail, and a fabulous place to spy shorebirds and wading birds along the shoreline of its namesake lagoon. Dozens of ospreys make their nests each spring in the tall

BEST BEACHES

For dogs: Pensacola Dog Beach
For people-watching: Pensacola Beach
For shelling: west end of Fort Pickens
For solitude: east end of Perdido Key
For sunbathing: Navarre Beach, Langdon Beach
For swimming: Opal Beach, Langdon Beach
For walking: east of Opal Beach to Navarre Beach

Public beaches along the Gulf of Mexico have powdery white sands and emerald waters. Parking is free at beach parking areas along CR 399 on Santa Rosa Island and FL 292 on Perdido Key.

LANGDON BEACH FROM BATTERY LANGDON, GULF ISLANDS NATIONAL SEASHORE

trees found at the western tip of the **Fort Pickens Unit, Gulf Islands National Seashore**, and songbirds seek the deep cover of a coastal forest at **Naval Live Oaks Preserve**.

    ♿ Just east of the Seville Historic District along Pensacola Bay, **Hawkshaw Lagoon Memorial Park** (850-434-1234) is a perfect location for spotting cormorants, pelicans, and great blue herons. The pedestrian bridge spanning the lagoon serves as a platform for the memorial sculpture *The Sanctuary*, the National Memorial for Missing Children.

    A 1.5-mile boardwalk through a wetlands park provides another birding opportunity at the **Bayou Marcus Nature Trail** (850-476-0480; ecua.fl.gov/green/bayou-marcus-nature-trail-walk). Woodpeckers, raptors, and songbirds are always in evidence along the trails of **Blackwater River State Forest**. See *Parks, Preserves, and Camping* for specific locations.

DIVING For underwater exploration of an aircraft-carrier-size artificial reef, **Dr. Dive** (850-932-6602; drdive.com), 600 S. Barracks Street, Pensacola, leads tours to the **USS Oriskany**, sunk in 2006, a good 25 miles offshore from Pensacola Bay. This combat naval vessel, built in the 1940s and in service in Vietnam, now provides a tableau for barracuda, amberjack, sharks, and reef fish. Depths range from 80 to 170 feet, so diving this site requires technical skills and advanced certification, including experience in open-water dives. Dive trips and scuba certifications are also offered at **MBT Dive and Surf** (850-455-7702; mbtdivers.com), 3920 Barrancas Avenue, Pensacola, which leads snorkeling trips and dives to historic shipwrecks in as little as 15 feet of water.

ECOTOURS ♂ Captain Kirk at **Condor Sailing Adventures** (850-637-SAIL; condor sailingadventures.com) offers two-hour dolphin cruises on Pensacola Bay and sunset cruises each evening. Multiple trips daily, departing from the Palafox Pier Yacht Harbor at the end of Palafox Street, downtown Pensacola, $85 adult, $60 ages 12 and under.

At Navarre Beach, a guided tour with **Navarre Beach Eco-Tours** (850-939-7734; navarrebeachkayaks.com/eco-tours) at the Navarre Pier gets you out on the gentle waters of Santa Rosa Sound for four hours of exploration in a small-group setting, $50 and up. Kayak rentals available.

FAMILY ACTIVITIES ♬ At the **Panhandle Butterfly House** (panhandlebutterflyhouse .org), 8581 Navarre Parkway, pop in for a visit with native caterpillars and butterflies, and discover what plants make the best butterfly habitat. May–August, Thursday–Saturday 10 AM–3 PM. Donation.

At the east end of Santa Rosa Island, Navarre Beach Park, 8579 Gulf Boulevard, Navarre Beach, is home to the new **Navarre Beach Sea Turtle Conservation Center** (850-499-6774; navarrebeachseaturtles.org), 8740 Gulf Boulevard. Seaside picnic pavilions are surrounded by sand drifts as white as snow.

♬ Immersing the little ones in history, the **Pensacola Children's Museum** (850-595-1559; historicpensacola.org), 115 E. Zaragoza Street, is part of the downtown complex of historic sites. But this one is aimed at the 10-and-under crowd, interpreting colonial and Native American life with play areas and artifacts; fee.

♬ Hit **Fast Eddie's Fun Center** (850-433-7735; fasteddiesfuncenter.com), 505 W. Michigan Street, for go-carts, mini golf, and video games. One of Pensacola's oldest family-fun parks, it features four different go-cart tracks—including one gentle enough for four-year-olds—and a serious competition speedway for mature racers. Open daily.

♬ At **Sam's Fun City** (850-505-0800; samsfuncity.com), 6709 Pensacola Boulevard, Pensacola, you stay dry or get as wet as you like. At Surf City you'll be soaked on four thrilling waterslides, two interactive children's pools with mini slides, and a 750-foot winding lazy river, and then dry off at Fun City, which features go-carts, mini golf, and more than a dozen amusement rides. Fun City also has bumper boats if you want to get a bit of a splash. The only park of its type in the area, it's open daily year-round; fee.

♬ Strap on a pair of skates at **Skateland** (850-623-9415; facebook.com/Skateland OfMilton), 6056 N. Stewart Street, Milton, a massive roller rink that's popular with the younger set.

FISHING At **Brown's Inshore Guide Service** (877-981-6246; brownsinshore.net), Captain Dave Brown will customize your charter trip, even an excellent fly-fishing trip, around Perdido Bay and vicinity. Day or night fishing on four- to six-hour trips

FISHING IS GREAT AT THE NAVARRE BEACH PIER

including licenses for Florida and Alabama fishing, bait, and tackle. $400–600 for two passengers. Families welcome.

Go for the big one with **Captain Wes Rozier** (850-982-7858; captwesrozier.com), who'll regale you with fish tales and local lore. Search out trout hidden in the grass flats or flounder in the mudflats; these are just some of the many species of fish you'll catch. Trips from 3–5 hours, rates $240–400.

For fly-fishing the Gulf of Mexico, **Gulf Breeze Guide Services** (850-934-3292; gulfbreezeguideservice.com) connects you with Captain Baz, whose passion for fly fishing, especially for false albacore and redfish, is infectious. An expert who knows the seasons and the species, he'll plan a memorable trip for you. Inshore, $400–500 for 1–2 anglers, 4 to 6 hours; offshore, $600 for 6 hours.

GOLF Tee off at the legendary 18-hole, par-72 course **Lost Key Golf Club** (888-256-7853; lostkey.com), 625 Lost Key Drive, Perdido Key. Designed by Arnold Palmer, the heavily wooded course is so challenging that golf carts with a GPS yardage system are mandatory. Established in 1926, Pensacola's most historic course is the **Osceola Municipal Golf Course** (850-453-7599; osceolagolf.com), 300 Tonawanda Drive. It has green fees as low as $16 (including cart) for 9 holes, and a long and storied history with the PGA Tour. Home of the Pensacola Open for a decade, the **Perdido Bay Golf Club** (850-492-1223; perdidobaygolf.com), 1 Doug Ford Drive, Pensacola, offers an extensive practice facility in addition to its greens.

HIKING The **Florida Trail** (floridahikes.com/floridatrail/seashore) is the country's only National Scenic Trail to traverse a beach—and not just any beach, but the sparkling white-sand strands of Santa Rosa Island, right up to the trail's northern terminus at **Fort Pickens**. Normally you can't walk on sand dunes, but the Florida Trail also traverses several miles of undulating dunes inside the **UWF /SRIA Dunes Preserve** (floridahikes.com/floridatrail/uwf-dunes-preserve) along CR 399, north of the paved Pensacola Beach Trail. **Blackwater River State Forest** offers many excellent places to hike, including a loop around Bear Lake and more than 50 miles of the **Florida Trail** (floridahikes.com/floridatrail/blackwater), following the rivers and creeks that flow through it. See *Parks, Preserves, and Camping* for more locations.

PADDLING **Adventures Unlimited Outdoor Center** (800-239-6864 or 850-623-6197; adventuresunlimited.com), 8974 Tomahawk Landing Road, Milton, has offered canoe-ing, tubing, and kayaking down Coldwater Creek, Juniper Creek, and the Blackwater River since 1975. You can also enjoy land activities such as the ropes course, canopy walks, zipline, hiking, biking, and hayrides. Founder Jack Sanborn was stationed at Whiting Field and decided he wanted to start a business that kept him outdoors. He's parlayed his original 12 canoes into a complex where guests can stay in relocated, ren-ovated historic cabins; a campground; and even a schoolhouse (see *Lodging*). Paddling excursions start at $25 per person and can run from 4 to 18 miles for a day trip. The staff can also arrange overnight trips of up to 3 days.

Whether you want a short or long canoe or kayak trip or just want to go tubing, **Blackwater Canoe Rental** (850-623-0235; blackwatercanoe.com), 6974 Deaton Bridge Road, Milton, has several options to enjoy the pristine Blackwater River. The snow-white sandbars are graced on each side by magnolias and river cedars. Consider a multiday trip with camping on the sandbars, a day trip at your own pace, or a lazy float down the shallow, clear river.

At **Bob's Canoe Rental** (850-623-5457), 7525 Munson Highway, Milton, rent canoes and kayaks for a paddle down Coldwater Creek, one of the most beautiful of the Black-water River's tributaries; shuttles included in price.

PARKS, PRESERVES, AND CAMPING ☀ With at least a mile of strenuous board-walks and staircases swarming up and down bluffs that tower as much as 85 feet above the water below, **Bay Bluffs Preserve** (850-436-5510; playpensacola.com), 3400 Scenic Highway, Pensacola, makes a good personal training ground for hill-climbing stamina. The views across Escambia Bay are nice, too. Several parking areas along the Scenic Highway (US 90) east of downtown provide access. Dogs are welcome off-leash on a dedicated beach provided for them.

🐾⛄ One of the best places in the region for birding, **Big Lagoon State Park** (850-492-1595; floridastateparks.org/park/Big-Lagoon), 12301 Gulf Beach Highway, Pensacola, surrounds its namesake lagoon. Kayak the shallow waters of several linked lagoons; camp in the middle of a coastal scrub forest, $20+, on sites that can handle RVs; or meander along miles of trails across the dunes. A tall observation tower provides a bird's-eye view from which you can see the distant whitecaps of the Gulf of Mexico. Fee.

🐾 ☀ At **Blackwater River State Forest** (850-957-6140; freshfromflorida.com), 11650 Munson Highway, Milton, immerse yourself in the largest state forest in Flor-ida—190,000 acres surrounding the Blackwater River and its tributaries. Fingers of red clay seep down from Alabama, exposed in outcroppings like the tall cliffs above Juni-per Creek. With high ground topped with longleaf pine and wiregrass, the undulating landscape seems to stretch on forever. Paddling, hiking, and hunting are the major draws to this vast wilderness. Of the forest's six campgrounds, our favorite is **Bear Lake**, a scenic spot near Munson, but the bathhouse at **North Hurricane Lake** can't be beat. Each campground is centered on a recreation area along one of the "lakes" (reser-voirs, really) and offers electric and water at sites tucked beneath the forest canopy, as well as direct access to hiking trails, paddling, and fishing; sites $10+. The other camp-grounds are **South Hurricane Lake** (tents only), **North & South Karick Lake**, and **Krul Recreation Area**. Primitive camping is permitted along the Florida Trail (see *Hiking*), with two camping shelters along the route.

At **Blackwater River State Park** (850-983-5363; floridastateparks.org/park/Blackwater-River), 7720 Deaton Bridge Road, Holt, bask on a sandy freshwater beach, hike the Chain of Lakes Trail along ancient oxbows in the floodplain, find the champion Atlantic White Cedar tree, or drop your kayak in for a scenic trip along one of the purest sand-bottomed rivers in the world. Thirty campsites with electric and water hookups offer easy access to paddling and hiking expeditions, $20+.

 Broken into seven segments along Florida's coast, **Gulf Islands National Seashore** (850-934-2600; nps.gov/guis), 1801 Gulf Breeze Parkway, Pensacola Beach, encompasses Pensacola's historic forts as well as great swimming beaches on Santa Rosa Island at Opal Beach and Fort Pickens and on Perdido Key. The **Naval Live Oaks Area** straddles US 98 in Gulf Breeze, where the visitors center explains the strategic and historic significance of this site: it's the country's first federally protected forest, a tree farm established in 1828 by President John Quincy Adams and overseen by Henry Breckenridge, our first federal forester. Ancient live oaks were felled to make wooden sailing ships to ensure the fledgling United States would have a strong navy. The **Fort Pickens Unit** has the most extensive and lonely stretches of beaches in the region, as well as the 200-site **Fort Pickens Campground** (877-444-6777 or 850-934-2656; recreation.gov), Pensacola Beach 32561, which has bathhouses and a camp store but little shade. However, it's a short walk to the beach. Tents, trailers, and RVs welcome. Sites are $26 per night with water and electric, but must be reserved in advance.

 Well north of Pensacola, **Lake Stone Campground** (850-256-5555; myescambia.com/our-services/parks-and-recreation/lake-stone-campground), 801 W FL 4, is a 100-acre, county-run campground centered on Lake Stone. The 77 broad, mostly shaded campsites are ideal for large RVs and can handle tent campers as well. $15 and up, including electric and water hookups.

 At **Perdido Key State Park** (850-492-1595; floridastateparks.org/park/Perdido-Key), 12301 Gulf Beach Highway, Pensacola, the coastal scrub and beaches preserved here are home to the tiny, federally listed endangered Santa Rosa beach mouse.

SCENIC DRIVES Designated a Scenic Byway in April 1998, **Pensacola Scenic Bluffs Highway** (pensacolascenicbluffs.org) leads you beneath moss-draped oaks and stately magnolias with scenic vistas along the way. At one point you'll reach the highest point along the entire coastline of Florida!

Two beachfront drives await on Santa Rosa Island. Follow **Fort Pickens Drive** west through Gulf Islands National Seashore to Fort Pickens (see *Historic Sites*) for broad views of beaches and dunes on both sides of the rebuilt highway. **CR 399** offers a sweeping vista of sparkling sands and dunes in all directions as you head east from Pensacola Beach to Navarre Beach through a string of public lands protecting these fragile, windswept landscapes.

TUBING **Coldwater Creek** in Blackwater River State Forest (see *Parks, Preserves, and Camping*) is *the* destination for floating down a lazy creek in an inner tube. Check with the outfitters listed under *Paddling* for logistics, or bring your own when staying at Coldwater Gardens (see *Campgrounds*) to play along the big sandbars at the camping areas.

WALKING TOURS Talk a stroll along the beautiful banks of the Blackwater River in historic **Bagdad Village** (850-623-8493). Listed on the National Register of Historic Places with 143 buildings, the Village's frame vernacular and Greek revival architecture dates back to the mid-1800s. Built with Creole elements by former slaves, Bagdad Village is located just north of Milton. Maps and guided tours are available through the

PITCHER PLANTS

If you're as obsessed with carnivorous pitcher plants as we are, welcome to Nirvana. This portion of the Gulf Coast has the most diverse assortment of pitcher plant species that you'll find in Florida, and if you arrive between late March and mid-April, you'll catch them in their showiest finery. While Blackwater River State Forest has hundreds of small bogs with showy flowers, here are some of the places you'll find pitcher plants more easily.

🐾 The mother lode of beauty is along the **Clear Creek Nature Trail** (floridahikes.com/clearcreek) just outside the gates at Whiting NAS [30.710586, -87.032572], FL 87, Milton, which leads to a boardwalk surrounded by thousands upon thousands of pitcher plants; free.

🐾 **Garcon Point Preserve** (850-539-5999; nwfwater.com/Lands/Recreation/Area/Garcon-Point), FL 191 just north of the Garcon Point Bridge tollbooth [30.459067,-87.092433], offers more than 4 miles of trails through open prairies and pine flatwoods, providing panoramic views of Blackwater Bay and close encounters with carnivorous pitcher plants. Open sunrise–sunset; free.

🐾♿ Walk through wild wet pine flatwoods on a mild paved pathway at **Tarkiln Bayou State Park** (850-492-1595; floridastateparks.org/park/Tarkiln-Bayou), CR 293 south of US 98, Pensacola, or jump off the easy route and explore the soggy forest on 7 miles of old jeep trails. At the end of the paved path, the Emma Claire Boardwalk of Hope stretches across a colorful pitcher plant bog and ends at a scenic overlook on the bayou. Fee.

🐾 Florida's largest pitcher plant prairie is protected at **Yellow River Marsh Preserve State Park** (850-983-5363; floridastateparks.org/park/Yellow-River), FL 191, south of Bagdad at Dickerson City Road [30.484300, -87.071500]. There are no formal trails, but there is a parking area; there are also plenty of colorful blooms to see in April—bring your GPS to find your way back. Open sunrise–sunset; free.

PITCHER PLANTS ALONG FL 191 IN BLACKWATER RIVER STATE FOREST

Santa Rosa County Tourist and Development Council (see *Guidance*). Pick up a walking tour brochure for the **Milton Historic District**, also listed on the National Register of Historic Places, with homes and structures dating from 1850 to 1945.

At **Historic Pensacola Village** (see *Museums*), the walking tours are a thorough and important part of learning about the many historic homes in the historic district. Tours start at the **Tivoli High House**—home to the ticket office and gift shop—and proceed through a parade of house museums.

ZIPLINE The extensive zipline and canopy walk course at **Zip Adventures** (850-613-6197; floridaziplineadventures.com), part of Adventures Unlimited (see *Paddling*), encompasses three separate routes through the forests surrounding Coldwater Creek. You must do them in sequence, since each one is progressively more difficult. The "Ultimate Zip Adventure" includes nearly a mile's worth of ziplines over Wolfe Creek and Big Coldwater Creek, and takes five hours to complete. Rates run $89–129, two-person minimum.

✳ Lodging

BED & BREAKFASTS (✺) Located in historic North Hill, **Noble Manor Bed & Breakfast** (850-434-9544; noblemanor .com), 110 W. Strong Street, Pensacola 32501 is a Tudor revival home designed by Charlie Hill Turner in 1905. Classy contemporary decor and furnishings, cable, and Wi-Fi bring four spacious historic guest rooms up to date, $145–195. The Carriage House Suite, with its own separate entrance, sits in the yard. $160–195. Guests can enjoy a heated pool and outdoor hot tub.

🍴 ♿ (✺) ♂ Overlooking the sweep of Pensacola Bay, **Lee House & Cottages** (850-912-8770; leehousepensacola.com), 400 Bayfront Parkway, Pensacola 32501 is an elegant inn across from Seville Square. It captures the essence of place while providing modern accommodations downtown. Each suite ($160–255) features its own unique contemporary decor; some have two beds, sleeping up to four guests. Business travelers will appreciate the work desks in each room. Two historic cottages, the Pi Cottage and the 1879 Sweet Shop Cottage, cater to families. Your stay includes a continental breakfast, parking, and numerous on-site amenities.

(✺) The Queen Anne Victorian **Pensacola Victorian Bed & Breakfast** (850-434-2818; pensacolavictorian.com), 203 W. Gregory Avenue, Pensacola 32501 was once a ship captain's home. Awaken each morning to fresh fruit, waffles, omelets, or quiche; you'll also be treated to complimentary fresh-baked treats and beverages throughout your stay. $95–150.

COMFORT AND LUXURY ♂ ♿ (✺) Jimmy Buffet hasn't forgotten his roots here along the Gulf Coast, opening **Margaritaville Beach Hotel** (850-916-9755, margaritavillehotel.com), 165 Fort Pickens Road, Pensacola Beach 32561. Kick back and relax with one of Jimmy's margaritas at the rooftop pool or soak in the sun along the sparkling sands. The sleek, spacious rooms have a colonial Caribbean feel and ample space for kicking back and enjoying the view. Several eateries are on-site, making it an easy, laid-back destination with the beach, the drinks, the tunes, and the eats right here. You'll be humming "Creola" before you know it. $219 and up.

HISTORIC ♂ (✺) In the 1930s, it served as a working schoolhouse in Fidelis; now it provides a retreat in a most restful setting. Tucked away in the forest at Adventures Unlimited (see *Campgrounds*), **Old School House Inn** (850-623-6197; adventuresunlimited.com), 8974 Tomahawk Landing Road, Milton 32570 showcases original bead-board walls and ceiling and hardwood floors in each of its literary-themed rooms: Poets, Audubon, Faulkner, Dr. Seuss, Hemingway, Mitchell, Rawlings, and Twain. No phones and no television—but you'll appreciate the coffeemaker, microwave, and small fridge. $129 per night with a two-night minimum.

🦴 (ᵢₚ) Updated, cozy rooms and suites that feel just like home make **New World Landing** (850-432-4111; skopelosatnewworld.com/stay/rooms/), 600 S Palafox Street, Pensacola 32502 an appealing and historic destination for downtown accommodations, positioned nicely near the best museums, restaurants, and shopping. $159–249, includes deluxe continental breakfast and free downtown parking. The complex also caters to wedding parties with a large event venue on-site; relax after a busy day with a Classic Cosmo at Skopelos, a fine Greek restaurant.

RETRO AND ARTSY ♿ (ᵢₚ) A fine example of urban revitalization, **Sole Inn and Suites** (850-470-9298; soleinnandsuites .com), 200 N Palafox Street, Pensacola 32502 is a former Travelodge reincarnated as a hip boutique hotel. Having seen before and after, this transformation rates a huge "wow." The rooms have crisp, sleek, urban decor in tasteful black and white, with extras you appreciate in a walkable downtown, like a microwave, mini fridge, coffeemaker, and free parking. Rates start at $89 and include continental breakfast and Happy Hour each evening 5–7 PM.

🦴 A fun and funky place to stay when you're on a budget, the **Paradise Inn** (850-932-2319; paradiseinn-pb.com), 21 Via De Luna Drive, Pensacola Beach 32561 sits bayside, with its own beach where live music accompanies beach volleyball and diners chowing down on picnic tables outside the beach bar. There's even a pier out into the bay. The rooms are a cozy slice of Old Florida, and you can't beat the price, starting at $59 in the off-season.

TRIED AND TRUE 🦴 ♿ (ᵢₚ) ✈ Outside of downtown but still convenient to attractions, **Hilton Garden Inn** (850-479-8900; hiltongardeninnpensacola.com), 1144 Airport Boulevard, is near the airport and medical centers; has a pool, business center, and fitness center; and also includes all the amenities you'd expect under the Hilton banner. Close to the gates of Pensacola NAS, ♿ (ᵢₚ) **Holiday Inn Express & Suites West** (850-696-2800; ihg.com), 307 N New Warrington Road, provides a comfortable place to stay with many chain restaurants nearby. 🦴 ♿ 🐾 (ᵢₚ) ✈ The pet-friendly **Residence Inn Downtown** (850-432-0202; marriott .com), 601 E. Chase Street, provides comfortable accommodations near the bayfront in downtown Pensacola.

CAMPGROUNDS 🦴 🐾 **Adventures Unlimited** (800-239-6864 or 850-623-6197; adventuresunlimited.com), 8974 Tomahawk Landing Road, Milton 32570 offers a wide variety of accommodations. Choose from a variety of fully equipped cottages with country charm and sizes to fit every family, from Granny Peadon's Cottage, with period furnishings and a back porch overlooking Wolfe Creek, to the Fox Den Bungalow with its fireplace. Cabins with bath start at $119, while the more rustic Camping Style Cabins with no bath are $69–89. Pets are welcome in one of the two campgrounds that cater to Class A RVs, $45; tent campers and pop-up sites, $25–35, include hookups as well.

🦴 🦴 ⚲ Go on safari in the piney woods of Florida at **Coldwater Gardens** (850-426-1300; coldwatergardens.com), 7009 Creek Stone Road, Milton, a serene nature preserve and organic farm on 350 acres along beautiful Coldwater Creek. Perhaps it's the burble of the creek you prefer, setting up a tent on a sandbar or tent plaform to drink in the sound and provide easy access to launch your kayak. Or the unique adventure of taking the family glamping, staying in a giant safari tent with screening to keep the

GLAMPING TENT AT COLDWATER GARDENS

bugs out and a fan to keep you cool in a comfy bed. Or relaxing in tranquil surroundings on the deck of an eco-friendly cottage. Guests have room to roam on 6 miles of hiking trails across the property, including taking a peek into the greenhouses and gardens of the organic farm, or letting kids be kids on the playground near the terrace. Weddings, workshops, and retreats find a home in this expansive space, but it's the accommodations and their affordability for families that make this a great natural alternative to a beach getaway. Primitive camping, $20; platform camping, $35–50; glamping tents, $75–85; cabins, $135 and up. Reserve in advance online or by phone, and arrive well before dark.

🐾 ♂ (ⁱ᎐) Park your rig under the pines at **Navarre Beach Campground** (888-639-2188 or 850-939-2188; navbeach.com), 9201 Navarre Parkway, Navarre Beach 32566 where amenities include a fishing pier on Santa Rosa Sound, a heated pool and hot tub, a playground and game room for the kids, and a dog walk for your pooch. Sites come in 30- and 50-amp flavors ($60–90 depending on location), plus a couple of 20-amp sites

for tent campers ($49). No camper? No problem! Cabin rentals range from simple sleeping spaces with cold water to big three-bedroom family units, $79–168.

✳ Where to Eat

ELEGANT AND ROMANTIC For relaxed fine dining in the historic downtown, look no farther than **Blackwater Bistro** (850-623-1105; blackwaterbistro .com), 5147 Elmira Street, Milton, tucked inside a 1909 cottage within view of the river. Some of the restaurant's more unique offerings include an artichoke cheesecake appetizer, the Cajun county gumbo, and the Portobello Dagenheart, a grilled mushroom cap topped with carmelized onions, roasted red pepper, and melted goat cheese atop a grilled chicken breast. Veggies are locally sourced and everything, including the tender-aged Beef Wellington, tastes fresh—we've dined here several times. Sandwiches and salads, $8–13; entrées, $13–25. Pair with their selection of fine wines or their sweet sangria. Closed Monday, live music on weekends.

♿ **Jackson's Steakhouse** (850-469-9898; jacksonsrestaurant.com), 400 S Palafox Street, sits in the heart of downtown Pensacola's historic district, cozy in an 1860s mercantile building overlooking historic Plaza Ferdinand. Notable as one of Florida's top restaurants, it features grain-fed beef from the Midwest with a menu that offers wet-aged steaks and chops, including center-cut wagyu New York strip, double-cut lamb chops, and a bison rib-eye. Chef Irv's menu sports creative creations beyond these classics, which on any given night might include a guajillo-crusted gulf yellowfin tuna with cilantro guacamole or a double-cut Cheshire pork chop with chaurice stuffing. For a lighter palate, go for a half-portion of entrées or a mix of appetizers, including smoked duck pastrami and a pecanwood-smoked mullet dip. Entrées $12–69; a prix-fixe Prelude Menu served 5:30–6 PM Tuesday–Saturday, $29.

Featuring inspired creations and presentations of seafood with a menu that changes daily to reflect the freshest sources—yes, the source of your dinner is noted, so you don't have to ask—**The Grand Marlin** (850-677-9153; thegrandmarlin.com), 400 Pensacola Beach Boulevard, is the hot spot for fine dining at the beach. Typical dinner selections from Chef Gregg might include Grouper Picatta with a parmesan crust or Key Lime grilled lobster tail. A selection of grilled steaks, chops, and even a burger topped with Tillamook cheddar are available for those not so fond of the seafood that is this restaurant's forte. Entrées $15–37, lighter lunch fare $12–19.

CASUAL FARE Dining out with a group of friends, we were delighted to find **Grover T's BBQ** (850-564-1231; grovertbbq.com), 5887 US 90, Milton, had not only their classic smoked meats—the St. Louis–style ribs being the must-have, if they aren't all gone—but also a few New Orleans favorites like Etoufee and Catfish Orleans. Sandwiches and BBQ plates, $5 and up.

COMFORT FOOD Established in the 1940s in a onetime timber industry boomtown, **Ruth's Country Store** (850-957-4463), corner of FL 4 and CR 191, Munson, a rustic and quaint country store, has deep local roots—Bobby (Ruth's son) grew up sleeping under the cash register, and his wife, Patty, offers a great little breakfast in the back room. Gather around the picnic table and order up fresh pancakes, omelets, and eggs and bacon, or stop in for burgers and dogs at lunch on your way to Blackwater River State Forest. Pop in, and you might catch a bluegrass jam in session!

A stop at **Scenic 90 Cafe** (850-433-8844; scenic90cafe.com), 701 Scenic Highway, soothed our hunger. It's a cute diner with a 1950s feel, but you can skip the cute and relax out on the big covered patio if it's cool enough to catch a breeze. What's important here is the food, classic diner comfort food like big breakfasts (the Greek omelet and Stack of Jacks get a big thumbs-up), juicy burgers, ice cream sundaes, chocolate malts, and root beer floats. $5 and up.

ETHNIC EATS Lively Irish folk music and traditional fare are found at the original **McGuire's Irish Pub** (850-433-6789; mcguiresirishpub.com), 600 E Gregory Avenue, Pensacola. Sing-alongs are encouraged; if you don't learn the words, you'll have to kiss the moose, and that's no blarney. The senate bean soup is still only 18 cents, but if it's your only purchase, they'll charge $18. The extensive drink menu includes the full-on "Irish Wake," which you'll have to try to believe.

At **The Tuscan Oven** (850-484-6836; thetuscanoven.com), 4801 N 9th Avenue, the flicker of an authentic Italian wood-fired pizza oven reflects in the front window, drawing you in with the promise of warmth and a tantalizing smoky aroma. The restaurant makes its pasta fresh, and the antipasto is a vibrant mix of artichokes with Italian meats and cheeses. Save some room for dessert, which includes chocolate mousse cake, tiramisu torte, raspberry gelato, and dressy cannolis. Pizza $9–24; pasta $9–11.

HIP BISTRO-STYLE (ᵜ) Kick back at **The Leisure Club** (850-912-4229; theleisure club.net), 126 S Palafox Street, a trendy downtown meet-up spot within walking distance of entertainment venues, museums, and the Palafox Market. The art on the walls evokes the weirdness of Edward Gorey, as do the funky furnishings. Come early for coffee, late for wine, and anytime for Wi-Fi.

Sno-cones, Skee-Ball, and beer? You betcha, at **Play** (850-466-3080; iplaypensacola.com), 16 S Palafox Place, Suite 200, Pensacola, a different kind of sports bar downtown, where arcade games, air hockey, and big-screen televisions compete for attention. Ages 21 and older only.

QUICK BITES More than a baker's dozen of flavors awaits at **Bagelheads** (850-444-9661; bagelheads.com), 916 E Gregory Avenue, a busy breakfast stop between the bluffs, the beach, and downtown. Overlooking Pensacola Bay, it's a place to settle in, with their cinnamon-dressed mocha latte and a helping of steel-cut oatmeal with a variety of toppings. Open 6 AM–2 PM weekdays, 7 AM–2 PM weekends.

Stop for lunch at the colorful **Hip Pocket Deli** (850-455-9319; hippocketdeli.com), 4130 Barrancas Avenue, Warrington, featuring world-famous gyros, calzones, muffaletta, and more, $4–11. Open 10:30 AM–3 PM Monday–Saturday.

OCEANFRONT Established more than 50 years ago on the state line, **Flora-Bama Lounge & Oyster Bar** (850-492-3048; florabama.com), 17401 Perdido Key Drive, Perdido Key, prides itself on being the "last authentic American Roadhouse." Stop in for a brew and a stack of oysters, and you might stumble upon Jimmy Buffett playing acoustic out on the porch, unannounced. It's a laid-back, rambling beachside bar and grill serving burgers, seafood baskets, and fresh seafood platters for lunch and dinner, $8–12; it also hosts the Annual Interstate Mullet Toss, the first full weekend of April, with prizes for successful tosses across the river from Florida to Alabama (you have to see it to believe it!) and the International Songwriters Festival. Cover charge for bands and special events.

SEAFOOD 🦐 Seafood is what it's all about at **All About Food** (850-564-1442; allaboutfoodfl.net), 5701 US 90, Milton, where quantity and quality come in heaping amounts. One family's table hardly had enough room for their oyster platters, while another couple dug into deep bowls piled high with crawfish. Packed with locals comfortable with cracking, peeling, and piling, this is an unfussy restaurant with everything from parmesan asparagus to gumbo to go with your entrée. The half-portion options are quite satisfying. Choose from seafood, steaks, overloaded potatoes, and the reason we walked in out of curiosity: the Hwy 90 Pile-up; $7–19.

Featuring fresh Gulf seafood, **David's Catfish House** (850-626-1500; davidscatfishhousemilton.com), 5129 Dogwood Drive, Milton, proves you don't have to be overlooking the water to serve up a perfect fish dinner. The lightest of batters coats the fried seafood, making it quite tasty. We honed in on their big seafood platter after a long day of hiking, but they have lighter options as well, including shrimp-topped salads, Po'Boys, and baskets, $7–18.

🦐 Fried mullet? Fresh local oysters plucked from nearby East Bay? **Nichol's Seafood** (850-623-3410), 3966 Avalon Boulevard, is a local favorite with these and more, where whatever's fresh from local fisherman—cobia, amberjack, flounder—shows up as the special of the night. Fresh-shucked raw oysters and satisfying seafood for $9–20, lunch and dinner. Seniors get to share the kids' menu, too!

With a funky Florida Cracker atmosphere, **Peg Leg Pete's** (850-932-4139; peglegpetes.com), 1010 Fort Pickens Road, Pensacola Beach at Lafitte Cove Marina remains a favorite getaway for us, especially for the oysters. Enjoy a constant sea breeze while savoring baked oysters (pick your style, from Buffalo Blue to Spicy Lafitte) or a plate of crab legs; entrées $13–30.

WATERFRONT ⚓ **Flounder's Chowder House** (850-932-2003; flounderschowder house.com), CR 399 at Fort Pickens Road. Since 1979 this casual beach bar has been a Pensacola favorite, set in a playful tropical atmosphere befitting its setting on Santa Rosa Sound—right down to a lively pirate ship playground for the kids. From their award-winning flounder chowder to "Floyd Flounder's Flawless Full Flavored Florida Flash Fried Fish," you won't go wrong with the fresh seafood cramming the menu, entrées $15–29. Here for the band? Hoist a "dirty old Mason jar" full of "Diesel Fuel" or one of their potent margaritas while you toast your buddies over platters of baked oysters, Pensacola Beach style, and seafood nachos. Add speedy, friendly service for lunch and dinner daily, and this one's a winner.

♿ Don't miss **The Fish House** (850-470-0003; fishhousepensacola.com), 600 S Barracks Street, a local institution with a menu that leans toward Asian fusion. A personal favorite is Grits à Ya Ya—jumbo spiced Gulf shrimp atop a sauté of spinach, portobello mushrooms, applewood-smoked bacon, garlic, shallots, and cream; all this lies atop a heaping bed of smoked Gouda grits. For those wanting something lighter, try the sushi or the cashew-and-Vidalia-crusted soft-shell crab salad. Save room for a piece of Florida key lime pie, served naturally yellow. Entrées $18–29; sushi starts at $8.

BAKERIES Stop in for a donut, a cupcake, or a slice of pie at the sweet-scented **Milton Quality Bakery** (850-623-3676), 6727 Caroline Street; the only disappointment comes when you realize you didn't get there early enough for your favorite treat. Opens at 4 AM every morning.

For freshly baked breads and hot coffee, start your mornings at **Sailors' Grill & Bakery** (850-939-1092; juanaspagodas .com/restaurant.htm), 1451 Navarre Beach Boulevard (corner of Gulf Boulevard), with tasty treats like cinnamon raisin French toast. Breakfast served 8 AM–11 PM Monday–Saturday, 8 AM–noon Sunday. Pizza, nachos, and other "Galley Grub" are served until closing.

✳ Selective Shopping

ANTIQUES While you won't go wrong buying a birdhouse from the hundreds decorating the porch at **Blackwater Trail Antiques** (850-898-1008; blackwatertrail antiques.com), 6705 Berryhill Road, Milton, it's worth a walk inside to see their wares, from farm-fresh eggs to artisanal soaps, vintage Florida souvenirs, seashells, and antique furniture. As for the name, yes, they're within sight of the Blackwater River Heritage Trail (see *Greenways*).

With dozens of dealer booths spaciously spread out beneath one roof, **The Copper Possum** (850-626-4492; thecopperpossum.com), 7060 US 90, Milton, is a pleasure to explore. First, it's fully air-conditioned. The booths contain all sorts of treasures, from a 1963 Chevy owner's guide to chewing tobacco molds, quilts, artifacts for historic home restoration of windows and sinks, fine antique furniture, and Floridiana.

Along US 29 north of I-10, **Dixie's Antiques & Collectibles** (850-484-6899; dixies-antiques.com), 10100 Pensacola Boulevard, Pensacola, brings together 50-plus dealers under one roof. Expect to find Fenton and Vaseline glass, antique clocks, colorful old bottles, record albums, folk art, and much more.

BOOKS AND GIFTS Delicate angels in porcelain and glass. Inspirational figurines by Willow Tree. At **Angel's Garden Unique Gifts** (850-435-9555; facebook.com/AngelsGarden), 1208 N 12th Avenue, Pensacola, you'll find the perfect expression of faith, hope, or love for a wedding, confirmation, or baby shower gift.

FARMERS' MARKETS On Saturdays 9 AM–2 PM, **Palafox Market** (palafoxmarket.com) is a sprawling farmers'-and-arts market in the heart of downtown Pensacola, with a dash of antiques for good measure. Here's where you'll find farm-fresh produce from Coldwater Gardens (see *Campgrounds*). Pick up local produce at the **Riverwalk Farmers' Market** (850-855-6420; mainstreetmilton.org/Market.htm), at the intersection of Berryhill, Willing, and Broad streets north of Riverwalk Park in Milton. Handmade crafts and green products are part of the mix, held seasonally.

FLEA MARKET Near Gary Park just northwest of downtown, the crowds pack in at **T&W Flea Market** (850-433-4315; tandwfleamarket.com), 1717 N T Street at W Street, "Pensacola's Largest Flea Market." Open Saturday–Sunday 7 AM–5 PM.

HOME DECOR In a historic gingerbread-trimmed cottage, **Artesana** (850-433-4001; artesanaimports.com), 242 W Garden Street, Pensacola, pulls together beauty and function. Browse through their extensive selections of wooden tableware, handcrafted pottery, and bespeckled German enamelware. If that's not enough, they delve into many more of the finer things that make a house a home, along with stationery, fragrances, and gift items.

SPECIALTY FOODS For the freshest seafood in the region, head to **Joe Patti's** (800-500-9929 or 850-432-3315; joepattis.com), S A Street and Main Street on the waterfront, Pensacola. Drawing clients from around the world, this frenetic fish house has been in business since 1931, offering the best from local fishermen and shrimpers. Open daily at 7:30 AM.

Pick the finest pecans at **J. W. Renfroe Pecan Company** (800-874-1929 or 850-432-2083; renfroepecan.com), 2400 W. Fairfield Drive. In business since 1956—when it was all strictly nuts—this family operation has expanded to include related food items such as pecan fudge, fresh pralines, divinity, pecan logs, and nut mixes. Coffee, too. Select from plenty of fancy gift packages online or pop in the store to make up your own. Open Monday–Friday 9 AM–5 PM.

Just off the I-10 exit for Bagdad, **Stuckey's** (850-623-2522), 3675 Garcon Point Road, is one of the last of its breed. Back in the 1960s, these restaurants were everywhere along the growing interstate system in Florida. But today this is the state's only honest-to-goodness Stuckey's, in sparkling shape in its original building, shared with a Dairy Queen. It retains the kitschy ambience and Southern charm—and all that classic candy we remember as kids.

BLACKWATER TRAIL ANTIQUES, MILTON

✳ Special Events

FALL/WINTER Don't miss the **Pensacola Seafood Festival** (fiestaoffiveflags.org), centered on Seville Square in late September. Now more than 40 years running, it showcases the best that local fishermen and chefs have to offer, with samples of delicacies like oyster croquettes, bang bang shrimp, and grilled conch available at vendor booths.

For nearly 80 years, the Annual **Pensacola Interstate Fair** (850-944-4500; pensacolafair.com), 6655 W Mobile Highway—bigger than a county fair and smaller than a state fair—has brought farmers and city families together to enjoy exhibits, competitions, fair food, and midway rides. Mid-October.

A true farmers' festival, the **Jay Peanut Festival** (facebook.com/pages/Jay-Peanut-Festival/146168972093600) the first weekend of October, Jay, has delighted large crowds for more than 25 years with live music, pig chases, a tractor pull, pet parade, and peanuts any way you could dream of eating them.

𝒫 The **Munson Heritage Festival** (munsonheritagefestival.com) highlights traditional folkways of Northwest Florida, with storytelling and folksingers, traditional crafters and history displays. Second weekend of October, Blackwater River State Forest.

One of Florida's must-see aviation events, the **NAS Pensacola Air Show** (850-452-2583; naspensacolaairshow.com) showcases naval aeronautics and acrobatics at the home of the Blue Angels as they finish out their touring season, Veterans Day weekend.

Santa comes to the seashore with a beachy touch, arriving in early December with the **Lighted Boat Parade** (850-932-1500; visitpensacolabeach.com), the first Saturday, and presiding over the **Surfing Santa Parade** soon after. Look for him at the **Downtown Christmas Parade** (coxpensacolachristmasparade.org) as well.

Ring in the New Year with the **Pelican Drop** (850-435-1603; pensacolapelicandrop.com), a Pensacola tradition in which a 10-foot, half-ton pelican is dropped 100 feet at midnight while fireworks illuminate the skies.

Don't miss the popular **Polar Bear Dip** (florabama.com/events/polar-bear-dip) at Flora-Bama Lounge (see *Eating Out*). This annual splash in Santa Rosa Sound on New Year's Day isn't as cold as its New England counterparts, but it can be chilly by Florida standards! Afterward, join in the southern tradition of eating black-eyed peas. Whoever finds a dime in his or her peas has good luck for the year.

Pensacola Mardi Gras (850-434-1234; pensacolamardigras.com) encompasses celebrations during the traditional Lenten season with numerous parades. Just like in New Orleans, people toss beads and treats from floats decorated and manned by creative krewes who keep the annual tradition colorful and vibrant. Perdido Beach flaunts a street party, while the celebrations in Pensacola and Pensacola Beach cater to families.

At the **Gulf Coast Renaissance Fair and Pirate Festival** (850-429-8462; gcrf.us), 6655 Mobile Highway at the fairgrounds each March, expect madrigals and magicians, storytellers and jesters, for an anachronistic mix of family entertainment.

SPRING/SUMMER The **Annual Interstate Mullet Toss** (850-492-6838; florabama.com) at Flora-Bama Lounge (see *Where to Eat*), the first weekend of April, is not to be missed. This wacky tournament is a local tradition, with real mullet tossing, live music, food, and drinks throughout the weekend.

The **Annual Pensacola Crawfish Festival** (850-433-6512; fiestaoffiveflags.org) celebrates Cajun influence in Northwest Florida. The three-day crawfish boil is one of the largest in the state, with Cajun fare like spicy chicken and red beans and rice. Last weekend of April.

✐ Milton's own **Scratch Ankle Festival** (850-626-6246; facebook.com/ScratchAnkle) in mid-April is nearly 50 years old and features a nice slice of Americana, including bake-offs, live music, craft vendors, carnival rides, and the "Little Mr. and Miss" pageant.

Pensacola's biggest and oldest annual bash is the **Fiesta of Five Flags** (fiestaoffiveflags.org), held in mid-June to commemorate the landing of Don Tristán de Luna in 1559 and the founding of the first settlement of Pensacola. Events during the fiesta include a boat parade, an airplane meet, a coronation ball, and the Fiesta Parade.

The **Pensacola Beach Air Show** (850-932-2257; visitpensacolabeach.com) features the aeronautic talents of the famous Blue Angels, stationed here at Pensacola Naval Air Station, as part of an extended 4th of July celebration.

DESTIN—FORT WALTON

Okaloosa, Holmes, and Walton Counties
Emerald Coast/South Walton

When southerners head for the beach, they head for this stretch of sugary white sand sweeping east through Okaloosa and Walton counties from Okaloosa Island to Seaside, a place of emerald waters, fine museums, historic towns, and outdoor adventure. Covered in pure Appalachian quartz, with tiny crystals that resemble powdered sugar, these beaches are baby-powder soft, and they are surprisingly cool to walk on with bare feet. You'll want to keep your sunglasses handy while collecting the plentiful seashells; the sand is as white and bright as newly fallen snow.

The area's roots, however, are much deeper than the shifting sands. At the Indian Temple Mound and Museum in **Fort Walton Beach**, a massive earthen mound around which the first settlements arose was built between 700–1650 AD. Archaeological digs have uncovered a variety of durable pieces of pottery, including animal effigies. The first Europeans to see this coast were part of the ill-fated Narváez expedition in the

PRISTINE BEACH AT TOPSAIL HILL PRESERVE STATE PARK

fall of 1528, but not until 1559 did the Spanish set foot on these shores, as they surveyed the region while establishing a short-lived colony at Pensacola Bay under Tristan de Luna. Once western Florida was no longer under the flag of a foreign power, settlers tempted by the Armed Occupation Act came south from the Carolinas and Georgia to stake their homestead claims. Established in the early 1800s, the communities of Isagora and Pittman—in fertile lands near the Choctawhatchee River in what is now Holmes County—drew farming families with Scottish roots. Along the coast, Connecticut shipmaster Captain Leonard Destin, impressed with the bounty of fish and the deep protected bay, settled down in 1845 in what is now **Destin**, home to Florida's largest charter fishing fleet.

Chartered in 1881 to connect the existing cities of Pensacola and Apalachicola, the Pensacola and Atlantic Railroad—later absorbed into the Louisville and Nashville system, or L&N—opened the floodgates of settlement along the rail line. Founded in 1881, **DeFuniak Springs** is the county seat of Walton County, its historic residential district clustered around a perfectly round, spring-fed lake

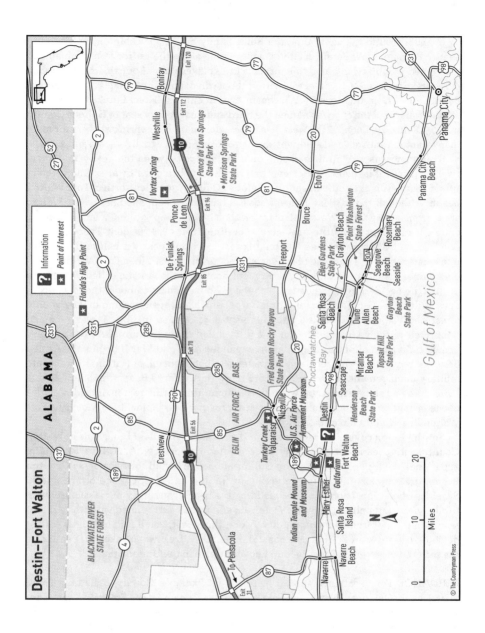

exactly a mile in circumference. The town is named for Fred R. DeFuniak, general manager of the railroad, but the community was intentionally planned—with the influence
of Fredrick Law Olmstead's designs of the era—as an educational campus to bring the
Chautauqua movement from its upstate New York home to the balmy Florida winters.
Hundreds of thousands of people visited the "education resort of the south," but land
lots around Lake DeFuniak were strictly sold to the well-to-do, hence the spectacular
Victorian homes that still anchor Circle Drive. Operating between 1884 and 1927, the
Florida Chautauqua was one of the most successful of its time, and it was resurrected
in 1993 with a modern twist. To the city's north, near the Alabama border, **Florida's
high point** is the lowest point in the United States, at 345 feet.

In 1886, around the same time the Keith family built their cabin on their farm in nearby Pittman, G.W. Banfill platted a square mile along the railroad on the map and christened it **Bonifay,** in a nod to Pensacola brickmaker Frank Bonifay, who'd bought a major stake in the L&N. If you're wondering about why Waukesha Street is the main road, Banfill hailed from that town in Wisconsin. Banfill built the Hotel Eureka to capitalize on rail traffic, and the city was named the third and final county seat of **Holmes County** in 1905. **Ponce De Leon**, to the west, has been a destination for spring-seekers for more than a century, with several ebullient springs offering a place to dive, soak, and swim.

Crestview was also a railroad stop on a high ridge between the Yellow and Shoal rivers, a place for farmers, timbermen, and ranchers to bring their wares. Chartered in 1916, Crestview is the county seat for **Okaloosa County**, 30 miles north of **Fort Walton Beach**. Although the earliest signs of coastal habitation happened here, Fort Walton arose from a post–Civil War settlement on the site of Camp Walton, a small Confederate encampment along the protected shoreline. In 1908, President Theodore Roosevelt signed Choctawhatchee National Forest, covering nearly a half million acres, into existence for the purpose of timbering and naval stores. When Fort Walton developer James Plew started building retirement homes on the land he called **Valparaiso** in 1922, he decided to set aside land for the US government to boost the local economy. Built by the Civilian Conservation Corps, which had been working in the national forest, the Valparaiso Bombing and Gunnery Base opened in 1934. It was renamed Eglin Field three years later to honor a pilot killed during training. As the military bomb-testing and pilot training mission expanded as World War II began, the Armed Services requested—and received—transfer of Choctawhatchee National Forest into military management. It became the core of **Eglin Air Force Base**, which now covers more than 640 square miles between the communities of this region, including miles of oceanfront on **Okaloosa Island**, restricting further development for **Niceville**, Fort Walton Beach, and Valparaiso as well.

South Walton covers the region east of Destin along 26 miles of coastline in **Walton County**, with oceanfront communities connected by Scenic 30A. At **Blue Mountain**, experience the highest point on the Gulf of Mexico; in small towns such as **Grayton Beach**, great opportunities for antiquing or finding an eclectic piece of art; and in **Seaside**, where *The Truman Show* was filmed, a beachfront array of classic architectural styles—antebellum, revivial, Victorian, and more—surrounded with white picket fences in a New Urbanism community. Along this coast, you'll find one of the rarest geologic treasures in Florida, the coastal dune lakes, freshwater lakes that spill into the sea (and vice-versa). They're found nowhere else in the United States.

GUIDANCE For vacation planning in towns in Okaloosa County, including Crestview, Destin, Okaloosa Island, and Fort Walton Beach, contact the **Emerald Coast Convention & Visitors Bureau** (800-322-3319 or 850-651-7131; destin-fwb.com), which has a welcome center at 1540 Miracle Strip Parkway SE, Fort Walton Beach. You'll also find valuable resources at the **Greater Fort Walton Beach Chamber of Commerce** (850-244-8191; fwbchamber.org), 34 Miracle Strip Parkway SE, the **Destin Chamber of Commerce** (850-837-6241; destinchamber.com), 4484 Legendary Drive, Suite A, and the **Crestview Chamber of Commerce** (850-682-3212), 1447 Commerce Drive.

The **Walton County Chamber of Commerce** (850-892-3191; waltoncountychamber .com), 63 South Centre Trail, Santa Rosa Beach, covers all of Walton County, but you can pick up local brochures for DeFuniak Springs at the **Walton County Heritage Museum** (see *Museums*) and find information for beachfront communities at **Visit South Walton** (800-822-6877 or 850-267-1216; visitsouthwalton.com), 25777 US 331 S, Santa Rosa Beach.

A log cabin houses the **Holmes County Visitor Center** (850-547-6153; holmes countyonline.com/tourism-development), 748 E Byrd Avenue, **Bonifay**. Pop in to ask questions, pick up brochures or maps, and see the quilt that's a map of communities and historic buildings throughout the county. Get off I-10 and see the beauty of the rural areas of this region with maps, directions, and planning information from **Riverway South** (rwsfl.org), a team of Northwest Florida counties including Holmes and North Walton.

GETTING THERE *By air:* **Destin-Fort Walton Beach Airport** (850-651-7160; flyvps .com), 1701 FL 85 N, Eglin Air Force Base, is served by Allegiant, American, Delta, and United. Delta, Southwest, and United serve **Northwest Florida Beaches International Airport** (850-763-6751; iflybeaches.com), 6300 West Bay Parkway, Panama City Beach.

By bus: **Greyhound** (800-231-2222 or 850-243-1940; greyhound.com), 101 Perry Avenue SE, Fort Walton Beach.

By car: **I-10** and **US 90** run east–west through the northern portion of this region. **FL 85** will take you from Crestview south through the region, connecting Niceville, Valparaiso, and Fort Walton Beach; **FL 123** is a more direct route to the airport and Fort Walton Beach, while **FL 293**—a toll road—acts as a beltway to the east around Niceville to lead to Destin. **US 331** connects DeFuniak Springs, Freeport, and Santa Rosa Beach. **US 98** runs east–west from Panama City Beach through Santa Rosa Beach, Destin, and Fort Walton Beach. **Scenic 30A** connects the small beach communities of South Walton.

GETTING AROUND **Destin Airport Shuttle & Taxi Service** (850-533-0022; destin airportshuttleandtaxi.com) provides service between the region's airports as well as the communities between, and local taxi service in Destin. **Destin Shuttle-Beachside Express** (850-685-3586; destinshuttle.com) provides minivan taxi service between the Destin-Fort Walton Beach airport and all beach communities to the east on a sliding scale by distance, $50/55 for Destin, $95 for Rosemary Beach, $115/130 for Panama City.

  ♿ **Okaloosa County Transit/The WAVE** (850-833-9168; ecrider.org) provides public bus routes in Crestview, Destin, Fort Walton Beach, and Okaloosa Island. No charge to bring a bicycle, which gets loaded on the front rack. Fare $1.50/2.00, half for ages 65+ and disabled. Route 14 is an express between Crestview and Fort Walton Beach. The Wave operates Monday–Friday 8 AM–7 PM, every 20 minutes; no service on holidays.

PARKING **Crestview** has free street parking along Main Street, and **DeFuniak Springs** offers ample free parking in the downtown shopping district and in the historic district around the lake. Parking lots and garages provide parking in the shopping areas throughout **Destin**, although you need to be mindful of parking restrictions in residential beachfront areas. Look for free street parking (2-hour limit) in the downtown shopping district of **Fort Walton Beach** along US 98 and side streets including Perry Avenue SE. Don't be tempted when you see others parking along the scenic stretch of US 98 along the beaches of **Okaloosa Island**—you'll either sink in the soft sand or get towed (or both) if you park there. There are beach lots along Okaloosa Island; see *Beaches.*

MEDICAL EMERGENCIES Crestview has **North Okaloosa Medical Center** (850-689-8100; northokaloosa.com), 151 E Redstone Avenue, while DeFuniak Springs has **Healthmark Regional Medical Center** (850-951-4500; healthmarkregional.com), 4413 US Highway 331 S. In Niceville, look for **Twin Cities Hospital** (850-678-4131; tchospital

.com), 2190 FL 85 N. Along the coast, **Fort Walton Beach Medical Center** (850-862-1111; fwbmc.com), 1000 Mar-Walt Drive, Fort Walton Beach, and their **Destin ER** (850-837-9194), 200 Tequesta Drive, Destin. For the coastal communities along 30A, **Sacred Heart Hospital on the Emerald Coast** (850-278-3000; sacredheartemerald.org), 7800 US 98 W. Always call 911 for major emergencies.

✳ To See

ARCHAEOLOGICAL SITE A National Historic Landmark, the **Indian Temple Mound** (850-243-6521; fwb.org/museums/indian-temple-mound-museum), 139 Miracle Strip Parkway, is the central feature in Heritage Park & Cultural Center (see *Museums*) in downtown Fort Walton Beach. More than 200,000 baskets of earth were placed here by Mississippian culture peoples to build this major ceremonial center between CE 800 and 1400. The adjoining museum has one of the best collections of prehistoric ceramics in the Southeast. Open Monday–Saturday 10 AM–4:30 PM; fee.

ARCHITECTURE Built in 1947, **Fox Theatre**, 382 Main Street, Crestview, premiered the movie *12 O'Clock High*, filmed in and around the area with Gregory Peck. It's now home to **Peaden Brothers Distillery** (850-306-1344; peadenbrothersdistillery.com), a whisky and rum distillery with its roots in fine moonshine concocted along the Blackwater River during prohibition. The theater is part of the **Crestview Commercial Historic District**, which lines this portion of Main Street and is obvious through the architecture of the buildings.

A two-story Mediterranean revival home built in the early 1920s, the **Waits Mansion**, 209 West Kansas Avenue, Bonifay, stands head and shoulders above the surrounding neighborhood. Constructed for George Orkney Waits, manager of the local sawmill, it has heart of pine floors and a central grand staircase leading to sizable bedrooms on the second story. Recently renovated, this private home opens on occasion for community events.

♂ Tour the antebellum **Wesley House** and gardens at Eden Gardens State Park (see *Gardens*), Point Washington. Built in 1898, the seven-bedroom mansion belonged to William Henry Wesley, who owned Wesley Lumber Company; the mill itself was nearby, with a dock to load barges at Tucker Bayou to ship lumber. In 1963, socialite Lois Maxon purchased the home from the family and designed the surrounding gardens. On a house tour, you'll see her pride and joy—the second-largest collection of Louis XVI furniture in the United States. Guided tours through the home begin on the hour, Thursday–Monday 10 AM–3 PM, and cost an additional fee beyond park admission.

ART GALLERIES At the **Arts and Design Society of Fort Walton Beach** (850-244-1271; artsdesignsociety.org), 17 First Street SE, enjoy the creativity of member artists showcased in the historic city hall complex. 12–4 PM. Tuesday–Friday, 1–4 PM Saturday.

The **DeFuniak Springs Art Co-op** (850-419-3007; facebook.com/defuniaksprings artcoop), 782 Baldwin Avenue, DeFuniak Springs, highlights local artists like Kristina Perry, who came to Florida from Lapland. Photography, ceramics, and lapidary share space with acrylics and oils; juried shows showcase themed works. Workshops are held in the back of the store and art supplies are sold near the front; the unexpected juxtaposition of antiques in the room is from Big Store Antiques, which shares a portion of this former department store's space. Monday–Saturday 10 AM–5 PM.

View international and national exhibitions at the **Mattie Kelly Fine & Performing Arts Center** (850-729-6000; mattiekellyartscenter.org), 100 College Boulevard,

DEFUNIAK SPRINGS: THE WINTER CHAUTAUQUA

The city of DeFuniak Springs is a must for architecture buffs, as it boasts more than 250 buildings on the National Register of Historic Places, most clustered around circular Lake DeFuniak. They are privately owned but can be enjoyed from Circle Drive or the sidewalk on a walking tour (see *Walking Tours*). You'll find the **DeFuniak Springs Historic District** roughly bounded by Nelson and Park avenues and 2nd and 12th streets. Several notable homes include **The Verandas**, 262 Circle Drive, a 1904 "steamboat"-style folk Victorian with wraparound porches; the **Dream Cottage**, 404 Circle Drive; and the turreted **Thomas House**, 188 Circle Drive, an elaborately decorated 1895 three-story Queen Anne. Serving as the Art Department for the Florida Chautauqua in 1884, the uniquely shaped **Octagon House**, 1259 Circle Drive, has gone through five owners. The first to live here was Wallace Bruce, author and president of the Florida Chautauqua Association in 1889 when he was named US Consul to Scotland. Returning to Florida several years later, he resided here while managing and growing the Chautauqua until his death; his son and family moved it afterward, followed by prominent businessman R.E.L. McCaskill. Today, the private property, owned by Dennis Ray, is maintained as a time capsule of the history of the community and opens occasionally for tours during special events.

Built in 1909, the **Chautauqua Hall of Brotherhood**, 95 Circle Drive, DeFuniak Springs, remains an imposing structure along Lake DeFuniak. Seating more than 4,000, it attracted visitors for its broad slate of cultural programs, which were discontinued during the Great Depression. In 1976 and again in 1993, local citizens revived the Chautauqua tradition (see *What's Happening*), and this hall is once more used for major events. Headquartered in the historic Lakeside Hospital, the **Florida Chautauqua Association** (850-892-7613; floridachautauquaassembly.org), 1290 Circle Drive, maintains the history of the Chautauqua movement as well as the history of DeFuniak Springs in its history research library and archives. Call ahead to arrange a visit.

CHAUTAUQUA HALL OF BROTHERHOOD

Niceville. The center houses two galleries: the Holzhauer and the McIlroy. Between the two sits *The Sculpture of the Seven Dancers*, an exquisite example of the creative talents of internationally famous sculptor Esther Wertheimer. Open Monday–Thursday 10 AM–4 PM and prior to performances in the mainstage theater.

At the heart of the storybook town of Seaside is the **Ruskin Place Artist Colony** (Ruskin, Quincy, and Central Square area), 120 Quincy Circle, where you'll find a nice collection of arts, crafts, and galleries, such as superior blown glass at **Fusion Art Glass Gallery** (850-231-5405; fusionartglass.com), 55 Central Square. Pieces by Josh Simpson are especially mesmerizing, with entire planetary scenes inside each globe.

AQUARIUM ✍ ⛛ ⚥ Opened in 1955, the **Gulfarium Marine Adventure Park** (800-243-9046 or 800-247-8575; gulfarium.com), 1010 Miracle Strip Parkway SE, Okaloosa Island, is the largest aquarium complex in Florida's Panhandle and is one of the world's oldest marine animal parks. Marvel at vibrant tropical fish swimming through the reef inside the 33-million-gallon Living Sea, watch dolphins being trained in the Dolphin Theater, and peek in the Penguin Preserve, home to African penguins who don't mind Florida's heat. It's a compact but thorough exploration of aquatic life, in both freshwater and saltwater. For an extra fee above general admission ($15–379), optional Animal Encounters enable close-up and hands-on time with stingrays, baby alligators, loggerhead turtles, dolphins, and more; you can even snorkel with the stingrays of Stingray Bay. You'll keep cool under the comfortably shaded exhibits and from occasional splashes from playful dolphins. Open daily 9 AM–5:30 PM; $22 adults, $14 ages 3–12.

CHURCHES ⚥ A Carpenter Gothic church completed in 1895 to house a congregation that began meeting in 1892, **St. Agatha's Episcopal Church** (850-892-9754), 144 Circle Drive, greeted its early parishoners with flowers filling the lathe before the doors and windows were added in 1896. Thanks to the Chautauqua movement, it was one of the first congregations to embrace both lay preachers and women leaders, which did not always sit well with the bishop. Light and bright inside, it features an unusual and elaborate organ built by a local boat captain; the church offers a free concert series, and you can always walk in when the doors are open.

Shapenotes have lifted to the heavens since 1906 at **New Effort Congregational Christian Church** (850-547-2996) 2679 New Effort Church Road, Bonifay. A singing school founded by T.O. Phillips began what is now known as the Mothers Day Sing, always held the second Saturday of May as an all-day event. A graveyard with interments dating back to the founding of Bonifay adjoins the historic church.

NEW EFFORT CHURCH, BONIFAY

GARDENS 🐾 ✍ ⛛ A century ago the grand plantation that is now **Eden Gardens State Park** (850-231-4214; floridastateparks.org/park/Eden-Gardens), 181 Eden Gardens Road, Point Washington, belonged to the William Henry Wesley family. Tour the manor—which holds the second-largest collection of Louis XVI furnishings in the United States—by candlelight, picnic at the old mill, a walk through the garden paths to enjoy the fragrant camellia blooms each spring under a canopy of moss-draped oaks, pause beside a tranquil reflection pool. The gardens surrounding the home include a rose garden, azalea garden, camellia garden, and a "hidden garden" in the forest. Note the unusual monkey puzzle trees near the ranger's office; they are native to Patagonia. Natural habitats buffer the gardens, with a nature trail leading along the edge of the bayou.

Adjoining the Walton-DeFuniak Public Library (see *Museums and Historic Sites*), the **Library Reading Garden** is a tranquil and colorful place with a lovely view of Lake DeFuniak and plenty of benches for readers to sit on. The massive concrete chess board/picnic table, an Eagle Scout project, is a recent addition. Young trees along the slope to the lake have been planted by keynote speakers at the Chatauqua on Arbor Day in recent years; check the granite markers at their bases for some surprises, like a red maple planted by "Leave it to Beaver" star Jerry Mathers.

MURALS In downtown **Crestview**, local history pops up on the brick walls of the historic commercial district downtown in a series of murals. Peek down the side streets to see them.

Crossing the Mid-Bay Bridge (FL 293) from Niceville to **Destin**, you can't help but notice the largest mural in the region, **Whaling Wall #88** by Wyland, on the side of Mid-Bay Marina. What you can't see—but the pilots training out of Eglin Air Force Base can—is the 290-by-150-foot American flag that Wyland painted on the roof of the marina. Both were dedicated on October 17, 2001.

MUSEUMS AND HISTORIC SITES ♿ A century's worth of aviation warfare history is on display at the **Air Force Armament Museum** (850-882-4062, afarmamentmuseum .com), 100 Museum Drive, Eglin Air Force Base. You'll find an impressive selection of US aircraft and weaponry, along with similar items from around the world. Outside, walk or drive on a tour past two dozen aircraft, including a SR-71A Blackbird and a Soviet MIG-21. Inside the museum you can walk around carefully restored planes representing several war periods, such as the P-51 Mustang and F-105 Thunderchief. Monday–Saturday 9:30 AM–4:30 PM; closed federal holidays. Free.

North of Crestview in the small town of Baker, the **Baker Block Museum** (850-537-5714; bakerblockmuseum.org), 1307 Georgia Avenue (corner of FL 189 and CR 189), provides a pictorial history of rural Okaloosa County's cotton and lumber heritage with a dramatic mural; inside, browse through artifacts and archives, including extensive genealogical records. Historic farm buildings were brought in from their original rural settings surround the museum. Open Tuesday–Friday 10 AM–3:30 PM and third Saturday of the month. Free; donations appreciated.

♿ Consolidating regional history around the most notable feature in Fort Walton Beach, the Indian Temple Mound (see *Archaeological Sites*), **Heritage Park & Cultural Center** (850-833-9595; fwb.org/museums), 127 Miracle Strip Parkway SE, is the oldest and most extensive municipal museum in Florida. In addition to the notable ceremonial mound and its adjoining **Indian Temple Mound Museum**, the park includes the **Camp Walton Schoolhouse Museum**, a two-room schoolhouse that was part of the original community at Fort Walton between 1912 and 1936, with exhibits on Camp Walton's history; the **Garnier Post Office Museum**, opened in 1918 at Garnier, interpreting early postal history in the region; and the **Civil War Exhibit Building**, explaining the history of the Walton Guards and Camp Walton, the Battle of Santa Rosa Sound, and Pensacola's important role in the war. All museums (and temple mound) included in admission fee. 1–3 PM Monday–Saturday for historic structires, 10 AM–4:30 PM Monday–Saturday for Indian Temple Mound Museum.

One of the biggest surprises inside the extensive **Holmes County Historical Museum** (holmescountyhistory.com), 412 W Kansas Avenue, Bonifay, was Laura's

Room, telling the story of Laura Ingalls Wilder in Florida. In 1891, she and her husband Alonzo and daughter Rose moved to the rural community of New Hope near Westville, west of Bonifay, living with her cousin Peter, leaving a year later because the humidity was too much for them. The museum offers much more in the way of exhibits, from the art of turpentine collecting to the connection between moonshine and auto racing, and the history of the "Diver Down" flag. Artifacts like a vintage voting machine and medical equipment share a room with research materials and maps. Open second Saturday of each month 10 AM–2 PM, or by appointment.

&. ♂ Dig 12,000 years into the past at the **Heritage Museum of Northwest Florida** (850-678-2615; heritage-museum.org), 115 Westview Avenue, Valparaiso, which covers the sweeping history of this region, from prehistoric times to early pioneer families to military history, which you'd expect right outside the gates of Eglin AFB. A Discovery Room has hands-on displays for children. Open 10 AM–4 PM Tuesday–Saturday, fee.

An 1886 pioneer cabin on a rural family farm, **Keith Cabin** (561-549-9213; keithcabinfoundation.org), 1324 CR 179, Pittman, is Florida's only residential log home listed on the National Register of Historic Places. Managed by the Keith Cabin Foundation, it is still in a pastoral setting and used as the backdrop for special events.

Inside the L&N Train Depot (see *Railroadiana*), the **Walton County Heritage Museum** (850-951-2127), 1140 Circle Drive, leans toward interpretation of historic DeFuniak Springs because of its location, with exhibits on how the town grew out of the Chautauqua movement. But every nook and cranny of this train station has something in it, including a genealogical library and depictions of rural life in a region where farming is still big business. Tuesday–Saturday 1–4 PM. Free; donations appreciated.

&. ♂ Founded by the Ladies Library Association in 1886, the **Walton-DeFuniak Public Library** (850-892-3624), 3 Circle Drive, is Florida's oldest continuously operating library. The compact exterior belies a spacious interior with a wall of windows

MILITARY UNIFORMS AT THE HERITAGE MUSEUM OF NORTHWEST FLORIDA

affording a view of Lake DeFuniak. Inside its doors are not just books from every vintage, but some unusual artifacts gifted by the library by the Bruce family, including an outstanding collection of medieval armor and armaments. 9 AM–5 PM Wednesday–Monday, 9 AM–8 PM Tuesday.

Just off US 90 at Westville, FL 10A leads you past a tall wooden structure at the railroad tracks that was once the **Westville Post Office**. It's significance is tied to literary history, since Laura Ingalls Wilder posted letters to family from here while living in the region between 1891 and 1892. Continue north to Poplar Head to find the **Laura Ingalls Wilder Home Site**, 1225 CR 163 [30.962333, -85.919267], with its historic marker and picnic tables near where the "little gray house in the piney woods" once stood.

PERFORMING ARTS Broadway shows and musical events take center stage at the two-tiered, 1,650-seat Mainstage Theater at the **Mattie Kelly Fine & Performing Arts Center** at Northwest Florida State College (850-729-6000; mattiekellyartscenter.org), 100 College Boulevard, Niceville. Take particular note of the walls in the lobby, which are covered with fossilized Mexican limestone. The deep theater seating ensures that everyone is within 100 feet of the stage. For smaller performances on the square, 195-seat Sprint Theater offers options—show seating on two or three sides of the theater or an intimate theater in the round. Outside, the OWC Amphitheater houses up to 4,000 on sloping grounds for concerts and shows.

The Repertory Theatre (850-231-0733; lovetherep.com), 216 Quincy Circle, has been Seaside's place to go for live performances since 2001. Not only does this professional theatre company regularly perform inside the Seaside Meeting Hall Theatre, they do pop-up performances in public spaces in neighboring beach communities, ranging from improv and magic to classic tales and thoughtful plays.

RAILROADIANA Along Main Street in **Crestview**, watch for the **railroad mural** fronting the railroad tracks that cross the street. An **L&N caboose** sits on a siding adjoining the **L&N Train Depot** in DeFuniak Springs, where trains still fly through on an adjacent working track. Built in 1882, the depot was expanded in 1909 and once hosted more than 4,000 passengers a day. A nearby nondescript walkway used to lead disembarking passengers off the train and toward the hotels used by visitors to the Chautauqua. The depot is now home to the Walton County Heritage Museum.

STATE HIGH POINT At 345 feet, it's not rarified air. But Florida's high point—which is almost at the Alabama border—contains enough signs and monuments on **Britton Hill** that you'll need to decide which one makes the best backdrop for a selfie. A nature trail loops through Lakewood Park (floridahikes.com/lakewood-park), and here's the secret (shh!): the real highest elevation in the state is not where the markers are at the front of the park, but in the woods near a bench sponsored by highpointers.org.

WINERIES With its prominent location along Interstate 10, you can't miss **Chautauqua Vineyards** (850-892-5887; chautauquawinery.com), 364 Hugh Adams Road, DeFuniak Springs. Taking advantage of the ideal climate for growing native muscadine grapes, their vineyard is located 12 miles north, close to the state high point; the processing, blending, and aging happens here, as well as your opportunity to taste their products. Made from thicker-skinned grapes, their Noble Muscadine has a velvet-smooth taste. Blended with the white Carlos grape, it makes a lovely Blush Muscadine. The tasting room overlooks the production space with its stainless steel tanks; oak barrel aging is used as well. During the winter, enjoy a bit of wine with mulling spice, or sip a sangria

FLORIDA'S HIGH POINT AT LAKEWOOD PARK ON BRITTON HILL

slushie during the warmer months. Browse the gift shop for the full wine selection and related goodies like etched glassware, jams, and grapeseed oil. Open daily.

Emerald Coast Wine Cellars (850-837-9500; emeraldcoastwinecellars.com), 1708 Scenic Gulf Drive, Miramar Beach, features the wines of Chautauqua Vineyards minus the production facility. Instead, it's a boutique shop where you can taste the wines and learn more about them. Beach Berry is a perennial favorite at this seaside location.

✳ To Do

BIKING Sea breezes filter through the pines at **Point Washington State Forest** (850-267-8325; freshfromflorida.com), 5865 E US 98, Santa Rosa Beach, which protects more than 15,000 acres of South Walton County and is home to the **Eastern Lake Bike/Hike Trail**, with up to 10 miles of doubletrack riding through natural areas. The trailhead is on CR 395, 1 mile south of US 98. Primitive camping available along Eastern Lake. Fee.

On the southern portion of Eglin Air Force Base (see *Parks, Preserves, and Camping*), the **Timberlake Mountain Bike Trails** (850-882-4164; eglin.isportsman.net/MTB.aspx) include 21 miles of true mountain bike fun on rolling hills and through ravines with elevation changes of up to 50 feet. Nearly 20 named trails, color-coded for difficulty, extend from the Timberlake and Ranger trailheads off FL 189 and RR 234. Bikepackers: camping is permitted at Timberlake Camp. Before using the trails, you must stop by the Jackson Guard to get a recreational permit.

Adjoining 30A for most of its length, the 18-mile **Timpoochee Trail** (visitsouthwalton .com/tips-trips/a-guide-to-the-timpoochee-trail) starts in Dune Allen and ends in Rosemary Beach. It connects both beach access points and the parks of the coastal dune lakes (see *Coastal Dune Lakes*), sometimes even crossing the lakes along bridges, while leading you through coastal communities with restaurants and shops. Rent bikes or take a guided tour with 30A Bike Rentals (850-807-0597; 30Atours.com), $35+, bikes delivered to accommodations.

BIRDING 🐾 ♿ Perhaps the broadest stretch of marshlands for birding along this coast is Tucker Bayou; you can sit beside the bayou or walk along it on the trails of **Eden**

For dogs: Liza Jackson Park, Fort Walton Beach (bayside)
For kids: James Lee Park, Destin
For people-watching: Wayside Park, Okaloosa Island
For shelling: Seagrove Beach
For solitude: Topsail Hill State Park, Destin
For sunbathing: Grayton Beach
For walking: Okaloosa Island east of John Beasley Park

Except for dogs owned by residents of Walton County who can apply for a county dog permit, dogs are not permitted on the Gulf of Mexico beaches in this region.

Gardens State Park (see *Gardens*). Little **Laird Park** [30.50162, -86.145784], just west of downtown Freeport along FL 20, is a pretty spot for a picnic lunch and a bit of birding along the boardwalks above a clear, shallow creek. ♿ **Turkey Creek Park** (see *Tubing*) is another pleasant boardwalk along a winding waterway, an excellent spot for songbirds. And of course, the edges of the coastal dune lakes (see *Parks, Preserves, and Camping*) afford plenty of places to spot wading birds; Topsail Hill has the most extensive natural shorelines that you can follow along its trails.

DIVING Experienced divers enjoy exploring **Morrison Springs** (see *Springs*), a cypress-lined bowl of beauty feeding the Choctawhatchee River with three major vents in the spring descending to 50 feet; cave diving extends 300 feet underground.

At **Vortex Spring** (see *Dive Resort*), the PADI Discover Scuba Experience ($150) gets you into the water with an instructor before committing to a full certification course. The 28-million-gallon spring is a beautiful place for open-water divers to explore. If you're cavern-certified, you can go deep to see the spring basin 50 feet down, lit well through the gin-clear water. Gear rentals are available. Nondiving visitors are welcome to snorkel the spring and lengthy spring run. Fee; additional diving pass, $20, allows night dives up until 11 PM for guests staying at the resort.

ECOTOURS 🐟 Take the family on a boat trip they won't forget—a glass-bottom boat for dolphin watching out of Destin Harbor at **Boogies Watersports** (850-654-4497; boogieswatersports.com), 2 Harbor Boulevard at the foot of Destin Bridge. Narrated cruises sail three times daily at 10 AM, 2 PM, and 6 PM, $29 adults, $16 ages 3–14. For a more unique experience, take a two-hour guided Waverunner tour to follow the dolphins, 9–11 AM daily; $145 for up to 3 passengers or 400 lbs.

FAMILY ACTIVITIES 🐟 Part water, all adventure, **Big Kahuna's Water & Adventure Park** (850-837-8319; bigkahunas.com), 1007 US 98 E, Destin, is a splash park with a twist. There's something for everyone, with high-adrenaline pipeline speed slides, spectacular splash fountains, a lazy river, and a pirate ship splash zone for the little ones. At the adventure side of the park you can play aerial daredevil on the Skycoaster or Cyclone, putt through the mini golf on a tropically landscaped course, or hang ten on a body board on the Honolulu Half Pipe. It's worth buying the season pass ($65) if you plan more than one visit; daily tickets are $33/$43. Open daily.

🐟 Go retro at **Downtown Cinema Plus** (850-200-4707; downtowncinemaplus.com), 174 Miracle Strip Parkway SE, Fort Walton Beach, with first-run movies in the 1940s-era Tringa's Theatre. It's a cozy space that still shows off those original lines, with one exception: the seats have been changed out for tables and chairs so you can nosh and drink as you enjoy the show. Tickets $5.

✐ Get the kids interested in science at the **Emerald Coast Science Center** (850-664-1261; ecscience.org), 139 Brooks Street, Fort Walton Beach, with hands-on activities in robotics, physics, color, and light; the new Emerald Coast Ecosystem Exhibit includes a pitcher plant toss, sand dune model, and augmented reality sandbox to play in as you learn how rainfall erodes a landscape. Monday–Saturday 10 AM–4 PM, fee.

✐ It's so old-fashioned even grandparents will want to stop for this one: **Goofy Golf** (850-862-4922; goofygolffwb.com), 401 Eglin Parkway NE, opened in 1958, and features Hammy the T-Rex for a Flintstones feel; the twin mini-golf courses are open late; $1.50 ages 12 and under, $3 adults, cash only.

✐ At **The Track Destin** (850-654-5832; funatthetrack.com/parks/destin), 1125 US 98 E, Destin, take a spin on the classic Family Track or put your go-cart to an old-fashioned seaside thrill with the multilevel Wild Woody, a wooden track. The Slick Track ensures plenty of spins and caroms off the walls. But this isn't just about go-carts. Bumper Cars and Blaster Boats offer silly family fun; more serious thrill-seekers can go for the SkyFlyer, with its views of the beach, or take a spin on the Hurricane 360, a ride that'll have you in knots. Sweet kiddie rides like the Groovy Bus are just perfect for tiny tots. Open daily except major holidays; rides cost $1 "per point," so check their online points chart to purchase a package that works for your family.

✐ A Bass Pro spinoff, **Uncle Buck's Fish Bowl and Grill** (850-269-6100; restaurants .basspro.com/UncleBucksFishBowl/Destin) at Destin Commons (see *Shopping*) has to be seen to be believed. It mixes family dining with 16 lanes of bowling, sporting a unique underwater theme. Unlike traditional bowling alleys, you rent the lane (up to eight can play) for $35/hour, shoe rental extra.

FISHING Given that **Destin** was founded as a fishing village, you won't find a better place to locate a captain than on a walk through **HarborWalk Marina** (850-650-2400; harborwalkmarina.net). Have your plan in mind before choosing one: offshore/deep-water fishing means more time on the boat, less time casting; inshore means more opportunities to catch fish. When going on an excursion, no fishing license is required; bait, tackle, and ice are provided, and some outfitters will clean and filet your catch for you. For a custom-tailored experience, **HarborWalk Charters** (888-976-4568; harbor walkfishingcharters.com), 10 Harbor Boulevard, will match you up with the right captain and others interested in fishing at the location to which you're headed; group charters start at $125/person for 4 hours.

✐ Head offshore aboard the ***American Spirit*** (850-837-1293; americanspiritparty boatfishing.com), 116 Harbor Boulevard, with Captain Jim Green guiding the largest fishing vessel in the Destin fleet out into open waters for snapper, triggerfish, sea bass, flounder, and grouper. Up to 80 people can fish off the 92-foot craft, with trips starting at $50 adults, $25 ages 12 and under for 4 hours on the water.

For inshore fishing, **Backcountry Outfitters** (850-391-5566; backcountry outfittersdestin.com), 214 Harbor Boulevard, will take you into the shallow flats to fish for speckled trout, redfish, and tarpon, day or night.

Deep sea fishing boats ***Swoop I & II*** (850-337-8250; swooppartyboat.com), 66 Harbor Boulevard, depart on 5- to 8-hour trips with up to 45 passengers on board, seeking amberjack, snapper, cobia, and more. Adult rates start at $69; private charters available.

GOLF ⛳ Enjoy the sweeping view of Choctawhatchee Bay at Fred Couple's signature par-72, 18-hole golf course at **Kelly Plantation** (850-650-7600; kellyplantationgolf

.com), 307 Kelly Plantation Drive, Destin, just west of Mid Bay Bridge, a challenging 7,099-yard course. At **Indian Bayou Golf Club** (850-837-6192; indianbayougolf.com), 1 Country Club Drive, choose from three courses to play a quick nine-hole game or combine any two for a more relaxed 18 holes of golf.

HIKING Thanks to the hilly nature of the landscape through this region—this is the home of Florida's high point (see *State High Point*), after all—backpackers experience an elevation-rich traverse of the **Florida Trail** through **Eglin Air Force Base** (floridahikes .com/floridatrail/eglin) for more than 40 miles; Eglin recreation permit required. In adjoining **Nokuse Plantation** (floridahikes.com/floridatrail/tag/nokuse), day-hike or backpack through ravines, across swamps, and beneath tall longleaf pines for nearly 30 miles. Shorter hikes are otherwise the norm, although **Topsail Hill Preserve** (see *Coastal Dune Lakes*) distinguishes itself with more than 10 miles of meandering roads and footpaths.

PADDLING The unique **coastal dune lakes** of this region are perfect for kayak or SUP; the state parks along their shores ask that you use their rentals rather than bring your own, to avoid introducing non-native vegetation or bacteria.

More than 100 miles of paddling trails span the backcountry of **Eglin Air Force Base** (eglin.isportsman.net/CanoeKayak.aspx), with some of them open to overnight camping. Popular runs include the 9.5-mile **Titi Creek**, up to 6 miles on **Turkey Creek** (see *Tubing*), the crystal-clear 5-mile **Boiling Creek**, and the multiday 34-mile **Shoal River** paddle. An Eglin recreation permit is required.

PARASAILING At **Sun Dogs Parasail** (850-259-1898; sundogsparasaildestin.com), 116 Harbor Boulevard, Destin, you can float unbelievably high—at the end of 1,200 feet of line!—above the Gulf or the bay on single, double, or triple parasails, $45–65. **Boogies Watersports** (see *Ecotours*) also offers parasailing.

PARKS, PRESERVES, AND CAMPING Originally the Choctawhatchee National Forest, established in 1908 by executive order by Theodore Roosevelt, **Eglin Air Force Base** became the prime use for what was working federally owned timberland at the start of World War II. Encompassing most of the forested land between Crestview, DeFuniak Springs, Niceville, and Freeport, it offers public recreation at a variety of locations, all of which require an Eglin Recreation Permit (eglin.isportsman.net), which can be obtained online or in person at the Jackson Guard/Eglin Natural Resources (850-882-4165; jacksonguard.com), 107 FL 85 North, Niceville. Some permits, such as those for camping, must be obtained in person at this office, which has displays about recreation and the role of the Jackson Guard. Before heading to the base for any type of recreational activity, consult the daily Public Access Map posted on the Jackson Guard website or call their office to ensure where you're headed isn't closed for military training. Base recreation encompasses campgrounds, hiking and biking trails, and paddling trails.

🎪 ⚒ ✒ Scenic nature trails and great fishing on the tidal bayou draw visitors to **Fred Gannon Rocky Bayou State Park** (850-833-9144; floridastateparks.org/park/Rocky -Bayou), 4281 FL 20, Niceville, on an arm of Choctawhatchee Bay. Their campground balances amenities, settings, and distances in a perfect mix. A cool breeze off the bayou combines with the low sand live oak canopy to keep the 42 well-shaded campsites naturally pleasant. Walk in either direction, and you'll find trails. Fish right off the beach or take the kids over to the playground on the bluffs. Add a camp chair and a good book to relax and enjoy, $16+.

OCEANFRONT AT HENDERSON BEACH STATE PARK

On the south side of Choctawhatchee Bay, **Gulf Islands National Seashore Okaloosa Day Use Area** (850-934-2600; nps.gov/guis/planyourvisit/okaloosa-day-use-area.htm), 1801 Gulf Breeze Parkway, is a popular swimming beach and a launch point for windsurfing.

   Sandwiched by the unrelenting press of urban development, **Henderson Beach State Park** (850-837-7550; floridastateparks.org/park/Henderson-Beach), 17000 Emerald Coast Parkway, Destin is an oasis on the ocean where the boom of the surf can drown out traffic noise along more than a mile of beach. Pets are welcome on the nature trail that loops the dunes, but not on the beach. Camp in a full-service campground: the 54 sites are tucked behind the dunes, so you see neither the hustle and bustle nor Destin nor the beach, but you can hear the waves roar when the surf is up, $30+. Fee.

SCENIC DRIVE Take a drive along **Scenic CR 30A** for an overview of the rare coastal dune lakes found along this coastline between Destin and Panama City Beach; it's the only place in the United States with these unique ecosystems. There are 17 dune lakes along this route, starting at the western end with Stalworth Lake, the focal point in Dune Allen. Oyster Lake is named for its oyster-like shape. The highest point on the Gulf of Mexico in the United States is at Blue Mountain Beach; it's 62 feet above sea level.

SPRINGS At **Morrison Springs** (850-892-8108; co.walton.fl.us/523/Morrison-Springs), 874 Morrison Springs Road, a 161-acre county park encompassing the haunting spring and its run, ancient cypress trees tower over the turquoise waters, a popular swimming and diving destination (see *Diving*). Paddlers can put in at the boat ramp farther down the run for a trip to the Choctawhatchee; GPS advised for navigating the sometimes-confusing floodplain. Sunrise–sunset daily, free.

Chalky blue 68-degree water tempts swimmers to take a chilly dip at **Ponce de Leon Springs State Park** (850-836-4281; floridastateparks.org/poncedeleon springs), 2860 Ponce de Leon Springs Road, in this first-magnitude spring, gushing forth 14 million gallons of water daily. Fish, picnic, or walk the nature trails through the lush hardwood forest. Fee.

Vortex Spring (850-836-4979), 1517 Vortex Spring Road, Ponce De Leon, open since 1972 as a diver's destination (see *Dive Resort*) with a campground, is an expansive natural water park as well. The swimming section—open for summer fun—is delightful for families, with high dives and swings into the spring run, water toys, and even a treehouse in the woods with a slide down to the water. Nature trails loop through the Otter Creek floodplain, and they're happy to launch you on a kayak or canoe trip down Blue Creek. Fee; $20 for a dive pass. Open daily.

THE SWIMMING AREA AT VORTEX SPRINGS, OPEN SEASONALLY

KITEBOARDING At Gulf Islands National Seashore on Okaloosa Island (see *Parks, Preserves, and Camping*), the winds on **Choctawhatchee Bay** draw kiteboarders and wind-surfers. Learn the craft first from **Liquid Surf & Sail** (850-664-5731; flkiteboarding.com), where lessons from qualified instructors will get you shooting the breeze in no time. $75 for a rental, $250 for three hours of semiprivate lessons.

TUBING ✎ Bring-your-own-tube family fun awaits at **Turkey Creek Park** (850-729-4062; floridahikes.com/turkeycreek), 340 John Sims Parkway W, Niceville, where during daylight hours you can walk on the boardwalk out to any of several launch points and float down the chilly, clear stream to the final take-out. Swimming, snorkeling, and paddling are part of the fun, too, and it's a pleasant, breezy walk on a warm day. Open from 6:30 AM; closes before sunset. Free.

WALKING TOURS With our guide Christopher Mitchell in period garb, we took a stroll back in time along the residential streets of **DeFuniak Springs** (defuniaksprings.com/walking-tour), a virtual cornucopia of Victoriana surrounding Lake DeFuniak. Intentionally established as the winter home for the New York Chautauqua program, the community reflects the grand ideals of the day. Departing from the Walton County Heritage Museum (see *Museums and Historic Sites*) at the L&N Train Depot, we visited the Octagon House, the Library, St. Agatha's, and the Pansy House with stops along the way in front of numerous Victorian homes. Check with the museum regarding guided tours, or use their outline online to circle the lake yourself. In October of each year, the **Haunted History Tours of Downtown Fort Walton Beach** (downtownfwb.com) takes you inside the community's mysterious past on a 90-minute tour.

COASTAL DUNE LAKES

Unique to this section of Florida's coastline—and to the United States, at that—are a series of freshwater lakes known as the coastal dune lakes. While each is fed by streams and rainfall, it isn't until the lake level reaches a certain tipping point that the tannic water flows across the beach and out into the sea, called an outfall. Conversely, a

WESTERN LAKE, ONE OF THE COASTAL DUNE LAKES

✳ Lodging

BED & BREAKFASTS 🐾 🏕 🛶 ♿ ♂ **Hibiscus Coffee & Guesthouse** (850-231-2733; hibiscusflorida.com), 85 DeFuniak Street, Grayton Beach 32459, is a slice of Old Florida with a room for everyone among the dozen rooms within this inn. Couples will want the Romance Room, with its king-size bed and supersize Jacuzzi for two. In the Hibiscus Room, you'll find an antique clawfoot tub in the bathroom. More than a century ago, the now-wheelchair-accessible Big Easy Room was the kitchen; it currently sits detached from the house. The Woodpecker Cottage is a cozy suite looking out over the garden. Pets are welcome in the Art Deco and the Funky Bird rooms; five of the rooms are child friendly, with

cots or cribs provided. Enjoy a hot breakfast in the morning or pop in the coffeeshop during the day. Rooms $135–285, minimum two-night stays on weekends.

Lisbeth's (850-231-1577; lisbethsbb .com), 3501 E CR 30A, Seagrove Beach 32459, offers a view of the Gulf of Mexico from its verandas and a short walk to either the beach or the picturesque town of Seaside. "We are not the Ritz Carlton," says Lisbeth, "but my house is clean, the beds are soft, and our breakfasts are hot." Five themed, spacious rooms, $110–285, have queen and king brass canopied and poster beds; some offer a Jacuzzi and fireplace. Minimum weekend stays apply to some rooms.

TRIED AND TRUE Chain motels and brand-name resorts are the mainstays of the smaller communities, with a

high tide or storm surge will push saltwater into these freshwater lakes, creating periods of brackishness. Recognizing their rarity, both state and county began to preserve land around them, although a few have been lost to development. There are 15 named coastal dune lakes along the 26 miles of coastline in Walton County (co.walton.fl.us), some of which you'll find within these oceanfront parks.

Watching the outfall at **Deer Lake State Park** (850-267-8300; floridastateparks.org/park/Deer-Lake), 6350 E CR 30-A, the contrast of this wild space is striking against the development up to the lake's western edge. Rare spoonflower and Gulf Coast lupine grow in the coastal habitats surrounding the dunes. A boardwalk across the dunes provides beach access and sweeping views of the dunes; walk west on the beach to see the outfall. Fee.

   With nearly 2,000 acres of coastal dunes, coastal scrub, pine flatwoods, and beachfront, **Grayton Beach State Park** (850-231-4210; floridastateparks.org/park/Grayton-Beach), 357 Main Park Road, is one of Northwest Florida's most beautiful state parks. Paddle across Western Lake or walk the nature trail to scenic overlooks from the dunes. Offering both cabins and campsites, the 37-site campground also has 30 fully furnished cabins. Either way, you'll have early access to sunrise watching over the dune lakes. Campsites $24–30, cabins $130. Fee.

   It's the dunes that give **Topsail Hill Preserve State Park** (877-232-2478; floridastateparks.org/park/Topsail-Hill), 7525 W CR 30A, its name, some topping 25 feet. Cradled between them are two of the larger coastal dune lakes, Campbell Lake and Morris Lake, edged by a surprising diversity of habitats that include pitcher plant bogs and cypress swamps. Rent bikes, canoes, kayaks, and paddleboards to explore around the lakes. The campground, a former RV park, is a destination in itself—Gregory E. Moore RV Campground off CR 30A has 156 sites with full hookups including cable, set in a diminutive coastal scrub forest and pine flatwoods, $42. Amenities include a heated swimming pool, shuffleboard, and private tram access to the beach. If you don't have a big rig, consider renting one of their 29 cabins or bungalows, available daily or weekly, $120–145. Tent campers are also welcome, $24. Fee.

densely packed collection of brands at the Crestview interchange on I-10 and along US 98 on Okaloosa Island and Destin. The **Ramada Plaza Fort Walton Beach** (850-243-9161; wyndhamhotels.com), 1500 Miracle Strip Parkway SE, is within a safe walk of the Gulfarium Marine Adventure Park (see *Aquarium*), has two large pools, and is on the beach, making it a nice choice for families. Chain lodgings we like in Destin include **Home2 Suites Destin** (850-650-3500; hilton.com), 14060 Emerald Coast Parkway, with family-friendly spaces with urban chic decor and moveable furnishings; and **Fairfield Inn** (850-654-8611; marriott.com), 19001 Emerald Coast Parkway, across from Henderson Beach State Park. Another that's recommended is the **Holiday Inn Express**

Niceville (850-678-9131; ihg.com), 106 Bayshore Drive, Niceville.

Since the last edition, we've stayed at the **Comfort Inn & Suites** (850-682-1481; choicehotels.com), 900 Southcrest Drive, Crestview, which sits uphill from the crowd of accomodations along busy SR 85; the **Holiday Inn Express DeFuniak** (850-520-4660; ihg.com), 326 Coy Burgess Loop, DeFuniak Springs, with large comfortable rooms and a friendly staff; and the **Best Western Crossroads Inn** (850-892-5111; bestwestern.com), 2343 US 331, DeFuniak Springs, the original hotel at the same interchange of I-10, with smaller but still clean rooms and the convenience of parking outside your door.

VACATION RENTALS For Destin and the oceanfront communities of 30A, vacation rentals, both homes and condos, dominate the scene, with **Emerald Grande** (800-676-0091; emeraldgrande .com) and **Sandestin Golf and Beach Resort** (800-622-1038; sandestin.com) in the thick of the all-inclusive action. See *What's Where* in the front of the book to find out how to navigate this complex accommodation market, as well as how to read any leases carefully.

CAMPGROUNDS (y) 🐾 🦴 ♿ Bring your rig or settle into a cabin with a private bath at **Camp Gulf** (850-837-6334; campgulf.com), 10005 Emerald Coast Parkway, Destin 32541. Located centrally in Destin with its own beach access, it makes a good base camp for exploring the area with your family. The kids will love the sleeping lofts in the cabins and two pools for swimming. Pets are welcome in some cabins; request in advance. Campsites start at $64, cabins at $130, with the highest pricing in spring.

🐾 🦴 (y) **Sunset King Lake RV Resort** (850-892-7229 or 800-774-5454; sunsetking.com), 366 Paradise Island Drive, DeFuniak Springs 32433, has direct access to King Lake and is a favorite of folks seeking big bass from their boat. Campsites are set in a forested area, with all hookups (including cable) and pull-through sites available ($40). Rental units include beautiful log cabins and cottages, fully furnished, for $80 (two-night minimum for weekends).

DIVE RESORT **Vortex Spring** (850-836-4979; vortexspring.com), 1517 Vortex Spring Lane, Ponce de Leon 32455, is the largest private diving facility in Florida, owned and operated by active divers. The 420-acre complex includes the 68-degree spring, a campground, and five lodges. **The Pinewood Lodge** has eight 4-person rooms ($75 per room) upstairs with private bath and television, with 20-person shared-bath dorms ($80 + $12 per person, bring your own linens) below. **Otter Creek Lodge** offers six kitchenettes ($96) and a variety of large

bunkrooms sleeping up to six, each with private baths. The **Grandview Lodge** has two home-away-from-home kitchenettes sleeping up to four ($120) and **The Treasure Chest** is a home, four-bedroom/ two-bath with full kitchen, accommodating 20 for $275 and up. Add in campsites ranging from full hookups to primitive, $23–32, beneath the pines, and three large camping cabins along the waterfront, $90, and you should be able to find the rustic experience you're looking for on a getaway to the spring.

✳ Where to Eat

ELEGANT AND ROMANTIC Defining fine dining for DeFuniak Springs, **Bogey's Bar and Restaurant** (850-951-2233), 660 Baldwin Avenue, delights with Chef Brad Harding's creative preparations, with nine different ways to enjoy the catch of the day. Grouper Lorenzo, sautéed with a grilled lump blue crab cake that was mostly crab, topped with béarnaise sauce, made for a filling meal before we touched any sides. But we couldn't skip dessert, not with a Bananas Foster ice cream cake worth a dessert-and-coffee stop on any evening. Fine steaks, veal, and chicken ensure an array of choices for every palate; sandwiches and salads dominate the lunch menu. Entrées, $16–37. Open 11 AM–2 PM and 5–8 PM Tuesday–Friday, dinner only on Saturday.

🐾 Enjoy great gumbo in a historical 1910 Florida home at **Magnolia Grill** (850-302-0266; magnoliagrillfwb.com), 157 Brooks Street, Fort Walton Beach, "the museum that serves food." The house was one of many of the period that were mail-ordered and shipped by train in a complete kit ready for assembly, with bricks for the chimneys and cupboards for the kitchen. The home is still in pristine vintage condition with many original components, such as the brick fireplace and left-and-right bookcases, windows that still open with ropes and pulleys, and cupboards still containing the wavy glass typical of that period. You'll also want to take note of the board marked DR. G. G. FRENCH, CAMP WALTON, FLA., which was the mailing label for the assembly kit. The fine-dining eatery features dishes such as filet mignon served with green peppercorn and mushroom sauce, and blackened amberjack, a local fish, served with rice on a crawfish étouffée ($14–36). You'll also find more than a dozen Italian entrées on the menu. Lunch 11 AM–2 PM weekdays; dinner Monday–Thursday 5–8 PM, Friday and Saturday 5–9 PM.

BARBECUE Definitely delicious Tex-as-style barbecue awaits at **4C BBQ Family Restaurant** (850-892-4BBQ; 4CBBQ .com), 1045 US 331, DeFuniak Springs, at once laid-back *and* entertaining in its open space at the end of a strip mall. Live music takes center stage some nights, but you can't upstage the brisket, or the smoked wings, or the smoked tuna dip and fresh tortilla chips, for that matter. Sandwiches, salads, and platters, $7–18.

Savory smoked pork awaits at **Buck's Smokehouse** (850-837-3600; buckssmokehouse.com), 303 Harbor Boulevard, Destin. The daily lunch special, $10 for a BBQ pork sandwich with side and drink, makes for a quick stop during a busy day. This being Destin, smoked mullet is also on the menu, as is smoked tuna dip. Sandwiches and platters, $6–24.

Mac and cheese figures heavily on the menu at **M&W Smokehouse BBQ** (850-547-2200; facebook.com/mandw-barbecue), 609 W US 90, Bonifay, a down-home family barbecue on one side of Doc's Market, a rope's throw from the rodeo grounds in Bonifay. Eclectic choices include the Southern Comfort potato stuffed with mac and cheese, collard greens, and chicken tenders; the Mac Attack Sandwich with BBQ pork and mac and cheese on a bun; and the Smokehouse Salad with BBQ chicken, almonds, and grapes. Tuesday–Saturday 10:30 AM–9 PM.

CASUAL FARE Inside **Donut Hole Cafe & Bakery** (850-837-8824), 635 Harbor Boulevard, Destin, it's always time for breakfast, with selections like Gulf Coast Crabmeat Benedict, the Super Egg Sandwich, Texas Sweet Potato Pancakes, and a Bayou Omelet, $7–12; lunch sandwiches are on the menu, too. Grab a donut or a sticky bun for later!

🎣🍴 Established in 1964, **Ed's Restaurant** (850-892-5839), 1324 US 90 W, DeFuniak Springs, is the "home of the Pub Burger," so of course we had to join the lunch crowd for one. The burger was perfect—no oozing, firm and meaty, covered the plate, and no sides are needed unless you're ravenous or sharing. Walk down and order to go or sit inside and cool own on a hot day while savoring a butterscotch shake—this is a Tastee Freeze ice cream shop, too. The shakes are so thick you have to eat them with a spoon! 6:30 AM–9 PM; closed Sunday.

Part antique shop, part restaurant, **Red Clover Emporium & Café** (850-315-4952), 5 Racetrack Road NW, Fort Walton Beach, is a sweet lunch find. Try Shane's grilled cheese, bacon, and tomato, or a slice of the quiche of the day with soup and salad; we met up with friends there, and all of us were delighted with our meals. $6–9. Monday–Friday 10:30 AM–3-ish PM.

Grab breakfast or a healthy lunch of wraps, salads, or sandwiches at **Summer Kitchen** (850-231-6264; summerkitchencafe.blogspot.com), 60 N Barrett Square, Rosemary Beach, a delightful eatery boasting the best burgers around. Breakfast and lunch daily, dinners Wednesday–Sunday 5–9 PM.

COMFORT FOOD 🍴 **Bruce Café** (850-835-2946), corner of FL 20 and FL 81, Bruce. Generals and lumberjacks rub elbows at this great family café, where Lillie Mae serves up inexpensive specials like beef tips, fried chicken, and barbecued pork with three country-style veggies on the side. Seat yourself and look over the menu board, which includes burgers and a pork chop sandwich. Closed Sunday and Monday.

A 1950s-style lunch counter with a loyal following, **Desi's Downtown Restaurant** (850-682-5555), 197 N Main Street, Crestview, offers up an affordable lunch-only buffet laden with Southern favorites like roast chicken, ribs, fried fish, cheese grits, greens, and three kinds of peas: black-eyed, zipper, and field.

In a vintage home along the waterfront of Boggy Bayou, **Front Porch** (850-897-1027), 306 Bayshore Drive, dishes up delicious spins on comfort food. While the French Toast—made with cinnamon and cream in the batter—was divine, it was tempting to order the Taco Omelette, which had exactly what you'd expect in it, topped with homemade guacamole. Open for lunch and dinner, $7 and up.

For that morning cup, **Joe & Eddie's Family Restaurant** (850-243-0733; joeandeddies.com), 400 N Eglin Parkway, Fort Walton Beach, is a must for earlier risers, as they start serving breakfast ar 5:30 AM. A hometown diner that opened in 1954, it's still buzzing at every meal. Their lunch/dinner specials include perennial Southern favorites like country fried steak, fried or grilled catfish, chicken livers, and fried pork chops, $8–13.

After a long day of hiking, we adjourned with friends to **McLain's Family Steakhouse** (850-892-2402), 622 Hugh Adams Road, DeFuniak Springs. You can order from the menu or take the buffet, and given the wide range of foods you'll find on it—good traditional Southern foods, of course—the buffet is your best bet.

For good old-fashioned comfort food, step inside **Tropical Palm Restaurant** (850-682-5532), 286 N Main Street, Crestview, and order up a stack of pancakes or a BLT. It's been a local favorite for more than 40 years, and you'll find it quite busy at lunchtime. Open 5:30 AM–2 PM.

ETHNIC EATS For nouveau tastes with an Asian twist, **Fusion Bistro**

LUNCH AT RED CLOVER FORT WALTON BEACH

(850-460-7775; qfusionbistro.com), 4100 Legendary Drive at Destin Commons, serves up entrées like Tamarind Fish and Volcano Shrimp in "fusion boxes" with sides ranging from steamed rice to french fries and thai carrot soup, $10–12. Their cool smoothies are worth popping in for while you're shopping!

Perhaps it's the oversize 2-4-1 margaritas, or the extensive selection of Mexican entrées that you don't see at most Mexican restaurants, or the just plain goodness of their meals, but you'll rarely find **La Rumba** (850-951-2174), 1317 US 331, without a crowd inside. 11 AM–10 PM; closed Sunday.

The lively Irish folk music and traditional eats at **McGuire's Irish Pub and Brewery** (850-654-0567; mcguiresirishpub.com), 33 US 98, Destin, will keep you going until after midnight. You'll find healthy portions of traditional Irish pub fare along with a wide selection of seafood, steaks, and chops ($11–33); the Senate Bean Soup is still only 18¢, as long as it's purchased with something else! Sing-alongs are encouraged, and at times mandated. Daily 11 AM–11 PM; light fare served until 1:30 AM.

Tucked between buildings at **Main Street Eats**, 147 N Main Street,

Crestview, a food truck court featured Tony & Manolo's Curbside Cuban Concoctions and Mongo's Grill on our visit, with patio tables set out between them for you to enjoy Greek tacos and carnitas. Vendors may vary depending on the season.

Seafood dishes come in a surprising selection at **Peppers Mexican Grill and Cantina** (850-613-6970; peppersmexicangrillandcantina.com), 1176 Eglin Parkway, Fort Walton Beach, with a variety of preparations of fresh local shrimp and fresh grilled filets in familiar tortillas with traditional garnishes. The expected Mexican standards, from chimichangas to fajitas, are here as well, along with an overstuffed wet burrito, $7–26.

HIP BISTRO-STYLE When they bring out the skillet at **Asiago's Skillet** (850-586-7998; asiagoskillet.com), 110 Amberjack Drive, Okaloosa Island, it's full of breakfast delights, from a spicy chorizo omelet to country fried steak, seafood, Bananas foster French toast, and even the King of the Biscuits. This is not your typical breakfast place—they're open for the night shift, midnight to noon—but you won't walk away hungry. Breakfast only, $5–15.

🐾 🐙 The oldest restaurant in this newish town, **Bud & Alleys** (850-231-5900; budandalleys.com), 2236 CR 30A E, Seaside, consistently rates as one of Florida's top restaurants. The views from the rooftop bar are phenomenal. Founded by a couple of surfing buddies, the casual atmosphere and top-notch food seal the deal. Shrimp and grits, Bud & Alley's crabcakes, and grilled veggies from local farms make the lunch menu, at $10–18, pop. Dinner is meant to be savored with the sunset, featuring entrées like seared diver scallops with creamy grits, and grilled chicken breast with mashed Yukon Gold potatoes, $30–39. Looking for something more laid-back? Check out their Taco Bar and Pizza Bar, extensions of the restaurant complex that are lighter on the wallet and sure to please the picky eaters in your family.

🐾 At **The Red Bar / Piccolo's** (850-231-1008; theredbar.com), 70 Holz Avenue, Grayton Beach, capture the pre-condo past of this coastline, when this strip was all about surfing, fishing, and hanging out at the beach. Listen to live music—the Red Bar Jazz Band—while lounging in the red velvet living room. This comfy, kitschy restaurant serves some of the best burgers around, along with treats like baked eggplant, shrimp and crawfish, smoked salmon salad, and Belgian waffles, $9–22. Cash or check only, open daily for lunch and dinner.

At **Wild Olives Market & Cafe** (850-231-0065; wildolivesmarket.info), 29 Canal Street, Rosemary Beach, you can shop for specialty groceries or order lunch salads, sandwiches, pizza, and hot meals to go. The tapas menu is great for a late-afternoon snack.

OCEANFRONT ♿ 🦮 A 12-foot giraffe greets you at the door at **Harry T's** (850-654-4800; harryts.com), 46 Harbor Boulevard, Destin, a souvenir from the circus days of "Flying Harry T." Despite its playful feel, Harry T's is a fine dining destination with grown-up food like almond-crusted chicken salad, grouper florentine, cashew-crusted mahi, and classic seafood steamers. The sweeping ocean view makes this a perfect place to slowly savor a meal. Entrées $15–49; the weekend brunch includes creative breakfast offerings.

QUICK BITE 🐾 Since 1947, tiny **H&M Hot Dog** (850-892-9100), 43 S 9th Street, has been a place where you can walk right up to the lunch counter window and place your order. The hot dogs and hamburgers are cooked to order, and the sides are carefully handmade, carrying on the tradition that Harley and Margaret Broxson started. Enjoy your meal at the picnic table underneath the adjacent arbor. Open Monday–Saturday 10 AM–6 PM.

SEAFOOD Oysters, plain or dressed, are the pride and joy of **A.J.'s Oyster Shanty** (850-226-8108; oystershanty.com), 108 Santa Rosa Boulevard, Okaloosa Island, and in ways you wouldn't have imagined: Wild Buffalo; Oysters AJ's, topped with jalapenos, jack, and bacon; or BBQ Oysters baked in a New Orleans style barbecue sauce. Try a sampler of flavors, or go with the gentler Italiano for a hint of spice; all are fresh shucked on-site, $10–17. Seafood sandwiches and lunch plates, burgers, and New Orleans–inspired dishes extend the menu, which also includes steamed snow crab.

Soak in the view at **Nick's Seafood Restaurant** (850-835-2222; nicksseafoodrestaurant.com), 7585 FL 20 W, Freeport, but if you're not facing the picture windows overlooking the sweep of Choctawhatchee Bay at Basin Bayou, no problem—the real reason for eating at this family-owned restaurant established in 1963 is the seafood. Trey and Jennifer Nick oversee preparation of the fresh catch, which you can enjoy with their just-perfect cheese grits and fried okra. The Fat Hattie ($13)—a pick two out of three seafood options—is what most diners had on their table, including us. 11 AM–8:30 PM Tuesday–Sunday, closed Monday–Tuesday in January.

At **Stewby's Seafood Shanty** (850-586-7001; stewbys.com), 427 Racetrack Road NW, Fort Walton Beach, you step up to the window (or drive up to the drive-thru window) and order dinners or "samwiches," fried or grilled, then settle down on a picnic bench on the porch while you wait for some of the freshest seafood you'll find around here, served no-frills on plasticware. Light breading makes the fried options a delight. Pick cheese grits as one of your two dinner sides or check the specials, as the grilled zucchini is awesome too. $8–17.

WATERFRONT Relax at sunset along Cinco Bayou and listen to old-time rock 'n' roll as color fades across the water: that's what **AJ's on the Bayou** (850-226-7579; ajsonthebayou.com), 200 Eglin Parkway NE, is all about. You'll always find more patrons outside than inside when the weather's fine, nibbling on appetizers like smoked tuna dip or calamari or dining on chef's specials like a whole fried snapper with creole hollandaise, or smoked pulled pork tacos with pineapple slaw, served up with tropical drinks. Sandwiches, baskets, and entrées $11–29, live music nightly.

LOCAL WATERING HOLES Just 1 mile east of the Destin Bridge is the world-famous **Hog's Breath Café** (850-837-5991; hogsbreath.com), 541 US 98. Established in 1976, this is the original café with a cousin in Key West. The saloon features live music, a restaurant and raw bar, great beer, and even fishing charters. Open daily for lunch and dinner.

ICE CREAM AND SWEETS ✿ The "Grouchy Old Candymaker," Tom Ehlke, isn't so grumpy after all. Once he decided there had to be a better saltwater taffy, he set his sights on a shop up in Destin, **The Candymaker** (850-654-0833; thecandymaker.com), 757 US 98 E, and since 1992 he's been satisfying locals and tourists alike, not only with his saltwater taffy but other confections as well. You'll find sumptuous delights like crunchy, rich, South Georgia–style pralines; creamy, buttery fudge; and chewy caramels.

✿ For a cool treat, **Shake's Frozen Custard** (850-269-1111; shakesfrozencustard.com), 1065 US 98 E, Destin, is the place to be. Made fresh every hour, the smooth and creamy frozen concoction contains no fillers or preservatives and is never fluffed up with air. The signature Shake's Bopper contains a monstrous three scoops of creamy frozen custard, caramel, and hot fudge.

✱ Selective Shopping

ANTIQUES **De'France Indoor Flea Market Antiques & Collectibles** (850-314-7500;

defranceantiques.com), 230 Miracle Strip Parkway, Fort Walton Beach, is busy with furnishings and home decor that graced many a home during our childhoods, and it has a devout following for its ever-changing stock.

The **Fort Walton Beach Flea Market** (850-301-3729), 125 SE Eglin Parkway SE, Fort Walton Beach, is an antiques shop filled with the goodies we used to find at flea markets, including collectible coins, vintage clothing, and 45 rpm records.

At **Marilyn & Company Antique Mall** (850-243-4991), 151 SE Eglin Parkway, Fort Walton Beach, dig through stacks of books or look for fine glassware atop the many antique furnishings.

At **Nook and Cranny** (850-865-2976; facebook.com/gentlyusedconsignment), 676 Baldwin Avenue, DeFuniak Springs, the name befits this consignment store that's far larger inside than it appears from the outside, with every nook and cranny filled with antique furnishings, glassware, and ephemera on consignment. There's even an Art Nook, showcasing local artists in multiple media, including ceramics, photography, and acrylics.

A collection of cookie jars stretching back more than 50 years led to today's packed shelves of ceramics and glass at **Pappy T's** (850-758-6269), 388 N Main Street, Crestview. See if you can spot the original Dumbo, which came from the early years of Disneyland in California.

ARTS AND CRAFTS At **Big Mama's Hula Girl Gallery** (850-231-6201; bigmamashulagirlgallery.com), 30 Gardenia Street, Seaside, Laura Holthoff's colorful folk art defines the charm of this cottage full of arts and crafts in the Shops of Old Seaside. Exhibiting a wide range of creative talent from more than 30 local artists, this eclectic boutique is full of hidden treasures.

At **Rustic Reflections** (850-306-1500), 267 N Main Street, Crestview, the rustic dealer booths are artfully constructed from pallets and full of crafts and decor from local artisans. You'll find handmade soaps, hand-painted furnishings, artsy jewelry, chocolates, and even baklava on the shelves; there's an ice cream shop inside, too!

BOOKS AND GIFTS In the Oak Creek Shopping Center, **Bayou Book Co.** (850-678-1593; bayoubookcompany.com), 1118 John Sims Parkway E, Niceville, offers a staff-curated collection of literature, nonfiction, and children's books. Dig around for interesting gifts, and if you need a greeting card, part of the store is devoted to Hallmark cards.

THE LITTLE BIG STORE, DEFUNIAK SPRINGS

In DeFuniak Springs, **Beads & Such** (850-520-4461; facebook.com/BeadsN-Such), 766 Baldwin Avenue, has a wall of sparkly prom dresses for the locals, with the rest of the store given over to gift items, accessories, and soft feminine T-shirts.

The Book Store (850-892-3119), 640 6th Avenue, DeFuniak Springs, carries a large selection of used books, with trades welcome. Look for new titles near the front and freebie paperbacks on the bench outside.

Tuck into **The Hidden Lantern Bookstore** (850-231-0091; thehiddenlantern .com), 84 N Barrett Square, Rosemary Beach, to browse through more than 12,000 books to find just the right read for relaxation.

For nearly 20 years, Brenda Ray has been looking after **The Little Big Store** (850-892-6066), 35 S 8th Street, DeFuniak Springs, a delightful homage to days gone by. With local books and postcards, old-fashioned country store candies and foods, country goodies and gifts, it's the one place in town you'll be sure to find something to take home for the kids.

Sundog Books & Central Square Records (850-231-5481; sundogbooks .com), 89 Central Square, Seaside, is a great place to browse, with something for all ages.

One of those rare stores where nature steals the show, **The Rock Shop** (850-796-1000; therockshopfwb.com), 445 Eglin Parkway NE, has the best selection of fine mineral specimens you'll find in this part of Florida. Lapidary is an important part of the business too, with pendants, necklaces, and cabochons from which to choose.

DECOR AND MORE Inside **Vault 46** (850-520-4787), 46 S 8th Street, DeFuniak Springs, Margaret Hoffman showcases her talents with jewelry design, offering many one-of-a-kind pieces. She carefully curates the home decor items she sells, including lovely lamps, colorful floor mats, platters and icons from her native Lithuania, and prints by fellow artist Bruce Naylor, as well as her own vibrant art on pillows.

The beachside open-air market, **Perspicasity** (850-231-5829; perspicasity seaside.com), 2236 E CR 30A, started as a produce stand and now is a collection of cottages with clothing, decor, and art celebrating the beach lifestyle.

At **Shops of Grayton** (850-231-0880), 26 Logan Lane, Grayton Beach, you'll find home decor, art, antiques, and unique clothing in eight colorful cottages. While walking around the old town, note the buildings on Hotz Avenue, which date back to the early 1900s. Here you'll find the eclectic home and garden store **Zoo Gallery** (850-231-0777; thezoogallery.com), 89 Hotz Avenue, founded in 1979 to showcase contemporary American handcrafted goods, with everything from earrings to tree swings.

MALLS AND OUTLETS Set up like a small town surrounded by a sea of big parking lots, **Destin Commons** (850-337-8700; destincommons.com), 4100 Legendary Drive, is a sprawling outdoor mall of upscale boutiques, restaurants, and top-name retailers you won't find elsewhere in this region, from Abercrombie & Fitch and H&M to Whole Foods. Their largest anchor store is a sprawling branch of **Bass Pro Shops** (850-269-6200; basspro.com), 4301 Legendary Drive, with everything from hunting rifles to a fleet of sportfishing boats under cover. An AMC movie theater and a very unique bowling alley (see *Family Activities*) round out the complex. Chocoholics: you will find *both* **Kilwin's Fudge** (850-460-7868) and **Godiva Chocolatier** (850-654-1500) here!

To visit the **Shoppes of Baytowne Wharf** (850-267-8000; baytownewharf .com), 9300 Emerald Coast Parkway, you'll first need to pass through the Sandestin Resort guard gate. Tell them you are heading to Baytowne Wharf. Intermingled with restaurants that

OWNER/ARTIST MARGARET HOFFMAN AT VAULT 46

cater to folks staying at the resort, the boutiques are centered on a lagoon off the bay and offer a variety of interesting themes, from children's toys to seashells, upscale pet supplies, and resort wear.

At **Silver Sands Factory Stores** (850-654-9771; premiumoutlets.com), 10562 Emerald Coast Parkway, Destin, you'll find more than 100 designer-name stores in one of Florida's largest designer outlet complexes.

SPECIALTY FOODS **Modica Market** (850-231-1214; modicamarket.com), 109 Center Avenue, Seaside, has everything you might need to outfit your cottage while staying in the area, from fine foods to just dishes. And if the market looks vaguely familiar, it might be because you saw it in a scene from *The Truman Show*.

Ready to boil up a pound of shrimp or grill an amberjack? Then you'll want to stop by **Sextons Seafood** (850-837-3040), 601 US 98 E, Destin, for the freshest catch of the day.

❋ Special Events

FALL/WINTER ✐ Nearly 50 years old, the **Northwest Florida Tri-County Fair** (850-862-0211; nwffair.com), 1958 Lewis Turner Road, encompasses the agricultural bounty and country fun of several surrounding counties. It's a classic county fair with everything from livestock and children's art contests to fried Twinkies and a midway with rides. It takes place at the fairgrounds in Fort Walton Beach late September to early October.

✐ There's fun for all at the **Boggy Bayou Mullet Festival** (850-678-1615; mulletfestival.com), Niceville, a seafood and down-home country festival celebrating the roots of the town, originally founded as Boggy Bayou. Enjoy smoked mullet, baked mullet, and mullet chowder . . . mullet every way you can think of. Mullet is a fish that eats only plants, so it's always tasty. Major country music stars perform, and everyone has a fine old time. Third weekend in October.

A month-long fishing frenzy goes on every October at the **Destin Fishing Rodeo** (850-837-6734; destinfishingrodeo .org), one of the most prestigious fishing events in the world. It began in 1948 as a way to attract anglers to Destin, and it worked! The first prizewinner won a kitchen full of appliances; today's prizes lean more toward exotic fishing vacations, fast boats, and fast cars. Learn how the "luckiest fishing village in the world" can boost your luck on the water by booking a tournament charter or registering your boat for the event.

FRESH CATCH AT SEXTONS SEAFOOD, DESTIN

🐾 🐾 How could you miss doggy square dancing at the annual **Dog Daze** (850-244-8191; fwbchamber.org), Fort Walton Beach Landing? Field events and other doggy delights take place throughout this one-day event in October.

Started in 1944, the **Northwest Florida Championship Rodeo** (850-547-5363; bonifayrodeo.com), Bonifay, run by the Bonifay Kiwanis Club, takes over the town of Bonifay for a weekend in October, with a parade, 5k run, Western wear pageant, and some of the top riders in the nation. More than 25,000 enthusiasts attend each year, with ample camping available on the downtown rodeo grounds.

🐾 The **Thunderbird Intertribal Pow-wow** (850-822-1495; thunderbirdpowwow .org), Niceville, celebrates regional Native American culture during the first weekend of November with storytelling, Native American crafts, and intertribal dancing competitions.

🐾 **Christmas Reflections** (defuniaksprings.net), DeFuniak Springs. More than three million lights bring a storybook Christmas to the Victorian residential district along Circle Drive between Thanksgiving and Christmas, with Santa's workshop and a nativity scene; free.

Florida Chautauqua Assembly (850-892-7613; floridachautauquaassembly .org), 1290 Circle Drive, DeFuniak Springs, is a southern companion to the original New York Chautauqua, offering workshops, classes, lectures, and activities in the original Victorian setting established as a learning center in 1885. Classes continued through the 1920s. Revitalized and reborn in 1993, the Chautauqua tradition continues during this annual four-day event in January.

One of the craziest times to be on Okaloosa Island is during **Mardi Gras on the Island** (fwbchamber.org), a parade that kicks off the Mardi Gras season with echoes of New Orleans: floats, bands, and the ubiquitous beads. Mid-February.

SPRING/SUMMER 🐾 Go fly a kite at the annual **Fly into Spring Kite Festival** (kittyhawk.com/event/fly-spring-fort -walton-beach-fl/), a two-day event in April at The Boardwalk on Okaloosa

Island (theboardwalkoi.com) near the pier. Free kite making, along with exhibitions of stunt and giant kite flying.

At **Musical Echoes Native American Flute Festival** (850-243-4405; musicalechoes.com), you'll experience an authentic Native American flute gathering. This cultural event is a weekend-long festival in April of music, food, and performances presented by the Muscogee Nation of Florida.

Each June, the **Billy Bowlegs Pirate Festival** (billybowlegsfestival.com) in Fort Walton Beach is not to be missed, featuring a torchlight parade with "Captain Billy" and his "Queen and the Krewe of Bowlegs" throwing goodies to the kids. Billy Bowles, the charismatic scoundrel, from the year 1779, was one of this region's earliest renegades, capturing the shipping lanes and creating a band of pirates out of runaways and ne'er-do-wells. Only one other governing body—the independent Republic of Texas—outlives Captain Bowles's Independent State of Muskegee. Three days of activities involve a mock battle between the captain and city militia, which often includes the Fort Walton Beach mayor. Food, fun, music, and unique performances are celebrated in a festival atmosphere for all ages.

Started in 1952, the **Bonifay Southern Gospel Sing** (850-547-1356; facebook .com/Bonifay-Southern-Gospel-Sing -730770756947773) is also known as the "biggest all night singing in the world," hosting hundreds of gospel groups and performers over the years. Held in July at Memorial Field off FL 79, $20 adult, $5 ages 12 and under.

Beach volleyball is big in Destin, as evidenced by the **Emerald Coast Volleyball Fall Classic** (850-243-2555; emeraldcoastvolleyball.com/ffc.htm) each September.

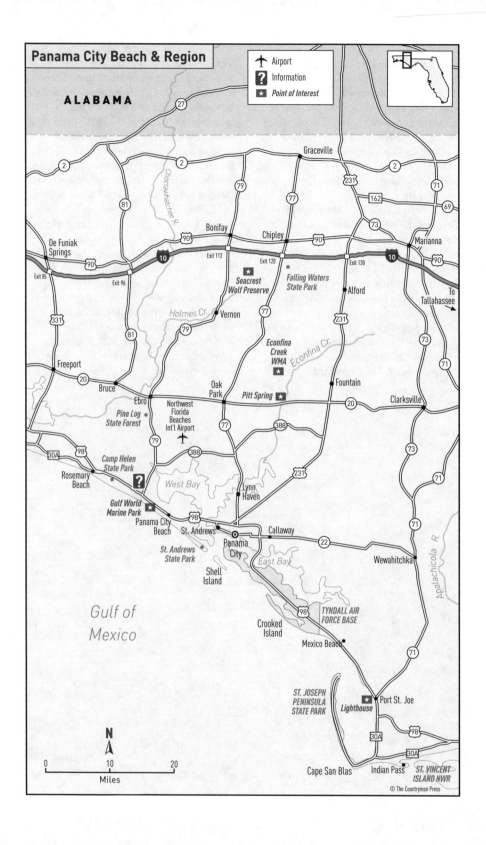

Panama City Beach & Region

✈ Airport
❓ Information
★ *Point of Interest*

ALABAMA

Graceville

De Funiak
Springs

Bonifay

Chipley

Marianna

To
Tallahassee

Exit 85

Exit 96

Exit 112

Exit 120

Exit 130

★ Seacrest
Wolf Preserve

Falling Waters
State Park

Alford

Holmes Cr.

Vernon

Freeport

Bruce

Econfina
Creek
WMA
★

Econfina Cr.

Fountain

Clarksville

Oak
Park

Ebro

Pitt Spring ★

Northwest
Florida
Beaches
Int'l Airport

*Pine Log
State Forest*

*Camp Helen
State Park*

Rosemary
Beach

❓

*Gulf World
Marine Park* ★

Panama City
Beach

St. Andrews

West Bay

Lynn
Haven

Callaway

*St. Andrews
State Park*

Panama
City

East Bay

Wewahitchka

Shell
Island

*Gulf of
Mexico*

Crooked
Island

*TYNDALL AIR
FORCE BASE*

Mexico Beach

*ST. JOSEPH
PENINSULA
STATE PARK*

★ *Lighthouse*

Port St. Joe

30A

98

N

Cape San Blas

Indian Pass

*ST. VINCENT
ISLAND NWR*

0   10   20
Miles

© The Countryman Press

PANAMA CITY BEACH, PANAMA CITY & REGION

Bay, Gulf, and Washington Counties
Cape San Blas, Port St. Joe, Mexico Beach,
and Chipley

More than 2,500 years ago, coastal tribes roamed the placid shores around St. Andrews Bay, discarding their oceanic bounty in middens and later building temple mounds. When the Spanish arrived in the mid-1500s, they found the Chatot people, who died off after European contact. The village of **St. Andrews** emerged in the 1820s, with a handful of people working year-round at fishing and salt-making. Around the same time, the settlement of Harrison, a commercial shipping port, developed just up the road. It became known as **Panama City**, established in 1906; St. Andrews, still growing, incorporated as a town in 1908. As the 1920s land boom swept through the area, residential neighborhoods filled in and the two communities met; Panama City annexed St. Andrews, along with several other towns, in 1927.

Panama City became an important port for shipbuilding and repairs during World War II, as up to 30,000 workers at the Wainwright Shipyard constructed 102 Liberty ships and six tankers. After the war ended, the shipyard stayed open, dismantling warships for scrap metal. Opened in 1941, Tyndall Air Force Base brought many servicemen and their families to the region for training during the war. Today the base is home to the 325th Fighter Wing, focusing on air education and training. The shipyards became the Port of Panama City and continue to be an important shipping and receiving complex for industry today. The county seat of **Bay County**, Panama City is the largest city between Tallahassee and Pensacola.

Panama City Beach came into being in 1936, incorporated after developer Gideon Thomas built the Panama City Hotel on the barrier island. The beach community—a separate municipality—has filled in rapidly, as dunes have given way to a skyscraper skyline not unlike that of Miami Beach. This 7-square-mile vacation destination draws crowds from

WATERSPORTS AND WATERFOWL ON THE GRAND LAGOON, PANAMA CITY BEACH

Alabama, Georgia, Tennessee, and Kentucky, especially during the summer and spring break seasons.

East of Tyndall is tiny **Mexico Beach**. Incorporated in 1966, Mexico Beach vowed to stay small. The town restricts building height to four stories; most shops, eateries, and lodgings are owned locally. Farther east along US 98, **Gulf County** touches the Apalachicola River but offers little river access; residents use much of its lands for farming and timber. Activities are centered around the county seat of **Port St. Joe**, one of the first cities established in Northwest Florida. Its marvelous beaches lie along the arc of **Cape San Blas**, out to the tip of the St. Joseph Peninsula, which forms the large, shallow St. Joseph Bay. The county is also Florida's home of tupelo honey, which you'll find in **Wewahitchka**. Gulf County is in the Eastern Time Zone.

While **Washington County** once reached to the sea, it was broken up as the communities along the coast grew faster. In 1825, settlers began to farm the region, growing pears, watermelons, sweet potatoes, and cotton. In 1882, the Pensacola & Atlantic Railroad was completed near present-day **Chipley**, and the small community was renamed from Orange to honor the railroad executive who brought it there. Chipley became the county seat by 1927; its first post office was located in one of the boxcars. With just a few hundred residents, **Ebro** is along the edge of Florida's oldest state forest, Pine Log. The sleepy village of **Vernon** sits along beautiful Holmes Creek, not far from **Wausau**, the Possum Capital of the World.

GUIDANCE Stop by the **Panama City Beach Convention and Visitors Bureau** (850-233-6503 or 800-722-3224; visitpanamacitybeach.com), 17001 Panama City Beach Parkway, 8 AM–5 PM daily, for brochures, attraction information, and hotel bookings. Inside the Bank of St. Andrews—built in 1908, the last old-style cement stone building in the county—**Destination Panama City** (850-215-1700; destinationpanamacity.com), 1000 Beck Avenue, welcomes you with brochures, maps, personal recommendations, and other helpful information for planning your stay. The **Mexico Beach Visitor Center** (850-648-8196 or 888-723-2546; mexicobeach.com), 102 Canal Parkway, covers this unique strand. For the communities of Gulf County—Port St. Joe, Indian Pass, Cape San Blas, and Wewahitchka—you'll find the **Gulf County Welcome Center** (800-482-GULF or 850-233-5070; visitgulf.com), 150 Captain Fred's Place, at the Port St. Joe marina, 8 AM–5 PM weekdays. To learn more about Chipley, Ebro, Vernon, and Wausau, contact the **Washington County Tourist Development Council** (850-638-6013; visitwcfla .com), 672 5th Street, Chipley, in a historic firehouse. Get off I-10 and see the beauty of Washington and Gulf counties, with maps, directions, and planning information from **Riverway South** (rwsfl.org).

GETTING THERE *By air:* Delta, Southwest, and United serve **Northwest Florida Beaches International Airport** (850-763-6751; iflybeaches.com), 6300 West Bay Parkway, Panama City Beach, one of the youngest international airports in the United States.

By bus: **Greyhound** (850-785-6111 or 800-231-2222; greyhound.com), 917 Harrison Avenue, Panama City.

By car: **I-10** and **US 90** run east to west along the northern part of the Panhandle. Chipley is at the intersection of **US 90** and **FL 77**. Following FL 77 south will lead you through Wausau to Lynn Haven until you reach Panama City. From Chipley, take **FL 277** south to Vernon to **FL 79** south to reach Ebro and Panama City Beach. **US 231** will take you from **I-10** south to Panama City, passing through the towns of Alford (see *Apalachicola River*) and Fountain en route, about a 45-minute drive. **US 98** runs east to west along the coast, connecting Port St. Joe with Mexico Beach, Panama City, and Panama City Beach, continuing west toward Destin-Fort Walton. **CR 30A west** of Panama City Beach leads to the beach communities of South Walton (see *Destin-Fort Walton*); **CR 30A east** of Port St. Joe leads to Indian Pass and Cape San Blas.

GETTING AROUND ♿ The **Bay Town Trolley** (850-769-0557; baytowntrolley.org), 919 Massalina Drive, Panama City, is the local public transportation service in and around Panama City and Panama City Beach, covering hundreds of stops for shopping, dining, and fun in the sun. Buses are equipped with bicycle racks and wheelchair lifts. Routes operate Mon–Sat 6 AM–8 PM. Full fare for bus or trolley is $1.50; 75¢ for seniors, persons with disabilities, and students; children under 5 ride free; day pass $4.

MEDICAL EMERGENCIES In the Panama City area, **Bay Medical Sacred Heart** (850-769-1511; baymedical.org), 615 N Bonita Avenue, and **Gulf Coast Medical Center** (850-769-8341; gcmc-pc.com), 449 W 23rd Street. For Gulf County, **Sacred Heart Hospital on the Gulf** (850-229-5600; sacred-heart.org/gulf), 3801 E US 98, Port St. Joe. Washington County is served by **Northwest Florida Community Hospital** (850-638-1610; nfch.org), 1360 Brickyard Road, Chipley. The center of the region in between the state line and the coastal communities (north to south) is quite rural and distant from emergency rooms. Always call 911 for major emergencies.

✳ To See

AQUARIUM ♺ ♿ Spend a day with the creatures of the sea at **Gulf World Marine Park** (850-234-5271; gulfworldmarinepark.com), 15412 Front Beach Road, Panama City Beach, where you can see a wide variety of shows. Marvel as spectacular bottlenose dolphins leap and flip, and streamlined rough-toothed dolphins show their great speed; learn about sharks and sea turtles when they have their daily feeding. Wander through lush tropical gardens where colorful macaws greet you with a loud squawk, or touch slippery stingrays in the petting pool. The well-kept facility, open since 1969, exhibits a variety of sharks, alligators, sea turtles, flamingos, and even penguins. Daily 9:30 AM–4:30 PM. The general admission price of $29 adults, $24 seniors, $19 ages 5–11, can be discounted by purchasing tickets online in advance. It includes all shows, exhibits, and parking. More than a dozen interactive programs, from snorkeling with stingrays to swimming with dolphins to being a trainer for a day, cost $79 and up.

ART GALLERIES ♿ ♺ Modern and eclectic, **Floriopolis Art Gallery** (850-249-9295; facebook.com/floriopolis), 1125 Beck Avenue, St. Andrews, is a gathering place for local artists and a garden in which to grow more budding artists. Outside, the public art courtyard is a nice place to take a pause; inside, see the works of more than a hundred local artists, or the current exhibit, or plunge into making your own art with their "Art on the Spot." Tuesday and Saturday 10 AM–8 PM, Wednesday–Friday 12–6 PM.

Featuring the truly offbeat—including original works by Peter Max, Purvis Young, Howard Finster, and Thorton Dial—in addition to classic movie posters from the 1940s, **Gallery 721** (954-765-0721; Gallery721.com), 445 Harrison Avenue, Panama City, is a one-of-a-kind collection of artwork assembled by Larry Clemons over 25 years in Fort Lauderdale and recently moved to this location.

Inside **The Light Room** (850-818-0475; thelightroompc.com), 306 Harrison Avenue, Panama City, the focus is fine art photography. Gallery shows last one to two months and feature both individual artists and clubs. Studio space is available for professionals, and newbies can take photography classes.

Step inside **Native Spirit Museum and Gallery** (850-890-9905; facebook.com/nativespiritpc), 1101 Beck Avenue, St. Andrews, for showy displays of arrowheads, hand-carved bows and arrows, woven baskets, and other Native American art, plus fine art inspired by Native American themes.

  ♿ ✒ **Panama City Center for the Arts** (850-640-3670; centerfortheartspc.com), 19 E 4th Street, Panama City, is itself is a piece of art. Built in the 1920s, the Spanish revival style reveals art deco influences, combining neoclassical, Gothic, and baroque features. Visual artists are featured in juried exhibitions along with permanent displays; the Bay Arts Alliance holds shows and workshops on-site. The Music in the Main concert series offers evening events on a regular basis, and special presentations highlight filmmakers. The galleries are free; check their website for event tickets.

The gallery and studio of internationally known watercolor artist **Paul Brent** (850-785-2684; paulbrent.com), 413 W 5th Street, Panama City, features originals and prints of coastal scenes and wildlife art, along with pottery, jewelry, and glassware from other talented artists.

Peeking into the **Randy Johnson Art Gallery** (facebook.com/RandyJohnsonArtGallery), 535 Harrison Avenue, while visiting the adjoining antique shop, we saw the impressionist landscapes that have characterized his long career.

The art cars lend a clue to what's inside the **UnReal ARTists Gallery** (850-215-0705; mermaidsdontcook.com), 839 Oak Avenue, Panama City, a 1920s cottage that opens Thursday–Friday 11 AM–2 PM as a local artists' hangout and cauldron of creativity. It's the brainchild and base camp of artist Paulette Perlman, whose whimsical style rolls with her when she's driving her decorated VW Westy.

LIGHTHOUSE Capricious weather and beach erosion meant one more move for the historic **Cape San Blas Lighthouse** (850-229-8261; capesanblaslight.org), 200 Miss Zola's Drive, Port St. Joe, since our last edition—it's now firmly planted at George Core Park along Harborview Drive in downtown Port St. Joe, overlooking St. Joseph Sound and Cape San Blas. First lit in 1885, it was the third lighthouse for the cape. The Keepers' Quarters contain some restored rooms, offices, and a gift shop with a museum upstairs recounting the history of the lighthouses on the cape. Thursday–Saturday 12–5 PM; fee charged for lighthouse climb.

MONUMENTS Founded as a retirement community of Union soliders, **Lynn Haven** boasts a statue of a Union soldier, corner of W 8th Street and George Avenue. Paid for and installed by the community in 1920, it was the southernmost tribute to a Union soldier at that time.

In tiny Wausau, south of Chipley, blink and you'll miss the **Possum Monument**, across from the post office along FL 77 at 2nd Avenue. Installed in 1982 to commemorate the value of the noble possum, it also kicked off the annual Possum Festival (see *What's Happening*) in this self-proclaimed Possum Capital of the World.

MUSEUMS AND HISTORIC SITES At **Constitution Convention Museum State Park** (850-229-8029; floridastateparks.org/park/Constitution-Convention), 200 Allen Memorial Way, Port St. Joe, exhibits and artifacts put a face on Florida's frontier days. In 1838, the coastal city of St. Joe hosted Florida's Constitutional Convention. A stone marker commemorates the signers; inside the museum, a replica meeting room has biographies of all of the delegates and gives a nice glimpse into a time when Mosquito County took up most of the southern Florida peninsula. Thursday–Monday 9–5 PM; fee.

✒ The **Museum of Man in the Sea** (850-235-4101; maninthesea.org), 17314 Panama City Beach Parkway, Panama City Beach, showcases the history of diving and work

MONUMENT HONORING THE SIGNERS OF THE FLORIDA CONSTITUTION IN 1838

in the ocean. This fascinating museum includes artifacts like SEALAB-1, the first-ever underwater living environment, early submarines and both human-powered and remote submersibles, antique diving equipment from 1837 and 1913, and other items that illustrate the long and storied history of underwater exploration. Open Tuesday–Saturday 10 AM–4 PM; fee.

Home of Panama City's first newspaper in 1920, the **Panama City Publishing Museum** (850-872-7208; historicstandrews.com/publishing-museum-visitor-center), 1134 Beck Avenue, Panama City, is filled with ephemera from the days when inked metal met paper to make a newspaper. Some of the presses, including an original Heidelberg, are fired up now and again to make art cards and posters. Tuesday–Friday 1–5:30 PM. Saturday 10 AM–1 PM. Free.

Established in 1827, **St. Andrews** (historicstandrews.com) is the oldest waterfront community along the coast. A stroll around its original downtown and a drive east along Business US 98 will give you a taste of its history. One of only five surviving two-masted schooners in the United States, the 1877 Schooner *Governor Stone* (governorstone.org) is moored at the marina. The 66-foot-long, wooden-hull vessel has masts made of longleaf yellow pine. It's considered the oldest operating sailing vessel in the American South. Driving along the bayfront toward downtown Panama City, stop at Asbell Park, E Beach Drive at 701 E Caroline Boulevard, for a pause at what was **St. Andrews Saltworks** during the Civil War. A skirmish happened nearby as Confederate soliders worked to protect the valuable commodity (the government shipped salt to the troops for meat preservation).

After a visit to the **Washington County Historical Society Museum** (850-638-0358), 686 7th Avenue, Chipley, take a walk through the **South 3rd Street Historic District, Chipley** (circa 1887–1938). It contains 16 private residences of historical interest, built in the Frame Vernacular style. The **1857 Moss Hill Church** at the corner of Vernon and Greenhead Road is another fine Frame Vernacular construction. The one-story church is the oldest unaltered building in Washington County and is an excellent example of local preservation efforts.

One of the region's oldest cemeteries, the **West Bay Cemetery**, 6446 Memorial Circle, Panama City Beach [30.293539, -85.864037] is particularly fascinating for its many shell-topped graves. In Victorian times, loved ones sent off family, particularly those who worked on the water, with a blanket of conchs or cockle shells atop their final resting place. This is the best place we've found in Florida that illustrates that tradition; some graves are topped with broken crockery and glassware as well. Many Confederate soldiers are buried here, some in unmarked graves.

PERFORMING ARTS The art deco **Ritz-Martin Theatre** (850-763-8080; martintheatre .com), 409 Harrison Avenue, Panama City, opened in 1936 as part of a movie house chain. In the 1950s, the Martin family purchased the aging facility and operated it for more than 20 years. The state-of-the-art facility now serves the community as an intimate venue for comedy, plays, and musical performances.

Established in 1962, the **Spanish Trail Playhouse** (850-638-9133; spanishtrail playhouse.com), 680 2nd Street, Chipley, is a charter member of the Florida Arts Council. An all-volunteer community theater, it offers several plays—often with a Southern twist—each season, along with concerts and special events.

RAILROADIANA Chipley owes its existence to the Pensacola & Atlantic Railroad, which later became the L&N. The mainline divides the town in two and is still busy with train traffic. The historic **Louisville & Nashville Depot**, 685 7th Street, sits half a block away from the current tracks and houses the local historical museum as well as a farmers' market. Within the same grassy block, you'll find the small white **Bill Lee Station**, which was an Amtrak stop until Hurricane Katrina shut down service on the

THE MARTIN THEATRE, DOWNTOWN PANAMA CITY

SEACREST WOLF PRESERVE

We were only seated for a minute or two on a great big log when I felt something big squeeze between us. I'd worried when Ricky Quick, our guide, told us we'd be less intimidating if we were seated. *Us* intimidating *them*? Imagine being face-to-face for the first time in your life with a timber wolf. Now that's intimidating. But our fears melted away as the wolves wove between us. As big as they were, they were puppies, and curious. Since 1999, **Seacrest Wolf Preserve** (850-773-2897; seacrestwolfpreserve.org), 3449 Bonnett Pond Road, Chipley, founded by Cynthia and Wayne Watkins, has taught guests that wolves should be respected, not feared. Their tagline, "preservation through education," reflects their focus on teaching people to understand wolf behavior, which will make them more likely to help with preservation efforts throughout the country. Wolves have a bad rap, and as Ricky, a former dog trainer, told us, that isn't fair.

As he led us through enclosures where each wolf pack lived, he pointed out specific behaviors of both individuals and families. Most of the wolves at Seacrest were hand-raised as pups by Cynthia, which is why they aren't fearful of visitors, but wary. They're also hand-fed by caretakers such as Ricky, who walked around with "meat cookies"—raw hamburgers—that attracted the younger wolves over to us. At one point we were allowed to feed the nearly full-size 10-month-old pups. Across more than 480 acres are five multi-acre enclosures, each housing a single family in a natural habitat. Both timber wolves and Arctic wolves are represented. A separate enclosure houses small mammals such as foxes and raccoons, cared for as rescues.

Reservations are required for all tours. Inexpensive general tours are offered on Saturdays, while more leisurely VIP tours like ours are handled during the week. There are specific restrictions on what you can wear and take into the enclosures, to protect the wolves from harm if they grab something from you. Cameras and other electronics are generally forbidden, although on VIP tours the guide will snap photos of you with your camera or phone. If you've never heard a wolf howl from inside your tent, the Preserve offers camping, too (see *Campgrounds*). Tours for ages 10 and up only; check their website for clothing restrictions before you visit. Saturday group tours $25; VIP tours $200 first two guests, $75 thereafter.

SANDRA AND JOHN INTERACTING WITH A WOLF PUP AT SEACREST WOLF PRESERVE

Sunset Limited, and an **L&N caboose** sitting by itself on a piece of track. Look west down the tracks toward downtown to find the railroad mural.

Inside the **Constitution Convention Museum** in Port St. Joe, you'll find a scale replica of Florida's first steam engine, which ran on an 8-mile route, the St. Joseph & Lake Wimico Canal & Railroad, between St. Joseph and Depot Creek in 1836. Outside the museum, look for a 1915 steam engine that belonged to the St. Joe Lumber Company. It sits at the terminus of the Port City Trail (see *Biking*).

ZOO ✦ ⅃ At **ZooWorld Zoological and Botanical Conservatory** (850-230-1243; zooworldpcb.net), 9008 Front Beach Road, Panama City Beach, you'll get closer to the animals than at any other zoo. With more than 200 animals, including big cats, giraffes, and orangutans, this zoo is also one of the cleanest. Through the glass windows at the Tilghman Infant Care Facility, you can view the care and feeding of newborn baby animals. Your little ones will enjoy the friendly Gentle Jungle Petting Zoo. Daily 9:30 AM–5 PM; adults $17, seniors $16, ages 2–12 $13, with additional fees for optional experiences like feeding the giraffes, holding an alligator, or getting close to a lemur.

✳ To Do

BIKING Panama City Beach has an unexpected bounty of bicycle paths just north of and accessible from US 98. With more than 24 miles of off-road, mostly gravel trails on 2,900 acres, **Conservation Park** (850-233-5045; pcbgov.com) 100 Conservation Drive, can be challenging thanks to its swampy nature, its primarily flat and coastal landscape rife with planted pines between swamps and bogs. Be sure to download a map before trying the trails.

To rent a bike to explore Conservation Park and the linked paved network of **Gayle's Trails** to **Frank Brown Park** (see *Swimming*), stop in at **Barley's Bike Rentals** (850-234-2453; barleysbikerental.com), 169 Griffin Boulevard #113, Panama City Beach, where you can ride right out the door and up the trails. Rent daily for $25 or weekly for $55; they provide delivery and pick-up for weekly rentals. **Gayle's Trails** allow both visitors and residents to cycle nearly 20 miles on flat, easy trails.

For more rugged off-road cycling, head to **Pine Log State Forest** (see *Parks, Preserves, and Camping*), where the 5-mile **Faye & Dutch Trail**, making a big loop through sometimes-soggy habitats around Sand Pond, has been a favorite for decades. It's joined by the winding singletrack of the **Crooked Creek Trail** on the east side of SR 79, which shares a trailhead with the Old Sawhill Horse Trail. Ride up to 9 miles in the floodplain and uplands of Little Crooked Creek, or use the shortcut trail to cut the ride in half.

For 4 miles, the **Port City Trail** provides a paved biking surface for bicyclists through Port St. Joe, connecting the downtown restaurant and shopping district with Constitutional Convention Museum State Park on the east side of town.

BIRDING On the upper **Choctawhatchee River**, noted ornithologist Dr. Geoffrey Hill from Auburn claimed to have spotted an ivory-billed woodpecker in 2006. Local sightings persist, and Cornell University (birds.cornell.edu/ivory) volunteers make regular trips into the ancient cypress floodplain trying to capture a clear video or photo of the elusive birds that might indeed be the last stronghold of a species once thought extinct. Audio is available on the Auburn website.

BEST BEACHES

For dogs: Panama City Beach Dog Playground, Pier Park; Salinas Park
For people-watching: in front of hotels on Panama City Beach
For shelling: Shell Island
For solitude: St. Joseph Peninsula State Park Wilderness Area
For sunbathing: Mexico Beach
For swimming: Jetty Beach, St. Andrews State Park
For walking: St. Joseph Peninsula State Park

CROSSOVER 66, PANAMA CITY BEACH

The wetlands area along the edge of **St. Andrews Bay** is one of the better places to watch for wading birds on the coast. Walk down to the water at Oaks by the Bay, Abell Park, or St. Andrews State Park. Similarly, the parks of Cape San Blas are along extensive wetlands. See *Parks, Preserves, and Camping* for details and more locations.

BOATING **Captain Anderson's Marina** (800-874-2415 or 850-234-3435; captandersons marina.com), 5550 Lagoon Drive, Panama City Beach, is a central place for ecotours and fishing charters while you're in Panama City Beach. Take the time to walk around **St. Andrews Marina** (850-872-7240; pcgov.org), 3151 W 10th Street, Panama City, the hub of activity in the historic district. Live-aboards abound, but charter captains dock here, too (see *Fishing*). **Panama City Marina** (850-872-7272), 1 Harrison Avenue, provides dockage at the edge of the downtown commercial district, with restaurants and shopping an easy walk away.

Whether you need fuel for yourself or your craft, the knowledgeable staff at **Mexico Beach Marina** (850-648-8900; mexicobeachmarina.com), 3904 US 98, Mexico Beach, will help you stock up on supplies for your day of fishing or cruising the emerald-green waters of the Gulf of Mexico.

At Port St. Joe Marina, **Seahorse Water Safaris** (850-227-1099; seahorsewatersafaris .com), 340 Marina Drive, rents everything from a kayak to a 23-foot pontoon boat; they also lead snorkeling trips (see *Snorkeling*). Boat rentals and fishing guides are also available at **Presnell's Bayside Marina & RV Resort** (see *Campgrounds*) in Port St. Joe.

BOAT SHUTTLES To get to the barrier islands, you'll need a shuttle. Take **St. Vincent Island Shuttle Services** (850-229-1065; stvincentisland.com) at Indian Pass, where trips to the island run $7–10. The **Shell Island Shuttle** (850-233-0504 or 850-235-4004; shellislandshuttle.com), 4607 State Park Circle, at St. Andrews State Park (see *Parks, Preserves, and Camping*) departs on regular trips across the bay to the 700-acre barrier island that's part of the park; $19 adults, $10 children. If you're staying at **Sheraton Bay Point Resort** (see *Lodging*), their shuttle to Shell Island costs $10 for adults, $5 for children.

BOAT TOURS Swashbucklers will want to step back in time aboard authentic 85-foot pirate ship the *Sea Dragon* (850-234-7400; piratecruise.net), 5325 N Lagoon Drive, Panama City Beach. You'll enjoy cruising the Gulf for two hours while pirates blast cannons, hang from the rigging, and then have a sword fight, which you might be asked to join! Reservations recommended. $25 adults, $21 seniors, $19 ages 14 and under.

Take a sunset cruise across the shallows of St. Joseph Bay with **Seahorse Water Safaris** (850-227-1099; seahorsewatersafaris.com), departing from Port St. Joe Marina, to watch the colors fade over Cape San Blas, $24. Seasonal wildlife and photography excursions are also offered in the spring and fall.

DIVING The area of the water off Panama City Beach is known as the **Wreck Capital of the South**. You can swim among sea turtles, rays, catfish, flounder, grouper, and curious puffer fish in a half-dozen historic wrecks in natural reefs reaching 100 feet a few miles offshore, or in 50 artificial reefs set just offshore. The famous 465-foot *Empire Mica* is there; dive down 75 feet to reach a 184-foot-long naval mine sweeper. Or inspect a 100-foot aluminum hovercraft, also sitting under 75 feet of water. A favorite dive is the *Black Bart*. The intact 185-foot oil-field supply ship offers an abundance of fish and turtles and is a great spot for underwater photography. Explore cargo holds, the wheelhouse, the galley, and even the heads. Sitting in 75 feet of water, the bridge is at 40 feet, the main deck at 66. **Divers Den** (850-234-8717; diversdenpcb.com), 3120 Thomas

Drive, Panama City Beach, provides both custom dive trips and daily diver charters. Their Delta dive boat accommodates up to 13 divers on each trip, and it's docked at Capt. Anderson's Marina (see *Boating*) between trips that range from inshore wreck and reef divers to deepwater dives on the big wrecks, $89–119. They also run snorkeling trips and scuba certification courses.

ECOTOURS ✎ Board the *Capt. Anderson III* for the **Shell Island Eco-tour & Dolphin Encounter** (850-234-3435; captandersonsmarina.com/shell-island-dolphin-tours), a trip across St. Andrews Bay to see the dolphins at play. The 3.5-hour narrated tour includes Grand Lagoon and the bay, as well as a visit to Shell Island to search for seashells. It departs Capt. Anderson's Marina (see *Boating*) multiple times daily. $23 adult, $20 seniors/military, $12 ages 2–11.

✎ At **Water Planet** (850-230-6030 or 866-449-5591; waterplanetusa.com), 5605 Sunset Avenue, Panama City Beach, one-day, three-day, and weeklong programs teach you about ecology, dolphin physiology, and how to interact with wild dolphins both socially and legally. Only six guests per excursion; you'll travel on a 24-foot pontoon boat around Shell Island for an unforgettable experience with wild bottlenose dolphins. Later, the team will take you on a walk in the shallows for a marine ecology wet lab, where you'll learn about crustaceans and local fish. Prices start at $98 for a one-day excursion.

FAMILY ACTIVITIES ✎ For a retro evening on the mini-golf course, head for the original **Goofy Golf** (850-234-6403; goofygolfpc.com), 12206 Front Beach Road, Panama City Beach, a beachfront classic built in 1959, still run by the same family, with dinosaurs dominating a crazy playland between the putting greens. Swashbuckling golfers will want to head for **Pirate's Island Adventure Golf** (850-235-1171; piratesislandgolf .com/panama-city-beach-fl-pirates-island), 9518 Front Beach Road, Panama City Beach, for a pirate-themed adventure with commanding views.

✎ Drive extreme go-carts at **Cobra Adventure Park** (850-235-0321), 9323 Front Beach Road, Panama City Beach, where 9-horsepower go-carts race up and down three-story coils. There's also a kid's roller coaster called the Dragon Wagon, several thrill rides, and an 18-hole pirate themed mini-golf course, Smuggler's Cove.

✎ One of the country's most-challenging mazes is at **Coconut Creek Family Fun Park** (850-234-2625; coconutcreekfun.com), 9807 Front Beach Road, Panama City Beach. Longer than a football field, the Gran Maze has doors that are changed often so you can never memorize the routes. When you've completed it, head over to the safari-style mini-golf course and bumper boats for more family fun. Tickets $12.

✎ Race on a mile-long track at **Hidden Lagoon Super Golf & Super Racetrack** (850-233-1825; hiddenlagoongolfandracetrack.com), 14414 Front Beach Road, Panama City Beach. The two 18-hole mini-golf courses will guarantee you're splashed by waterfall spray and fountains, perfect for a hot day. $10 and up for tickets.

✎ At **Race City** (850-234-1588; racecitypcb.com), 9523 Front Beach Road, Panama City Beach, there's fun for everyone, from a go-cart track that's a replica of the Golden Gate Bridge to a swirling sea maze that will take the wiles of the entire family to escape.

✎ ♿ The curious and weird can be found at cartoonist's **Robert Ripley's Believe It or Not! Museum** (850-230-6113; ripleys.com/panamacitybeach), 9907 Front Beach Road, Panama City Beach. This counterpart to the original in St. Augustine will have you walking through spinning tunnels and displays of the bizarre in the Odditorium. On the Moving Theater 7D, you'll experience a mine shaft or cosmic galaxy—a great roller-coaster experience for those wanting a virtual thrill without the physical dips and turns. Find your way through the Mirror Maze Challenge, and then show you have the stealth of a jewel thief by working your way between laser beams in the Impossible LaseRace. Open daily 9 AM–10 PM; combo tickets $23–29 adults, $18–24 children, under 5 free.

🐾 ♿ An upside-down building. A rollicking family funhouse. **Wonderworks** (850-249-7000; wonderworkspcb.com), 9910 Front Beach Road, Panama City Beach, is where kids won't even realize they're learning about science as they're having fun. Hang out in the Hurricane Shack to learn what Category One is all about. Try the three-story indoor glow-in-the-dark ropes course. Lie down on a bed of nails or design your own roller coaster and ride it in a simulator. Open daily 10 AM–11 PM; $28–35 adults, $22–29 for children and seniors.

FISHING For a serene place to drop a line, walk out on the **Mexico Beach Fishing Pier** at 37th St. Bait, licenses, and gear can be purchased nearby at Cathey's Ace Hardware (850-648-5242), 3000 US 98, which also rents some equipment.

While the simplest thing to do at Panama City Beach is to head for the **Russell-Fields Pier** (850-233-5080), 16201 Front Beach Road—it stretches 1,500 feet into the Gulf of Mexico—Panama City is known for its offshore fishing. For deep-sea—and it can get rough out there—**Tomcat Fishing Charters** (850-303-2210; tomcatfishingcharters.com) represents a group of captains who run trips from half a day to several days on the water. Rates are hourly ($150–160) for up to 18 passengers, and you can review the boats online before you book. **Capt. Anderson's Marina** (850-234-3435; captandersonsmarina.com/deep-sea-fishing) hooks you up with local captains who run deep-sea trips day and night, ranging from 3 hours to overnight; vessels spend about half their time getting offshore and back and have meal service available onboard. Rates run from $65–105, and some trips allow non-fishing riders for $35, so families are welcome. Prices include bait & tackle and license. Captain B. J. Burkett runs **Hook 'em Up Charters** (850-774-8333; pcbeachfishingcharters.com), focused on taking the whole family out fishing, as does Captain Don Williams with **Cynthia Lynn Charters** (850-249-5813; cynthialynncharters.net), 825 Linda Lane.

St. Joseph Bay is famous for its scalloping and oyster beds, but there are plenty of fish to fry. Family expeditions are encouraged by **Perfect Cast Charters** (850-227-5149; perfectcastcharters.com), 1311 McClelland Avenue, starting at $400 for inshore.

Trophy-size lunkers lurk along the **Dead Lakes** at Dead Lakes Recreation Area (see *Parks, Preserves, and Camping*); check with local fish camps (see *Fish Camps*) if you need outfitting or guiding.

GOLFING Panama City Beach offers five challenging courses. The area's oldest golf course, built in 1962, is **Signal Hill** (850-234-3218; signalhillgolfcourse.com), 9615 N Thomas Drive, originally built on rolling dunes not far from the sea. One of the most challenging courses in the United States is the intimidating par-72 **Nicklaus Course** at the **Bay Point Golf & Tennis Club** (850-235-6950; baypointgolf.com), 4701 Baypoint Road. Measuring more than 7,100 yards and with a slope rating of 152, it's the only Nicklaus-designed course in Northwest Florida. If you find it tough, you'll never be bored at the **Meadows Course** in the same complex. Easy enough for beginners, the course still offers enough challenges for experienced golfers. The 18-hole, par-72 course at **Holiday Golf Club** (850-234-1800; holidaygolfclub.com), 100 Fairway Boulevard, is only a mile from the beach. At **Hombre Golf Club** (850-234-3673; hombregolfclub.com), 120 Coyote Pass, wetlands and water holes are favorites among the 27 holes, which can give you three different 18-hole games.

HIKING One of Florida's finest **backpacking trips** is an 18-mile overnighter on the **Florida Trail** through **Econfina Creek WMA** (floridahikes.com/floridatrail/econfina

-creek). Heading west from the Scott Road trailhead [30.548914,-85.435829] near Fountain, you're instantly immersed in the dense bluff forests along this picturesque creek, with challenging hills, high bluffs, swinging bridges, springs, and even water-falls. Once the trail leaves the creek, rolling hills and picturesque lakes keep the hike fun up to its conclusion at the SR 20 trailhead [30.428308,-85.60968].

For one of Florida's more picturesque nature trails, follow the blazes between Pitt Spring and Williford Spring (see *Swimming*) on the **Econfina Nature Trail** (floridahikes .com/econfina-nature-trail) to experience springs, high bluffs, and a long switchback down to creek level. Hikers are welcome on the trails of **Conservation Park** (see *Biking*); your best choices are to take the Green (1.7 miles) or Yellow (4–6 miles) Trails for loops that include long boardwalks winding through cypress domes.

✐ Short but pleasant nature trails offer visitors to **Camp Helen State Park** and **St. Andrews State Park** the opportunity to learn about coastal habitats, and **Falling Waters State Park** showcases the state's tallest waterfall, dropping into a deep cylin-drical sinkhole. See *Parks, Preserves, and Camping* for locations.

HORSEBACK RIDING Cape San Blas is one of the few places in Florida where you can go horseback riding on the beach with an approved outfitter. Your ride starts at Sali-nas Park, near the beginning of the sweep of the cape. Outfitters include **Two Bit Stable** (850-227-4744; twobitstable.com) and **Broke a Toe** (850-899-7433; brokeatoe.com). Rates start at $50–60 per hour, depending on season. Private inland rides can also be arranged with Broke a Toe.

NATURE CENTER ✐ ♿ At the **Science & Discovery Center** (850-769-6128; science anddiscoverycenter.org), 308 Airport Road, Panama City, children learn and play in a variety of exhibits, ranging from a Digital Wall live video funhouse to a virtual Shark Tank to the Dino Dig, where children can excavate "dinosaur bones," to a big play pirate ship outside. A nature trail winds through natural habitats behind the buildings, includ-ing a boardwalk leading into a cypress swamp. Open 10 AM–5 PM Tuesday–Saturday, fee.

OFF-ROADING Off-road trails mean family fun for dirt bike enthusiasts at **Hard Labor Creek Off-Road Park** (850-527-6063; hlcorpark.com), 2009 FL 277 [30.706028, -85.620685], with a trail system carefully designed for safety and fun by Dexter Lead-beater, an expert racer and lifelong enthusiast who manages the park and oversees competitive races held several times a year. The Beginner and Pee Wee trails near the campground are perfect for new riders and young riders; more extensive well-groomed trails wind through more than 700 acres. Trails open on weekends; $20 ages 13+, $15 ages 5–12, under 5 free, non-riders $5. Campground with bathhouse open daily, $10 tents, $15 camper, $25–30 for RV sites with electricity.

PADDLING One of Florida's most unusual paddling destinations, the **Dead Lakes** make up a strangely tangled maze of swamp forest and open water formed when a dam blocked the flow of the Chipola River into the Apalachicola River for nearly 30 years. The cypresses here have fluted, buttressed bases unlike those you see on shorelines, and while you're in a kayak, you simply won't see a shoreline at all, just a dense swamp forest surrounding the lakes. Bring a GPS, as it's easy to get lost. Launch from Dead Lakes Recreation Area (see *Parks, Preserves, and Camping*). Guided tours available from **Off the Map Expeditions** (850-819-3053; offthemapexpeditions.com), $50 for a 3–4 hour tour; pontoon boat tours available for groups.

Econfina Creek is one of Florida's most spectacular places to paddle. From high clay bluffs with splashing waterfalls to gentle floodplains where springs bubble up along the sides of the creek, it is a beautiful waterway well worth your exploration. Plan your trip with **Econfina Canoe Livery** (850-722-9032; canoeeconfinacreek.net), Strickland Road, Youngstown. $40 kayak, $50 canoe for the 3–4 hour trip. Bring your own craft and pay $5 to launch or $35 for shuttle service. Cash only.

Explore the needlerush marshes along **St. Joseph Bay** by launching at St. Joseph Peninsula State Park (see *Parks, Preserves, and Camping*) or at the public launch. Rent kayaks and SUP at **Happy Ours** (850-229-1991; happyourskayak.com), 775 Cape San Blas Road, $35–50. Guided excursions available.

PARKS, PRESERVES, AND CAMPING ﴾ The beach at **Camp Helen State Park** (850-233-5059; floridastateparks.org/park/Camp-Helen), 23937 Panama City Beach Parkway, is particularly interesting because of the outfall of Lake Powell, one of the chain of coastal dune lakes that stretches west to Destin (see *Coastal Dune Lakes* in the previous chapter). When it overflows into the Gulf, the tannic water etches pathways through the white sand, and birds, especially seagulls and plovers, race to it looking for tidbits to eat. Employees of an Alabama textile mill enjoyed the lodge and cottages as their getaway from 1945 until 1987; the structures are in the process of being restored. An accessible nature trail on the north side of US 98 showcases coastal habitats. Don't miss the story of the sea monster of Lake Powell! Fee.

🏕 𝒜 At **Dead Lakes Recreation Area** (850-258-3466; floridahikes.com/dead-lakes -recreation-area), 416 Gary Rowell Road, Wewahitchka, the centerpiece is a hauntingly beautiful 6,700-acre lake, with dark tannic waters and wizened ancient cypresses. The tupelo and cypress offer cover for the fish, so the fishing and kayaking are superb.

SUNSET OVER LAKE POWELL OUTFALL, CAMP HELEN STATE PARK

PADDLING HOLMES CREEK

With a stroke of two paddles against the current, we were headed upstream in a canoe with **Old Cypress Canoe Rentals** (850-388-2072; oldcypresscanoe.org), 2728 Traverse Drive, Vernon, with owner Dana Phillips leading our tour group. Our destination? **Cypress Springs**, a crystalline pool of fresh water pouring into **Holmes Creek**. As we discovered on the downstream journey, which continued miles past our put-in point, you'll rarely see a house along the cypress-lined creek, although there are more than 15 springs along the 16-mile paddling run. A rustic sign pointed into the swamp forest toward a spring, and we just had to follow, emerging at a broad opening below a grassy bluff. Sure enough, the spring boil of **Beckton Spring** was obvious. Ours was a two-hour trip, and we saw a lot. A four-hour trip will get you even more. Looking for an overnight trip with plenty of time for swimming in the springs? Old Cypress Canoe Rentals can help you find the places to camp; reserve in advance. For those with their own kayaks and canoes, download Designated Paddling Trails (dep.state.fl.us/gwt/guide/paddle.htm) from the Florida Park Service, which includes a blueway along the mighty **Choctawhatchee River**, home to dense cypress swamps throughout its broad floodplain.

PADDLING ACROSS CYPRESS SPRING IN HOLMES CREEK

Care should be taken when operating a motorboat in this lake—it's filled with cypress snags and stumps. Once a state park, the recreation area also has fishing ponds, a hiking trail, and pleasant campsites under the pines, first-come, first-served. Twenty-one campsites with electric and water, $14; 8 tent-only sites $10.

☀ Covering more than 41,000 acres, **Econfina Creek Water Management Area** (850-539-5999; nwfwater.com/Lands/Recreation/Area/Econfina-Creek) offers dozens of recreation areas and trails from which to explore the outdoors. Interior roads—which lead to camping areas, lakes for fishing, and launch points for paddling—are unpaved and sometimes rough. You can backpack the Florida Trail across the entire WMA (see *Hiking*); search out **Devil's Hole**, a natural spring-fed bowl above the creek; or camp out at any of the many free primitive campgrounds. Some, like Walsingham Park, showcase the creek itself, while others, like Rattlesnake Lake South, are simply beauty spots. Their amenities vary; some have portable toilets and picnic pavilions, while others just have a picnic table in the woods. Overnight camping is by online reservation. Our favorite is Rattlesnake Lake, a gorgeous lakefront campground for tent camping. Obtain free camping permits online.

♿ Along the waterfront in St. Andrews, the 5-acre **Oaks by the Bay Park** (floridahikes .com/oaks-by-the-bay-park), 1000 Beck Avenue, Panama City, protects a quiet shoreline and the massive live oaks for which it's named. Among the surprises you'll find walking around the park are a four-headed pindo palm, historic exhibits on salt-making along this coast, and a boardwalk that leads down to the edge of St. Andrews Bay, where you can walk along the shore and watch for wading birds plucking fish from the shallows.

☀ Established in 1936, **Pine Log State Forest** (850-872-4175; freshfromflorida.com), FL 79, Ebro, is Florida's oldest state forest, protecting 7,000 acres of sandhills, flatwoods, cypress-lined ponds, and titi swamps. Bring your canoe and paddle across the lakes or fish in the natural streams and ponds. Horseback riding is permitted on designated equestrian trails. Bikers have a bonanza of trails to ride (see *Biking*), and hikers can cross the forest on 7.8 miles of the Florida Trail. Sand Pond Campground provides respite beneath the pines with 20 campsites, electric and water, $14–23.

☀ ⚲ A longtime local park and beach access point, **Salinas Park** (floridahikes.com/ salinas-park) 240 Cape San Blas Road, Cape San Blas, provides a picnic grove with small wooden pavilions in a pine forest. It's the primary access point for equestrians headed to the beach. Although the sands here aren't as lovely as at St. Joseph Peninsula State Park, the beach is busy (access is free), and leashed pets are welcome. Across the street, **Salinas Park Bayside** offers a playground, fire pit, screened rooms for picnicking, and a long pier for fishing and dropping your kayak into the sound.

☀ ⚲ ♿ One of Florida's busiest state parks, **St. Andrews State Park** (850-233-5140; floridastateparks.org/park/St-Andrews), FL 392, Panama City Beach, got that way because of its beaches. Encompassing 1,200 acres of undisturbed forests and sand dunes, the park has miles of beaches; you can swim and snorkel in the protected pool behind the jetty or cast a line off one of two fishing piers. It's the only place along Panama City Beach where condos won't be crowding your ocean views. For the best beaches, go to the very east end of the park. From the bayside parking area near the replica turpentine mill, follow the Heron Pond Trail to reach the sweeping bayfront shoreline that extends to **Sandy Point**, the tip of the barrier island separating Grand Lagoon from St. Andrews Bay. Paths cross the island and lead you to a pretty white strand. Behind the jetty where anglers hang out at the far end of the park, **Jetty Beach** offers a mellow, protected lagoon behind the dunes, with shallows good for kids, and surfing opportunities on the ocean side. Mind the flags—red truly means "don't go" into the surf, which can be rough at times. Two beautiful campgrounds under the pines have sea breezes as a bonus. The 176 sites in the park come with water and electric hookups, and they give you the opportunity to park your rig or pitch your tent within walking distance of the beach. $28+.

♟ ✍ ♿ **St. Joseph Peninsula State Park** (850-227-1327; floridastateparks.org/park/St-Joseph), 8899 Cape San Blas Road, Cape San Blas, is far and away a top choice for a beach destination vacation. This slender peninsula offers everything you could ask for: big dunes protecting the most stunning undisturbed white-sand beaches on the coast, with no homes or towering condos to sully the view; two campgrounds that accommodate RVs, trailers, and tent campers; a sweep of coastline along St. Joseph Bay, perfect for scalloping, snorkeling, and sea kayaking; nature trails that showcase fragile coastal habitats; a backpacking trail that lets you head out into the wilderness area at the tip of the peninsula and pitch your tent on a lonely beach; and A-frame cabins nestled in the coastal scrub forest on high bluffs with a sweeping view. Bring a week's worth of food and drinks, a few books, beach towels, an easel, and paints. Relaxation is assured. Sites $24 and up, cabins $100. Day-use fee.

Offshore from Indian Pass, **St. Vincent National Wildlife Refuge** (850-653-8808; fws.gov/refuge/St_Vincent) is one of Florida's wilder barrier islands, 12,000 acres of forests, marshes, and coastal habitats. Most visitors roam the lonely beaches, where shelling is fantastic. The island is home to sambar deer imported from Asia more than a century ago, as well as a breeding pair of red wolves that are part of the Red Wolf Recovery Program. Be prepared for outrageous numbers of mosquitoes. You can kayak over from Indian Pass, take your own boat to the dock, or use the shuttle service from Indian Pass (see *Boat Shuttles*). Overnight stays are not permitted, and you must bring water with you, as there is none on the island.

SCALLOPING Scallop season runs July through mid-September in St. Joseph Bay, one of the best destinations in Florida for bay scallops. You can wade in at any of the bayside public beaches and sift through the shallows for free or book a charter—check in at **Port St. Joe Marina** (850-227-9393; psjmarina.com), 340 Marina Drive, or drop in at **Scallop Cove** (850-227-1573; scallopcove.com), 4310 Cape San Blas Road, where they also rent kayaks and SUP. Captain Dan Van Treese of **Perfect Cast Charters** (see *Fishing*) leads scallop trips for 2–4 people, $350–550.

SHELLING Shelling can be good on any beach, especially after a storm. Several tours will take you to **Shell Island** across from St. Andrews State Park (see *Boat Shuttles*). Paddling across is not recommended due to rough open water, submerged rocks, and treacherous shipping lanes. **Mexico Beach** offers a quiet place to search for sand dollars, fragile paper fig shells, and the rare brown speckled junonia. Removal of live shells is prohibited.

SNORKELING Snorkel the gentle shallows of **St. Joseph Bay** from the bayside beach at **St. Joseph Peninsula State Park** (see *Parks, Preserves, and Camping*) or from a boat. **Seahorse Water Safaris** (see *Boat Tours*) runs two 3-hour snorkel trips each day, perfect for family fun as you poke into the sea grass beds to see what's there. They supply masks, snorkels, and fins; $44, children 6 and under $29. Call for 850-227-1099 for reservations.

SPA It didn't take long to settle into relaxation at **Serenity Spa** (850-236-6028; sheratonbaypoint.com/panama-city-beach-spa) at Sheraton Bay Point Resort (see *Lodging*), after a whiff of aromatherapy and a well-needed knead of the muscles by Virginia, my masseuse. When you sign up for a treatment, you get the run of the house, from the sauna, private lounges, whirlpools, and aromatherapy showers to

JETTY BEACH AT ST ANDREWS STATE PARK

the expansive zero-entry pool overlooking the bay. Treatments—which include massages, wraps, and skin care—start at $119, with nail care $20–75. Book appointments in advance.

SURFING Surf's often up at **St. Andrews State Park** (see *Parks, Preserves, and Camping*), where wave action is almost guaranteed along the zone between the jetty and fishing pier.

SPRINGS Accessible only by paddling upstream from Vernon (see *Paddling*), **Cypress Spring** is a bowl of natural beauty pouring its turquoise waters into **Holmes Creek**, which has 15 named springs along its length. **Brunson Landing Springs** are down a footpath from Brunson Landing, 3112 Brunson Landing Road, Vernon, and flow into the creek; **Hightower Spring** isn't far by water from Hightower Landing, 3107 Hightower Springs Road, Vernon.

Lower Econfina Creek is also a beautiful spot for springs to swim and snorkel in, centered on public access at **Pitt Spring Recreation Area**, 6315 FL 20, Youngstown. Swim in the swimming-pool-size natural spring, or bring a kayak to paddle downstream to the showy **Gainer Springs Group** and upstream to pretty **Sylvan Springs**, which can also be viewed from a boardwalk above. A nature trail (see *Hiking*) connects Sylvan Springs to **Williford Spring**, 5647 Porter Pond Road, Youngstown, another recreation area along the creek. Both Pitt and Willford Springs have parking, picnic pavilions, and composting toilets.

SWIMMING ✎ 🐾 A large recreational complex with an aquatic center, ballfields, and a fishing pond, **Frank Brown Park** (850-233-5045; panamacitybeachparksandrecreation

.com), 16200 Panama City Beach Parkway, offers summer swimming. The seasonal 5,000-square-foot Kids Pool (fee) features a playground and slides into the water, plus a big looping waterslide that drops kids into the water under the watchful eye of a lifeguard. The park is also a trailhead for biking Gayle's Trails (see *Biking*).

WATERFALL ♪ It's the lure of seeing Florida's tallest waterfall that brings most visitors to **Falling Waters State Park** (850-638-6130; floridastateparks.org/fallingwaters), 1130 State Park Road, Chipley, but it's not what you'd expect. Atop a high ridge, the park drops down a steep slope punctuated with a long line of sinkholes. It's in one of these that the outflow of a stream drops 67 feet into a perfectly cylindrical sinkhole. Yes, the stream can dry up, so call ahead or show up in the rainy season to take in this unusual geologic site, which also offers nature trails, a picnic area, a playground, and a campground. Fee.

WATER PARK ♪ Families will love swimming around the Great Shipwreck or riding the White Knuckle Rapids at **Shipwreck Island** (850-234-3333; shipwreckisland.com), 12201 Middle Beach Road, Panama City Beach. Little ones will delight at Tadpole Hole, where they can slide down a toad's tongue into a few inches of water while the thrill seekers scream as they descend the 65-foot Tree Top Drop. Those needing to relax can float on tubes down the scenic Lazy River. For the most part, fees are measured in inches, not age. Guests 50 inches and above $36, 35–50 inches $30, under 35 inches free. Guests over age 62 get in for $25, regardless of height.

✽ Lodging

BED & BREAKFASTS (ᵗᵖ) Along a tiny finger of St. Joseph Bay, **Cape San Blas Inn** (800-315-1965; capesanblasinn.com), 4950 Cape San Blas Road, Port St. Joe 32456 offers seven spacious guest rooms ($200–320) with DVD players, phones, small refrigerators, and extraordinarily comfortable beds. Stroll down to the dock and put in your kayak for a paddle, or head up the road to one of the top beaches in the United States. The private courtyard out back is a perfect place for relaxation, but the rooms are roomy enough that you might just stay in on a lazy day. Minimum stays required for weekends and holidays.

♂ (ᵗᵖ) ⇸ ♿ On a stretch of remote Gulf beachfront near Indian Pass, **Turtle Beach Inn & Cottages** (850-229-9366; turtlebeachinn.com), 140 Painted Pony Drive, Port St. Joe 32456, features four comfy modern rooms ($200–220); enjoy a full breakfast with an ocean view and private entrances from the oceanfront decks. Three cottage units with full kitchens are also available; the two-bedroom Sand Dollar Cottage is wheelchair accessible. Cottage rates start at $250. The large wooden sea turtles set amid the pines and palms remind you that in the proper season you can watch loggerheads nesting or hatching. Walk by moonlight—no lights, please!

🦐 ☀ (ᵗᵖ) Bring your pups along to **Wisteria Inn** (850-234-0557; wisteria-inn.com), 20404 Front Beach Road, Panama City Beach 32413 where you might just find homemade dog biscuits in the lobby. The pool—where mimosas are served at noon—and oversize hot tub are set inside a private courtyard with lush landscaping and a koi pond. The garden behind the property is for pets and their owners to enjoy. Guests meet up in the evenings over wine and in the mornings for breakfast before heading out to the beach. You'll spend more time outdoors than in, but each of the cozy rooms has its own specialized decor and unique flair; some offer two doubles. $79–159, depending on season; minimum stay required on certain weekends.

COMFORT AND LUXURY 🐾 ⚲ ((•))

You'll find a relaxed atmosphere at **Driftwood Inn** (850-648-5126; driftwoodinn.com), 2105 US 98, Mexico Beach 32456, where kicking back is the number one activity. The inn evokes turn-of-the-last-century summer getaways, with grand architecture, spacious verandas, and carefully trimmed lawns. Stay in an efficiency in the main house, or in a spacious Victorian house or cottage with multiple bedrooms and a full kitchen, if you're moving in for a while. Rates start at $110 for rooms, $130 for cottages.

🌹 ♿ ((•)) The snazzy little **Port Inn** (866-825-7175; portinnfl.com), 501 Monument Avenue, Port St. Joe 32456, honors the memory of the original, circa 1913, with 21 spacious rooms reflecting modern sensibilities such as cable TV, Internet access, and a sparkling pool. But you can still sit on the front-porch rocking chairs and dine on the complimentary breakfast while watching the fishing boats on St. Joseph Bay. Rates $79–209 rooms, $269–309 cottages.

DESTINATION RESORT 🌹 ♿ ⚲ 🐾 ((•))

For nature-lovers like ourselves, **Sheraton Bay Point Resort** (850-236-6000; sheratonbaypoint.com), 4114 Jan Cooley Drive, is a compelling place to stay thanks to its setting: it sits where Lower Grand Lagoon and St. Andrews Bay meet, looking out over the forested shore of St. Andrews State Park. While this site has been under other brand banners in the past, $30 million invested in a total makeover makes this a top Starwood Resort. Settling into our spacious room, we realized there wasn't any reason to leave the property. With the upscale **Tides** (see *Where to Eat*) and two casual restaurants within an easy stroll, dinner plans were taken care of. Sunset drew us to the long boardwalk along the clear shallows of the lagoon, where we watched herons and fish outsmarting each other. At boardwalk's end is a

BOARDWALK ON THE BAY AT SHERATON BAY POINT RESORT

private beach on the bay, a sandy sweep along shallows where children might happily splash, immersed in nature. Throughout our stay, we watched families enjoying each other's company at the beach and the pool, while dining and while heading down to the shuttle to **Shell Island** (see *Boat Shuttles*) for a day on a wild shore. Free use of bicycles and paddleboard rentals added to the outdoor fun. Adults have additional diversions, from tennis lessons to golfing at **Bay Point Golf** (see *Golf*) to relaxing at the private pool outside **Serenity Spa** (see *Spa*) after a treatment. Pets are welcome. Rates start at $124, inclusive of a $25 daily resort fee.

OCEANFRONT   ♿ 🐾 ⚲ 🛜 The **Boardwalk Beach Resort Hotel** (800-224-4853; boardwalkbeachresort.com/hotel-amenities), 9600 S Thomas Drive, Panama City Beach 32413, features an oceanfront tropical paradise with lots of water activities. Relax as you float down the lazy river pool, lounge around the lagoon pool, or let the kids splash in the kiddie pool. Then head to the beach, where you can splash in the surf or hunt for shells. The cheerful rooms include family-friendly bunk/futon configurations, rates starting at $79.

⚲ ♿ 🛜 Right on the beautiful Gulf of Mexico, **The Driftwood Lodge** (800-442-6601 or 850-234-6601; driftwoodpcb.com) 15811 Front Beach Road, Panama City Beach 32413, built in 1957, is a perennial favorite for families looking for a laid-back place to stay. The rooms in this refreshingly low-rise hotel rate highly and come in sizes from a simple double to a 900-square-foot Cabana Suite. The pool deck looks right out on the beach and provides direct access to it. Both the pier and Pier Park are nearby. $73 and up.

⚲ Every room at the beachfront **El Governor Motel** (888-648-5757; elgovernormotel.net), 1701 W US 98, Mexico Beach 32456, overlooks the blue-green waters of the Gulf of Mexico.

Breathe in the fresh air from your own private balcony, curl your toes in the sugary sand, take a dip in the ocean or pool, and then sip a cool drink at the beachside pool bar. The not-fancy but spacious rooms ($129 and up), with double or king-size beds, offer cable TV and kitchenettes. Daily and monthly rates available.

⚲ ♿ 🛜 A stay at **Osprey on the Gulf** (800-338-2659 or 850-234-0303; ospreyonthegulf.com), 15801 Front Beach Road, Panama City Beach 32413, keeps you in the middle of the action while off to the west of the party crowd you'll find at certain times of the year (especially spring break) along this beach. Parents and kids love the beachfront playground and planned children's activities. A sister property to Driftwood Lodge, it offers a choice of kitchenettes or suites. $105 and up.

🐾 ⚲ ♿ 🛜 **Palmetto Inn & Suites** (850-234-2121; palmettomotel.com), 17255 Front Beach Road, Panama City Beach 32413, is one of the more popular non-chain, noncondo properties on the beach, with a big thumbs-up from folks who stay here. Rooms include kitchenettes as well as traditional-size hotel rooms; all of the Beachside rooms in the seven-story hotel include balconies, $95 and up. A pool, kiddie pools, and hot tub are right above the beach. The original motel is now the Northside, on the opposite side of the street, and it has its own indoor pool and solarium; $75 and up. Minimum stays apply during certain parts of the year.

TRIED AND TRUE 🛜 🐾 Across from the beach, the **Gulf View Motel** (850-648-5955), 1404 W US 98 and 15th Street, Mexico Beach 32456, offers an affordable option at a 1950s mom-and-pop motel with a devoted following. Rooms are simple and clean. Rates vary by season, starting around $50, with weekly rates available.

As chain lodgings go, we've stayed at 🛜 ⚲ ♿ **Hilton Garden Inn** (850-392-1093; hilton.com), 1101 US 231, Panama

City 32405, a central location from which to explore the region. A restful night in Chipley at (((•))) & **Comfort Inn & Suites** (850-415-1111; choicehotels.com), 1140 Motel Drive, made it easy for us to get to outdoor activities in this rural region.

CAMPGROUNDS 🐾 At the end of CR 30A, **Indian Pass Campground** (850-227-7203; indianpasscamp.com), 2817 Indian Pass Road, Port St. Joe, encompasses a small peninsula surrounded by an estuary, with sites set under gnarled oaks. There's plenty to do, with a pool, fishing charters (they'll set you up with a local guide), excursions to St. Vincent Island, canoe and kayak rentals, and bike rentals. Choose from RV sites with water and electric for $36–42, waterfront tent camping for $25–36, or the Stewart Lodge camping cabins for $100 and up.

At **Presnell's Bayside Marina & RV Resort** (850-229-9229; presnells.com), 2115 CR 30A, Port St. Joe, their RV sites are right on the rim of St. Joseph Bay. Bring your boat and launch here for scalloping expeditions and flats fishing. RV sites $50–60; cottages and park rentals, $125 and up.

🐾 🏕 (((•))) Right around the corner from Shipwreck Island (see *Water Park*), **Raccoon River Campground** (850-234-0181; raccoonriver.net), 2209 Hutchison Boulevard, Panama City Beach, sits in a lovely pine forest with a sea breeze. Deeply shaded and family friendly, with a pool and playground to keep the kids happy, it offers tent sites ($32) and full hookup RV sites, 30/50 amp with cable and Wi-Fi, $56–65, some of which are pull-through. The camp store out front also serves as the registration desk.

🐾 🏕 For a night under the stars with the howls of wolves in the background, camping at **Seacrest Wolf Preserve** (850-773-2897; seacrestwolfpreserve .org/camping), 3449 Bonnett Pond Road, Chipley, is a one-of-a-kind experience. Primitive tent sites and electrical sites for RVs or campers sit on a hill above the enclosures, with a tidy

bathhouse nearby and dark skies above. A nature trail loops through the woods behind the camping area, $20–25. One important rule among many: stay away from the wolf enclosures. Take a tour (see *Wolf Preserve*) to see the wolves up close.

✳ Where to Eat

ELEGANT AND ROMANTIC Since 1978 the Old English–style **Boars Head Restaurant & Tavern** (850-234-6628; boarsheadrestaurant.com), 17290 Front Beach Road, Panama City Beach, has been serving up great prime rib and fresh Gulf seafood. They're proud to feature "wild" Florida shrimp—caught by Florida shrimpers—on the menu, along with an array of signature fish dishes such as Paneed Grouper (pan-fried, topped with lump crabmeat and béarnaise) and Grouper Picatta (lightly floured and sautéed in olive oil, lemon juice, and capers). Their char-grilled steaks include a mouthwatering "Greek" Petite stuffed with feta cheese, smoked bacon, and chopped Greek peppers. Venison and quail are on the menu, too. Entrées $12–49. Open daily 4:30–9 PM.

🐾 & A wall of saltwater greets you when you walk into **Saltwater Grill** (850-230-2739; saltwatergrillpcb.com), 11040 Hutchison Boulevard, Panama City Beach, a floor-to-ceiling tropical fish tank guarantees fascination as you wait to be seated. The extensive seafood menu provides many gluten-free options, such as the pan-seared U-10 diver scallops presented on a bed of Parmesan risotto with braised grape tomatoes, shallots, and basil. Any salad can be topped with fresh shrimp or lump crabmeat. A pianist adds atmosphere most evenings. Entrées, $19–43.

CASUAL FARE At **Katie's Kafe** (850-638-8998), 2184 Pioneer Road, Wausau, the local mascot is in evidence, peeping its head out of a knothole in a tree. Filling the inside of a historic brick building, this family-owned diner offers up big sandwiches like "The Pig"—with ham, pork shoulder, *and* bacon—alongside its big burgers, as well as tasty Chicken Philly, each with hand-cut fries on the side. They have gourmet pizzas, too, and a prime rib special dinner twice a week. Save room for a slice of coconut cream pie! Lunch and dinner, $8–15.

Craving a blueberry waffle? Seafood omelet? **Mike's Diner** (850-234-1942; eatatmikes.com), 17554 Front Beach Road, Panama City Beach, is worth skipping the continental breakfast at the hotel for a real sit-down breakfast. And their Beach Lover's Lunch hits the high notes on diner classics such as beef tips over rice, country-fried steak, and liver and onions, served with fresh corn bread and grits, two veggies, and a dessert. Meals under $10.

🍴 Locals love **Sharon's Café** (850-648-8634), 1100 US 98, Mexico Beach, a mom-and-pop place at the beach, for breakfast: kids of all ages take delight in their fluffy pancakes, which come decorated with a happy face. And yes, those are real blueberries in your pancakes, a tough thing to find these days! Cash only.

A downtown Port St. Joe favorite, **Sisters' Restaurant** (850-229-9151), 236 Reid Avenue, serves up tasty lunches like the Port Special, a turkey-bacon-Swiss BLT mash-up, and Carolina Chicken Salad, with slices of southern fried chicken atop fresh garden veggies. Meals under $10, open for dinner Thursday–Friday.

COMFORT FOOD 🍴 When you order a loaded baked potato at **Skins & Bubba's Family Restaurant** (850-638-4227), 1458 Main Street, Chipley, expect it to be your whole meal. We marveled at the size of the thing, an oversize Idaho that filled the dinner plate. While barbecue is their mainstay, good Southern cooking prevails on the menu, which kicks off with a late breakfast at 11 AM; sandwiches, salads, and entrées $4–18. Closed Tuesday.

HIP BISTRO-STYLE 🍴 ♿ The aroma of freshly baked bread and muffins will grab you when you step into **Andy's Flour Power Cafe** (850-230-0014; andysflourpower.com), 2629 Thomas Drive, Panama City Beach, but it's their homemade French toast that wows, on thick but perfectly softened French bread dipped in cinnamon and brown sugar, grilled and topped with toasted walnuts and strawberries. It's so good you won't need syrup or butter for it! Brunch and lunch daily, $4–9, plus baked goods to go.

((•)) ♿ Small but bustling, **St. Andrews Coffee House & Bistro** (850-215-0669), 1006 Beck Avenue, St. Andrews, is a place to savor a cup o'joe, a tasty breakfast, or a light lunch. Enjoy a variety of omelettes, freshly made biscuits, and tasty desserts. Monday–Saturday 7 AM–3 PM.

♿ At **Tides** (sheratonbaypoint.com/panama-city-beach-restaurants#tides) at Sheraton Bay Point Resort (see *Lodging*), the artful presentation of each bold entrée created by Executive Chef Shane Miller accents the modern setting; walls of windows provide a panorama of pines framing the bay. The rich lobster bisque had a hint of tomato; the house roasted chicken was accented with tasty brussel crisps and carrot souffle. Choose from Sea, Land, or Air entrées, $18–36, or mix and match lighter items for a filling meal. Open for all meals, daily.

QUICK BITE Anchored just outside the gates of St. Joseph Peninsula State Park (see *Beaches*), **Coneheads** (850-229-5252; coneheadseightytwenty.com), 8020 Cape San Blas Road, Cape San Blas, has tasty "world famous burgers," hand-pattied and seasoned. Enjoy yours inside a little niche indoors or outdoors with a sea breeze. Other lunch treats include seafood baskets and seafood chowder, $7–15. Don't forget the ice cream, or at least try a big banana split. Open 11:30 AM–9 PM. Closed Wednesday and Sunday.

🍴🍴 Jump back in time with **Tally-Ho Drive In** (850-769-2436; tallyhopanamacity.com), 1449 Harrison Avenue, Panama

City, a vintage drive-in restaurant that's always been the local hot spot for fast food. It opened in 1949 with curb service, and that hasn't changed today. You can also sit at a picnic table and enjoy your burger and milkshake, $3 and up.

🍩 **Thomas' Donut and Snack Shop** (850-234-8039; thomasdonutandsnack shop.com), 19208 Front Beach Road, Panama City Beach, has a long line at the take-out window at sunrise; the breakfast room is packed, too. While you can take your pick of the scrumptious fresh donuts in the window and walk off with a pink boxful in a jiffy, their diner food is great, too, including hot country biscuits all dressed up with your choice of sausage, ham, chicken, steak, pork chops, eggs, or gravy. Mealtime means delights like a shrimp melt with pimento cheese, corn dogs, and pizza, $3 and up. 6 AM–10 PM daily.

The top dog in town is at **Tom's Hot Dogs** (850-769-8890; tomsdowntown .com), 555 Harrison Avenue, Panama City, consistently voted best hot dog year after year. The secret is in the sauce—get your dog (under $3) topped with "Tom's Sauce" for the authentic taste. That's not all they dish up, however; try their famous chili on a cheeseburger or in a chili pie, or opt for a BLT or chicken salad boat, $5–8.

OCEANFRONT ⚤ Relax after a long day at **Toucan's** (850-648-8207; toucansmexicobeachfl.com), 812 US 98, Mexico Beach, while enjoying a breath-taking view of the Gulf of Mexico from the restaurant or the tiki bar. Fresh local seafood comes steamed, broiled, or fried. You're close enough to the famed bay for a mouth-watering plate of Apalachicola oysters baked several ways—try them Monterey style, with lump crab, sherry, and Monterey cheese. Entrées $14–30; Breakfast on the Beach buffets every Friday–Sunday 8 AM–10:45 AM.

SEAFOOD We popped in to the decid-edly unfussy **Captain's Table Fish House Restaurant** (850-767-9933), 1110 Beck Avenue, St. Andrews, to grab a late lunch and were delighted by both the speed of service and the quality of the seafood. It's not often you can order mullet, but it's on the menu along with amberjack, mahi, flounder, and shellfish. Lunch plates and sandwiches, $10–15; grilled or broiled seafood, $12–16. Closed Sunday.

Their tag line—"The Freshest Seafood from the Gulf of Mexico!"—is what they stand behind at **Fish House Restaurant** (850-648-8950; fishhousemexicobeach .com), 3006 US 98, Mexico Beach, where you can feed your family great seafood at reasonable pieces. Their array of seafood options includes grouper, bay scallops, oysters, mahi-mahi, crab, and shrimp several ways ($15–25), with half-orders as an option. A popcorn shrimp basket with fries and slaw is only $8 from 11 AM to 4 PM daily. Open for lunch and dinner, and for breakfast on weekends.

Indian Pass Raw Bar (850-227-1670; indianpassrawbar.com), 8391 CR 30A, Indian Pass, looks like an old general store where folks hang out drinking cold beer while chowing down on some of the freshest seafood in these parts. Live music is often on offer. Grab oysters and shrimp by the dozen, try steamed crab legs, or get the kids corn dogs. Tuesday–Saturday noon–9 PM.

The in-town cousin, **Indian Pass Raw Bar-Uptown** (850-899-9001; indianpassrawbaruptown.com), 411 Reid Avenue, Port St. Joe, expands the orig-inal menu in a bistro-style atmosphere to include daily creations shared on the blackboard, such as grilled oysters and Kickin Crab & Corn Chowder. Every-thing is prepared fresh, and it's up to you to keep your own tab at the bar. Meals $9–25. Monday–Saturday 11 AM–9 PM.

For a fabulous fish taco, stop at **Killer Seafood** (850-648-6565; killerseafood .net), 820 US 98, Mexico Beach. If you love seafood, you'll be salivating over everything from smoked tuna dip to shrimp or scallops simmered in their own special "Killer Seafood Simmerin'

Sauce." Platters, baskets, salads, and even burgers, $7–21.

TEAROOM (symbols) Inside the charming **Willows British Tea Room** (850-747-1004; willowstea.com), 6320 FL 22, Panama City, British favorites like the Ploughman's Lunch and shepherd's pie join the delicacies you'd expect in a tearoom—scones with cream and jam, finger sandwiches, and crumpets, $3–12; children's portions are available. Open Tuesday–Saturday 11 AM–5 PM. High Tea and Afternoon Tea are available by reservation, Sunday 12–5 PM.

WATERFRONT **Bayou Joe's** (850-763-6442; bayoujoes.com), 112A E 3rd Court, Panama City, serves all three meals daily—homemade jam in the morning, Cajun cookin' in the evening—with a side order of a blissful view of Massalina Bayou. Hearty breakfast options include the Bayou Omelet, Tom's Trash with Class, Garbage Grits, and Catfish & Eggs; dinner brings out the house favorite Pecan Encrusted Fillet O' Fish (cod or grouper, your choice), Papaya Marinated Steak, and a dozen other temptations, $18–28. Opens 7 AM daily.

Settle in for a sunset dinner at **Boon Docks** (850-230-0005; boondocksfl.com), 14854 Bay View Circle, Panama City Beach, a funky fish camp turned seafood dive along the Intracoastal Waterway at West Bay. No matter what we order each time we visit, fried or broiled, we're never disappointed—the sweet Grilled Bay Scallops, with a side of grilled peppers and onions, are a favorite. Sandwiches and entrées, $9 at market price, with several seafood platter combos including "Boat Trash" and "Big Catch." Show up early or expect a long wait, but no worries—you can browse through the gift shop, hang out on the porch, or take an airboat ride before dining. Opens at 11 AM Thursday–Sunday, 4 PM Monday–Wednesday.

Enjoy the view as well as the food at **Dockside Seafood & Oyster House**

(850-249-5500; facebook.com/dock sidepcb), 5550 N Lagoon Drive, upstairs at Capt. Anderson's Marina (see *Fishing*). Parmesan garlic oysters make a great companion to their signature margaritas, but the mainstay here is the collection of seafood platters, from a Captain's Platter to an Admiral's Platter, where the bounty of the sea will sate your appetite, $19–34.

Your burgers are made just offshore at **Just The Cook** (850-610-1775; justthecook.com), 3151 W 10th Street, St. Andrews Marina, a funky little houseboat that's a floating kitchen. With less than a dozen items on the menu ($9–16), the Dan-D Donut, a rosemary-seasoned burger set between two grilled donut slices, has a devoted following. We opted for simpler but still tasty fare: the Cilantro Slaw Burger is a Swiss cheeseburger topped with their signature slaw, and the all Grown Up Grilled Cheese has pesto and tomato. Chow down at picnic tables in the shade on the shore, with the breeze off the water and classic rock in the air. Everything's made fresh, so it's not fast food.

Settle back and watch the sun set over the bay in the New Orleans–influenced **Sunset Coastal Grill** (850-227-7900; sunsetcoastalgrill.com), 602 Monument Avenue, Port St. Joe, where fresh, local seafood has a twist of Cajun spice and hand-cut steaks sate the hungry landlubbers. Signature dishes include "Such Gouda" scallops and shrimp, catfish with crawfish gravy, and their twist on country fried chicken, Panko-crusted chicken. Lunch and dinner, entrées, $14–32.

Right on the waterfront at the historic St. Andrews Marina, **Uncle Ernie's Bayfront Grill & Brew House** (850-763-8427; uncleerniesbayfrontgrill.com), 1151 Bayview Avenue, treats diners to an excellent view and the sparkle of history—this restaurant is centered around a home built in the late 1800s and moved here from nearby. Seafood is the primary focus, with soft-shell crab, grilled sea scallops, and Grouper Imperial—where lump crab meat in Crab Imperial sauce adorns a grouper fillet—are among the many delights on the menu. It's easier to grab a table at lunchtime, but dinner ($19–40) is worth the wait. Tuesday–Sunday 11 AM–10 PM.

ICE CREAM AND SWEETS Watch fudge being made on the giant marble slabs at **Kilwins** (850-230-4177; kilwins .com/panamacitybeach), 821 Pier Park Drive, Suite 100, as you wait to order ice cream, and you'll find yourself walking out with a fresh slab for later. Their ice cream has a nice light taste. Try the cherry, and enjoy.

Go for cold at **Shoobie's Frozen Treats** (shoobies.us), 402 Reid Avenue, Port St. Joe, in a food truck just off the main block. Their locally themed ice cream sundaes rate rave reviews, and their colorful Jersey Gelato mixes water ice atop vanilla soft-serve.

Blame great-grandma for the name **Sugar Boogers** (850-640-0790; sugar boogerspanamacity.com), 556 Harrison Avenue—she was a war bride from Germany and that was her grandpa's pet name for her. The great-grandkids love to share the story, along with their fancifully frosted gourmet cupcakes and ice cream.

Follow your sweet tooth to **Sugeez Sweets** (850-215-3790), 1105 Beck Avenue, St. Andrews, for cookies, cupcakes, pies, and ice cream.

✳ Selective Shopping

ANTIQUES Inside **Bay Breeze Antiques** (850-229-7774), 219 Reid Avenue, Port St. Joe, you'll find an array of nautical items and beer steins that could brighten up any man cave.

From a 1950s fridge full of vintage bowls to fine mineral specimens and hand-turned wood bowls, **Clara Jean's Antiques** (850-640-2106; clarajeansantiques.com), Harrison Street, Panama City, offers an eclectic mix of collectibles, gift items, and home decor.

With walls of glassware and display cases filled floor-to-ceiling with everything from dolls to dishes, **Elegant Endeavors Antique Emporium** (850-769-1707; elegantendeavorsantiqueemporium .com), 551 Harrison Avenue, Panama City, fills two stories of the former G.C. Murphy department store with an outstanding array of collectibles.

At **The Loft on Reid** (850-227-8669), 207 Reid Avenue, Port St. Joe, antiques and vintage furnishings provide a backdrop for local artists to provide painting classes.

We had to step inside **Main Street Antiques** (850-640-3390; mainstreet antiquesonharrison.com), 535 Harrison Avenue, Panama City, when we saw an assortment of none-too-common antique clocks. Their ever-changing stock often includes consignments and estate sale finds, with glassware, coins, jewelry, and railroad memorabilia among the dozens of rooms and cabinets within.

A classic VW bug drew our attention to **The Shadow Box** (850-249-1388), 1711 Thomas Drive, Panama City Beach. Inside, it's a funky meld of seaside shabby chic and modern antiques, where mermaid pillows nestle near cornflower-blue Pyrex bowls and wooden blocks, antique farm implements sit below cast nets, and a beaded purse is draped over an antlered skull. The crunch of gravel underfoot indoors was a surprise as we poked about in the maze of rooms.

ARTS AND CRAFTS Prepare to be delighted with funky furnishings and coastal-inspired art at **Turtle Girls Market** (850-775-4101; turtlegirlsmarket .com), 7930 Front Beach Road, Panama City Beach, where beyond the expected shabby chic tables and chairs, you'll find fine art pieces and art glass.

BOOKS AND GIFTS **No Name Café** (850-229-9277), 325 Reid Avenue, Port St. Joe, may highlight the café on their door, but we know a bookstore when we see one. This is the "everything" shop of Port

NO NAME CAFÉ AND BOOKS

St. Joe, from toys to new fiction and Floridiana, art by local artists, a big space in which art classes are held, and the namesake coffee shop—which serves up lunch as well.

Filled with cute beachy gifts and coastal decor, **Footprints** (850-236-3332; footprintscoastal.com), 800 Pier Park Drive #120, Panama City Beach, has lovely turtle bracelets and necklaces, sunglasses in loud beach colors, and plenty of pithy sayings on wooden signs.

Dainty ceramic bud vase clusters set a tone for **Joseph's Cottage** (850-227-7877; josephscottage.com), 403 Reid Avenue, Port St. Joe, where you'll find upscale souvenirs, fine homemade soaps and candles, and vintage items turned into creative gifts.

The **Markets at Mexico Beach**, 2802 US 98, offer shopping in a collection of cute pastel-colored cottages, which include **Splendiferous** (850-648-2020), Unit C, full of beachy Ts and gift items, and **Two Gulls at the Beach** (850-648-1122), Unit D, with its colorful flags and souvenirs.

Breathe deep and enjoy the soothing aroma of **Naples Soap Company** (850-708-3220; naplessoap.com), 701 Pier Park Drive #125, Panama City Beach, before selecting the perfect handmade soap slab or bath bomb.

CLOTHING A nice selection of gifts and beachwear can be found at **Beachwalk** (850-648-4200; mexicobeachgifts.com), 3102 US 98, featuring some of the top casual names like Life is Good, Columbia, Santiki, and Teva.

Ladies should peek into **The Crystal Pistol** (850-541-3892; extrabeans.net/thecrystalpistol), 1012 Beck Avenue, St. Andrews, not just for the custom cowgirl boots but for unique jewelry, fancy photo frames, and clothing that says "country with attitude."

The outdoor brands sold by **Hy's Toggery** (850-235-1177; hystoggery.com), 700 S Pier Park Drive #165, Panama City Beach, made it a natural for us to browse through, and wouldn't you know, we found the perfect fit for an upgrade on some comfortable technical clothing.

PIER PARK, SHOPPING MECCA IN PANAMA CITY BEACH

Cute outfits for tiny tots fill **The Maddie Hatter** (850-252-6039), 314 Harrison Avenue, Panama City.

A sweet little boutique in the historic McKenzie Building adjoining McKenzie Park, **Salty Marsh Mercantile** (850-571-2033; saltymarshmercantile.com), 228 Harrison Avenue, Panama City, features breezy clothes and jewelry.

DECOR AND MORE Inside **About Beach** (850-229-2500), 234 Reid Avenue, Port St. Joe, you'll find beach-theme home decor and functional items like artsy pillows, pottery, and glassware; photography and paintings by local artists grace the walls.

Adirondack chairs in bold patriotic colors caught our attention at **The Grove** (850-648-4445), 2700 US 98, Mexico Beach, for long enough to reveal the array of coastal furnishings and artwork displayed inside.

Vintage items and creativity mingle at **The Little Mustard Seed** (850-818-0691; thelittlemustardseedpc.com), 437 Harrison Avenue, Panama City. Inside

the walls of this former downtown J.C. Penney, a collection of dealer booths contains a fascinating array of decorative objects, from rustic furnishings to classic glassware, lamps and mirrors, and artfully repurposed tools.

Coastal chic is what you'll find at **Pieces on the Beach** (850-234-6277; piecesonthebeach.squarespace.com), 2505 Thomas Drive, Panama City Beach, where vintage furnishings provide a backdrop for decor items. Pop in to purchase seashells and driftwood to make your own craft project or add to your budding collection.

🐾 **Two Sisters** (850-785-1899), 1010 Beck Avenue, St. Andrews, shares its love of coastal life with decorative items ranging from flags, ceramic art, and framed photography to functional items like breezy clothing and necklaces.

FARMERS' MARKET In downtown Chipley at the historic depot, the **Chipley Farmers' Market** draws together farmers from the region in summer and fall, Tuesday and Thursday 12–4 PM and

Saturday 8 AM–12 PM; sometimes, as we did, you'll find locals with home-canned preserves, pies, and pastries as well.

Gathering at Parker Park on the second Saturday of each month, the **Mexico Beach Farmers' & Craft Market** (facebook.com/mexicobeachfarmers market), 2500 US 98, provides open-air shopping for produce and baked goods along with arts and crafts.

MALLS AND OUTLETS An open-air Caribbean-theme shopping mall by the sea, **Pier Park** (850-236-9974; simon .com/mall/pier-park), 600 Pier Park Drive, was the site of a classic amusement park. It does retain a smattering of amusements—mainly simulators—that make it popular with the younger crowd. Pop into Jimmy Buffett's Margaritaville for a bite, catch a movie at the Grand 16, or check out Chico's for cute resort wear. Dillards, J.C. Penney, and Target anchor the complex, which also has a Ron Jon's Surf Shop surfside.

OUTDOOR GEAR When we met Ron Pekrul at **Sunjammers Watersports** (850-235-2281; sunjammers.com), 1129 Beck Avenue, St. Andrews, we could tell he loved paddling. The store may be more than half full of apparel, but we migrated with him to the back corner, learning that the new Hobie Mirage Eclipse SUP—a wide paddleboard with pedals and handlebars, which we'd just seen at an outdoor writers conference—was their hottest seller. Check in here for accessories, gear, and bug juice for your outdoor outings.

SPECIALTY FOODS Walk right up to **Smiley's Apiaries** (850-639-5672; smileyhoney.com), 163 Bozeman Circle, Wewahitchka, for some of the freshest, most delicious honey in Florida. We did, and, catching the bottling facility in operation, we got the grand tour, tasting many of their varieties. While best known for their tupelo honey, they produce holly, orange blossom, and other

SUNJAMMERS, ST ANDREWS

TUPELO HONEY AT SMILEY APIARIES

honeys, as well as selling exotic honey from around the world. Open Monday–Friday, 8 AM–4 PM.

Learn some new recipes and then pick up a fine wine to complement your new culinary skills at **Somethin's Cookin'** (850-769-8979; somethinscookin.com), 93 E 11th Street, Panama City, a gourmet grocery store with a broad range of international products, or just stop in for a tasty European-influenced lunch at their Bistro Gardens Cafe.

St. Patrick's Seafood Market (850-229-8070), 405 Woodward Avenue along FL 71, packs your shrimp, oysters, and other seafood treats for travel.

✳ Special Events

FALL/WINTER A regional favorite since 1996, the **Florida Scallop & Music Festival** (850-227-1223; gulfchamber.org/scallopfestival), George Core Park, Port St. Joe, mixes major music acts with Southern foods, arts and crafts, as well as everything you ever wanted to know about scallops and scalloping along the bay.

Don't miss the annual **Mexico Beach Art & Wine Festival** (888-723-2546; mexicobeach.com), when the tiny oceanfront town presents juried artists, fine wines, unusual beers, and live jazz and blues at The Driftwood Inn, mid-October.

A highlight of the holiday season, the **Holly Fair**, features crafts, choirs, and culinary delights at Boardwalk Beach Resort (850-785-7870; boardwalkbeachresort.com) in Panama City Beach, benefiting the Junior Service League.

Just for fun, **celebrate New Year's Eve twice** in one night! That's what you can do when you stay near the edge of the time zone: Mexico Beach is in Central Time, while Port St. Joe is in Eastern Time. **Celebrate Twice** (celebratetwice.com) holds fireworks and a scavenger hunt, with free shuttles between the towns from 8 PM EST (7 PM CST) to 3 AM EST (2 AM CST) on New Year's Eve.

Chefs from all over the United States compete annually at the Mardi Gras–style **Mexico Beach Gumbo Cook Off** (888-723-2546; mexicobeach.com) every Febuary; proceeds subsidize the town's Independence Day celebration.

SPRING/SUMMER The **Ironman 70.3 Gulf Coast** (gulfcoasttriathlon.com) kicks off in May in Panama City Beach, when athletes from all over the United States and abroad compete in a flat, fast race.

They've been making tupelo honey in Wewahitchka for more than a century, and the **Annual Tupelo Festival** (tupelohoneyfestival.com), in late May, celebrates this heritage with food, crafts, and entertainment in Lake Alice Park.

🖋 One of Northwest Florida's longest running festivals, the **Panhandle Watermelon Festival** (panhandlewatermelon.com) started celebrating the fruit of the harvest in 1956. Gospel and bluegrass bands provide the backdrop to a day of beauty queens, antique cars, arts and crafts, and free watermelon slices for all. Events go on at Pals Park and the Ag Center in Chipley, in late June.

🖋 **Best Blast on the Beach** (888-723-2546; mexicobeach.com). Expect a fun beach party for the Fourth of July with lots of entertainment for the kids. A beach trolley runs up and down the 3-mile stretch in town, for easy transportation from your hotel or campground.

☊ **Vernon Firecracker Day** (facebook .com/VernonFirecrackerDay) offers an authentic slice of Americana and apple pie for July 4, with Little Miss and Mister Firecracker presiding, pony rides, a car show, arts and crafts, and fireworks at night.

☊ Anglers of all ages will want to compete in the largest kingfish tournament in the region. Sponsored by the Mexico Beach Artificial Reef Association, the annual **MBARA Kingfish Tournament** (888-723-2546; mbara.org) takes place during the weekend before Labor Day.

There's lots of music, fun, and food, including a fish fry. Cash prizes are awarded for the largest king mackerel, Spanish mackerel, and wahoo. The proceeds benefit artificial reef and fisheries habitat education, research, and local fishery habitat improvements.

For nearly 50 years, the **Wausau Possum Festival** (850-638-1781; wausaupossumfestival.com) has shone a spotlight on farm life in rural Washington County. Come meet the Possum King and Queen, join a sack race, climb a greased pole, and try calling the hogs in. Gospel, bluegrass, and country bands join in the fun. First Saturday of August.

APALACHICOLA RIVER

Calhoun, Franklin, Jackson, Liberty, and
Western Gadsden Counties
Apalachicola, Blountstown, Marianna, and Quincy

The ages-old superhighway of the region, the meandering 108-mile Apalachicola River, begins at the confluence of the Flint and Chattahoochee rivers, where Georgia and Florida meet. It marks the divide between Eastern and Central time zones—except for the town of **Apalachicola**, which is rooted, as the seat of Franklin County, in Eastern Standard Time. Along the lower Apalachicola River are remains of aboriginal sites, where the first peoples of this area gathered oysters and clams and left mounds called middens. The Creek Indians followed the river's course and settled here in the 1700s, coining the name, which means "the people on the other side." Fighting the British in the War of 1812 and the Creeks during the Creek War of 1813–1814, Andrew Jackson moved his interests into western Florida to fight the British and their Indian allies. In 1816, under Jackson's command, American colonel Duncan Clinch led a force to take the fort upriver from Apalachicola, at Prospect Bluff. A single cannonball hit the ammunition pile inside, causing a massive explosion that blew apart the fort and instantly killed most of its defenders. Now known as Fort Gadsden, it's a significant historic site along the river.

River traffic grew tremendously from 1829 onward, with upward of 200 riverboats making the 262-mile journey between the towns of Columbus, Georgia, and Apalachicola, with more than 240 docks and landings between them. As plantations rose on the bluffs, commerce kicked into gear, with shipments of cotton and produce bound for distant ports. As the port city incorporated in 1829, Apalachicola thrived. Shipping cotton, it became the third-largest port on the Gulf Coast by 1836, after New Orleans and Mobile. The bustling city attracted enterprising folks of all types, including the celebrated Dr. John Gorrie, who applied his engineering know-how to keeping his recovering malaria patients cool. He developed the world's first system for mechanical refrigeration, patented in May 1851: it was a forerunner to the air conditioner.

During the Civil War, Apalachicola was under heavy siege by the Union Blockading Squad. The river's strategic importance was key to Confederate naval efforts, as shipbuilding for the fleet occurred in Columbus. Timbering became the mainstay of trade after the war. Oyster harvesting hit its stride by 1896, when three canneries shipped more than 50,000 tins of oysters nationwide daily, and a sponge industry took hold. But as railroads started carrying more commercial freight, Apalachicola declined, and by 1927 steamboat traffic had ceased due to unpredictable water levels. Between 1935 and 1946, the Army Corps of Engineers built upstream dams and dredged navigational channels; they dumped spoil on fragile habitats, leading to a decline in the fisheries that has accelerated in modern times as Georgia has held back the river's flow to provide for Atlanta's growing population.

Today, 246,000 acres at the river's mouth are under state and federal protection and are named a United Nations Biosphere Reserve, surrounding **Apalachicola**, the vibrant heart of the region; **Eastpoint**, a community defined by its shrinking numbers of working shrimpers and oystermen (90 percent of Florida's oysters are harvested from Apalachicola Bay); and **St. George Island**, with its white-sand beaches and rolling

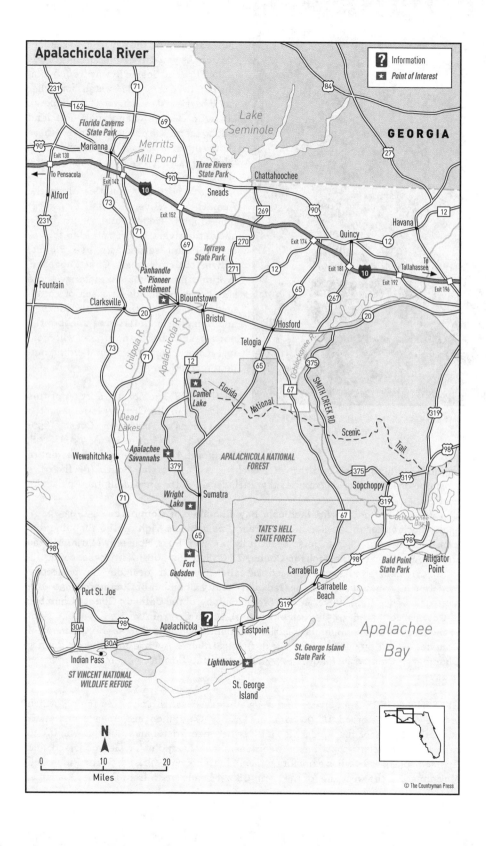

CAVE DIVERS ON MERRITTS MILL POND, MARIANNA

dunes separating the bay from the Gulf of Mexico. As you drive the shoreline bends of the Big Bend Scenic Byway from Apalachicola to Carrabelle, watch for other small barrier islands in the Gulf shallows, **Little St. George Island** and **Dog Island** among them. The public lands along these shores mean an immersion into authentic Old Florida as you enjoy the beauty of the "Forgotten Coast."

In the northerly counties along the Apalachicola River watershed, expect pine-topped ridges and high bluffs above the rivers, where rural life thrives in river-bluff settlements like **Blountstown**, **Bristol**, and **Chattahoochee**. Working downtowns characterize these small towns—islands in a sea of cotton fields, pine plantations, cattle ranches, and dairy farms. **Marianna** anchors the northwest corner of the region, with genteel historic homes and outstanding outdoor recreation.

GUIDANCE The coastal portion of this region (Franklin County) is represented by **Florida's Forgotten Coast** (850-670-3474; saltyflorida.com), 731 US 98, Eastpoint. For an overview of the entire region—including maps and directions—check with **Riverway South** (rwsfl.org), a team of Northwest Florida counties that includes all of the ones along the Apalachicola River.

You'll easily find the **Apalachicola Bay Chamber of Commerce** (850-653-9419; apalachicolabay.org), 122 Commerce Street, Apalachicola, right in the shopping district. Similarly, it's hard to miss beautifully restored Russ House in Marianna (see *Historic Sites*), where the **Jackson County TDC** (850-482-8061; visitjacksoncountyfla .com), 4318 Lafayette Street, is housed and can help you with local tourism and accommodation information. Stop in the **Gadsden County Chamber of Commerce** (850-627-9231; gadsdencc.com), 208 N Adams Street, Quincy, or the **Calhoun County Chamber of Commerce** (850-674-4519; calhounco.org), 20816 Central Avenue E, Suite 2, right in the heart of the commercial district of Blountstown. The **Carrabelle Chamber of Commerce** (850-697-2585; carrabelle.org), 105 St. James Avenue, and **Liberty County Chamber of Commerce** (850-643-2359; libertycountyflorida.com) are best contacted in advance.

GETTING THERE Four major highways run east–west through this region, which is taller than it is broad. **US 90** connects Quincy, Chattahoochee, Sneads, and Marianna; **FL 20** crosses the Apalachicola River between Bristol and Blountstown; **US 98** runs along the scenic coastline between Carrabelle, Eastpoint/St. George Island, and Apalachicola; and **I-10** has exits for Quincy, Chattahoochee/Bristol, Grand Ridge, and Marianna. On the west side of the river, **US 231** heads south from Dothan, Alabama, through Jackson County—Campbellton, Cottondale, and Alford—toward Panama City Beach; **FL 71** will get you to Apalachicola from I-10 at Marianna via Blountstown, and **US 98** east from Port St. Joe (see the *Panama City* chapter); **FL 65** is the scenic route through Liberty County to US 98 between Carrabelle and Eastpoint (head west for Eastpoint and Apalachicola, east for Carrabelle), and **FL 67** is the scenic direct route from FL 20 to Carrabelle. Virtually every route through the region will delight you with rural scenery or forested landscapes.

MEDICAL EMERGENCIES Emergency treatment can be received at **George E. Weems Memorial Hospital** (850-653-8853; weemsmemorial.com), 135 Avenue G, Apalachicola, and at **Jackson Hospital** (850-526-2200; jacksonhosp.com), 4250 Hospital Drive, Marianna. Most of this region is very remote, and cell phone service isn't guaranteed in the vast forests south between FL 20 and US 98 on the east side of the Apalachicola River.

✳ To See

ARCHITECTURE **Downtown Apalachicola** is a Florida treasure, with more than 900 homes and buildings on the National Register of Historic Places. Pick up a walking tour map at the Chamber of Commerce (see *Guidance*) and explore the many unique sites, such as the 1836 **Sponge Exchange**, the 1831 **Chestnut Street Cemetery**, and this port city's **Customs House** from 1923, now a US post office.

Circa 1904, the old **Calhoun County Courthouse**, 314 Central Avenue, Blountstown, is a picturesque sight along FL 20 as you drive into town from the river, especially in spring when the cherry trees around it are covered in blossoms. An excellent example of Romanesque revival architecture, it is on the National Register of Historic Places.

In **Marianna's historic districts**, fine architecture surrounds the downtown area. The distinctively rounded **Russ House**, built in 1895 by prominent merchant Joseph W. Russ, had its fancy neoclassical pillars added in 1910. It now houses the Jackson County TDC (see *Guidance*), where you can pick up a walking tour guide to Marianna's many other historic structures. One of the more prominent structures is the **Marianna Post Office**, 439 Lafayette Street, an elegant Spanish revival built in 1928 to house both the post office and the Federal Building. It's still the post office today.

  ♿ On a high bluff above the Apalachicola River, **Orman House** (850-653-1209; floridastateparks.org/park/Orman-House), 177 5th Street, Apalachicola, was built by early settler and shipping magnate Thomas Orman with wood shipped from Syracuse, New York, in 1838. A tour through the mansion, which served as a bed and breakfast for some years and is now furnished with non-original period antiques, evokes the period in which cotton was king in Apalachicola. The dining area has a small alcove with exhibits about Orman. Ranger-led tours are offered periodically, or you can take a self-guided tour. Open Thursday–Monday 9 AM–5 PM; fee.

Established in 1869, **Pender's Store** (850-594-3304), 4208 Bryan Street, Greenwood, is one of the oldest continuously operated stores in Florida, retaining its original shelving and heart pine floors. On the way there, you'll pass stately **Great Oaks**, known as Bryan Plantation during the Civil War. The **Erwin House** on Fort Road, east of FL 71, is perhaps the oldest structure in Jackson County, circa 1830. All three structures are on the National Register of Historic Places.

The **Raney House** (850-653-1700), corner of Market Street and Avenue F, Apalachicola, is a Greek revival home built for prominent cotton merchant David Raney in 1825. Docents with extensive knowledge of the Raney family and the city of Apalachicola during their lifetimes guide you through the rooms of the home, which is furnished with many original pieces on both stories. Free, donations appreciated. Open Tuesday–Friday 1 AM–4 PM, Saturday 9 AM–5 PM.

ART GALLERIES Inside the beautifully restored Fry-Conter House, built in 1845 by Captain Daniel Fry, the **Apalachicola Museum of Art** (850-653-2090; apalachicolamuseumofart.org), 96 5th Street, Apalachicola, showcases changing exhibitions of the visual arts.

Florida landscapes, especially watercolors and acrylics of the iconic Apalachicola River, will draw you in the door at **Artemis Gallery** (850-653-2030; shopartemis.com), 127 Commerce Street, Apalachicola. Their shop competes with the gallery space, with handmade soaps, racks of colorful women's resort wear, and unique gifts from local artists.

🐾 The place for fine arts and crafts, the **Bowery Art Gallery** (850-653-2425; boweryartgallery.com), 149 Commerce Street, Apalachicola, is a collaborative effort among local artists who work in a variety of media, including fiber, pottery, and wood. You can tell their love of pets by the fun sculptures within (by Leslie Wallace-Coon) and the water bowl on the porch.

Richard Bickel Photography (850-653-2828; richardbickelphotography.com), 81 Market Street, Apalachicola, is the showcase for this outstanding photographer's haunting black-and-white images of daily life that capture the soul of this region.

Sea Oats Gallery (850-927-2303; forgottencoastart.com), 128 E Pine Street, St. George Island, has four rooms filled with scenes of Apalachicola and the Panhandle, featuring artists like Roger Leonard, who deftly captures the coastal light, and Carol Nahoom, who creates colorful fused glass.

DAIRY FARMS At Shady Nook Farm's **Ocheesee Creamery** (850-674-8620; ocheeseecreamery.com), 28367 NE FL 69, Grand Ridge, the Jersey cows—which roam the pastoral landscape until milking time—provide the natural goodness that goes into every old-fashioned recyclable glass bottle of Ocheesee milk . . . remember milk bottles? You can watch the pasteurized milk being bottled; they make their own butter and cheese, too. The best reason to stop in is for fresh ice cream; the sweet cream flavor is pure magic.

In Cottondale, **Mosier's Family Farm** (850-326-6168; mo-ganics.com), 2565 Standland Road, has 90 cows pastured on their 64 acres. Stop in to check out their farm market, which features a broad range of organic goods from neighboring farms, as well as fresh milk, of course.

GARDEN Part of Orman House Historic State Park (see *Architecture*) and accessed from the same parking area, the **Chapman Botanical Garden** honors Dr. Alvin Wentworth Chapman (1809–1899), a medical doctor and botanist who spent most of his life in Apalachicola and defined 144 plant species during his research of regional botanicals. In 1860 he published *Flora of the Southern United States*. He is buried at nearby Chestnut Street Cemetery, surrounded by some of the many plants named for him. Volunteers have made the park into a pleasant place to take a walk or read a book, with its gazebos, benches, and quiet nooks. Free.

LIGHTHOUSES ⚓ **Cape St. George Light** (850-927-7744; stgeorgelight.org), 2 E Gulf Beach Drive, now sits prominently in the center of St. George Island, moved and reconstructed from its original components after a hurricane toppled the historic structure into the Gulf in 2005. Dating back to 1852 and rebuilt with a sturdy, broad interior staircase, the lighthouse no longer has a lens inside, but that means you can crawl right up into the top (dexterity on a narrow ladder required) and look out across the island below. Adjoining structures illustrate the lighthouse keeper's quarters and provide a museum of artifacts from the lighthouse. Tours Monday–Wednesday and Saturday 10 AM–5 PM, Sunday noon–5 PM; fee.

↯ Built in 1895 to replace a lighthouse destroyed in a hurricane on Dog Island, the newly restored **Crooked River Lighthouse** (850-697-2732; crookedriverlighthouse .org) along US 98 west of Carrabelle is the centerpiece of a pretty park. Decommissioned from service in 1995, the lighthouse is now on the National Register of Historic Places and adjoins the Keeper's House Museum and a gift shop, open Wednesday–Sunday noon–5 PM. Depending on the weather, you can climb up the very narrow staircase to the top of the lighthouse, Wednesday–Sunday, 1–4 PM, if you are 44 inches or taller. Fee.

MEMORIAL At the base of the bluff below the Orman House (see *Museums and Historic Sites*), **Veteran's Memorial Plaza**, 230 Market Street, honors area veterans. This landscaped space features a Circle of Freedom walkway and the bronze *Three Servicemen Statue*, a tribute to Vietnam veterans by Fredrick Hart.

MURALS Local history is illustrated through the use of murals in several downtowns throughout the region. In Chattahoochee, the prominent **J. W. Callahan Riverboat Mural** by Von Tipton, gracing a brick building at Heritage Park, 400 W Washington Street, reminds westbound travelers on US 90 of the importance of riverboats to the history of the Apalachicola River. Blountstown sports three showy murals, the work of our talented friend, local artist Jeff Vickery. The **Snowden Land Surveying Mural** near FL 20 and Pear Street, behind the Preble-Rish Building, greets visitors driving through downtown with historical surveying scenes and a detailed map of the city; the **Diamond Corner Mural** on the northeast corner of FL 20 and FL 71 focuses on historic architecture from around the area; and one building along FL 20 at the west edge of Blountstown shows a wilderness scene from the nearby Chipola River.

MUSEUMS AND HISTORIC SITES Built above the strategic confluence of the Flint and Chattahoochee rivers between 1834 and 1839, the historic **Apalachicola Arsenal**, Florida's first military arsenal, was an important US Army depot when Florida was still a territory. After the Civil War, the complex was used as a prison and later as part of the Florida State Hospital, a sanitarium. The restored powder magazine is now a conference center, and the ornate officer's quarters are still in place. Enter through the main gate of Florida State Hospital, North Main Street, Chattahoochee. Historic markers interpret the site; interiors are not open to the public.

Learn about the Gulf Coast's long and storied maritime history through the permanent and changing exhibits at the **Apalachicola Maritime Museum** (850-653-2500; ammfl.org), 103 Water Street, open Monday–Saturday 10 AM–5 PM. A second location is being constructed along the Apalachicola River in Chattahoochee at River Landing Park (see *Parks, Preserves, and Camping*).

♿ Bet you didn't know that the first amphibious landing craft didn't land at Utah Beach on D-Day: they tried them out in Carrabelle first! From 1942 to 1946, the Gulf Coast from Ochlocknee Bay to Eastport was Camp Gordon Johnston, a training facility for more than 250,000 amphibious soldiers as they practiced storming beaches. The **Camp Gordon Johnston Museum** (850-697-8575; campgordonjohnston.com), 1001 Gray Avenue, Carrabelle, honors the World War II troops who trained here, preserving the history of that important effort, which clinched the Allied liberation of France, via

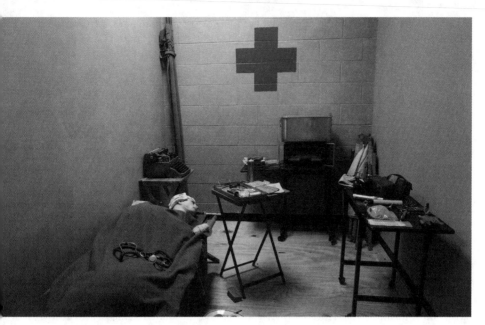

ONE OF THE DISPLAYS AT THE CAMP GORDON JOHNSON MUSEUM

artifacts and archives of special interest to vets and history buffs. Monday–Thursday 1–4 PM; Friday noon–4 PM; Saturday 10 AM–2 PM. Donation.

🐾 South of Sumatra, **Fort Gadsden** in the Apalachicola National Forest (850-643-2282; fs.usda.gov/apalachicola) is tricky to find [29.940383,-85.011233] but worth the effort for history buffs. Constructed during the War of 1812 to defend British colonial interests, the original fortress along the Apalachicola River served as a base to recruit runaway slaves and Indians to the British cause of wresting control of Florida from the Spanish. When the British abandoned this effort in 1815, they left behind 300 former slaves and Seminoles to oversee what they called the "Negro Fort." Only 30 survived a direct hit from a cannonade on July 27, 1816. General Andrew Jackson ordered a new fortress erected on the spot as a base of operations for his missions during the First Seminole War. Lieutenant James Gadsden and his men held the fort until Florida became a US territory in 1821. The fort was briefly occupied by Confederate troops. It's reached by dirt roads from FL 65—follow the signs. A mile-long interpretive and nature trail showcases the key points. Open sunrise–sunset; fee.

At **Historic Heritage Village**, on the grounds of the Baptist College of Florida (850-263-3261; baptistcollege.edu), Sanders Avenue, Graceville, a collection of historic homes, churches, and a one-room schoolhouse surround a central commons; restoration was accomplished by students and faculty. The buildings can be viewed any time, but are only open for special events such as their annual Village Christmas.

Learn about the birth of air conditioning at **John Gorrie Museum State Park** (850-653-9347; floridastateparks.org/park/John-Gorrie-Museum), 46 6th Street, Apalachicola. Living in malaria-stricken Florida in the 1850s, Dr. John Gorrie had a problem: how to keep recovering patients cool? Gorrie found a way to use compressed air and condensation to make ice, and then he ran a fan across the ice to keep his infirmary cool. In May 1851, he patented the world's first system for mechanical refrigeration: an ice maker. Although he died in obscurity, his patent led to the design of air conditioners.

Gorrie is buried in Gorrie Square, within sight of his old hospital, which is now the museum. Open Thursday–Monday 9 AM–5 PM; fee.

First settled in the 1820s, **Marianna** formed the commercial center for a hub of busy plantations, including **Sylvania**, the home of Civil War–era governor John Milton, near what is now the grounds of Blue Springs Recreation Area (see *Parks, Preserves, and Camping*). During the war, Marianna was a target because it was the governor's hometown. On September 17, 1864, the **Battle of Marianna** pitted the Home Guard (a militia of old men and teenagers) against invading Union troops. They fought in and around **St. Luke's Episcopal Church**, which was burned during the conflict. A Union officer preserved and returned the Holy Bible to the church, where it remains on display. Faced with surrendering the state to the Union army, Governor Milton returned home on April 1, 1865, and shot himself, eight days before Lee surrendered the Confederacy. Milton is buried at St. Luke's.

For interpretation of early Spanish colonial history, follow the **Jackson County Spanish Heritage Trail** (visitjacksoncountyfla.com/heritage/spanish-heritage-trail) where significant historic sites surrounding Marianna, such as the original Old Spanish Trail and Misson San Carlos, a Spanish mission established around 1680, are explained in detail at interpretive kiosks.

☙ A desire to save the Yon House, an 1897 wood-frame pioneer farmhouse, gave birth to Willard and Linda Smith's collection of important structures of the past at the **Panhandle Pioneer Settlement** (850-674-3050; panhandlepioneer.org), 17869 NW Pioneer Settlement Road, Sam Atkins Park, Blountstown. Opening in 1995, it was Calhoun County's first tourist attraction. Nearly 20 buildings—from 1820 to the 1940s—sit in this living history village and farmstead, all donated and carefully restored by volunteers. Each building has artifacts that make it look like someone just stepped out the door a moment ago. Offering periodic classes in pioneer basics—like blacksmithing and jelly making—they also hold annual festivals (see *Special Events*). Volunteer docents lead guided tours 10 AM–2 PM Tuesday/Thursday–Saturday; fee.

Although the police force has outgrown its old digs in Carrabelle, the **World's Smallest Police Station**, a phone booth downtown, remains, with a squad car always parked next door. It dates back to 1963.

PERFORMING ARTS **Chipola College** (850-718-2301; chipola.edu/fine-and-performing-arts), 3094 Indian Circle, Marianna, sponsors an annual performing arts series that includes Broadway shows, musicians, choral groups, and opera.

The beautifully restored **Dixie Theatre** (850-653-3200; dixietheatre.com), 21 Avenue E, Apalachicola, hosts musicals, plays, jazz and folk concerts, and ballroom dancing. There's hardly a week when there isn't an event going on; check their website for the upcoming schedule.

RAILROADIANA ☙ In downtown Blountstown, you can't miss the railroad history at **Depot Park**, with the big M&B steam engine, tender, and caboose—aka Old 444—on what used to be the main line between N Pear Street and N Main Street (FL 71), in the middle of, fittingly, Railroad Avenue and along the Blountstown Greenway (see *Biking*). On the opposite side of N Pear Street, Depot Park includes the original Blountstown Depot, restored by the local historical society to house the **M&B Railroad Museum** (850-674-5040; facebook.com/MBRRDepot), filled with artifacts from the railroad days. Adjoining it is a city park with a railroad-theme playground and direct access to the greenway.

A visit to Hinson Conservation Area (see *Parks, Preserves, and Camping*) in Marianna will let you trace a part of the old **M&B rail line** along tracks still in the woods. At

29 miles, the M&B was Florida's shortest short line. Also in Marianna, the **L&N Railroad Depot** was the eastern terminus of that east-west railroad line when it was built. It dates back to 1881 and has been used for various functions since, including being used as a bank.

In Chattahoochee, Heritage Park has a **red caboose** parked next to a beautiful mural of the John W. Callahan steamboat on the Apalachicola River. ⚓ Nearby Greensboro is home to the **Greensboro Depot Railroad Museum** (850-442-6434; gadsdenhistory .com/greensboro-depot.html), at the corner of Selman Street and Duffle Avenue, Saturday 1–4 PM; free.

⚓ At Veterans Memorial Park, 10561 NW Theo Jacobs Way, Bristol, hop aboard the **Veterans Memorial Railroad** (850-643-6646; veteransmemorialrailroad.org) for a ride through woods and wetlands on scale model railcars powered by a coal-fired, 2-foot gauge Crown live steam locomotive. There is also a 1950s model Century Flyer diesel engine. Both operate out of a small depot and museum. A volunteer-run project, this extensive model railroad opens monthly for public trips and for special holiday events; see their website for dates.

✳ To Do

BIKING 🌑 ⚓ ♿ Park your car at Depot Park (see *Railroadiana*) or at Sam Atkins Park and walk, bike, or in-line skate the scenic and historic **Blountstown Greenway**, a 5-mile paved trail that connects the community to Apalachicola Landing along the Apalachicola River. Another terminus is a trailhead for the Florida Trail along FL 71. A dedicated bicycle path runs down the middle of St. George Island; rent bicycles at Journeys of St. George Island (see *Ecotours*). The region's scenic rural roads lend themselves to long-distance excursions as well.

BIRDING Along nearly 100 miles of back roads in the **Apalachicola River Wildlife and Environmental Area** (see *Parks, Preserves, and Camping*), look for hundreds of bird species, including swallow-tailed and Mississippi kites roosting in tall cypresses. Shorebirds abound on the tidal flats of the barrier islands. Inland, the **Apalachicola River basin** lies along a flyway for migratory birds, so you can spot Baltimore orioles, winter wrens, and goldfinches. Both the wrens and brown creepers like the old-growth trees along the **Chipola River basin,** as do warblers. On **Lake Seminole**, look for tens of thousands of American coots on the placid surface in the wintertime; canvasbacks can be seen here as well. Painted white bands mark nesting trees in the **Apalachicola National Forest** for the endangered red-cockaded woodpecker.

BOAT EXCURSIONS Two of the region's wildest places are barrier islands accessible only by boat. **Cape St. George Island**, a 9-mile stretch of beach sheltering Apalachicola Bay, plays host to families of red wolves being acclimated to the wild. Off Carrabelle, **Dog Island Preserve** is home to coastal scrub and a stand of mangroves. To get to the remote islands, you'll need a shuttle, such as one run by **All Aboard Cruise & Tow** (850-697-8909), Carrabelle, to Dog Island. At **Journeys of St. George Island** (see *Ecotours*), you can rent your own boat to putter around Apalachicola Bay.

BOATING Because the quickest way between two points along this coast can be by boat, there are marinas and boat ramps along the way. In Apalachicola, **City Marina** hides well beneath the big bridge depositing drivers westbound on US 98 into downtown, adjoining Battery Park. **Scipio Creek Marina** (850-653-8030; scipiocreekmarina

BEST BEACHES

For dogs: Alligator Point, St. George Island main beach
For shelling: Little St. George Island
For solitude: eastern end of Dog Island
For sunbathing: St. George Island State Park
For swimming: Bald Point State Park, Carrabelle Beach
For walking: eastern end of St. George Island State Park
For wheelchairs: St. George Island State Park

BEACHFRONT AT ST GEORGE ISLAND STATE PARK

CAVE TOUR

At Florida Caverns State Park (see *Parks, Preserves, and Camping*), prepare for a cool experience—and we mean that in every sense. On Florida's only show cave tour, the difference between the outside air and the underground climate can be a real relief. Discovered in 1937 when tree roots exposed the entrance, the caverns became a tourist attraction thanks to the Civilian Conservation Corps' "Gopher Gang" digging through the earth from 1938 to 1942. Still used today, the tour route they created curves past a South America-shaped rimstone pool, ribbons of cave bacon, the tight squeeze of the Catacombs, and the colorful Round Room, bathed in pools of light. It's a live cave, dripping water on us from the stalactites above. Our guide, Park Specialist Kelly Banta, grew up in Marianna; she travels worldwide to explore caves. She talks about how weather patterns can be interpreted through calcite crystals, and points out an endangered gray bat. "I love bringing kids down here," said Kelly. "They think they're the first to ever see this." The walking tour requires you to climb stairs and duck low, and you might get your shoes wet and muddy. For claustrophobic visitors, a video tour plays constantly in a big theater at the visitors center, where informative exhibits explain the unique habitats found in the park. Tours run Thursday–Monday and require a separate fee from park admission; call ahead at 850-482-1228 to ensure tours are not sold out for the day. ✐

ON THE FLORIDA CAVERNS STATE PARK CAVERNS TOUR

.com), 301 Market Street, has slips, dockage, showers, gas/diesel, and a ship's store, and is within walking distance of downtown. In Eastpoint, **Wefing's Marine** (850-670-8100; apalachicolaboatrentals.com), 131 US 98, offers boat rentals; they'll meet you at a boat ramp right on Apalachicola Bay. Choose from cats, skiffs, or flats boats starting at

$225 a day, plus launch fees and fuel. Proof of boating experience required. **Moorings of Carrabelle** (see *Lodging*) provides dockage and onshore amenities in a hotel/condo complex.

CAVE DIVING After Edd Sorrenson first dove the crystalline waters of Jackson Blue Springs, he packed his bags and moved to Marianna. His guide service, **Cave Adventurers** (850-482-6016; caveadventurers.com), 5211 Limestone Lane, serves as the gatekeeper for county permits for dives at Jackson Blue Spring and can introduce you to the dozen springs of Merritt Mill Pond. Need dive instruction? They do that too. Their shop rents and sells diving essentials—including tanks, lights, scooters, and pontoon boats—and has a continuous blend nitrox mixing station for filling your tanks. Nondivers can rent canoes, kayaks, or pontoon boats to explore the beautiful spring-fed pond.

DIVING Go offshore diving with **Carrabelle Charters** (850-528-1926; scubadive charters.com) to explore artificial reefs and wrecks along the Forgotten Coast; trips start from two tanks/two dives up to an overnighter with six dives in up to 115 feet of water.

ECOTOURS Most interior excursions through this region are on your own, but on the coast, you can pick up a guide. For a closer look at the Apalachicola River estuary, cruise with **Book Me A Charter** (850-653-2622, bookmeacharter.com) for general sightseeing, starting at $350; they also run inshore fishing charters and evening flounder gigging.

    Captain Chester Reese (850-228-9060; naturalworldcharters.com) of Carrabelle can get you out to Dog Island for a day of exploration and adventure. $225 for up to 6 passengers to go shelling along the open beaches of this barrier island; $400 for the grand tour with historic and ecologic details shared as your captain shows you around.

    ⚓ **Journeys of St. George Island** (850-927-3259; sgislandjourneys.com), 240 E 3rd Street, has a complete menu of tours ranging from guided paddling trips to ecotours to Little St. George Island to deep-sea and bay fishing. They also rent sailboats, motorboats, SUP, and kayaks, and they run environmental summer camps and special kid-oriented trips. Kayak and SUP ecotours start at $50.

FISHING The Apalachicola River watershed is a huge destination for sport fishing, with tournaments held nearly every month. In Carrabelle ask about fishing guides at **C-Quarters Marina** (850-697-8400; c-quartersmarina.com), 501 St. James Avenue. Ask around Apalachicola for top guides like the **Robinson Brothers Guide Service** (850-653-8896; floridaredfish.com), or **Boss Charters** (850-853-8055; bosscharters .com), 150 Bay City Road, for inshore, light-tackle bay fishing, or offshore fishing with Dennis Crosby. Depending on the guide, length of trip, and location, you'll pay $400 and up for a trip. To fish the Apalachicola River on your own, put your boat in the river at any of many ramps along FL 71 or FL 67; you can rent a fishing boat from **Wefing's Marine** (see *Boating*). Stop in at **Forgotten Coast Outfitters** (850-653-9669), 94 Market Street, Apalachicola, for fly-fishing tackle and homespun advice.

    Lake Seminole is the hot spot for bass fishing in the region, splitting the state line between Georgia and Florida as the Flint and Chattahoochee rivers come together to form the Apalachicola. Our friends tend to head for **Seminole Lodge** (see *Fish Camps*), a storied institution along the southern shore. For day trips with your own boat, **Three Rivers State Park** (see *Parks*) provides access as well. To its west, you won't want to miss the serenity of cypress-lined **Merritts Mill Pond** along US 90, Marianna, or **Spring Creek** for fly fishing.

GOLF Built by the Civilian Conservation Corps in the 1930s, the Robert Trent Jones–designed **Florida Caverns Golf Course** (850-482-4257), 3309 Caverns Road, has nine holes on hilly terrain under the tall pines adjoining the state park and is managed by a local club, not the state park. Off US 90 east of Marianna, **Indian Springs Golf Club** (800-587-6257; indianspringsgolfcourse.net), 5248 Club House Drive, offers 18 holes, par 72.

HIKING **Apalachicola Bluffs and Ravines Preserve** (850-643-2756; tnc.org), CR 12, Bristol, provides hikers with a look at unique natural areas along the bluffs of the Apalachicola River along the extremely rugged 3.5-mile Garden of Eden Trail. Along this footpath, you'll see the world's most endangered conifer, the torreya tree, along with unusual species of magnolias and the showy Florida anise—look for bright red blooms in spring. The hike has a big payoff beyond the botanical wonders: great views from Alum Bluff above the Apalachicola River.

The nature trails adjoining the caverns parking area at **Florida Caverns State Park** (see *Parks, Preserves, and Camping*) are a must for day hikers because of unusual geology, rugged bluffs, and colorful wildflowers in spring. One of the trails even leads through a cave!

For a scenic hike to the famed Look and Tremble rapids of the Chipola River, follow the Altha section of the **Florida Trail** (see *What's Where*) westward from the north shore of the river at Willis Bridge Park, CR 274 [30.5341, -85.164767]. The Florida Trail also traverses true wilderness in the Apalachicola National Forest between Porter Lake and Camel lakes, with dozens of swamps amid the vast pine forests, and rare pitcher plant bogs (best seen during their blooming period in early April) between Vilas and Shuler Bay. To see more extensive pitcher plant savannas, hike the **Wright Lake Trail** around Wright Lake Recreation Area, Sumatra.

INSIDE THE APALACHICOLA NATIONAL ESTUARINE RESEARCH RESERVE VISITOR CENTER

PADDLING THE CHIPOLA

The Chipola River (nwfwater.com/Lands/Recreation/Area/Chipola-River) flows 51 miles south to Dead Lakes at Wewahitchka, a three-day trip with a stretch of whitewater (portage recommended) at the Look and Tremble rapids. Along its length, there are more than 60 springs, the most found along a river in Northwest Florida.

For canoe rentals and shuttling, try Scott's Ferry General Store & Campground (see *Campgrounds*) or Bear Paw Adventures (850-482-4948; bearpawescape.com), Magnolia Road off FL 71; they provide kayak and canoe rentals ($35–50) and shuttles. Based in Altha, Chipola River Outfitters (850-762-2800; chipolariveroutfitters.com) meets you at the landings of the Middle Chipola—Peacock Bridge, Willis Bridge, Johnny Boy, and Lamb Eddy—with your rentals, $35–55.

For day trips on the Upper Chipola, rent a canoe at Florida Caverns State Park (see *Parks, Preserves, and Camping*) or check in with Lily Pad Adventures (see *Campgrounds*) for put-in at a secluded spring even farther north, plus pick-up downriver; your kayak or theirs. Kayak and canoe rentals, $35–50, include shuttles. Half-day trips are playtime on the water, while a full-day trip is a workout. Most outfitters only run seasonally and are closed during the winter months; call ahead to check.

Backpackers won't want to miss the challenges of **Torreya State Park** (see *Parks, Preserves, and Camping*), where, during the winter months, you have ridgeline views from the 14-mile, double-loop trail system. A primitive campsite perched in a quiet spot well above the river is worth the hike—in fact, the hike itself, physically challenging and visually diverse, is worth the trip to this lushly forested park.

NATURE CENTER ⌀ ♿ A half-mile of interpretive boardwalks meander around the **Apalachicola National Estuarine Research Reserve Visitor Center** (850-670-7700; apalachicolareserve.com), 108 Island Drive, Eastpoint, where visitors can explore coastal habitats along St. George Sound. Inside the building are aquariums with aquatic life and interactive exhibits about the history of commercial fishing and timbering, as well as shells and fossils common to this region. Tuesday–Saturday 9 AM–4 PM; free.

PADDLING Nonprofit guardians of the health of the river and bay, **Apalachicola Riverkeeper** (850-653-8936; apalachicolariverkeeper.org), 232-B Water Street, Apalachicola, runs guided paddling trips on the fourth Saturday of every month in the Apalachicola watershed. The trips are free to members and $30 for non-members. For saltwater adventure in Apalachicola Bay, **Journeys of St. George Island** (see *Ecotours*) rents kayaks—single and tandem—and stand-up paddleboards, in addition to running guided trips.

For a hauntingly beautiful paddle on a calm day, the cypress-lined spring-fed waters of **Merritts Mill Pond** should not be missed. Rent canoes in the summer months at Jackson Blue Spring (see *Springs*) or year-round at Cave Adventures (see *Cave Diving*).

Along FL 65 you'll find numerous put-ins for paddling adventures into **Tate's Hell** and on the **Apalachicola River**; watch for the yellow-and-black signs at places like Graham Creek. Eleven such routes are outlined in the free **Apalachicola River Paddling Trail System** map, available from the Apalachicola River WEA office; see *Parks, Preserves, and Camping*.

PARKS, PRESERVES, AND CAMPING The **Apalachicola National Forest** (850-643-2282; fs.usda.gov/apalachicola) encompasses more than half of Liberty County, with some of the world's finest pitcher plant savannas on its western edge, surrounding Sumatra. This is the most rugged and wild portion of Florida's largest national forest, best enjoyed in its major recreation areas—Camel Lake and Wright Lake, which offer tent and RV sites for $10–15—as well as along its very scenic highways, including Apalachee Savannahs Scenic Byway, which branches south from CR 12 south of Bristol. The forest offers many quiet primitive getaways for hikers, anglers, and hunters; four-wheel drive is recommended on most unpaved forest roads.

✦ **Bald Point State Park** (850-349-9146; floridastateparks.org/park/Bald-Point), 146 Box Cut Road, provides Alligator Point with a quiet sweep of sandy beach along a peninsula of scrub oaks and pines. It's perfect for kids, thanks to the lack of waves and the gentle shallow slope. Nature trails and bicycle paths following old roads wind through the coastal hammocks of the park. Fee.

✦ ♿ 🐾 At **Florida Caverns State Park** (850-482-9598; floridastateparks.org/park/Florida-Caverns), 3345 Caverns Road, most visitors come for the show cave (see *Cave Tour*), but if that's all you do, you're missing out. Rugged limestone bluffs above the cave and the Chipola River floodplain offer some truly fun and scenic hiking, with a profusion of wildflowers in early spring. Rent a canoe to paddle on the cypress-lined Chipola River, which vanishes underground for a stretch (you do not). The parking area at Blue Hole accesses picnic pavilions and is the saddle-up point for equestrians and mountain bikers headed out on the Upper Chipola Trail System. The deeply shaded campground is within walking distance of the swimming area at Blue Hole; sites for $20. Fee.

🐾 **Hinson Conservation & Recreation Area** (850-482-4353; floridahikes.com/hinson-trail), SR 73, Marianna [30.757621,-85.213923], protects the western shore of the Chipola River and its extensive karst formations, including large sinkholes and a natural bridge over Alamo Cave. A 4-mile hiking and biking trail loops the 266-acre preserve, with shorter options available; there are picnic tables and a put-in on the river below a well-known karst feature called The Ovens.

♿ Unless you go for a stroll in the historic residential district to the west of Apalachicola's downtown, you might miss **Lafayette Park** (850-653-9319), 13th Street and Avenue B, and that would be a shame. Dating back to 1832, this park is on a bluff well above the bay, with a long fishing pier that stretches out over the placid waters. Period lamps and an old-fashioned gazebo remind you of a bygone era, as do the many beautiful Victorian homes around the park's edges.

✦ **River Landing Park** (850-663-2123), 269 River Landing Road, has access to the Apalachicola River for anglers and boaters as well as a playground and a large midden along the river. At the top of the hill is the county-run **Chattahoochee RV Campground & Fishing Resort** (850-663-4475; cityofchattahoochee.com/rv&fishing.html), with an RV park and cabins. Tent/trailer sites $11; full hookups with 30 amp service $19. Cash or check only.

✦ ♿ 🐾 Occupying the purely natural eastern end of St. George Island, **St. George Island State Park** (850-927-2111; floridastateparks.org/park/St-George-Island), 1900 E Gulf Beach Drive, has a pleasant 60-site campground ($24) nestled in among the pines at the east end of the island, and primitive camping for folks who hike the Gap Point Trail. A wheelchair-accessible trail connects beach to bay. But the big draw here is the miles and miles of unspoiled white-sand beaches with a backdrop, behind the scenic park road, of tall dunes. Pets welcome on the trails and in the campground but not on the beach. Fee.

🐾 With nearly 150,000 acres of mostly wetlands, **Tate's Hell State Forest** (850-697-3734; freshfromflorida.com), 1621 US 98, Carrabelle, is one helluva swamp. Hunting, fishing, and paddling are the main recreation here, but hikers have two spots to explore:

the short ♿ wheelchair-accessible Ralph G. Kendrick Dwarf Cypress Boardwalk (look for signs on FL 67) leading out over a rare (for North Florida) dwarf cypress swamp and the High Bluff Coastal Nature Trail along US 98. Roads are rough; high-clearance or 4WD vehicle recommended.

♿ 🐾 🏕 ↝ The expansive **Three Rivers State Park** (850-482-9006; floridastateparks .org/park/Three-Rivers), 7908 Three Rivers Park Road, Sneads, edges Lake Seminole, a top-notch bass fishing destination. Hiking trails extend across the hilly terrain above the lake. The lakeside campground has shaded sites ($16) and a wheelchair-accessible rental cabin ($65), picnic pavilions, and canoe rentals.

♿ 🏕 🐾 ↝ From the 150-foot bluffs above the Apalachicola River at **Torreya State Park** (850-643-2674; floridastateparks.org/park/Torreya), 2576 NW Torreya Park Road/FL 271 between Bristol and Greensboro, you can see for miles. An 1849 mansion, the Gregory House, dominates the skyline. It's getting harder to find the namesake of the park, the torreya tree—also known as the stinking cedar—because a blight keeps the young trees from maturing. But you can find them along the trails. Enjoy the scenic developed campground, where you can pitch a tent, pull in an RV, settle into a camping cabin, or try out Florida's only state park yurt, $16–50.

SCENIC DRIVES One of Florida's best scenic drives, once a little-known treasure, is now part of the nationally acclaimed **Florida Big Bend Scenic Byway** (floridabigbendscenicbyway.com). Start at FL 20 in Bristol; head south on CR 12 into the Apalachicola National Forest. This designated scenic route merges with FL 65 and continues south through nearly 50 miles of unspoiled old-growth longleaf pine forest as the road parallels the Apalachicola River. When the road ends, turn left. Atop a high sand bluff, US 98 offers sweeping views of St. George Sound for the next 22 miles.

A SWARM OF YELLOW PITCHER PLANTS IN THE APALACHEE SAVANNAHS

At Carrabelle, head north on FL 67 through the national forest to return to FL 20 at Hosford. Total drive time: 3 hours. Alternatively, CR 379 south of Bristol is **Apalachee Savannahs Scenic Byway**, which dovetails with the route above onto FL 65 at Sumatra. Along this route, you'll see vast pitcher plant savannas blooming each spring.

SPRINGS With Jackson Blue Spring at its head and nearly a dozen more, like Shangri-La and Indian Springs feeding its length, **Merritts Mill Pond** is a must-visit for serious spring hunters. You can snorkel at **Blue Springs Recreation Area** or from a kayak or canoe, or you can rent a pontoon from **Cave Adventures** (see *Cave Diving*) to spend a day on the water with friends. If you're scuba-certified, Cave Adventures can also outfit you and drop you off for a drift dive.

Marianna's **Blue Springs Recreation Area** (850-482-9637; jacksoncountyfl.com), 5461 Blue Springs Highway, offers a sandy beach, diving boards, and playground surrounding Jackson Blue Spring, a 70-degree, first-magnitude spring bubbling more than 64 million gallons of water daily. Open Memorial Day–Labor Day. Fee.

SWIMMING ✍ Used for D-Day invasion practice in 1942, **Carrabelle Beach**, US 98 west of Carrabelle, tends to be busy because of its easy-to-reach location along this scenic stretch of coastal highway. It has restrooms, shaded picnic shelters, and a panoramic view that includes Dog Island in the distance. Waters are shallow and gentle here, perfect for youngsters. Free.

TUBING **Bear Paw Adventures** sets up 4-mile tubing trips down crystal-clear, cypress-lined Spring Creek; March–September, $15 and up. **Chipola River Outfitters** offers tubing and river rafting on the middle Chipola, right through the Look and Tremble rapids, $15–25, April–October. See *Paddling the Chipola* for contact information.

WALKING TOURS Stop at the Apalachicola Bay Chamber of Commerce for a copy of their historic walking tour booklet that highlights **downtown Apalachicola** sites, most within seven blocks of Market Street. In Marianna, or pick up a self-guided tour of **historic sites in Jackson County**, which you can use to explore downtown on foot.

WATER SPORTS Check at the beach in front of the Blue Parrot on **St. George Island** for summer-season stands with Hobie Cat rentals and parasail rides, and at **Journeys of St. George Island** (see *Ecotours*) for water sports rentals.

❋ Lodging

BED & BREAKFASTS ♂ (ᵗᵖ) **Coombs Inn & Suites** (850-653-9199; coombsinnandsuites.com), 80 6th Street, Apalachicola 32320. One of the grandest restored mansions in the South (circa 1905) and one of the nation's top inns, the pride of lumber baron James Coombs will amaze you. Step inside the doorway into a grand hall lined with black cypress walls and a high-beamed ceiling. Some suites offer spacious Victorian elegance with careful restorative touches, such as the gleaming colored tile on the coal-fired fireplaces (a relic of the days when ships from Liverpool swapped coal ballast for cotton) and built-in cabinets. Breakfast includes hot dishes, and in the afternoon, enjoy tea and cookies or a glass of wine before dinner. Twenty-three rooms across three grand Victorian mansions, each room with private bath, some with whirlpools; multiroom suites available. $89–160.

🐾 (ᵗᵖ) Relax at **The Hinson House** (850-526-1500; thehinsonhouse.com),

4338 Lafayette Street, Marianna 32446, a classic 1922 bungalow in Marianna's historic residential district. Now in its third generation of hospitality from the same family, it's a comfortable place to settle in after a long day of paddling, hiking, or exploring; Rachel, who whips up an excellent breakfast from locally sourced organic foods, is also a mountain biker. Choose from two regular rooms or three spacious suites (including the Home Guard Suite, which overlooks the site of the Battle of Marianna), with your choice of multiple beds—great for families, friends, and relatives traveling together. $79–139.

🐾 Built in 1890, **The Old Carrabelle Hotel** (850-528-3983; oldcarrabellehotel.com), 201 Tallahassee Street, Carrabelle 32322, is a former railroad hotel lovingly restored by Skip and Kathy Frink. Like a sea captain's home (which it also was), it's filled with treasures from abroad as well as fine art from the tropics and from Florida's coasts. Curl up with a good book in the Hemingway Room, with its literary theme and decor evoking dreams of Africa. Each room is a quiet, private retreat, or you can mingle with your fellow guests in the parlor or on the veranda and watch the sunset shimmer on the Carrabelle River, $87–97.

COTTAGE **Winchester Cottage** (850-697-9010; oldcarrabellehotel.com/Winchester), 506 Tallahassee Street, Carrabelle 32322, is a restored 1933 coastal cottage made of tongue-and-groove pine. A breezy screened porch fronts the cottage, which has three bedrooms, a bath, and a full kitchen. $350–400 for three nights, or $500–700 per week, just 2 miles from Carrabelle Beach.

HISTORIC 🐾 ⚓ (📶) At **The Gibson Inn** (850-653-2191; gibsoninn.com), 51 Avenue C, Apalachicola 32320, the hallways and doorjambs are a little out of kilter and the solid wood floors creak a bit underfoot, but it's all part of the charm of this meticulously restored hotel in the heart of downtown. Known as the Franklin Hotel when it opened in 1907, it was constructed by James Fulton Buck, who hand-selected the tongue-and-groove paneling used as wainscoting throughout the structure. Built of heart pine and black cypress three stories tall with wraparound porches, it offers exterior halls and doors on upper floors, which are put to good use as pet-friendly rooms. On the National Register of Historic Places, the inn has 31 rooms and suites. Some rooms are cozy, others spacious. Some are known for their ghosts. Opt for a corner room to throw your windows open and catch the cool salt breezes, or settle down in a rocking chair on the shaded broad wraparound porch to watch the world go by. $140–170 rooms, $260–285 suites.

COMFORT AND LUXURY (📶) **The Consulate** (800-341-2021 or 850-927-2282; consulatesuites.com), 76 Water Street, Apalachicola 32320, consists of four apartment-size suites above the J. E. Grady & Company Market. The brick walls, 10-foot-high tin-plated ceilings, and heart pine floors remind you you're in a historic building; in the early 1900s, this was the French consulate in Florida. The artistic touches and views are a reminder that you're in Apalachicola. The complex has a private garden entrance off Commerce Streetand private balconies for each suite, which range in size up to 1,300 square feet. Amenities include washer/dryer, fully equipped kitchen, and cable TV. Right in the heart of downtown, this classy choice lets you wander down the staircase and into the action in moments. $175–305; discounts for longer stays.

RETRO AND ARTSY ♿ (📶) **St. George Inn** (850-927-2903; stgeorgeinn.com), 135 Franklin Boulevard. Built to look like a turn-of-the-twentieth-century hotel, this pleasant, modern inn is a short walk from both beach and bay. Rooms range in size from spacious to cozy, including the hostel-like SGI Xpress with its twin bunk beds, and their rates reflect size, starting at $105–140 for a queen and $115–155 for a king. Discounts for weekly stays.

WATERFRONT 🐾 📶 At **Apalachicola River Inn** at Oystertown (850-653-8139; apalachicolariverinn.com), 123 Water Street, Apalachicola 32320, all of the spacious rooms come with a river view and a cooked-to-order breakfast at adjoining Caroline's Restaurant, as well as a happy-hour drink at the Spoonbill Lounge. Kick back on your riverfront balcony and watch the shrimpers come in. $149–179, discount for winter months.

🐾 **Moorings of Carrabelle** (866-821-2248 or 850-697-2800; mooringsofcarrabelle.com), 1000 US 98, Carrabelle 32322. This popular full-service marina overlooking the Carrabelle River offers large waterfront condos (one, two, and three bedrooms) with docking slip included (up to 25 feet) just outside your door, $119–140; or standard large hotel rooms, $90. Smoking and non-smoking units; weekly rates available. Swimming pool, dive shop, and charter captains on-site.

🐾 📶 All rooms are on the Apalachicola River at **Water Street Hotel** (850-653-3700; waterstreethotel.com), 329 Water Street. Decked out in Caribbean colonial style, these apartment-size rooms are big enough to move in for the season, with a full kitchen and full-size appliances, a screened deck overlooking the river, and accents like shiny hardwood floors and wall-mounted flat-screen televisions. A dock runs along the front of the hotel, but it doesn't obstruct your view of the river and its vast estuary; on the back side of the complex, a pool with sunning deck is surrounded by the marsh that wraps around the property. Starting at $169–189.

TRIED AND TRUE On trips to Marianna, we've stayed at the pet-friendly 📶 🐾 ♿ **Microtel** (850-633-1825; wyndam hotels.com), 4959 Whitetail Drive, and the adjacent 📶 ♿ **Fairfield Inn and Suites** (850-482-0012; marriott.com), 4966 Whitetail Drive. 📶 ♿ **Best Western Apalach Inn** (850-653-9131; bestwestern .com), 249 US 98, Apalachicola, is an inexpensive option west of downtown.

CAMPGROUNDS 🐟 On beautiful cypress-lined Merritts Mill Pond, **Arrowhead Campground** (850-482-5583; arrowheadcamp.com), 4820 US 90, Marianna 32446, has several rental cabins with baths in addition to its full-hookup spaces shaded by tall pines. Swimming pool and general store; canoe rentals available.

🐾 📶 **Ho Hum RV Park** (850-697-3926; hohumrvpark.com), 2132 US 98, Carrabelle 32322, offers free cable and Wi-Fi with their sites, many of which face right out on the Gulf of Mexico. Full hookups, pull-throughs for RVs, recreation hall, and laundry facilities. $34–43, discount for Good Sam, AAA, Escapees. Weekly and monthly rates available.

📶 Offering family-friendly cabins ($89) as well as campsites ($7–30) for tents, RVs, and pop-ups, **Lily Pad Adventures** (850-326-4884; lilypadadventures .com), 3150 FL 2, Campbellton 32446, sits on a spring run connecting to the Chipola River, making it a perfect launch point for spring hunters and avid paddlers.

Scott's Ferry Landing and General Store (850-674-2900; facebook.com/ Scottsferrycampground), 6648 FL 71, Blountstown 32424, offers a back-to-nature campground under the pines along the Chipola River, with RV and tent sites ($20–25), and basic cabins ($55–75) built on stilts above flood level. They also rent canoes (see *Paddling*), and there's a fish-cleaning station and boat launch.

FISH CAMPS 🐾 The legendary **Seminole Lodge** (800-410-5209 or 850-593-6886; seminolelodge.com), 2360 Legion Road, Sneads 32460, is an angler's getaway along the shores of Lake Seminole, the best place for bass fishing in

Northwest Florida. The complex includes a nine-room waterfront motel ($55–65, some units with kitchenettes), marina with full-service fuel ($5 a day for slips), campground ($15–22), and bait-and-tackle shop/store.

☂ Offbeat and Old Florida, the funky **Sportsman's Lodge Motel** (850-670-8423; sportsmanslodgeonthebay.blogspot .com), 99 N Bayshore Drive, Eastpoint 32328, caters to the get-off-the-beaten-path and love-to-fish crowd. It sits directly on the bay across from downtown Apalachicola but worlds apart, a small complex with a tropical exterior and basic rooms inside. Smoking, kids, and pets permitted, $62–85.

✳ Where to Eat

ELEGANT AND ROMANTIC The she-crab soup at **Caroline's Dining on the River** (850-653-8139; apalachicolariver inn.com) at Apalachicola River Inn (see *Lodging*) was a delicious delight, especially when coupled with the gorgeous view of the river through the picture windows. Don't plan to hurry through dinner, especially while the sun is setting. Fresh local oysters come in several preparations, and the dinner menu has its own vegetarian section. Entrées, $12 and up, range from pastas to a grilled filet mignon, with many seafood choices on the menu. Reservations suggested.

The Owl Cafe & Wine Room (850-653-9888; owlcafeflorida.com), 15 Avenue D, Apalachicola, treats your taste buds upstairs with fun dishes like 13 Mile Apalachicola Deep Fried Oyster salad; Melty Danish Brie with fruit compote; and lump blue crab cakes with spicy tartar sauce. Richard Bickel's scenes of Apalachicola add moodiness to the room. Savor fine wines downstairs in The Wine Room. Lunch and dinner, $10–28.

CASUAL FARE Inside a former Coca Cola bottling plant, **Madison's Warehouse** (850-526-4000; madisons

warehouse.com), 2881 Madison Street, Marianna, is a delightful steakhouse with a broad menu. Chef Mark's chef salad doesn't fill you up with lunchmeats—hearty grilled steak and chicken sit with your greens and eggs. We enjoyed the Center Cut Pork Chop, with its light apple glaze, and Chicken Portabella, topped with a massive mushroom, spinach, red peppers, and cheese. Speaking of mushrooms, the fresh-battered fried mushrooms almost stole our appetite for dinner. Come hungry! Entrées, $13–24.

🚂 For railroad buffs, **Main Street Station** (850-237-1500), 17415 Main Street N, Blountstown, lets you sit at big picture windows and stare at a historic steam engine (see *Railroadiana*) while chowing down on fish tacos, authentic Cuban sandwiches, and burgers, $7 and up. A small ice cream parlor in the back caters to folks right off the Blountstown Greenway.

COMFORT FOOD **Bobbie's Waffle Iron** (850-526-5055), 4509 Lafayette Street, Marianna, a little country diner with home cooking, is your best bet for a cheap, hearty breakfast. Don't miss the home-cooked hash browns! Open **6 AM–2 PM** daily, with a Blue Plate Special at lunch.

🍽 **Gazebo Coffee Shop & Deli** (850-526-1276), 4412 Lafayette Street, Marianna, is a popular downtown coffee and lunch stop. Here in farm country, their eggs are farm fresh, so order up an omelet or one of their famed sandwiches, like the Flying Floss—a scoop of shrimp salad with garlic mayonnaise, melted Swiss cheese, and tomato slices atop a croissant. Lunch $5 and up; open Monday–Friday 10 AM–3 PM.

Genuinely unfussy and busy as all get out despite being hidden in a shopping center, **The Oaks** (850-526-1114), 4727 US 90, Marianna, packs them in with just down-home Southern cooking like catfish and grits or broiled steak tips with peppers and onions and cheese grits. All shrimp is local, and it is the go-to pick if you're not doing the buffet. Another must is cake. Piled high on metal shelves, you'll find flavors and styles to please everyone, from butternut to seven-layer and red velvet. Entrées $12 and up.

ETHNIC EATS 🍴 The hopping spot downtown after dark, **El Jalisco** (850-674-3411; eljalisco.com/store_locator/el-jalisco-blountstown), 16919 Pear Street, Blountstown, fills a former IGA supermarket. A festive Mexican restaurant with authentic dishes and a menu that goes on and on and on, they'll fill you up—and still keep the chips and salsa coming. Entrées include grilled rib-eye steaks prepared Mexican style, mole and adobe chicken, and platters with half a dozen delights, $9 and up.

🍴 A delightful Mediterranean treat, **Mashawy Grill** (850-526-1578), 3297 Caverns Road, Marianna, wowed our taste buds with their kafta kabob and moussaka. Entrées come with fresh fattoush and hummus with pita ($12–20), or you can nibble away at a collection of appetizers that include sambousa and falafel. Trying their freshly made juices, we found the lime/mint an unexpectedly cool combination. Finish off with a unique dessert like konafa (a creamy cheese-filled cake) or basbousa (a sweet cake soaked in syrup) for a most eclectic and tasty meal.

HIP BISTRO-STYLE 🍴 🍷 ((ᵖ)) Enjoy your gourmet panini with a side of smooth jazz at **Bistro Palms** (850-526-2226; bistropalms.com), 2865 McPherson Street, Marianna, a downtown lunch favorite serving up generous portions of soups, salad, and sandwiches, $5–7. Watch the world go by while dining out on the deck, but save room for their amazing peanut butter pie! Monday–Friday 10:30 AM–2 PM.

Tamara's Cafe Floridita (850-653-4111; tamarascafe.com), 71 Market Street, Apalachicola serves up funky fusion foods orchestrated by its South American owner. Look for tapas (on Wednesday evenings), paella, pecan-crusted grouper, and grouper tacos with fresh cilantro sauce. Trust us, they're fabulous! Lunch and dinner, most entrées under $30, and open for breakfast, too. Closed Monday.

OCEANFRONT The casual **Blue Parrot Cafe** (850-927-2987; blueparrotcafe.net), 68 W Gorrie Street, St. George Island, offers oceanfront dining; feast on oyster and grouper while the sea breeze blows in your face. Try a heaping platter of seafood on their "World Famous" Blue Parrot Seafood Platter, or the delicious Seafood Marguarite, with grouper, shrimp, scallops, and crabmeat covered in a cream sauce and cheddar cheese and then baked. Lunch specials 11 AM–4 PM. Sandwiches and entrées, $10–32.

QUICK BITE 🍴 🍷 Offering up a triple scoop of nostalgia: old-fashioned soda parlor, quirky Florida memorabilia and postcards, and recollections of when this was Camp Gordon Johnson, **Carrabelle Junction** (850-697-9550), 88 Tallahassee Street, Carrabelle, has that time-travel feel, thanks to antique signs and ephemera adding to the original 1940s soda fountain decor. Grab a sundae or a sandwich, or enjoy one of the nicely done salads or made-from-scratch soups; $3 and up for lunch or ice cream.

🍴 🍷 Homemade cakes tempt at the **Country Creamery** (850-674-4663), 20755 Central Avenue E, Blountstown. Stop in for a hearty Navajo sandwich on 12-grain bread, with grilled chicken, tomato, romaine, banana peppers, onions, provolone, and chili mayonnaise—it's a handful! The kids will appreciate this downtown ice cream stop, too. Lunch, $2–7.

SEAFOOD With the best people-watching view in town (big picture windows and an unobstructed view down to the shrimp boats) and fabulous fresh fish, **Apalachicola Seafood Grill** (850-653-9510), 100 Market Street, Apalachicola, is a century-old landmark in a city best known for its seafood. Of course the oysters were perfect, but you won't go wrong with shrimp, grouper, or "the world's largest fried fish sandwich." Sandwiches and baskets, $7–18. Closed Sunday.

At **Papa Joe's** (850-653-1189; papajoesoysterbar.com), 45 Avenue D, Apalachicola, there are always oysters on ice behind the bar and they serve them up 14 different ways, including baked and topped with capers and feta cheese. Order them fried and they come Southern-style with a big bowl of cheese grits and hush puppies. Shrimp, scallops, crab, and grouper are fresh choices, $9 and up, or opt for some beef; the steak-and-shrimp combo is the best of both worlds. Closed Sunday.

LOCAL WATERING HOLES Catch the spirit of the Gulf at **Harry's Bar** (850-697-3420), 306 Marine Street, Carrabelle, an old-time fisherman's hangout; shoot some pool and shoot the breeze 10 AM–12 PM daily.

ICE CREAM AND SWEETS Satisfy your sweet tooth at **Apalachicola Chocolate & Coffee Company** (850-653-1025), 75 Market Street, Apalachicola, where you can try a tupelo honey walnut caramel, bourbon pecan truffles, fresh divinity, or dozens of other tasty creations. Too hot for sweets? Cool down with their homemade gelato.

The **Old Time Soda Fountain** (850-653-2606), 93 Market Street, Apalachicola, is arguably the state's oldest, in business since 1905. Sit at the 1940s-style luncheonette counter (from the days when this still was a drugstore with a soda fountain) and slurp down an egg cream or a big chocolate milkshake, or order up a giant ice cream sundae, hand-scooped and prepared right in front of your eyes. Touristy gifts like T-shirts and coconut monkeys fill the remainder of the shop, which is open daily.

✻ Selective Shopping

ANTIQUES **The Tin Shed** (850-653-3635), 170 Water Street, Apalachicola, has everything from portholes and ship's

LOCAL ART GRACES THE SIDE OF DOWNTOWN BOOKS & PURL

bells to lobster traps and even a ship's binnacle or two, as well as modern home decor items and seashells. Be sure to step out back, where the collection of buoys is quite the artistic show.

ARTS AND CRAFTS At **All That Jazz** (850-653-4800), 84 Market Street, Apalachicola, peruse local arts and crafts, especially the clever coin catchers: socks topped with open-mouthed ceramic faces. Crème brûlée coffee tempts, too.

With creative art—from pastels to recycled found items—along with interesting books and gifts, **Olio Art and Gift Gallery** (850-557-8886), 2869 Jefferson Street, Marianna, is a delightful place to stop in and browse around. Don't forget to ask about the luscious Southern Craft Creamery ice cream they sell by the pint, in flavors like Sweet Corn & Blackberry, Buttermilk, and Raspberry Basil.

BOOKS AND GIFTS Step through the back door into busy **Downtown Books & Purl** (850-653-1290), 67 Commerce Street, Apalachicola, which features an excellent range of literary fiction, Florida books, and a small newsstand; luxurious yarn and knitting supplies fill out the store, with local artwork displayed outdoors.

Golden Pharmacy (850-674-4557), 17324 Main Street N, Blountstown, is one of those old-fashioned drugstores you'll find in a small town—they used to have a soda fountain, and folks still rest on seats while waiting for their prescriptions. You'll find local art and cute gifts, soy candles, great greeting cards, and tasty treats like slushies and tupelo honey made just down the road in Wewahitchka.

On the waterfront, the renovated **J. E. Grady & Co. Market** (850-653-4099), 76 Water Street, Apalachicola's ship's chandlery circa 1884, is now a department store with tin ceilings and its original wooden floor. Browse for everything from dressy apparel and classic reproduction toys to "Wild Women" gear.

CLOTHING **Journeys of St. George Island** (850-927-3259; sgislandjourneys .com), 240 E 3rd Street, is part outfitter (see *Ecotours*) and part beach shop, with kayaks for sale under one roof and sarongs, teeny dresses, and Hawaiian shirts in the next room. Closed Sunday.

Riverlily (850-653-2600), 78 Commerce Street, Apalachicola is filled with delightful feminine items—dresses, scarves, purple satin slippers, aromatherapy, incense, and candles—to uplift a woman's spirit. Need mermaids? You'll find them in every shape and size here.

DECOR AND MORE Sponges from the Gulf of Mexico—harvested just like in olden times from offshore beds—are the heart of **Apalachicola Sponge Company** (850-653-3550; apalachspongecompany .com), 14 Avenue D, Apalachicola. Select one for scrubbing, or a few to heighten your nautical decor. Handmade olive oils and soaps also hark to the Greek influence on this port city.

Inside **The Stuffed Owl** (850-653-9888), 15 Avenue D, Apalachicola, are gourmet goodies and everything you need to set the perfect table.

FARMERS' MARKETS Each Wednesday from 9 AM–1 PM, **Bowery Market** (844-272-2523), Commerce Street between Avenue F & G, Apalachicola, is in full swing, with live music, fine BBQ, and fresh veggies.

Buddy's Picked Fresh Produce (850-593-9977), 8082 US 90, Sneads, stand offers farm-fresh fruits and vegetables all year long, as well as seafood from the coast.

On Saturday mornings, the **Downtown Farmers' Market** (along FL 20, adjoining Wakulla Bank) in Blountstown brings in the rural goodness of the surrounding area, including fresh cheese and milk from Ocheesee Creamery (see *Dairy Farms*), succulent barbecue, in-season produce, and creative crafts.

Held downtown at Madison Street Park (atop the bluff), the **Marianna City Farmers**

Market (mariannacityfarmersmarket.net), 2844 Madison Street, is one of the best places for fresh produce in the region. That's because the area is all about agriculture, and only local farmers are invited to sell their wares here. The market is open May–August every Tuesday, Thursday, and Saturday 7 AM–noon.

MALLS AND OUTLETS This little town along FL 77 is home to ♿ **Factory Stores of America** (factorystores.com), 950 Prim Avenue, Graceville, the only factory outlet mall we know of in a truly rural area. Why here? It's halfway between Dothan, Georgia, and Panama City Beach. Merchants include Corningware, Bon Worth, and more. Open daily.

NURSERIES You've seen the signs along I-10—$20 BONSAI! Now go take a peek at **Bonsai by Dori** (850-352-4390), 3089 Main Street, Cottondale, purveyor of diminutive trees along US 231, to fall in love with a miniature tree of your own.

Our Secret Garden (850-482-6034; secretgardenrareplants.com), 5005 Old Spanish Trail, Marianna, has been in business since 1968, selling both native and unusual plants, including bonsai, water gardens, ferns, and bog plants. Friday–Saturday 8 AM–2 PM.

OUTDOOR GEAR One of the most intriguing outdoor stores in Florida, **McCoy's Outdoors** (850-526-2082; mccoysoutdoors.com), 2823 Jefferson Street, is a sprawling hunting and fishing mecca hidden in plain sight. Walk through the original gas station and convenience store to discover a maze of rooms stocked with outdoor apparel, camo for kids, an indoor archery range, and a gun shop.

SPECIALTY FOODS At **Buddy Ward & Sons Seafood** (850-653-1399; 13milebrand.com), 227 Water Street, Apalachicola, four generations of Buddy Ward's family have worked the waters here, bringing the fine taste of the coast to you. Coolers available.

Grab your oysters right along the bay at **Lynn's Quality Oysters** (850-670-8796; lynnsqualityoysters.com), 402 US 98, Eastpoint, where today's catch comes directly off the boats—it doesn't get any fresher, especially if you chow down on them in their new raw bar. Open daily.

Amid the cotton and cane fields of northern Jackson County, the tiny town of Two Egg has a dozen explanations for its very odd name. Take away a piece of its history from **Robert E. Long Cane Syrup** (850-592-8012), a roadside stand along CR 69 selling fresh cane syrup by the quart and gallon. If you stop in at the crack of dawn on the first Saturday of December, you'll catch the crew grinding cane and cooking up a big breakfast for visitors.

Sometimes It's Hotter (888-468-8372; sometimesitshotter.com), 112 Gulf Beach Drive, St. George Island, showcases spicy, unusual foods, including boutique beers, private-label hot sauces, and their own award-winning seasonings. Open daily.

✻ Special Events

FALL/WINTER Greased pigs. Chicken races. Cane boil. A parade. Goat Day (blountstownrotary.com/goat-day) is Blountstown's biggest celebration of family and community, held at the **Panhandle Pioneer Settlement** (see *Museums*) during their fall Pioneer Days. Third Saturday of October, fee.

At **Lantern Fest**, celebrate the birthday of the 1895 Crooked River Lighthouse (see *Lighthouses*) after dark and enjoy shipwreck tales, music, seafood, and glowing lanterns to evoke the past as you climb to the top. Fourth Saturday of October.

For a humorous afternoon on the water, be a part of the annual **Whatever Floats Your Boat Regatta** (marinelab.fsu.edu/outreach/special-events/regatta), where participants "build boats out of stuff that any normal person would take to the dump." Watch these crazy craft sail or sink slowly into Apalachee Bay. First Saturday of October, noon–3 PM, at the FSU Coastal & Marine Lab in Alligator Point.

Florida Seafood Festival (850-653-4720; floridaseafoodfestival.com), Apalachicola. Held at Battery Park every November, this granddaddy of seafood festivals is more than 50 years old and simply shouldn't be missed—from oyster shucking to the annual blessing of the fleet, it's a *huge* event.

🐾 ✎ Luminaries and Christmas lights settle holiday magic on Apalachicola during the **Apalachicola Historic Downtown Christmas Celebration** (apalachicolabay.org) on Thanksgiving weekend. Costumed docents in historic finery bring a touch of history to town, and Santa arrives on a shrimp boat at the City Dock to kick off the celebration.

Show up at the **Apalachicola Oyster Cook-Off**, Apalachicola Riverfront Park, and prepare to eat not just oysters but all sorts of great seafood. Held Friday and Saturday before Martin Luther King Jr. Day.

Since 1996, the annual **Forgotten Coast Chef Sampler** (850-653-9419; apalachicolabay.org) has paired epicureans with the finest chefs of the region.

Show up at the historic Fort Coombs Armory, 4th Street, to sample their best; tickets $60.

SPRING/SUMMER **Apalachicola Boat & Car Show** (850-653-9419; apalachicolabay.org), showcases both vintage marine equipment and classic automobiles, plus boat-building demonstrations. Held at Riverfront Park the third Saturday of April.

✎ At the **North Florida Wildflower Festival** (facebook.com/NFLWildflowerFest), Magnolia Square, Blountstown, learn all about native wildflowers in the region during the prime spring blooming season. Last Saturday of April.

✎ **Carrabelle Riverfront Festival** (850-697-2585; carrabelleriverfrontfestival .com), last weekend of April, features arts and crafts, lots of fresh seafood, music, and a vintage car show.

✎ **Panhandle Folk Life Days** (850-674-3050). Demonstration of traditional arts and crafts at the Panhandle Pioneer Settlement (see *Museums and Historic Sites*). Late April, free.

On the **Apalachicola Historic Home & Garden Tour** (850-653-9550), visit a dozen or more historic private homes on a self-guided walking tour route. Donations benefit the historic Trinity Episcopal Church. First weekend of May.

TALLAHASSEE &
THE BIG BEND

*Jefferson, Leon, Taylor, Wakulla, and
Eastern Gadsden Counties*

On March 4, 1824, Florida's politicos decided on a meeting place halfway between the thriving cities of Pensacola and St. Augustine, and they dubbed it **Tallahassee**—a corruption of the Creek word for "abandoned village." A log cabin served as the first capitol building, replaced by a more grandiose structure completed just in time for Florida's induction into the Union in 1845. Tallahassee's classy downtown, a mix of old brick buildings and modern architecture with side alleys just wide enough for a horse and carriage, has incredible hills for a Florida city—you'll think you're in New England.

Atop the tallest hill in **Monticello**, the Jefferson County Courthouse evokes déjà vu: It's a replica of Thomas Jefferson's famous home. The namesake of **Havana** is indeed Cuba, as the Red Hills region supplied the Cuban cigar industry with tobacco until Fidel Castro came to power. The old tobacco-drying barns and downtown infrastructure now make up the region's top antiquing town. Several generations ago folks in the

ST. MARKS NATIONAL WILDLIFE REFUGE

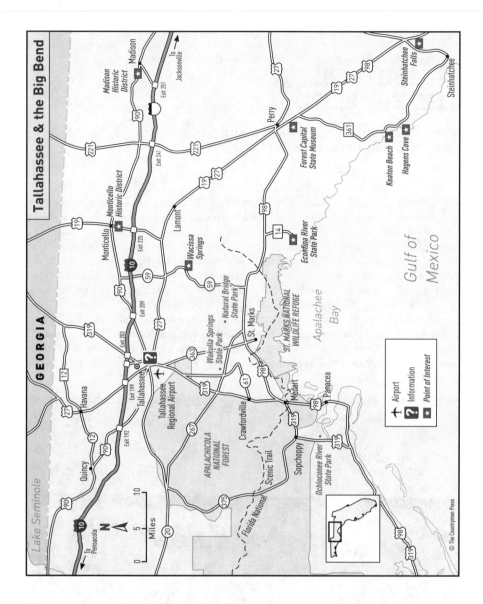

nearby tobacco community of **Quincy** invested in a young company called Coca-Cola, and their dividends show in the Victorian homes that dominate this artistic town.

As you head toward the Gulf of Mexico, red clay hills give way to the densely forested Woodville Karst Plain, a wonderland of sinkholes and springs defining **Wakulla County**. It's a green, wet place, with lushly canopied roads edged by floodplain forests and salt marshes. The medicinal qualities of the sulfur and magnesium springs near **Panacea** led to its unusual name, but this coastal town is best known for its seafood. Buy it roadside direct from the fishermen, or have it fried or broiled at one of the local eateries. The fishing village of **St. Marks** sits along the St. Marks River and the vast estuaries where it meets the Gulf of Mexico. Congress created this town in 1830 as a port of entry to the United States before Florida's first major railroad, the Tallahassee & St. Marks, joined the two cities in 1837.

Continuing along the sweep of the Big Bend southeast, **Perry**, the seat of Taylor County, grew up around farming in the 1860s, but the economy shifted to lumber and turpentine after the Civil War. Timber companies removed vast tracts of virgin pines and cypress, processing the harvest in two enormous timber mills. Along this coastal puzzle of swamp forests and estuary, you'll find the small communities of Adams Beach and **Keaton Beach**, and the more well-known **Steinhatchee** along the Steinhatchee River, founded by settlers looking for cedar to feed the pencil factories in the Cedar Keys (see *Lower Suwannee*). In the 1940s Greek sponge divers moved into the area to work the vast sponge beds in the Gulf of Mexico, and the fishermen followed. Although the sponge divers are long gone, you can see reminders of Greek culture in the offerings on local menus.

GUIDANCE For an overview of the region's natural wonders and history, the collaborative multicounty center **Natural North Florida** (877-955-2199; naturalnorthflorida .com) provides visitor information and links to all local visitors services. **Visit Tallahassee** (visittallahassee.com) has a prominent Downtown Visitor Information Center (800-628-2866 or 850-606-2305), 106 E Jefferson Street, with a wall of brochures and a gift shop serving free iced tea, Monday–Friday 8 AM–5 PM. Street parking may be tricky, so head to nearby Kleman Plaza. Stop in the **Gadsden County Chamber of Commerce** (850-627-9231; gadsdencc.com), 208 N Adams Street, Quincy, when you're exploring downtown Quincy.

Along US 98 in Panacea, the **Wakulla County Welcome Center** (850-984-3966; visitwakulla.com), 1493 Coastal Highway, sits across from Panacea Mineral Springs and has exhibits about local history and nature in addition to general travel information. In Monticello, stop by the **Jefferson County TDC** (850-997-5552; visitjeffersoncountyflorida.org), 420 W Washington Street, for information on this county that stretches from the Georgia border to the Gulf of Mexico. In Perry, **Taylor County Tourism Development** (850-584-5366; taylorflorida.com), 428 N Jefferson Street, can help you with exploring the Big Bend.

GETTING THERE *By air:* **Tallahassee Regional Airport** (850-891-7800; talgov.com/airport), 3300 Capital Circle SW, has commuter service on America, Delta, and Silver Airways.

By bus: **Greyhound** (850-222-4240; greyhound.com) pulls into 112 W Tennessee Street, downtown Tallahassee.

By car: **I-10** is the major east–west corridor through Florida's Panhandle, with **US 98** providing the scenic route connecting coastal communities between Panacea and Perry, and **US 90** running through the northerly Red Hills region from Monticello through Tallahassee to Quincy. **US 27** connects Havana and Perry with Tallahassee.

GETTING AROUND *By car:* With its many one-way streets, downtown Tallahassee can be a bit confusing; watch for signs that direct you to points of interest. Roads radiate out of Tallahassee like spokes on a wheel: **US 27** leads northwest to Havana, southeast to Perry; **US 319**, north to Thomasville, Georgia, and south to Crawfordville; **FL 363** south to St. Marks; **US 90** northeast to Monticello, northwest to Quincy. **Capital Circle** defines the wheel's rim. From Monticello, **US 19** heads south through Perry to pass by Steinhatchee on its way to the towns of the Lower Suwannee.

By bus: Weekdays (except in summer) catch a free ride between downtown Tallahassee points of interest on the **Old Town Trolley** (talgov.com/trolley) every 20 minutes, 11:45 AM–2:15 PM and Friday–Saturday evenings 4:30–1 PM. **StarMetro** (850-891-5200;

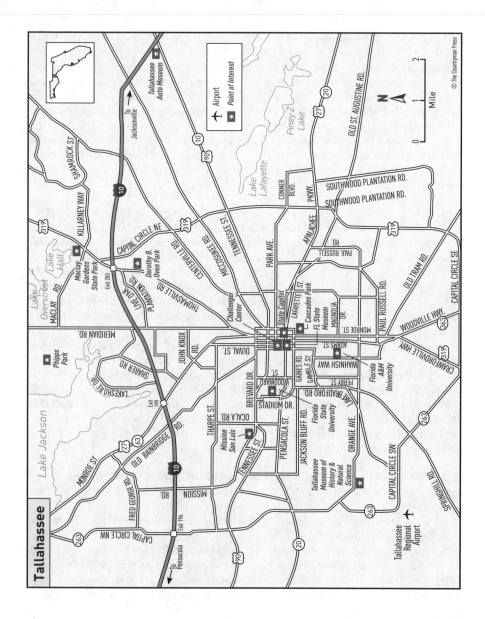

talgov.com/starmetro), the public bus service, runs routes to suburban neighborhoods; fares $1.25, or $3 for a one-day pass.

By taxi: **City Taxi** (850-575-7575; taxitallahassee.com) and **Yellow Cab** (850-999-9999; tallahasseeyellowcab.com).

PARKING Havana, Monticello, Perry, St. Marks, and Quincy have free street parking for shopping and dining. But in busy Tallahassee, metered on-street spaces have time limits from 30 minutes to 10 hours. If you're visiting a museum or restaurant, it's best to pop into a parking garage. **Kleman Plaza Parking Garage** (850-561-3066) between Bronough and Duval, is roomier than **Eastside Parking Garage** on Calhoun and offers easy access to museums and downtown historic sites. Weekday rates range from $2 for one hour to $6 per day, and only $1 for all day on weekends.

MEDICAL EMERGENCIES **Tallahassee Memorial Hospital** (850-431-1155; tmh.org), 1300 Miccosukee Road, Tallahassee, **Capital Regional Medical Center** (850-325-5000; capitalregionalmedicalcenter.com), 2626 Capital Medical Boulevard, Tallahassee, and **Doctor's Memorial Hospital** (850-584-0800; tmh.org/doctors-memorial-hospital), 333 N Byron Butler Parkway (US 27), Perry. Call 911 for all major emergencies. From rural/ coastal areas, it may take up to an hour to reach an emergency room.

✳ To See

ANTEBELLUM PLANTATIONS Most of Florida's remaining antebellum plantations are found in the Capital Region—the visitors bureau lays claim to 100 plantations between Tallahassee, Thomasville, and Perry, as well as many still-working farms, some owned by folks like Ted Turner. Although specifically noted for its formal gardens, the grounds of **Alfred B. Maclay Gardens State Park** (see *Gardens*) comprise an antebellum plantation; fee.

Once the center of a corn-and-cotton plantation from the 1830s, **Goodwood** (850-877-4202; goodwoodmuseum.org), 1600 Miccosukee Road, is the most accessible and the oldest of the region's plantation homes. With period furnishings, including many European antiques from when Senator William C. Hodges owned the home, its classy interior is beautiful to behold. The ceiling in the salon is thought to be the oldest fresco in Florida. There are 16 buildings surrounded by historic gardens and ancient live oaks, but the main house is the focus of tours Tuesday–Saturday 10–2. Admission $12, $10 seniors/military/students, $6 ages 6–12.

In 1895, **Hickory Hill Plantation** changed hands, as New York architect Edward Beadel moved in, building the **Beadel House**, a vernacular colonial revival home overlooking Lake Iamonia. In 1919, Beadel's nephew Henry purchased the place and expanded the house; the addition has the feel of an Adirondack-style hunting lodge. Concerned about the long-term health of quail populations, Henry's legacy was to found **Tall Timbers Research Station** (850-893-4153; talltimbers.org/beadel-house), 13093 Henry Beadel Drive, in 1958. It is a scientific facility for research into the use of fire to regenerate habitats. While visitors are welcome to roam the grounds, the home typically opens for tours on the second Sunday of each month; free.

Dixie Plantation (850-997-1957; dixieplantation.org), 1583 Livingston Road, Greenville, was originally called Cedars when owned by General William Bellamy. Purchased in 1926 by Gerald Livingston, the governor of the New York Stock Exchange, the holdings were expanded to more than 18,000 acres across the Florida–Georgia border. Livingston commissioned noted architect John Russell Pope to design a 14,200-square-foot neoclassical revival brick mansion to replace the old hunting lodge. This is Pope's only design in Florida; he's also the architect of the National Archives, the Washington Mall, and the Jefferson Memorial. An avid sportsman, Livingston began hosting the nation's top field trial for wild quail pointing dogs, the Continental Field Trial, in 1937, and it is still held here today. Now under the stewardship of Tall Timbers Research Station, the plantation—which is under a conservation easement with Suwannee River Water Management District—is open to visitors; restoration of the mansion is ongoing.

ARCHAEOLOGICAL SITES Two extraordinary earthen temple sites in the region are at **Lake Jackson Mounds Archaeological State Park** (850-922-6007; floridastateparks

INTERPRETIVE PAVILION AND PAVED TRAIL LEADING TO THE LETCHWORTH-LOVE MOUNDS

.org/park/Lake-Jackson), 3600 Indian Mounds Road, and **Leitchworth/Love Mounds Archaeological State Park** (floridastateparks.org/park/Letchworth) off US 90 west of Monticello. On the north shore of Lake Jackson, the temple complex of Lake Jackson Mounds consists of six earthen temple mounds and a burial mound, part of a CE 1200–1500 village. At Leitchworth Mounds you can walk around the base of the tallest and most complex ceremonial mound in Florida, 46 feet high, from the Woodland Period circa CE 500. In addition to excellent interpretations of the sites, both parks also offer picnic grounds and nature trails.

ARCHITECTURE Downtown **Tallahassee** contains many treasures, including some narrow old brick alleyways reminiscent of those in New England cities. Tallahassee's two universities, Florida A&M and Florida State, merit their own historic districts, and both the Park Avenue and Calhoun Street historic districts are lined with antebellum and early-1900s homes. Some of the more notable buildings include the **Brokaw-McDougall House** (850-891-3900), 329 N Meridian Avenue, which shows off its 1850 classical revival charm with its balcony and verandas behind the Corinthian columns, and **The Columns**, 100 N Duval Street, where the Greek revival columns say it all: it was built for the first president of the Bank of Florida, William Williams, in 1830. Built in 1838, the **First Presbyterian Church** (850-222-4504; oldfirstchurch.org), 102 N Adams Street, is Tallahassee's only church remaining from territorial days, complete with frontier accoutrements like rifle slits in the basement. The massive pipe organ was built to fit the building, and the North Gallery served as a segregated congregation for plantation owners' slaves.

A Florida Heritage downtown, **Monticello** has more than 40 historic buildings, including the 1908 county courthouse that mimics Thomas Jefferson's grand home. Since 1890, **Monticello Opera House** (see *Performing Arts*) has dominated the town square. Attend one of their shows to enjoy the outstanding acoustics from a time before electronic amplification existed. Built in 1852, **Monticello High School**, west on US 90, is Florida's oldest brick school building. Walk around downtown to enjoy other

HOUSE TOURS

In downtown Tallahassee, **The Grove** (850-577-0228; thegrovemuseum.com), with parking at 902 N Monroe Street, was home to two of Florida's governors. The ten acres centers on a grand home built in 1840 for Florida's first territorial governor, Richard Keith Call; a century later, state senator Leroy Collins, related to the Calls via marriage, purchased the home and became governor while living there. Open Wednesday–Saturday, grounds open 10 AM–4 PM; free. Adjacent to The Grove, the **Governor's Mansion** (850-488-4661; floridagovernorsmansion .com), 700 N Adams Street, is not an antebellum home, but it looks like one. Thanks to Governor Collins and his wife Mary Call Collins, it was rebuilt in 1957 and patterned after Andrew Jackson's Hermitage. It's open for free tours; see their website for dates and times.

At the **Knott House** (850-922-2459; museumoffloridahistory.com/about/sites), 301 E Park Avenue, Tallahassee, step into 1928 and learn about the lives of William Knott, a former state treasurer, and his wife, Luella, a temperance advocate and whimsical published poet who wrote about and attached short poems to virtually every piece of the home's original furnishings, earning the home the nickname "The House that Rhymes." The home was designed by George Proctor, a free black builder, commissioned in 1843 as a wedding gift for Catherine Gamble from her husband-to-be, attorney Thomas Hagner. On May 20, 1865, the Emancipation Proclamation was read from its front steps. Tours on the hour Wednesday–Friday 1–3 PM, Saturday 10 AM–3 PM; closed in August. Free, donations appreciated.

While Frank Lloyd Wright was the architect behind Florida Southern College in Lakeland, the only Florida home built from his designs during his lifetime is in Tallahassee. Built for George and Clifton Lewis in 1954, **Spring House** (850-321-6417; preservespringhouse.org), 3117 Okeeheepkee Road, is one of only two pod-shape houses that Wright designed. Before Clifton died, she established the nonprofit Spring House Institute to preserve and restore the home as a permanent museum. Public tours are held the second Sunday of each month, 2–4 PM; $15 adults, 12 and under free. Private tours are also available by reservation.

THE GROVE, TALLAHASSEE'S FIRST GOVERNOR'S MANSION

residential and business structures with fine classical and Greek revival architecture, including the 1833 **Wirick-Simmons House**.

Stop by the **United Methodist Church**, 206 N Madison Street, Quincy, to see the handiwork of Louis Comfort Tiffany, who also installed windows in homes around town. Around the corner, the **White House**, constructed in the early 1840s, became the home of Pleasants Woodson White, chief commissary officer for the Confederate army in Florida. Both the **Allison House** and **McFarlin House** (see *Lodging*) offer glimpses into Quincy's storied past.

Built in 1894, the **Wakulla County Courthouse** (850-926-1848), 23 High Drive, Crawfordville, is one of only three remaining wooden courthouses in Florida. Replaced in 1948 by a brick courthouse built nearby, this classic structure and its prominent cupola is still the most eye-catching building in Crawfordville as you drive down US 319. Across the street, the art deco **Old Wakulla County Jail** (850-926-1110; wakullahistory .org/museum.html), 24 High Drive, built in 1949, is home to a small regional history museum, historic archives, and gift shop. Dating back to 1936, **Bo-Lynn's Grocery** (850-925-6156), 850 Port Leon Drive, St. Marks, is an old-time grocer that was just added to the National Register of Historic Places. Stop in to meet "Miss Joy" and grab a cold drink or an ice cream!

ART GALLERIES **Gadsden Arts Center & Museum** (850-875-4866; gadsdenarts.org), 13 N Madison Street, Quincy, showcases fine visual arts in a 1910 hardware store; this is one of the top art centers in rural Northwest Florida, with a significant permanent collection of Southern vernacular art. Rotating exhibitions include some of the finest traveling displays, such as Florida's First Highwaymen. Don't miss the gift shop, with its one-of-a-kind works of art. Open Tuesday–Saturday 10 AM–5 PM. Fee; children 17 and under free.

The **LeMoyne Art Foundation** (850-222-8800; lemoyne.org), 125 N Gadsden Street, Tallahassee, encompasses a complex of three major buildings connected with a sculpture garden, where fine arts from local, regional, and national artists fill the galleries and gardens. Tuesday–Saturday 10 AM–5 PM; donation. Near Florida State University, **Railroad Square Art Park** (850-224-1308; railroadsquare.com), 567 Industrial Drive, contains a cluster of art galleries, studios, and gift shops surrounding a sculpture garden and a diner inside a caboose. The **Museum of Fine Arts Florida State University** (850-644-6836; mofa.fsu.edu), 250 Fine Arts Building, features changing exhibits from students and national artists, and the **Foster Tanner Fine Arts Gallery** (850-599-3161; famu.edu) at Florida A&M focuses on world art, with an emphasis on African American artists.

BLUES AND BLUEGRASS The Apalachee Blues Society meets at the **Bradfordville Blues Club** (850-906-0766; bradfordvilleblues.com), 7152 Moses Lane off Bradfordville Road, where you can catch live blues concerts on Friday and Saturday evenings at a modern-day juke joint. At **Sopchoppy Opry** (850-962-3711; sopchoppyopry.com), 164 Yellow Jacket Avenue, a bluegrass jam and country music venue at the historic Sopchoppy High School Auditorium, country legend Tom T. Hall would often pop in and play in the past.

FLORIDA STATE CAPITOL Tallahassee is the place where you can both see how sausage is made (see Bradley's Country Store, *Shopping*) and how our government works. After you go through security at the Florida State Capitol (850-488-6167; floridacapitol.myflorida.com), 400 S Monroe Street, Tallahassee, go to the gallery and see if there is room for you to visit. Watching legislators at work can be surprisingly entertaining, although you do have to follow rules of decorum and keep your mouth shut as you ponder the inner workings of goverment. Even when the legislature is not in session, stop by for a self-guided tour or a formal tour, so you can see what the chambers look like and also see the Florida Artists Hall of Fame wall in the rotunda. Take the elevator to the 22nd floor for the view from the observation deck, which, at 512 feet exceeds the highest point in Florida. Open Monday–Friday 8 AM–5 PM, except state holidays; free.

Florida Historic Capitol Museum (850-487-1902; flhistoriccapitol.gov), 400 S Monroe Street, Tallahassee. Construction began in 1839 to replace the old log cabin used as a meeting place for Florida's first legislators. Although the new capitol opened in 1845, a hurricane damaged it in 1851. Restoration and expansion followed; the building continued to sprawl until the 1970s, when the state replaced it with a tall modern structure next door. Saved from the wrecking ball by public support, the Old Capitol, restored to its 1902 classical revival glory, is now a museum devoted to Florida's legislative history. Monday–Friday 9 AM–4:30 PM, Saturday 10 AM–4:30 PM, Sunday noon–4:30 PM. Free, donations appreciated.

GARDENS Walk through the iron gate at **Alfred B. Maclay Gardens State Park** (850-487-4556; floridastateparks.org/park/Maclay-Gardens), 3540 Thomasville Road, and up the brick drive—the azaleas are in bloom, and the air is strong with their sweet fragrance; a thousand shades of green march down the hill to Lake Hall. It's spring, and it's just as New York financier Alfred Maclay envisioned: his retirement home is surrounded by blooms. When Maclay purchased the antebellum quail hunting lodge in 1923, he turned his landscape design skills to the surrounding hills. Several years after he died, his widow opened the formal gardens as a tourist attraction, turning them over to the state a decade later. The flow of form is subtle: as you approach the house, the grounds yield from wild woodlands to formal Italianate walled gardens, with burbling fountains and stands of cypress. Prime blooming months run from December to early summer, but the gardens are a joy to explore any time of year. Adjacent Lake Overstreet is a wild, wooded addition to the park with miles of hiking and biking trails. The antebellum home, furnished in antiques bought and used by the family, is open for tours 9 AM–5 PM. January–April. Fee.

♂ A hidden gem owned by the city of Tallahassee, **Dorothy B. Oven Park** (850-891-3915; talgov.com/parks/centers-oven.aspx) 3205 Thomasville Road, has a series of formal gardens, including extensive azalea and camellia plantings, on six acres surrounding a manor house designed by Alfred Maclay. Located on an original 1824 land grant within the city, its quiet niches offer spaces to relax, walk, or read.

LIGHTHOUSE One of the most photographed structures in the region is **St. Marks Lighthouse** (fws.gov/saintmarks/lighthouse.html) built in 1842. It's at the end of the road in St. Marks National Wildlife Refuge (see *Parks, Preserves, and Camping*) and looks over its own beach. During the Civil War, the Fresnel lens was removed and hidden in the salt marsh to make the lighthouse useless to the Union Blockading Squadron. Lighthouse keepers and their families lived in the structure until 1960, when the US Coast Guard automated the beacon. It remains a working lighthouse, opening for visitors to explore on Florida Lighthouse Day (floridalighthouses.org) and during other special events at the refuge.

MARINE SCIENCE CENTER ♂ Part aquarium, part scientific lab, the **Gulf Specimen Marine Lab** (850-984-5297; gulfspecimen.org) off US 98, Panacea, is a place where you can interact with the native marine life of the Gulf estuary—and see the efforts in place to preserve them, such as the sea turtle hospital. The aquarium has a primary focus on the small side of Florida sea life—scallops and crabs, snails and lobsters, sea fans and sea urchins, shrimp and oysters, and other tiny denizens of the coastline, although you will see sharks and stingrays here as well. Monday–Friday 9 AM–5 PM, Saturday 10 AM–5 PM, Sunday noon–5 PM; $10 adults, $9 seniors, $8 ages 3–11.

MUSEUMS AND HISTORIC SITES ♿ In addition to commemorating the former senator's accomplishments, the **Claude Pepper Center** (850-644-9311; claudepepper center.fsu.edu), 636 W Call Street, Tallahassee, contains research materials dating back to the New Deal era and an art gallery with a focus on political activism. A true believer in liberalism, Senator Pepper received the Presidential Medal of Freedom while working to improve life for his fellow Americans. Open Monday–Friday 9 AM–5 PM; free.

♿ In Florida's heart of forestry, **Forest Capital Museum State Park** (850-584-3227; floridastateparks.org/park/Forest-Capital), 204 Forest Park Drive, Perry, focuses on the importance of Florida's timber, particularly its pine forests. In addition to a diorama on the historic turpentine and naval stores industries, there are life-size replica habitats and a talking tree to teach the kids about the life cycle of Florida's trees. The jewel of the complex is a reconstructed Cracker homestead, with an original dogtrot home and farm outbuildings moved here from a variety of locations. Decorated with period furnishings, they remind you of the hardships of life for Florida's pioneers. Thursday–Monday 9 AM–5 PM; museum fee.

♿ **Mission San Luis** (850-487-3711; missionsanluis.org), 2020 Mission Road, Tallahassee, once oversaw the operation of more than 100 missions throughout Spanish Florida from 1656 to 1704. This robust living history museum now includes Florida's only fully reconstructed Spanish mission, complete with fortress, church with

CRACKER HOMESTEAD BARN AT THE FOREST CAPITAL MUSEUM

living quarters, tradespeople, and village homes where you'll find occupants grinding corn or working on corn husk dolls. The Jesuit priests settled among the Apalachee, so the site interpets the original indigenous village as well, with its most notable feature being the mighty Apalachee council house. The original held up to 3,000 people and was one of the largest indigenous structures in the southeastern United States. Tuesday–Sunday 10 AM–4 PM; fee.

& ♂ At the **Museum of Florida History** (850-245-6400; museumoffloridahistory .com), 500 S Bronough Street, Tallahassee, prepare to have your eyes opened about Florida's rich and colorful past. It's one of the most immersive places to learn about the state. In addition to rotating thematic exhibits, the state's official history museum includes a climb-aboard replica of an early steamboat, tales of buried treasure, a citrus-packing house from the 1930s, information on Florida's role in the Civil War, and many interactive exhibits that'll keep the kids hopping. The adjoining History Shop contains classy reproductions and a great selection of Florida books. Open Monday–Friday 9–4:30 PM, Saturday 10–4:30 PM, Sunday noon–4:30 PM. Free, donations appreciated.

An important site in Florida's Civil War history, **Natural Bridge Battlefield Historic State Park** (850-922-6007; floridastateparks.org/park/Natural-Bridge), 7502 Natural Bridge Road, Woodville, speaks to a time when the Confederacy was close to collapse. On March 6, 1865, Union troops marching north from their landing point at St. Marks Lighthouse met the Florida Fifth Cavalry and cadets from the West Florida Seminary (now Florida State University). Confederate troops routed the Union attack and are credited with keeping Tallahassee the only Confederate capital east of the Mississippi that did not fall into Union hands during the war. Some historians surmise that the Union objective was to capture the key port of St. Marks rather than invade the capital city, and they came to this spot to utilize the Natural Bridge, a place where the St. Marks River dives underground at a river sink and reemerges less than a quarter mile south at a spring. A battle re-enactment is held the first full weekend of March. Free.

The **John G. Riley Center/Museum** (850-681-7881; rileymuseum.org), 412 E Jefferson Street, Tallahassee, is in an 1890 home designed by John G. Riley, a black architect of the time. Inside, you'll find a museum of regional African American history from Reconstruction through the civil rights movement, with a special focus on historic cemeteries. Monday–Friday 10 AM–4 PM, Saturday 10 AM–2 PM; fee.

The site of the first fortress built along Florida's northern coast, **San Marcos de Apalache Historic State Park** (850-925-6216; floridastateparks.org/park/San-Marcos), 148 Old Fort Road, St. Marks, protects several generations of battlements, from the faint tracings of the original wooden stockade fort completed by the Spanish in 1679 at the confluence of the St. Marks and Wakulla rivers to the remains of the masonry structure occupied up through the Civil War. Visit the museum before walking the interpretive trail along the rivers. 9 AM–5 PM Thursday–Monday; fee for museum.

♂ & **Tallahassee Museum of History & Natural Science** (850-575-8684; tallahassee museum.org), 3945 Museum Drive, Tallahassee, isn't at all what you'd expect from a museum. On its 52 acres along Lake Bradford, gentle footpaths and boardwalks blend into the natural surroundings, winding through Florida habitats alive with native wildlife like bald eagles, alligators, Florida panthers, and river otters. On their Big Bend Farm, living history shows what farm life was like in the 1880s, from livestock pens to cotton patches; volunteers demonstrate shucking corn, turpentining, and pressing cane for sugar. Walk into Old Florida to discover several historic buildings moved here from around the region, including the 1897 Concord Schoolhouse, the first post-Reconstruction school where blacks were taught, and Catherine Murat's 1850s manor

CARS AND COLLECTIBLES

While I was admiring a blacksmithing wagon at the **Tallahassee Automobile and Collectibles Museum** (850-942-0137; tacm.com), 6800 Mahan Drive, Tallahassee, two men approached to discuss it; one of them turned out to be museum owner and entrepreneur Devoe Moore, who was a blacksmith well before getting into auto parts, truck sales, and real estate. Sometimes outbidding Jay Leno at car auctions, Moore has had a lifelong love of both collecting and automobiles, as evidenced by the expansive spread in his museum. Among nearly 100 vehicles, there's a 1931 Duesenburg Model J worth more than a million, a 1948 Tucker Torpedo, the hearse that carried Abraham Lincoln, and the first steam-powered car ever built, the 1894 Dureyea, with handwritten instructions from J. Frank Duryea under the seat. But cars aren't Moore's only passion. He's a collector of collections, so the two cavernous stories are filled with impressive ephemera—mostly mechanical in nature—from toy trucks, pocket knives, and cash registers to Steinway pianos, pedal cars, brass fans, and model trains. The sheer volume of items in this museum is mind-boggling. Visit with a friend or your family, so you can share "remember when . . ." stories as you browse. Monday–Friday 8 AM–5 PM, Saturday 10 AM–5 PM, Sunday noon–5 PM; $15–18 adults, $12 students, $8 ages 5–9. ♿ ✍

A FRACTION OF THE COLLECTIBLES INSIDE THE TALLAHASSEE AUTOMOBILE AND COLLECTIBLES MUSEUM

home, moved here from the Bellevue Plantation. There's even a 1924 Seaboard Air Line caboose. The newly added Tree to Tree Adventures (see *Zipline*) adds another layer of fun—62 feet in the air. Monday–Saturday 9 AM–5 PM, Sunday 11 AM–5 PM; $11–12 adults, $9 ages 4–15.

PERFORMING ARTS Go for Baroque with **The Tallahassee Bach Parley** (tallahasseebachparley.org), which features Baroque music concerts at Goodwood (see *Antebellum Plantations*). **Tallahassee Symphony Orchestra** (850-224-0461; tallahasseesymphony.org), 515 Park Avenue, plays a concert series every September to May, with concert-goers encouraged to come as you are, just come and enjoy. **Big Bend Community Orchestra** (850-893-9934; bbcorch.org), 690 Industrial Avenue, offers seasonal Sunday-afternoon classical and "pops" in area parks, and the **Artist Series of Tallahassee** (850-224-9934; theartistseries.org), 1897 Capital Circle NE, brings in philharmonic orchestras and soloists from around the globe. **Theatre A La Carte** (850-224-8474; theatrealacarte.org) bills itself as North Florida's premiere musical theater company, putting on two musicals each year, and the **Tallahassee Film Society** (850-386-4404; tallahasseefilms.com) shows indie, art, and retro films twice monthly at the All Saint Cinema, 918½ Railroad Avenue, in the Tallahassee Amtrak station.

 ♂ At **Monticello Opera House** (850-997-4242; monticellooperahouse.org), 185 W Washington Street, Monticello, folk artists, mystery nights, and an annual performance season are all part of the fun in this classy turn-of-the-last-century brick theater, with amazing acoustics and a massive stage.

RAILROADIANA In Tallahassee, in addition to **Railroad Square** (see *Art Galleries*) near FSU, be sure to see the **railroad exhibit** at Tallahassee Museum of History & Natural Science. The **Tallahassee–St. Marks Historic Railroad State Trail** (see *Biking*) traces the route of Florida's earliest lengthy railroad, circa 1837.

For classic depots, downtown Perry has a beautifully renovated **passenger station** from the Live Oak, Perry & Georgia Railroad, now housing shops and restaurants. In downtown Sopchoppy, the vintage wooden **Sopchoppy Railroad Depot** has been restored to its former glory.

WATERFALL **Steinhatchee Falls** [29.74635, -83.342608] rates as Florida's broadest and most interesting waterfall. This limestone shelf along the Steinhatchee River served as a crossing point for wagons as settlers pushed their way south along the Gulf Coast, and the wagon ruts are still visible in the limestone on both sides of the river. A

STEINHATCHEE FALLS

riverside park has interpretive information, picnic tables, and a boat launch; a hiking trail loops upriver and a multi-use trail leads several miles up to a trailhead at CR 51. The falls are off CR 51, down unpaved roads 2 miles west of US 19/27; follow signs.

WINERY **Monticello Vineyards & Winery** (850-294-9463; monticellowinery.com), 1211 Waukeenah Highway, is a small operation at Ladybird Organics on CR 259 south of Monticello. All wines are certified organic, processed from muscadine grapes grown on site. Saturday–Monday 8 AM–6 PM; during harvest months, August–September, visitors can pick fresh grapes.

✳ To Do

BIKING Although the **Tallahassee–St. Marks Historic Railroad State Trail** (850-519-6594; floridastateparks.org/trail/Tallahassee-St-Marks), 1358 Old Woodville Road, runs up into the southern suburbs of Tallahassee, the trailhead along FL 363 provides ample parking, restrooms, picnic tables, and a historic marker that explains it all: The Tallahassee–St. Marks Railroad began operation in 1837 with mule-drawn cars and switched to steam locomotives in 1839, connecting ships coming into Port Leon with Tallahassee. This paved bike trail runs through wilderness areas along its 23-mile route to its southern terminus in St. Marks, so take plenty of water and ride with a friend if possible. An equestrian trail runs parallel to the forested right-of-way. At its south end, rent bicycles from Shields Marina (see *Boating*).

The **Miccosukee Canopy Road Greenway**, 5600 Miccosukee Road, parallels Miccosukee Road, with four entrances offering bicyclists, hikers, and equestrians 6 miles of canopied trail and open spaces. The **J. R. Alford Greenway**, 2500 S. Pedrick Road, covers 800 acres with rambling trails. Both are in Tallahassee and managed by Leon County.

The **Capital City to the Sea Trails** (cc2st.com/about) is an ambitous project to link paved bike paths to create a 120-mile bike touring loop through the region. The Tallahassee–St. Marks Historic Railroad State Trail has long been in place; the **Capital Circle Connector Trail** stretches 6 miles northeast from it; and the **Capital Cascades Trail** from Cascades Park, in downtown Tallahassee, is being extended to reach it as well. The **Ochlockonee Bay Bike Trail** (mywakulla.com) offers 13 miles of paved bike path between Mashes Sands Park (see *Beaches*) and Sopchoppy; the **Coastal Trail** from Mashes Sands to the St. Marks River is in the planning stages; and a 2.4-mile portion of the **GF&A Trail** (fs.usda.gov/recarea/apalachicola) has been paved through the Apalachicola National Forest near Tallahassee at Trout Pond. It will eventually extend to Sopchoppy. In Crawfordville, the Wakulla Environmental Institute (850-558-3500), 170 Preservation Way, is an official trailhead for the CC2ST and offers on-campus camping for bike tourists; call ahead.

In the Apalachicola National Forest (see *Parks, Preserves, and Camping*), the **Munson Off-Road Bicycle Trail** attracts mountain bikers from around the region to ride the rolling sandhills. Mountain bikers have fun inside city limits, too. Winding mountain bike paths on rugged terrain can be found in the **Lake Overstreet Trails** portion of Alfred B. Maclay Gardens State Park and at **Phipps Park**.

BIRDING With hundreds of excellent birding spots throughout the region, it's tough to pick just a few. **St. Marks National Wildlife Refuge** (see *Parks, Preserves, and Camping*) can't be beat for the number of species to spot during the winter migration. Stop by the **Henry M. Stevenson Memorial Bird Trail** at Tall Timbers Research Station (see

BIG BEND BEACHES

The Big Bend isn't known for its beaches—the waters of Apalachee Bay along the Gulf of Mexico are quite shallow. But the vast salt marshes do yield to a few remote beaches accessed from US 98 or, in Taylor County, off CR 361. Some of the better-known spots are **Mashes Sands Beach** at Panacea; near Spring Creek, **Shell Point Beach** and **Wakulla Beach**. Our favorite strands are on **Dickerson Bay** at the end of Bottoms Road, and the wild shore behind **St. Marks Lighthouse** (see *Lighthouse*). Near Steinhatchee, families will enjoy a soft white strand at **Hodges Park** in Keaton Beach, complete with picnic pavilion and playground. Between Steinhatchee and Keaton Beach on CR 361 in the Tide Swamp Unit of Big Bend WMA, **Hagens Cove** is a prime destination for scalloping, especially for families with small children. Don't expect a beautiful white sand beach here. It's an accessible piece of shoreline along an infinite stretch of mudflats, a beautiful place to sit and watch the sunset.

SANDY STRAND ON THE GULF AT THE ST. MARKS LIGHTHOUSE

Antebellum Plantations) for prime birding along Lake Iamonia. Along US 90 between Tallahassee and Monticello, park at the boat ramp for **Lake Miccosukee** and walk out on the boardwalk paralleling the highway for a panoramic view of this cypress-lined lake; it's a great place to watch ducks, coots, herons, and osprey. You'll have excellent opportunities to see wading bird behavior while on the tour boat at **Wakulla Springs State Park** (see *Springs*). Hang out at **Hagens Cove** (see *Beaches*) to watch flocks of shorebirds, including black skimmers.

BOATING **Shields Marina** (850-925-6158; shieldsmarina.com), 95 Riverside Drive, in St. Marks is the largest marina along the Big Bend, well sheltered from the sea up the St. Marks River. With a well-stocked ship's store, fuel, dockage, mechanics on-site, and rentals—boat, kayak, SUP, and bike—it's a must-visit if you want to take a pontoon ($150–200) out into the estuaries. In Steinhatchee you can rent 24-foot Carolina skiffs at **Sea Hag** (352-498-3008; seahag.com) for $125–199.

ECOTOURS The long-standing Florida Green Guide program in Wakulla County has certified numerous homegrown experts on the wild spaces that make up more than 70 percent of this coastal county. Under the umbrella of **Palmetto Expeditions** (850-926-3376; palmettoexpeditions.com), you can arrange a broad variety of tours with local Green Guides. Woody and Kathy Lewis lead kayak and canoe tours for wildlife watching along the St. Marks River. Debbi Clifford leads "Nature on the Beach" interpretive walks, or join Marie Anne Luber for an exploration of the region's sinkholes and springs. Tours start at $20 per person.

Don't miss the boat tour at **Wakulla Springs State Park** (see *Swimming*), an excellent introduction to the beauty and wildlife of the Wakulla River. For a morning on the area's riding trails, contact **Russ Peters** (850-926-4348; cypressrunfarm.com).

FAMILY ACTIVITIES *✐* At the **Challenger Learning Center and IMAX Theatre** (850-645-7827; challengertlh.com), 210 S Duval Street, Tallahassee, most visitors are there for the big-screen IMAX, with 20,000 watts of sound and the incredibly crisp digital planetarium with dazzling, immersive graphics in its 50-foot dome. But inside this science center you'll find ongoing STEM programs for kids; an exhibit on the History of Florida as the Space State, with vintage items that flew in space plus one-third-scale models of the Mercury and Gemini capsules and the Apollo Lunar Module; and a Space Mission Simulator, where groups of nine can work through simulated missions using mockups of the International Space Station and NASA Johnson Space Center. This collaborative effort between the FSU College of Engineering and NASA is a living memorial to the Space Shuttle *Challenger* crew. Open daily, varying hours; fee.

✐ At **Cross Creek Driving Range** (850-656-4653), 6701 Mahan Drive, Tallahassee, practice your putts on the driving range, or challenge the kids to a round of par-3. Open daily at 8 AM.

✐ **Tallahassee Rock Gym** (850-224-7625; tallyrockgym.com), 629-F Industrial Drive, Railroad Square, Tallahassee, offers a popular climbing wall in a historic railroad warehouse. Take lessons, or practice your skills!

FISHING With more than 60 miles of wilderness coastline, the Big Bend has always attracted a steady clientele of saltwater anglers in search of grouper, cobia, and trout. Toward that end, you'll find plenty of fishing guides, especially around **Steinhatchee**. Ask around at the marinas regarding specific captains' specialties and expect a day's worth of guided fishing (which includes your license) to cost $400–800, depending on what you're after. At **Keaton Beach**, a lengthy fishing pier provides a quiet place to drop a line.

Around Tallahassee, saltwater anglers head for St. Marks, the nearest launch point into the Gulf of Mexico; ask after guides at **Shell Island Fish Camp** (see *Fish Camps*) and **Shields Marina** (see *Boating*). Inland, **Lake Talquin**, a hydroelectric reservoir on the Ochlockonee River, has plenty of speckled perch, sunfish, and tantalizing, trophy-size largemouth bass for the patient angler. There are numerous fish camps off FL 267 and several off FL 20 on the Upper Ochlockonee River, along with many boat ramps around the lake.

GENEALOGICAL RESEARCH You'll hit the jackpot for all sorts of historical research at the **Florida State Archives** (850-245-6700; dos.myflorida.com/library-archives), 500 S Bronough Street, but most folks who quietly sit at the long tables inside are digging through their ancestors' roots. Tip: Use their online resources first, and then come to Tallahassee to look through manuscripts and letters you couldn't otherwise view.

GOLF Playing a round on the gently rolling greens at the par-72 **Wildwood Golf & RV Resort** (850-926-4653; wildwoodgolfrvresort.com), 3870 Coastal Highway, Crawfordville, is like taking a walk in the woods, with each fairway fringed with a forest of oaks and pines. The club includes a driving range, putting green and at the 19th hole, The Seinyard at Wildwood (see *Where to Eat*). Non-member fees include cart and green fee. Magnuson Wildwood Inn (see *Lodging*) is next door.

In Tallahassee, enjoy a round at **Hilaman Golf Course** (850-891-2560; hilaman golfcourse.com), 2737 Blair Stone Road, a municipal course with 18 holes and a driving range, $15–48. **Jake Gaither Golf Course** (850-891-3942; hilaman.com/jake_gaither), 801 Bragg Drive, is a city

LILIES BLOOM IN SUMMER ON LAKE JACKSON

course with nine holes. Owned by FSU, the **Don Veller Seminole Golf Course and Club** (850-644-2582; seminolegolfcourse.com), 2550 Pottsdamer Street, is a popular 18-hole course with lighted driving range, reservations required.

HIKING At **Aucilla Wildlife Management Area**, the **Florida Trail at Aucilla River Sinks** [30.20092,-83.92469; floridahikes.com/floridatrail/aucilla-sinks] provides access to one of the strangest rivers in Florida—after rushing across rapids, it vanishes beneath the limestone bedrock and pops up time and again in "windows" in the aquifer, deep sinkholes with water in motion. Hiking is the only way to explore this unique area, where the most ancient relics of human civilization in the Southeast have been found. Along with nearly 50 miles of the statewide **Florida Trail** (see *What's Where*) crossing St. Marks National Wildlife Refuge, miles of levees off Lighthouse Road provide easy walking for wildlife watching.

Bordering Lake Jackson's east shore on Meridian Road, **Eleanor Klapp-Phipps Park** (850-891-3975; talgov.com/parks/parks-phipps.aspx) has an excellent hiking loop as well as biking and equestrian trails. On the west shore of Lake Jackson, **J. Lee Vause Park** (850-606-1470), 6024 Old Bainbridge Road, has a boardwalk along the lake and nature trails as well as picnic shelters. There is also a small pull-off along

US 27 for access to Lake Jackson. See *Parks, Preserves, and Camping* for more hiking destinations.

PADDLING With the **Sopchoppy, Aucilla, Ochlockonee, St. Marks, Steinhatchee, Wacissa,** and **Wakulla** rivers sluicing through this region, paddlers will find plenty of challenges. The Aucilla offers rapids, the Steinhatchee a waterfall, and the Sopchoppy a twisting, winding, blackwater river. The Ochlockonee, St. Marks, and Wakulla rivers pour out into the Gulf of Mexico through a mazy meander of salt marshes, much fun for kayakers. **The Wilderness Way** (850-877-7200; thewildernessway.net), 3152 Shadeville Road, is an outfitter offering kayak rentals and guided trips. We've paddled with the folks at **TnT Hideaway** (850-925-6412; tnthideaway.com), 6527 Coastal Highway, to explore hidden springs and watch for manatees along the Wakulla River. **Shields Marina** (see *Boating*) offers kayak rentals on the St. Marks River. For a trip on the beautiful and little-known Wacissa River, **Wacissa River Canoe Rentals** (850-997-5023; wacissarivercanoerentals.com), 290 Wacissa Springs Road, is just up the road from the springs and rents canoes daily.

For a tiny taste of whitewater, head to **Steinhatchee** with your kayak to leap the Steinhatchee Falls (see *Waterfall*). The 8-mile trip from the falls to Steinhatchee along this obsidian-color waterway winds through dark river hammocks and forested residential areas before meeting the tidal basin, offering several Class I rapids. Kayak rentals and shuttles are available at **River Haven Marina** (352-498-0709; riverhavenmarine.com/Kayaking.html).

Estuary dominates the central and most remote portion of a rough but scenic 91-mile saltwater paddle attempted by a handful of people every year: the **Historic Big Bend Saltwater Paddling Trail** (a segment of the Florida Circumnavigational Trail; see *The Lower Suwannee* chapter). Paddlers on this segment can find services at Steinhatchee, Keaton Beach, and Econfina, where sea kayakers put in at Econfina River State Park (see *Parks, Preserves, and Camping*) for easy access to the Gulf of Mexico. On US 98 you'll find picnic tables and a boat ramp on the **Econfina River Paddling Trail**, a jungle-like paddling route that heads south 6 miles to the state park. A little farther west, paddlers can also put in at the Aucilla River and head upstream along the **Wacissa River Paddling Trail** into Jefferson County; the Aucilla quickly peters out as it disappears through its famed sinks.

PARKS, PRESERVES, AND CAMPING The **Apalachicola National Forest** (850-643-2282; fs.usda.gov/apalachicola) is one of the wildest places in Northwest Florida. Sweeping around the southern and eastern sides of Tallahassee, it's also Florida's largest national forest. Some of its special spots include **Leon Sinks Geological Area**, which showcases karst features along its hiking trails; **Bradwell Bay**, a wild and lonely wilderness area along the Florida National Scenic Trail; **Silver Lake**, a nice fishing and picnic area; and the cypress-lined **Sopchoppy River**, a great paddling route. Its full-hookup recreation areas are located on the western side of the forest (see the *Apalachicola River* chapter), but simpler camping can be found at many designated primitive sites along its creeks and the easily accessible **Porter Lake Recreation Area** off FR 13. Free random camping is permitted throughout the forest except during the fall deer hunting season.

✒ 🏕 ♿ A new 12-acre park in the heart of Tallahassee, **Cascades Park** (850-891-3866; talgov.com/parks/parks-cascades.aspx), 1001 S Gadsden Street, transformed an abandoned hollow where there was once a waterfall into a delightful green space along St. Augustine Branch. The park includes the Capital City Amphitheatre, where public performances are held; commemorative spaces for the former locations of Centennial

Field and Smokey Hollow; a Korean War memorial; and 2.3 miles of paved trails. Along the pathways are several places for kids to play, including the Discovery play area, with nature-inspired playground equipment, and the Imagination Fountain, a splash playground by day, light show with dancing fountains by night. The Capital Cascades Trail (see *Biking*) leads south out of the park along St. Augustine Branch to Lake Munson, and will eventually connect to the St. Marks Historic Railroad Trail.

At the end of CR 14 in coastal Jefferson County, **Econfina River State Park** (850-922-6007; floridastateparks.org/park/Econfina-River) gives paddlers and boaters a put-in to the vast Gulf estuary and offers loop trails through uplands along the marsh. Two rustic rooms are available for rent.

West of Tallahassee along FL 20, **Lake Talquin State Park** (850-922-6007; floridastateparks.org/park/Lake-Talquin) gives you a scenic panorama of Lake Talquin with a picnic pavilion, fishing dock, and nature trail; fee.

Encompassing more than 16,000 acres, **Lake Talquin State Forest** (850-487-3766; freshfromflorida.com) is spread across 10 tracts on the shores of the Ochlockonee River and Lake Talquin. You can hike through forests of magnolia and beech along trails on the Fort Braden Tract and Bear Creek Tract or ride horses on the equestrian trails. Biking is permitted on forest roads, numerous boat ramps allow access for anglers, and seasonal hunting is allowed in some of the tracts.

Set along the Sopchoppy River, **Myron B. Hodge Park** (850-962-4611), 220 Park Avenue, Sopchoppy, is a city-owned campground with riverfront campsites ($15) and a bathhouse. The 35-acre park has an extensive nature trail along the river, a boat ramp, and fishing docks.

🦫 At deeply shaded **Newport Park** (850-926-7227 or 850-925-4530; mywakulla.com), 8046 Coastal Highway, St. Marks 32355, choose from full hookup or primitive sites under the pines with access to the St. Marks River for boaters. This county campground sits right across from the main entrance to St. Marks National Wildlife Refuge, where camping is not permitted. $11 for tent sites, $22 for water and electric, $27 full hookup.

Just south of Sopchoppy, **Ochlockonee River State Park** (850-962-2771; floridastateparks.org/park/Ochlockonee-River), 429 State Park Road off US 321, sits at the confluence of the Ochlockonee and Dead rivers, with access upriver to the Sopchoppy and downriver to the bay. Two loop trails showcase the mature pine flatwoods and the riverfront, and the campground—accommodating tents or RVs, $18—is well shaded, with a cool river breeze. Fee.

Established in 1931 to protect the fragile Gulf estuaries, **St. Marks National Wildlife Refuge** (850-925-6121; fws.gov/refuge/st_marks), 1255 Lighthouse Road, St. Marks, spans three counties and is the best birding destination in the region. Monarch butterflies rest here in October on their annual migration to Mexico, carpeting shrubs in orange and black. Although the refuge is broken up into several units, most folks arrive at the visitors center south of Newport off US 98. Browse the exhibits and learn about this mosaic of habitats before setting off down the road. The Florida Trail (see *Hiking*) crosses the entire width of the refuge. Shorter nature trails give you a taste of the salt marshes, pine flatwoods, and swamps. Drive to the end of the road to visit the historic St. Marks Lighthouse (see *Lighthouse*).

SCALLOPING Florida's number one scalloping destination, **Steinhatchee** remains the destination of choice for serious shellfish harvesters. Your success is in direct proportion to the weather: Too much rain and the scallop population suffers. The season runs mid-June to mid-September, and you must abide by state-mandated limits of 2 gallons of whole scallops per person per day. If you snorkel from your own boat, you must have a saltwater fishing license and display a DIVER DOWN flag. Some local marinas arrange charters; **Captain Mark Brady** (352-354-0067; steinhatcheescalloping.com) specializes in scalloping trips, $350 for 4–6 people for 4 hours. No fishing license is required when you scallop with a charter, nor if you head for **Hagens Cove** (see *Big Bend Beaches*), where you can wade into the Gulf and collect to your heart's content.

SCENIC DRIVES The 220-mile-long **Big Bend Scenic Byway** (floridabigbendscenic byway.com) knits together a network of scenic roads throughout the region and extends west to the Apalachicola River (see the *Apalachicola River* chapter).

In addition to cruising Tallahassee's many "official" canopy roads, such as **Meridian Road**—which is wonderful in late March when azaleas and wisteria are in bloom—follow rural FL 12 and FL 269 across Gadsden County from Havana through Quincy, Greensboro, and Chattahoochee to enjoy the rolling farmland. **The Loop** in Taylor County is a nearly 100-mile circuit taking you through the scenic fishing villages along the Gulf Coast, via US 19, FL 51, and CR 361, through the heart of the "Forest Capital of Florida."

SPRINGS 🐚 ♿ Showcasing Florida's deepest spring, where the water is sometimes clear enough to see the bones of mastodons and giant sloth resting at the bottom of the 180-foot pool, **Edward Ball Wakulla Springs State Park** (850-224-5950; floridastateparks .org/park/Wakulla-Springs), 550 Wakulla Park Drive, Wakulla Springs, offers swimming facilities (69 degrees year-round) with a high diving platform, more than 10 miles of shaded nature trails and hiking trails, and daily boat tours where you're bound to see dozens of alligators and innumerable waterfowl. At the center of it all is the classic Wakulla Lodge (see *Lodging*); don't miss the marble-topped soda fountain in the gift shop! Fee.

Lesser-known **Wacissa Springs** [30.340389, -83.991268], at the end of Wacissa Springs Road in Jefferson County, has the expansive feel of Wakulla Springs without any development of the spring basin. It's rustic—there's a dirt parking lot, boat ramp, and ladder out of the water where you can jump into the spring. Canoe rentals are available just up the road (see *Paddling*). But it's a gorgeous and wild place, especially from the water, where there are multiple springs downriver only accessible by water.

WALKING TOURS In Tallahassee, grab a map at the visitors center and hit the bricks for a self-guided walk around more than **60 historic sites downtown**, or join **Tours in Tallahassee** (850-212-2063; toursintallahassee.com) for their Capital City Tours or Ghost Walking Tours. You can watch the Florida Legislature at work while taking a self-guided **walking tour at the Capitol** (myfloridacapitol.com/tours). Don't miss the view from the 22nd-floor observation deck! **Quincy** has a self-guided walking tour booklet of 55 historic homes and churches; drop by Gadsden Arts Center & Museum (see *Art Galleries*) for a copy. **Monticello** offers a historic walking tour following numbered posts in front of significant buildings; drop in at the Chamber of Commerce for a guide. Also check in with Palmetto Expeditions (see *Ecotours*) for walking tours in Wakulla County, including a lively exploration of **Sopchoppy**.

ZIPLINES 🐾 At Tallahassee Museum of History & Natural Science (see *Museums and Historic Sites*), **Tree to Tree Adventures** gets you more than 60 feet up into the dense tree canopy along Lake Bradford on a series of challenging canopy walks and ziplines. Canopy Crossing, the 45-minute beginner's course, sticks close to the museum's main area and gets 20 feet in the air, $28; Soaring Cypress climbs high among the old-growth cypress above the wildlife enclosures for 2–3 hours, $45. Treemendous Adventures is for the little ones, with bridges, tightropes, and a zipline near Big Bend Farm, $17. Discounts for museum members.

✳ Lodging

BED & BREAKFASTS 🏠 🐾 ((ᵠ)) The former home of General A. K. Allison, who stepped into office as governor of Florida at the end of the Civil War, **Allison House Inn** (888-904-2511; allisonhouseinn.com), 215 N Madison Street, Quincy, an 1843 Georgian-style house, is one of the oldest in North Florida. Extensive renovation in 1925 added a story to the house and gave it an English country look. Step into Florida's genteel past and enjoy one of the six spacious guest rooms and fine crumpets and orange marmalade offered by innkeepers Stuart and Eileen Johnson. Many of the rooms have multiple beds in this family-friendly inn, $95–140.

♂ ((ᵠ)) 🏠 A visit to the **Avera-Clarke House** (850-997-5007; averaclarke.com), 580 W Washington Street, Monticello 32344, will make you fall in love with Southern hospitality. The main house is an 1890 Victorian with four elegant bedrooms; in the expansive yard is The Cottage, a favorite of happy honeymooners. It's thought to be the oldest building in Jefferson County, circa 1821, moved here in 2006 and renovated as a romantic hideaway.

((ᵠ)) **Buckhorn Creek Lodge** (airbnb .com/rooms/1381930), 367 Buckhorn Creek Road, Sopchoppy 32358, is one of those places you settle in and enjoy your surroundings. Bicycles await your use for a ride down the Ochlockonee Bay Trail (see *Biking*), kayaks out back for exploring the Sopchoppy River basin, and you can wander right in to St. Marks NWR to bird. Your hosts, our friends Robert and Laura, are outstanding resources to point you to natural areas nearby. Two rooms on the third floor share a common bath and sitting area; guests have the run of the house and grounds, including use of the gourmet-style kitchen and big porches. $95 and up, all bookings through AirBnB.

🏠 🐾 ((ᵠ)) The **John Denham House** (850-997-4568; johndenhamhouse.com),

555 Palmer Mill Road, Monticello 32344, is a classic piece of history, built by a Scottish immigrant in 1872. Luxuriate in the silky sheets under a down comforter, or relax in a clawfoot tub. Each of the five large rooms has a fireplace accented with candles. $110–125; children and pets are welcome in a safe, family-friendly environment. Two historic four-bedroom homes, the 1895 J.M. Henry House and the Jackson Lake House, are an option for families or private gatherings; they are rented by the house, two-night minimum, $250–349.

♂ ((ᵠ)) **McFarlin House** (850-524-0640; mcfarlinhouse.com), 305 E King Street, Quincy 32351. Decorated with Tiffany windows original to the home and 11,000 square feet of imported Italian tile, this century-old Queen Anne Victorian showcases the good life that Quincy's well-to-do gentry enjoyed. With renovations completed in 1996, this was a finalist for an award as one of the top homes in the United States. The three-story mansion has nine elegant rooms, each unique in size, shape, and decor, offering romantic amenities such as Jacuzzi and fireplace; $109–239.

♂ **Sweet Magnolia Inn** (850-925-7670; sweetmagnoliainnbandb.com), 803 Port Leon Drive, St. Marks 32355, offers an interesting meld of old-fashioned charm and updated facilities; it's a former railroad boardinghouse from 1923, but the interiors are sparkling new. Of the seven roomy bedrooms ($149–215), five offer a Jacuzzi for two. The beautiful water gardens behind the home are a perfect place to settle in and read a book, and the comfy back porch is great for just hanging out. Gourmet breakfasts served for guests; the dining room opens for lunch on weekends with live jazz to liven up the day.

HISTORIC 🦅 ♿ 🐾 ♂ **The Lodge at Wakulla Springs** (850-421-2000; wakullalodge.com), 550 Wakulla Park Drive, is Florida's only state park lodge and a true step into the past, with gleaming Tennessee marble floors and period furnishings in each of the 27 rooms, $129–169. Designed in 1937 as a corporate retreat by businessman Edward Ball, it overlooks the fabulous springs at Wakulla Springs State Park (see *Swimming*), which is what you'll see from the lobby and The Ball Room (see *Where to Eat*) during dinner. Look up and take in the artistic beauty of the hand-decorated wooden beams, completed by a Bavarian artist. This remains a retreat, with no television—except in the lobby, where guests mingle as they enjoy checkers, cards, and conversation at the marble tables in front of "Old Joe," an 11-foot alligator shot by a poacher in 1966. Surrounding the lodge are the woods and waters of the state park, which you can enjoy on foot or on a boat tour.

COMFORT AND LUXURY 🍴 (ᵖ) ♂ A 41-room boutique hotel, **The Governors Inn** (800-342-7717 or 850-681-6855; thegovinn.org), 209 S Adams Street, Tallahassee, created in the heart of a historic warehouse and stable in the shadow of the Capitol, showcases the finest that Tallahassee has to offer. Learn a little history, too—each room is named for one of Florida's former governors. The refined atmosphere extends from the common spaces into the rooms, which are furnished with antiques but have flat-screen televisions and iPod docks for music, along with writing desks. Rooms and suites, $99 and up.

🍴 ♿ (ᵖ) At **Hotel Duval** (866-957-4001 or 850-224-6000; hotelduval.com), 415 N Monroe Street, Tallahassee, in a total makeover of the 1951 original, each spacious room has a sleek, modern feel, the perfect meld of function and beauty. When we were nestled in this downtown boutique hotel for a conference, it was hard to leave. The modern bathroom, with a clear sink and pebbled shower room, was a work of art. An easy chair adjoining the bed had perfect ambience for reading; the desk felt just right, and

the upstairs lounge had a bustling bar with a killer view of the city. Bonus: since they're part of the Marriott chain, you still score hotel points. Rooms and suites, $136 and up.

RETRO AND ARTSY Go for funky with the **Shacks at Sea Hag** (352-498-3008; seahag.com/lodging), 322 Riverside Drive, part of Sea Hag Marina (see *Boating*). This eclectic collection of colorful shanties features cottages that date back to the 1940s and '50s, all fully renovated, and includes some tasteful coastal houses with multiple bedrooms. Enjoy the pool by the marina and the ambiance of grilling freshly caught fish outside. Smaller units start at $69 for a one-bedroom up to $349 for a 6-bedroom house; rates rise significantly during the summer scalloping season.

TRIED AND TRUE (ᵖ) ♿ ✎ At **Best Western Wakulla Inn & Suites** (850-926-3737; wwakullainn.com), 3292 Coastal Highway, Crawfordville 32327, all of the nicely sized rooms are centered around a large common courtyard with a fountain and a gazebo. Breakfast selections are outstanding, and the breakfast room looks out on the peaceful gardens of the courtyard. A pool is behind the hotel, and there is a fitness center on-site. $97 and up.

🍴 (ᵖ) 🐾 ♿ For spacious pet-friendly accomodations in the heart of the region's outdoor recreation, head to **Magnuson Wildwood Inn** (800-878-1546 or 850-926-4455; innatwildwood.com), 3896 Coastal Highway, Crawfordville 32327. Art reflects nature in details throughout the common areas, from the etched-glass doors to paintings and drawings of local wildlife and the large breakfast area with a wood-and-stone fireplace. Each guest room features a writing desk and luxury linens; there is also a fitness center and pool. The inn adjoins Wildwood Golf & RV Resort (see *Golf*) and The Seineyard Seafood Restaurant (see *Where to Eat*). $89 and up.

As the hub of regional activity, Tallahassee boasts a large number of chain hotels and motels. Over the years, we've had pleasant stays at ♿ (ᵞᵖ) ⊙ **Hampton Inn Tallahassee-Central** (850-309-1300; hilton.com), 2979 Apalachee Parkway; ♿ (ᵞᵖ) **Candlewood Suites** (850-597-7000; ihg.com), 2815 Lakeshore Drive; and ♿ (ᵞᵖ) **Holiday Inn Express Tallahassee I-10 E** (850-386-7500; ihg.com), 1653 Raymond Diehl Road. Despite the many choices, it can still be hard to find a room in town—lobbyists and football fans often book the place full. Your best bet is to call Visit Tallahassee (see *Guidance*) for recommendations when rooms are tight. The best downtown rates are during the summer months, when the colleges are empty and the legislature is not in session.

VACATION RENTALS 🐾 𝒮 ♿ 𝒮 Built in the 1980s as a gathering place for families, **Steinhatchee Landing Resort** (352-498-0696; steinhatcheelanding.com), 315 NE FL 51, is a village of Victorian and Florida Cracker-style cottages in a lovely, lush setting under a canopy of live oaks along the Steinhatchee River. Guests are free to roam and enjoy the riverside pool, health center, petting farm, children's playground, and miles of walking trails; they can rent bikes, canoes, and kayaks to explore the area. Most of the homes are owned privately and leased for rental through the 35-acre resort, so quality from cottage to cottage will vary. Read any lease agreement carefully. Rates start at $146 off-season, two-night minimum, for the smallest of the accommodations, the Spice Cottages.

WATERFRONT (ᵞᵖ) **Fiddler's Motel** (352-498-7427; fiddlersrestaurant.com), 1306 SE Riverside Drive, offers a riverfront view on the Steinhatchee River, adjacent to Fiddler's Restaurant (see *Where to Eat*). Amenities vary, but all of the spacious rooms and suites have Dish TV and a screened balcony; $110–169.

🐾 𝒮 (ᵞᵖ) ⊙ **Steinhatchee River Inn** (352-498-4049; steinhatcheeriverinn

.net), 1111 Riverside Drive SE, has 17 large and tidy suites on a hillside above the river, offering a variety of room configurations for $109–149. The swimming pool and the entire motel overlook the river.

CAMPGROUNDS 🐾 (ᵞᵖ) **Big Oak RV Park** (850-562-4660; bigoakrv.com), 4024 N Monroe Street, Tallahassee 32303, offers shady spaces under grand old oaks just north of Tallahassee, perfect for antiquing excursions and a favorite for legislators living on a budget, offering a mix of back-in and pull-through, 50-amp full-hookup sites for campers and self-contained RVs only, $45–50.

🐟 🐾 𝒮 (ᵞᵖ) **Holiday Campground** (850-984-5757; holidaycampground.com), 14 Coastal Highway, Panacea 32346, is a large family campground with a steady breeze off Ochlocknee Bay and great views from many of its sites. They can accommodate anything from a tent to a big rig and offer full 30- and 50-amp service, nice bathhouses, a playground, a 200-foot pier for fishing the bay, a swimming pool, and a camp store. Dump station available. $30–40, weekly and monthly rates available.

𝒮 🐾 (ᵞᵖ) **Perry KOA** (850-838-3221; koa.com/campgrounds/perry), 3641 S Byron Butler Parkway, Perry 32348, provides a mix of shady and sunny pull-through sites with full hookups or tent sites and camping cabins, $23–50. Amenities include a swimming pool (open seasonally) and a hot tub.

🐾 Adjoining their expansive convenience store—worth a stop in itself—**Rocky's Campground** (850-584-6600; rockyscampground.com), 5175 US 98, Perry 32348, has a pleasant loop in a wooded area with both primitive camping and full hookups, $7–30. Grab hot food or deli items inside the store.

Steinhatchee Outpost Campground (352-498-5111; outpostcampground.com), 24123 US 19 at the junction of US 19 and FL 51, Steinhatchee 32359, has 13 acres adjacent to the Steinhatchee River. They offer open and shaded sites for tents and RVs ($20–30) with fire rings and picnic tables. The only convenience store along US 19 between Cross City and Perry sits out front.

🏕 (((•))) **Tallahassee RV Park** (850-878-7641; tallahasseervpark.com), 6504 Mahan Drive, Tallahassee 32301, has azalea-lined roads with shaded spaces, picnic tables, full hookups at each site, and a swimming pool, $45–50.

🏕 (((•))) At **Wildwood Golf & RV Resort** (see *Golf*), Crawfordville 32327, pull in for the night for $45 or stay the week or the month. Greens fees are included in your stay, as are access to the swimming pool, catch-and-release fishing, laundry, and a dog park.

FISH CAMPS Six fish camps cluster around Lake Talquin off FL 267, offering anglers a place to retreat from busy Tallahassee. The busiest is (((•))) ✒ **Whippoorwill Sportsman's Lodge** (850-875-2605; fishthewhip.com), 3129 Cooks Landing Road, Quincy 32351, which has cottages, chalets, and cabins sleeping up to 10 people, $115–299, and RV sites with full hookups, $25.

✒ For saltwater fishing, visit **Shell Island Fish Camp** (850-925-6226; shellislandfishcamp.com), 440 Shell Island Road, St. Marks 32355, a comfy family getaway on the Wakulla River. They offer basic, clean motel rooms with a small fridge, cable TV, no phones, $55–68; larger cabins and spiffy no-smoking park models, $60–96; and a small amount of small camper and tent space with a river view, $10–20. The marina store/bait shop always has fishermen hanging out and swapping stories. Ask about renting a boat or hiring a guide to get you out on the flats. Brought your own boat? Ramp and dockage are available for a fee.

❋ Where to Eat

TRADITION 🍴 ✒ Large windows open out onto a view of the Wakulla Springs as you settle back into a casual fine dining experience at **The Ball Room** at The Lodge at Wakulla Springs (see *Lodging*) where they've served guests since 1937. Entrées that have pleased patrons for decades remain on the menu, including the navy bean soup, Apalachicola oysters, pan-fried beef liver, and Old South fried chicken, now joined by more modern creations like steak and portobello tacos, Drunken Duck, and orange coconut shrimp, $10–35. While it's far more casual than it was decades ago, reservations are still suggested for dinner.

BARBECUE (((•))) At **Goodman's Real Pit Bar-B-Que** (850-584-3751; goodmansbbq .com), 2429 S Byron Butler Parkway, Perry, you will be delighted at the selection and the speed of service for smoky, succulent pork on a platter. Opened in 1977, it remains a local favorite for meat lovers, with dinners under $12.

🍴 ✒ It's rare that you'd consider ordering meat—and only meat—at a restaurant, but **Hamaknockers** (850-926-4737), 2837 Coastal Highway, makes it a compelling choice with their richly smoked pork and nearly two dozen barbecue sauces to taste test. We've done this more than once, with friends leading the way, and we always walked away satisfied. Grab a pound of pulled pork to share for $12 or a sandwich platter for $6 and up.

CASUAL FARE ✒ At **Andrew's Capital Grill & Bar** (850-224-2935; andrews downtown.com/grill.php), 228 S Adams Street, Tallahassee, the sandwiches come named for Florida politicos and local celebs—try Coach Jimbo's Truffle Melt or the "Marco Cubio" Cuban for lunch, $10–13, or their signature Haight Ashbury, with roasted turkey breast. Looking for something more substantial? Entrées include cedar plank salmon, fresh Florida grouper, and filet medallions, $13–26. It's one of the few places left where you can find a slice of classic Florida Orange Sunshine Cake.

🍴 Dark, rich coffee and simply perfect cheese grits start the day right with a "Simple Breakfast" at **Havana Eatery** (850-445-5940), 204 8th Avenue W, Havana. This homey diner dishes up a few tasty options for breakfast, but their forte lies with sandwiches and salads, with offerings like Purple Chicken, glazed with a sweet Vidalia raspberry vinegarette, grilled and chilled and served in a tortilla; ham, bacon, and Swiss grilled cheese pressed on an inside-out hoagie roll; and their secret recipe Flat Iron Mac & Cheese, $4–10.

You'll miss neither the full-size gorilla outside nor the barnacle-encrusted bicycle in the front window of **Sopchoppy Pizza Company** (850-962-1155), 106 Municipal Avenue, Sopchoppy, housed in the renovated 1912 drugstore that served this once-bustling railroad town. Choose from specialty pizzas like the Tree Hugger, Sopchoppy Supreme, or Carnivore, $11–20, or try the sandwiches, salads, and lasagna, too.

Since Ted Turner owns a massive plantation down by Lamont, it's no surprise that **Ted's Montana Grill** (850-561-8337; tedsmontanagrill.com), 1954 Village Green Way off Capital Circle NE, popped up in Tallahassee. Turner's own steak house chain, drawing on his cattle ranches out West, serves up fresh juicy Angus beef or bison steaks and burgers, $15 and up.

Established in 1983, **Uptown Cafe** (850-218-9800; uptowncafeandcatering.com), 1325 Miccosukee Road, Tallahassee, serves omelets, scrambles, smoked salmon hash, and made-from-scratch brunch delights, including banana bread French toast, buttermilk biscuits, and hearty blueberry pancakes, $4–11.

COMFORT FOOD 🍴 For burgers, fries, and milkshakes straight out of the 1950s, go retro at **Graves Drive In** (850-584-3669; gravesdrivein.com), 1974 US 221, Perry, with hand-patted patties, beloved slaw dogs, shrimp and clam dinners, and a Friday special dinner of fried mullet

with swamp cabbage. Most meals under $10 including drink. Eat-in or drive-thru, Tuesday–Saturday 10 AM–9 PM.

🍴🥄 Since 1985, **Myra Jean's Restaurant** (850-926-7530; myrajeansrestaurant.com), 2669 Crawfordville Highway, has been feeding the whole family for a small price while keeping them entertained with the suspended G-scale model railroad running way up over the tables. Their homemade home fries come as a side, cooked up with peppers and onions, and the burgers are handmade, including the 5-pound Behemoth. Enjoy a hearty meal for under $10, and don't forget the ice cream counter—grab a chocolate shake on your way out. Open daily, breakfast served until 11 AM; closes at 3 PM on Saturdays.

We're pleased as punch that a visit to **Pouncey's Restaurant** (850-584-9942), 2186 Highway 19 S, Perry, revealed a redo of the interior and the same excellent meals and service we've enjoyed in the past. Hand-cut fries accompany the hearty burgers, and daily lunch specials like the shrimp basket come with fries and a drink for $7. Dinners are just as filling, from the fried catfish or fried quail to sirloin tips and New York strip, $9–18, or for the really big appetite, the "Big Johnson," a 1½ pound ribeye for $29. Daily 6 AM–9 PM.

ETHNIC EATS Melding Chinese and Thai cuisine, **Bahn Thai Restaurant** (850-224-4765; bahnthai.org), 1319 S Monroe Street, Tallahassee, presents a wide array of fresh Asian food for discriminating palates in an unassuming locale. Nothing is precooked, and there are more than 126 menu options, including an extensive selection of vegetarian dishes, entrées $12–30. The convivial staff can occasionally be caught breaking into traditional song and dance in honor of their patrons' birthdays. Open for lunch on weekdays, dinner daily.

🍴🥄 At **Riccardo's** (850-386-3988; riccardostallahassee.online), 1950 Thomasville Road, Tallahassee, the menu is primarily Italian, and delicious. Eggplant Parmesan comes with a very light breading, and the tiramasu is delicate. The recipe for their bread is a family secret, and the entrées are very reasonable, $9–14. Thursday is German night, with rouladen and schnitzel on the menu. It's a busy family restaurant, so you might want to call ahead for weekend reservations.

🦐 Tucked into an urban Tallahassee stripmall backing up on FSU, **Pitaria** (352-412-7482; thepitaria.com), 631 W Tennessee Street, Tallahassee, is a grill shop serving up souvlaki, pita, dolmades, and other Greek standards in veg and non-veg versions, $6–9. Established in 1991, it's an FSU tradition, as it gets pretty busy when the back-to-college crowd files in. Falafel, hummus, and fava beans accent the menu.

San Miguel (352-385-3346; sanmiguel mexicanrestaurant.weebly.com), 200 W Tharpe Street, Tallahassee. Authentic Mexican in a comfortable atmosphere, with à la carte items $2 and up and entrées $7–13, like the tasty enchiladas verdes, smothered in spicy green tomatillo sauce. Murals brighten the intimate spaces.

HIP BISTRO-STYLE **Andrew's 228** (850-224-2935; andrewsdowntown.com/228 .php), 228 S Adams Street, Tallahassee. The upscale big brother to Andrew's Capital Grill & Bar (see *Eating Out*) presents a very different face from its neighbor, featuring a fine fusion of Italian and American cuisine, with entrées like Dijon Brie chicken, Quinoa Paella, and Bronzed Snapper, $16–44.

Moving out of its roots in Sopchoppy and into the big city, **Backwoods Bistro** (850-320-6345; thebackwoodsbistro .com), 401 E Tennessee Street, Tallahassee, expands upon its humble origins with some mighty fine creations like the Bay-N-Hay, a strip steak and cream cheese-stuffed crab ball skewer on basil-mash, and the Crabby Grouper, almond-encrusted, stuffed with crab

cake, and set in a puddle of blue crab bisque. Creative salads, sandwiches, and entrées, $9–26.

Always reserve ahead at the **Cypress Restaurant** (850-513-1100), 1350 W Tennessee Street, Tallahassee, as it's a favorite of the local politicos. Chef-proprietor David Gwynn serves up creations like oysters and biscuits, sugar cane-mopped ribeye, and low country bouillabaisse, $24–38.

A farm-to-table approach means local products make the meals special at **Flying Bear** (850-320-6132; flyingbearusa .com), 6265 Old Water Oak Road, Tallahassee, and we were here to try out Bradley's sausage after a visit to their store (see *Shopping*). We spoiled our appetites with a mound of 'Your Fly' Cheesy Fries smothered in cheese and bacon, but we still made it through the White Gumbo with sausage and shrimp—unexpectedly creamy like a clam chowder but with a spicy kick—and the Cheese Griller, featuring Bradley's sausage on a grilled cheese with tomato. Pizzas, wings, and burgers join sandwiches with a twist, like the Mac Attack Wrap stuffed with mac and cheese; Kodiak salmon and ribeye steak kick the entrée choices up a notch. Sandwiches, salads, and entrées, $9–28.

QUICK BITE Since 1942, **Metro Deli** (850-224-6870; metrodelitally.com), 104½ S Monroe Street, Tallahassee, a tiny downtown sub shop, has been packing 'em in at lunchtime with its full slate of deli sandwiches, hot subs, melts, and grinders, $7–10. The aroma of cheddar bacon soup will draw you in! You can now grab breakfast melts and wraps here as well, $5–6, Monday–Friday 7:30 AM–5 PM; Saturday 11 AM–4 PM.

ORGANIC AND VEGETARIAN Moving from their old lunchtime pushcart at Kleman Plaza into a nearby storefront, **Soul Vegetarian Restaurant** (850-893-8208; soulvegtallahassee.com), 1205 S Adams Street, Tallahassee, still serves up delicious vegan and gluten-free meals to busy downtowners, $4–12.

SEAFOOD For mouthwatering fresh oysters, pull in to **Outz Too** (850-925-6448; ouztstoo.com), 7968 Coastal Highway at the St. Marks River. On weekends, the place is packed, thanks to live music outdoors. It's easier to grab a table on a weekday, but you will wait for any oyster dishes, as they are pure Apalachicola magic, hand-shucked at the bar on the spot before they're broiled, fried, or served up raw—shooters $2, half-dozen $7, dozen broiled with toppings $12. Enjoy locally caught smoked mullet, too, or pick from a couple dozen other menu items. Plan for a relaxed time chowing down on appetizers (gumbo, mullet, fried green beans, and more) while you wait for your oysters. The results are well worth it.

Serving up sandwiches, steamed shrimp, and snow crab, or baskets of fried seafood including grouper fingers, oysters, and jumbo lump crabmeat—the best crabcake ever!—**Posey's Up the Creek** (850-984-5243), 1506 Coastal Highway, Panacea, is still a winner after all these years. Dinners under $25.

No matter the hour, **The Seineyard Seafood Restaurant** (850-421-9191; theseineyard.com), 8159 Woodville Highway, Woodville, is a busy dining spot—we have friends who'll drive two hours to have dinner here. Fresh Gulf shrimp is featured prominently on the menu; have your seafood fried, broiled, or blackened to taste. Sandwiches, baskets, and entrées, $9–19; this is one of the rare places where you can have a mullet sandwich for lunch, and their fried mushrooms are among the best anywhere. Open daily.

At **The Seineyard at Wildwood** (850-926-919; theseineyardatwildwood.com), 3870 Coastal Highway, Crawfordville, a spinoff of the Woodville original, their seafood is just as scrumptious and, as we learned, it's dangerous to order the ample appetizers, as they'll sate your appetite before the main course arrives. Fried seafood is their specialty, but you can get it grilled or blackened, too. Baskets and dinners, $9–19. Open Thursday–Sunday.

🦪 Opened in 1945, **Shell Oyster Bar** (850-224-9919), 114 Oakland Avenue, Tallahassee, has outlasted most politicians who've made their mark at the Capitol. It's a no-frills, bring cash kind of place, a family-owned business that serves fish and nothing but, from peel-and-eat shrimp to steamed oysters, $6–15.

🦪 Do go out of your way to visit **Spring Creek Restaurant** (850-926-3751), 33 Ben Willis Road, end of CR 365 in Wakulla County, one of Florida's finest down-home seafood restaurants. Tended by the Lovel family since 1977, this off-the-beaten-path seafood restaurant is filled with artifacts recounting history along the Forgotten Coast. The crab chowder is superb, but that's just the beginning of your meal. Fresh, locally caught seafood on the menu includes grouper, mullet, shrimp, and soft-shell crabs. Tuesday–Friday 5–9 PM, Saturday–Sunday noon–9 PM.

WATERFRONT 🦪 **Angelo & Sons Seafood Restaurant** (850-984-5168; angeloandsonsseafoodrestaurant.com), 5 Mashes Sands Road, Panacea, stretches out over Ochlockonee Bay into the next county, providing gorgeous waterfront views while you dine on sumptuous seafood dishes with a Greek flair. A family-run business since 1945, it's an elegant place for less common seafood dishes like char-broiled octopus or amberjack, crab meat au gratin, shrimp creole, snapper, and a variety of stuffed seafood dishes, as well as regional favorites. Entrées $10–28.

Kick back and enjoy the view at **Fiddler's Restaurant** (352-498-7427; fiddlersrestaurant.com), 1306 SE Riverside Drive, Steinhatchee, as you feast on specialties like grilled grouper with caper sauce, lime & dill grouper, and Greek shrimp with feta over linguine. The steaks are fantastic: Delmonico, prime rib, New York strip, and filet mignon. Entrées $16–26. For breakfast and then lunch, they morph into Cackleberry's, "Home of the famous Steinhatchee Sabertooth Sand Gnat Sandwich," with soft-shell crab, blackened grouper, smoked prime rib, and burgers, $6–9.

Riverside Cafe (850-925-5668; riversidebay.com), 69 Riverside Drive, is the epitome of Old Florida waterfront dining: open air, the breeze coming right in off the river. Chow down on a variety of sandwiches from oyster to BLT, or savor a dinner of stone crab claws in-season or any of several vegetarian specialties. The dining room has expanded beyond the cozy entrance into a massive chickee, so they can handle the crowds. Breakfast served daily 9–11 AM, lunch and dinner thereafter, $9–28.

Everyone raves about **Roy's** (352-498-5000; roys-restaurant.com), 100 1st Avenue SW, Steinhatchee, a fixture since 1969 with a killer view of a Steinhatchee sunset. Their mashed potato salad goes down smooth as silk, and the barbecue attracts folks from several counties. Offering a wide variety of steaks and seafood, Roy's is a place for fresh, locally caught specialties, including bay scallops, shrimp, oysters, and tender mullet. Entrées $15–29.

LOCAL WATERING HOLES ((y)) Bigband music drifts into **Black Dog Cafe** (850-224-2518; blackdogcafefl.wixsite .com/blackdogcafe), 229 Lake Ella Drive, Tallahassee, from the adjoining American Legion, filling this hangout where friends chat and singles tap on their laptops, hoping to be noticed. Be the scene: order up a latte, a pinot grigio, or a beer and settle into a comfortable chair. Anywhere that hosts Scrabble Nights is all right by us! Open until midnight most nights.

You'll find Florida legislators hanging loose downtown at **Clyde's and Costello's** (850-224-2173), 210 S Adams Street, Tallahassee, a city pub with pool tables.

ICE CREAM AND SWEETS Cranking out the candy, **Barb's Gourmet Brittles** (850-385-9839; barbsbrittles.com), 1671 N Monroe Street, Tallahassee, have been a longtime institution at the Cottages at Lake Ella. In addition to her fine brittles, Barb now offers fancy brittle ice cream, in flavors like hot chocolate, banana nut, and orange cream pecan.

𝒮 Mix toys with candy-making and an ice cream fountain, and **Lofty Pursuits** (850-521-0091; loftypursuits.com), 1355 Market Street #A11, Tallahassee, is just plain fun. You can buy a kite, a yo-yo, or a board game, or just stop in for an ice cream cone.

✱ Selective Shopping

ANTIQUES Havana is the region's antiques hub, with more than 20 small shops filling the downtown buildings, old railroad station, and tobacco barns to overflowing with a little bit of everything country. One of our favorites is **Mirror Image Antiques** (850-539-7422), 303 1st Street NW, Havana, a sprawling complex with an eclectic selection of items—it's not just antiques. You'll find an art gallery, a gourmet food room stocked with British imports, rooms filled with books, and intriguing items from the Far East, like a Vietnamese Buddha. Antiquarian tomes are offered along with the Peterson Asian Collection and other vintage items.

At **Old Bank Antiques** (850-997-9669), 100 N Jefferson Street, Monticello, look for collectibles and not-so-antiques along with classic items.

A rambling building along the railroad tracks, **The Planters Exchange** (850-539-6343; theplantersexchange.com), 204 NW 2nd Street, Havana, sweeps you back through the past century in a series of dealer booth settings that'll have you thinking about your next home decorating project, with everything from vintage glass, games, books, and art to very fine furnishings.

Something Nice (850-562-4167), 206 E 6th Avenue, Tallahassee, is a collection of gallery shops filled with antiques, collectibles, and handcrafted children's furniture.

ARTS AND CRAFTS Entering **George Griffin Pottery** (850-962-9311), 1 Suncat Ridge Road, Sopchoppy, you're swept into a world of creativity. George has practiced his art here for more than four decades, and his pottery is a wonderful, fluid thing, natural sculpture in a very natural setting, reflective of his inherent love of the craft. After you've looked for the perfect piece on his shelves, stroll the shaded grounds and enjoy the art that emerges from his Florida stewardship forest. The sign out front announces when the gallery is open.

It feels like the '50s inside **Jackson's Drug Store** (850-997-3553), 166 E Dogwood, Monticello, where local art spruces up the walls along the corridor off Jefferson Street.

A mix of vintage and modern, **Two Sisters** (850-997-2550), 170 N Jefferson Street, Monticello, offers up both treasured finds and handcrafted goods.

BOOKS AND GIFTS You'll find both old and new books at **Book Mart** (850-584-4969), 1708 S Byron Butler Parkway, Perry. Among the titles in the Florida section is an essential book for learning about this region, *Along the Edge of America* by Peter Jenkins.

Simply Entertaining (850-668-1167; simplyentertainingtallahassee.com), 1355 Market Street #A10, Tallahassee, is a fun stop for culinary items: gourmet foods and wines, plus kitchen accessories that would make a chef proud.

The Tallahassee **Visitor Information Center** (see *Guidance*) has its own shop, featuring art, books, and CDs from Tallahassee artists, including photo cards, primitives, bold acrylics, fiber arts, paintings on slate, and more.

CLOTHING A great Western wear shop, **Michelle's Bull Pen** (850-584-3098), 3180 S Byron Butler Parkway, Perry, has moccasins, boots, hats, and jewelry, as well as tack for your steeds.

DECOR AND MORE Inside a little Cracker home, **My Secret Garden** (850-926-9355), 3299 Crawfordville Highway, Crawfordville, has fine home decor, pretty pottery and garden statues, and all the little (and big) things you need to plan a fancy party or outdoor wedding.

The most colorful occupant of the Cottages at Lake Ella is **Quarter Moon Imports** (850-222-2254; quartermoonimports.com), 1641 N Monroe Street, Tallahassee, filled with fair trade exotica like lush tapestries from India, sensuous sushi platters, Moroccan tea sets, and stylish dresses.

Part of the 1906 Havana depot, **Wanderings** (850-539-7711; thewanderings .com), 312 1st Street NW, Havana, is a roomy shop dealing in exotic home decor and primitives—arts, crafts, and furnishings.

FARMERS' MARKET 🌱 Don't miss the **Tallahassee Downtown Market** (850-224-3252; downtownmarket.com) in Ponce de Leon Park (Park Avenue between Monroe and Adams), where vendors haul in the freshest of local produce while local musicians play on stage, poets and authors offer readings under the grand live oaks, and kids can join in fun activities like pumpkin carving, sidewalk chalk art, and other hands-on arts and crafts. Saturday 9 AM–2 PM, March–November; free.

NURSERIES **Just Fruits & Exotics** (850-926-5644; justfruitsandexotics.com), 30 St. Francis Street, Crawfordville. Along US 98 east of Medart, this sprawling native plant and exotic fruit emporium has everything from ferns and *Sarracenia* (carnivorous pitcher plants) to persimmon and guava trees. A must-stop for the serious gardener.

🌿 **Native Nurseries** (850-386-8882; nativenurseries.com), 1661 Centerville Road, Tallahassee, is a nursery for nature lovers, a shop where you'll learn about native plants and animals as you browse. Be sure to check out the Children's Nature Nook and the Wren's Nest Nature Shop, and if you're in town for a while, sign up for one of the many free workshops on native creatures and gardening.

OUTDOOR GEAR With more than 40 years serving Tallahassee, **Trail & Ski** (850-531-9001; trailandski.com), 2748 Capital Circle NE, is the shop where backpackers and campers head when they're gearing up for a trip. The store features a fine selection of outdoor guidebooks, travel items, and technical clothing; rental gear available.

SPECIALTY FOODS A drive up Centerville Road from Tallahassee will take you to **Bradley's Country Store** (850-893-4742; bradleyscountrystore.com), 10655 Centerville Road, a general store in continuous operation since 1927. Stop in for their signature country-smoked sausage and milled grits—both made right here on the farm—as well as tasty coffee, local history books, and country-theme gifts. Just poking around the store is a delight, thanks to the antiques, some of which have been in use here for decades.

Lighthouse Seafood Market (850-925-6221), 720 Port Leon Drive, St. Marks, features fresh fish and shellfish caught and gathered daily by local fishermen.

A community co-op, **New Leaf Market** (850-942-2557; newleafmarket.coop), 1235 Apalachee Parkway, Tallahassee, is nearly 40 years old and invites the public in to shop for organic produce, ecofriendly household goods, alternative diet foods, and more. They've opened a second store northeast of downtown at 6668-0 Thomasville Road; both are open daily.

Known for its fresh fine seafood, the stretch of highway between

PART OF THE SELECTION INSIDE THE BRADLEY COUNTRY STORE

ARTHUR ROBINSON AT ROBINSON PECANS

Crawfordville and the fishing village of Panacea boasts the largest number of roadside seafood stands in Wakulla County. In addition to folks selling shrimp and oysters out of the backs of their trucks, some of the old standbys with storefronts include **Brown's Seafood** (850-962-3981), 84 Sopchoppy Highway, and **Nichols & Son's Seafood** (850-962-2800), 564 Sopchoppy Highway (on US 319 toward Sopchoppy), plus **My Way Seafood** (850-984-0164), 1249 Coastal Highway.

Along the side of US 27, the bright yellow signs with black-and-red hand-lettered print draw your attention to a longstanding roadside stand that Arthur Robinson started 50 years ago. **Robinson Pecan House** (850-997-5330), 3621 E Capps Highway, Monticello, is a simple place, but the wares they carry speak of the bounty of this region—mayhaw jelly, cane syrup, tupelo honey, and of course, pecans. Open seasonally.

Where FL 267 meets US 98 in Newport, you'll find "**The Tupelo Honey Man**," Preston Bozeman, a longtime local vendor selling tupelo honey, mayhaw jelly, and cane syrup out of the back of his pickup truck on weekends year-round.

✳ Special Events

FALL/WINTER 🖊 Since 1956, the biggest annual celebration of the forestry industry in Florida has been in Perry at the **Florida Forest Festival** (850-584-8733; floridaforestfestival.org), at Forest Capital State Park (see *Museums and Historic Sites*). It happens the fourth Saturday of October with the world's largest free fish fry, lumberjack competitions, heavy equipment exhibits, an antique car show, arts and crafts, and plenty of fun and games for the kids. Of course, there's always a parade to kick it all off.

🖊 At St. Marks National Wildlife Refuge (see *Parks, Preserves, and Camping*), the **Monarch Butterfly Festival** (floridabirdingtrail.com/event/

monarch-butterfly-festival), in the last weekend of October, offers guided naturalist tours to view butterflies along hiking trails, environmental exhibits (including a butterfly tent for the kids), arts and crafts, and the opportunity for you to volunteer to tag butterflies for research. During the same weekend, the **St. Marks Stone Crab Festival** (stmarksstonecrabfest.com) draws visitors to riverside restaurants with massive fixed-price feeds, live bluegrass, and a small arts and crafts festival.

𝒮 Founded more than 75 years ago, the **North Florida Fair** (850-878-3247; northfloridafair.com), 441 E Paul Russell Road, Tallahassee, is the Red Hills region's largest agricultural fair, featuring major country music acts, midway rides, agricultural competitions, and food vendors over the span of two weeks in October–November. Fee.

Held since 1937 at Dixie Plantation (see *Antebellum Plantations*), the **Continental Field Trials** (dixieplantation .org) show off the working qualities of bird dogs trained to point at quail. Third Monday of January.

Step into Civil War history at the **Natural Bridge Civil War Reenactment**, first full weekend of March at Natural Bridge Historic State Park, Woodville (see *Museums and Historic Sites*) to revisit the last battle in Florida during the Civil War.

𝒮 A nationally recognized equestrian competition with Olympic riders, the **Red Hills Horse Trials** (850-893-2497; rhht .org), is held at Eleanor Klapp-Phipps Park (see *Hiking*) in Tallahassee. It includes educational exhibits and special activities for the kids. Fee.

SPRING/SUMMER If you didn't know the proper way to extract an earthworm from the ground, the **Sopchoppy Worm Grunting Festival** (wormgruntinfestival .com) will show you how. The festival also features live bluegrass, arts and crafts, and the annual worm grunters' ball. No jokes, folks—this is an honest profession in the Apalachicola woods! First Saturday in April.

Established in 1991, the **Tallahassee Jazz and Blues Festival** (tallahassee museum.org) brings together the finest Dixieland, swing, big band, and smooth jazz musicians in the region for a weekend during the month; fee.

𝒮The annual **Wakulla Wildlife Festival** (850-561-7286; wakullawildlifefestival.com), usually held in April, gets you into the woods and out on the waters of Wakulla County on guided expeditions for birding and wildlife-watching.

Panacea Blue Crab Festival (850-984-2722; bluecrabfest.com), first weekend of May. A parade and craft booths are an adjunct to seafood, seafood, and more seafood from the folks who know crabs! Held at Wooley Park on Dickerson Bay. Fee.

NORTH FLORIDA

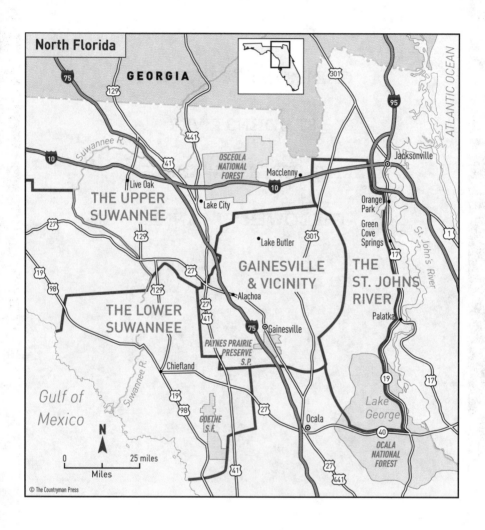

North Florida

GEORGIA

ATLANTIC OCEAN

Suwannee R.

OSCEOLA
NATIONAL
FOREST

Live Oak

Macclenny

Jacksonville

THE UPPER
SUWANNEE

Lake City

Orange
Park

Green
Cove
Springs

Lake Butler

St. John's River

GAINESVILLE
& VICINITY

THE
ST. JOHNS
RIVER

Alachoa

THE LOWER
SUWANNEE

Gainesville

Palatka

PAYNES PRAIRIE
PRESERVE
S.P.

Suwannee R.

Chiefland

Gulf of
Mexico

Lake
George

GOETHE
S.F.

Ocala

N

OCALA
NATIONAL
FOREST

0   25 miles

Miles

© The Countryman Press

GAINESVILLE & VICINITY

Alachua, Bradford, and Union Counties

In 1765, botanist William Bartram described a visit to the village of Cuscowilla, on the edge of a vast prairie, where he met with the great chief Cowkeeper. Cowkeeper's descendants, the Seminoles, were pushed south off their ancestral lands by settlers eager to claim the rich prairies, oak hammocks, and pine flatwoods as their own. After Florida became a US territory in 1821, Congress authorized the construction of the Bellamy Road, a wagon route from St. Augustine to Tallahassee, leading settlers to this region. But it was not until the establishment of the University of Florida in 1853 that **Gainesville**, now the largest and most vibrant city in the region, became a major population center. All three counties maintain their rural roots, where farming and ranching surround small historic communities.

Gainesville started out as Hogtown, an 1824 settlement of 14 inhabitants on a creek that snaked its way into the vast prairie south of town. Named for General Edmund Gaines, a commander of US Army troops in Florida during the Second Seminole War, Gainesville won out over Lake City for the location of the newly formed University of Florida, becoming the county seat in 1854. Civil War skirmishes in the downtown streets added a touch of excitement in the 1860s, but it wasn't enough to discourage a steady stream of settlers. Gainesville incorporated as a city in 1869.

"Historic but hip" describes the towns north along US 441, mingling old and new, with historic structures reinvented as cafés, art galleries, and theaters. Settlers coming down the Bellamy Road moved into **High Springs** on the Santa Fe River as early as the 1830s; Florida's phosphate boom accelerated the town's growth in the 1870s; the town retains that turn-of-the-century feel. The Bellamy Road also brought settlers to the pastoral town of **Alachua**, founded in 1905. Blink and you'll miss the turnoff from US 441 onto Alachua's Main Street, just a mile south of I-75. But it's worth the stop. Although only a few blocks long, downtown Alachua is crammed with unique shops and restaurants.

In Bradford County, the county seat of **Starke** lives in infamy as the home of the Florida State Prison and its electric chair, but downtown Call Street shows the genteel side of this historic city. South of Starke on US 301 is **Waldo**, founded in 1858 as a railroad town. Starting in the 1960s, Waldo became infamous for speed traps along US 301. To this day, *Waldo* remains a synonym for *speed trap* in Florida, so watch that gas pedal when you drive through!

The railroads also ran through **Hawthorne**, established in 1880 as a junction for trains from Gainesville to Ocala and Waldo. The Lake District continues in a sweep southward past Newnans Lake and the historic village of **Rochelle,** down to Lake Lochloosa and Orange Lake, where Pulitzer Prize–winning author Marjorie Kinnan Rawlings put the fishing village of **Cross Creek** on the map. Nearby **Evinston**, established in 1882 on the Marion County border, was a major citrus center until the deep freezes of the 1890s killed the groves. And **Micanopy**, founded in 1821 near Paynes Prairie, is one of Florida's top destinations for antiques shopping, its downtown a snapshot of the late 1800s. In western Alachua County, history buffs will appreciate tiny **Archer** for its railroad museum and Civil War history. Florida's 1870 phosphate boom built the town of

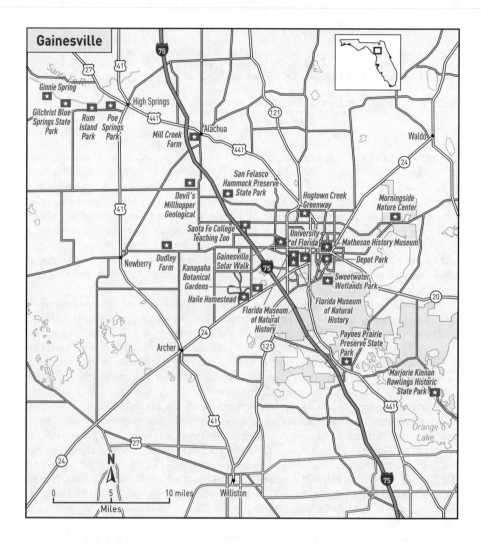

Newberry, where workers dug deep pits to extract the black nuggets used for fertilizer. In more recent times, paleontologists have had a field day in Newberry's phosphate pits, pulling out fossilized crocodiles, turtles, and other creatures whose bones are on display at the Florida Natural History Museum in Gainesville.

GUIDANCE Stop in at the Gainesville/Alachua County Visitors & Convention Bureau (352-374-5260 or 1-866-778-5002; visitgainesville.com), 30 E University Avenue, Gainesville 32801. For points east and north of Gainesville, visit the **North Florida Regional Chamber of Commerce** (904-964-5278; northfloridachamber.com), 100 E Call Street, Starke 32091. In addition, Gainesville-based **Natural North Florida** (877-955-2199; naturalnorthflorida.com), 2009 NW 67th Place, Gainesville, offers tourism information and advice for the 13-county region that encompasses this area plus the Upper Suwannee, the Lower Suwannee, and the Big Bend.

GETTING THERE *By air:* American and Delta provide daily commuter service to **Gainesville Regional Airport** (352-373-0249; gra-gnv.com), located east of town off FL 20.

By bus: **Greyhound** (352-376-5252), 516 SW 4th Avenue, Gainesville.

By car: **I-75** runs through the heart of Gainesville and Alachua County, paralleled by **US 441; US 301** passes through major towns in Bradford and Union counties.

GETTING AROUND *By bicycle:* Gainesville is one of Florida's most **bicycle-friendly** cities, with rail-trails, dedicated urban bike paths, and bike lanes connecting the city core and the University of Florida with the suburbs. **FL 20, 24,** and **26** radiate out of Gainesville to reach points east and west in Alachua County, and **US 41** provides an often-canopied scenic rural route between High Springs, Williston, and Archer. **FL 121** connects Gainesville with Lake Butler to the north.

By bus: Given the University of Florida's large student population, local bus service via **Regional Transit System** (352-334-2600; go-rts.com) is frequent and comprehensive. Adults $1.50; half fare for students, seniors, military; children and disabled free.

By taxi: **A1 Yellow Cab** (352-374-9696), **Gator Cab US** (352-336-8484), **Commuter Taxi & Shuttle** (352-256-1086).

SPRING RUN FLOWING OUT OF POE SPRINGS

PARKING Although there are some free parking spaces in downtown Gainesville (two-hour limit), it's mostly **metered parking, with a two-hour limit** in most places. **Two parking garages** serve the downtown district, one along University Avenue and the other near the Hippodrome Theatre. At the University of Florida, if you can't find metered parking along the edge of campus, it's essential to pick up a visitors pass (free) at one of the staffed parking permit kiosks off University Boulevard or SW 13th Street. Park only in **permit areas** that match the color of your pass—even in metered areas—or you'll face a parking ticket, payable immediately at the main parking office on North-South Road. In all other communities, you'll have no problem finding free street parking within easy walking distance of shops and restaurants.

MEDICAL EMERGENCIES In Gainesville, **UF Health** (352-265-0111; ufhealth.org), 1600 SW Archer Road, formerly Shands Hospital, is one of the nation's top medical facilities. You also have the option of **North Florida Regional Medical Center** (352-333-4000; nfrmc.com), 6500 W Newberry Road.

✳ To See

ARCHAEOLOGICAL SITES Thanks to the archaeologists of the University of Florida–Gainesville, many significant sites have been identified throughout Alachua County. Some, like the **Law School Burial Mound**, are open to public inspection. Located on the University of Florida campus near Lake Alice, this burial mound dates back to CE 1000. It contains the remains of the ancestors of the Potano culture, also known as the Alachua Tradition peoples. The **Moon Lake Villages** were a series of Alachua Tradition villages on the site now occupied by Buchholz High School in Gainesville.

Accessed by the trails in **Gum Root Swamp Conservation Area** (see *Parks, Preserves, and Camping*), villages along **Newnans Lake** were occupied as early as 3000 BCE, and more recently by the Seminoles, who called the lake Pithlachocco, the place where boats are made. More than 100 aboriginal canoes were unearthed from the lake in 2000, the largest such find in Florida's history. Most remain buried in the mud.

At **San Felasco Hammock Preserve State Park** (see *Parks, Preserves, and Camping*) one of the first Spanish missions in North America was established in 1608 and occupied until 1706. Its exact location is not marked, but you can walk through the woods around the mission along the Old Spanish Way trail, where Alachua County's original seat, Spring Grove, vanished under the thick cover of hardwood forest. The rim of **Paynes Prairie** (see *Parks, Preserves, and Camping*) is also dotted with village sites, including one near the boardwalk on US 441.

ARCHITECTURE Several historic districts surround the city core of downtown Gainesville, where the original **Courthouse Clock** (circa 1885) resides in a new housing at the corner of University and 1st Street in front of the new courthouse. B&Bs (see *Lodging*) stake a claim in the historic **Southeast Residential District**, Gainesville's earliest suburb, settled in the 1880s. Wander through these streets for some fine examples of Victorian and Cracker architecture. In the lushly canopied **Northeast Historic District**, covering a few blocks around the Thomas Center, 12 historic homes show off their Victorian charm beneath the live oaks and magnolias. Start your tour there at the **Thomas Center** (see *Art Galleries*). Built in 1906, this restored Mediterranean revival hotel began as the home of Major William Reuben Thomas, the man instrumental in attracting the University of Florida to Gainesville. Founded in 1853, the **University of Florida** boasts its own historic center. In 1989 the **Pleasant Street District** was placed on the National Register of Historic Places, the first predominantly African American community in Florida to gain that designation. Comprised of a 20-block area to the northwest of downtown, it contains 35 points of historical interest, including the **St. Augustine Day School**, 405 NW 4th Avenue, an 1892 mission for African Americans, and the **Dunbar Hotel**, 732 NW 4th Street, a favorite of jazz musicians and the only Gainesville lodging available to African American travelers from the 1930s through the 1950s.

High Springs is a historic downtown; many of its buildings date back to the late 1800s and remain in use as commercial establishments (see *Shopping*). The 1902 **Bradford County Courthouse** anchors the west end of Call Street to US 301 in **Starke**, where a trip up Walnut Street north of Call reveals a row of Victorian-era homes.

More than 35 historic buildings crowd Micanopy's small downtown, best enjoyed as a self-guided walking tour (see *Walking Tours*). Some don't-miss stops include the **Old Presbyterian Church**, built in 1870; the 1890 **Thrasher Warehouse**, housing the Micanopy Historical Society Museum (see *Museums and Historic Sites*); the 1880 **Calvin Merry House**, the oldest home on the east side of the street; the Victorian Gothic

MURAL IN HIGH SPRINGS

revival **Powell House**, from 1866; the 1895 **Brick School House**; the 1875 **Simon-ton-Herlong House** (see *Lodging*); and the **Stewart-Merry House**, built around the 1855 log cabin where Dr. James Stewart practiced medicine. None of the homes are open for public inspection, although many of the historic business buildings now house the town's shops.

ART GALLERIES Our friend Jeff Ripple returned to his roots with **Ripple Effect Studio & Gallery** (352-398-3375; jeffrippleart.com), 112 NE Hunter Avenue, Micanopy, behind the Old Florida Cafe (see *Where to Eat*). Displaying both his outstanding outdoor photography and his plein air interpretations of Florida scenes in oils, it'll stir your heart to see nature the way Jeff does in the field—and yes, he does offer photographic workshops.

    ☯ ♿ **Samuel P. Harn Museum of Art** (352-392-9826; harn.ufl.edu), SW 34th Street and Hull Road, Gainesville, showcases thematic exhibits of fine arts from their extensive collections as well as rotating traveling exhibits. The tall, open rotunda provides access to the main galleries. In the Richardson Gallery, you might encounter an exhibit of fine turn-of-the-twentieth-century American oils, but you'll always find the museum's masterpiece on display—Monet's *Champ d'avoine*. Take a seat and enjoy some quiet time studying this impressionist masterpiece. Looking for more to aid your art appreciation? Stop in the Bishop Study Center to peruse their library of fine art books or examine the computers for exhibits from virtual galleries. The David A. Cofrin Asian Art Wing enables the museum to finally showcase the best of more than 2,000 works from Japan, China, India, and Southeast Asia. In addition to books, jewelry, and fine art reproductions, the Museum Shop carries artsy games and toys for kids, as well as the artistic works of several local artisans. Tuesday–Friday 11 AM–5 PM, Saturday 10 AM–5 PM, Sunday 1–5 PM. Closed on state holidays. Free; donations appreciated.

Santa Fe Art Gallery (352-395-5621; sfcollege.edu/finearts/gallery), 3000 NW 83rd Street, Building P, Room 201, Gainesville. Approved for loans of high-security exhibits from the National Gallery of Art and the Smithsonian Institution, Santa Fe College displays rotating exhibits of contemporary art in their galleries. Monday–Friday noon–4 PM. Free.

Thomas Center Galleries (352-334-2787; gvlculturalaffairs.org), 302 NE 6th Avenue, Gainesville. Serving the community as the Hotel Thomas from 1928 to 1968, this is now a cultural center housing a small history museum, two art galleries with rotating exhibits, and the city's Department of Cultural Affairs. Roam the galleries and enjoy the beautiful surrounding gardens. Monday–Friday 8 AM–5 PM, Saturday 1–4 PM; free.

University of Florida Galleries (352-273-3000; arts.ufl.edu/galleries), 400 SW 13th Street, Gainesville, include the University Gallery (Tuesday–Saturday) in Fine Arts Building B, with contemporary national and regional art displays; the Gary R. Libby Gallery (Monday–Friday) in Fine Arts Building C, with exhibitions organized by graduate student curators; and the Grinter Gallery (Monday–Friday) in Grinter Hall, with its international and multicultural art displays. Free.

BUTTERFLIES Butterflies float like autumn leaves across a backdrop of tropical forest at **Butterfly Rainforest** (floridamuseum.ufl.edu/exhibits/butterfly-rainforest), a permanent conservatory at the Florida Museum of Natural History (see *Museums and Historic Sites*). Bright blossoms and the constant movement of color through the air make this a magical place to stroll, best enjoyed on weekdays when the crowds are lighter. The conservatory is part of the McGuire Center for Lepidoptera and Biodiversity, hosting the world's second-largest collection of mounted specimens amid 39,000 square feet of research labs. What will catch your eye from the museum floor and draw you into this space is the Wall of Wings, with thousands of colorful and unique specimens. Outdoors, enjoy the Florida Wildflowers & Butterflies Garden. Open Monday–Saturday 10 AM–5 PM, Sunday 1–5 PM. Adults $13, Florida residents/students/seniors $11, ages 3–17 $6.

GARDENS ✍ ♿ A walk around the **Jean Klein Rock Cycle Garden** (sfcollege.edu/rockcycle/index), Santa Fe College Department of Natural Sciences, 3000 NW 83rd Street, Gainesville isn't just a pretty walk through a garden, it's an instruction in geology. Twenty massive boulders—from basalt to migmatite—brought in from around the United States are arranged in sequence of rock formation from igneous to sedimentary and metamorphic, with interpretive information to lead you through the cycle. In addition to this oversize rock collection, the college is the recipient of one of Florida's largest private mineral and fossil collections, some of which may be on display inside.

🐾 ✍ ♿ With more than 14 distinct garden areas spread across 62 acres bordering Lake Kanapaha, **Kanapaha Botanical Gardens** (352-372-4981; kanapaha.org), 4700 SW 58th Drive, provides a peaceful retreat on the western edge of Gainesville. One of the top gardens in America for bamboo species, they're known for their annual bamboo sales. In late winter, trillium—at the southernmost point of its range—fills hillsides with blooms. By spring, you can revel in the aromas of azalea and camellia. Come any time to walk more than a mile of pathways between the burbling water gardens, the palm hammock, and the woodland gardens, where you can pause and sit on a bench next to a reflective pool, lose yourself in a Celtic labyrinth, or watch an artist at work painting one of many lovely garden scenes. Plant identifications add to your understanding of native plants and popular botanicals. Kids will appreciate the expansive children's garden, as well as the many places to duck beneath bowers of plants. Art-glass aficionados should note the collection assembled in the gift shop; you'll always find fine art on display in the Summer House, as well as plants available from the on-site nursery. Managed by the North Florida Botanical Society, this is one of Florida's little-known beauty spots. Dogs on leash permitted. Closed Thursday and on Christmas, opens 9 AM all other days; fee.

MOVIES Florida's oldest operational movie theater, built in 1926 as a minstrel and vaudeville venue, is **The Priest Theater** (386-454-7469; facebook.com/priesttheater), 15 NW 1st Street, High Springs. Movies are shown here on vintage X-16 projectors from the 1940s, on Monday, Friday, and Saturday evenings for $5.

MUSEUMS AND HISTORIC SITES In addition to its interpretation of Alachua County's history, the **Alachua County Historic Trust** and **Matheson Museum** (352-378-2280; mathesonmuseum.org), 513 E University Avenue, Gainesville, has a historical library and archives, with an extensive collection of Florida history books and documents. Open 11 AM–4 PM, Tuesday–Saturday. Free; donations encouraged. The trust also administers the historic **Matheson House**, the second-oldest residence in Gainesville, and the **Tison Tool Barn**, both open by appointment only. Fee.

In its showy new location anchoring a corner of Depot Park (see *Parks, Preserves, and Camping*), the **Cade Museum for Creativity & Invention** (352-371-8001; cademuseum .org), 904 S Main Street, hops into the spotlight with a new 26,000-square-foot space dedicated to the history of invention and inspiring visitors to take their ideas to new heights. Dr. J. Robert Cade was the lead inventor of Gatorade and lived a life of "purposeful creativity." The museum reflects his philosophy that science needs the arts to creatively transform ideas into reality. Exhibits on inventions and technology emerging from the University of Florida (including Gatorade), as well as creativity and fabrication labs, are central to the museum, where young people can attend STEAM (Science + Technology + Engineering + Arts + Math) workshops and meet living inventors.

Inside the Old Bradford County Courthouse, the **Eugene L. Matthews Bradford County Historical Museum** (904-964-4606), 201 E Call Street, Starke, showcases Bradford County's history, with a special emphasis on turpentine, logging, and railroads. Open Tuesday–Sunday 1–5 PM; free.

🐾 ♿ Interactive and engaging, the **Florida Museum of Natural History** (352-846-2000; floridamuseum.ufl.edu/), SW 34th Street and Hull Road, continues to evolve with picture-perfect 3-D dioramas and hands-on activities. Kids and adults love the walk-through Florida cave, which now funnels you into the permanent exhibit called Northwest Florida's Waterways and Wildlife, showcasing everything from karst topography and carnivorous plants to indigenous peoples and the creatures of the salt marsh. In the South Florida People and Environments gallery, shrink down to the size of a killifish to explore the world beneath the mangroves, and walk into the home of a Calusa chieftain. Dinosaurs never walked Florida's soil, but we've had saber-toothed tigers, mastodons, and shoveltuskers; learn more about them in the dynamic Florida Fossils exhibit. One of the museum's top attractions is the Butterfly Rainforest, a separate (fee-based) exhibit that will surround you with these winged wonders. Don't miss the Collectors Shop, a must for picking up educational toys and books for the kids. Monday–Saturday 10 AM–5 PM, Sunday 1–5 PM. Free (except for featured rotating exhibits); donations encouraged.

Housed in a restored 1907 church, the **Hawthorne Historical Museum** (352-481-4491), 7225 SE 221st Street, Hawthorne, illustrates the long history of this rural village through artifacts, exhibits, and primitive arts. Open 10 AM–2 PM Wednesday and Friday, 1–4 PM Saturday and Sunday. Free.

At **Marjorie Kinnan Rawlings Historic State Park** (352-466-9273; floridastateparks
.org/park/Marjorie-Kinnan-Rawlings), 18700 S CR 325, Cross Creek, house tours take
you through the living and working space of this Pulitzer Prize–winning novelist
beloved by regional historians for her accurate depictions of rural North Florida. Set in
what remains of her original orange grove from the 1940s, this dogtrot Cracker home
offers some quirks specific to its northern resident, including the "liquor cabinet" with
firewater on top and firewood on the bottom, as well as her use of inverted mixing
bowls as decorative fixtures for lights. Cary Grant, Spencer Tracy, and many other legends stayed in Marjorie's guest room. Costumed guides explain what life was like in
Cross Creek when Marjorie sat on the front porch and typed the drafts of her novels,
including *The Yearling*. Fee.

Housed in the Thrasher Warehouse (circa 1890), built along the railroad tracks—
the "Home Depot of its day," says volunteer Paul Oliver—the small but comprehensive **Micanopy Historical Society Museum** (352-466-3200; micanopyhistoricalsociety
.com), 607 NE Cholokka Boulevard, gives an overview of life in and around Micanopy,
from the ancient Timucua peoples and William Bartram's visit to Cuscowilla in 1774,
through the town's settlement as a trading post in 1821, and on into this century, with
special exhibits of historical railroad items, relics from the Thrasher Store, and period
pieces from the Simon H. Benjamin Collection. There's also a small gift shop and bookstore with historical tomes on the region. Open 1–4 PM daily. Donation.

A remnant of the original wagon road that brought settlers to this region, **Old Bellamy Road** can be accessed from US 41 north of High Springs: Follow Bellamy Road
east to the interpretive trailhead. Just south on US 41 is the **De Soto Trail monument**,
commemorating the route of explorer Hernando de Soto and his men as they traversed
the Florida peninsula in 1539.

Built in 1884 of heart pine, **Wood & Swink General Store** (352-591-1334;
woodandswink.org), 18320 SE CR 225, Evinston, is one of the few remaining historic
post offices in the United States, complete with original decorative postboxes. It's a
welcoming place, with a jumble of antiques, crafts, groceries, fresh produce, books on
local culture and history, and gift items. Stop by and say hello!

PERFORMING ARTS Dance aficionados enjoy the **Gainesville Ballet Theatre** (352-
372-9898; gainesville-ballet-theatre.org), 1501 NW 16th Avenue, a 45-year-old nonprofit regional ballet company. **Dance Alive!** (352-371-2986; dancealive.org), 1325
NW 2nd Street, the evolution of the Gainesville Civic Ballet, presents modern works
and classic ballet around the world. The **Gainesville Orchestra** (352-336-5448;
gainesvilleorchestra.com), founded in 1983 and performing at a variety of venues
around the city, continues to delight its fans. One of those venues, the **Curtis M. Phillips Center for the Performing Arts** (352-392-1900; performingarts.ufl.edu), 3201 Hull
Road, can be counted on for a wide variety of shows.

Since Gainesville is a university town, the place to see and be seen is downtown,
of course, on the patio bars and cafés surrounding Sun Center and **Hippodrome State
Theater** (352-375-4477; thehipp.org), 25 SE 2nd Place, where vibrant live productions
take the stage. Check with the **Gainesville Cultural Affairs Office** (352-334-ARTS;
gvlculturalaffairs.org) for their latest slate of free public concerts downtown on Friday
night, presented year-round at Bo Diddley Plaza.

PRAIRIE OVERLOOK **Paynes Prairie Overlook**, I-75 rest area southbound, Gainesville. Notice the DANGEROUS SNAKES warning signs around the rest area, discouraging
visitors from getting too close to the edge of Paynes Prairie, North Florida's largest prairie. Reflecting this theme, the Florida Department of Transportation built a

KANAPAHA PLANTATION

You've undoubtedly heard a tour guide a say "if these walls could talk . . ." At the **Historic Haile Homestead** (352-336-9096; hailehomestead.org), 8500 SW Archer Road, Gainesville, the walls do just that. The "talking walls," as the docents call them, are physical records of history left behind by the residents of this 6,200-square-foot home, the "writing on the wall" found in every room and closet. Our guide suggested the documentation of everything from household tips to guest lists and inventories might have started when paper was in short supply during the Civil War, then becoming a family tradition.

The Hailes were not a small family—Thomas and Serena, coming to Gainesville from South Carolina, had 15 children, most of them boys. Built in 1855 of cypress and heart pine hewn on the property, the home was the central point of Kanapaha, a 1,500-acre cotton plantation under cultivation by enslaved laborers, some of whom were excellent craftsmen. Once freed, some laborers stayed with the family as Serena Haile diversified the crops to include citrus and vegetables; an exhibit in the kitchen traces their descendents.

A handful of furnishings, including a crib and a dresser, are original to the home, which sat boarded up for more than 40 years until filmmaker Victor Nuñez was directed to it as a potential film location in the late 1970s. Based on a Marjorie Kinnan Rawlings short story, his film, *Gal Young'n*, was shot here and was the first feature film for Nuñez, who went on to become a founding member of the Sundance Film Festival and a member of the Florida Artists Hall of Fame. After the film came an interest in restoring the home, which is owned in partnership with the descendents of the Haile family and the Alachua Conservation Trust, which cares for the home. It has been on the National Register of Historic Places since 1986.

Tours start at the Allen & Ethel Graham Visitors Center, where exhibits document the period when the Haile family occupied Kanapaha. A short walk in the woods leads to the manor home, where you can peruse the "talking walls" up close, noting sketches in the music room and shopping lists in the kitchen. The most colorful time to visit is in December, when Christmas lights brighten the home and surrounding forest. Tours run weekends only, Saturday 10 AM–2 PM and Sunday 12–4 PM; fee.

TALKING WALLS AT HAILE HOMESTEAD

snake-shaped walkway out to an observation deck overlooking the prairie. To northbound travelers, the walkway and deck look like an enormous snake, complete with a ribbon of concrete creating a forked tongue.

RAILROADIANA Inside a historic railroad depot, the **Archer Historical Society Museum** (352-495-2310; sites.google.com/site/archerhistoricalsociety/museum), 16994 SW 134th Avenue, Archer, displays local history and railroad memorabilia, including a lab-model Edison phonograph, an original telephone and telegraph from the depot, and the curator's antique camera collection. A plaque on the depot tells the story of Archer's most famous resident, the founder of the Florida Railroad. In 1865, US Senator David Levy Yulee stashed the personal effects of Confederate president Jefferson Davis at his nearby Cottonwood Plantation while Davis attempted to flee to Florida after the surrender of the Confederacy. Yulee's servants led Union soldiers to the prize, and Yulee was detained here, jailed for treason. The museum is open September–May on the first and third Saturday of each month, 9 AM–1 PM; donation.

Visit the Micanopy Historical Society Museum (see *Museums and Historic Sites*) for historical information and relics from the **Gainesville, Rocky Point & Micanopy Railroad**, circa 1895. After it became the Tampa & Jackson Railroad, locals called the T&J the "Tug & Jerk." It stopped at Thrasher's Warehouse, which now houses the museum.

High Springs grew up around Henry Plant's Seaboard Air Line: the man credited with putting Tampa on the map selected High Springs as his distribution center. On Railroad Street (south of Main), look for the original **passenger depot**. To the west of the station, vast rail yards, roundhouses, and engine shops kept busy with mighty steam engines; the only reminder of their passing is a bright red **Seaboard Coast Line caboose** tucked behind City Hall.

Railroads shaped the towns of Starke, Waldo, and Hawthorne as well. You'll find a **railroad depot** at E Brownlee Street (FL 16) in Starke at the railroad crossing just west of US 301, and a retired **caboose** sitting on a siding southwest of the junction of US 301 and FL 20 in Waldo.

WATERFALLS Visit **Devil's Millhopper** (see *Parks, Preserves, and Camping*) during the rainy season, and you'll see cascades dropping more than 100 feet down the walls of this steep sinkhole, creating an atmosphere much like a tropical rain forest for Florida's southernmost natural waterfall.

ZOO 🐾 ♿ For more than 25 years, the 10-acre, hands-on **Santa Fe College Teaching Zoo** (352-395-5604; sfcollege.edu/zoo), 3000 NW 43rd Street, Gainesville has taught animal technicians (once known as zookeepers) how to create exhibits and handle animals. Ramble the walkways and boardwalks of this deeply forested complex and spend time in front of the enclosures, watching squirrel monkeys swing, turtles sun, and guanacos browse. Actively involved in the international Species Survival Plan, the zoo has endangered species from exotic locations, including Matschie's tree kangaroo and Asian small-clawed otters. A playground provides a place for small children to let off steam. While you visit, you may see students at work, learning how to care for their charges. Open daily 9 AM–2 PM, except for special events; fee.

✳ To Do

ALLIGATOR SPOTTING To see hundreds of live alligators, visit **Alachua Sink** in Paynes Prairie Preserve State Park (see *Parks, Preserves, and Camping*), which boasts

SWEETWATER WETLANDS PARK

the densest population of monster-size alligators in the state. Farther west along Paynes Prairie, alligators (and snakes) sun along the grassy slopes of the levees making up the impoundments and trails at **Sweetwater Wetlands Park**. On the University of Florida campus, a network of nature trails surrounds **Lake Alice**. Visitors get up close and personal with the university's real-life namesakes—but don't ramble down the pathways after dark! The daytime sightings of 10-foot alligators sunning themselves along the trail are thrill enough. Parking areas on Museum Road are restricted to student use until 3:30 PM.

BIKING Gainesville is a city for serious biking, as many eco- or cost-conscious residents use bikes as their sole means of transportation. For a map of the urban bikeway network, contact the **Gainesville Bicycle/Pedestrian Program** (352-334-5074; cityofgainesville.org), 306 NE 6th Avenue, Gainesville. Check on bike rentals at **Gator Cycle** (352-373-3962; gatorcycle.com/rentals), 3321 SW Archer Road, Gainesville.

The paved **Gainesville-Hawthorne State Trail** (352-466-3397; floridastateparks .org/trail/Gainesville-Hawthorne) runs along a 17-mile section of the old railroad line between the two towns, with termini at Boulware Springs Park in southwest Gainesville (although the trail extension continues into downtown to Depot Park) and in downtown Hawthorne, with additional parking areas at all major road crossings.

Passing through Hampton on US 301, the **Palatka–Lake Butler State Trail** (floridastateparks.org/trail/Palatka-Lake-Butler), connects these towns on a mostly unpaved route through rural Putnam, Bradford, and Union counties, right through the middle of downtown Lake Butler. The Florida Trail (see *What's Where*) also follows this route from Keystone Heights north to Lake Butler.

For the best off-road riding in the region, head to the northern end of **San Felasco Hammock Preserve State Park** (see *Parks, Preserves, and Camping*), with more than 12 miles of shady, hilly mountain biking routes radiating from its trailhead in Alachua.

BIRDING At **Paynes Prairie**, birders head for open ground—look for overlooks from Bolen's Bluff and the La Chua Trail, and along US 441. **Sweetwater Wetlands Park** (see *Parks, Preserves, and Camping*) provides a panoramic perspective on the prairie for birders and should not be missed. Encounter dozens of trilling species around the water gardens at **Kanapaha Botanical Gardens** (see *Gardens*). Any spot with a marsh is a major haven for birds, but these are prime places for birding.

DIVING Northwestern Alachua County lies along the spring belt, offering both open-water and cave diving at **Poe Springs** as well as underwater adventures in adjacent Gilchrist County at **Ginnie Springs** and **Blue Springs** (see *Springs*). At High Springs, check in at **Extreme Exposure Adventure Center** (800-574-6341 or 386-454-8158; extreme-exposure.com), 15 S Main Street, for rental equipment, instruction, and pointers on the area's best dives.

    Cave Country Dive Shop (386-454-4444; cavecountrydiving.com), 705 NW Santa Fe Boulevard, is a must-stop for your nitrox fill when you're en route to nearby dives. Kick back on the couch to grab pointers on local hot spots. Besides filling air, nitrox, oxygen, and helium, they offer rental tanks, wings, regulators, scooters, and lights.

    At **Lloyd Bailey Scuba and Watersports** (352-332-0378; lloydbaileysscuba.com), 3405-B NW 97th Avenue, Gainesville, go with a pro with more than 40 years of training experience; classes and guided trips are offered.

ECOTOURS Author and river rat Lars Andersen runs regular guided kayaking trips out of his **Adventure Outpost** in High Springs (see *Paddling*). At the **Lubee Bat Conservancy** (352-485-1250; lubee.org) north of Gainesville, researchers care for endangered fruit bats under the auspices of the Lubee Foundation, formed by rum magnate Louis Bacardi. Group tours are offered by reservation only.

FARMS ✎ ♿ A trip to **Dudley Farm Historic Site State Park** (352-472-1142; floridastateparks.org/park/Dudley-Farm), 18730 W Newberry Road, is one of the best ways to let the younger generations learn about life before electricity, city water, and motorized vehicles. The working nineteenth-century Florida farm belonged to the Dudley family, who settled here in the 1880s, building an entire complex to keep daily life going: canning shed, smithy, smokehouse, syrup house, barns and sheds, and even a general store along the highway, where folks stopped to pick up mail, swap stories, and buy household items. Each of the rooms in the well-preserved farmhouse gives a glimpse into the family's daily life. On weekends and during special events, park rangers in period costume present living history demonstrations of sugarcane harvesting and daily farm chores. Farm open Wednesday–Sunday 9 AM–5 PM, grounds 8 AM–5 PM. Guided tours available. Fee.

    ✎ Children love to feed animals. So it's no surprise that kids, with parents in tow, walk eagerly along the pasture fences at **Mill Creek Farm Retirement Home for Horses** (386-462-1001; millcreekfarm.org), 20307 NW CR 235A in Alachua, where two carrots will get you in the gate—and a bag of carrots will keep them busy feeding horses for an hour. There are 42 paddocks and meadows across this sprawling complex in the rolling hills north of Alachua, with 30 acres of woodlands and wetlands between them. From her golf cart, founder Mary Gregory checks on the groups of visitors rambling from paddock to paddock each Saturday. In 1984, she and her husband Peter created this

FEEDING TIME AT MILL CREEK FARM

haven for abandoned, old, and neglected horses, where their 130 equine guests range from blind Appaloosas to former mounted police patrol horses. Most are more than 20 years old; they will spend the remainder of their lives here and be buried at the farm. A private nonprofit, Mill Creek Farm provides regular care for their horses, thanks to their many volunteers and donations received. The farm only opens to the public once a week, Saturday 11 AM–3 PM, but the joy on visitors' faces—and the interest level of the horses in this interaction—makes this a one-of-a-kind experience for horse lovers and children alike.

🖋 In the 1840s farmstead at **Morningside Nature Center** (352-334-2170; Cityof GainesvilleParks.org), 3540 E University Avenue, kids learn what life in Old Florida was really like during living history demonstrations. Let them join in on a cane-grinding session or talk to the blacksmith. The farm is open daily for visitors to acquiant themselves with the resident sheep, cows, and chickens and to walk around the historic buildings. It's part of the greater urban forest of 278 acres on the eastern edge of Gainesville, the city's oldest nature preserve, with miles of hiking and biking trails. Free.

FISHING While there are many lakes in the region, two stand out as serious fishing destinations: **Lake Lochloosa** and **Orange Lake**, linked by Cross Creek. Cast for bass, bluegill, and speckled perch by slipping your boat into the water at busy **Lochloosa Park**, a favorite launch point in the tiny town of Lochloosa along US 301, or from one of the fish camps along the lake. **Newnan's Lake** is just east of downtown Gainesville between FL 20 and 26. A boat ramp and pier at **Earl P. Powers Park**, 5902 SE Hawthorne Road, Gainesville, provide direct access for fishing Newnan's Lake; if you're in need of a boat or some fishing advice, head just down the road to **Kate's Fish Camp** (see *Fish Camps*).

Have your own boat? Head for the quiet waters of **Lake Alto**, where a boat launch at **Lake Alto Park** (352-374-5245), 17800 NE 134th Place, Waldo provides access to the headwaters of the Santa Fe River, 573 acres surrounded by a cypress-lined shoreline.

Cast for bass, brim, catfish, and crappie. A man-made canal from the late 1800s connects to **Lake Santa Fe** in Melrose, which is ten times the size of Lake Alto and a hot spot for bass. There is a boat ramp for Lake Santa Fe just west of Melrose off FL26.

GOLF **Ironwood Golf Course** (352-334-3120; ironwoodgolfcourse.org), 2100 NE 39th Avenue, is a city-owned public course named one of Golf Digest's "Best Places to Play," with 18 holes, par 72, on an Audubon-approved natural course established in 1962. At **West End Golf Course** (352-332-2721; westendgolfclub.com), 12830 W Newberry Road, you can play day or night. Opened in 1969, it features a fully lighted course (18 holes, par 60), along with an illuminated driving range.

HIKING Home to the state office of the **Florida Trail Association** (352-378-8823; floridatrail.org), 5415 SW 13th Street—where you can pick up hiking guides and hiking-related gifts—Gainesville is ringed with dozens of excellent opportunities for hikers, including more than 20 miles of trails at **Paynes Prairie Preserve State Park** and another 12 miles of trails at **San Felasco Hammock Preserve State Park** (see *Parks, Preserves, and Camping*). Or opt for an easier stroll at one of the many parks, county preserves, or wilderness areas in the region. With both the nonprofit Alachua Conservation Trust and the county's Alachua Forever program setting aside lands for public use, the amount of hiking in the area has grown significantly since *50 Hikes in North Florida* was published. Other hiking destinations we recommend include **Mill Creek Preserve** [29.879407,-82.497118], CR 241 and CR 236, Alachua, where you can explore the southernmost beech forest in the United States along several miles of trails; 🐾 **Prairie Creek Preserve** [29.596357,-82.228401], CR 2082 and CR 234, Gainesville, with 5 miles of trails that lead into lush bottomland forest along a creek connecting Newnan's Lake and Paynes Prairie; and **Watermelon Pond WEA** [29.555754,-82.606814], SW 250th Street, Newberry, a wildlife-rich area with expansive views and more than six miles of trails.

PADDLING Several outfitters in High Springs can get you in the water and down the Santa Fe or the nearby Ichetucknee in Columbia County. At **Santa Fe Canoe Outpost** (386-454-2050; santaferiver.com), US 441 at the Santa Fe Bridge, rent a canoe (shuttle included) or take a guided trip (including overnights) on the Santa Fe or Ichetucknee rivers.

In addition to their "menu" of guided trips and a selection of canoes and kayaks for sale or rent, the **Adventure Outpost** (386-454-0611; adventureoutpost.net), 18238 NW US 441, High Springs, has technical clothing, camping equipment, and a nice selection of regional guidebooks.

Taking the time to match you up with the right craft, the friendly crew at **Rum 138 Outfitters** (386-454-4247; rum138.com), 2070 SW CR 138, rents SUPs, single and double kayaks, and canoes; offers shuttle services; and shows off nature-inspired art by local artists in their gallery. Open Wednesday–Monday 9 AM–5 PM for rentals. $15 shuttle, $40–60 for 4- or 8-hour rentals (includes shuttle).

PARKS, PRESERVES, AND CAMPING From its headquarters at the historic Prairie Creek Lodge, the **Alachua Conservation Trust** (352-373-1078; alachuaconservationtrust .org), 7204 SE CR 234, Gainesville, oversees a growing network of wild places throughout the region. Founded in the 1980s, this nonprofit land trust has helped set aside more than 50,000 acres of natural land throughout North Central Florida for future generations. While many of their projects, including the Historic Haile Homestead (see Historic Sites) and the Hogtown Creek Greenway (see *Parks*), were envisioned and managed as partnerships with other nonprofits and state and local government, there are some lands which are entirely under their care, including beautiful ☀ **Tuscawilla Preserve** [29.502246,-82.269881], under the ancient live oaks on the shores of Tuscawilla Prairie in Micanopy; ☀ **Little Orange Creek Preserve** [29.594297, -82.062618] in Hawthorne; and ☀ **Prairie Creek Preserve** [29.596357,-82.228401] in Gainesville. Among other conservation projects, they are actively involved in creating a greenway between Alachua and Lake Butler in this region.

Just west of Interstate 75, **Barr Hammock Preserve** [29.516451,-82.306449] (352-264-6800), 14920 SE 11th Drive, Micanopy, protects more than 5,700 acres with a massive open wetland, the Levy Prairie, a major landform along the 6.8-mile Levy Loop Trail. Newly opened trails on the south side give equestrians a good place to ride.

✐ ☀ As befits a city with a lot of tree canopy, Gainesville has an extraordinary number of small parks with picnicking, playgrounds, and other fun activities for the kids. One of the easiest to find is **Bivens Arm Nature Park** (352-334-3326), 3650 S Main Street, where nature trails and boardwalks circle a willow marsh and lead beneath tall longleaf pines. A playground and picnic area provide a gathering spot for families.

✐ ☀ An urban playground for all ages, **Depot Park** (depotpark.org), 200 SE Depot Avenue, Gainsville, revitalized what was long a rundown factory district along the railroad. The children's playground draws on natural elements, as does the free children's splash park, Blue Grotto, with its hidden fossils, water jets, and caves. A promenade leads around the big pond access to food truck gatherings and festivals that happen in this new gathering space, while more natural paths offer birding opportunities in the wetlands. Big open lawns invite Frisbee players and offer a place to romp with your dog. The Pop-A-Top General Store has soft drinks and snacks; the Box Car Wine & Beer Garden offers adult beverages. Anchored on its south end by the new Cade Museum (see *Museums and Historic Sites*), this is a clever and expansive addition to the edge of downtown. Cyclists will appreciate the connectivity to the Gainesville-Hawthorne Trail (see *Biking*) and will note the sobering Share the Road Memorial, perhaps the only such bicycle safety memorial of its kind. Play areas and natural areas open dawn–dusk; lighted areas open dawn until 11:30 PM.

✐ One of Florida's more unusual parks is **Devil's Millhopper Geological State Park** (352-955-2008; floridastateparks.org/park/Devils-Millhopper), 4732 Millhopper Road, Gainesville, where you can walk down 232 steps to the bottom of a 120-foot sinkhole lush with vegetation. In the rainy season, tall waterfalls cascade down its sides.

☀ At **Little Orange Creek Nature Park** (352-481-2432; littleorangecreek.org), 24115 SE Hawthorne Road, Hawthorne, this rural city park shows off a gem of a waterway that's been restored over the past five years through a massive volunteer effort. Remains of a historic gristmill sit along one of the hiking loops; picnic tables crowd around the future enviromental education center. Across the highway, the adjoining Little Orange Creek Preserve offers several miles of hiking out to scenic Fowlers Prairie.

For sheer scale of an open landscape, nowhere else in North Florida can compare to **Paynes Prairie Preserve State Park** (352-466-3397; floridastateparks.org/park/Paynes-Prairie), 100 Savannah Boulevard, a 22,000-acre wet prairie defining the southern edge of Gainesville. Herds of bison and wild horses roam the vast open spaces, while alligators collect en masse in La Chua Sink at the north end of the prairie. With more than 20 miles of hiking, biking, and equestrian trails, it's one of the best places in the region for wildlife-watching. Deeply shaded and within walking distance of a playground, boat ramp, and boardwalk along Lake Wauberg, Puc Puggy Campground accommodates tents, trailers, or RVs, $18+. Open 8 AM–sunset daily; fee.

Enjoy many miles of rugged mountain biking and hiking trails through the hills of **San Felasco Hammock Preserve State Park** (386-462-7905; floridastateparks

.org/park/San-Felasco-Hammock) on Millhopper Road, a lush preserve with Appalachian-like landscapes formed by the southernmost large tract of Eastern deciduous forest growing atop Florida's limestone karst. Open 9 AM–5 PM daily; fee.

♿ Wildlife is abundant at **Sweetwater Wetlands Park** (352-393-8520; sweetwater wetlands.org), 325 SW Williston Road, Gainesville, which hugs the north rim of Paynes Prairie. Unlike many wetland parks in Florida—which are generally built to treat wastewater—this park allows the tainted waters of Sweetwater Branch, which flows through the city and gets fed by storm drains, to settle out nutrients that would otherwise harm the fragile prairie habitats. Graveled paths and boardwalks provide nearly four miles to roam, which you'll do slowly while watching for alligators, deer, and the famed bison of Paynes Prairie. Open 7 AM to dusk daily, it is the only city park with an entrance fee.

Conservation areas are some of the wilder spots around the region's lakes, where hikers, bikers, and equestrians can roam through miles of old forest roads and developed trails through floodplain forests. Visit **Gum Root Swamp Conservation Area** on FL 26 for a glimpse of Newnans Lake; **Newnans Lake Conservation Area** (with three tracts: Hatchet Creek, North, and South) off CR 234 and FL 26; and **Lochloosa Conservation Area**, where you can hike out to an observation platform on Lake Lochloosa from a trailhead adjoining the fire station in Cross Creek. All are managed by the St. Johns Water Management District (386-329-4483; sjrwmd.com).

SCENIC DRIVES **Old Florida Heritage Highway** (scenicus441.com), a Florida Scenic Highway, circles the Gainesville area, using US 441, CR 346, CR 325, and CR 2082 to create a beautiful drive around Paynes Prairie and along canopied roads. Along CR 234, from FL 26 south through Rochelle to Micanopy along the east side of Newnans Lake, you'll cruise past historic homes under a canopy of ancient live oaks.

SOLAR WALK It's humbling to find your place in the universe, even as a scale model. On the **Gainesville Solar Walk**, pedestrians along NW 8th Avenue experience our solar system at a 4 billion-to-1 scale by walking east from NW 34th Street toward Loblolly Woods Nature Park (see *Parks*). The sun and each of the planets are represented by an artistic monument with a plaque containing statistics and data for the celestial body. The distance from the sun is represented by the placement of the monument; Jupiter sits across from the best parking along NW 31st Drive, near the pedestrian crossing of NW 8th Avenue for park visitors.

SPRINGS Gainesville once pulled its municipal water supply from **Boulware Springs** (352-334-5067), 3300 SE 15th Street, where you can visit the historic waterworks and see the spring pumping. The park is also a trailhead for the Gainesville-Hawthorne Trail (see *Biking*).

☜ Protecting the springs that were the reason for settlement in this rural area, **Chastain-Seay Park**, 3210 SW 118th Road, Worthington Springs, surrounds the waterway; you can look at, but can't enter, the spring. However, this expansive park has a boardwalk trail that leads down to sandy beaches along the Santa Fe River, where you can fish or swim or swing into the water.

WALKING TOURS Check with the Matheson Museum (see *Museums and Historic Sites*) for brochures outlining walking tours of historic Gainesville, such as the **Pleasant Street Historic Walking Tour** and **Historic Gainesville: A Walking Tour**, which covers the Northeast Historic District around the Matheson Museum. Stop in at the **Micanopy Historical Society Museum** to purchase an inexpensive walking tour booklet that details the history and location of 38 significant sites in the historic district.

HOGTOWN CREEK GREENWAY

The City of Gainesville (352-334-5000; cityofgainesvilleparks.org) has made an import-ant effort to preserve natural lands along **Hogtown Creek**, the waterway that gave the city its original name. While none of these parks are truly wild—all are surrounded by neighborhoods and subdivisions—they are not developed, either. All of them provide places inside Gainesville city limits for hikers to immerse themselves in the deciduous forest on natural pathways. At the north end of the chain is **Hogtown Creek Headwaters Nature Park** [29.696516, -82.342923], 1500 NW 45th Avenue, on 70 acres that were part of Hartman's Dairy for more than a century. Old-growth trees on deeply shaded trails along the narrow creek give no clue about the land's long agricultural use. Next up is **29th Road Nature Park** [29.696516, -82.342923], end of NW 14th Street, a tiny patch of beautiful slope and bottomland forest with many ferns. The two most popular parks along the creek are along its middle and are the easiest to find. **Alfred Ring Park** [29.674283,-82.347019], 1801 NW 23rd Boulevard, lets you ramble through a ravine lined with trout lily and false Solomon's seal beneath tall magnolias; a boardwalk provides nice views of Hogtown Creek. At the confluence with Possum Creek, **Loblolly Woods Nature Park** [29.655222, -82.371825] lies between 5th Avenue and 8th Ave-nue, with trails meandering into the lush forest off a linear path called the Hogtown Creek Greenway. Finally, Hogtown Creek nourishes a large prairie before it vanishes into the Flori-dan aquifer through a sinkhole. Both prairie and sink are protected within the 241-acre **Split Rock Conservation Area** [29.639295, -82.410380] off SW 20th Avenue, along RTS Route 75 (no nearby parking). All of the Hogtown Creek parks are open dawn to dusk. 🐾

HOGTOWN CREEK IN LOBLOLLY WOODS NATURE PARK

SPRINGS OF THE SANTA FE

In the Florida peninsula, no waterway has such an outstanding number of springs feeding its flow in such a short distance as does the **Santa Fe River**, with more than 50 springs along a ten-mile stretch. With such a bounty of cool, clear waters, it's no surprise that High Springs is a mecca for springs enthusiasts. Four parks flanking the river provide public access to major springs. Pets are not allowed at any of these parks.

Closest to town is 🛶 **Poe Springs Park** (386-454-1992; visitgainesville.com/attractions/poe-springs-park), 28800 NW 182nd Avenue, High Springs, with 202 acres of forested and grassy hillsides and steep bluffs heading down to the river. Its namesake spring is a clear pool pumping 45 million gallons of water daily from a spring vent 25 feet deep, and stairs making for easy entry to the natural sandy pool, which is shallow enough along most of its length for young ones. Open 9 AM–6 PM Thursday–Sunday; free.

On the north side of the river, **Rum Island Park** (386-719-7545), 1447 SW Rum Island Terrace, Fort White, is centered around Rum Island Spring, a second-magnitude spring. The island sits in the river between two counties, and back during Prohibition, neither sheriff paid it any attention. With clear spring water and a still, a local business was born. Today, it's a county park, popular for a put-in or take-out for paddling trips along the Santa Fe as well as for its river and spring access for swimmers. Open 7 AM–10 PM Wednesday–Monday, 12 AM–9 PM Tuesday; free.

It's a quick paddle downstream along the 55-mile Gilchrist Blueway to 🛶 **Gilchrist Blue Springs** (386-454-1369; floridastateparks.org/park/Gilchrist-Blue-Springs-State-Park), 7450 NE 60th Street, High Springs, home to five named springs, including second-magnitude Blue Spring. Most visitors arrive via the main gate off FL 236 on the south side of the river. Permanently protected as a state park in 2017, it features swimming in the springs, picnicking, and nature trails, with plans for its popular campground to reopen in the future. Fee.

Finally, also off FL 236, privately owned (📶) **Ginnie Springs Outdoors** (386-454-7188; ginniespringsoutdoors.com), 5000 NE 60th Avenue, High Springs, is an international destination for divers because of the clarity of the water, according to Jacques Cousteau, "visibility forever." Both open-water divers and certified cave divers have several spring systems to explore. While dive training is also offered at Ginnie Springs, those of us with simpler aspirations can snorkel the springs and swim in them as well. There are five spring runs flowing into the Santa Fe from this park, some of which are fed by multiple springs. General admission is $14 adults, $4 ages 6–12; divers pay $22 or $30. Tubes (for tubing the Santa Fe River), canoes, kayaks, and paddleboards are also available for rent. They also have plenty of tent camping space—sites have grills and picnic tables—all first come, first served, plus 90 sites with hookups for $10 a night extra. Per-person camping fees are $22 adults (senior discount), $7 ages 7–14, free for younger guests. The on-site laundry and Wi-Fi near the camp store are great amenities for a long stay. A three-bedroom, two-bath cottage is also available for $175 for up to four adults, minimum two-night stay.

✳ Lodging

BED & BREAKFASTS (📶) Enjoy spacious accommodations in a romantic setting at **Grady House** (386-454-2206; gradyhouse.com), 420 NW 1st Avenue, High Springs 32643, a charming two-story mansion from 1917 with intimate formal gardens in the backyard. The aroma of home-cooked muffins wafts through the dining room; settle down by the fireplace and read a book. Choose from five rooms, $140–170; or Skeet's Cottage with two bedrooms sleeping four, $280 and up (two-night minimum).

🦴 (📶) On Lake Hampton north of Waldo, **Hampton Lake Bed & Breakfast**

(800-480-4522; hamptonlakebb.com), 9138 S W 71st Avenue, Hampton 32091, a massive winged A-frame with a native stone fireplace and pecky cypress walls, is the dream home of Paula Register; the antique gas pumps were handed down from Grandpa, the local Gulf Oil distributor in the 1930s. This is a retreat for those who love the outdoors, with fishing tackle and a pedal boat waiting at the pier, walking trails winding through 18 acres of pines, a porch swing and rockers overlooking the lake, and a hot tub for relaxing after play. Outdoorsy decor accentuates the spacious Wade Room, big enough for an entire family. Four rooms of varying sizes, $99–169. Full breakfast provided.

♂ When guests come to the **Herlong Mansion** (800-HERLONG; herlong.com), 402 NE Cholokka Boulevard, Micanopy 32667, a neoclassical 1875 mansion, they take to the verandas, where comfortable chairs overlook the expansive lawns. Of the four suites, five rooms, and two private outbuildings, sisters and girlfriends traveling together will especially appreciate Pink's Room, with its two antique cast-iron beds and a daybed; brothers will like the masculine Brothers' Room, with a double bed and a daybed. For your own private space, try the Pump House Cottage in the garden. The mansion features private baths, classy antiques, and original push-button electric switches throughout. For a touch of history, settle back in the Music Room and watch *The Yearling* or any of several other movies filmed in the region. If the house looks vaguely familiar, have you perhaps seen *Doc Hollywood*, which was filmed on-site with Michael J. Fox? There are ghosts, although we didn't hear any bumps in the night. Full breakfasts on weekends; continental breakfasts weekdays; no special orders. No children, no pets, no smoking on premises. $119–189.

♿ ♂ (ᵞ) One of the anchors of the bed-and-breakfast district of Gainesville, **Laurel Oak Inn** (352-373-4535; laureloakinn.com), 221 SE 7th Street, Gainesville 32601, is a place to unwind. Sit on the spacious porches of the roomy 1885 Queen Anne and watch the owls from the comfort of your rocking chair, or enjoy the pampering afforded by the soft robes, fragrant lotions, and candles that accompany your in-room hydro-jet massage tub. It's a hit with honeymoon couples, and business travelers appreciate Internet access in every room ($135–200). You won't go away hungry, as innkeepers Monta and Peggy Burt ensure that a steady parade of artfully presented gourmet treats appears on your breakfast plate. A ground-floor room accommodates wheelchairs with an appropriately sized wheel-in shower.

🐾 ♪ ♂ (ᵞ) At **The Magnolia Plantation Inn** (800-201-2379 or 352-375-6653; magnoliabnb.com), 309 SE 7th Street, Gainesville 32601, relax in a private tropical oasis. In 1991 Joe and Cindy Montalto opened the Baird Mansion, an 1885 Victorian painted lady, as the first bed and breakfast in Gainesville. In addition to the five lavish rooms in the main house, each with private bath ($186–218), their plantation now encompasses nine lovingly restored cottages ($230–280) connected by lush, shaded gardens developed by Joe, a landscape architect. Full breakfast served where you'd like it, whether in the lovely Baird House dining room or outdoors on a porch or gazebo. Pets and children welcome in some of the cottages; call ahead for details.

🍴 Set on a 7-acre mini-ranch, **The Rustic Inn** (386-454-1223; rusticinn.net), 15529 NW SR 45, High Springs 32643 is where Tom and Wendy Solomon offer relaxation in six modern rooms ($89–139) with nature themes, from the Everglades to sea mammals; the Zebra Room comes with a hot tub on the deck (additional fee). Settle into a rocking chair on the porch or take a lap around the pool. A continental breakfast basket is left at your room each evening so you can set your own pace in the morning.

♂ ♪ 🐾 (ᵞ) In a glass-walled conservatory, surrounded by a thick screen of greenery, the Piccadilly Suite at **Sweetwater Branch Inn** (800-595-7760; sweetwaterinn.com), 625 E University Avenue, Gainesville 32601, is a calm place to sit and catch up on writing. Although it's just a few blocks from the heart of downtown, the hum of the air conditioner and the chirps of birds mask the sounds of the city. Laughter, however, floats through the air. This is a busy place on weekends, with frequent weddings, but the atmosphere is one of cheer and relaxation. Guests gather in this Victorian home after 5 PM to enjoy a wine-and-cheese break before dinner, to mix and mingle in the parlor, and to meet up with old friends and family members here for the weddings. Built in 1895, the McKenzie House is one of Gainesville's earliest and largest Victorian homes. Proprietor Cornelia Holbrook's mother, Giovanna, purchased the house in 1978 and spent three years returning it to its former glory while her daughter dreamed up decor and amenities. In 1992, she purchased the adjoining Cushman-Colson House, built in 1885, and the duo began the renovations that led to the core of this comfortable complex. Anchored by these two historic homes, six cottages—perfect for families with children—surround the gardens of the complex, which covers a block and a half. Carefully crafted as a wedding venue, the gardens

PICCADILLY SUITE AT SWEETWATER BRANCH INN

are adjoined by a large reception hall on the back of the McKenzie House, which hosts the Sweet Tea Restaurant, a tearoom, during weekday afternoons. This is a family-friendly venue with a pool. Children are welcome but must be supervised; pets are permitted in cottages for a fee. Rooms $144–199; cottages $164–229.

ALUMNI AND STUDENTS 🦟 🍸 ♿ (ᵞₚ) ⊸ You gotta be a Gator—or know one—to book a room at the **Reitz Union Hotel** (352-392-2151; union.ufl.edu/Union Hotel), 655 Reitz Union Drive, but having that in makes a comfortable stay all yours. Occupying the top two floors of the Reitz Student Union on the University of Florida campus, this under-the-radar student-run hotel offers ecofriendly rooms and suites with a bird's-eye view of the campus; $99 and up. Reservations recommended, parents of students welcome.

RETRO AND ARTSY 🦟 (ᵞₚ) The updated 1960s family-run **High Springs Country Inn** (386-454-1565; highspringsinn.com), 520 NW Santa Fe Boulevard, High Springs 32643, has cute landscaping outside its period rooms ($52–604, which vary in size from small to suite; each is sparkling clean, with a small tiled bathroom, a mini-fridge, a microwave, and cable TV.

TRIED AND TRUE As a university town—and a sports town—Gainesville has pretty much every major chain hotel up and down the four exits of I-75, plus a handful around downtown, including ♿ 🍸 **Hampton Inn & Suites Downtown** (352-240-9300; hamptoninnandsuites gainesville.com), 101 SE 1st Avenue, Gainesville 32601, which blends in nicely into the downtown district and is right in the heart of Gainesville nightlife. Near the on-campus museums you'll find the ♿ 🍸 (ᵞₚ) ⊸ **University of Florida Hilton** (352-371-3600; www.hilton.com), 1714 SW 34th Place, Gainesville 32601. This is a top-notch chain hotel conference center that we've stayed in time and again, with comfortable rooms with free Wi-Fi, fitness center, heated pool, and spa; visit **Albert's Restaurant** for fine dining, American-style, including a Sunday brunch with complimentary mimosas. Shuttle provided to airport. At the north edge of Gainesville, & ☀ (ŋ) ⌁ **Best Western Gateway Grand** (352-331-3336; gatewaygrand.com), 4200 NW 97th Boulevard, provided a great launch point for us to explore San Felasco Preserve and the springs of the Santa Fe River, and they offer an airport and medical center shuttle as well.

CAMPGROUNDS ⌁ ☀ (ŋ) **High Springs Campground** (386-454-1688; highsprings campground.com), 24004 NW Old Bellamy Road, High Springs 32643, provides camping in a family-oriented atmosphere, with playground, swimming pool, tent sites, and full hookups, $22–33, discounts for AAA and many camping clubs.

⌁ ☀ (ŋ) With horseback riding, camping, canoeing, swimming, and nearby hiking trails, **River Rise Resort** (352-318-4602; passport-america.com), 252 SE Riverview Circle, High Springs 32643 is a centrally located destination for outdoor recreation along the Santa Fe River. $35–48, half price for Passport America members.

⌁ ☀ (ŋ) **Starke KOA** (904-964-8484; starkekoa.com), 1475 US 301, Starke 32091, is a large campground, partially shaded, with exceptional amenities like free wireless Internet and wide, grassy, 70-foot pull-through spaces ($38–48). Heated swimming pool, playground, one-room camping cabins with no bath ($50); no tenting permitted.

FISH CAMPS Around a campfire many years ago at **Kate's Fish Camp** (352-372-1026; katesfishcamp.com), 6518 Hawthorne Road, J. T. Glisson told tale after tale of being a young boy growing up in Cross Creek when "Miss Rawlins" was

around. There's something about a fish camp that brings on this sort of camaraderie, and Kate's has been sparking that magic since the 1950s. With access to Prairie Creek, Newnan's Lake, and the Gainesville-Hawthorne Trail just off FL 20, Kate's is a piece of Old Florida that locals cherish. Stop here to rent a boat ($45) or a canoe or kayak ($20), or just camp on the property ($9 tents, up to $30 for big campers with electric) and explore the local wilds.

Once owned by baseball legend Wade Boggs, ☀ **Lochloosa Harbor Fish Camp** (352-481-2114; lochloosaharbor.com), 15008 SE US 301, Hawthorne, has the best views of and access to Lake Lochloosa. Bring your RV or a tent, or rent a cabin ($62) so you can head out before daybreak on this placid lake and land your own lunkers at this tournament destination. Boat rentals and a small diner on-site. Full hookups available, as well as tent sites with water and electric, $30. Small pets welcome.

Secret River Lodge/Yearling Cabins (352-466-3999), 14531 S CR 325, Cross Creek 32640, is an eclectic collection of restored fish camp cabins providing a quiet venue for relaxing in a sleepy little town. Each cabin is named for a book by Marjorie Kinnan Rawlings and ranges in amenities from a simple bedroom with bath to a two-bedroom cabin with a full kitchen. $89–129.

Right on historic Cross Creek, (ŋ) **Twin Lakes Fish Camp** (352-466-3194; twinlakesfishcamp.com), 17105 S CR 325, lets you settle in and enjoy the two best lakes to fish in the area. Rent a boat or pontoon, $60, or a canoe, $20, to explore the lakes—Lochloosa tends to hold more water than Orange Lake in a dry year—camp for $24 or rent one of their cabins (satellite TV provided), $86–96.

✳ Where to Eat

TRADITION Although the outside looks like an old shack, **Yearling Restaurant**

(352-466-3999; yearlingrestaurant.net), 14531 E CR 325, Cross Creek, has a dining room that features dark, rich wood and windows on the creek. This is a funky place celebrating the legacy of their neighbor Marjorie Kinnan Rawlings, where you're as likely to rub elbows with the poet laureate of Tennessee as you are with local fishermen. "Cross Creek Traditions" include crawdad, alligator, frog legs, venison, soft-shell crab, catfish, and pan-fried quail, as well as a variety of steaks and combination platters. Coated in a light breading, the fresh venison medallions are surprisingly tender and juicy; the stuffed flounder contains a mass of succulent buttery crabmeat. Lighter fare is available before 5 PM, including a "Creek Boy" sandwich served up with your choice of fried shrimp, oyster, or alligator with coleslaw and Jack cheese. Entrées $15 and up. Thursday noon–9 PM, Friday–Saturday noon–10 PM, Sunday noon–8 PM; Live music Friday and Saturday.

ELEGANT AND ROMANTIC Gainesville's top pick for fine Italian cuisine, **Amelia's Restaurant** (352-373-1919; ameliasgainesville.com), 235 S Main Street #107, entices you off the street with the aromas of fresh sauces bubbling in the kitchen, ready to become part of your Penne alla Sorrentino or Capellini Puttanesca. It's Italian dining at its finest, with extensive seafood and chicken options. Top off your dinner with a gorgeous dessert like their bittersweet chocolate torte. Entrées $18–27.

For fine downtown dining, **Mark's Prime** (352-336-0077; marksprime steakhouse.com), 201 SE 2nd Avenue, offers a cut well above your typical steakhouse. Try your filet mignon crusted with Maytag Bleu Cheese, or enjoy a Surf and Turf petit filet with a butter poached lobster tail. Chef's specials may include inspired creations like sea bass with cabbage palm, caper berries, and roasted peppers, or a mocha macchiato cheesecake. Expect to drop a couple of

Benjamins on a romantic dinner for two. Monday–Saturday 5–10 PM; reservations recommended.

In his sophisticated downtown, European-style bistro, chef-owner Clif Nelson draws on more than 25 years of local experience to create provocative fusion food at **Paramount Grill** (352-378-3398; paramountgrill.com), 12 SW 1st Avenue, Gainesville. Chilled cucumber, yogurt, and almond soup du jour was artfully presented with a salad with four types of farm-fresh berries and baby asparagus over baby greens. Their menus change often; entrées may include creative gems such as spicy Thai-style prawns with Asian vegetables, linguine, fresh basil, and coriander; stir-fried curried tofu with chick peas and vegetables, cashews, biriyani rice and pappadum; and pan-roasted prime Angus fillet served over garlic mashed potatoes with shiitake mushroom sherry wine sauce. Entrées $15–39, with salads à la carte. Lunch Monday–Saturday 11 AM–2 PM, dinner daily at 5 PM; Sunday brunch 10 AM–3 PM. Reservations suggested.

BARBECUE Cheap, fast, and good: It's not supposed to be possible, but **David's Real Pit BBQ** (352-373-2002; davidsbbq .com), 5121 NW 39th Avenue, Gainesville, pulls it off. Plates of barbecued ribs, chicken, beef, turkey, and pork run $9–15, hearty sandwiches run $4–6, and you can choose your sauce from the "wall of fire." They even do omelets and pancakes for breakfast, $4–7. The surroundings are nothing fancy, but the food is sublime.

On the outside, it looks like your basic convenience store. But step inside **Pearl Country Store** (352-466-4025; pearlcountrystore.com), 106A NE US 441, Micanopy, and you'll be treated to down-home breakfast sandwiches, hotcakes, French toast, and omelets served 6–11 AM followed by a parade of barbecue ($5 and up): sandwiches, dinner platters, and barbecue-by-the-pound, as well as daily dinner specials. It's all tucked away in David and Peggy Carr's eclectic country store, where local baked goods, organic veggies, and books on natural Florida share the floor with more traditional convenience store fare. Barbecue served Monday–Thursday 11 AM–7 PM, Friday–Sunday 11 AM–8 PM.

CASUAL FARE 🦐 🍴 With nearly 30 years of pleasing their customers, **Conestogas Restaurant** (386-462-1294; conestogasrestaurant.com), 14920 Main Street, Alachua, is one of those longtime institutions everyone who's been there will go out of their way for. In this unpretentious Western-theme restaurant, you'll nibble on peanuts while waiting for one of the tender house sirloin or specialty steaks ($16–24), marinated in the family's secret marinade recipe. Burgers are their other big thing—big fresh handmade burgers ($10–14) cooked the way you want them. The Main Street Monster Burger ($30) challenges *Guinness Book of World Records* appetites with 48 ounces of beef on an extremely oversize bun; free T-shirt and a slice of key lime pie if you eat it, sides and all. Open Monday–Saturday at 11 AM for lunch and dinner; daily specials.

🍴 Dominating downtown High Springs, **Great Outdoors Restaurant** (386-454-1288; greatoutdoorsdining .com), 65 N Main Street, should not be missed. An excellent place to kick back and chill out after a day of paddling, swimming, hiking, or diving, it feels like a comfortable lodge. Hang out with friends and enjoy the live music. Select a Nut n' Berry Salad for lunch or a hearty Tennessee Top Sirloin, $9–24. Dinner, $15–29, requires a more relaxed pace to savor the standout on the menu, Naked Ed's Low Country Boil, with Gulf shrimp, snow crab legs, Georgia sausage, mussels, cobbed corn, and red-skin potatoes simmered in spices and Naked Ed's Pale Ale. For those in the know, Naked Ed was once a legendary fixture along the Santa Fe River, living in the woods near Lily Spring in the altogether.

A mashup of antique shop and restaurant under the shade of giant live oaks, **Old Florida Cafe** (352-466-3663), 203 NE Cholokka Boulevard, Micanopy, provides tasty homemade soup, black beans and rice, and chili as well as a gamut of "generous sandwiches," hot Cubans and Reubens, and fabulous thick BLTs ($5 and up). Browse the shelves while waiting for your order, or stake out a place on the front porch and watch the world wander past.

At **The Swamp** (352-377-9267; swamp restaurant.com), 1642 W University Avenue, Gainesville, enjoy a great lunch in a renovated 1915 professor's home right across from campus. With ahi tuna tacos, Argentine steak salad, and gator tail on the menu, it appeals to an eclectic Florida palate. With a sports-bar atmosphere, it's a raucous place, but the meals are great; $8–16. Open 11 AM–2 PM daily.

COMFORT FOOD Open all day, **Alice's Restaurant** (386-454-1166), 215 SW Santa Fe Boulevard, High Springs, is where the locals hang out. And why not? Breakfast is simple and cheap, and the rest of the day they serve up good homestyle Southern cooking, with fried chicken a favorite and beef tips over rice a staple. Meals under $15.

ETHNIC EATS Make ours sushi at the famed **Dragonfly Sushi & Sake Company** (352-371-3359; dragonflysushi.com), 201 SE 2nd Avenue #104, Gainesville. Purple walls and velvety black and red chairs accentuate the op-art feel of sushi. Lunch and dinner entrées; sushi served à la carte and as rolls ($5–16) and platters ($23–75). Consider the delicious Mango Tango, a roll with smoked salmon, cream cheese, avocado and mango strips, topped with tempura flakes and sweet potato curls, and served with a plum and apricot sauce.

With a daily selection of Spanish tapas, Cuban and Caribbean sandwiches, and Cuban entrées in a setting with a special Spanish-Caribbean flair, **Emiliano's Cafe** (352-375-7381; emilianoscafe.com), 7 SE 1st Avenue, provides Gainesville's best choice for fine Latin cuisine. Create your own combination Latin Lunch Bowl ($8–11) or pick a favorite off the chalkboard for dinner ($14–25).

Dining with a vegetarian friend at **Liquid Ginger** (352-371-2323; theliquidginger.com), 101 SE 2nd Place #118, we had no problem finding tasty creations to please both our palates. Having arrived straight from the Harn, it was a delight to settle into this artsy space and order up tea and tastings, including edamame, garlic eggplant, and Buddha rolls. Entrées come grilled or sautéed. $9–25 for entrées, or make a meal of the many tastings for a spin through Asia.

HIP BISTRO-STYLE **Bistro 1245** (352-376-0000; leonardosgainesville.com), 1245 W University Avenue, a tiny speck of a café near the busiest corner in Gainesville serves fabulous lunches in a classy atmosphere. Think grilled eggplant, fresh mozzarella and spinach, marinara and pesto on a baguette. Sandwiches run $9–14, dinner $12–18.

For flatbread and antipasto, it's worth the drive to **Blue Highway** (352-466-0062; bluehighwaypizza.com), 204 NE US 441, Micanopy, a bistro evoking a French country kitchen with its bold colors and bright local artwork. Their handcrafted pizzas come with creative but sensible combination toppings like Rustica, Greek, and BBQ Chicken; our fave is their Blue Highway Salad, crunchy with toasted pecans and feta, the best. Open Tuesday–Sunday for lunch and dinner; $5–20.

Winner of numerous awards, **Mildred's Big City Food** (352-371-1711; mildredsbigcityfood.com), 3445 W University Avenue, is a hot spot for those who enjoy good food beyond café fare. Sandwiches at lunchtime include grilled pimento cheese with bacon and tomato, lamb sliders with tzatziki sauce, and a shrimp roll; plus creative salads topped with chicken, tempeh, or seared tuna. Dinner starts at 5 PM, with three perfect courses to select from: perhaps escargot "Rockefeller," followed by a mushroom bisque, and a dry-aged New York Strip, paired with the perfect wine. $8–38.

Setting a mood with gleaming chrome, dark wood, and snappy 1940s jazz, **New Deal Cafe** (352-371-4418; thenewdealcafegainesville.com), 3443 W University Avenue, Gainesville, provides quick-stop diners with delicious organic food, including a seasonal hummus platter, beet and goat cheese salad, and Chef Bert's Veggie Burger (lunch $7–15). Monday–Thursday 11 AM–9 PM, Friday–Saturday 11 AM–10 PM.

ORGANIC AND VEGETARIAN **Harvest Thyme Cafe** (352-384-9497; harvestthyme cafe.com/), 2 W University Avenue, Gainesville, is somewhere to kick back and read the morning paper while sipping coffee, tea, or chai. Enjoy shakes and smoothies, fresh fruit, sandwiches, soups, salads, and wraps, $5–9. The menu is posted on a colorful chalkboard over the kitchen.

Mosswood Farm Store & Bakehouse (352-466-5002; mosswoodfarmstore .com), 703 NE Cholokka Boulevard, Micanopy, is a must-stop for guilt-free gluten-free baked goods. Besides the bakery, this is a sweet little coffeeshop, with a side room of simple living products and books to inspire you.

Think pop art and paint-by-number: **The Top** (352-337-1188), 40 N Main Street, Gainesville, is a step back into the 1970s, with chairs like our 1975 high school cafeterias. But it's a hip young crowd that hangs here, with food to match, including vegetarian and vegan choices. Think spinach salad with scallops, roasted peppers, onions, pecans, goat cheese, and a mango vinaigrette, or crispy tofu triangles with peanut sauce. Lunch $7–12; dinner entrées like pecan-crusted tofu and ginger chimichurri grill with tempeh show off the chef's creativity, $11–25.

QUICK BITE ✍ Aunt Sherry's chicken salad is the must-have at **Coffee n' Cream** (352-466-1101; micanopycoffeeshop .com), 201 Cholokka Boulevard, Micanopy, where you can sit out on the shaded porch and enjoy the sunshine. Other favorites from the chalkboard menu include the Frito Pie and Kelly's Chicken & Dumplings (Thursdays only). It's not just a café, but also a busy ice cream parlor—a good selection of ice cream and fresh lemonade guarantees return customers. Grab breakfast, lunch, or a coffee, $3–10.

✍ **The Station Bakery & Cafe** (386-454-4943, stationbakery.com), 19327 NW US 441, High Springs, offers great sandwiches on freshly baked bread ($6), including a fabulous Roast Beef & Horseradish Cheddar Melt, as well as salads, ice cream, and baked goods.

✳ Selective Shopping

ANTIQUES High Springs, Micanopy, and Waldo have attracted antique shoppers for decades. Micanopy is considered one of the top antiquing destinations in Florida, with enough shops crowding Cholokka Boulevard (Micanopy's "Main Street") to allow you to spend the entire day looking for that perfect find.

At **Decades on Main** (386-454-8525), 15 Main Street, High Springs, a search through their wall of old Florida books was rewarded with several new-to-us classic titles at affordable prices. Vintage furnishings are shown off in a series of open rooms in the back of the store.

It's not just about the cameos, although **Delectable Collectibles** (352-466-3327), 112 NE Cholokka Boulevard, Micanopy, has one of the largest displays of these vintage pieces of art that we've ever seen. From Arts and Crafts-period pottery to Magellan dinner plates, the collectibles here are of the highest quality.

In **The Garage** (352-288-8485), 212 Cholokka Boulevard, Micanopy, fun ephemera fills the booths, from figurines and postcards to toys and glassware at reasonable prices.

Main Street Antique Mall (386-454-2700), 10 S Main Street, High Springs, is a maze of dealer booths that runs along the railroad tracks. Some are chock-full of small items like saltcellars, antique glassware, and kitchen items; others have furniture, books, record albums, and more. Although it doesn't say so on the door, be sure to bring cash for transactions here.

Seeking that '60s look for your retro loft? Or an original Star Wars figurine? Try **Micanopy Modern** (305-321-1098), 118 NE Cholokka Boulevard, for the sleek and funky lines of our childhoods.

Among the many fine pieces of antique furniture at **Micanopy Outpost** (352-466-0010), 205 NE Cholokka Boulevard, was a mahogany Duncan Phyfe table and chair set. Had we not just purchased a dining room set, it would have followed us home. Stop in here for some amazing furniture finds.

At Thornebrook Village, **The Painted Table** (352-371-1555), 2441 NW 43rd Street# 5A, Gainesville, is full of delightful vintage collectibles, pottery, furnishings, and books.

Micanopy's oldest antiques store is still full of fun finds, especially Floridiana. At **Stagecoach Stop** (352-466-3456), 110 NE Cholokka Boulevard, classy glass is on the shelves too: carnival glass, Vaseline glass glowing under blacklights, and a wall of old-time Coca Cola bottles with their city of origin stamped on the bottom.

An old-fashioned flea market started in 1975 and the main reason to stop in Waldo, the **Waldo Farmers' and Flea Market** (352-468-2255; waldofleamarket .com), 17805 US 301, is a successful, sprawling complex of more than 800 vendors across 50 acres on both sides of the highway. Not only does it showcase the best produce that North Florida has to offer, but you can find livestock and old farm tools as well. The flea market is open on the west side of US 301 on Saturday and Sunday 7 AM–4 PM, varying by vendor. On the east side of the highway, there are daily vendors, as well as the massive **Waldo Antique Village** (352-468-3111; waldofleamarket.com/antique-village). The large farm implements outside are just a sample of the primitives and country items you'll find here. Bargain hunters can browse for hours through nearly 80 dealer booths with everything from classic rock albums to Vaseline glass glowing under fluorescent lamps. With multiple staircases running up and down the two floors inside the 24,000-square-foot building, it's a destination. Open daily 9 AM–6 PM.

ARTS AND CRAFTS Art glass aficionados and stained glass artists will want to stop at **McIntyre Stained Glass Studio & Art Gallery** (352-372-2752; mcintyrestudio.com), 2441 NW 43rd Street, Gainesville, a working studio since 1976. You'll find creative stained glass art, pottery, watercolors, and more by a variety of local artists.

"Art for Life" is the theme of **Paddiwhack** (352-336-3175; paddiwhack.com), 1510 NW 13th Street, Gainesville, the most eclectic of art shops, where creativity molds colorful, playful, functional pieces ranging from mirrors and wall hangings to large pieces of furniture, each signed by one of the many artists represented.

For fabulous Tiffany-style lamps, visit **Shady Oak Gallery & Stained Glass Studio** (352-466-3476; shadyoak.com), 201 Cholokka Boulevard, Micanopy. In addition to selling both serious and whimsical creations from local artists, they teach hands-on art glass courses at very reasonable prices.

Sweetwater Picture Framing (352-373-5745; sweetwaterpictureframing.com), 101 SE 2nd Place, showcases stunning images of natural Florida by local photographers, including some of our favorites by nature photographer John Moran; his work is interspersed throughout **Sun**

Plaza, a dining and shopping complex that surrounds the Hippodrome.

A commercial gallery with an outstanding collection of Florida artists, **Thornebrook Gallery** (352 378-4947; thornebrookgallery.com), 2441 NW 43rd Street, Gainesville, founded in 1981, is one of the cornerstones of Thornebrook Village. Fine art glass, artisan jewelry, and sculptures are displayed as well as original and limited-edition oils, acrylics, and photography. Closed Sunday.

BOOKS AND GIFTS Delightful aromas fill **Buffalo Girl Soaps** (541-314-3603; buffalogirlsoaps.com), 23641 W US 27, High Springs, a cute shop with lotions and potions, goat's milk artisanal soaps, and essential oils.

High Springs Emporium (386-454-8657; highspringsemporium.net), 19765 NW US 441, is the region's only rock and mineral shop, offering everything from New Age quartz points to assemblages of crystals that would impress the most serious mineral collector—as would Sharon Britton, the owner, who knows her stuff about geology.

It's loud, it's proud, and it's Florida's only feminist bookstore. The merchandise at **Wild Iris Books** (352-375-7477; wildirisbooks.com), 22 SE 5th Avenue Suite D, Gainesville, runs the gamut from hand-beaded jewelery and artisanal soaps to tomes on Zen Buddhism, Wicca, and artistic inspiration. Their inventory of books contains a special emphasis on strong female and queer voices in fiction and nonfiction. Open Friday 1–5 PM, Saturday 12–5 PM.

A true period piece, **Wisteria Cottage** (386-454-8447), 225 N Main Street, High Springs, a tin-roofed Cracker home with bead-board walls and ceilings, has numerous spacious rooms filled with country crafts and collectibles, a kitchen filled with gourmet foods, and an Americana room.

BOUTIQUE The warble of finches—live, in a massive bird cage—and the air of

SUN PLAZA, GAINESVILLE

stepping into a Paris boutique belies the name on the shop. At **Dakota Mercantile** (352-466-5005; dakotamercantile.com), 114 NE Cholokka Boulevard, Micanopy, all is swaddled in white. A hint of fragrance rises from fine soaps and lotions; here you'll find clothing for the children, tiaras for that young princess, and charms for her bracelet. A secret garden lies beyond the back doors.

DECOR AND MORE Soft and feminine, **Bird Nest Vintage Market** (386-454-2200), 18 Main Street, High Springs, has blueware displayed atop elegant antique dressers and inspiring home decor items to match, including cute curio cabinets and cedar chests.

Losing yourself in a rambling collecting of rooms is the norm on a visit to **The Shop** (352-466-4031; theshopinmicanopy .com), 210 NE Cholokka Boulevard, Micanopy, where both bright baubles

and delicate fairy lights soften and illuminate the corners of every little nook. This surprisingly large shop is tastefully filled with both antique and new home and garden decor, with everything from gnome homes to vintage tables for your interior design.

FARMERS' MARKETS Residents line up every Saturday morning before 8:30 AM, waiting for the bell at the **Alachua County Farmers' Market** (352-371-8236; 441market.com), 5920 NW 13th Street, corner of US 441 and FL 121, Gainesville. Buy fresh produce straight from local growers—only farmers who grow their own crops are permitted to sell here. Held every Saturday until 1 PM or until everything is sold.

Make a stop at **Brown's Farm** (352-475-2015), FL 26 just east of US 301, Orange Heights, a permanent roadside stand, to buy straight from the farm;

look for fresh honey, veggies, and fruits, including strawberries, peaches, and onions in-season.

The weekly **High Springs Farmers' Market** (386-454-1416; farmersmarket.highsprings.com), 115 NE Railroad Avenue, goes on along the railroad tracks downtown by the Chamber of Commerce. Local farmers with seasonal fresh veggies offer their bounty, making this a prime place for produce. Thursday 12–4 PM, first Saturday 10 AM–2 PM.

Kings Kountry Produce (904-964-2552), 18079 US 301 N, Starke, offers up the bounty of Bradford County at a permanent roadside stand. Since this is a major strawberry growing region, be sure to show up in March for the bounty of their crop. Jellies, jams, salsa, and pickles are available year-round.

Founded in 1996, the **Union Street Farmers' Market** (352-462-3192; unionstreetfarmersmkt.com), is a downtown Gainesville tradition, now in a new location at Bo Diddley Community Plaza along University Avenue. As a producer's market, the only foodsellers are those who grow or make their own, from fruits and vegetables to dairy, honey, baked goods, and ice cream; they're joined by artists in this lively venue, often accompanied by live acoustic music. Wednesday 4–7:30 PM.

SPECIALTY FOODS One of the last "orange shops" that once dotted Florida's highways, **Cross Creek Groves** (352-481-2000; crosscreekgroves.com), 6609 SE US 301, has grove-fresh oranges and grapefruit in season—which they'll ship anywhere for you—and tropical fruits and wines year-round. Buy them roadside at one of the northernmost places in Florida where you can grab a big bag of fresh citrus.

More than 4,000 types of wine line the floor-to-ceiling shelves at **Downtown Wine & Cheese** (352-222-1348; dwacgainesvilleshop.com), 133 N Main Street, a fixture in downtown Gainesville and a necessary stop for the discriminating gourmand. In addition to the perfect wine, you'll find imported chocolates, microbrew beers, and a wide array of gourmet food items. Under new ownership and an updated name after a 42-year run, it features a wine bar and wine school as well.

It's hard to walk out of the heavenly scented **Thornebrook Chocolates** (352-371-0800; thornebrookchocolates.com), 2441 NW 43rd Street #21, Gainesville, without a bagful of fresh truffles or other melt-in-your-mouth treats.

✳ Special Events

FALL/WINTER Drift into ᪣ **Butterflyfest** (floridamuseum.ufl.edu/event/butterflyfest), Florida Museum of Natural History (see *Museums and Historic Sites*), the first Sunday of September, for live native butterfly exhibits, a photography contest, lectures, field trips, and on-site vendors.

Sweep in the Halloween season with the ᪣ **Florida Bat Festival** (lubee.org/event/florida-bat-festival), held in late October at the Lubee Bat Conservancy (see *Ecotours*).

᪣ The **Alachua County Fair** (352-354-3708; alachuacountyfair.com), the first week of November, at the fairgrounds on NE 39th Avenue, Gainesville, is a traditional county fair attracting farmers from around the region, showing off their cattle, chickens, vegetables, and more in friendly competition. Top country music acts and exhibitions from vendors; fee.

Micanopy Fall Harvest Festival (352-466-7026; micanopyfallfestival.org), Micanopy. Since 1973, this end-of-November celebration brings together artisans, craftspeople, and musicians with more than 200 display booths throughout town.

The largest and longest-running Renaissance faire in Florida, the **Hoggtown Medieval Faire** (352-393-8536; hoggetownefaire.com), at the Alachua County Fairgrounds, on 39th Avenue,

Gainesville, kicked off in 1985 and spans two weekends each February. What makes it fun is that more than a third of the people on-site are dressed in medieval costumes and in character; the fair has themed carnival games, manually powered amusement sides, and plenty of artisans.

SPRING/SUMMER The **Spring Garden Festival**, held each March at Kanapaha Botanical Gardens (see *Gardens*), is a weekend's worth of gardening tips, landscaping tricks, and environmental awareness set in the beauty of the region's largest garden, bringing together more than 175 exhibitors.

🖌 The **Farm and Forest Festival**, Morningside Nature Center (see *Farms*), features cane grinding, a cane boil, and other pioneer crafts; displays of antique fire engines; and hands-on activities for the kids. End of April.

Swarming the Northeast Gainesville Historic District with more than 100,000 artists and art aficionados at the beginning of April, the **Santa Fe College**

Spring Arts Festival (sfcollege.edu/spring-arts/index) is one of the largest and oldest events of its kind in the region, launched in 1969. Musicians join in for the weekend at a variety of stages, and artists come from around the country to be a part of this April event.

May is harvest time in North Florida! Spit seeds at a slice of Americana during the 🖌 **Newberry Watermelon Festival** (newberrywatermelonfestival.com), the third Saturday, or commemorate a noble vegetable at the 🖌 **Windsor Zucchini Festival** (afn.org/~windsor/page2.html), the second weekend. These are two of the longest-running farm festivals in Florida.

Yulee Railroad Days Celebration (sites.google.com/site/archerhistorical society/yulee-day), Archer, the second Saturday of June. Celebrating the birthday of David Levy Yulee, Florida's first US senator and founder of the Florida Railroad, the town that was his home hosts exhibits, crafts, and vendors at the historic railroad depot.

ST. JOHNS RIVER

Clay and Putnam Counties
Green Cove Springs, Palatka, and Orange Park

Designated an American Heritage River, the St. Johns River is a compelling destination for those who like a slower pace. In this two-county region, it's the central feature among more than 70 square miles of rivers and lakes south of Jacksonville and east of Gainesville. These are the lands that botanist William Bartram roamed before the American Revolution, documenting encounters with indigenous peoples while collecting interesting plants to take to his patron. Where the Timucua once built villages on the riverbanks, anglers now slip past cypress-lined shores, looking for quiet coves to spend the morning. Where plantation owners carved out their empires on land grants from the King of Spain, farms (and later, subdivisions) sprouted. Where steamboats once chugged upriver, guiding Florida's earliest tourists to Silver Springs and Sanford, Spanish moss sways from the branches of ancient oaks. Things are pretty quiet on this part of the St. Johns, mostly rural or residential, depending on where you go.

With its county seat of **Palatka**, Putnam County spans both sides of the river and encompasses the northernmost part of the Ocala National Forest. Clay County hugs the western shore of the river just south of Jacksonville. Its northernmost cities, **Orange Park** and **Middleburg**, have the Jacksonville metro lapping at their shores. North of **Doctors Lake**, Orange Park was plotted in 1877 by developers from Boston as a planned community atop a former Civil War–era plantation. An 1816 Spanish land grant surrounding a bubbling spring along the shores of the St. Johns River became White Sulfur Springs, and then the more-marketable **Green Cove Springs** in 1866; it's the county seat of Clay County. Established in 1823, Hibernia eventually became **Fleming Island**.

The communities of the region have long and storied histories, from Palatka's role in the Civil War to J.C. Penney's dream of a Florida retirement village—**Penney Farms**— for his employees, from the original Kingsley Plantation at the headwaters of **Black Creek**, to the first Girl Scout camp in Florida, **Camp Chowenwaw**, established in 1932 near the mouth of Black Creek. **Melrose** was established along Bellamy Road—Florida's first significant cross-peninsula road—in 1887, and you won't find a better place to study early Florida architecture. There are nearly 80 buildings in Melrose on the National Register of Historic Places. Originally called Brooklyn before it was renamed by a promoter from Pittsburgh, **Keystone Heights** shows off the natural side of Florida at **Mike Roess Gold Head Branch State Park**, built by the Civilian Conservation Corps as one of Florida's first state parks.

History buffs will appreciate the broad spectrum of museums in the region, including military and aerospace displays found nowhere else in Florida. Nature lovers have massive wild spaces to immerse themselves in, trails to wander, waterways to paddle, and treehouses in which to camp. A quiet getaway is what you'll find when exploring this region.

GUIDANCE **Clay County Tourism** (claycountygov.com/departments/tourism) can help you with your travel planning for Orange Park, Fleming Island, Green Cove

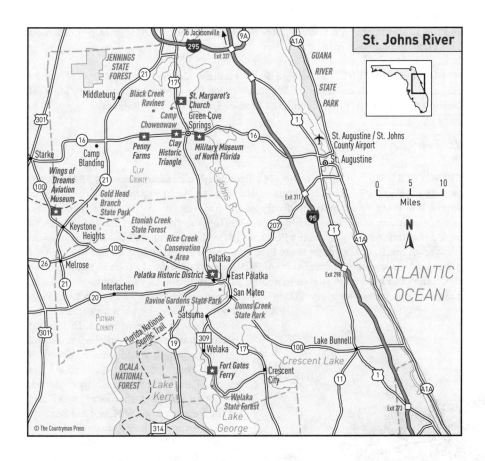

Springs, Keystone Heights, and Middleburg. In Palatka stop by the **Putnam County Chamber of Commerce** (386-328-1503; putnamcountychamber.com), 1100 Reid Street, Palatka 32178.

GETTING THERE *By air:* **Jacksonville International Airport** (see the *Jacksonville* chapter) or **Gainesville Regional Airport** (see the *Gainesville & Vicinity* chapter) are the nearest major airports.

By bus: **Greyhound** (800-231-2222; greyhound.com).

By car: From Jacksonville, take **US 17** south of I-295. From the St. Augustine area, take **FL 16** from I-95 to Green Cove Springs. **FL 207** connects St. Augustine and Palatka.

By train: The **Amtrak** station in Palatka (800-872-7245; amtrak.com), 220 N 11th Street, is one of the few remaining active passenger train stations in North Florida. It's served by the Silver Service/Palmetto, which runs from New York City and Washington DC, to Jacksonville, Orlando, Tampa, and Miami.

GETTING AROUND **US 17** runs from Orange Park south along the St. Johns River past Green Cove Springs into Palatka, where it crosses to the east side of the river and continues south through Crescent City, passing Welaka. **FL 19** heads south from Palatka along the west side of the St. Johns River to reach the Ocala National Forest. **FL 16** runs east–west from Green Cove Springs past Penney Farms and Camp Blanding to Starke in Bradford County. Take **FL 21** from Orange Park south to reach Middleburg and Keystone Heights. **FL 100** connects Palatka with Keystone Heights, or branch off onto **FL 26** to reach Melrose.

MEDICAL EMERGENCIES **Orange Park Medical Center** (904-639-8500; orange parkmedical.com), 2001 Kingsley Avenue, Orange Park. **Putnam Community Medical Center** (386-328-5711; pcmcfl.com), 611 Zeagler Drive off FL 20, Palatka.

✱ To See

ARCHITECTURE ♿ ♂ Inside the 1854 **Bronson-Mulholland House** (386-326-2704; palatka-fl.gov/239/Bronson-Mulholland-House), 100 Madison Street, Palatka, a grand antebellum plantation home, the finery of the past—including exquisite furnishings and art—is full of tales, as is your docent. The Greek revival mansion sat on what was once a plantation known as Sunny Point, which in turn was carved out of a prior Spanish land grant. Built for Judge Isaac Bronson, one of Florida's first circuit judges, this grand home is where the modern city of Palatka was born, thanks to Bronson's sterling reputation and business acumen in selling property in the city he had been given as compensation for his services. While the home was abandoned during the Civil War, it was occupied by both sides as a command post at different times. In 1866, it became a school for freed slave children, and during both world wars it served as a Red Cross center. Now owned by the city of Palatka and beautifully restored, it is open for tours, thanks to the efforts of the Putnam County Historical Society, who ensured the home was saved. Their museum (see *Museums and Historic Sites*) sits next door. Open Saturday 10–4, first Sunday 1–4, or by appointment.

BIKING THE PALATKA-LAKE BUTLER STATE TRAIL AT CARRAWAY

The grounds of **Club Continental** (see *Lodging*) in Orange Park evoke an era when travel to Florida meant settling in for the season. Built in 1923 as Mira Rio, a grand estate for the heir of the Palmolive Soap Company, it morphed into classy accommodations a generation later. Next door, their wedding venue, **Winterbourne**, is one of the oldest remaining homes in the area, built in 1870.

The Gilded Age is beautifully represented in **Crescent City** (crescentcity-fl .com), whose streets are lined with nearly two dozen ornately decorated Victorian homes under a canopy of ancient live oaks. Among them are the **Charles & Emily Cheatham House**, 102 Main St. Emphasizing horizontal planes and wide eaves, this 1911 Prairie-style house plays homage to the horizontal lines that Frank

Lloyd Wright first popularized. Horticulturalist Henry G. Hubbard built the **Hubbard House**, 600 N Park St. The circa-1879 dwelling was once surrounded by botanical gardens, where he grew plants he had collected abroad; today, you can see a line of well-established camphor trees that got their start here. Also a noted entomologist, Hubbard studied insects attacking cotton and orange crops and later worked for the USDA.

One of Florida's first state parks, **Gold Head Branch** (see *Parks, Preserves, and Camping*), showcases the work of the Civilian Conservation Corps. Established in June 1935, CCC Company 2444 completed their work at the park in May 1941. They built the park from the ground up, constructing everything from the ranger station, equipment sheds, and picnic areas to roads and fire lanes, natural trails—including the steps down into the steep ravine—and a cluster of cabins along Little Lake Johnson, in which you can still stay.

After the Civil War interrupted the 1854 attempt to make **Green Cove Springs** (see *Springs*) a tourist destination, promotion of the medicinal qualities of this sulfurous spring drew droves of northern visitors by steamboat in the 1880s. They were met at the long dock by a trolley car, which took them to their chosen hotel for the winter—perhaps The Morganza, or The Cherokee, or the Magnolia Springs Hotel. Nearly a dozen hotels and boarding homes catered to visitors, who often bathed daily in the pool for their health. You'll find 85 structures in the **Green Cove Springs Historic District**, mostly around Walnut Street and bounded by Bay Street, the CSX railroad tracks, Center Street, Orange Avenue, St. Elcom Street, and the St. Johns River.

Boasting one of the highest concentrations of historic architecture in Florida, with 79 vintage homes and businesses, **Melrose** is a town where history is part of everyday life. Many buildings are more than a century old but remain well kept and occupied as residences. One of the more unique ones is the **Sexton House**, a vacation home built in 1893 for Capt. Dowling Sexton; the top story looks like the bridge of a ship. To help

CABIN CONSTRUCTED BY THE CCC AT MIKE ROESS GOLD HEAD BRANCH STATE PARK

you explore the town, Alachua County provides a map and a little history of most of the historic sites on their website (growth-management.alachuacounty.us).

Palatka rapidly grew after the Civil War when it became a major transportation and freight distribution center, thanks to steamboats plying the St. Johns River. Both the commercial downtown and upscale residental neighborhoods blossomed. Reid's Garden, now called the **North Historic District**, developed in the beautifully cano-pied woodlands that were once part of Sunny Point, boasting the larger and finer homes. The more pragmatic **South Historic District** grew along the waterfront upriver from the city center, sprouting more tightly packed Victorian homes. Both districts are on the National Register of Historic Places and well worth a drive through them to enjoy the architecture; signs along US 17 direct you to each one, just before you reach the Palatka Memorial Bridge. Built by the Atlantic Coast Line in 1908, the **Historic Union Station** (see *Railroadiana*) in Palatka showcases the architectural style of H. H. Richardson with its random window openings and hexagonal dormered bays. The Georgian-style **Tilghman House** (386-325-8750), 324 River Street, Palatka, built around 1887, now operates as the home of the Palatka Art League. Note the half-gabled veranda supported by Greek Doric columns and the Palladian window in the gable dormer. Open Monday–Friday 9 AM–5 PM.

One of the oldest operating wooden churches in America closed its doors in 2012. **St. Margaret's Episcopal Church**, 6874 Old Church Road, Fleming Island, is a tes-tament to its storied past. George Fleming emigrated from Ireland and established Hibernia (Latin for "Ireland") Plantation on the 1,000 acres now known as Fleming Island. The church, a gift for his wife, Margaret Seton Fleming, was completed in 1878. The Carpenter Gothic-style sanctuary has only 50 seats and is adjoined by a cemetery; it is on the National Register of Historic Places.

The 1847 **Middleburg United Methodist Church** and its cemetery adjoin the Mid-dleburg Historical Museum (see *Museums and Historic Sites*). There are a dozen build-ings in the **Middleburg Historical District** along Main and Wharf streets.

ART GALLERIES **Bellamy Road** (352-283-9700; facebook.com/bellamydtw), 309 SR 26, Melrose, is a nonprofit that focuses on the region's artists, who capture the soul of Florida in music, paintings, and other media, by providing space for artists' studios and the occasional film screening.

Embracing both performing and visual arts, **Florida School of the Arts** (386-328-1571; floarts.org), 5001 St. Johns Avenue, Palatka, has gallery space showcasing stu-dents and local artists in its downtown location.

Serving as a public library until the 1980s, the **Larimer Arts Center** (386-328-8998; artsinputnam.org/gallery.html), 216 Reid Street, Palatka, is the home of the Arts Coun-cil of Greater Palatka and their monthly exhibits.

Melrose Bay Gallery (352-475-3866; melrosebayartgallery.com), 103 FL 26, Mel-rose, represents fine regional artists in a variety of media.

At **Mossman Hall** (352-475-2924), 301 FL 26, Melrose, stop in to see works by local artists and cultural events inside a restored 1920s missonary church along the edge of Melrose Heritage Park.

FOLKLORE While driving through the small community of Bardin off FL 100, peer into the piney woods; you might just catch a glimpse of the **Bardin Booger**. Local leg-end has it that a giant, shaggy-haired creature, much like the elusive Sasquatch, was first sighted here in the 1940s. Said to smell much like rotting cabbage and stand 10 feet tall, the ape-like creature has been touted as Northeast Florida's Bigfoot, drawn to Etonia Creek. The curious and the disbelievers can view a scrapbook filled with news clippings and illustrations at **Bud's Store** (386-328-4257), 341 Bardin Road, the Bardin community gathering spot.

GARDEN Home of the Florida Azalea Festival, **Ravine Gardens State Park** (386-329-3721; floridastateparks.org/park/Ravine-Gardens), 1600 Twigg Street, Palatka, is one of Florida's finest places to see spring put on a show. Constructed in and around a steephead ravine by the Civilian Conservation Corps in 1933 with 250,000 ornamental plants and 95,000 azaleas, it was Palatka's first and foremost tourist attraction. Drive 1.8 miles around the rim of the ravines through canopies of live oaks surrounded by thick blankets of tropical and subtropical flora, or stroll the walkways through the 182-acre park, where the kids will love bouncing across the swaying pedestrian suspension bridges. A rose garden and a collection of unusual plants, including endemic East Palatka holly and a double-trunk cabbage palm, are at the top, next to the visitors center and parking areas. Open daily 8 AM–sunset; fee.

MEMORIALS Dedicated in 1927 at the ends of the original bridge over the St. Johns in Palatka, four **E.M. Viquesney "doughboy" statues**—depicting a sailor, a soldier on parade, a soldier with dynamite, and another at arms—memorialized World War I veterans.

MURALS Pick up a map at the Putnam County Chamber of Commerce (see *Guidance*) and stroll through the "Mural City of Northeast Florida" seeking out the murals scattered throughout the downtown historic district. These building-size, breathtaking murals beautifully depict the history, landscape, and culture of **Palatka**. Among them, you'll find a cattle drive, a St. Johns River steamboat, sailboats from the annual Mug Race, and a collection of identified wildflowers. Look for the tiny gray church mouse in the Billy Graham mural (it's on the church porch).

MUSEUMS AND HISTORIC SITES Fans of Lynyrd Skynyrd will want to find **Brickyard Road** in Green Cove Springs, where Ronnie Van Zant lived before his untimely death. Unfortunately, other fans kept stealing the sign, so the county erected a concrete pillar with the street name painted on it.

On 170,000 acres of sand pine and scrub oak in the heart of the Florida wilderness, Camp Blanding was home to 800,000 World War II soldiers from 1940 to 1945. Nine infantry divisions prepared for conflict in ankle-deep sand on arguably one of the toughest training grounds anywhere. **Camp Blanding Museum and Memorial Park** (904-682-3196; campblanding-museum.org), 5629 FL 16 W, Keystone Heights, is dedicated to these soldiers, but it also honors all who have served since. Life at Camp Blanding during the 1940s is depicted in the museum through colorful displays of weaponry, photos, memorabilia, and even a life-size bunkhouse. In Memorial Park, monuments honor the original nine army infantry divisions and the 508th Parachute Infantry Regiment; several World War II aircraft and vehicles are on display. Open noon–4 daily except holidays. Free; donations accepted.

At the **Clay County Historic Triangle**, three significant buildings from local history now serve as repositories of regional history. First raised in 1874, soon after the city became the county seat, and rebuilt in brick in 1889, the **old Clay County Courthouse** houses the **Clay County Historical Museum** (904-219-5196), 915 Walnut St. Built in 1894, the imposing two-story brick old county jail now serves as the county's archives and historical resource center. Between them sits a relic of the busy railroad era, the **Atlantic Coast Line station** for Green Cove Springs. With the addition of the former passenger depot, artifacts now include fine china and silverware, step boxes,

CLAY HISTORIC TRIANGLE

and baggage tags from the railroad. Open the first and third Sundays of each month from 2–5 PM or by appointment. Free, donations appreciated.

The **Hilltop Black Heritage Education Center** (904-282-4168), Longmire Road at Hunter-Douglas Park, Middleburg, is a sensitive and thought-provoking view of African American culture during the late 1800s, displayed in a one-room schoolhouse. Call with two days' notice to arrange a tour with a docent knowledgable in local history.

Built in 1892, **Interlachen Town Hall,** on the National Register of Historic Places, was the city's social center in the early 1900s, holding town hall activities such as dances, ladies' society meetings, and voting. It hosts the **Interlachen Museum** (inter lachen-fl.gov), 201 Commonwealth Avenue, which provides a picture of this once-bustling winter resort, a major destination in the 1890s, with three hotels on its lakes. Run by the Historical Society of Interlachen, the museum is open every Saturday 10 AM–2 PM. Free, donations appreciated.

The Crescent City Women's Club takes on a labor of love, filling the **Little Blue House Heritage Museum and Art Center** (386-698-4711), 602 N Summit Street, Crescent City, with pieces of the past. The former home, dating back to 1871, showcases the history and art of South Putnam. Open Tuesday–Saturday 2:30–5 PM.

Developed as a winter resort and residential community in the 1920s, **Keystone Heights** had its own hotel, The Keystone Inn, up through the 1950s. It sat on the hill above Keystone Beach (see *Swimming*), where the historic **bathhouse and dance hall,** built in 1928, still perches over the ever-shrinking waters of Lake Geneva.

Photographs and displays of the early turpentine, timber, and phosphate industries depict one of the oldest continuous communities in Florida at the **Middleburg Historic Museum** (904-282-5357), 3912 Section St. Open Sunday 2–4 PM. Donations appreciated.

&. ♫ As you're driving FL 16 east toward the St. Johns River, a massive troop carrier draws your attention to the **Military Museum of North Florida** (904-718-5571), 1

Bunker Avenue at Reynolds Park, on the site of Benjamin Lee Field, a Naval air station during World War II. The base was where pilots for the F6F Helicat trained and also where the 600-ship Atlantic fleet was "mothballed" after the war. Support vehicles, uniforms, weapons, and artifacts date from World War II to the modern day. Open 10 AM–3 PM Tuesday–Friday. Fee.

Established in 1921 as a retirement village along the St. Johns River, **Moosehaven** (moosehaven.org), 1701 Park Avenue, covers 63 acres. The Loyal Order of Moose bettered the community of Orange Park at the same time by donating buildings that became the town hall, fire station, and library.

Founded as a retirement community "for Christian people whose lives had been devoted to Christian service" by department store founder J. C. Penney, **Penney Farms** (penneyretirementcommunity.org) dates back to 1927. It is centered on the **J. C. Penney Memorial Church** (904-529-9078), which at the time was surrounded by 98 cottage apartments. Hundreds of Southern magnolias were planted when the community was founded. They now form a spectacular canopy, helping earn that portion of FL 16 designation as **J.C. Penney Memorial Scenic Highway** (see *Scenic Drives*).

Originally part of Fort Shannon during the Seminole Indian Wars (1832–1845), the **Putnam Historic Museum** (386-325-9825), 100 Madison Street, Palatka, is the oldest dwelling in the area. Open Tuesday, Thursday, and Sunday 2–5 PM.

In addition to preserving the rich history of Keystone Army Airfield, where fighter squadrons prepared for the Normandy invasion, the **Wings of Dreams Aviation Museum** (352-256-8037; wingsofdreams.org), 7100 Airport Road, Keystone Heights, also boasts quite a collection of aerospace artifacts, thanks to Executive Director and Co-founder Bob Oehl. His father, Don, was on the team that helped guide Apollo 13 home safely. Saving space history from salvage, Bob has picked up a 75,000-pound space shuttle guidance and navigation simulator and a full-scale model of the shuttle's external fuel tank, as well as many smaller artifacts. The hangars also house a collection of vintage aircraft, from a Douglas C-47 Skytrain that was in Europe on D-Day to a Lockheed T-33 Shooting Star. Watch their website for open house events, and call ahead to arrange a tour or to visit their library. Free; donations accepted.

PERFORMING ARTS **Thrasher Horne Center for Performing Arts** (904-276-6815; thcenter.org), 283 College Drive, Orange Park. This state-of-the-art 84,666-square-foot theater is fully equipped with a multi-use theater and two art galleries. Performances include professional theater, dance, and music, along with visual art exhibits.

RAILROADIANA ✒ ♿ All aboard at the **Historic Union Station** and **David Browning Railroad Museum** (386-328-15395; railsofpalatka.org), 222 N 11th Street, Palatka, managed by the Palatka Railroad Preservation Society, at the corner of 11th and Reid. The Union Depot is open daily with railroad memorabilia, historical documents, and photographs of the Palatka area; it's also a working Amtrak station. But you'll want to plan your visit when all the members run their trains at the Browning Museum—on the first Sunday and third Saturday of the month. Look for the 31-foot HO-scale model train, one of the longest in the world, chugging along the tracks for the enjoyment of young and old. Open the first and third Saturday of each month, 1–4 PM, or call to schedule a personal tour.

Both the **Atlantic Coast Line big red caboose** and the **ACL Passenger Depot** are compelling reasons to stop at the Clay County Historic Triangle (see *Museums and Historic Sites*), even when they aren't open for inspections. These colorful reminders of Florida's railroad heyday make a great backdrop for photos.

✳ To Do

AGRICULTURAL TOURS Working with Jacksonville's sister city of Masan, Korea, **Jaxma Orchids** (904-284-4442; jaxma.com), 6440 US 17 S, south of FL 16, grows and distributes six different types of orchids, including *Phalaenopsis* and *Dendrobium*. Their 110,000-square-foot greenhouses are open for public viewing Monday–Friday 8 AM–close; free.

Learn about warm-water fish production and native Florida fish conservation at **Welaka National Fish Hatchery** (386-467-2374; fws.gov/welaka), CR 309, Welaka. The facility, built in 1926, now focuses on breeding and restoration of Gulf Coast striped bass. Open daily 7 AM–4 PM; guided group tours available, or wander the facility on your own; free.

BIKING Thanks to the long-term efforts of former Putnam County resident and cycling advocate Herb Hiller, the southern part of this region has a network of mapped **road rides and paved bicycle paths** easily accessed for bicycle tourism by arriving in Palatka via Amtrak with your bike. The longest multi-use trail under development in the Southeast, the 260-mile **St. Johns River-to-Sea Loop** (sjr2c.org) comes through East Palatka and continues south through the county, with completed paved portions paralelling US 17 between Crescent City and Seville.

Stretching across the region from US 17 in Palatka to Lake Butler (see *Gainesville & Vicinity*) north of Gainesville along what was once the right of way for the Norfolk Southern, the **Palatka-Lake Butler State Trail** (floridastateparks.org/trail/Palat-ka-Lake-Butler) is a 47-mile multi-use corridor roughly paralleling SR 100 through this region. Nineteen miles of paved trail offer an easy cycling route between Carraway, Florahome, Putnam Hall, and Keystone Heights, with trailheads at Twin Lakes Park [29.4551,-81.5934] in Keystone Heights, at a public ballfield in Florahome off E Michigan Street [29.733175, -81.886347], and at a parking area at Roberts Ln along SR 100 in Carraway [29.705752, -81.780349]. The long-awaited connection between Palaka and Carraway is slated to be completed in 2018.

North of downtown Keystone Heights alongside FL 21, the **Keystone Bike Path** enables campers at Gold Head Branch State Park (see *Parks, Preserves, and Camping*) to access services in town. There is also a paved bicycle path paralleling US 17 along **Fleming Island** from Doctors Lake south about 7 miles; you can veer off onto Pine Avenue for views of the St. Johns River. Many local parks have bike paths, and the unpaved back roads and Jeep trails of the Ocala National Forest are little used and open for off-road cycling.

BIRDING Hundreds of osprey nests top the trees and beacon markers along the St. Johns River. Great blue herons and snowy egrets are a common sight along the banks, especially around the fish camps. The roadside observation tower at **Welaka National Fish Hatchery** provides excellent viewing (winter and spring) of sandhill cranes, bald eagles, and a variety of egrets and herons. **Welaka State Forest** (see *Parks, Preserves, and Camping*) is a good place to see woodpeckers, Osceola turkeys, and owls. Thousands of azaleas bloom in spring, making **Ravine Gardens State Park** (see *Gardens*) a great place to view cedar waxwings, cardinals, hummingbirds, and a variety of butterflies. View limpkins, gallinules, anhingas, and white ibises along Lake Ocklawaha at the Rodman Recreation Area off US 19 in the **Ocala National Forest**, which is also home, in its vast strands of longleaf pine between Rodman and Lake Delancy, to colonies of endangered red-cockaded woodpeckers.

SWINGING BRIDGE AT RAVINE GARDENS STATE PARK

BOATING Along the St. Johns River in Palatka, ((ᵖ)) **The Boathouse Marina** (386-328-2944; boathousemarina.com), 329 River Street, is an easy walk into downtown for eateries when you rent one of the 40 wet slips, each with its own in-slip pumpout. Nightly fee is $1/foot ($30 minimum), weekly $150 plus tax and electric. Cruisers call ((ᵖ)) **Green Cove Springs Marina** (904-284-1811; gcsmarina.com), 851 Bulkheard Road, home, as live-aboards are welcome. They offer long-term low cost drydock, so you can work on your boat or let others do so. Overnight dockage $10/night plus electric; floating dock slips $7/ft per month.

On Doctor's Lake in Fleming Island, **Whitey's Fish Camp** (see *Where to Eat*) rents 14-foot boats for fishing on the lake—$15–20 without a motor, $45–65 with one.

Welaka Charters (386-559-1957; welakacharters.com) 10 Boston Street, Welaka, focuses on boat rentals for your exploration of the St. Johns, either by pontoon or with a fishing boat. Reserve for a half or full day, $125–250.

FERRY A narrows in the St. Johns River attracted settlers to Fort Gates, a 1780 military outpost expanded during the Third Seminole War. Soldiers began being transported across in 1835. The first ferryboat operators used long poles. By 1856, a neighborhood of homes rose beneath the canopy of ancient oaks on the western shore, and crossings became more frequent. The modern-day **Fort Gates Ferry** isn't really modern at all, but it is a one-of-a-kind experience. A 1910 Sharpie sailboat pilots a 1930s barge, its brief crossing saving nearly 60 miles of driving. It can hold up to two cars side by side, and drifts softly across the cypress-lined river as ospreys wheel overhead and you slip back in time. Now that the ferry is part of Florida Black Bear Scenic Byway (see *Scenic Drives*), the road in the Ocala National Forest to Fort Gates is maintained more frequently, but it is still rough and unpaved. Ferry crossings are on demand, 7–5:30 Wednesday–Monday, $10 per car. It operates out of Fort Gates Fish Camp (see *Fish Camps*) on the eastern shore. If you arrive at Fort Gates and the ferry is on the east side

HISTORIC BARGE AND SAILBOAT THAT MAKE UP THE FORT GATES FERRY

of the river, pull up on the loading ramp and turn on your headlights. On the Welaka side of the river, the ferry operator is right at the dock.

FISHING While the **St. Johns River** is well known for its bass fishing, and **Rodman Reservoir** draws a crowd daily at the George Kirkpatrick Dam outflow, don't pass up the deep waters of **Crescent Lake**. Often neglected by anglers, this 12-mile body of water quickly drops from the 3-foot shoreline flats to depths reaching 14 feet. You may want a depth finder to locate the 12- and 13-pound bass lurking under the tea-color water, or you can catch them as they move to the shallows to feed in places such as Shell Bluff and Sling Shot Creek. Off CR 309, several marinas and fish camps (see *Fish Camps*) lead down to the St. Johns River; bait and tackle is plentiful, and you can rent boats and find local guides.

GOLF Adjoining Ravine Gardens State Park, **Palatka Golf Club** (386-329-0141; palatkagolfclub.com), 1715 Moseley Avenue, is a Donald Ross–designed gem from 1925. Tee off with a sense of history as you enjoy 9 or 18 holes on rolling terrain, $10–32.

HIKING With so many wild places throughout the region, this is an excellent area for backpackers and day hikers to roam during hiking season, October–April. The common thread through many public lands is the **Florida Trail** (see *What's Where*), as the 1,400-mile National Scenic Trail slips through forests and swamps on its way between the Ocala National Forest and the Suwannee River. Our favorite segments include hiking through a cathedral of longleaf pines between Lake Delancy West and Rodman Reservoir; hiking beneath ancient cypress along Rice Creek; the views from the bluffs above Etoniah Creek; and taking the trail across Gold Head Branch State Park. Both Rice Creek Conservation Area and Etoniah Creek State Forest offer screened camping shelters for backpackers. For day hiking, don't miss the beautiful Fern Loop at the bottom of the ravine in Gold Head Branch State Park, the stroll to Mud Spring in Welaka

State Forest, and the rugged, botanically diverse loop around Black Creek Ravines (see *Parks, Preserves, and Camping*).

NATURE CENTER ✒ The kids will enjoy hands-on activities as they learn about the St. Johns River's habitats, history, and creatures at the **St. Johns River Center** (382-328-2704; palatka-fl.gov/256/St-Johns-River-Center), 102 N First Street, Palatka, right across from the clock tower in Riverfront Park. Tuesday–Saturday 11 AM–4 PM, Sunday 1–4 PM.

OFF-ROADING With more than 125 miles of designated off-road trails looping through the northern part of the Ocala National Forest (see *Parks, Preserves, and Camping*), the **Ocala North OHV Trail System** is a major destination for ATV enthusiasts. The system is made up of the Motorcycle Loops, 14 miles for off-road dirt bikes only; 35 miles more just for unlicensed vehicles less than 50 inches wide; and 76 miles where jeeps and other all-terrain licensed vehicles can snake through the woods on narrow tracks. A three-day pass is $10, $5 for drivers under 15; annual pass $75.

PADDLING **Black Creek** meanders through Middleburg for many miles from its source up at Kingley Lake near Jennings State Forest toward the St. Johns River at Hibernia, with put-ins at Master Sergeant John E. Hayes Memorial Park along Main Street in Middleburg [30.072775, -81.852475] and at both Black Creek Park and Camp Chowenwaw Park off US 17.

One of the wildest scenic waterways in the region, the **Ocklawaha River** will take you back to a time when steamboats puffed their way up the St. Johns to visit Silver Springs. Cypress lined and winding, it can be accessed at two points in the northern part of the Ocala National Forest—a dirt ramp on the west side of the George Kirkpatrick Dam at Rodman Reservoir, Kirkpatrick Dam Road, and at the bridge farther south along FL 19.

✒ For an easy paddling outing, rent a canoe at Gold Head Branch State Park (see *Parks, Preserves, and Camping*) to explore **Little Lake Johnson** and its wetlands.

PARKS, PRESERVES, AND CAMPING 🐾 Access the 10,000-acre **Bayard Point Conservation Area** (386-329-4404; sjrwmd.com/recreationguide/bayard), FL 16, Green Cove Springs, from the John P. Hall Sr. Nature Preserve entrance off FL 16 near the St. Johns River Bridge to follow the trails through pine flatwoods and scrub out to a beautiful campsite on the banks of the St. Johns River. It's a popular place for horseback riding and fishing, and it's used for environmental education classes for the local school district.

🐾 To see pitcher plants in bloom, stop at **Black Creek Ravines Conservation Area** (386-329-4404; sjrwmd.com/recreationguide/blackcreekravines), Green Road north of CR 218, Middleburg, and walk the trails out to the vast bogs beneath the high-tension lines. The reason for this preserve, however, is the rugged terrain—bluffs up to 90 feet above sea level, deeply cut with ravines that channel rainwater down to Black Creek. Primitive camping, biking, and horseback riding are permitted; bring your camera for the showy parade of spring wildflowers!

A segment of the **Cross Florida Greenway** (floridastateparks.org/trail/Cross-Florida) straddles Buckman Lock on the Cross Florida Barge Canal and continues down toward Rodman Reservoir, hugging both shores of the reservoir and the Upper Ocklawaha River. On the south side of the canal, the Florida Trail (see *Hiking*) connects Buckman Lock with the George Kirkpatrick Dam area before heading south deep into the Ocala National Forest. **Rodman Campground** (386-326-2846; reserveamerica .com), 410 Kirkpatrick Dam Road, Palatka 32134, has 34 full-hookup campsites tucked

BACK TO NATURE AT CAMP CHOWENWAW

Built during the Depression under a Hoover-era re-employment program, 🔗 🐾 Camp Chowenwaw opened in 1932 along Black Creek as Florida's first Girl Scout camp. By utilizing resources found at the camp, workers built cabins from hand-processed pine trees, whittled pegs as a cheaper alternative to nails, dug pits to have clay for chinking, made shingles from cypress trees, and felled magnolias to make handcrafted furniture. Renovated in the past decade, their largest piece of work, **Big Cabin**, is a testament to innovative craftsmanship.

In 2006, Clay County bought the longtime camp and christened it **Camp Chowenwaw Park** (904-529-8058; claycountygov.com), 1517 Ball Road, Green Cove Springs. It's not your typical county park, by any means, although several miles of trails wind beneath a towering canopy of magnolias, oaks, and hickories. The oldest of the trails, the ♿ Jungle Trail, is a historic boardwalk leading from the modern pool complex, where Big Cabin looks over Black Creek, where the Scouts once swam. There is a canoe launch and picnic tables along the creek behind Big Cabin. The camp also features the Kiwita Nature Center, and a historic Girl Scout camp cabin houses the **Camp Chowenwaw Park History Museum**, a small but information-packed museum recounting the camp's more than 70 years of service to the Girl Scouts. Camp Chowenwaw was the first purpose-built Girl Scout camp in Florida, opening in 1932. Dioramas, artifacts, books, and binders full of historic information tell its sweeping story. Open the third Saturday monthly, 9–11 AM, or by appointment.

The biggest bounty in this park is the availability of places to camp, especially for large groups or families. The Hickory Trails loop around clusters of cabins that are available for overnight or longer stays. The **Ahwenassa cabins** look just like camping cabins at a KOA; both they and the block cabins at **Squirrel Run** are air-conditioned. If you've ever wanted to camp in a treehouse, here's your chance: the Treehouse Trail ends at a group of 1970s-vintage treehouses built for the Scouts. Each cabin at Treehouse Point is up on stilts and screened so the breeze through the tree canopy washes over the four bunks. Each cabin cluster has a

under the pines and oaks not far from Rodman Reservoir, $22. Tent campers can choose a primitive site, $12; there's a bathhouse nearby.

🐾 **Dunns Creek State Park** (386-329-3721; floridastateparks.org/park/Dunns-Creek), 320 Sisco Road, Pomona Park, protects sandhills and scrub along a sharp bend in the St. Johns River. Stop for a picnic, or follow the 1.5-mile nature trail to Blue Pond.

Etoniah Creek State Forest (386-329-2552; freshfromflorida.com), FL 100 N, Florahome, protects one of Florida's most beautiful ravines at Etoniah Creek, where hikers can look down a 40-foot bluff to see tapegrass waving in the current of the stream at the bottom; visit in springtime, when the azaleas and dogwoods put on a show. The Florida Trail (see *Hiking*) runs through the state forest, with designated campsites and a screened-room camping shelter at Iron Bridge, and a nature trail leads to the shores of George's Lake. Fee.

The easiest place for visitors to see the St. Johns River in Palatka is **James C. Godwin Riverfront Park** (386-329-0107), 100 Memorial Parkway, where a brick walkway, public art, and benches liven up the green space connecting downtown with Boathouse Marina (see *Boating*) and the Riverfront ampitheater, which hosts special events and concerts.

🐾 Popular with equestrians for its dozens of miles of riding trails, **Jennings State Forest** (904-291-5530; freshfromflorida.com), 1337 Long Horn Road, Middleburg, also offers several hiking trails; try out the Fire & Water Nature Trail for an interpretive introduction to the habitats found here, including seepage slopes with pitcher plants.

bathhouse with hot showers and a screened room shared by each group of campers, and they are as rustic as you'd expect at a historic Scout camp. Rates start at $20/night per cabin. Tent campers can choose from two walk-in camping areas, both deeply shaded—Hickory Flats and Magnolia Hill—for $15/night. The park is open 9 AM–sunset daily. Pets are not allowed in cabins but are welcome on the trails. Call ahead to make camping reservations.

1970S TREEHOUSES ARE ONE OF MANY CAMPING OPTIONS AT CAMP CHOWENWAW PARK

The North Fork Black Creek Trail offers primitive camping within a stone's throw of the waterway. Fee.

🚲🐾♿⚓ **Mike Roess Gold Head Branch State Park** (352-473-4701; floridastateparks .org/park/Mike-Roess), 6239 FL 21, Keystone Heights, centers on an incredible ravine dripping with ferns, from which the sand-bottomed Gold Head Branch is born. Nature trails let you climb down into the deep ravine and follow the stream's course to Little Lake Johnson, where you can grab a canoe and paddle across the expanse. More than five miles of the Florida Trail pass through the park, with a primitive campsite along the way. The park is one of North Florida's top getaways for camping, thanks to 73 campsites on its three campground loops and the most cabins you'll find in a Florida state park: 16 cabins, 9 of which were built by the Civilian Conservation Corps, overlook the lake. Bring your bike to get around; you'll be glad you did. Cabins $65–100, with a two-day minimum stay required on weekends and holidays; campsites $20 and up. Pets permitted in campground but not in cabins.

The granddaddy of wilderness areas in this region is the **Ocala National Forest** (352-236-0288; fs.usda.gov/ocala), established by Theodore Roosevelt as one of the first National Forests in America and occupying the southwest end of Putnam County south of Palatka. Covering more than 400,000 acres, the forest extends across four counties. In this region, popular recreation sites include Rodman Reservoir and Kirkpatrick Dam for fishing; the Florida Trail for hiking; the Ocklawaha River for paddling; and a vast system of purpose-built OHV trails stretching from Rodman Reservoir to

Salt Springs, with trailheads at Rodman and along FL 19 south. On Lake Delancy, two National Forest campgrounds cater to different camping crowds. Open year-round, **Lake Delancy West** is a launch point for ATVs onto the Ocala North OHV Trail System through the forest, and sits within an easy walk of the Florida Trail. Shaded sites look out onto the lake. No hookups, small campers and tents only, 30 sites at $6 per site plus $6 day-use fee; portable toilets. On the east side of the lake, the seasonally open (October–June) **Lake Delancy East** has no nearby trails, so it's focused on fishing, boating, and relaxing. There are 29 sites at $10 per site, no hookups, portable toilets; small trailers and tents only. Both are accessed off FL 19; watch for signs south of the Ocklawaha River.

   Rice Creek Conservation Area (386-329-4404; sjrwmd.com/recreationguide/rice creek) is a very special preserve off FL 100 N, 3 miles west of Palatka. A loop off the Florida Trail (see *Hiking*) follows impoundments built in the 1700s by British settlers who scraped an indigo and rice plantation from the floodplain forest. Dozens of bridges and a quarter-mile boardwalk carry you across blackwater waterways between ancient cypresses.

   ✥ 🐾 ♿ On 90 acres donated to the county by Judy Van Zant in memory of her late husband and Southern rock legend, **Ronnie Van Zant Park** (904-284-6378; claycountygov .com), 2760 Sandridge Road, Penney Farms, has a fishing pond with four piers as well as nature trails, playground, and a Frisbee golf course along with a full sports complex. Free.

   Home to pretty Mud Spring, **Welaka State Forest** (386-467-2388; freshfromflorida .com), CR 309 south of Welaka, is a nice place for a remote overnight campout. Grab your backpack and walk 4 miles along the Johns Landing Trail to one of two scenic primitive campsites right on the St. Johns River.

SCENIC DRIVES Although much of its route is south of Putnam County, **Florida Black Bear Scenic Byway** (floridablackbearscenicbyway.org) extends up into the Ocala National Forest to Buckman Lock and across the Fort Gates Ferry (see *Ferryboat*) to loop back down through Welaka to Volusia County. **J.C. Penney Memorial Scenic Highway** (jcpenneyscenichighway.org) encompasses the best part of FL 16 and a loop through historic Penney Farms.

SPRINGS Pouring out of a cavern on a bluff above the St. Johns River, the moder- ately sulphuric waters of **Green Cove Spring** became the focal point of a "health spa" craze in the late 1800s, drawing winter residents from the Northeast to come "take the waters" for their health. Inside **Spring Park** (904-297-7500), 106 St. Johns Avenue, a formal green space around the spring, the fully renovated historic pool complex is where you can enjoy the 72°F waters, which then flow on down a spring run through the park into the river. Gentle breezes blow through the shady canopy of tall and graceful live oaks covering the children's play area.

   At **Ravine Gardens State Park** (see *Garden*), sulfur springs bubble out of the ground at the bottom of the steephead ravine, just as small springs do to form Gold Head Branch at **Gold Head Branch State Park**. Large enough to have its own short spring run flowing out into the St. Johns River, **Mud Spring** in Welaka State Forest (see *Parks, Preserves, and Camping*) shimmers like an underwater garden, an aquatic pool teeming with life.

SWIMMING The constant 72-degree water of Green Cove Springs feeds directly into the renovated historic **Green Cove Springs City Pool** (904-495-6087; greencovesprings .com), 106 St. Johns Avenue, and then out to the St. Johns River, ensuring clean, mineral-rich water with a hint of sulfur. The pool is open Tuesday–Sunday 11–7, with an adjoining Splash Park for the kids open an hour later. Fee.

Step back in time at **Keystone Beach** (352-473-4807; keystoneheights.us), 565 S Lawrence Boulevard, Keystone Heights. Established in 1924, it's a park where you can splash around on a sandy beach below the historic dance hall on Lake Geneva, and it has one heck of a wooden playground for the kids to lose themselves in. You'll also find a swimming beach on **Little Lake Johnson** at nearby Gold Head Branch State Park on the north end of town.

✳ Lodging

B&B Take in the cool breeze off the St. Johns River while sitting on the veranda of an 1887 inn perched above a spring. **River Park Inn** (904-284-2994; riverpark inn.com), 103 S Magnolia Avenue, Green Cove Springs 32043, is the last of the accommodations standing that once served visitors coming to the theraputic spring. This three-story Frame Vernacular home has five guest rooms, all with private bath and vintage decor. The master suite has a two-person Jacuzzi and sitting room. Part of the historic district, the inn is within easy walking distance of the fishing pier and restaurants. Rooms with breakfast $94–139.

HISTORIC 🐾 ♂ (ᵞ) With seven rooms in the former Mira Rio, a Mediterranean revival gem built in 1923 for Palmolive Soap Company heir Caleb Johnson at the cost of more than $700,000, **Club Continental and River Suites** (800-877-6070 or 904-264-6070; clubcontinental.com), 2143 Astor Street, Orange Park 32073 is a fascinating piece of Florida history. Still owned by the same family after several generations, this historic 27-acre estate centers on a top-notch private, members-only dining club that you get to enjoy as an overnight guest. Set among the splendor of carefully manicured gardens and fountains set in intimate courtyards along the St. Johns River, where centuries-old live oaks bend to frame the three swimming pools, it's one of the most elegant historic hotels in North Florida. Each of the seven original rooms ($115–225) are themed around classic travel destinations that 1920s guests might have visited on their grand tours, such as Spain, France, and Italy. An adjoining 1870 home, Winterbourne, is used for weddings and receptions. Fifteen spacious ♿ (ᵞ) River Suites ($140–215), each with a European flair, overlook the St. Johns River.

WATERFRONT (ᵞ) Right on the St. Johns River in Palatka but out of the mainstream, **Crystal Cove Riverfront Resort** (386-325-1055), 133 Crystal Cove Drive, comes recommended from friends who spent a week there. It's an older waterfront property with a pool overlooking a marina, a popular spot for boaters thanks to ample parking; $79 and up.

TRIED AND TRUE As Orange Park is right on the edge of the Jacksonville metro, there are plenty of top brands to choose from, including the ♿ (ᵞ) **Courtyard by Marriott** (904-854-1500; marriott.com), 610 Wells Road, and the ♿ (ᵞ) **Hilton Garden Inn** (904-458-1577; hilton.com), 145 Park Avenue. Most viable options in Palatka are chain hotels as well, including a brand-new (ᵞ) ♿ **Hampton Inn** (386-530-2420; hilton.com), 100 Memorial Parkway, overlooking the St. Johns River in Riverfront Park. We've spent many nights at the pet-friendly (ᵞ) 🐾♿ ♂ **Sleep Inn & Suites** (866-538-0187; choicehotels.com/florida/palatka/sleep-inn-hotels/fl906), 3805 Reid Street, where the beds are comfortable and you can take free popcorn and DVDs from the lobby up to your room and watch; $74 and up.

CAMPGROUND Along the St. Johns River, **Lynchs Landing** (386-546-0546;

lynchslandingrvpark.com), 129 Troupe Road, San Mateo 32187, has a place for you to park your trailer under the trees and walk over to their dock to fish; 30- or 50-amp hookups, cable TV included, $35–45/night.

FISH CAMPS Quiet and rustic, **Fort Gates Fish Camp** (386-467-2411), 229 Fort Gates Ferry Road, Crescent City 32112, is located in the heart of bass fishing country, between Little Lake George and Lake George. Stay in the air-conditioned cottages, where you can fry up your catch of the day. Fish off the private boat ramp or take to the river in a rental boat. Cottages $40–55 daily, $240–330 weekly, full hookup sites $17. Boat slips available. It's also the gateway to the Ocala National Forest via the Fort Gates Ferry (see *Ferryboat*), which they operate Wednesday–Monday 7 AM–5:30 PM.

🐾 Step into the 1940s at **Stegbone's** (386-467-2464; stegbones.com), 144 Norton Fish Camp Road, Satsuma 32189. On the St. Johns River near Marker 41, with the wilds of the Ocala National Forest on the far shore, is a place to retreat with your buddies or your family of anglers and go fish. It offers quiet accommodations in one of five classic Florida cabins, the upscale three-bedroom Riverfront Getaway cottage, or a single-wide trailer ($90–250). Boat rentals to guests only, $80 half day, $125 dusk til dawn.

An angler's getaway since 1963, **Whitey's Fish Camp** (904-269-4198; whiteysfishcamp.com), 2032 CR 220, Orange Park 32003, has 44 RV sites with full hookups ($50), a restaurant (see *Where to Eat*), boat rentals, and, of course, fishing.

✳ Where to Eat

BARBECUE Just the name should have you hitting the brakes for **G's Slow Smoked BBQ** (904-531-5980; gsslow smokedbbq.com) 414 Walnut Street, where the owner, Gary, keeps a close watch on making his customers happy. Try the award-winning beef brisket or smoked spare ribs; fresh smoked sausage is a temptation too. Weekdays 11 AM–2 PM.

🐾♿ Eat in, walk up, or drive through **Johnny's Bar-B-Q Restaurant** (352-473-4445; johnnysbbqcatering.com), 7411 FL 21, Keystone Heights, where families gather for great barbecue and burgers. The waitresses know everyone by name, and service is in a snap, even during the lunch rush. Historic photos and memorabilia from the community line the walls. Lunch ($4–8) and dinner plates ($9–13) pack in the crowds; salads (with your choice of barbecue meat) appeal to the lighter palate.

CASUAL FARE A former Huddle House repurposed to a hometown diner, **Sunrise to Sunset** (904-531-9624), 618 Orange Avenue, dishes up breakfast real fast; one of the more intriguing items on the menu is grit cakes with sausage gravy. Since they're near the courthouse, they keep busy at breakfast and lunch, but pop in during the between hours for real milkshakes and ice cream cones.

COMFORT FOOD Since 1932, **Angel's Dining Car** (386-325-3927), 209 Reid Street, Palatka, Florida's oldest operating diner, stays crowded at breakfast and lunch. It's a tight squeeze inside, but they do offer curb service. To enjoy the dining car, you'll want to come during the lulls between. Their signature fountain drink is the Pusalow, made with chocolate milk over ice laced with a dash of vanilla syrup. Serving up standard Southern diner fare, from scrambled eggs and hash browns in the morning to fried catfish and big burgers in the afternoon, it's a place to stop with an appetite, say, after a hike. Meals under $10, 6 AM–9 PM.

A homespun diner that's always busy for lunch, **Carol's Melrose Café** (352-475-2626), 886 N FL 21, Melrose, serves up meals in mere minutes. Grab the daily special or some classic diner fare like a BLT, tuna melt, or grilled cheese. An alligator skin and photos of alligators cruising nearby Lake Santa Fe decorate the walls. Open **7 AM–3 PM**.

Evoking memories of old Keystone Heights, **The Keystone Inn** (352-473-3331), 208 FL 100, is an unstuffy nod to the past, with Southern comfort food—including outstanding fried chicken—served up on a daily buffet or from the menu. Daily specials draw in a big local crowd, especially for the AYCE smoked ribs on Thursdays. We stop here for a meal on almost every visit to the area, as it's down-home and inexpensive. Open daily for breakfast, lunch, and dinner.

ETHNIC EATS Delighting us with two different takes on Caprese—as salad and sandwich—tiny **D' Fontana Pizzeria & Ristorante** (904-529-5515), 324 Ferris Street, Green Cove Springs, is primarily a busy pizza shop but served up a satisfying lunch for under $20 for two. Monday–Saturday **11 AM–9 PM**.

A frequent stop for us in Palatka, **Niko's Pizza** (386-328-8559), 804 FL 19, doesn't have a big dining room but it's always bustling. Melding Greek and Italian on their menu, it's the place to grab a gyro, Greek salad, or share a hearty meat-loaded pizza with your family. Meals under $15.

HIP BISTRO-STYLE ♿ A classy café in the heart of downtown Palatka, **The Magnolia Café** (386-530-2740), 705 St. Johns Avenue, serves up fresh favorites with a Florida twist, like shrimp & grits for breakfast (don't worry, biscuits & gravy are on the menu too) and crab cake Benedict, $8–14. Lunches include shrimp po' boy, paninis, and a harvest salad laden with seasonal fruit. Wednesday–Monday **7 AM–2 PM**.

((ꜜ)) ♿ In an elegant coffeehouse just steps from the springs, **Spring Park Coffee** (904-531-9391; springparkcoffee.com), 328 Ferris Street, Green Cove Springs, baristas serve up both the classics—Americano, cappuccino, machhiato, chai—and a fun variety of seasonal lattes

like the Ice Princess, with peppermint, raspberry, and white chocolate on a base of espresso. In the morning, enjoy classic New York bagels shipped in from Brooklyn, or waffles with berry compote; otherwise, food is limited to freshly baked goods. The relaxing atmosphere makes this a great place to connect with friends.

SEAFOOD ♟ With a formal dining room in shades of oceanic blue, the classy **Blue Water Bay** (352-475-1928; thebluewaterbay.com), 319 FL 26, Melrose, pulls in patrons all the way from Gainesville and Jacksonville with entrées ($13–20) like lemon-steamed snow crab legs, Cajun crawfish étouffée, and farm-raised gator tail. Prime rib night is Thursday; "Gourmet Buffets" on Friday and Saturday at 5 PM, drawing from local organic growers. Their desserts—especially the sour orange pie and Chocolate Kahlua Mousse Bombe—are some of the best we've ever sampled. Lunch 12–3 PM, dinner 3–10 PM. Reservations suggested.

♟ ♿ ✍ The family-owned **Musselwhite's Seafood & Grill** (386-326-9111; musselwhitesseafood.com), 125 US 17 S, Palatka, serves up seafood favorites like fresh sea scallops with homemade tartar sauce; tangerine tuna marinated with citrus, soy, ginger, and honey; and also steak and chops, like New York strip cut and grilled to your liking. Entrées $10–24, plus some market price, like the fresh catch of the day. Save room for dessert: their Key lime pie and chocolate peanut butter pie are delicious. Open Thursday–Sun, serving dinner only on Saturday.

Catfish with Florida flair is the specialty at **Whitey's Fish Camp** (904-269-4198; whiteysfishcamp.com), 2032 CR 220, Orange Park, founded in 1963 and still going strong. The nightly all-you-can-eat catfish ($18) is only for those with big appetites. Petite eaters can order a basket with slaw, fries, and hush puppies. If you're not into catfish, then there's just about any other type of fish you can think of—have it grilled, blackened, broiled, fried, or pecan-crusted. Seafood platters include shrimp, oysters, scallops, and grouper. Fear not, landlubbers: you can get a 16-ounce rib eye or marinated chicken breast. Sandwiches and baskets $8–13, entrées $14–24.

WATERFRONT Kick back on the shores of Crescent Lake and enjoy the view at **3 Bananas** (386-698-2861; 3bananas.com), 11 S Lake Street, Crescent City. This tropical paradise offers up peel-and-eat shrimp, Caribbean jerk chicken, lightly fried Crescent City catfish, and a half-pound of grilled sirloin on their Paradise Burger, plus hand-cut prime rib on Saturday nights. Sit at the tiki bar and look for the sunken pirate ship while drinking rum runners and piña coladas. Lunch and dinner; closed Tuesday.

  ♿ We've always enjoyed **Corky Bell's** (386-325-1094; corkybellsseafood.com), 185 US 17, Palatka, so when this new one rose along the riverfront, it was good to see Gator Landing put to perfect use. Approach by river or by car to dine out on the patio along Devil's Elbow while nibbling on crab-stuffed mushrooms and fried squash, then dig into one of their groaning seafood platters, or lighter fare like shrimp scampi. Be sure to order the cheese grits as a side! Entrées $11 and up.

LOCAL WATERING HOLES Find an excuse to stop in **Chiappini's** (352-475-9496), 326 FL 26, just because. When I picked up a drink and mentioned I was looking for antiques, the clerk said "just wait around a few minutes, they'll be filing in the door!" The heart of town since 1935, they dispense bait and beer, gasoline and Dom Pérignon, and a sense of a time gone by. A park just behind the store at a small veteran's memorial hosts impromptu music jams.

✳ Selective Shopping

ANTIQUES At **Elsie Bell's Antique Mall** (386-329-9669), 111 N 4th Street, Palatka, we were looking for a music stand—and

they'd just sold out. Filled with vintage furnishings that would look good in any home, it's a collection of dealer spaces with a little bit of everything, including old-fashioned candy that your kids will love.

  The bright red building housing **Florahome Station** (386-659-1999; florahomestation.com), 105 Coral Farms Road, originally built in 1904, served as general store and post office during the early days of the community. Inside and out, you'll find fresh local produce, collectible books by Joseph Lippincott—who penned some of his books while wintering in Florida and set *The Wahoo Bobcat* in Florahome—as well as antiques and vintage clothing.

  Inside **River City Antiques & Collectibles** (386-546-4217), 717 St. Johns Avenue, Palatka, dealer booths span two storefronts, offering vintage glass and vases, a smattering of books, and some apparel along with plenty of knick-knacks and home decor items.

ARTS AND CRAFTS In the lovely 1886 Hilton-Brinson House, **Artisan's Way** (352-639-0730; artisansway.org), 5910 Hampton Street, Melrose, is a co-op that showcases the work of member artists, including the fine lapidary settings of Paula Phillips and Tea's Chirren, delightful dolls with their own personalities.

  Quilters will appreciate the fabric selection at **Miss D's Quilts** (386-385-5678; missdsquilts.com), 305 St. Johns Avenue, Palatka, as well as the availability of a long-arm machine. They can do the quilting for you, or you can learn how to use their machine and rent time on it by the hour.

  For Christmas shopping, don't miss the open house at the **Palatka Art League**, when the Tilghman House (see *Museums and Historic Sites*) is filled with cheery Christmas crafts and fine pieces by local artisans.

BOOKS AND GIFTS ⟪(ᵼ)⟫ At **Read Think Books** (386-227-7752; readthinkbooks

DOWNTOWN PALATKA

.com), 627 St. Johns Avenue, staff picks of new books, Florida authors, and children's books get front-room billing at a sunny street corner. Kristen welcomes book groups and writers to mingle and linger. Trades are welcome, as the second part of the story is a fine collection of used books. Spread the word! Monday–Saturday 10 AM–5 PM.

DECOR AND MORE **Ann Lowry Antiques** (352-475-2924), 1658 SE 5th Avenue, Melrose, showcases classy home decor items and furnishings.

Handcrafted quilts bulge from the shelves at **Country Charm Mercantile** (904-282-4512), 4544 Alligator Boulevard, Middleburg; wind chimes dangle from the ceiling. This five-room home is jam-packed with gift items and home decor, from Heritage Village miniatures to Yankee Candles, gourmet foods, and Beanie Babies.

FARMERS' MARKETS For more than 50 years, **County Line Produce** (904-692-9400; facebook.com/countylineproduce), 848 FL 207, Hastings, has been the place to go for fresh produce from this potato- and cabbage-producing area. As one of their signs says, "slaw down!"

SPECIALTY FOODS Get buzzing and head to the self-serve **Honey Stand** (386-749-3562), 303 E FL 100, San Mateo, where you'll find pure, raw Florida honey. Choose from orange blossom, gallberry, or wildflower in 1-, 2-, and 5-pound jars. Run by Barberville Produce, it's been a local tradition since 1947.

✳ Special Events

FALL/WINTER Try some sweet potato pie the first Saturday of October at the **Soul Food Festival and Parade**, Vera Francis Hall Park on Palmetto Avenue, Green Cove Springs.

Get your caboose to the **Palatka Railfest** (386-649-6137; railsofpalatka.org), Union Station, corner of 11th and Reid, where you can learn about model and full-scale trains or enhance your HO, S, and N collection at the many railroad exhibits. Held in October.

↪ The annual **Christmas on Walnut Street** draws attention to downtown

Green Cove Springs as the Jingle Bell Fun Run, the Parade of Trees—trees decorated by different citizens and businesses throughout town—and a Christmas parade usher in Santa's arrival. First Saturday of December.

At Christmas, take a tour through **Crescent City**, where many of the grand and glorious homes are decorated in holiday splendor. During the **Clay County Historical Society Holiday Tour of Homes** (claycountyhistoricalsociety .org), walk through Green Cove Springs's authentic Victorian homes decorated for the holidays; fee.

Each February, taste a bit of Scottish culture at the **Northeast Florida Scottish Games & Festival** (904-725-5744; neflgames.com), the last Saturday, Clay County Fairgrounds, Green Cove Springs.

Ravine Gardens State Park (see *Garden*) and downtown Palatka host the annual **Florida Azalea Festival** (386-326-4001; flazaleafest.com), started in 1945. Always held the second weekend of March, with arts, crafts, music, and food, it's always an excellent reason to come to town.

✒ The annual **Railroad and History Festival** (904-284-9644; claycountyhistoricalsociety.org) makes the Clay County Historic Triangle (see *Historic Sites*) come alive each March with pioneer craftspeople, Civil War reenactors, and an antique car show. Tour the museums and even walk inside the big red caboose. Free.

You'll find traditional agricultural exhibits, entertainment, and midway rides during March at the **Putnam County Fair** (386-329-0318; putnamfairandexpo.com), Putnam County Fairgrounds, East Palatka, a local tradition since 1926.

SPRING/SUMMER The biggest **Bluegrass Gospel Festival** in the region is held at Rodeheaver Boys Ranch

(386-328-1281; rbr.org), on the St. Johns River, with an all-star jam of nationally notable musicians all day long. Camping available, call for reservations. Fourth Saturday in April.

Keep the rural fun rolling with a visit to the **Clay County Fair** (904-284-1615; claycountyfair.org), 2493 FL 16 W, Green Cove Springs, held each April.

The best place to learn to skin a catfish is at the **Florida Catfish Festival** (386-698-1666; rotaryclubcrescentcity .com), Crescent City, run by the local Rotary Club, the first Saturday of April. The championship catfish-skinning contest is one of many events, including the catfish run, a parade (led by King Catfish), a bluegrass concert, an antiques show, and an arts and crafts fair.

One of this region's major events, the 42-nautical-mile **Mug Race** (904-264-4094; rudderclub.com/mug-race.html) is the world's longest river race, founded in 1954 and overseen by the Rudder Club, a sailing club. Event participants set sail from the Palatka riverfront and race to Jacksonville along the St. Johns River, the first Saturday of May.

Wake up early and head to the **Bostwick Blueberry Festival** (386-329-2658) for the blueberry pancake breakfast, where you can pick up blueberry-related foods, arts, and crafts; it's held in May.

You'll find not only hot steaming blue crabs at the annual **Blue Crab Festival** (386-325-4406; bluecrabfestival.com), downtown Palatka, but also delights such as soft-shell crabs, shrimp, and alligator. Four days of entertainment, rides, and arts and crafts. Always on Memorial Day weekend.

✒ At **Riverfest**, held each Memorial Day, Spring Park (see *Springs*) is packed with food and craft vendors. Bring your lawn chair for the day to enjoy live music, children's activities, a hotdog eating contest, fireworks over the river, and a ceremony to honor fallen veterans.

THE UPPER SUWANNEE

Baker, Columbia, Hamilton, Lafayette,
Madison, and Suwannee Counties
Lake City, Live Oak, Madison, and White Springs

As the frontier territory of Florida opened for settlement in 1820, families migrating south found the red hills, deep ravines, and high bluffs along the Suwannee River and its tributaries reminiscent of the landscapes they'd left behind in Georgia and the Carolinas. Building farms and large plantations, they planted cotton, corn, and sugarcane and used the river for trade. Shallow-draft steamboats plied the waterway from the Gulf of Mexico up to White Springs, where the shoals of the Suwannee made farther passage impossible.

The heart of the region was Alpata Telophka, or "Alligator Town," a Seminole village ruled by the powerful chief Alligator in the 1830s. To the north, settlers Bryant and Elizabeth Sheffield built a log hotel at White Sulphur Springs in 1835, entertaining the first tourists along the Suwannee River. The city of **Madison**, based on the Seminole village of "Hickstown," was founded in 1838 and has a core historic district of homes and churches originally built as early as the 1850s, with 50 historic structures on the National Register of Historic Places. **Fort White** grew up around a frontier fortress from the Second Seminole War.

As more settlers moved into the Suwannee Valley and traded with the Seminoles, the village of Alligator was founded between several lakes adjacent to the Seminole community. It became incorporated as **Lake City** in 1856. Lake City was the original site for the University of Florida, but the Gators were lured to Gainesville by supporters with political clout.

Ocean Pond became a massing ground for Confederate troops with a mission to protect the rail line leading west toward Florida's capital, Tallahassee. On February 20, 1864, a westward push of Union troops met the Confederate pickets near the town of **Olustee**. A full-scale battle erupted in the thick pine forest, with both sides utilizing the rail line to move cannons and troops. After four hours, more

THE SUWANNEE RIVER AT WHITE SPRINGS

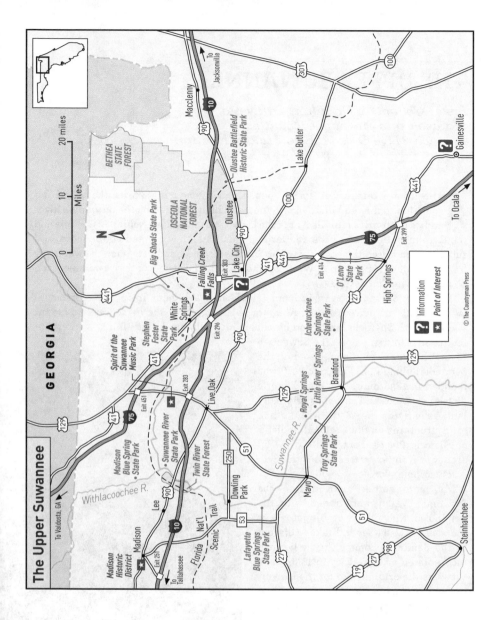

The Upper Suwannee

than 2,000 lay dead and dying; the Union troops retreated to Jacksonville. It was Florida's largest Civil War battle.

During the steamboat era, the region flourished. **White Springs** had 14 hotels catering to tourists who came to "take the waters" at the springs. Along the banks of the Suwannee much farther south, **Branford** was an important steamboat-building town. **Mayo** became the county seat of agrarian Lafayette County in 1893. Covering only 1 square mile, **Lee** is one of the state's smallest incorporated towns. **Macclenny**, the seat of rural Baker County, dates back to 1886 and was once known as the horticultural capital of Florida; the Glen St. Mary Nursery, established 1907, was responsible for the citrus industry's standardization of orange varieties.

Railroads soon crisscrossed the region after the Civil War. Full-scale logging of the surrounding pine woods brought prosperity to Lake City and **Live Oak**, with a building boom that set the tone for the feel of their downtowns today. But the end of the steamboat era left White Springs and others along the Suwannee behind the march of progress. Those that didn't vanish into ghost towns—like Columbus, unearthed at Suwannee River State Park at the confluence of the Suwannee and Withlacoochee rivers—settled into a relaxed pace. Ongoing preservation efforts ensure the splendor of these classic old Florida small towns and of downtown Lake City and Madison. The youngest community in the region is **Dowling Park**, established in 1913 along the Suwannee River by the Advent Christian Church, first as an orphanage and then as a retirement village for its members.

GUIDANCE At the upper end of the Suwannee River, **Visit Columbia County** (386-758-1312; springsrus.com), 971 W Duval Street, Lake City, is your top source of information, particularly through the interactive maps on their website. **Hamilton County TDC** (386-792-6829; hamiltontdc.org) encompasses the area north from White Springs between the Suwannee and Withlacoochee rivers. East of the Suwannee River, the **Baker County Chamber of Commerce** (904-259-6433; bakerchamberflorida.com), 20 E Macclenny Avenue, provides information on the outdoors and heritage attractions of the area. The Osceola National Forest sprawls across both counties. Walk into the **Osecola Ranger Station** (386-752-2577; fs.usda.gov/osceola), 24874 US 90, 8:30 AM–4 PM Monday–Friday for maps, permits, and campground reservations.

On the western side of the region, stop by the **Madison County Chamber of Commerce** (850-973-2788; madisonfl.org), 316 SW Pinckney Street, Madison, for walking tour brochures and more, and check in with the **Suwannee County Chamber of Commerce** (386-362-3071; suwanneechamber.com), 212 N Ohio Avenue, Live Oak, for things to see and do along the biggest arc of the Suwannee River through the region. **Natural North Florida** (naturalnorthflorida.com) is a coalition that provides information for many of the communities found in the region.

If you're headed out on the Suwannee River, you'll want a map showing boating access and springs. Contact the **Suwannee River Water Management District** (386-362-1001; srwmd.state.fl.us), 9225 CR 49, Live Oak 32060; you can also download their recreational guide from the website.

GETTING THERE *By air:* The nearest commuter service comes into **Tallahassee** (see the *Tallahassee & The Big Bend* chapter) and **Gainesville** (see the *Gainesville & Vicinity* chapter); **Jacksonville International Airport** (see the *Jacksonville* chapter) provides a broader choice of carriers and is only an hour and 10 minutes from Lake City via Interstate 10.

By bus: **Greyhound** (800-231-2222; greyhound.com) stops in Lake City.

By car: **I-75** and **I-10** provide quick access to most of the region, but you'll want to wander the back roads to see the sights.

GETTING AROUND Heading north from High Springs, **US 41** passes through downtown Lake City before becoming Hamilton County's "Main Street," running through its three towns—White Springs, Jasper, and Jennings. **US 129** also runs north–south, linking Branford, Live Oak, and Jasper. For the scenic east–west route, take **US 90** from Olustee west to Lake City, Live Oak, Lee, Madison, and Greenville; **US 27** takes a more southerly route, tying together High Springs, Fort White, and Branford on its way to Tallahassee. **FL 51** and **US 27** meet at Mayo, the center of Lafayette County, passing through all of its major towns.

MEDICAL EMERGENCIES Regional hospitals include **Shands Lake Shore** (386-292-8000; shandslakeshore.com), 560 E Franklin Street, Lake City; **Shands Live Oak** (386-362-0800; shandsliveoak.com), 1100 11th Street SW, Live Oak; and **Madison County Memorial Hospital** (850-973-2271; mcmh.us), 24 NW Crane Avenue, Madison.

✻ To See

ARCHITECTURE Now serving as the town's library, the original **Baker County Courthouse** is an architectural landmark at the corner of 5th and McIver streets. The old **Baker County Jail**, built 1911–1913 (see *Genealogical Research*), is next door. The sheriff's family lived on-site and prepared food for inmates. Stop in at the Macclenny Chamber of Commerce, 20 E Macclenny Avenue, to browse through their book of historic sites and to get directions to see the town's historic homes from the late 1800s, all privately owned.

In downtown Lake City, check out the old **Columbia County Courthouse**, circa 1902. The Columbia County Historical Society (see *Museums and Historic Sites*) sits in a neighborhood dominated by beautiful 1890s Victorian houses, including the **Chalker-Turner House**, 104 E St. Johns, Lake City. Stop at the historical society for information on walking tours in the city's antebellum neighborhoods.

First established as a Baptist congregation in a log cabin prior to 1866, **Falling Creek Methodist Church and Cemetery**, 1290 Falling Creek Road, dates back to the 1880s, the land having been donated to the church after 1855 by heirs of one of the original settlers of the area, Thomas D. Dicks from South Carolina. Its wood frame is weathered

ANTIQUE AUTO PARTS GARDEN ALONG US 90, LAKE CITY

by age; it contains original water glass; it is shaded by ancient live oaks and southern magnolias. The deep gorge of Falling Creek rings the property (see *Waterfalls*).

Built in 1893 in **Jasper**, the red brick **Old Jail** (386-792-1300), 501 NE 1st Avenue, functioned as a prison until 1984. It gives a glimpse into what it was like on both sides of the bars—the sheriff and his family occupied living quarters connected to the jail. Saved from the wrecking ball by a determined group of women, the structure is still undergoing restoration, as is the adjoining **Heritage Village** complex, which includes a cotton gin, a small church, and two shotgun houses.

In Live Oak, take a look at that Wrigley's ad painted on the side of a brick building behind the Blue Star Memorial on Pine Avenue: It's been there since 1909. Driving south to the 1915 post office, still in operation, you pass a cell phone place inside a **1960s Sinclair gas station**. Architectural landmarks remain utilitarian, from the **1890s downtown block** filled with businesses to the pillared **Thomas Dowling House** on CR 136, renovated into a community center.

At the City Hall Complex in Lee, 286 NE CR 255, the 1850s **McMullen House**, a log farmstead, was once part of a larger antebellum plantation along the Suwannee River, moved here to Louis Demotsis Park as part of a pioneer Florida display. Surrounding it are a corncrib, outhouse, smokehouse, and external kitchen.

With more than 30 buildings from the 1800s and nearly 50 historic sites dating to 1936, downtown **Madison** has the highest concentration of historical architecture in the region. The **Wardlaw-Smith-Goza Mansion**, 103 N Washington Street, is a classical revival mansion built in 1860, once known as Whitehall. Other historic homes of note include the **W. H. Dial House**, 105 E Marion Street, a Victorian mansion circa 1880; the **J. E. Hardee House**, 107 E Marion Street, a two-story Mediterranean villa from 1918 designed by Lloyd Barton Greer (who also designed the classy **Madison County Courthouse**); and the **Livingston House**, 501 N Range Street, Madison's oldest home, from 1836. In continuous use for worship services since 1881, the small wood frame **St. Mary's Episcopal Church** (850-973-8338), 108 N Horry Street, permits tours by appointment.

Dominating downtown Mayo, the neoclassical **Lafayette County Courthouse**, 120 W Main Street, Mayo, dates back to 1908 and is still in use as a courthouse today.

White Springs is a beautiful historic town; take the time to walk down River Street and its adjoining blocks to see many homes from the late 1800s. Interpretive signs in front of homes and businesses discuss local history.

BLUEGRASS AND FOLK Entertainment in this region mainly comes in the form of music—see *Music Festivals* for the full scoop. At **Thayer's Grove** (904-755-9035; southwestfloridabluegrass.org/fljams.html), Mikesville, enjoy free bluegrass and folk music jams on Wednesday at 1 PM, off FL 18 just west of I-75.

DE SOTO TRAIL In 1539 Spanish explorer Hernando de Soto and his troops crossed Florida in pursuit of gold. Roadside markers (floridadesototrail.com) interpret his route; see the website for a map of locations.

EQUESTRIAN EVENTS **Suwannee River Riding Club, Inc.** (386-935-0447; srrc branford.com), 9132 254th Terrace (US 129) north of Branford. Stop by their arena to watch team roping (first and third Fridays) and speed events (first and third Saturdays) each month; they also hold an annual rodeo.

GARDEN **O'Toole's Herb Farm** (850-973-1280), 305 NE Artemesia Trail, Madison. Culinary herbs and flowers grown organically—that's the mainstay of Betty O'Toole's

REMEMBERING RAY CHARLES

Music would not be the same without Ray Charles, and his hometown of Greenville hopes you'll remember that. A community effort resulted in reconstruction of **Ray Charles Childhood Home** (850-948-2251), 465 SW Ray Charles Avenue, along with a state historic marker installed on the property. The town park has also memorialized their most notable citizen with a bronze statue of "RC," who learned to play the piano thanks to Wiley Pitman, owner of the Red Wing Café, in a prominent spot at Haffye Hays Park, visible from US 90 just west of Broad Street.

RAY CHARLES MEMORIAL IN GREENVILLE

lovely gardens, and their greens garnish platters in fine restaurants around the region. This 150-year-old family farm is open by appointment or during Friday Morning Yoga or their festival weekends; call for details.

GHOST TOWNS The towns of **Columbus** and **Ellaville** vanished not long after steamboats stopped running along the Suwannee; railroads had taken their place. You'll find Columbus Cemetery within Suwannee River State Park (see *Parks, Preserves, and Camping*). Directly across the Suwannee, the remains of Ellaville (primarily foundations and loose bricks) lie along the Florida Trail through Twin Rivers State Forest (see *Hiking*) north of US 90. In 1870 **New Troy**, near Troy Springs (see *Springs*), boasted busy steamboat docks and steady commerce. It was the seat of Lafayette County, but after an arsonist torched the courthouse in 1892, county residents voted to move the courthouse to Mayo.

MONUMENTS Dedicated in memory to Captain Colin P. Kelly Jr., a Madison resident and the first American casualty of World War II on December 9, 1941, at Clark Field in the Philippines, the **Four Freedoms Monument**, downtown, reflects on the "Four Freedoms" speech made by President Franklin Delano Roosevelt prior to the outbreak of the war.

MUSEUMS AND HISTORIC SITES Located along the rail line, **Heritage Park Village** (904-259-7275; heritagepark.cityofmacclenny.com), 102 S Lowder Street, Macclenny, holds a collection of historic buildings from around the county as well as the historic depot and a caboose. Guided tours available for a small fee; call ahead to arrange. Open **7 AM–9 PM** daily.

In downtown Lake City, the **Lake City–Columbia County Historical Museum** (386-755-9096; lccchm.org), 157 SE Hernando Avenue, offers exhibit rooms with furnishings that capture the period of this southern Italianate manor circa 1870, including artifacts from the Civil War. Thursday and Saturday **10 AM–1 PM**.

Near the old **Madison Depot**, a giant steam engine sits along Range Road at 109 W Rutledge, Madison. It's a relic of what was once the **largest cotton gin in the world**, combing through Sea Island cotton at the Florida Manufacturing Company in the 1880s.

At **Olustee Battlefield Historic State Park** (386-758-0400; floridastateparks.org/park/Olustee-Battlefield), 5815 Battlefield Trail Road off US 90, learn the story of Florida's largest and most deadly Civil War battle. Preserved as a memorial by the 1899 Florida Legislature, it is also Florida's oldest piece of state-protected public land. While the Battlefield Trail leads you on a well-documented interpretive walk through the combat that happened in this haunting pine forest, the most compelling time to visit is during the annual reenactment in February (see *What's Happening*), one of the South's largest encampments. A new interpretive center is in the works. Daily **9 AM–5 PM**, free.

After you learn about Florida's largest Civil War battle at the visitors center at Olustee Battlefield, stop in the **Olustee Visitor's Center and Museum** at the old railroad depot (off US 90) for an interactive walk through life in this logging and railroad community.

Housed in the 1903 Atlantic Coast Line freight depot, the **Suwannee County Historical Museum** (386-362-1776), 208 N Ohio Avenue, Live Oak, presents dioramas and an extensive collection of historic objects—including a working telephone switching station—to bring history alive. In the former Jasper High School agricultural building, the **Hamilton County Historical Society Museum** (386-792-1668), 3113 Hatley Street NE, Jasper, shows off historical documents, display cases with exhibits, and photos of historical structures throughout the county, along with a small gift shop with local art. Tuesday and Thursday and the first Saturday, **10 AM–3 PM**.

A repository of Madison County history, with information on long-lost historic sites like the San Pedro Mission and the Drew Mansion, is the **Treasures of Madison County Museum** (850-973-3661; treasuresofmadisoncounty.com), 194 SW Range Avenue, in the beautiful W. T. Davis Building, one of only three metal-front commercial buildings remaining from its era. Open Tuesday–Friday **10 AM–2 PM**, Saturday **11 AM–1 PM**.

In **Veterans Memorial Park**, 123 CR 300, Mayo, a **Cracker homestead** sits beneath the ancient live oak trees. The park is home to the annual Pioneer Day Festival (see *What's Happening*).

Just inside Stephen Foster Folk Culture State Park (see *Parks, Preserves, and Camping*) is the original **White Sulfur Springs Spa**, built in the late 1800s. Standing on its balcony, you can look down into the spa, and down along the rapid flow of the Suwannee River. During World War II the spa and its grounds served as an internment camp for German prisoners of war.

MUSIC FESTIVALS Thank Stephen Foster for singing about the Suwannee River: this region is a magnet for music festivals. It all started with the **Florida Folk Festival** (see *What's Happening*) nearly 60 years ago, the grandaddy of all folk festivals with nearly a dozen stages going simltaneously over Memorial Day weekend at Stephen Foster Folk Culture State Park in White Springs. Over the years, the festival has headlined greats such as Bill Monroe, Rosanne Cash, Bo Diddley, Mel Tillis, and Arlo Guthrie, while the heartwarming music of renowned Florida folk singer/songwriters rings out throughout the park all weekend. When the **Spirit of the Suwannee Music Park** (see *Campgrounds*) opened, they started bringing in big name acts to the region, from Tim McGraw to Phish. While there are concerts there all year long, they also host many popular annual music festivals like the **Suwannee River Jam** (suwanneeriverjam .com), **Suwannee Roots Revival** (suwanneerootsrevival.com), and the **Wanee Festival** (waneefestival.com). More recently, Bienville Plantation (see *Hunting Lodge*) has launched the **Party in the Pines** (partyinthepines.com); their 2017 festival featured Keith Urban and Miranda Lambert as headliners.

PERFORMING ARTS At Florida Gateway College, the **Levy Performing Arts Center** (386-754-4340; fgc.edu), 149 SE College Place, Lake City, is a venue for concerts, plays, and art exhibitions during the school year.

RAILROADIANA Many settlements of the Upper Suwannee started as railroad towns, and so their railroad history remains. You'll find **turn-of-the-twentieth-century railroad depots** still standing in Fort White, Live Oak, and Madison, and restored depots at **Olustee** (housing a beautiful national forest visitors center with regional railroad history) and **Macclenny** (with a red caboose outside the depot). A **historic iron boxwork bridge** crosses the Suwannee River at Dowling Park. The east–west main line paralleling US 90 through the region remains a busy thoroughfare, with great train spotting for rail fans from Suwannee River State Park (see *Parks, Preserves, and Camping*).

Stop in the **Suwannee County Historical Museum** (see *Museums and Historic Sites*) for information on Live Oak's railroading history. Live Oak grew up around the Seaboard Air Line railroad, which came through in 1903, and the locally owned **Live Oak, Perry & Gulf Railroad**, affectionately known as the "Lopin' Gopher." Railroad shops in Live Oak once turned out steam locomotives and parts for the Plant System.

✳ To Do

BIKING Mountain bikers have a blast on nearly 50 miles of rugged riverside trails built and maintained by the **Suwannee Bicycle Association** (386-397-2347; suwanneebike.org), 10561 Bridge Street, White Springs, hosts of the **Suwannee Fat Tire Festival** (see *Special Events*) each fall. Stop by to pick up maps of local biking routes, including the popular Swift Creek, Gar Pond, Disappearing Creek, and Big Shoals routes. Each provides challenges to bikers with the undulating terrain along the Suwannee River and its tributaries; trails are posted for three levels of difficulty, from beginner to gung-ho.

Perfect for beginning mountain bikers, the **Allen Mill Pond Bike Trail** runs 4.2 miles between Allen Mill Pond and Lafayette Blue Springs (see *Springs*) along the Suwannee River. Madison County boasts **The Loop**, a 100-mile marked road biking route running down paved rural byways; pick up a map from the Chamber of Commerce (see *Guidance*).

A paved bike path in Live Oak, the **Heritage Trail** (386-362-3004; suwanneeparks .com) has a trailhead off US 90 at Cooper Street SE and connects to Heritage Park, 1004 Helvenston Street, which boasts a big colorful playground.

✐ For tamer outings, the paved 3.5-mile **Woodpecker Trail** at Big Shoals State Park (see *Parks, Preserves, and Camping*) is a gentle-enough ride for the kids through some beautiful river bluff forest. Connecting Little River Springs and the Ichetucknee River, the **Suwannee River Greenway** parallels US 129 and US 27 with a paved bicycle path along an old railroad route; parking is provided in downtown Branford. In Madison, the paved 12-mile **Four Freedoms Trail** (madisoncountyfl.com) starts at the north edge of town and heads to the state border at the Withlacoochee River.

BIRDING Top sites in the region include **Alligator Lake**, where colonies of nesting egrets occupy the islands, and the **Nice Wander Trail** and **Mount Carrie Wayside** in the Osceola National Forest (see *Parks, Preserves, and Camping*), where an early-morning visit lets you watch rare red-cockaded woodpeckers, marked with white bands, emerging from their holes in longleaf pines. Part of the Florida Trail (see *Hiking*), which also affords access to red-cockaded woodpecker colonies much deeper in the forest, the 2-mile, accessible-with-assistance Nice Wander Trail starts at a trailhead at Olustee Battlefield Historic State Park. Mount Carrie Wayside is along US 90. At the **Ladell Brothers Environmental Center** in Madison (see *Nature Centers*), go birding in this oasis on the North Florida Community College campus. **Cooks Hammock**, hidden in a maze of forest roads off FL 51 south of Mayo at the Lafayette Hunt Club, has a colony of white and glossy ibises.

BOATING Most of the rivers in this region have shallows, sandbars, and rapids, and even go dry at times. Unless your craft has a very shallow draft, don't put in any farther north on the Suwannee than Branford, and don't take it any farther upriver than its confluence with the Withlacoochee—snags and sandbars are very real hazards, as are giant sturgeon. See *Paddling* for details on the best river routes in the region. See *Fishing* for locations of the best lakes for boaters.

CAVE DIVING Where the Santa Fe meets the Suwannee, the town of Branford calls itself the "**Spring Diving Capital of the World**." Stop in at Steamboat Dive Inn (see *Dive Resorts*) for information about open-water dive sites. Cave divers also flock here for both **spring diving in the Suwannee River** and the extensive underwater cave system at **Peacock Springs** (see *Springs*). For cold air, gear rentals, instruction, and a friendly chat, stop at **Dive Outpost** (386-776-1449; diveoutpost.com), 20148 180th Street, en route to the park. Important note: Many open-water divers have died in this region while attempting cave diving. Do not enter an underwater cave or spring unless you are a certified cave diver. Most springs must be accessed by boat, and a DIVER DOWN flag is necessary while diving the river.

FISHING From **Ocean Pond** at Olustee (see *Campgrounds*) to **Watertown Lake** [030.193332, -82.603032] on the edge of Lake City, you'll find plenty of stillwater opportunities. Don't miss **Cherry Lake**, a WPA reservoir popular for bass fishing north of Madison off FL 253; launch at Cherry Lake Beach (see *Swimming*). Looking for bream? Head for the **Aucilla River**, west of Greenville.

If you're fishing along the banks of the **Suwannee River**, stop in at **Rooster's Outfitters** (386-234-0851), 10606 Bridge Street, White Springs, to talk to Keith "Rooster" Knipp; he has an artist's touch with custom bamboo fly rods, and he can point you to some good spots. Target sunfish around the snags and channel catfish in the deep holes. John M. Bethea State Forest has numerous places for anglers to access the **St. Mary's River** and its tributaries.

GENEALOGICAL RESEARCH Housed in the old Baker County Jail in Macclenny, the **Baker County Historical Society Family History Library** (904-259-0587), 42 W McIver, opens Saturday 1–4 PM for folks doing historical and genealogical research; you can also make an appointment to visit.

GOLF With three 9-hole, par-36 courses on their property, **Quail Heights Country Club** (386-752-3339; quailheightscc.com), 161 Quail Heights Terrace, Lake City, is a golfer's destination. Condos and efficiencies on-site enable them to offer "Stay and Play" packages, $82–118.

HIKING From Olustee Battlefield, you can backpack west on the **Florida Trail** (see *What's Where*), 20 miles through Osceola National Forest and another 70 miles following the bluffs of the Suwannee River from Bell Spring to Mill Creek in Twin Rivers State Forest; Swift Creek, Camp Branch, and Holton Creek are all don't-miss sections. To pass through pieces of private land along the river, you must be a member of the Florida Trail Association (877-HIKE-FLA; floridatrail.org). American Canoe Adventures (see *Paddling*) offers shuttle services.

You can find other great hiking at **Suwannee River State Park**, **O'Leno State Park**, and numerous other locations detailed in *50 Hikes in North Florida*. Don't miss the easy, 2-mile round-trip to Big Shoals from **Big Shoals State Park** (see *Parks*) north of White Springs, where you can watch Class III rapids froth like cola, and the quarter-mile walk to **Falling Creek Falls** (see *Waterfalls*). Pursue your Florida State Forests Trailwalker patch with several qualifying trails in **Twin Rivers State Forest** (see *Parks, Preserves, and Camping*) or take a scenic amble along the Suwannee River on the **Milford Clark Nature Trail** at Dowling Park, a 4-mile round-trip starting near the Village Lodge (see *Lodging*).

HORSEBACK RIDING At **Windmill Ranch & Stables** (386-935-2278), 11300 NW 15th Avenue, Branford, trail rides are offered daily in summer, weekends in winter, $30 per hour. Camping available. In Jasper, **McCulley Farms** (386-938-1147; mcculleyfarms .com), 6415 NE CR 143, a historic farmstead, holds the equestrian equivalent of RV rallies—guided group trail rides along the Withlacoochee River, with on-site camping and meals—twice a year. **R. O. Ranch Equestrian Park** (386-294-1475; roranch.org), 10807 S FL 51, Mayo, has 14 miles of trails on their property plus more riding nearby, with a campground on-site. Equestrian trails wind through **Big Shoals State Park**, **Twin Rivers State Forest** in Madison County, and the **Osceola National Forest**, with opportunities for overnight camping.

NATURE CENTER At North Florida Community College in Madison, the **Ladell Brothers Outdoor Environmental Center** (850-973-1645; nfcc.edu/visitors/nature-center), 1000 Turner Davis Drive, occupies the west side of campus, on the far side of the lake. Interpretive walking trails and boardwalks lead through a variety of North Florida habitats; the Wood Duck Pond is an excellent birding stop.

PADDLING The **Ichetucknee River** is closed to paddlers upstream from US 27 during the summer months to allow tubing. But in all other seasons, it's a compelling trip. Canoeists interested in the **Ichetucknee** or **Santa Fe River** can contact the **Santa Fe Canoe Outpost** (386-454-2050; santaferiver.com), 21410 NW US 441, for rentals and

SUWANNEE RIVER WILDERNESS TRAIL

The Suwannee River is one of the top paddling destinations in Florida, thanks to its length and lack of commercial boat traffic—it has enough shoals and sandbars to discourage most motorboats from heading any farther north than Ellaville. It takes two weeks to paddle the river from its headwaters in the Okefenokee Swamp in Georgia to the town of Suwannee on the Gulf of Mexico. With its broad sand beaches and beautiful springs, the Suwannee is a perfect choice for a long-distance canoe outing. To guide you down the river, the **Suwannee River Wilderness Trail** (800-868-9914; floridastateparks.org/park/Suwannee -River-Wilderness-State-Trail) outlines the 170-mile route, providing multiple river camps and numerous access points along the way. A National Geographic map covers the entire route.

In White Springs, **American Canoe Adventures** (386-397-1309; aca1.com), 10610 Bridge Street, can set you up with a canoe or kayak and shuttle service, $35–65 for a day trip, or arrange a multiday outing. **Suwannee Canoe Outpost** (386-364-4991; suwanneeoutpost.com), 2461 95th Drive, Live Oak, provides canoe and kayak rentals and shuttles out of Spirit of the Suwannee Music Park (see *Campgrounds*). Their day trips, $13–26, are set up to end at their take-out. They also offer guided 3-to-5-day trips on the Suwannee River Wilderness Trail for $499 per person and up. For guided day trips, check with Chris Mericle at **Blackwater River Guide** (386-855-5096; blackwaterriverguide.com) in Jasper; he leads paddles for two or more on the Alapaha, Suwannee, and Withlacoochee rivers starting at $165 per person, including canoe or kayak rental.

CLEAR AND TANNIC WATERS MINGLE WHERE LITTLE RIVER SPRINGS POURS INTO THE SUWANNEE RIVER

shuttles; **Rum 138 Outfitters** (386-454-4247; rum138.com), 2070 SW CR 138, Fort White, focuses on the Santa Fe. See the Gainesville chapter for more about the Fort White/High Springs area, a popular paddler's destination. To the east of the Suwannee River basin, the headwaters of the **St. Mary's River** (sjrwmd.com/stmarysriverguide) starts within John M. Bethea State Forest (see *Parks, Preserves, and Camping*), where a put-in is available at Maple Set Recreation Area.

PARKS, PRESERVES, AND CAMPING More than 6 miles of hiking trails loop around **Alligator Lake Recreation Area** (386-719-7545; columbiacountyfla.com), 420 SE Alligator Glen, Lake City. Colonies of herons nest in the willows. Paddle a kayak across the placid water, or walk the gentle trails with your family. Closed Monday.

Along CR 135 north of White Springs, **Big Shoals State Park** (386-397-4331; floridastateparks.org/park/Big-Shoals), 18738 SE 94th Street, encompasses river bluffs and uplands overlooking the roughest whitewater on the Suwannee River. Hike or mountain bike trails along the river bluffs, or put in your kayak or canoe for a paddle down to the shoals. You should use the portage on the south shore if you're not experienced with whitewater; canoes have been ripped open on the rocks. The lower entrance of the park, with a "Little Shoals" sign at 11330 SE CR 135, is primarily for access to the Woodpecker Trail (see *Biking*). Fee.

Along the Florida-Georgia border, 37,736 acres surrounding the headwaters of the St. Mary's River are under the protection of **John M. Bethea State Forest** (904-259-2157; freshfromflorida.com), 11656 FL 2, Sanderson. Adjoining Osceola National Forest to the east while straddling FL 2 and CR 125, it offers unpaved access to a number of fishing holes and primitive camping areas while providing wildlife connectivity to the Okeefenokee Swamp.

✦ ♿ ☙ At one of Florida's oldest state parks, **O'Leno State Park** (386-454-1853; floridastateparks.org/park/Oleno), 410 SE O'Leno Park Road, High Springs, the Santa Fe River vanishes into a riversink and flows underground for several miles. A network of hiking trails winds through shady hardwood forests, leading to the river rise. A small museum recaps the history of the Civilian Conservation Corps's work on this and other state parks. There are two major camping loops, Magnolia and Dogwood, with 61 campsites under the canopy of the forest. There is also a large historic group camp with 1930-vintage cabins (no heat or A/C) and a capacity of 120 people, which sits above the river near the swinging bridge. Sites at the primitive backpack camping area on Sweetwater Lake are 3 miles in along the hiking trail and first-come, first-served; the camping area has a fire ring and a privy. Pay $5 at the park entrance for this backcountry site. Day-use fee.

Osceola National Forest (386-752-2577; fs.usda.gov/osceola) is the smallest of Florida's three national forests. For an orientation to recreation in the forest, stop at the ranger station (see *Guidance*). Walk the short nature trail at Mount Carrie Wayside for an introduction to the longleaf pine and wiregrass habitat, then head to Olustee Battlefield Historic State Park (see *Museums and Historic Sites*) to follow the **Nice Wander Trail**, a 2-mile loop along the Florida Trail through red-cockaded woodpecker habitat. To see the wilder side of the forest, visit the **Big Gum Swamp Wilderness**, where the Florida black bear roams. Another access point is from the Sanderson Rest Area on the westbound side of I-10, where the **Fanny Bay Trail** leads you half a mile to a boardwalk into Fanny Bay, a floodplain forest with giant cypresses. The **Florida Trail** (see *Hiking*) provides 20 miles of backpacking across the forest. Watch a picture-perfect sunset between the cypress trees at **Ocean Pond Campground** (386-752-2577; fs.usda.gov/osceola). The primary full-service campground inside the national forest, Ocean Pond has a special appeal thanks to its perch on its namesake lake, great for fishing, kayaking, and even a little swimming. The campground has both tent sites with a nearby bathhouse and RV sites, all situated in the shade of tall pine trees, $8–18. Osceola National Forest also has other limited-facility and primitive campgrounds scattered throughout the forest; see their website for locations.

With nearly 2,600 acres and several access points, **St. Marys Shoals Park** (904-259-3613), Odis Yarborough Road, Glen St. Mary, managed by Baker County, has both front-country and backcountry fun. Two miles of riverfront have white-sand shoals to swim from, but there are also historic trails to follow and deep, dark cypress swamps. Dedicated areas for equestrians as well as 17 miles of ATV trails [30.344069, -82.193670] open on weekends lead through both natural forests and planted pines.

✎ ♿ ☀ ✧ The mission of **Stephen Foster Folk Culture Center State Park** (386-397-4331; floridastateparks.org/park/Stephen-Foster), 11016 Lillian Saunders Drive, White Springs, is to preserve Florida's folk culture heritage. Home to the Florida Folk Festival (see *What's Happening*), the park holds folklore-oriented weekends throughout the year, along with a permanent crafts village. A museum recounts the musical heritage of Stephen Collins Foster, a Pittsburgh songwriter who never set foot here. A towering carillon, one of only two in Florida, chimes frequently and plays old-time tunes that ripple across the waters of the Suwannee River at the base of the bluff. The Florida Trail (see *Hiking*) passes right through the park, staying close to the river atop bluffs topped with fragrant blooms of wild azalea each March. Camping in this park is a delight, among its deeply shaded campground and quiet cabins perched above the river. Set up your tent at one of 45 sites under the ancient live oaks, $20, or rent one of their beautiful two-bedroom cabins with screened porch, $100. Leashed pets welcome in campground, not in cabins.

✎ ♿ ☀ ✧ Although **Suwannee River State Park** (386-362-2746; floridastateparks .org/park/Suwannee-River), 3631 201st Path, Live Oak, boasts some of the best views you'll get of the Suwannee River; you're missing out if you don't take them in from the hiking trails around the park, including the connector to the Florida Trail that crosses the old US 90 highway bridge, now a recreational corridor. Historic Civil War earthworks sit above the confluence of the Withlacoochee and Suwannee rivers. In addition to its RV and tent sites ($20) set in a lush forest not far from the river, the park also has modern cabins, $100.

Spanning both sides of the Suwannee at its confluence with the Withlacoochee, **Twin Rivers State Forest** (386-208-1460; freshfromflorida.com) covers nearly 15,000 acres of thick hardwood forest and timberlands. In addition to seasonal hunting, it provides access to the Suwannee River for anglers and boaters and hosts an extensive network of biking, equestrian, and hiking trails, including the Florida Trail.

SPRINGS In the town of Branford, **Branford Springs** is the centerpiece of **Ivey Memorial Park**, 614 SW Ivey Memorial Drive, downtown off US 27 at the Suwannee River bridge. Continue upriver via the Suwannee River Greenway or highway to reach lovely **Little River Springs**, 24891 105 Lane, O'Brien, set below steep-forested bluffs. Both it and nearby **Royal Springs**, 157th Lane, are excellent swimming holes managed by Suwannee Parks & Recreation (386-362-3004; suwanneeparks.com). Farther upriver, ☀ ♿ at **Wes Skiles Peacock Springs State Park** (386-776-2194; floridastateparks.org/park/Peacock-Springs), 18532 180th Street, Live Oak, a one-lane dirt road winds through deep woods past pull-offs leading to sinkholes that interconnect underground, forming a karst playground for cave divers. A nature trail traces aboveground the route that divers are following below. Fee.

On the opposite side of the Suwannee off US 27, **Ruth Springs** is a third-magnitude spring open for swimming and diving. You'll see a sign for it on the way to **Troy Springs**

DIVERS EMERGING FROM MADISON BLUE SPRING

State Park (386-935-4835; floridastateparks.org/park/Troy-Spring), 674 NE Troy Springs Road, Branford. The water here is nearly 75 feet deep and contains the remains of the *Madison*, a steamboat scuttled in 1861 when her owner left to fight for the Confederacy in Virginia. There are ♿ ⚓ rental cabins on stilts at **Lafayette Blue Springs** (386-294-1617; floridastateparks.org park/Lafayette-Blue-Springs), 799 NW Blue Spring Road, Mayo, available for $100 per night, as well as a simple campground for paddlers and car campers with tents, $10. But the springs are the primary feature of this park, both above and below a bluff, with a limestone bridge between the two lower pools.

♿ **Madison Blue Spring State Park** (850-971-5003; floridastateparks.org/park/Madison-Blue-Spring) provides visitors a cool natural pool along the Withlacoochee River at FL 6; fee. ⚓ At **Suwannee Springs** (north of Live Oak off US 129 before the river bridge), a warm sulfur spring pours into a turn-of-the-twentieth-century spa building before flowing out into the river. Expansive beaches make this a cool weekend hangout. Along US 90 east of Suwannee River State Park, **Falmouth Spring** [30.362018, -83.134861] is an unusual geologic formation called "the shortest river in the world," 450 feet from spring rise to river sink.

♿ Powder-blue hues across limestone rocks in a natural basin define **Ichetucknee Spring**, found at the north end of **Ichetucknee Springs State Park** (386-497-4690; floridastateparks.org/park/Ichetucknee-Springs), 8294 SW Elim Church Road. It's the headwaters of a wild and scenic river popular for tubing and paddling; fee.

SKYDIVING Jump out of an airplane at **Squires Aviation Ranch** (386-938-4800; squiresar.com), 3502 NW 44th Street, Jasper, where they offer tandem skydiving. If you already have skydiving experience, this is your kind of place. They have four dedicated jump planes they use during the week to let you jump solo for fun, as well as training courses in wingsuit, canopy, and water training. Rental gear available, and cabins on site so you can fly in to stay and play.

SWIMMING Not all of the springs (see *Springs*) in the area are appealing or acccessible for swimming, but the ones that are do get busy in the summer months. In Branford, **Little River Springs** is close to town and has shallows on the rocks, with several entrances into the spring basin. For those who like to leap, **Royal Springs** has an outstanding high jump that can accommodate two or three jumpers holding hands to plunge into its 42-depths. Both are free. While you pay to enter **Ichetucknee Springs State Park**, the head spring is a beautiful place to swim around and observe the water's flow; both swimmers and divers are permitted in Blue Hole.

Bob's River Place (352-542-7363; bobsriverplace.com), 2878 CR 340, Branford, is an old-fashioned swimming hole on the Suwannee River, with metal slides, rope swings, swimming platforms, and sandy beaches. 11 AM–6 PM during season, fee.

✎ Head to **Suwannee Springs** for some freebie swimming and sunning on the **natural white-sand beaches of the Suwannee River**. For a lakefront swimming beach, try **Cherry Lake Beach** (850-973-4640; madisoncountyfl.com), CR 253 [30.621959, -83.419840], Madison.

TUBING The most popular tubing run in the state, the Ichetucknee River flows forth from **Ichetucknee Springs** (see *Springs*) to create a 6-mile crystalline stream that winds through deep, dark hardwood forests. Pick up a rental tube at any of the many small shops along US 27; **Ichetucknee Tube Center** (386-497-2929; ichetucknee-tube-center .com), 7354 SW Elim Church Road, is near the park's north entrance/put-in. Leave your rental tube in the tube corral at the end of the day for the outfitters to reclaim. A shuttle service gets you back to your car; fee. Tubing season runs from the end of May through early September.

TUBERS FLOATING DOWN THE SPRING-FED ICHETUCKNEE RIVER

U-PICK ✐ At **Rooney's Front Porch Farm** (386-590-9053; rooneyfarm.com), 8611 47th Drive, Lake City, show up in late spring to pick your own blueberries and thornless blackberries. Monday–Saturday 7 AM–8 PM during picking season.

Scott's Blueberry Farm (386-963-4952), 4984 124th Street, Wellborn. Watch for the signs off US 90 that say FOLLOW THE YELLOW DIRT ROAD and do just that, to one of the region's most popular U-picks. In season mid- to late May.

WALKING TOURS In Lake City, the **Lake Isabella Residential District** covers 30 blocks, and the downtown historic district encompasses another 15 blocks. Pick up a walking tour brochure at the Columbia County Historical Museum (see *Museums and Historic Sites*). The **Madison County Chamber of Commerce** can also provide you with a walking tour brochure for their extensive historic downtown.

WATERFALLS While Florida isn't known for its waterfalls, the Upper Suwannee has them! Start with the showiest and easiest to reach, **Falling Creek Falls** (386-758-2123; floridahikes.com/fallingcreek) off Falling Creek Road, Lake City [30.257817, -82.668633]. A quarter-mile, accessible boardwalk leads to the root-beer-color cascade, which plummets ten feet over a deep lip of limestone.

Visit **Robinson Branch Falls** (floridahikes.com/florida-trail-big-shoals) to the north of here by driving to Bell Springs [30.329298,-82.689613] and following the blue blazes north for a mile; the creek pours over an escarpment and into a ravine to the river.

In **Camp Branch Conservation Area** along CR 25A [30.3778,-82.8789] north of White Springs, a 2-mile walk gets you views of the disappearing creek (floridahikes .com/disappearingcreek) churning through hydraulics before plunging into a deep sinkhole.

WATER PARK ✐ At the **water park at Jellystone Campground** (see *Campgrounds*) in Madison, a 60-foot-tall, 300-foot-long spiral waterslide splashes down into a small lake lined with kids' activities, from playground equipment, boats, and water sprinklers to the nearby mini golf, train ride, lazy river, and kayaks in the lake. $20 per person for day use. Water park and other kids' activities are seasonal, so call ahead.

❋ Lodging

BED & BREAKFASTS ♂ ((ᵍ)) 🐾 ✐ In the historic Bishop-Andrews Hotel, **Grace Manor** (888-294-8839 or 850-948-5352; gracemanorinn.com), 117 SW US 221, Greenville 32331, is the grand dame of Ray Charles's hometown, a romantic 1898 Queen Anne Victorian with sweeping porches. Four double guest rooms, including a Honeymoon Suite, offer old-time charm with modern upgrades, $85–125. Innkeeper Brenda Graham takes your needs into consideration as she plans each healthful gourmet breakfast; optional dinners available. A swimming pool sits in the gardens, where a two-bedroom, pet-friendly cottage is perfect for families, $135.

♂ A 1905 boardinghouse, **White Springs Bed & Breakfast** (386-397-4252; whitespringsbnb.com), 16630 Spring Street, White Springs 32096, offers a casual getaway with historic touches, from the heart pine floors and pillared main fireplace to the restored 200-year-old antique German beds. Six spacious rooms come in various shapes and shades; a favorite is the Magnolia Room, with its canopied bed and tiled fireplace. $85 and up.

QUIET RETREAT 🌸 ♿ With its porches and rocking chairs overlooking the Suwannee River, **Village Lodge**

(800-371-8381 or 386-658-5200; acvillage
.net), 11097 Dowling Park Drive, Dowling
Park 32060, is a tranquil getaway in the
heart of Advent Christian Village, the
state's oldest retirement community. Follow the walkways to enjoy the chapel,
find an observation deck over the river,
or walk the Milford Clark Nature Trail
(see *Hiking*). Large, immaculate rooms,
$85 and up; no pets or alcohol.

RETRO AND ARTSY (ᵒ) ✿ **Cindy's
Motel** (386-294-1212; cindysmotel.com),
487 W Main Street, Mayo 32066,
reminds us of the places we stayed as
kids when traveling through Florida, and
indeed, it's straight from the 1960s,
although the rooms have been updated.
The nine-room motel is tucked under a
lovely canopy of live oaks, where they
also have a few RV sites available.

TRIED AND TRUE A crossroads where
I-10 and I-75 meet, Lake City has plenty
of chain hotels and motels to choose
from. Some of our go-to choices over the
years have been the ♿ (ᵒ) ↬ **Holiday Inn
Hotel & Suites Lake City** (386-754-1411;
ihg.com), 213 SW Commerce Drive; ✿ ♿
✿ (ᵒ) **Home2 Suites** (386-487-9890;
hilton.com), 414 SW Florida Gateway
Drive; ♿ (ᵒ) **Hampton Inn & Suites** (386-
487-0580; hilton.com), 450 SW Florida
Gateway Drive; and ♿ (ᵒ) **Country Inn &
Suites** (386-754-5944; countryinns.com),
350 SW Florida Gateway Drive.

DIVE RESORTS (ᵒ) Cave divers visiting
Branford stay at (ᵒ) **Steamboat Dive Inn**
(386-935-2283; steamboatdiveinn.com),
corner of US 129 and US 27, Branford
32008, which provides basic motel
accommodations and suites ($50–80)
with dive instructors and "ice cold air"
on-site.
    At (ᵒ) **Suwannee River Rendezvous
Resort** (see *Campgrounds*), the Hilltop
Motel and Lodge rooms ($70) are diver-
friendly; step out and walk down the
path, and there you are at Convict Spring
along the Suwannee River. Consider it

inspiration and a swimming hole rather
than a dive spot; the owners can show
you a video of this dangerous route,
with a restricted entrance that requires
sidemounts. Ask about canoe rentals to
explore nearby springs.

HUNTING LODGE ♂ (ᵒ) Set on nearly
15,000 acres, **Bienville Plantation** (386-
397-1989; bienville.com), 16673 SE 81st
Drive, White Springs, provides a place
for hunters and anglers to get outdoors
no matter the season. Their primary
focus is guided Southern-style quail
hunting, but they also offer trophy alligator hunts, guided fishing, skeet shooting,
and falconry training. Rent the full
White Tail Lodge with 10 beds for $400,
or a room with two double beds in a cabin
with shared great room and full kitchen,
$195. Meal plans available. In addition to
their sportsman's focus, they host the
Party in the Pines, an outdoor music festival (see *Music Festivals*), and provide a
beautiful backdrop and amenities for
weddings.

COTTAGES ✿ ♂ A collection of six
cottages, each with its own full kitchen
and screened porch, **Ichetucknee Hideaway Cottages** (386-935-0844;
ichetuckneehideawaycottages.com),
22665 35th Drive, Lake City 32024, $90–
120, provide a quiet, genteel retreat
within a few minutes, drive of Ichetucknee Springs State Park (see *Springs*),
closer to Branford than Lake City.

CAMPGROUNDS ♂ (ᵒ) The closest
camping to Ichetucknee Springs is **Ichetucknee Family Canoe & Cabins** (866-224-
2064 or 386-497-2150; ichetuckneecanoe
andcabins.com), 8587 SW Elim Church
Road, Fort White 32038, just west of the
state park. Rustic cabins ($50–60) sleep
up to 6, and camping for tenters and RVs
($16–22) is just upstream from one of the
region's most beautiful springs; they provide tube rentals and offer float trips
with pickup at the take-out, for easy
return to your car.

CABINS ON STILTS AT LAFAYETTE BLUE SPRINGS STATE PARK

🐾 ⚓ ♿ The family-oriented **Jellystone Park Campground** (850-973-8269 or 800-347-0174; jellystoneflorida.com), 1051 Old St. Augustine Road, Madison 32340, is a camping resort with its own water park (see *Water Park*) and has a little something for everyone, with campsites and cabins to accommodate all needs and special events held almost every weekend. $45–95 for campsites; $85–350 for cabins, which range from a playful chuck wagon with bunk beds to comfortably refurbished portable classrooms with enough space for the entire family. Two- to three-night minimum required for holidays and special events. No bathrooms provided in low-end cabins; nearby bathhouses are shared with campers. Pets permitted, but not in cabins.

🐾 **Kelly's RV Park** (844-695-7527; kellysrvpark.com), 142 NW Kelly Lane, White Springs 32096 off US 41 south of town, has sites for RVs and tents ($31), and roomy rental cabins ($62) with screened porch, air-conditioning, and heat set in a deeply shaded park with nature trails that lead to the adjoining Gar Pond Tract. Wi-Fi available at the clubhouse. Pets welcome for a fee.

🐾 ⚓ (ᵂⁱ) North of I-10, **Lake City Campground** (386-752-9131; lakecitycampground.com), 4743 N US 441, Lake City 32055, is a former KOA with sites nicely tucked into the woods and family-friendly amenities like a pool, playground, nature trail, and fishing pond. With easy access to both downtown shopping and outdoor recreation in the Osceola National Forest, it's a nice choice for a getaway. Camping options include pull-through RV or tent sites, $20–38; rustic cabins near the bathhouse, $38–40; cottages with bunk beds, $58; and lodges with full kitchen, $85.

🐾 (ᵂⁱ) ♿ ⚓ Under the canopy of live oaks along the river at **Suwannee River Rendezvous Resort & Campground** (386-294-2510; suwanneeriverrendezvous .com), 828 NE Primrose Road, Mayo 32066, this expansive riverfront resort features a large playground, swimming

SPIRIT OF THE SUWANNEE

Both a campground and a concert venue, 🚣 🐾 ♿ Spirit of the Suwannee Music Park and Campground (800-224-5656 or 386-364-1683; musicliveshere.com), 3076 95th Drive, Live Oak 32060 off US 129 at the Suwannee River, is a gathering place, no matter why you're here. Spread out across 700 thickly wooded acres along the Suwannee River, they hold events that draw up to 20,000 people and they still don't run out of space. There are 14 different camping styles and areas on their reservation form, starting with simply pitching your tent, no frills but a bathhouse, $25. Depending on the hookups you need, camping rates run $30–45. Equestrians have their own camping area, with stall rentals available. Cabin rentals include bath and kitchen, $85–140. Some cabins (and all campsites) are pet friendly. Pets are welcome, except during festivals and other special events.

And then there are the treehouses. The **Spirit Treehouse**, which in 1998 was Oregon treehouse architect Michael Garnier's first commission for a client, sits in the middle of the concert grounds and can be rented for $165, except during concerts. That's when the Cornett family, who founded this park more than 30 years ago, get to enjoy it. Jean Cornett asked Michael to come back in 2015 to build a second treehouse, an elegant three-story home in a 175-year-old live oak rising above the riverbank. They called the tree the **Mother Tree**. Before the treehouse was complete, Jean passed away, but the house is a lovely legacy to her family. Construction of this unique 450-square-foot treehouse was documented on the DIY Network *Treehouse Guys* show. We had the delight of touring it soon after it was completed. This new treehouse is for family use, although they admit someday they may open it to the public. Tours may be available.

Weekly rates are available for all camping, and for good reason: this is a destination with so much to do, even if you're not here for a concert. There are many miles of trails for equestrians and hikers, with connections to public lands so you can roam all day. A **Craft Village** is open on weekends, and it's adjoined by the **Boatright Barn Museum**, full of old-time farm implements. Birders can ramble the quiet bird sanctuary on Rees Lake, where catch-and-release fishing is also welcome. An on-site outfitter, **Suwannee Canoe Outpost** (see *Paddling*) can assist with rentals and shuttles. Rent bikes for $25 per day or bring your own. Campers often gather at dusk to watch the bats fly from the largest known bat house in the United States; they estimate half a million bats can roost here during the day. Families appreciate the swimming pool, which isn't far away from an old-fashioned arcade room complete with pinball machines and PacMan. The park has its own restaurant, **SOS Cafe**, serving all meals six days a week. And since this is a music park, don't be surprised to stumble across impromptu jams at campsites and pavilions; the **Suwannee River Bluegrass Association** meets every Saturday night at 6 in the Pickin' Shed.

area, canoe and kayak rentals, and a swimming spring—Convict Spring—right on the site. For lodging, take your pick from tenting under the oaks, $20–30; 136 full-hookup sites, $35–40, with weekly and monthly rates available; basic rooms in the motel, $70; and a broad variety of rental cabins, which range from pretty log cabins ($100) to full houses, including an A-frame, $190. Pet owners will appreciate the dog washing station and dog park. Rent kayaks and canoes on-site.

✳ Where to Eat

BARBECUE With several locations around the region, including three in Lake City, **Ken's Bar-B-Que** (386-752-5919), 1659 US 90, Lake City, is a favorite when we roll through town. In addition to the usual smoked fare, they have marinated grilled chicken, New York strip, and a nice selection of light platters and BBQ-topped jumbo tossed salads. Sandwiches and lunch specials, $4–10;

platters and dinners, $8–15. Closed Tuesday and Sunday.

CASUAL FARE When friends took us to **The Brown Lantern** (386-362-1133), 417 E Howard Street, it was a new find hidden in plain sight—it's closed on weekends, so we were never in town when it was open! The atmosphere is pure pub, with a porch out front, and as the shrimp came recommended, we feasted on it. Get the grilled veggies as a side. It can take time to get your meal, as everything is made to order. Sandwiches and salads, $8–13; entrées, $9–19. Monday–Friday 11 AM–9:30 PM.

Unpretentious but delicious, **Chasteen's** (386-752-7504; chasteens downtown.com), 204 N Marion Avenue, established in 1978, is *the* gathering place in downtown Lake City, being across from City Hall. For something light, go with delicious Fandangled Salad—spring greens, feta, toasted pecans, and seasonal fruit—or enjoy a trio of Bam Bam Chicken sliders. You can make a meal of sides like the sweet potato patties, broccoli salad, congealed salad, and corn nuggets. Of course, there are classics like a grilled pork chop or cod filet, hamburgers, and Boar's Head deli sandwiches. Serving lunch 11 AM–2 PM Monday–Friday, $3–12. Save room for their freshly baked cookies, cakes, and pie!

🍴 With mouthwatering pies on display when you walk in, you know you'll save room for dessert. The **Dixie Grill & Steer Room** (386-364-2810; thedixiegrill .com), 101 Dowling Avenue, Live Oak, is where the politics of Suwannee County get resolved over coffee. Breakfasts—served all day—range from Bubba's Basic to a Bananas Foster waffle topped with ice cream, and their French toast is made with custard batter. Lunches and dinners offer up buttermilk-dipped fried pork chops, beef liver, chicken gizzards, and their famous fried chicken. While the menu tips to mainstream Southern, there are some creative breakouts like the James Brown—panko-breaded chicken breast with sriracha, bacon,

avocado, and swiss; Mom's Salad with artisanal lettuce, sunflower seeds, and green peas; and the FGTBLT, melding fried green tomatoes to a saucy BLT. Enjoy a hearty meal for $11 and under, 5:30 AM–9 PM daily.

Inside a former drugstore, the nifty **Norris Cafe** (850-973-2552; facebook .com/norriscafemadison), 140 Range Street, serves up breakfast in the morning, followed by a bevy of sandwiches and salads that satisfy, from turkey & cheese to French dip and BLTs, and even PB&J, $3–6. Closed Sunday.

COMFORT FOOD 🍴 The Stormant family serves up fine Southern fare at **Fat Belly's** (386-397-2040), 16750 Spring Street, White Springs. Barbecue is the mainstay here, but they open early for breakfast for folks headed out to enjoy the outdoors, and they make great pancakes, eggs, and grits. Stop by and fill yourself up! Meals mostly under $10. Monday–Saturday 5 AM–9 PM.

At 3 PM on a Monday, the parking lot is packed. That's because everyone in the tri-county area knows that **Mayo Cafe** (386-294-2127), 850 Main Street(US 27), Mayo, has great home cooking, buffet style. Try the wide variety of chilled salads at the salad bar as well as southern comfort foods like fried chicken, fried okra, and collard greens. Make a meal of the lunch or dinner buffet for under $10; breakfasts are standards off the menu, $2–13. Daily 7 AM–9 PM.

🍴 Now, *this* is an all-you-can-eat. **O'Neal's Country Buffet** (850-973-6400), 558 Base Street, Madison, offers a spread under $15 that boggles the mind with great Southern cooking. Start with ribs, catfish, whitefish, or fried chicken and pile on the creamed corn, yams, cheese grits, sour cream potatoes, and baked beans. Your waitress will bring you crystal-clear homemade lemonade or perfect sweet tea, and you can finish up with cherry cobbler or banana pudding. There are dozens of other choices, too, but come early or late—this place is packed at noon!

Sunday–Thursday 10:30 AM–2:30 PM, Friday until 9 PM, Saturday 4–9 PM.

 Open early for breakfast, **Shirley's Restaurant** (386-755-9130), 746 E Duval, Lake City, is a go-to place for hearty country breakfasts—yes, you can get your country fried steak with sausage gravy, eggs, and grits. Their "metal wallpaper," an outstanding collection of antique auto license plates, will please any car buff. Most meals under $10. Open 5 PM–2 AM, closed Sunday.

Southern cooking is the theme of **Sisters Cafe** (386-935-6989), 26804 FL 247, Branford, home of the local country buffet. Fridays they feature seafood, and you'll usually find Southern fried chicken; you can order meals from the menu as well. Sandwiches, salads, and baskets, $5–7; Lunch buffet $5–8, Friday evening seafood buffet $12.

QUICK BITE Boasting "World Famous Subs," the **Live Oak Sub Shop** (386-362-6503), 511 S Ohio Avenue, Live Oak, a local landmark, piles it on with massive sandwiches ($4–9) good for a picnic on the Suwannee River. Open 10 AM–4 PM Monday–Friday.

SEAFOOD **Pier 6 Seafood & Steak House** (904-259-6123), 853 S 6th Street, Macclenny, has a loyal clientele devoted to their heaping seafood platters for two: Order fried or steamed, with shrimp, oysters, scallops, crab, and fish filets, $31. The variety of seafood is pretty broad across their entrées, from whole catfish to gator tail and frog legs, mahi, pollock, tilapia, and stuffed cod or flounder, $12–16, and fried baskets for $7. Mix and match chicken or steak with your seafood, too. Daily 11 AM–9 PM.

✳ Selective Shopping

ANTIQUES The building has dominated downtown White Springs for more than a century, but only in the past decade has it come to life again. **Adams Country Store**

(813-986-3597), 16536 Spring Street, White Springs, is both a landmark and a lovely collection of antiques, showcased in vignettes that honor the past of this historic town. Need a spinning wheel, a hand-carved wooden bedframe, a quilt, or an antique wardrobe? You'll find it here. Thursday–Saturday 10 AM–4 PM.

Antiques North-South Connection (386-758-9280), 248 SW Webbs Glen at I-75 and US 441 exit 414, Lake City. Five thousand square feet. One owner. Loads of antiques. Literally: a new truckload comes in every week. Look for beaded Victorian lamps, quilts, milk bottles and country kitchen implements, Christmas decor, and row upon row of funky saltcellars.

For summer fun, **Madison Antiques Market & Interiors** (850-973-9000; madisonantiquesmarket.com), 197 SW Range Avenue, Madison, had an entire tableau of water-skiers in vintage swimsuits filling their front window. This large downtown store is chock-full of treasures, including vintage clothing, fine antique furnishings, and classy glassware. Wednesday–Saturday 10 AM–5 PM.

Rachel's Farmhouse (904-259-2990), 238 E Macclenny Avenue, Macclenny. Step inside this old-time mercantile set in a historic home to browse primitives, local crafts, and old-fashioned farm implements. Antique furniture in various stages of restoration is scattered throughout the house and the porches.

Webb's Antique Mall (386-758-5564; webbsantiquemallfl.com), 245 SW Webbs Glen, Lake City at US 441/41 and I-10. With 300 dealer booths to roam, you can get lost in here for days, checking out items ranging from vintage tools and golf clubs to fine china, collectible Barbies, and church pews.

ARTS AND CRAFTS **Cousin Thelma's** is the gift shop at Stephen Foster Folk Culture Center State Park (see *Parks, Preserves, and Camping*) in White Springs, and thanks to the focus of the park, it's a shop full of Florida folk music, crafts, and books like the ones we write. There are turquoise-inlaid fine wood turnings by Tony Cortese, pine needle baskets, painted window folk art, and quilts by "Artist Lady" Ann Opgenorth. We find new treasures on every visit!

In the shops of Village Landing, the **Rustic Shop** (386-658-5273), 11097 Dowling Park Drive, Dowling Park, stands out with its mix of antiques, import items, and crafts, including fine quilts, pillows, and crocheted baby sets made by local residents. Open 10 AM–5 PM; closed Sunday.

BOOKS AND GIFTS **Franklin Mercantile** (904-566-1932), 7184 E Franklin Street, Glen St. Mary, is an old-time general store and post office in this once thriving citrus town. Step back a century as you browse through antiques, local crafts, and gifts.

Founded in 1951, **Ward's Jewelry & Gifts** (386-752-5470; wardsjewelry andgifts.com), 156 N Marion Avenue, Lake City, is one of the last remaining merchants downtown. They've always been the place for fine jewelry in the region, but they also carry a nice selection of china and servingware thanks to their bridal registry.

FARMERS' MARKETS **K. C.'s Produce** (386-752-1449), 1149 SE Baya, Lake City, is the most popular spot in Lake City to pick up a bunch of bananas or a pound of peppers—a great selection of fresh fruits and vegetables sold wholesale and retail. Closed Sunday.

Lake DeSoto Farmers Market (386-719-5766; market.lcfla.com), Marion & Duval, downtown Lake City, is a weekly market with produce and dairy from local farmers, Saturday 9 AM–1 PM.

SPECIALTY FOODS You'll never think the same of a convenience store again after a visit to **Busy Bee** (386-487-2935; shopthebusybee.com), 6458 US 129, Live Oak, at the I-10 interchange. This particular 24-hour gas station/truck stop/food court is the largest in this regional chain,

but when you walk inside, what a surprise. They have fresh fudge, a jerky bar, and baked goods made locally, plus their own in-house snacks, Bee Bits. Barrels of candy await for the pickin' by the pound, and there are plenty of gifts to take home, like jellies and sauces. The restrooms are over-the-top on how squeaky clean and fancy they are. Around the edges are convenience store basics like soda and freeze fountains, coffee, and snacks. Stop in and be surprised. The one at the Lake City I-10/US 41 exit is a smaller version but just as packed with cool stuff; there are more than a dozen such stores in the region, but this one is the king of the road.

✳ Special Events

FALL/WINTER The **Columbia County Fair** (386-752-8822; columbiacountyfair .org), 438 FL 247, a traditional agricultural fair with livestock judging, a barbecue festival, a midway, and a pro rodeo at the county fairgrounds, happens every fall between September and November. Check their website for exact dates.

Alligator Warrior Festival (alligatorfest.org), O'Leno State Park (see *Parks, Preserves, and Camping*), mid-October, celebrates the heritage of Columbia County, where the first settlement (now Lake City) was called Alligator Town. The event includes a reenactment of the 1836 Seminole War Battle of San Felasco Hammock and a Native American gathering with foods and crafts, with living history in a variety of history camps from the early days of Florida. During the festival, Lake City officially returns to its original name for the week by mayoral proclamation.

Pioneer Day Festival (386-590-7263), Veterans Town Park, Mayo, the second Saturday in October. This pioneer-theme event mixes up history and fun: Southern belles drift through town as staged gunfights rage; the crowd whoops and hollers at the rodeo while more sedate

REENACTMENT OF THE BATTLE OF OLUSTEE

visitors amble through hundreds of craft booths and an arts show.

Sponsored by the Suwannee Bicycle Association, the **Suwannee Fat Tire Festival** (suwanneebike.org) treats riders to mountain bike clinics, group rides, more than 50 miles of off-road riding, and paddling on the river. Held mid-October; register in advance online.

One of the top quilters gatherings in the Southeast, the **Suwannee River Quilt Show and Sale** (386-397-7009; whitesprings.org), held at Stephen Foster Folk Culture Center State Park (see *Parks, Preserves, and Camping*) each October, showcases quilting demonstrations, displays of quilts from regional guilds, and a mall of quilts for sale; fee.

⚓ Join Hamilton County in a celebration of the past during November at **Pioneer Days** (386-792-1668) at the Historical Museum and Heritage Center (see *Museums*) in Jasper, with antique farm equipment on display, horse-drawn wagon rides, and living history demonstrations.

⚓ The forest sparkles during the **Christmas Festival of Lights**, Stephen Foster Folk Culture Center State Park (see *Parks*), held throughout December. From dusk through 9 PM, take a horse-drawn carriage through the wonderland of more than four million Christmas lights, or ride in a slow line of vehicles along the park's looping road and wish you'd taken the carriage ride. Shops in the Craft Village will be open and selling their wares. Fee.

Suwannee Lights, Live Oak. A drive-through wonderland of light in Spirit of the Suwannee Music Park (see *Campgrounds*), including a miniature Victorian Christmas village and Santa's workshop. All December; fee.

Greenville Country Christmas (mygreenvillefl.com), Greenville, is held mid-December with a parade, bake-off, art contest, community caroling, and live entertainment centered around Haffye Hayes Park.

The **Battle of Olustee** (battleofolustee .org/reenactment.html), Olustee, the third weekend in February, is the largest Civil War reenactment in the Southeast, featuring living history encampments, a large sutlers' (period shopping) area, and battle reenactments on Saturday and Sunday; fee.

Lee Days (850-971-5867), Lee. A celebration of the heritage of this tiny Florida town, with arts and crafts and food vendors at the park. Mid-March.

SPRING/SUMMER **Suwannee County Fair** (386-362-7366; suwanneecountyfair.com), 1302 11th Street, at the Suwannee County Fairgrounds, held late March. A traditional, old-time county fair with judged livestock and vegetables; quilting, fine arts, and other crafts; commercial and educational exhibits; a popular midway; a talent show, and more.

Wild Azalea Festival (386-234-0817; whitesprings.org), the third Saturday in March, White Springs. Celebrate the fragrant blossoms that usher in spring on the Suwannee with arts, crafts, music, and food.

Step back in time at **Down Home Days** (850-973-2788; madisonfl.org/festivals.php), Madison, the third weekend of May, with a parade, traditional crafts and foods, a 5K, barbecue cookoff, antique auto show, and a frog hop that Mark Twain would be proud of. Early May.

Held at the Hamilton County Arena Complex, 165 Robin Avenue SW, Jasper, the annual **Hamilton County Championship Rodeo** encompasses all traditional rodeo events from barrel racing to bull riding and a drill team performance. Presented by the Hamilton County Riding Club, the second weekend May.

The annual **Florida Folk Festival** (877-635-3655; floridastateparks.org/folkfest), Memorial Day weekend at Stephen Foster Folk Culture State Park (see *Parks*) in White Springs, will get you in touch with the soul of Florida. In addition to more than 300 performances on over a dozen stages, you'll learn about Florida folklife traditions from all walks of life, pioneer to immigrant. Nationally acclaimed acts take the main stage in the evenings. More than 65 years old, it's one of the largest and most compelling music festivals for anyone who loves folk music: see *Music Festivals* for why.

✿ The **Wellborn Blueberry Festival** (386-963-1157; wellborncommunityassociation.com) celebrates the fruits of the harvest in June with a parade, talent content, live entertainment, and, of course, a blueberry bake-off. Free wholesome family fun!

✿ The **Wild Blackberry Festival** in downtown Jasper features a pancake breakfast, 5K run, live music, jams and jellies, and fun for the kids during the heart of blackberry season in the piney woods; the second weekend of June.

THE LOWER SUWANNEE

Dixie, Levy, and Gilchrist Counties
Cedar Key, Chiefland, and Trenton

I f you've come to Florida for peace and quiet, you'll find it "way down upon the Suwannee River" in a region known best for its rivers, springs, and estuaries, part of the laid-back western shore of Florida known as the Nature Coast. Settlers trickled into the region in the 1850s when state senator David Levy Yulee (son of Moses Levy, founder of Levy County) ran his Florida Railroad from Fernandina Beach to **Cedar Key,** providing the first shipping link across Florida. In 1867 naturalist John Muir followed the path of the Florida Railroad on his 1,000-mile walk to the Gulf of Mexico. Arriving at the Cedar Keys, he fell ill with malaria and spent several months living in the village, which had a booming pencil industry. The fine southern red cedars and white cedars growing on scattered islands throughout the Gulf made the perfect housing for pencil leads. The original settlement on Atsena Otie Key included several houses and the Eberhard Faber Pencil Mill. After the island was devastated by a tidal surge in 1896, business shifted to Depot Key, today's downtown Cedar Key.

Cedar Key sits between the mouth of the Withlacoochee River, where the towns of **Yankeetown** and **Inglis** sprang up, and the mouth of the Suwannee River, home to the fishing village of **Suwannee**. The railroad line (now the Nature Coast State Trail, a rail-trail) connected **Fanning Springs**, where Fort Fannin was built along the river in 1838 as part of a chain of forts during the Seminole Wars, with turpentine and lumber towns **Chiefland**, **Old Town**, and **Cross City**.

On the southern shore of the Steinhatchee River, the fishing village of **Jena** grew up around the abundant mullet and crab, with packinghouses shipping out seafood to distant ports. Dixie County boasts the lowest per-capita population in the state, and Gilchrist County has only a single traffic light, at the crossroads in the county seat of **Trenton**. Sleepy riverside hamlets and end-of-the-road fishing villages like **Suwannee** provide a natural charm found only in rural Florida.

GUIDANCE **Levy County Visitors Bureau** (877-387-5673; visitnaturecoast.com), 620 N Hathaway Avenue, Bronson, covers the coast from Inglis and Yankeetown to Cedar Key and Chiefland, and the inland communities of Bronson and Williston. **Gilchrist County TDC** (352-463-3467; visitgilchristcounty.com), 209 SE 1st Street, Trenton, provides information for their county on the east side of the Suwannee River, which includes the towns of Fanning Springs, Trenton, and Bell. On the west side of the river down to the Gulf of Mexico, Dixie County TDC (352-498-1403; visitdixie.com) showcases the natural side of their area online. **Natural North Florida** (naturalnorthflorida .com) is a coalition that provides information for this region as well.

GETTING THERE *By air:* **Gainesville Regional Airport** (352-373-0249; gra-gnv.com; see *Gainesville & Vicinity* chapter) provides the only "nearby" commuter access, an hour or more from most points on the Nature Coast.

By bus: **Greyhound** (352-493-4954), 1904 N Young Boulevard, stops along US 19 in Chiefland.

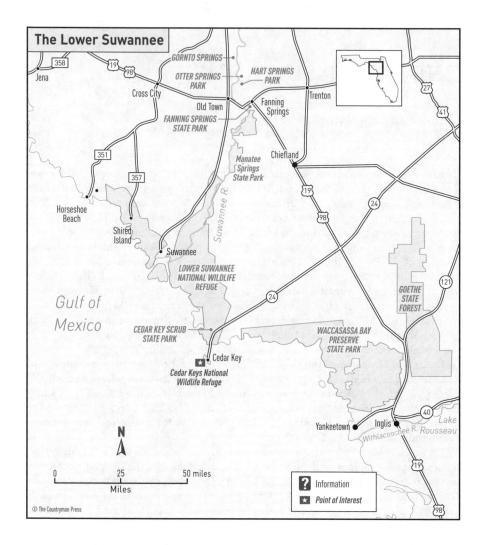

The Lower Suwannee

GORNTO SPRINGS
Jena
Cross City
Otter Springs Park
Hart Springs Park
Trenton
Old Town
Fanning Springs
FANNING SPRINGS STATE PARK
Chiefland
Manatee Springs State Park
Suwannee R.
Horseshoe Beach
Shired Island
Suwannee
LOWER SUWANNEE NATIONAL WILDLIFE REFUGE
Gulf of Mexico
GOETHE STATE FOREST
CEDAR KEY SCRUB STATE PARK
WACCASASSA BAY PRESERVE STATE PARK
Cedar Key
Cedar Keys National Wildlife Refuge
Yankeetown
Inglis
Lake Rousseau
Withlacoochee R.

N

0   25   50 miles
Miles

© The Countryman Press

Information
Point of Interest

By car: **Alt US 27**, **US 129**, and **US 19** are the major north–south routes through this trio of rural counties. To reach them from **I-75**, use **US 27** from Ocala or High Springs, or **FL 24** or **FL 26** west out of Gainesville.

GETTING AROUND This is a large rural area with many dead-end roads (some with no services) to the coast and to the Suwannee River. Make sure you have adequate gas in your tank before heading down the long roads to Cedar Key, Suwannee, Shired Island, and Horseshoe Beach. **Driving is a must** between points, unless you're **paddling** the coastline on the Historic Big Bend Saltwater Paddling Trail (a segment of the Florida Circumnavigational Trail; see *Paddling*) or **biking** the trails of the region (see *Biking*).

MEDICAL EMERGENCIES **Nature Coast Regional Hospital** (352-528-2801; regionalgeneral.com), 125 SW 7th Street, Williston, has a 24-hour ER. It's a small hospital but the only one in the region. Call 911 for emergencies—if you can get a signal—and realize that some points in this region are an hour or more away from medical help. Heading to Gainesville (see the *Gainesville* chapter) for non-emergencies may be the best choice if you're in Gilchrist or Dixie County.

✳ To See

ARCHAEOLOGICAL SITES At the end of CR 347 in Lower Suwannee NWR (see *Parks, Preserves, and Camping*), the quarter-mile **Shell Mound Trail** takes you to the most significant archaeological feature in this region, a 28-foot-tall shell midden created between 2500 BCE and CE 1000 by the ancestors of the Timucua who once inhabited this coastline. Just off CR 351 at Old Railroad Grade in Dixie County, the **Garden Patch Archaeological Site** at Horseshoe Beach has several burial and ceremonial mounds and two large middens from the Middle Woodland period, CE 100–500.

SNORKELING IN MANATEE SPRINGS

ART GALLERIES Intrigued by the stacks of driftwood outside **Catch the Drift** (352-542-7770), 26652 US 19, Old Town, I stopped to take a look and was glad I did. C. Emery Mills's longstanding gallery is all about nature as art, with local artists creating sculptures from wood, shells, and coral.

Adjoined by a whimsical art park created by its members, **The Cedar Keyhole** (352-543-5801), 457 2nd Street, Cedar Key, represents more than 20 local artists and a handful of consignments. Their gallery tempts with art in virtually every medium. Fused art glass captures the motion of ocean waves, and Cindy's gourd handbags add a touch of humor. Despite ceramic slugs and hand-painted dresses, the art reflects island themes. On the top floor is the **Cedar Key Arts Center** (cedarkeyartscenter.org), with ongoing gallery events, including nationally juried exhibits, and artist workshops.

ELEPHANTS 🐾 Since 1984, more than 200 elephants have called **Two Tails Ranch** (352-359-6676; allaboutelephants.com), 18655 NE 81st Street, Williston, home, but only in recent years has the public been able to meet the elephants boarded with exotic animal trainer Patricia Zerbini. On a tour of the 67-acre ranch, guests visit with the elephants, learn about elephant behavior, and see other exotic animals, such as zebras and ostriches. Tours $20 adult, $10 child, Friday–Wednesday; call ahead to schedule your visit.

GARDEN ♂ 🐾 The creative transformation of a limestone quarry into a series of gardens and ponds led to **Cedar Lakes Woods and Gardens** (352-529-0055;

cedarlakeswoodsandgarden.com), 4990 NE 180th Avenue, Williston, 20 acres of botanical beauty to roam. Thursday–Tuesday, 9:30 AM–5 PM; $12 adults, $7 ages 6–13.

MUSEUMS AND HISTORIC SITES **Atsena Otie Key**, abandoned by most of its settlers after an 1896 hurricane-driven storm surge, is now part of Cedar Key National Wildlife Refuge (see *Parks, Preserves, and Camping*), only accessible by boat. It was the "original Cedar Key," with a robust community and an Eberhard Faber Pencil Mill that relied on the bountiful coastal cedars for pencil making. Tombstones in the cemetery date back to 1882. **Seahorse Key**, also part of the island chain, has a small cemetery with Union soldiers who died while occupying Seahorse Key Lighthouse. The island can only be visited on open-house days announced by the refuge.

    ♻ At the **Cedar Key Historical Society Museum** (352-543-5549; cedarkeyhistorical museum.org), 609 2nd Street, Cedar Key, exhibits and artifacts trace the history of this coastal town from its founding through Civil War occupation, the rise and fall of the pencil industry, and advances in aquaculture. Sunday–Friday 1–4 PM, Saturday 11 AM–5 PM; donation.

    ♻ **Cedar Key Museum Historic State Park** (352-543-5340; floridastateparks.org/park/Cedar-Key-Museum), 12231 SW 166 Court, grew out of an effort by St. Clair Whitman, a colorful local man, who started his own museum in the 1920s. His house has been restored back to how it looked in his day. Open Thursday–Monday; fee.

    ♻ In Fanning Springs, **Fort Fanning Park** [29.591737, -82.936024], just north of US 19 at the Suwannee River, marks the site of the wooden 1838 US Army fort built at the river crossing as part of a string of defenses during the Second Seminole War. Nearly 200 men garrisoned the fort in 1843; it was abandoned in 1849.

    ♻ Amid the farms and fields of Levy County, quilting is one of the favored pastimes. Inside the **Levy County Quilt Museum** (352-493-2801), 11050 NW 10th Avenue, Chiefland, quilters come together to perfect their craft. The modern log structure contains plenty of space for active quilting while displaying prizewinning quilts around the rooms.

    Inside the 1910 Wade Building at the Suwannee Valley Shops is the emerging **Florida Quilt Museum** (352-316-3656), 409 N Main Street, Trenton, a display space for quilting shows as well as headquarters for the Florida Quilt Trail (floridaquilttrail.com) and the Suwannee Valley Quilt Festival (trentonquiltfestival.com). Monday–Saturday 11 AM–3 PM.

RAILROADIANA Although the railroad no longer carries cypress logs through Chiefland, Trenton, and Bell, these **train depots** along US 129 are put to good use. In Chiefland, the depot is the centerpiece of a small park that's the southern terminus of the Nature Coast Trail (see *Biking*). Call ahead to arrange a tour of the **City of Chiefland Trail Depot Museum** (352-493-1849; chieflandtraindepot.com), 23 SE 2nd Avenue, a collection of railroad ephemera and artifacts in this 1913 station. Monday–Friday, 10 AM–2 PM.

    The 1906 **Trenton Railroad Depot** serves as another trail terminus in a city park in Trenton, while the **Bell Trail Depot**, built in 1905, serves as Bell Town Hall. On US 19 in Cross City, the old **railway freight station** marks another end of the Nature Coast Trail near Barber Avenue.

    Along US 19, watch for "3 Spot," a **steam engine circa 1915**, in a small wayside park just north of the blinker at Gulf Hammock. One of the few pieces of original rolling stock displayed in Florida, it pulled logging cars to the Patterson-McInnes sawmill.

    At Cedar Key the **depot** marking the historic western terminus of the Florida Railroad is still on Railroad Street, but the trestle leading to the coast has been obliterated by condos. You can walk along the old railroad line on the **Cedar Key Railroad Trestle Nature Trail** off Grove Street [29.144801, -83.032668].

In Williston, chug into the past on a steam train ride at **Kirby Family Farm** (see *Train Rides*) as they hold periodic themed events for Easter, Halloween, Christmas, and more.

WINERY ♿ Established in 1985, **Dakotah Winery & Vineyards** (352-493-9309; dakotahwinery.com), 14365 NW US 19, Chiefland, features wines and other products produced from cultivated Carlos and Noble muscadine grapes. Antique windmills stand tall over the vineyard, and visitors relax under an arbor overlooking the vines and a duck pond. Inside the tasting room, owner Rob Rittgers buzzes around, answering questions and pouring wine for each new group of guests. Open Monday–Saturday.

✳ To Do

BIKING From its start in Dixie County at Cross City, the 32-mile **Nature Coast Trail** (352-535-5181; floridastateparks.org/trail/Nature-Coast) forks in Fanning Springs. One prong heads east to Trenton, ending at their historic train depot; the other heads south to end at the Chiefland railroad depot. Equestrians may use the grassy strip parallel to the paved biking trail.

Mountain bikers frequent the trail system at **Manatee Springs State Park** (see *Springs*). Off-road biking is also welcome on the unpaved Dixie Mainline Trail through California Swamp in Lower Suwannee NWR (see *Parks, Preserves, and Camping*), and touring riders will appreciate the many low-traffic rural routes through the region.

BIRDING You'll always see pelicans at the **Cedar Key dock**—just beware of getting too close! At **Cedar Key NWR**, each island has colonial bird rookeries and beautiful beaches; watch out for the high snake population in forested areas. **Seahorse Key** is off-limits to all visitors March–June due to its fragile pelican rookery. **Lower Suwannee NWR** offers great birding opportunities along the trails at Shell Island, where you'll see Louisiana herons, willets, and other wading birds in shallow saline ponds near Dennis Creek, and belted kingfishers along the hammocks in the **California Swamp**. In spring follow the **Road to Nowhere** (see *Scenic Drives*) through the **Jena Unit of Big Bend WMA**, and take the side roads (if wet, only navigable by four-wheel drive or on foot) west to the Gulf hammocks to see seaside sparrows, clouds of migratory birds (from robins to vireos and warblers), and nesting pairs of black rails. At any time, you'll see wading birds by the roadside in the salt marshes.

BOATING For a map of boat ramps along the **Suwannee River**, contact the Suwannee River Water Management District (386-362-1001; srwmd.state.fl.us); one of the easiest to access is off US 19 at the Gilchrist–Dixie county line in the old roadside picnic area. Recreational boaters enjoy playing on a segment of the **Cross Florida Barge Canal** accessed at Inglis off US 19. In Cedar Key parking gets tight around the **public marina** (downtown) on weekend mornings. **Island Tours** (352-231-4435 or 352-278-0065; cedar keyboatrentalsandislandtours.com), City Marina, rents boats and provides guided tours and island drop-offs on the Gulf of Mexico.

At Suwannee, the full-service **Gateway Marina** (352-542-7349; gatewaymarina.us), 90 SE 910th Avenue, has dockage, a ship's store, wet slips, and houseboat rentals (see *Houseboating*); there is also a boat ramp in town.

NEAR THE MOUTH OF THE SUWANNEE RIVER AT SHELL MOUND PARK

The main reason to head to **Horseshoe Beach** is to get on the water, and **The Marina in Horseshoe Beach** (352-498-5405; themarinainhorseshoebeach.com), 262 3rd Street, can help with their boat lift. They have dockage, marine gas, a marina store, and waterfront lounge. At Jena, Good Times Motel and Marina (352-498-8088;goodtimesmot elandmarina.com), 7022 CR 358, is on the Steinhatchee River, offering wet slips and pontoon boat rentals.

DIVING Scuba divers have several unique venues to try out their skills. At **Devil's Den** near Williston (see *Dive Resort*), a shimmering pool of 72-degree, ice-blue water fills an ancient cave. As you descend stone steps to access the open water underground, a chandelier of ivy dangles down through the sinkhole, with rays of sunlight filtering through the opening. It's a surreal and beautiful scene. Divers delight in discovering prehistoric fossils on the limestone bottom. Dive fee $38, gear rental $40 for full kit. Cave certification not required. Full dive shop and instruction on-site. Snorkelers pay $15–20; gear rentals $10.

At **Blue Grotto Springs** (352-528-5770; divebluegrotto.com), 3852 NE 172nd Court, cave-certified divers can descend up to 100 feet into the Floridan aquifer, dropping down into a cave system from the bottom of a sinkhole; dive shop with rentals on-site. Daily 8–5, night dives by appointment. $45 per diver, $90 if renting gear. Snorklers $15, only welcome if accompanying divers.

The many springs of the Suwannee River are open to open-water diving, but *only* cave-certified divers should venture into the crevices from which the waters pour. At **Manatee Springs**, both open water and cave diving is available to visitors who bring their gear and check in for a $10 dive fee. Both the head spring and a nearby karst window, Catfish Sink, are open to divers. Open-water divers are welcome at **Fanning**

Springs as well. Check the *Springs* section for these and other springs popular with divers.

Wreck diving on the Suwannee is a popular pastime, as divers can visit sunken steamboats such as the *City of Hawkinsville* (nps.gov/articles/cityofhawk.htm). Built in 1886, it was the very last of the Suwannee River steamboats, sunk just south of Fanning Springs in 1922. It's a designated underwater archaeological preserve.

ECOTOURS ⅏ **Captain Doug's Tidewater Tours** (352-543-9523; tidewatertours.com), Cedar Key, takes you out from City Marina on a catamaran for an interpretive cruise of Cedar Key from the water, followed by your choice of tours, including a cruise up the Suwannee River or through the islands that make up the Cedar Keys. $26–45 with discounts for ages 10 and under.

⚓ Catch a ride out to the outer islands of the Cedar Keys with **Island Tours** (see *Boating*), offering island drop-offs (perfect for exploring Atsena Otie or Seahorse Key), shelling tours, two-hour scenic cruises, and sunset cruises. $25 adults, $15 children under 12.

Explore the Withlacoochee River with **Osprey Tours** (352-400-0133; ospreyguides .com), 6115 Riverside Drive, on a seven-mile loop through the wildlife-rich estuary between Yankeetown and the river's mouth at the Gulf of Mexico. $25 per person, minimum 2; reservations suggested.

Paddle with knowledgeable local guide Brack Barker at **Wild Florida Adventures** (352-215-4396; wild-florida.com), where you'll explore the region's estuaries and waterways at a leisurely pace on a custom-tailored trip. Destinations include Cedar Key, Steinhatchee, Waccassa, and Suwannee, $50.

FISHING For recommended fishing guides and charters in **Cedar Key**, check in at the marina. **Lady Pirate Fishing** (352-486-4413) will take you out on their 22-foot pontoon for half a day of inshore fishing, $60 per person—or you can rent the whole boat and crew for $295/half day. **Grouper Therapy** (352-363-0244; groupertherapy.net) gets you out deep sea fishing with Captain GT. At **Hooked Up Charters** (352-949-0721; hookedupcharters.us), Captain John will fish either nearshore or offshore (30–50 miles out) sites, your choice, $475–925.

At Inglis, **Lake Rousseau** is a hot spot for bass anglers; check in at the fish camps (see *Fish Camps*) along CR 40 for guides.

HIKING The best hikes in this region—many of which are detailed in *50 Hikes in North Florida*—lead to scenic points along the Suwannee River and the Gulf of Mexico. Some of our favorites include the trail system and boardwalks at **Manatee Springs State Park**, the Dennis Creek Trail at **Lower Suwannee NWR**, and the boardwalk loop at **Hart Springs**. The **Cedar Key Railroad Trestle Nature Trail** (see *Railroadiana*) offers great views and birding with a different take on Cedar Key. One of our more recent finds, **Withlacoochee Gulf Preserve** (see *Parks, Preserves, and Camping*), has several miles of trails though the coastal estuary at Yankeetown. One constant about hiking anywhere near the Lower Suwannee River—ticks are a common problem except in the dead of winter. Use big doses of insect repellent before you hit the trails.

HORSEBACK RIDING With more than 100 miles of equestrian trails, **Goethe State Forest** (see *Parks, Preserves, and Camping*) is a major destination for riders. Look for trailheads at the Black Prong, Apex, and Tidewater Units along CR 336. Take a guided trail ride with Roberta Cogswell from **North Star Acres** (352-489-9848; dunnellonbusiness .com/northstar.htm), 9950 SE 125th Court, Dunnellon; call to reserve.

GOETHE TRAILHEAD RANCH

Camp across the street from the Apex trailhead with your horse at **Goethe Trail-head Ranch** (352-489-8545; goethetrailcamping.com), 9171 SE CR 337, $20 for stalls, $35–38 for full-hookup RV sites, and $65–95 for cabins.

♂ ☗ **Black Prong Equestrian Center** (352-486-1234; blackprong.com), 450 CR 337, serves the traveling equestrian community with access to the Goethe trails as well as a full training facility for dressage and obstacle events. $32–40 for stalls, $90–129 for apartments, $15–40 for campsites.

Cedar Ridge Ranch (352-325-0305; cedarkeycedarridgeranch.com), 13950 SW 77th Place, Cedar Key, boards horses ($10/night) while you visit Cedar Key and provides direct access for riding the trails of adjacent Cedar Key Scrub State Reserve.

HOUSEBOATING At **Gateway Marina** (352-542-7349; suwanneehouseboats.com), 90 SE 910th Avenue, Suwannee, rents a houseboat for a cruise up the 70-mile meander of the Suwannee River from Suwannee to Fanning Springs—head out for an overnight, a few days, or a week. In these 44-foot houseboats, you have all the amenities of home (minus the yard) as you drift past shorelines crowded with red maple and sweetgum and count the manatees. Rates vary by season and number of days, starting at $599 for two days and going up to $1,799 for a week.

PADDLING Two major paddling trails meet in this region. The lower Big Bend section of the **Florida Circumnavigational Saltwater Paddling Trail** (dep.state.fl.us/gwt/paddling/saltwater.htm) stretches 101 miles from Steinhatchee to Yankeetown. If that sounds like a lot of paddling, you're right, and it's extraordinarily remote. Don't set out unless you have the appropriate maps and navigational aids, camping gear, and plenty of fresh water and food. Logistics can be found on the trail's website. **The Marina in Horseshoe Beach** (see *Boating*) rents kayaks for day explorations on this coastal trail.

Along the **Suwannee River Wilderness Trail** (800-868-9914; floridastateparks .org/parks/suwannee-river-wilderness-trail), it's 55 miles from Gornto Spring to the mouth of the Suwannee alone. En route, five sites provide a place for you to launch from or camp overnight. Based where these two major paddling trails meet, **Suwannee Guides & Outfitters** (352-542-8331; suwanneeguides.com), Suwannee, can help you with rentals, logistics, and shuttles for any length of paddling expedition. Rentals $30/ day or $40/two days.

Anderson's Outdoor Adventures (352-507-0059; andersonsoutdooradventures .com) offers rentals of canoes, kayaks, and SUP ($15–35) as well as shuttles at parks along the Santa Fe and Suwannee rivers, including Manatee Springs, Hart Springs, Gilchrist Blue Springs (see *Springs*), and Santa Fe River Park, 8500 NE SR 47, High Springs. At Hart Springs, ask about their shuttle up to Otter Springs, so you can take it there and then paddle downriver between the two parks.

Kayak Cedar Keys (352-543-9447; kayakcedarkeys.com) rents kayaks and pad-dleboards ($25 and up) you can launch from the City Beach in downtown Cedar Key to explore the estuary or paddle over to Atsenie Otie Key. Since so many motels and campgrounds are on the water, there's a chance your lodging rents kayaks or canoes, too. Just ask.

PARKS, PRESERVES, AND CAMPING Most parks in this region are tied to springs (see *Springs*). But there are many wild spaces to roam, too. Along the Suwannee River, 5,000 acres of shoreline and uplands are a part of **Log Landing WMA** (386-362-1001; srwmd.state.fl.us), where spring wildflowers put on a show beneath a lush canopy of old-growth forest along the river floodplain [29.750916, -82.941745].

At Fanning Springs, **Andrews WMA** (386-758-0525; myfwc.com) is notable for the number of national and state champion trees in its dark riverside forests.

SPRING BLOOMS AT LOG LANDING

Inland, you'll find one of Florida's largest cypress trees among the 53,000 acres of **Goethe State Forest** (352-465-8585; freshfromflorida.com), which includes some of the oldest growth inland forest in the state. With multiple trailheads, it's a popular destination for hikers and equestrians (see *Horseback Riding*).

Along FL 24 on the way to Cedar Key, **Cedar Key Scrub State Reserve** (386-543-5567; floridastateparks.org/park/Cedar-Key-Scrub) has miles of sandy trails leading through Florida scrub-jay habitat and into coastal pine flatwoods overlooking the estuary [29.204539, -82.987923].

SCENIC DRIVES The **Dixie Mainline Trail** is a one-of-a-kind scenic drive, a 9-mile, one-lane, hard-packed limestone road through the wilds of the cypress-and-gum floodplain of the California Swamp in Lower Suwannee NWR (see *Parks, Preserves, and Camping*). Don't expect to drive more than 20 mph, and watch for oncoming traffic. There are pull-offs every mile to allow vehicles to pass. Check with the refuge before you go to make sure it's not flooded.

The **Road to Nowhere** doesn't lead to a home or a fishing pier: It was a clandestine airstrip for drug runners in the 1970s and '80s. Now part of Big Bend Aquatic Preserve, with unparalleled views of the salt marshes, it's an amazing place for photography, birding, and fishing. If you drive down it, go slow and pay careful attention—the road ends in the salt marsh without any warning. It's most easily accessed from CR 358 in Jena via Steinhatchee (see the *Tallahassee* chapter).

SPRINGS Freshwater bubbles up all along the Suwannee River and its tributaries, so this region is a big draw for spring hunters. Along the Santa Fe River, **Gilchrist Blue Springs** and **Ginnie Springs** are spectacular destinations with multiple springs; since they are close to the town of High Springs, see the *Gainesville & Vicinity* chapter for details. At Ellie Ray's RV Resort (see *Campgrounds*) on the Santa Fe north of Bell, grab a day pass to swim in the spring. Not far downstream, the Santa Fe flows into the Suwannee.

On the west side of the Suwannee River, **Gornto Springs**, off CR 349 and Rock Sink Church Road [29.779457, -82.940365], is a county park centered on an old-fashioned swimming hole, with a platform where folks jump into the 10-foot-deep water. A stop along the Suwannee River Wilderness Trail, it also has a small tent campground. Free.

✧ (((•))) On the east side of the Suwannee River, the spring in the most natural setting is **Otter Springs Park & Campground** (352-463-0800; ottersprings.com), 6470 SW 80th Avenue, Trenton 32693, and it will take your breath away with the setting of a spring surrounded by a canopy of ancient live oaks. Four cozy cabins with bath make the perfect getaway for couples or small families; bring your own linens and cleaning supplies, $82–93. A large stilt house with a screened porch in the trees sleeps up to 8, $115. Tent campers can pitch for $24, and full-hookup sites for RVs, trailers, and tents are $31. It's a pleasant walk down to the spring, but campers also enjoy access to a heated pool in a gigantic screen room, where Wi-Fi is available. Day-use fee.

✧ 🏕 **Hart Springs** (352-463-3444; hartsprings.com), 4240 SW 86th Avenue, Bell 32619, is a family-friendly swimming hole with a long boardwalk along the Suwannee River. You can rent canoes here as well, and you can arrange to be shuttled back to Otter Springs if you rented them there. Within sight of its namesake, the campground has a gorgeous primitive tent camping area beneath a canopy of ancient live oaks, not far from the spring, $20. A separate RV campground, connected to the springs area via a walking trail, offers full hookups and a heated pool, $25. Pets are permitted at the RV campground but not at the springs. Two three-bedroom house rentals are also available at $150, sleeping 6–8; two-night minimum. Day-use fee.

FLORIDA'S WILDEST SHORE

Most of this region has a wild and remote shoreline, for it's here that vast swamps edge the Gulf of Mexico. Almost a million acres of submerged shallows along the coast are managed as **Big Bend Seagrasses Aquatic Preserve** (dep.state.fl.us/coastal/sites/bigbend), essential habitat for fish and shellfish. Along the vast estuaries on its edge, **Big Bend WMA** (myfwc.com) stretches from Jena south through Horseshoe Beach, with limited access at places like the Road to Nowhere (see *Scenic Drives*).

Lower Suwannee National Wildlife Refuge (352-493-0238; fws.gov/refuge/lower_suwannee) protects the floodplain of the Suwannee River as it reaches the Gulf of Mexico. Most of the refuge is inaccessible except by boat, although there are short hiking trails at Shell Mound and the park headquarters; additionally, the Dixie Mainline Trail (see *Scenic Drives*) goes through the California Swamp.

Established in 1929, **Cedar Keys National Wildlife Refuge** (352-493-0238; fws.gov/refuge/cedar_keys) protects the offshore islands that are a critical habitat for colonial nesting birds. **Waccasassa Bay Preserve State Park** (352-493-0238; floridastateparks.org/park/Waccasassa-Bay), stretches across 31,000 acres of estuary and swamp forest in Gulf Hammock between Cedar Key and Yankeetown, and it is only accessible by boat [29.214050, -82.763564].

The final piece of the coastal puzzle is **Withlacoochee Gulf Preserve** (352-447-2511; wgpfl.org), 1001 Old Rock Road, Yankeetown, managed by the town itself. It provides the best spot to explore this wild coast, with a tall observation tower and miles of hiking trails with panoramic views of the estuary and coastal pine flatwoods.

COASTAL MARSHES AT WITHLACOOCHEE GULF PRESERVE

✒ ♿ ⚓ At **Fanning Springs State Park** (352-463-3420; floridastateparks.org/park/Fanning-Springs), 18020 NW US 19, Fanning Springs 32693, the spring and its swimming area are the focal points, but some visitors just come for a quiet stay. Their modern two-bedroom cabins include linens and dishes, but you're unplugged—no television, phone, or Wi-Fi. Read a book on the screened porch or watch the sun set over the spring basin. When you rise in the morning, you'll have the swimming hole all to yourself. $100. Day-use fee.

✒ ♿ 🎪 It's the spring that compels you to stare into its aqua depths at **Manatee Springs State Park** (352-493-6072; floridastateparks.org/park/Manatee-Springs), 11650 NW 115th Street, Chiefland, although the spring run, which you can follow on a boardwalk through a cypress swamp, is gorgeous too. True to the name of the place, manatees flock here in winter, and paddlers can see them along the spring run. With one of the more beautiful campgrounds in the region, the park tends to fill up quickly, despite there being 80 campsites along the three loops through the forest near the spring. Some sites are for tent camping only, others are gravel pads. All have electric and water, $20. Leashed pets are permitted, but not at the springs. Day-use fee.

Nearly 8,000 acres of the Waccasassa River's headwaters and floodplain are within **Devil's Hammock WMA** (386-758-0525; myfwc.com), which has miles of roads for biking, horseback riding, and hiking—and one major spring you can swim in. **Blue Springs** (352-486-3303), 4550 NE 94th PL, Bronson, creates a natural 72-degree pool as it feeds the Waccasassa River; fee. Near Williston, **Blue Grotto Springs** and **Devil's Den** cater to divers (see *Diving*).

SWIMMING For refreshing plunges into cool water, visit the region's springs (see *Springs*) at any time of year. Adjoining City Marina, **Cedar Key City Park** provides

PADDLERS AMONG THE MANATEES AT MANATEE SPRINGS STATE PARK

the village's only **public beach** on the Gulf of Mexico. Several motels in Cedar Key have their own private beaches, but the best beaches are found on the outer islands, accessed only by boat. Shallow Gulf waters invite bathers to small beaches at **Shired Island** (end of CR 357) and **Horseshoe Beach** (end of CR 351), both accessible via Cross City.

TRAIN RIDES ♪ When rail fan Daryl Kirby found an abandoned steam engine and rail cars, it was love at first sight—and a lot of mechanical work to get it running. The shocker? It was once part of the Denver & Rio Grande narrow gauge railroad, and dated back to the late 1800s. It's now the centerpiece of a life-size railroad layout at **Kirby Family Farm** (352-812-7435; kirbyfarm.com), 19630 NE 30th Street, Williston, home of the largest railroad on private land in the state of Florida. Founded in 2012, it's now home to five locomotives and six open-air passenger cars running on more than a mile of track. While their primary work is to host at-risk children, the farm opens to the public at least four times a year for themed events like the Christmas Express, $20–25 donation, and hosts small groups by prior arrangement.

WALKING TOURS Stop in at the Cedar Key Historical Society Museum (see *Museums and Historic Sites*) for the official **walking tour of Cedar Key**, which leads you past sites in the old town and explains the history of the outlying islands.

✳ Lodging

BED & BREAKFASTS ♪ ♿ 🐾 ♂ ((ᵖ))
Cedar Key Bed & Breakfast (352-543-9000; cedarkeybedandbreakfast.com), 810 3rd Street, Cedar Key 32625, takes you back to the era when the islands exported fine cedar for buildings and pencils. Built in 1880, this home was used as a boardinghouse by the daughter of one of Florida's first senators, David Levy Yulee. Within an easy walk of shopping and the docks, it's an ideal place to unwind under the paddle fans with a good book. Six romantic rooms with TV, two suites, and a Honeymoon Cottage, $110–200.

((ᵖ)) **Nature Coast Inn** (352-388-8044; naturecoastinn.com), 649 W CR 40, Inglis 34449. Enjoy lazy days and quiet nights amid romantic decor in Old Crackertown, with a selection of four rooms inside the main house or five nearby cottages, $130–165. A beautiful sunset is just steps away on the antique porch rockers, and a hearty country breakfast awaits you in the morning. Elvis fans will appreciate being immersed in part of the set of *Follow That Dream*, which was filmed along this highway out to the Gulf.

HISTORIC ((ᵖ)) Don't look for right angles in the **Island Hotel** (352-543-5111; island-hotel-cedarkey.com), 373 2nd Street, Cedar Key 32625. This historic tabby-and-oak hotel was built just before the Civil War and is the perfect place in town to sleep with history. Each room has a private bath; full breakfast in the restaurant downstairs is included with your stay, $90–155.

((ᵖ)) ♂ 🐾 Built in 1928, **Putnam Lodge** (352-440-0414; putnamlodge.com), 15487 NW US 19, Cross City, once hosted executives of the Putnam Lumber Company. Now fully restored and renovated, it's reopened as a historic hotel, the hand-stenciled pecky cypress walls of the dining room and lobby a work of art. An in-house restaurant is available to guests, along with a spa. Twenty-five rooms and suites, $110–150.

COMFORT AND LUXURY For spacious accommodations in the center of it all, **Harbour Master Suites** (352-543-9146;

cedarkeyharbourmaster.com), 390 Dock Street, offers a broad selection of well-appointed suites with apartment-style amenities. Most are dockside along the historic waterfront, with views of the Gulf of Mexico. $90–145.

RETRO & ARTSY 🦮 ((ɲ)) **Carriage Inn** (352-498-3910; carriage-inn-motel.com), 16872 SE US 19, Cross City 32628. At this family motel, the wrought-iron railings are reminiscent of the French Quarter. Enjoy well-kept, reasonably sized 1960s-style rooms, $45–57, with a swimming pool, shuffleboard court, and adjacent restaurant; it's across the road from the Nature Coast Trail.

🦮 🐾 A colorful place with character, **Faraway Inn Motel & Cottages** (352-543-5330; farawayinn.com), 847 3rd Street, sweeps you back into the great age of Florida tourism—the funky beach cottages and motels of the 1940s. $100–160.

COTTAGES 🦮 The brightly colored waterfront cottages of **Mermaid's Landing** (877-543-5949; mermaidscottages.com), 12717 FL 24, Cedar Key 32625, are an easy stroll from town and a great place to launch a kayak. Set in a funky beach atmosphere, each of the nine 1940s cottages has its own charm and a variety of sleeping arrangements; the larger ones have a full kitchen. $75–94, weekly rentals available.

((ɲ)) 🐾 At **Pirates Cove** (352-543-5141; piratescovecottages.com), 12633 FL 24, Cedar Key 32625, each of the seven cottages in the waterfront complex comes fully equipped with dishes and linens and a gas grill for cooking outdoors. Borrow the canoe when the tide is in to explore the area. $79–99.

CAMPGROUNDS 🐾 ((ɲ)) **B's Marina and Campground** (352-447-5888; bmarinacampground.net), 6621 Riverside Drive, Yankeetown 34498. Tent and RV site, $28–35, along the pine-and-palm-lined Withlacoochee River, with paved pads and picnic tables, or sleep on

a sailboat at their dock for $77. Bring your boat and take advantage of the dock, or come by boat and arrange overnight dockage. It's a great place to launch a kayak and head out to the Gulf, with kayak and boat rentals available.

🦮 ((ɲ)) 🐾 The lush riverside forest and its own spring along the Santa Fe River makes **Ellie Ray's River Landing Campground** (386-935-9518; ellieraysriverlanding.com), 3349 NW 110th Street, Branford 32008, a compelling destination for a getaway. Swim at the pool or the spring, kayak down to the Suwannee River, or walk the nature trails. Tents $35, RVs $40–55, and riverside cabins with bath for $89–150.

🐾 ((ɲ)) **Old Town Campground** (352-542-9500; oldtowncampground.com), 2241 SE CR 349, Old Town 32680, provides a quiet place to tuck your tent or RV under the trees and dream Suwannee dreams. $15–35, closed June 1–September 15.

🐾 Surrounded by Lower Suwannee NWR, **Shell Mound County Park** (352-221-4466), 17650 SW 78 Place, Cedar Key 32625, is a surprising beauty spot in a remote location, cooled by breezes off the salt marsh. It's a true nature-lovers' destination. Many of the sites are in the shade, so you will be fighting off no-see-ums; be prepared. $5–15 cash only, full hookups available.

🐾 Along the estuary, **Sunset Isle Motel & RV Park** (352-543-5375; cedarkeyrv.com), 11850 FL 24, Cedar Key 32625, is a longtime waterfront RV park with a four-room motel. Campsites include full hookups, $43–50. The motel rooms have a fridge and microwave, $75–85. A park model and a cottage are also available for guests, $85–149; the cottage is pet friendly but the other rooms are not.

🦮 🐾 ((ɲ)) At **Suwannee River Hideaway Campground** (352-542-7800; riverhideaway.com), 1218 SE CR 346-A, Old Town 32680, you're greeted by a 1920s general store at check-in. The full-hookup spaces are under a canopy of pines and oaks. A pool and clubhouse with Wi-Fi are available to all campers. During the busy winter months, campers enjoy weekly potluck dinners, game nights, and other activities. Primitive tent campers get primo access to the river; a quarter-mile boardwalk leads from the bathhouse area through the cypress floodplain down to the water. Sites $26–39.

 **Yellow Jacket Campground** (352-542-8365; yellowjacketcampground .com), 55 SE 503rd Avenue (FL 349), blends well into its natural surroundings. A rope swing with a grand view of the Suwannee River hangs off an ancient live oak tree next to shady riverside campsites; guests enjoy a beautiful swimming pool and spa area. $35 and up, cottages also available.

DIVE RESORT Surrounding its world-renowned dive venue (see *Diving*), **Devil's Den** (352-528-3344; devilsden.com), 5390 NE 180th Avenue, Williston 32696, provides a full-service dive resort. Pop up a tent for $10 per person, bring your

RV for $24 (full hookups), or rent a cabin or park model for $110–145, all linens and dishes included. Campers enjoy use of bathhouses and a heated pool on-site; diving fees are separate. No pets permitted.

FISH CAMP Plan your next fishing expedition on the Gulf at **Bill's Fish Camp** (352-542-7086; billsfishcamp.com), 63 219th Street, Suwannee 32692, where you can settle into a basic motel room ($65), bring in your RV ($30, full hookups), or pitch a tent. Fish-cleaning room available and a cookhouse. Bill's also maintains the adjacent free river camp on the Suwannee River Wilderness Trail (see *Paddling*), Anderson River Camp.

✳ Where To Eat

TRADITION 🍴 Since 1928, **Cypress Inn Restaurant** (352-498-7211), 15568 US19, Cross City, has been serving up heaping helpings of Southern cooking in this beautiful pecky cypress building; sit

CYPRESS INN, CROSS CITY

down and make yourself at home. Pick from the prime rib special, Southern fried quail, seafood dinners (including fresh mullet and grouper), and much more, $10 and up. Everything comes with your choice of home-style sides like fresh acre peas, baby limas, fried okra, and corn nuggets.

ELEGANT AND ROMANTIC ♂ Featuring recipes handed down through the Hale family for more than 50 years, **The Ivy House** (352-528-5410; ivyhousefl .com), 108 NW Main Street, Williston, presents gourmet Southern cooking in a 1912 Victorian home. From Southern-fried scallops to baked "Krispy Chicken" to a Big South sampler of a 12-oz Delmonico steak, fried shrimp, and cod, you'll find something to fit every appetite. Leave room for their classic milk cake! Entrées $13–27.

BARBECUE In the mood for mounds of food? Stop by **Akins Bar-B-Q & Grill**, (352-463-6859; akinsbbq.com), 1159 S Main Street, Bell, where the locals gather for heaping helpings of country cooking. Entrées $6–20.

🐷 **Bar-B-Q Bill's** (352-493-4444), 1901 N Young Boulevard, Chiefland, is always packed, and it took one meal to understand why: fine barbecue that even impressed friends from Texas. Served with traditional fixings, sandwiches and plates run $6–18. Daily lunch and meal specials and breakfast, too.

Barbecue with attitude is the key to **BubbaQues** (352-528-4227; bubbaquesbbq.com), 143 E Noble Avenue, Williston, with menu items like Redneck Nachos made with fries instead of corn chips, Fried Green Beans, the Motherclucker: "Smoked chicken breast topped with Tractor Grease . . ." This small Florida chain pushes the redneck theme pretty hard but the food's dang good, and that's what matters most. Opens at breakfast, meals $4 and up, plus smoked meat to go.

CASUAL FARE Inside the spacious Suwannee Valley Quilt Shop (see *Shopping*), **The Suwannee Rose Cafe** (352-463-3842; suwanneeshops.com), 517 N Main, Trenton, offers delightful daily specials like crab salad on croissant and the quiche of the day, sweet little gourmet meals under $15. You'll be tempted by slices of pie—like cashew, sawdust, and tin roof—displayed prominently in a bakery case on the edge of this garden-like space inside the historic Coca-Cola bottling plant.

COMFORT FOOD It looks like a truck stop, but **Bett's Big T Restaurant** (352-490-4906), 12351 NW US 19, Chiefland, was a real surprise. Inside, it's quite a contrast to the exterior, with fresh Cedar Key mullet on the menu among other local favorites like Southern fried chicken and steak. Served up with Southern sides, it was perfect, as was their sweet tea. Meals $8 and up.

SEAFOOD 🦪 For a taste of what Cedar Key does best—raising clams—stop in **Big Deck Raw Bar** (352-543-9992), 331 Dock Street, for local clams, oysters, and fresh Gulf shrimp steamed and grilled, $10–28. Live music Thursday–Sunday.

Salt Creek Restaurant (352-542-7072), 23440 SE CR 349, Suwannee, is a spacious restaurant with seating overlooking the Gulf estuary. It's worth the drive to the end of the road for their succulent seafood, including fresh oysters, mullet, bay scallops, and gator tail. Entrées, including a Fisherman's Platter with blue crab, $14–28.

You must try the clam chowder at **Tony's Seafood Restaurant** (352-543-0022; tonyschowder.com), 597 2nd Street, Cedar Key, as Tony is the king of chowder makers and his ingredients can't get fresher. Savor a Low Country boil with all the fixin's, or try shrimp or steamed clams Tony's way and you won't be disappointed. Entrées $7–20.

WATERFRONT ♨ **Annie's Cafe** (352-543-6141), FL 24 and 6th Street, Cedar Key, is a quiet little place down by the clam farms with that pop of protein you need in the morning, like omelets and French toast, under $10. Come at lunchtime to savor seafood on the deck with a view of the mangrove marshes. Cash only.

♂ Dine in a historic setting at the **Riverside Inn at Izaak Walton Lodge** (352-447-2595; izaakwaltonlodge.com), 6301 Riverside Drive, Yankeetown. Sitting along the Withlacoochee River, this is the location where the original lodge was established in 1924, catering to anglers and hunters coming down from "up north" during the winter months. While the lodge burned down in 1999, its replacement pays homage to its predecessor. The menu, while seasonal, is heavy on seafood, as befits its location, with smoked fish spread, peel-and-eat shrimp, and scallops all excellent choices, meals $9–16.

✳ Selective Shopping

ANTIQUES **Dixie's Antiques** (352-528-2338), 131 E Noble Avenue, Williston, is a mini mall overflowing with antiques and collectibles, with a heavy emphasis on kitchenware and dishes—look for your missing Fenton glass, Fiestaware, and enamelware here. But you'll also find country crafts, Western home decor, rustic wooden furniture, and ironworking by a local blacksmith in among the stacks of paperbacks, Hardy Boys mysteries, and soda pop bottles—a little something for everyone.

Magnolia Mist (352-493-7877), 711 N Main, stands out along US 19 in downtown Chiefland with a good selection of antiques and gift items.

With wagon wheels piled outside a pecky cypress building, **Manatee Antiques** (352-493-4043), 121 S Main Street, Chiefland, draws your attention with a porchful of farm implements and country fare.

ARTS AND CRAFTS A complex of artsy shops and eateries, **Suwannee Valley Shops** (352-463-3842; suwanneeshops.com), 517 N Main Street is a destination all its own. It started with **The Suwannee Valley Quilt Shoppe** inside the renovated Coca-Cola bottling plant. Inside you'll find the most amazing array of fabrics you've seen in years. Next door, the Crystal Ice House is now **The Suwannee Valley Antique Gallery**, filled with fine furnishings, antique sewing machines, classic glass, and, of course, beautiful quilts on the walls. Walk to the far back of the building to see a long-arm machine for quilting.

BOOKS AND GIFTS Every little town needs an independent bookstore, and none so much as Cedar Key, being an enclave of artists and writers. **Curmudgeonalia** (352-543-6789; curmudgeonalia.com), 598 2nd Street, Cedar Key, fills the niche, with an excellent selection of tomes on Florida and by Florida authors and a children's section that caters to inquisitive, outdoorsy kids.

DECOR AND MORE Dark woods accent the nautical theme at **Dilly Dally Gally** (352-543-9146; dillydallygally.com), 390 Dock Street, Cedar Key, with wooden signs, wood carvings, and antique ephemera tucked away in the back rooms.

FARMERS' MARKETS At the **Chiefland Farmers Flea Market** (352-493-2022; chieflandfleamarket.com), 316 NW 11th Avenue, comb through the stalls for country bargains! Friday–Sunday 8 AM–4 PM.

SPECIALTY FOODS **Williston Peanut Factory Outlet** (352-528-2388), 1309 US 41, is a small outlet with offerings of peanut goodies made on-site, from roasted peanuts to peanut butter and peanut brittle. They're open during production hours.

✳ Special Events

FALL/WINTER Thousands converge on this tiny village for samplings of local seafood during the **Cedar Key Seafood Festival** (352-543-5600; cedarkey.org), the third weekend in October, along with a large arts and crafts show and special tours of Seahorse Key Lighthouse.

Nearly 60 years running, the **Suwannee River Fair** (352-486-5131; mysrf .org), 17851 90 Avenue, Fanning Springs, is the combined county fair for the three-county region, with livestock and vegetable judging, rides and crafts, and more. Held each March.

The **Suwannee Valley Quilt Festival** (trentonquiltfestival.com), mid-March, brings together quilting guilds from around the South to display and admire more than 400 quilts around downtown Trenton. Centered on the Old Railroad Depot, the festival also features craft vendors, quilting demonstrations, live music, and an antique auto show.

SPRING/SUMMER Started in 1963, the **Old Florida Celebration of the Arts** (352-543-5400; cedarkeyartsfestival.com) lets you enjoy the works of local artists in April, with a taste of seafood for good measure.

THE ATLANTIC COAST

■

JACKSONVILLE

AMELIA ISLAND

ST. AUGUSTINE

FLAGLER COUNTY

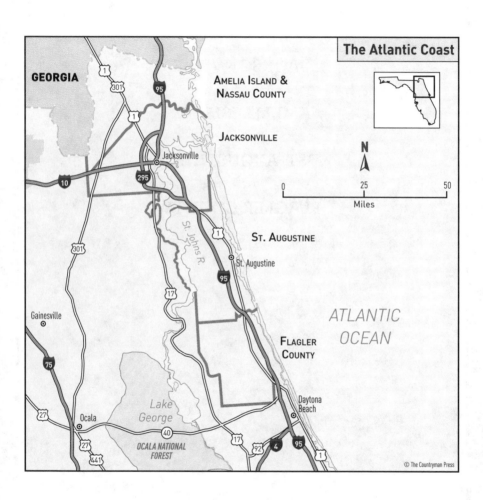

The Atlantic Coast

GEORGIA

AMELIA ISLAND &
NASSAU COUNTY

JACKSONVILLE

Jacksonville

St. Johns R.

ST. AUGUSTINE

St. Augustine

Gainesville

FLAGLER
COUNTY

ATLANTIC
OCEAN

Lake
George

Daytona
Beach

Ocala

OCALA NATIONAL
FOREST

N

0   25   50
Miles

© The Countryman Press

JACKSONVILLE

The place known as "Cowford" by early Florida settlers who drove their cattle across the shallows of the St. Johns River has grown up into **Jacksonville**, one of the financial centers of the Southeast. The heart of the region, its lifeblood, has always been the St. Johns River. One of the nation's only north-flowing rivers, it springs from the marshes of Central Florida, its 310-mile length lying two dozen miles or less west of the Atlantic Ocean's shoreline. By the time the St. Johns reaches Mandarin Point, Jacksonville's southernmost outpost on the river, it widens to a mighty channel, perfect for commercial shipping.

The earliest human habitation along the river, indicated by the massive shell middens (oyster-shell landfills) along the St. Johns, came from the Timucua and their forefathers more than a thousand years before the first Europeans set foot in Florida. On May 1, 1562, three years before the founding of the Spanish colony at St. Augustine, French Huguenots landed along the shores of "the River of May"; their leader, Jean Ribault, claimed this land for France and began a small colony at what is now Fort Caroline. In 1564 more than 200 soldiers, artisans, and civilians settled on the St. Johns' bluff in protection of the new fort. But just a year later, Pedro Menendez de Aviles, founder of St. Augustine, marched here with 500 troops and massacred most of the French settlers; the colony was abandoned.

The region stood under many flags. British loyalists settled here during the American Revolution, and American patriots sent them packing. But the Spanish held on to this portion of Florida for nearly 200 years before ceding it to the United States in 1821. "Cowford" was christened "Jacksonville" in honor of territorial governor General Andrew Jackson in 1822.

A thriving commercial center by the time the state of Florida was established in 1845, Jacksonville saw a great deal of action during the Civil War, as both Union and Confederate forces took, abandoned, and retook the city. When in federal hands, Jacksonville was a launch point for Union raids up the St. Johns River and along the Florida Railroad west to Olustee. By the late 1800s, the city became a place for northerners to escape the cold and to convalesce. Author Harriet

MOUNTAIN BIKE TRAIL AT HANNAH PARK

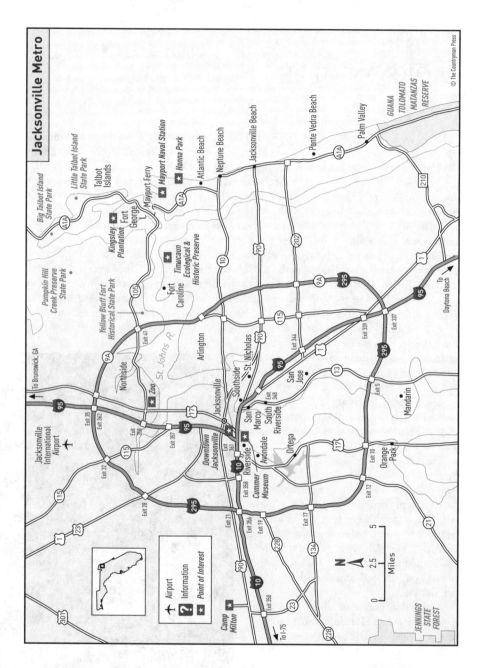

Jacksonville Metro

Beecher Stowe held court on her front porch in **Mandarin**, where passing steamboats would point out her house to passengers and sometimes stop for a visit. **Jacksonville Beach** blossomed into a turn-of-the-twentieth-century tourist destination with many oceanfront hotels, while **Atlantic Beach** and **Neptune Beach** split the bounty of a bustling seaside business district and older, more established hotels. **Mayport**, home to the shrimping fleet and to Mayport Naval Station, comissioned in 1942, sits at the mouth of the St. Johns River.

For downtown Jacksonville, the Great Fire of 1901 marked a turning point. In less than 8 hours, it wiped out 2 square miles of wooden buildings in what was the largest-ever city fire in the South. With 10,000 people homeless and 2,600 buildings gone, the city immediately began to rebuild. More than 20 distinct communities—including the popular shopping districts of **Avondale, Riverside**, and **San Marco**—emerged, graced with homes and businesses designed using new architectural styles in stone and brick, not wood. Historic districts highlight classic architecture from the 1920s through the '40s.

All of Duval County is within the city of Jacksonville's jurisdiction, a point it's tough to believe as you're driving on US 301 on the county's western rural fringe or along the salt marshes paralleling Heckscher Drive north of the St. Johns River. For that reason, destinations within this chapter are broken out under their neighborhoods or traditional community names.

GUIDANCE The primary source of tourism information for the region is **Visit Jacksonville** (800-733-2668 or 904-798-9111; visitjacksonville.com), 208 N Laura Street, Suite 102, Jacksonville 32202. **Walk-in visitor information centers** are on the lower levels of the Jacksonville Landing (904-791-4305), 2 Independent Drive, Monday–Tuesday 11 AM–3 PM, Wednesday–Saturday 10 AM–7 PM, Sunday 12–5 PM; Jacksonville International Airport baggage claim area (904-741-3044), daily 9 AM–10 PM; and the Beaches Visitor Center (904-242-0024), 381 Beach Boulevard, Jacksonville Beach, Tuesday–Saturday 10 AM–4 PM, Sunday 12–4 PM.

GETTING THERE *By air:* **Jacksonville International Airport** (904-741-4902; flyjacksonville.com), 2400 Yankee Clipper Drive, Jacksonville, is the region's major airport, with a full schedule of flights by major carriers.

By bus: **Greyhound** (904-356-9976; greyhound.com) takes you into downtown Jacksonville, where transfers to city buses and JTA Skyway are nearby.

By car: **I-95** runs north–south through the heart of Jacksonville, with **I-10** coming in from the west to meet **I-295**, the beltway around the west side of the city.

By train: **Amtrak** (904-766-5110; amtrak.com), 3570 Clifford Lane on the north side of Jacksonville, 7 miles from the downtown area, has an ♿ enclosed waiting room and parking.

GETTING AROUND *By public transportation:* **JTA Skyway, JTA Trolley, Community Shuttles**, and **JTA buses** (904-743-3582 or 904-RIDE-JTA; jtafla.com). The free Skyway peoplemover weaves through the downtown area from Kings Avenue Garage to the FCCJ campus and the Convention Center on Bay Street, Monday–Friday 6 AM–9 PM and on weekends for special events only. During peak hours it runs every 4 minutes; off-peak, every 8. Buses take you east to the beach or southwest to Orange Park for $1.50 and up, depending on distance; discounts for disabled, seniors, and youth. JTA's Community Shuttles act like regular bus routes but focus on small neighborhood areas. Two trolley buses help visitors get around popular destinations. The **Beaches Trolley** runs between South Beach Regional Shopping Center and Atlantic Boulevard on weekends and late into the evening Friday–Saturday past closing time at popular bars; the Riverside-Avondale Night Trolley hits Five Points, Riverside, Avondale, the Brewery District, and St. Johns Village on weekends from 6 AM–2 PM. A one-day pass is recommended for on-off privileges, otherwise it's $1.50/trip. Exact fares are required, but fare cards can be bought in advance at automated machines or through the MyJTA app (myjta.com) on your phone.

By car: There are four main highways that take you from Jacksonville's neighborhoods east to the coast. North of the St. Johns River, follow **Heckscher Drive** (FL 105)

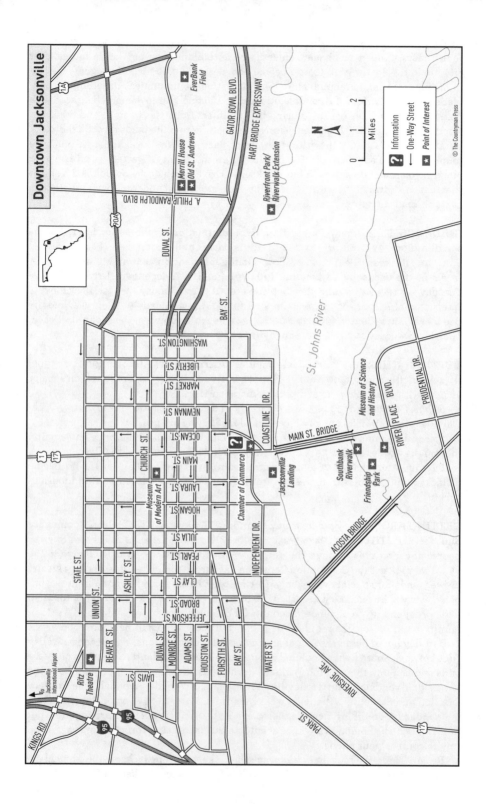

Downtown Jacksonville

Miles
0 1 2

? Information
← One-Way Street
★ Point of Interest

© The Countryman Press

east to A1A, which comes north on the **Mayport Ferry** (see *Ferry*) and continues north to the Talbot Islands. From downtown, follow **Atlantic Boulevard** (FL 10) to Atlantic Beach/Neptune Beach. US 90, **Beach Boulevard**, connects downtown with Jacksonville Beach. From the Southside, follow **J. Turner Butler Boulevard** (FL 202) to Ponte Vedra. I-95 and US 1 head north–south through the heart of the city, with I-295 forming a beltway out to Orange Park, I-10, and the airport. In town, **Roosevelt Boulevard** (US 17) parallels the west side of the St. Johns River south from downtown past Riverside, Five Points, Avondale, and St. Johns Park to I-295; **San Marco Boulevard** (US 13) does the same on the east side of the river from downtown through San Marco and San Jose to Mandarin.

By boat: **St. Johns River Taxi & Tours** (904-860-8924; jaxrivertaxi.com) shuttles you across the river between downtown hotels and popular Northside destinations, including Jacksonville Landing, the Metropolitan Marina, Riverside Arts Market, and Jacksonville Zoo & Gardens (Saturday only); pick it up downtown at the Friendship Fountain, the Doubletree, or the Lexington. Runs Tuesday–Thursday 11 AM–9 PM, Friday–Saturday and holidays 11 AM–11 PM. All day pass $10 adult, $8 child; tours offered on Mondays and zoo packages on Saturdays.

PARKING **Parking garages** are your best bet downtown; rates vary. The shopping districts of Avondale, Five Points, Riverside, and San Marco have done away with metered parking and now have **free parking with a 3-hour limit** from 8 AM–6 PM, but it can be tough to find a space during the lunch rush. Large public lots in Jacksonville Beach and Atlantic Beach are free, as is street parking along A1A and in the shopping areas.

MEDICAL EMERGENCIES For general emergencies, visit **Memorial Hospital Jacksonville** (904-702-6111; memorialhospitaljax.com), 3625 University Boulevard S. A medical destination within the city is the world-renowned **Mayo Clinic Jacksonville** (904-953-2000; mayoclinic.org/jacksonville), 4500 San Pablo Road.

✳ To See

ARCHITECTURE Thanks to their vibrant business districts, **Avondale and Riverside** are well traveled and well known. Get a block or two off the busier roads to see some of the architectural marvels of its residential areas. The **Riverside/Avondale Historic District** (riversideavondale.org), which also includes the St. Johns Quarter, is heavily influenced by the bungalow style, but you'll also find Mediterranean revival, Tudor revival, and even Art Moderne.

After the 1901 fire, **downtown Jacksonville** sprouted skyscrapers befitting a growing center of commerce. Most have been demolished over the years, but the "Laura Street Trio," three classic office buildings from 1908–1909, remain. They include the narrow 11-story **Florida Life building**, 117 N Laura Street, with Chicago-style windows; the **Bisbee Building**, 47 W Forsyth Street, Florida's first reinforced-concrete skyscraper; and the **Marble Bank**, 51 W Forsyth Street, with its stunning marble façade.

Home to the Jacksonville Historical Society, **Old St. Andrews Episcopal Church** (904-665-0064; jaxhistory.org), 317 A. Philip Randolph Boulevard, opened in 1888 and was the largest house of worship in the city prior to the Great Fire of 1901. Designed by architect Robert S. Schuyler in the Gothic revival style, with a brick exterior, Gothic spires, and Florida yellow pine interior, it was considered one of the "most satisfying pieces of architecture in the South" in 1889. Dilapidated by the 1990s, it was located on land purchased by the city for their new football stadium and given to the historical

1920S LION FOUNTAIN IN SAN MARCO SQUARE

society with the provision that it would be restored. With restoration completed in 1998, it is now on the National Register of Historic Places. Learn about life in Jacksonville circa 1903 at the adjoining **Merrill House Museum** (904-665-0054; jaxhistory .org/merrill-museum-house-tours), 317 A Philip Randolph Boulevard, Midtown. Inside this Victorian house museum, a docent will guide you through the life of the James Merrill family and its intersection with important events in Jacksonville. Reserve tours online or by phone; $10 donation suggested.

Old St. Luke's (904-374-0296; jaxhistory.org), 314 Palmetto Street, was built in 1878. It first served as a hospital and then as the first modern nursing school in Florida. Both it and the adjoining **Florida Casket Company** (circa 1924) were also purchased and restored for the Jacksonville Historical Society to preserve, curate, and open to the public their historical archives. Call ahead for access.

♂ ᨔ Along the driving loop on Fort George Island, **Ribault Club** (904-251-1050; theribaultclub.com) stands out. Established in 1928 as a getaway for the affluent, the club once boasted a yacht basin, lawn bowling courses, and a nine-hole golf course. Beautifully restored, it's part of Fort George Island Cultural State Park (see *Parks, Preserves, and Camping*) and contains a museum inside that shows off both the club's and the island's history. It's a popular venue for retreats and weddings.

Built around the Venetian-style lion fountain of **San Marco Square** in the 1920s, San Marco's distinctive triangular shopping district was one of the earliest "town center" developments, based on its namesake plaza in Venice, Italy. Entertainment was as important then as now, so two art deco theaters opened in the 1930s—the San Marcos Theater and the Little Theater, both on San Marcos Boulevard (see *Performing Arts*).

♂ **Old St. Paul's Episcopal Church**, a Carpenter Gothic from 1888, is the centerpiece of tiny Fletcher Park (904-396-4737; smpsjax.com/san-marco/preservation-hall), 1652 Atlantic Boulevard, and home to the San Marco Preservation Hall.

Established in 1869, the northerly neighborhood of **Springfield** didn't suffer from the Great Fire of 1901—in fact, it grew, as residents exited the charred city and built uptown homes. The Springfield Historic District (sparcouncil.org) covers a square mile between Hogan's Creek, Ionia Street, and 12th Street, created to inspire and assist residents to maintain the architectural glory of this residential district. While no homes are open for tours, you can drive around and see Queen Anne Victorians, Craftsman bungalows, Prairie School structures, and other magnificent architectural styles.

A beautiful example of Carpenter Gothic architecture described as a "standing sermon," **St. George Episcopal Church** (904-251-9272; saintgeorgejax.org), 10560 Fort George Road, Fort George Island, was designed by Robert S. Schuyler and built in 1882. A Florida heritage site, it still houses the island's congregation, which pre-dates the church by a few years, and it is one of the historic river mission churches founded by the second Episcopal bishop of Florida, John Freeman Young.

ART GALLERIES Inside **Anazao Galleries** (904-588-2575; anazao.com), 3568 St. Johns Avenue, Avondale, vintage gilded Greek icons and pages from centuries-old illuminated manuscripts are juxtaposed with fine art oil paintings and blown glass art by Robert Held Art Glass. Fine jewelry and crafts, including colorful, clever recycled scarves made of strips of other scarves, make for easy gifts.

Set in the oak-shaded shopping district, **The Avondale Gallery** (904-389-6712), 3545 St. Johns Avenue, Avondale, showcases paintings of estuarine and beach scenes by local artists as well as palm tree pop art.

We couldn't browse **First Street Gallery** (904-241-6928; firststreetgalleryart.com), 216-B First Street, Neptune Beach, without falling in love with the glass fish swimming across the windows of this mostly beach-theme gallery representing regional artists. Only juried work is displayed, with a featured monthly artist or art group. In the end, it was one of Janet Mulligan's colorful snappers and a fun mosaic by Kevan Breitinger of St. Augustine that followed us home.

Emerging artists thrive at **Gallery 1037** (904-398-3161; reddiarts.com), 1037 Hendricks Avenue, San Marco, which presents bimonthly shows of local artists launching their careers. Open daily.

Gallery 725 (904-345-932; gallery725.com), 725-5 Atlantic Boulevard, Atlantic Beach, showcases works from fine local artists and from the art community at large, bringing in such notables as Peter Max for "meet the artist" receptions during exhibitions of the artists' works.

Local artists display landscapes and city scenes at **Gallery Framery** (904-398-6255; galleryframery.com), 4446 Hendricks Avenue, San Marco.

In an elegant, classical setting, **Stellers Gallery** (904-396-9492; stellersgallery .com), 1409 Atlantic Boulevard, San Marco, is one of Jacksonville's oldest galleries representing local fine artists, many of whom draw inspiration from the wild places along this coast.

ART MUSEUMS ✑ ♿ In 13 formal galleries, North Florida's largest fine art museum, the **Cummer Museum of Art and Gardens** (904-356-6857; cummer.org), 829 Riverside Avenue, Riverside, displays a broad permanent collection of art from the Middle Ages to the present, including original works from Glakens to Rubens. One of their more important pieces is Thomas Moran's oil painting *Ponce de Leon in Florida* (1878), which depicts the Spanish conquistador in the company of native Floridians deep in the mystical forests around the St. Johns River; the extensive Wark Collection of Early Meissen Porcelain, with pieces more than 250 years old, is an unexpected delight. One arm of the museum houses working studio spaces and a special children's section with hands-on activities. Between the museum and the St. Johns River lies this attraction's other major feature, an area of formal landscaped gardens dating back to 1903 (see *Gardens*). $10 adults, $6 seniors/military/students, 5 and under free. Tuesday 10 AM–9 PM, Wednesday–Saturday 10 AM–4 PM, Sunday 12–4 PM. A variety of free admissions are offered, including Tuesday evenings 4–9 PM; see their website for specifics.

Founded in 1924, the **Museum of Contemporary Art** (904-366-6911; moca jacksonville.unf.edu), 333 N Laura Street, was the first institution in the city devoted to visual arts. It displays a fine selection of modern and contemporary works by locally and nationally acclaimed artists. Ongoing changing exhibitions highlight photography as well as paintings, sculpture, and printmaking. Tuesday–Saturday 11 AM–5 PM, Sunday noon–5 PM, open until 9 PM on Thursday. Fee; free admissions available, see website for details.

DINNER THEATER For more than 50 years, **Alhambra Dinner Theatre** (904-641-1212; alhambrajax.com), 12000 Beach Boulevard, Jacksonville, has given Broadway-style performances like *Phantom of the Opera* coupled with a nice home-style dinner. Tuesday–Sunday, with matinees on weekends, $35–62.

FERRY In continuous operation since 1948, the **St. Johns River Ferry** (904-241-9969; stjohnsriverferry.com), one of Florida's last and certainly largest ferryboats, connects both A1A and the East Coast Greenway across the St. Johns River between Mayport and Fort George Island. The *Jean Ribault* departs at :30 after the hour in Mayport, :15 Fort George Island, and costs $1 per pedestrian or cyclist, $6 per car. Monday–Friday 6 AM–7 PM; Saturday–Sunday 7 AM–8:30 PM. Real-time schedule at ferry.jtafla.com.

FOOTBALL Fall and winter, catch North Florida's only NFL team, the **Jacksonville Jaguars** (904-633-2000; jaguars.com), One EverBank Field Drive near the Hart Bridge, downtown. Special water taxi and bus routes just for the games help lighten parking problems.

GARDENS At the **Cummer Museum of Art & Gardens** (see *Art Museums*), the formal gardens now complement one of Florida's finest art collections, but are much older than the museum itself. Having made their fortune in logging Florida's cypress, the Cummer family built a grand home on the St. Johns, with gardens landscaped to impress. The first garden, started in 1903, was the English Garden. In the 1930s both William Lyman Phillips and Ellen Biddle Shipman were hired—by different family members—to redesign the garden space. Those designs persist today, with Shipman's Italian Garden using arches to direct your gaze out over the St. Johns River. One of the oldest live oaks in the region, a landmark from the river, was incorporated into the design of the Upper Garden. Open in concert with the museum, the gardens are included in the admission price and are accessed via the loggia.

🐾 ♿ One of the more unusual arboretums in Florida is the **Camp Milton Historic Tree Grove** at Camp Milton Historic Preserve (see *Parks, Preserves, and Camping*). Located west of the city along the rail corridor where Camp Milton—an important Confederate encampment during the Civil War—was located, this grove of 58 young trees serves as a memorial of that difficult time. Each tree was propagated directly from trees that existed during the Civil War, from the Gettysburg Address honeylocust to the Fredrick Douglass White Oak.

🐾 ♂ A delightful urban forest, the privately managed 120-acre **Jacksonville Arboretum & Gardens** (jacksonvillearboretum.org), 1445 Millcoe Road, grew out of a piece of neglected public land that was once a titanium mine. Natural habitats are resilient when left alone, and it is in this context that the arboretum excels: it's a deeply wooded place, showing off an outstanding variety of natural habitats in a community that is otherwise heavily developed today. The terrain is surprisingly rugged. Nearly four miles of interpretive trails lead through natural ravines that feed a deep pond, past bogs and bottomland hardwoods, through wet pine flatwoods and a rare rosemary scrub, and even to the edge of an estuarine marsh. Gardens surround Lake Ray in a deep ravine, where a short boardwalk leads to the base of the National Champion lob-lolly bay tree. A pavilion along the pond provides the perfect backdrop for outdoor weddings. Free, open daily 8 AM–5 PM; $3 donation suggested.

LIGHTHOUSE Inside the Mayport Naval Station but visible from the St. Johns River and the streets of this small community, the 64-foot St. **Johns River Light** (floridalighthouses.org/page-1106684), Patrol Road, is a square white lighthouse with keeper's quarters that has marked the river's entrance since 1954. Grounds may be visited if you are visiting the Naval Station.

MOVIES The silver screen was the silent screen in the early 1900s, and Jacksonville was the **"Winter Film Capital of the World,"** thanks to Henry Flagler's railroad, which brought the industry south from New York into ideal conditions for shooting outdoors under the bright sun. The first of Jacksonville's many **film studios** opened in 1908, and Oliver Hardy of "Laurel and Hardy" fame became Jacksonville's most famous movie star. In 1920, Richard Norman of nearby Middleburg bought out Eagle Studios to found Norman Laboratories in Arlington. His was the first film studio to feature African American actors in non-stereotypical roles. It's the last studio standing. The **Norman Studios Silent Film Museum** (904-212-0105; normanstudios.org), 6337 Arlington Road, Arlington, encompasses the historic studio complex still under restoration. The non-profit holds Silent Sundays at a variety of locations in Jacksonville to raise funds and to showcase historic films.

One of Florida's last three remaining 1920s Mediterranean revival fantasy theaters, the beautifully refurbished **Florida Theatre** (904-355-5661; floridatheatre.com), 128 E Forsyth Street, takes center stage as the venue for summer movies, top-name concerts, and community events. It was the first major downtown building to be air-conditioned. Remember the national stir over Elvis and his on-stage gyrations in 1956? It started here!

An art deco treasure, **San Marco Theatre** (904-396-4845; sanmarcotheatre.com), 1996 San Marco Boulevard, designed by Roy A. Benjamin in 1938, is an elegant place to take a date as the centerpiece of an evening out on the town. The theater shows both art films and cult classics, and in addition to popcorn, they serve up beer and wine.

Catch indie films and midnight movies at **Sun-Ray Cinema** (904-359-0049; sunraycinema.com), 1028 Park Street, Five Points, a restored 1927 beauty that was built as Riverside Theatre, one of the first theaters in Florida to show "talkies," signaling the end of Jacksonville's golden age as a silent film production mecca.

MUSEUMS AND HISTORIC SITES At Jacksonville Beach, the landmark **American Red Cross Volunteer Life Saving Corps Building** (jaxbeachlifeguard.org) dates back to 1947. Established in 1912, the corps provides volunteer lifeguards for the beaches, and historically provides rescue teams in lifesaving boats for ships in distress. Still an important part of the local community, volunteer lifeguards have rescued more than 1,400 people from the surf.

🖉 ⬧ Learn all about regional history along the beaches at **Beaches Museum & History Park** (904-241-5657; beachesmuseum.org), 381 Beach Boulevard at Pablo

FORT CAROLINE: FLORIDA'S FRENCH COLONY

At Fort Caroline National Memorial (904-641-7155; nps.gov/foca), 12713 Fort Caroline Road, Arlington, a replica of Fort Caroline sits along the St. Johns River, its size and shape based on the paintings of French artist Jacques Le Moyne, one of the settlers who called Florida's first European colony home in June 1564. St. Augustine founder Pedro Menendez marched here just a week after establishing the Spanish colony, bringing 500 troops to roust the French from Florida under the orders of King Phillip II. Taking the fort by surprise, they murdered 140 settlers, sparing only the women and children. Nearly 50 settlers, including Le Moyne, escaped by boat and returned to France. An interpretive center tells the story, and nature trails through the deeply wooded preserve make this National Park a nice place for a gentle walk. Across the street from the main entrance is **Spanish Pond**, where the Spanish troops camped before attacking the colony. Open daily 9 AM–5 PM; free. A short drive to the end of Fort Caroline Road takes you to the **Ribault Monument** on St. Johns Bluff, commemorating where the French first landed; it is a replica of the stone originally erected by Jean Ribault in 1562, claiming this land for France. 🐾 ♿ 🚶

REPLICA OF FORT CAROLINE

Historical Park, Jacksonville Beach. The Mayport & Pablo Railway stretched out to the barrier island in the late 1800s, where the town of Pablo was first formed; the original post office is here to peek inside, as is one of the oldest churches in the area, St. Paul's By-the-Sea. Rail fans will appreciate the significant artifacts that are a central point of the collection (see *Railroadiana*). Open Tuesday–Saturday 10 AM–4 PM, Sunday 12–4 PM; free.

🐾 ✒ ♿ A significant Civil War historic site, **Camp Milton Historic Preserve** (904-255-7912; coj.net), 1175 Halsema Road N, northwest Jacksonville, has an educational center with artifacts and interpretive information about Camp Milton, one of the Confederacy's largest encampments in the region. Trails lead to defensive earthworks and McGirts Creek Bridge, a replica of a "Campaign Bridge" of the era. Its Historic Tree Grove (see *Gardens*) has a unique collection of trees tied to Civil War history. The preserve also offers recreational facilities as a stop along the Jacksonville-Baldwin Trail (see *Biking*), including an 1800s Florida farm to explore.

✒ The Great Fire of 1901 brought immediate attention to the need for Jacksonville's buildings to be sturdy brick and stone. At the **Jacksonville Fire Museum** (904-630-0618; coj.net/departments/fire-and-rescue/fire-museum), 1406 Gator Bowl Boulevard, Midtown, learn about the history of firefighting in Jacksonville inside a historic firehouse, complete with a 1902 American LaFrance horse-drawn fire engine. Open Monday–Friday 9 AM–4 PM.

Researchers will appreciate access to the **Karpeles Manuscript Library Museum** (904-356-2992; karpeles.weebly.com), 101 W 1st Street, Springfield, part of the world's largest private collection of important *original* manuscripts and art. Holdings across this library system include the writings of Sir Arthur Conan Doyle, The Lawrence Williams Presidential Collection of portraits, the Bill of Rights, Roget's *Thesaurus*, Einstein's *Theory of Relativity*, and many other treasures. Open Tuesday–Friday 10 AM–3 PM, Saturday 10 AM–4 PM.

🐾 ✒ Deep inside the forest that now covers much of Fort George Island, **Kingsley Plantation** (904-251-3537; nps.gov/timu/learn/historyculture/kp.htm), 11676 Palmetto Avenue, was established in 1791 by John McQueen on a Spanish land grant. His Sea Island cotton plantation passed into the hands of Zephaniah Kingsley, a slave trader, in 1812. Kingsley lived here with his wife, Anna Madgigine Jai, a slave he had bought in Senegal and later freed, and their children. Although Kingsley strove to establish

INSIDE A SLAVE CABIN AT KINGSLEY PLANTATION

liberal policies for the freeing of slaves and to ensure their rights and privileges after freedom, his efforts failed; he moved his family to Haiti in 1837. The modest planter's home fronts the Fort George River, as all transportation would have been by water. Interpretive information makes a self-guided tour of the kitchens, slave cabins, and other outbuildings easy; home tours are offered on weekends. Open daily 9 AM–5 PM; home tours offered on weekends at 11 AM and 3 PM; call for reservations. Free.

Not far from where Harriet Beecher Stowe waved to steamboats from her porch, the **Mandarin Museum,** tucked within **Walter Jones Historical Park** (904-268-0784; mandarinmuseum.net), 11964 Mandarin Road, is the 1873 homestead of Major William Webb and later Walter Jones, Mandarin's postmaster. The complex also includes the original Mandarin post office and the last one-room schoolhouse in Duval County, built in 1898. Guided tours through the home and historical park are offered Saturday 9 AM–4 PM. Free, donations appreciated.

✇ ᕐ The extensive **Museum of Science and History** (904-396-7062; themosh.org), 1025 Museum Circle, downtown, brings together science and local history into an entertaining and educational package that will take you most of a day to explore. Walk the Currents of Time, learning about local history through artifacts and interpretation, including Jacksonville's former role as the top silent movie producer of that era—yes, Laurel and Hardy hung out here along with hundreds of other early screen stars. Discover Northeast Florida's wildlife at the Florida Naturalist's Center. Play in the Space Science Gallery, launching a rocket or discovering magnetic attraction. Listen to music in the starry night with Cosmic Concerts at the Alexander Brest Planetarium. Tots can explore the treehouse in KidSpace, or you can settle in for a scientific lecture with the MOSH After Dark series. Open Monday–Thursday 10 AM–5 PM, Friday 10 AM–8 PM, Saturday 10 AM–6 PM, Sunday 12–5 PM; $12.50 adults, $10 seniors & military, $10 ages 3–12. Limited free parking.

Learn about the lifestyle and culture of the antebellum South at the **Museum of Southern History** (904-388-3574; museumsouthernhistory.com), 4304 Herschel Street, Avondale. While largely focused on the Civil War, exhibits and artifacts cover politics, fashion, home life, and military memorabilia of the day, as well as prehistoric Florida. Open Tuesday–Saturday 10 AM–4 PM; donation.

The history of African American life in Jacksonville is depicted at the beautifully restored **Ritz Theatre and Museum** (904-807-2010; jaxevents.com/venues/ritz-theatre-and-museum), 829 N Davis Street, in the heart of the century-old LaVilla district near downtown, once known as the "Harlem of the South." The 400-seat theater (see *Entertainment*) is home to exciting musicals and theatrical performances. Inside the 11,000-square-foot museum, learn from brave men and women who made a difference during a time of institutionalized racism, their stories told through artifacts, displays, and animatronic figures. Open Tuesday–Friday 10 AM–5 PM, Saturday 10 AM–2 PM; fee.

Florida's first naval warship museum which is actually a ship, the **USS *Adams* Museum** (904-910-5241; ussadams.com), 2 Independent Drive at the Jacksonville Landing, is steaming into place, with plans to open in spring of 2018. A guided missile destroyer commissioned in 1960, the ship was on active duty for the Cuban blockade in 1962 and participated in recovering astronauts during Project Mercury. She has served in Europe, the Middle East, the Mediterranean, and the Indian Ocean, with many deployments out of Mayport, where she was decommissioned in 1990. The Ship's Store is showcasing artifacts and shipboard equipment as the Landing awaits the Adams' arrival.

✤ There's not much to **Yellow Bluff Fort Historic State Park** (904-251-2320; floridastateparks.org/park/Yellow-Bluff), New Berlin Road [30.399745, -81.55564], save its storied history. The deep gouges in this hillside above the St. Johns River (now hidden by a screen of trees) were earthworks used by both Confederate and Union troops during the Civil War, an encampment from which big guns were trained on the river below. Some cannons remain, as well as a picnic spot. Free.

PERFORMING ARTS In a classic playhouse—the Adele Grage Cultural Center, 716 Ocean Boulevard, built in 1932—the **Atlantic Beach Experimental Theatre** (ABET) (904-249-7177; abettheatre.com) acts out September–May. In their 26th season in 2017, they stage classics like *Little Shop of Horrors* as well as edgy, experimental pieces. Visit their website for schedule and tickets.

In San Marco, the art deco **Little Theatre** (904-396-4425; theatrejax.com), 2032 San Marco Boulevard, offers a slate of live theater from **Theatre Jacksonville**, a theatrical company founded in 1919.

The vibrant **Ritz Theatre** (see *Museums and Historic Sites*), 829 N Davis Street, celebrates the richness of African American music and culture with stage shows, concerts, storytelling, theater, and dance. Home to both the Ritz Jazz Society and the Ritz Jazz Orchestra, it's a venue where you'll find something new going on every weekend.

Bringing world-class music to Jacksonville year-round, the **Riverside Fine Arts Series** (904-389-6222; riversidefinearts.org) is based in the sanctuary of the Episcopal Church of the Good Shepherd, 1100 Stockton Street, a venue that seats 550.

♿ At the **Times Union Center for the Performing Arts** (904-633-6110; jaxevents .com), 300 W Water Street, see major traveling shows like *Sesame Street Live*, *Dancing with the Stars*, and more. It is the home of the **Jacksonville Symphony Orchestra** (904-354-5547; jaxsymphony.org), with concerts year-round.

RAILROADIANA At the **Beaches Museum & History Park** (see *Museums*), railroad buffs will appreciate being able to walk around the relocated Mayport railroad depot from 1900, Florida East Coast Foreman's House #93 from the same year, and a 1911 Cummer and Sons steam locomotive from the cypress logging days, right off the Mayport & Pablo Railway, which once ran here.

✳ To Do

AMUSEMENTS **Mindbender Escape Rooms** (904-853-6192; mindbenderescaperooms .com), 1500 Beach Boulevard #212, offers a different kind of indoor challenge—one where you need to use your brain. Choose from four tricky escape games full of clues and puzzles that need to be solved within an hour, such as The Jewel Heist, where you must break into Ashton Manor and steal the Templar Ruby. It's an immersive way to take a break from the beach, $30–33.

BIKING Bikes and the beach? Jacksonville is an off-road cyclist's dream. Wicked twists and turns plus sudden ups and downs under a dense canopy of forest make the tightly winding **mountain bike trails at Kathryn Abbey Hanna Park** (see *Parks, Preserves, and Camping*) a challenge you won't forget. Cyclists can rent a Giant ATX mountain bike at the park at the Hanna Park campground store (904-404-6177), $10/hr or $50/day. Pay attention to trail signage: most trails are singletrack and must be ridden in the posted direction on certain days to avoid accidents with fellow riders, and the trails cross the hiking trail system frequently.

The 4-mile **off-road loop trail** at Fort George Island Cultural State Park (see *Parks, Preserves, and Camping*) is challenging in places due to the terrain; a more gentle and beautiful ride is on the **Saturiwa Trail**, tunneling deep into old-growth forest; vehicles

THE JACKSONVILLE ZOO

One of Florida's larger zoological parks, Jacksonville Zoo and Gardens (904-757-4463; jacksonvillezoo.org), 370 Zoo Parkway, blends formal gardens with thematically grouped animal enclosures across 92 acres near the confluence of the Trout River with the St. Johns River. Moved here from Springfield Park in 1925, the "Municipal Zoo" grew into the largest and most beloved of Jacksonville's attractions. ✐ ♿

Each part of the zoo flows into the next while retaining its distinct character. Rhinos, warthogs, and bongos inhabit the Plains of East Africa, crossed on a 1,400-foot boardwalk that also takes you under a rare nesting colony of native wood storks. Introspection is invited inside the lovely Monsoon Asia, with its lotus pool, koi pond, and bamboo forest. As gardens yield to habitats, the Komodo dragons look like dinosaurs walking the earth and the expansive Land of the Tiger surrounds you with a space where Malaysian and Sumatran tigers roam and splash, sometimes right over your head. The child-scaled Play Park includes a splash playground and a peek at Magellanic penguins. Of course there's a Wild Florida, where residents and visitors alike will see some of our more common fauna like gopher tortoises and alligators, and less-common fauna like the whooping crane and Florida black bear.

On a single day's visit, you'll walk several miles and still not catch all of the nuances of the gardens and exhibits; there are more than a dozen distinct exhibit areas. General admission $18 adult, $16 seniors, $13 ages 3–12; value tickets available to bundle extra cost items such as train and carousel rides, 4-D theater, and animal interaction exhibits like Butterfly Hollow and Stingray Bay; additional fees for special behind-the-scenes and guided tours. Open Sunday–Friday 9 AM–5 PM, Saturday 9 AM–6 PM.

TIGER EXHIBIT AT JACKSONVILLE ZOO

share the trail. Off-road opportunities are also available at Tillie K. Fowler Regional Park and the Theodore Roosevelt Area (see Parks). Rent beach-going bicycles at **Rent Beach Stuff** (904-305-6472; rentbeachstuff.com), 11 1st Street N, Jacksonville Beach for surfside rides.

Ray Greene Park (904-252-9923; coj.net), 1946 Ray Greene Drive, Northside, managed by Jacksonville BMX (jacksonvillebmx.com), lets you bring your own bike for **BMX** action or rent a bike and helmet on the spot. Your first practice and race is free. Open 5–10 PM; members only on Tuesday and Friday evenings.

For a paved ride by the sea, head for the **Timucuan Trail**, which is being established along the length of the Talbot Islands; it's part of the East Coast Greenway. The northern section in Big Talbot Island is nicely shaded and includes a boardwalk along the marshes. The southern section on Little Talbot Island is more open. You can rent a bike for that trip at the Little Talbot Island State Park ranger station ($2/hr, $10/day).

The **Jacksonville-Baldwin Rail Trail** (floridahikes.com/jacksonville-baldwin-trail) comprises 14.5 miles of an old CSX railway line through a dense canopy of forests, wetlands, and fields between Imeson Road and CR 121. There are three separate paths: one for walking, jogging, and in-line skating; one for mountain bikers; and one for horseback riding. This historic route was the path taken by Union soldiers en route to and in retreat from the Battle of Olustee (see *The Upper Suwannee* chapter).

BIRDING Birding sites are plentiful along the estuarine shorelines where the St. Johns River meets the sea. From the bluffs at **Pumpkin Hill Creek** and the **Theodore Roosevelt Area**, watch herons, ibis, and other wading birds in the tidal creeks and

JACKSONVILLE-BALDWIN RAIL TRAIL AT CAMP MILTON

BEST BEACHES

For dogs: Hanna Park
For families: Sea Walk/Oceanfront Park, Jacksonville Beach
For people-watching: Atlantic Beach/Neptune Beach
For solitude: Big Talbot Island
For sunbathing: Little Talbot Island
For walking: Little Talbot Island

This portion of Florida's coast is known for riptides, so it's best to swim only at beaches where lifeguards are present and follow the warning flags flying. Red means don't enter the water, yellow means it's risky. Wildly popular with the younger set, **Jacksonville Beach**, **Neptune Beach**, and **Atlantic Beach** all offer broad, sunny strands on which to nourish a tan, and lifeguards watch these beaches.

North of Fort George Island, A1A runs through **Little Talbot Island State Park** (904-251-2320; floridastateparks.org/parks/little-talbot-island-state-park), 12157 Heckscher Drive, Northside, and **Big Talbot Island State Park** (floridastateparks.org/parks/big-talbot-island-state-park), N A1A. These adjoining barrier islands provide an immersion into the wilds along two undeveloped Florida shorelines, estuary and oceanfront, which is a rare and glorious experience.

The beachfront at Little Talbot is a 5-mile-long swath of dunes and wilderness; walk north to stake out your own private piece of waterfront for the day. On Big Talbot, a short hiking trail leads out to one of Florida's most unusual beaches, Blackrock Beach. With offshore sandbars and black rocks in the foreground, it looks like a scene from Hawaii, but the lava-like "rocks" are made of naturally eroded peat and sand, with fallen trees from the bluffs creating a "boneyard." The Bluffs Picnic Area provides a promontory at the north end of the island and is great for surf fishing. The Timucuan Trail, a paved bike path that's part of the East Coast Greenway, slips through a stunning array of habitats across the length of both islands.

mudflats along with ospreys overhead. **Castaway Island Preserve** is busy with bird life along the Intracoastal Waterway, even in the heat of the day, with **Cradle Creek Preserve** and **Dutton Island Preserve** providing observation decks on the opposite shore. Migrants like the colorful painted bunting show up on the **Talbot Islands** each winter, and songbirds always echo through the forest at the **Sawmill Slough Preserve** on the University of North Florida campus. See *Parks, Preserves, and Camping* for details on these and many more locations.

BOATING **St. Johns River Taxi & Tours** (904-860-8924; jaxrivertaxi.com) offers a Zoo Cruise and MOSH History Cruise every Saturday, as well as their popular River Jam Sunset Cruise each evening. Narrated sightseeing tours are also available; cruise tickets run $15–40.

BREWERY TOURS Established in 1969, the **Budweiser Jacksonville Brewery** (904-751-8116; budweisertours.com), 111 Busch Drive, Jacksonville, is the granddaddy of local breweries, serving the South for Anheuser-Busch. You can pop in for a free self-guided tour; sign up for a more in-depth guided tour, which covers the history of the company pre-Prohibition; or join the Beermaster Tour for an in-depth look at the Brew Hall and the cellars, with a taste from a finishing tank. There's even a Beer School

✒ ♿ The campground on Little Talbot Island sits in a shady bowl created by the dunes of the maritime forest. It's across the street from the beach but in a perfect place, well hidden from the sun by a thick canopy of sand live oaks. Walk down to the Intracoastal and fish from the bank or explore the nature trail; canoe rentals are available at the boat ramp. There are 33 sites to choose from, $24.

BEACHGOERS AT LITTLE TALBOT ISLAND

where you sit on a taste test panel—one of the jobs Sandra did for a living in the 1980s. All tour guests 21 and over receive a free sample at the start of each tour, and of course you can sample more beer at the Tap Room. Guided tours, $10–30, include commemorative gifts. Check their website for specific footwear requirements for the paid tours and to purchase tickets/make reservations online. Of course, there's beer gear for sale, too. June–August 10 AM–5 PM daily, September–May 10 AM–4 PM, Thursday–Tuesday.

Microbrew enthusiasts rejoice: Jacksonville isn't a one-beer town. Although the Budweiser Jacksonville Brewery is the biggest and oldest brewery in the region, the **Jax Ale Trail** (visitjacksonville.com/jax-ale-trail) leads you beyond the obvious with a Brewery Passport to eight craft breweries. Five of the breweries have won medals at the Best Florida Beer Championship. Pick up your passport by stopping at the Visit Jacksonville Visitor Centers (see *Guidance*) or any of the breweries themselves; see the website for the list.

ECOTOURS Heading off-road at Fort George Island Cultural State Park, the **Segway Tours by Kayak Amelia** (904-251-0016; kayakamelia.com/segway.htm) are quite unique. First you learn how to guide the vehicle, then you glide across the grass and sand on an interpretive introduction to Florida as the Timucua knew it. The longer tour continues on to Kingsley Plantation for a ride around the historic site; $75–95.

FAMILY ACTIVITIES ✍ **Adventure Landing** (904-685-4343; jacksonville-beach
.adventurelanding.com), 1944 Beach Boulevard, Jacksonville Beach. Get wet at Shipwreck Island Water Park, and then compete with the kids on go-carts, miniature golf,
and laser tag. Full day admission $24–29, or come in after 3 PM for $20 to splash around
the waterpark.

✍ Eat, drink, and play at **Dave & Buster's** (904-296-1525; daveandbusters.com/
jacksonville), 7025 Salisbury Road, Jacksonville Beach. Interactive games, simulators,
arcades, and food and drink. After 10 PM, adults enjoy Happy Hour until close. Fee.

✍ Inside a cute castle that seems incongruous on this busy boulevard, the **Hands
On Children's Museum** (904-642-2688; handsonchildrensmuseumjax.startlogic.com),
8580 Beach Boulevard, Southside, offers hands-on adventures for small children. They
can make a deposit at the Mini Bank, be cashiers at the Winn-Dixie Little Grocery, or
play with the puppets. Tiny tots have their own adventure room to explore, and everyone gets soapy in the Bubble Room. Fee.

✍ A shady oasis in this urban area, **Tree Hill Nature Center** (904-724-4646; treehill
.org), 7152 Lone Star Road, Arlington, is a place for families to explore together, with
more than 53 acres in which you can roam on nature trails and boardwalks. Enjoy the
butterfly garden and explore their natural history museum, with its interactive exhibits on native wildlife, energy, and more; fee. Monday–Saturday 8 AM–4:30 PM.

FISHING **Captain Dave Sipler** (904-642-9546; captdaves.com) will take you up to the
Mayport Jetties and sometimes into nearby inlets and tidal creeks; his motto is "no
long boat rides" because he'd rather you spend your time fishing. Six-hour trips, $400
for 2 passengers, $600 for 4.

To cast off a pier, head to the **Jacksonville Beach Pier** (904-241-1515), 503 N 1st Street,
Jacksonville Beach, for salt water (no license required), fee; or **Mandarin Park** (904-630-
2489), 14780 Mandarin Road, for freshwater fishing in the St. Johns River, free.

GOLF While golfers tend to cast an eye south to the offerings around Ponte Vedra
(see the *St. Augustine* chapter), Jacksonville has its own charming courses. Rated as
one of the top golf courses in Florida by *Golf News*, **Windsor Parke Golf Club** (904-223-
4653; windsorparke.com), 13823 Sutton Park Drive N, Southside, is an 18-hole course
designed by Arthur Hills, considered the only beginner-friendly course in the area.
Run by the city of Jacksonville, **Bent Creek Golf Course** (904-779-0800; golfbentcreek
.com), 10440 Tournament Lane, Jacksonville Heights West, is a 6,620-yard par 71 with
meandering fairways edged by pine flatwoods. Offering the best tee times and rates,
Florida's First Coast of Golf (800-530-5248; florida-golf.org/teetimes) can book you
into any of the major courses between Amelia Island and St. Augustine.

HIKING In this urban area, Jacksonville's preserves, along with state and federal
lands, shine as destinations for hikers. None of the hikes are especially lengthy, but
scenic vistas are the norm; you'll find many recommendations in *50 Hikes in North
Florida*. One of our favorites is the **Island Hiking Trail** at Little Talbot Island State
Park, a 3.8-mile loop through coastal habitats and up and over sand dunes to end as a
beach walk back to the main part of the park. For a surprising bit of urban quiet that's
perfect for the kids, check out **Castaway Island Preserve** on the way to Jacksonville
Beach. In town, **Jacksonville Arboretum and Gardens** has a diverse trail system to
roam, and the **Theodore Roosevelt Area, Timucuan Ecological & Historic Preserve**
offers great views from its bluffs above the St. Johns River. Explore a surprising variety of habitats at **Sawmill Slough Preserve** on nearly 5 miles of trails on the University
of North Florida campus.

HORSEBACK RIDING Explore the bluffs above the Fort George River on a **guided trail ride with Happy Trails Walking Horses** (904-557-3126; happytrailswalkers.com) through Pumpkin Hill Preserve State Park and adjoining Betz Tiger Point Preserve. Call in advance to book, $88 per hour, ages 10 and up.

NIGHTLIFE On a Friday night, the in place to be is **Atlantic Boulevard**, with parties on both sides of the street where Atlantic Beach and Neptune Beach meet at the shore. With a few dozen places to hang out until all hours, it's easy to find a nightspot to fit your mood, or you can try a pub crawl—there's one taking place every few doors. Jazz lovers flock to **Ragtime** (904-241-7877; ragtimetavern.com), 207 Atlantic Boulevard, a New Orleans–style establishment that goes on and on and on down the street. Featuring handcrafted beers, it's not a bar but a series of intimate spaces (each with its own bar) evoking the French Quarter, and it offers a full dinner menu and plenty of appetizers till late.

PADDLING The extensive saltwater creeks and tidal marshes of the St. Johns River can only be seen by kayak. On the Northside and in the Talbot Islands, paddle these remote, scenic waterways with **Kayak Amelia** (904-251-0016; kayakamelia.com), the official outfitter for the state parks in that region. For trips south of downtown and along the Intracoastal Waterway, check with **Black Creek Guides** (blackcreekguides .com), a spin-off of local outfitter Black Creek Outfitters (see *Shopping*), for their list. Guided tours start at $65. Both outfitters also rent kayaks and SUP.

    Rent Beach Stuff (904-305-6472; rentbeachstuff.com), 11 1st Street N, Jacksonville Beach, offers **stand up paddleboards**; rentals run $25 per hour, $50 per day. Dutton Island is a great spot to launch into the winding tidal creeks.

PARKS, PRESERVES, AND CAMPING 🐾 ✎ ♿ One of the most pleasant coastal parks in the region, **Castaway Island Preserve** (floridahikes.com/castawayisland), 14548 San Pablo Drive N, Jacksonville, offers a gentle, paved nature trail with boardwalks for birding along the Intracoastal Waterway. At the end of a residental bike path, the preserve is a place where you can slip a canoe in the water, stop at the playground, or visit the nature center before communing with wildlife along the well-interpreted loop trail.

    ✎ 🐾 ♿ With tent sites (some with benches and fire rings) on an island in the Intracoastal Waterway, **Dutton Island Preserve** (904-247-5828; coab.us), 1921 Dutton Island Road [30.338324, -81.431651], is truly an island, reached by a long one-lane causeway paralleled with a bicycle path through the estuary. Boardwalks lead to scenic views and a kayak launch; wheelchairs available on request. It is a beautiful spot for camping, but here, you're roughing it. Choose from five campsites among the cedars and oaks; you must haul your gear in, but it's a short walk. Bathrooms are in one central location on the island. $26.75 per site per night. Nearby **Tideviews Preserve**, 1 Begonia Street, also a city park, has a boardwalk to an estuarine overlook and a place to launch your canoe.

    🐾 The site of tens of thousands of years of human habitation, **Fort George Island Cultural State Park** (904-251-2320; floridastateparks.org/park/Fort-George-Island), 12157 Heckscher Drive, shows more modern signs of the human touch—the former golf greens of the historic Ribault Club (see *Museums and Historic Sites*) are being reclaimed by coastal forest. Explore the park along its hiking or the Saturiwa Trail driving tour; guided cross-terrain Segway tours through the ancient forest are also available (see *Ecotours*).

    ✎ On a hot summer day, catch the mist off the world's first high-spraying fountains at **Friendship Park & Fountain** (jaxfountain.com), 1015 Museum Circle, Southbank

RIVERFRONT AT FORT GEORGE ISLAND STATE PARK

Riverwalk, downtown, on the St. Johns River. Refurbished in recent years to its former glory, it's the site of evening light and music shows.

Henry J. Klutho Park (coj.net), 204 W 3rd Street, was known as Springfield Park when it was created between 1899 and 1901 along Hogans Creek. Improved during the Great Depression with Klutho as architect, it features a Venetian-style promenade. The original municipal zoo opened here in 1914, as well as the city's first public swimming pool.

✍ Just across the St. George River from Little Talbot Island, perched at the mouth of the St. Johns, **Huguenot Memorial Park** (904-251-3335; coj.net), 10980 Heckscher Drive 32226, is one of the region's more popular remote beaches but is extra-special because it offers camping. Bounded by water on three sides, the size of the park expands and contracts with the tides, but the three campgrounds (inlet, river, and woods) remain the same—88 sites total. There are no hookups, but at $23–27/night, no need to complain. Tents and RVs welcome.

At **Jesse Ball DuPont Treaty Oak Park**, Prudential Drive at Main Street (FL 13), downtown, the ancient live oak that canopies much of the park boasts a spread of more than 160 feet. In 1907 the tree was festooned with electric lights as electricity came to Jacksonville for the first time.

South of the St. Johns River, 447-acre **Kathryn Abbey Hanna Park** (904-249-4700; coj.net), 500 Wonderwood Drive, honors Dr. Hanna, who served on the Florida Parks Board from 1953–1963 while encouraging historic preservation of natural areas in Florida. Boardwalks lead through gnarled forests of sand live oaks and over tall, windswept dunes topped with cabbage palms and sea oats to strands of white sand that attract surfers, anglers, and dog walkers from all over the region. The park also includes fishing ponds and hiking and biking trails through a dense coastal forest, as well as two campgrounds with 300 wonderfully wooded sites. Sites come with electric and water and cost $20/tent, $34/camper or RV, $34/camping cabin (two-day minimum stay).

Between Riverside and Avondale, **Memorial Park** (904-630-2489; coj.net), 1620 Riverside Avenue, was the city's first major park, dedicated in 1924. Designed by the prestigious Olmsted Brothers firm, it offers a broad open green space overlooking the St. Johns River, a gathering place for locals and a quiet place to read amid a neighborhood of stately 1920s homes. A central piece of art in the park is the bronze sculpture *Life* by Charles Adrian Pillars.

Within city limits yet certifiably wild, **Pumpkin Hill Creek Preserve State Park** (904-696-5980; floridastateparks.org/park/Pumpkin-Hill), 13802 Pumpkin Hill Road, Northside, lies north of the St. Johns River off a maze of roads off Heckscher Drive (follow the signs). The park is adjoined by **Betz Tiger Point Preserve** (coj.net), 13990 Pumpkin Hill Road, surrounded by Pumpkin Hill Creek and a vast estuary. More than 4,000 acres are protected along the Nassau River, encompassing tall bluffs, scrub, and salt marshes.

♿ More than 300 acres of upland and floodplain habitats are protected as **Sawmill Slough Preserve**, University of North Florida (904-620-2998), 4567 St. Johns Bluff Road, Southside. An extensive, well-marked trail system guides you through the preserve, with a portion of it a wheelchair-accessible boardwalk through the heart of a cypress swamp. Deeper in the woods, one of Florida's more ancient cypresses can be seen from an overlook. A parking pass is required on weekdays; fee.

🐾 **Theodore Roosevelt Area, Timucuan Ecological & Historic Preserve** (904-221-5568; nps.gov/timu), 13165 Mt. Pleasant Road, Arlington, is both a wild shore and a preserve of archaeological and historic importance due to its massive Timucuan middens and a trail on which the Spanish trod en route to Fort Caroline. This deeply shaded National Park Service unit encompasses coastal scrub, freshwater wetlands, shady oak hammocks, and saltwater marshes, with several miles of biking and hiking trails. Open daily 9 AM–4:45 PM; free.

✎ ♿ In the heart of Jacksonville Beach, the **Seawalk Festival Area** (904-247-6100; jacksonvillebeach.org) consists of two blocks of open green space between A1A and the oceanfront, with open grassy squares, walkways, and a pavilion for concerts. Bring your beach chair or blanket and join the locals for arts festivals, the Summer Jazz Concert, and classic car cruises held each month on the third Thursday.

🐾 ✎ ♿ Covering 509 acres across US 17 from the Jacksonville Naval Air Station, **Tillie K. Fowler Regional Park** (904-573-2498; coj.net), Ortega, is a park you can get lost in. Its extensive trail system includes an off-road bicycle trail loop, an easy walk from the park's nature center to an observation tower overlooking the Ortega River floodplain, and the Island Trail, which heads out to an island in the river swamp and has so many side trails that you'll need a map or GPS to stay on track. Playgrounds and a picnic area sit beneath the pines.

SURFING At Kathryn Abbey Hanna Park, **"The Poles"** adjoin Mayport Naval Station. Breaking best on a low tide with clean lefthand lines, it's an experienced surfer's must. **Wave Masters** (floridasurfing.org/event/wavemasters) holds Florida's top amateur surfing event at the park each May. Check Surfline (surfline.com) for the best spots along the beaches, or consult the experts at **Austin's Surf Shop** (904-249-9848; austinssurfshop.com), 615 3rd Street S, Jacksonville Beach. They've offered up advice since 1972 and know the surf report; stop in for leashes, wax, and other essentials you may have forgotten. Established in 1974, **Fort George Surf Shop** (904-256-4151; ftgeorgesurfshop.com), 10030 Heckscher Drive, is en route to the **North Jetty** at **Huguenot Memorial Park**, another top surfing spot, a shifting sandbar at the mouth of the St. Johns River with a campground at the beach. It's considered one of the best places in the region to catch a wave.

U-PICK Rural Duval County is a hot spot for blueberries, thanks to the acidic soil. In June, pick your own at the **Dowless Blueberry Farm** (904-772-1369), 7010 Ricker Road, 2 miles south of 103rd Street off I-295.

✳ Lodging

BED & BREAKFASTS ⟮⟲⟯ ⤳ A 1925 Prairie School brick home, **The Jenks House** (904-387-2092; thejenkshouse.com), 2804 Post Street, Riverside 32204, still contains many original furnishings owned by the Jenks family and passed down to Ila Rae and Tom Merten, who've resided in and lovingly cared for this home for several decades. Two rooms invite you in: the Mission Room, with a cane-back headboard and modern 1920s flair, and the Live Oak Room, awakening your sense of style with classic art deco furnishings. $95–110, including gourmet breakfast.

☀ ⟮⟲⟯ In the romantic **Riverdale Inn** (904-354-5080; riverdaleinn.com), 1521 Riverside Avenue, Riverside 32204, a dash of period furnishings, as part of the soothing decor of each room, adds to the appeal of leaving the everyday world behind and cozying up in this 1901 Shingle-style mansion along "The Row," where turn-of-the-twentieth-century wealth built stately homes. This is one of only two remaining. With 10 guest rooms and suites, including accommodations in the mansion's Carriage House, an on-site restaurant and pub open for guests (and their friends), and a policy of permitting small dogs, the inn attracts a regular clientele. Jacuzzi tubs are featured in some of the larger rooms, and the Petit Lancaster room has two twin beds, perfect for sisters traveling together. The new Coach House Quarters offers the largest space in the complex, with two queen beds and a full kitchen; $155–285.

⟮⟲⟯ Built in 1914, **St. Johns House** (904-384-3724; stjohnshouse.com), 1718 Osceola Street, Riverside 32204, is an elegant Prairie School home that offers views of the river from its sunporch as you enjoy your breakfast. Innkeepers Joan Moore and Dan Schafer live on-site, attentive to your needs. Three spacious guest rooms provide amenities that business travelers will appreciate, including a coffeemaker, a hair dryer, an ironing board, an alarm clock, and Wi-Fi. The beautiful Barnett Room provides a writing table and a strong dose of natural light to get you going in the morning. Open November–May, closed March; $99 and up.

The well-to-do flocked to this new Spanish Mediterranean hotel in droves. A parade of famous folks has stayed here through the years, from Al Capone to Harry S. Truman. And like many of Florida's historic hotels, it was commandeered for the war effort during World War II to house troops. Not until 1991 did it reopen as a hotel with the elegance of its former glory, with 24 individually decorated rooms and suites providing a taste of the regal past. A member of the Historic Hotels of America, it's a destination that no classic-hotel buff should miss. $159 and up.

COMFORT AND LUXURY ✧ ♂ ⟮⟲⟯ ⤳ Walk into **One Ocean Resort** (904-249-7402; oneoceanresort.com), 1 Ocean Boulevard, Atlantic Beach 32233, and you'll immediately feel the touch of class. Stay in an oceanfront room or suite to be left breathless at the perfection of an Atlantic sunrise. It's the Sea Turtle rejuvenated and pushed up the high-society ladder, with appealing modern decor and a new sense of style. Some of the unique amenities include your own docent and guest historian, a personalized refreshment cabinet, complimentary snacks and beverages, iPod docking stations, ocean sound machines, and heat sensors that tell housekeeping whether you're in or out so you aren't disturbed by a knock on the door. Wi-Fi is included, but a resort fee is charged on top of your base room fee. Aspiring novelists, note: Each room has a writing desk. Read John Grisham's *The Brethren*, which he wrote here when this was the Sea Turtle Inn, and discover your inspiration, too. $194 and up.

RETRO AND ARTSY ☀ ♂ ⟮⟲⟯ Go retro at **The Hotel Palms** (904-241-7776; thehotel palms.com), 28 Sherry Drive, Atlantic

Beach 32233 a boutique beach hotel reborn from a 1947 motor court by the sea, the beach just a couple of blocks away. Chat with friends over drinks from the beer and wine lounge while relaxing in the private courtyard. Of the eleven rooms, one is a bunkhouse perfect for parents with a child or close friends; at the other end of the spectrum, The Suite has 475 sq ft of comfort with a desk and dining nook. Amentities include parking, a big plus when visiting in this busy seaside district. $149–209.

All rooms face the ocean at the **Sea Horse Oceanfront Inn** (800-881-2330 or 904-246-2175; jacksonvilleoceanfront hotel.com), 140 Atlantic Boulevard, Neptune Beach 32266, its exterior distinctively decorated with blue neon seahorses. Inside your room, savor the view, or better yet head down to the famous Lemon Bar, an oceanside tiki bar that gets rolling well after dark. Standard rooms offer a refrigerator and a coffeemaker; suites and a penthouse are available. $129–239.

TRIED AND TRUE As a financial center with many business travelers, Jacksonville has multiple locations of every major chain hotel scattered across the region; indeed, major brands dominate this market. & (ꜽ) **Holiday Inn Express & Suites Jacksonville South** (904-899-9000; ihg.com), 11262 Old St. Augustine Rd, is strategically located along the southern I-295 beltway, a good location for exploring San Marco, Mandarin, and Southside. We've stayed there as well as the & (ꜽ) **Hampton Inn & Suites Jacksonville South—Bartram Park** (904-268-6264; hilton.com), 13950 Village Lake Circle, which is not far from St. Johns Village and points north off I-295 like Jacksonville Arboretum & Gardens and Fort Caroline. & (ꜽ) **Holiday Inn Express Jacksonville East** (904-997-9190; ihg .com), 53 Jefferson Road, is right on top of those Arlington destinations with easy access to Mayport and the North Shore attractions, like the Jacksonville Zoo.

Near the airport, & (ꜽ) **Courtyard by Marriott Jacksonville Airport Northeast** (904-741-1122; marriott.com), 14668 Duval Road, Jacksonville 32218, is a comfortable option with an airport shuttle and guest laundry. On the west side, a budget-friendly stay at **Country Inn & Suites By Carlson, Jacksonville West** (904-786-0388; countryinns.com), 7035 Commonwealth Avenue, Jacksonville 32220, made it easy to explore the Cummer Museum and the shopping in Avondale, Five Points, and Riverside after rush hour had subsided.

& 🐾 🐕 (ꜽ) At the beach, **Four Points by Sheraton Jacksonville Beachfront** (904-435-3535; fourpoints.com), 11 1st Street N, Jacksonville Beach 32250, is a pet-friendly option that looks right out over the ocean. & 🐕 (ꜽ) Also oceanfront, the **Hampton Inn Jacksonville Beach/ Oceanfront** (904-241-2311; hilton.com), 1515 1st Street N, Jacksonville Beach 32250, offers the biggest pool on the beach, a meandering lagoon with four waterfalls and a whirlpool grotto.

& & (ꜽ) ⇲ From the **Hyatt Regency Jacksonville** (904-588-1234; jacksonville .regency.hyatt.com), 225 E Coastline Drive, Jacksonville 32202, you can stroll the Riverwalk to the Landing, downtown's hot gathering spot. Rooms come in two flavors: Riverview or Cityview. Suites are available on the Regency Club Level, where guests enjoy a private breakfast. The 19th floor has a rooftop fitness center, hot tub, and pool overlooking the river. There are two restaurants and two bars in the 951-room complex, which is a favorite for major conventions. $95–245.

CAMPGROUND 🐾 🐕 (ꜽ) **Flamingo Lake RV Resort** (800-782-4323; flamingolake .com), 3640 Newcomb Road 32218, is just off I-295 at Lem Turner Road. With 288 full-hookup sites, Wi-Fi included, this is one monster of an RV destination, complete with its own dog park. Kids will enjoy splashing into the lake at its little beach or fishing at the other end. Located next to the playground, a pool is open during the summer months. Sites $51–89, depending on location and surface; rental cabins with kitchen equipment and linens included, $90–140; and semi-primitive yurts with heat and A/C, $50–84. The on-site Flamingo Lake Café whips up breakfast, lunch, and dinner daily.

✳ Where to Eat

TRADITION Savor a slice of Floridiana at a funky fish camp—**Clark's Fish Camp Seafood Restaurant** (904-268-3474; clarksfishcamp.com), 12903 Hood Landing Road, Mandarin. With a menagerie of critters looking over your shoulder—one of the largest private taxidermy collections in the country—you'll savor Southern favorites like fried green tomatoes and fried dill pickles, or choose a less-common appetizer off their "Call of the Wild" menu: ostrich sausage or smoked eel, anyone? Their house special oysters are the cream of the crop. Their extensive entrée selection, $10–34, has "Nawlins" specialities like Boudin and Etoufee, and includes a big Low Country boiled platter for two if you have a sweetie to share that heap of steamed seafood.

ELEGANT AND ROMANTIC 🍴 Rated one of Jacksonville's best by its patrons, **Bistro Aix** (pronounced *X*, like the city in France) (904-398-1949; bistrox.com), 1440 San Marco Boulevard, melds French and Mediterranean influences for the best of both worlds. The 1940s brickwork and plush leather seats offer comfortable surroundings as you savor grilled tuna over whipped potatoes or a mushroom and Fontina wood-fired pizza; entrées $18–29, with half-portions of pasta available. At lunch, try the short rib grilled cheese or calamari salad, and don't miss the crispy homemade potato chips with warm blue cheese. It's a culinary experience you won't soon forget.

Gluten-free eaters rejoice: wine and food selections await.

♿ Sit and watch the river traffic at **River City Brewing Co.** (904-398-2299; rivercitybrew.com), 835 Museum Circle, downtown, where the five-star meals are as much a draw as the location. In casual but elegant surroundings, the restaurant's menu relies heavily on fresh seafood, starting with steamed tiger clams and calamari and moving on to jambalaya, tempura shrimp, and traditional gumbo, thick with oysters, shrimp, crab, crawfish, scallops, and andouille sausage. Local Mayport shrimp are featured as well, but landlubbers will appreciate the grilled New York strip and other beef and chicken choices. Salads and vegetables are à la carte, with entrées $15–34, so the $25 prix fixe menu—featuring seared salmon, roasted chicken, shrimp and grits, or meatloaf—is a good deal.

"Delicious ambience" awaits at the intimate **Ocean 60** (904-247-0060; ocean60.com), 60 Ocean Boulevard, Atlantic Beach, where the experience starts with select martinis and fine wines. Move along to the main dining room to savor the menu by owner and executive chef Daniel Groshell, which might offer crispy brussels sprouts and pork carnitas, Latin-style whole fried fish, or 1960s shrimp scampi made with Mayport royal reds. Entrées are $19–29, but you won't want to stop there, not with oh-so-special salads and mouthwatering desserts to bookend your meal. You can drop a bundle with your date, but call it an education in epicurean life. Reservations strongly recommended. Monday–Thursday 5–10 PM, Friday–Saturday 5–11 PM.

BARBECUE For more than 60 years, **Jenkins Quality Barbecue** (904-353-6388; jenkinsqualitybarbecue.com), 830 N Pearl Street, downtown, has served up the most succulent barbecue in the city, including a huge slab of ribs. Now under the third generation's care, this institution features meats smoked over a wood-fired pit and smothered in secret sauces; it'll have you coming back again and again. $8 and up.

CASUAL FARE Lunchtimes are busy at **Beach Diner** (904-399-1306; beachdiner .com/san-marco), 1965 San Marco Boulevard, San Marco, where it's a pleasure to dine al fresco with the sound of the Three Lions fountain as a backdrop. The menu includes big breakfasts, including "Eggs on the Bayou," a twist on Eggs Benedict, as well as steak and eggs or fish and grits. The tuna melt and grilled triple cheese are tasty lunch options, $8–12.

A classy diner at one of the busiest corners of the beach, **Ellen's Kitchen** (904-372-4099; ellenskitchenatbeaches .com), 241 3rd Street, Neptune Beach, has been around for more than 50 years, and they know how to please the breakfast crowd. The sweet North Beach omelet comes with fresh mushrooms, avocados, spinach, sweet onion, fresh tomatoes, and asiago; there's even house-made corned beef hash to be had. Breakfast and lunch, $6–13.

You're never far from sports action at **The Mudville Grille** (904-722-0008; themudvillegrill.com), 1301 Monument Road, Arlington, where Louis Joseph and his family have been dishing up pub fare in a decidedly non-chain restaurant for more than 25 years. Choose from hefty half-pound burgers, including a turkey burger option; smoked wings or ribs; tasty wraps; and a broad selection of "jump starters" including red chili poppers and sweet potato fries, $5–15.

COMFORT FOOD At **Beach Hut Café** (904-249-3516), 1281 3rd Street S, Jacksonville Beach, the chili comes thick and meaty, just like we'd make it at home. People greet each other as they come in the door, and the waitress knows almost everyone's name. Lunch is a bustling proposition, with daily specials posted above the kitchen window and a long list of Southern sides to go with your meal. $5 and up.

🍗 **Beach Road Chicken Dinners** (904-398-7980; facebook.com/BRCD1939), 4132 Atlantic Boulevard, St. Nicholas, is one of those places that if you crave fried chicken all the time, you'd move nearby. It's been here since 1939, and it's just plain good Southern cooking—mashed potatoes and creamed peas, soft biscuits, and sweet tea to go with your done-just-right chicken.

🍴 For comfort food, **Famous Amos** (904-268-6159; famousamos.bz), 10339 San Jose Boulevard, is like a Howard Johnson's of the 1960s, but with a Southern twist. Think breaded pork chops, ham and pinto beans, and gizzards. Each home-style entrée comes with your choice of three veggies or a slice of pie—you'll have a tough time deciding between chocolate cream pie and broccoli, right? Breakfast served 24 hours, including Southern fare like pecan waffles and fried tomatoes and grits. No matter what time of day, you'll walk out full for under $20.

A retro diner with booths and counter service, **Fox Restaurant** (904-387-2669), 3580 St. Johns Avenue, Avondale, should be your lunch stop for comfort food, from hand-patted hamburger patties to classic reubens and pimento and cheese sandwiches. Lunch for under $10 often means a line out the door for hearty fare.

ETHNIC EATS 🍴 Savor the aromas flowing from **Al's Pizza** (904-388-8384; alspizza.com), 1620 Margaret Street #201, Five Points, a local chain found all over the city. Settle into the snazzy bistro digs and order a to-die-for BLT pizza—we couldn't have believed how good it was until we polished one off. Al Mazur is the quintessential immigrant-makes-good success story, and he means a lot to the local community. New York–style pies run $12 and up, and the menu includes other Italian faves.

Under the deep shade of a live oak tree, guests partake in makdous and the hubble-bubble of a hookah pipe at **The Casbah** (904-981-9966; thecasbahcafe

.com), 3826 St. Johns Avenue, Avondale, where the ambience transports you to a secret hideaway deep within a Moroccan souk, complete with pillows on the floor and a belly dancer. Billing itself as "Jacksonville's Premier Original Hookah Lounge," it's quite the draw for the late-night crowd. The food is pure Middle Eastern. Order the mezze and share: hummus, stuffed grape leaves, falafel, and baba ghanouj (with a side of kebbe for the carnivores) make an interesting meal (three-mezze combo, $17).

🐾 Since 1956, **Joseph's Pizza** (904-270-1122; josephsitalian.com), 30 Ocean Boulevard, Atlantic Beach, home of the homemade crust, has fed a steady stream of satisfied customers. Bring Fido to the pet-friendly side patio to share your pizza pie, and leave a little room for the nightly gelato specials. Pizzas $9 and up. Three locations, including Southside and downtown.

Settle into a Mediterranean trattoria at **Mezza Restaurant & Bar** (904-249-5573; mezzarestaurantandbar.com), 110 1st Street, Neptune Beach, a place to relax over Thai steamed mussels or a hand-cut steak tartare, and watch the world drift by. Entrées ($19–39) include delights like diver scallops, pan-roasted Idaho trout, and Mayport shrimp spaghetti; smaller appetites and budgets will enjoy homemade pizzas from their aromatic wood-fired oven, $18–22.

For traditional Italian in a decidedly nontraditional setting, **Santioni's Cucina Italiana** (904-262-5190; santionisjax .com), 11531 San Jose Boulevard #6, Mandarin, delights with the classics, from a real shrimp cocktail to spaghetti carbonara. The atmosphere is old-school Italian with traditional Neapolitan entrées, $12 and up.

Since 1985, **Sorrento Italian Restaurant** (904-636-9196), 6943 St. Augustine Road, San Jose, has consistently delighted diners with fresh presentations of Neapolitan favorites such as sausage with peppers, veal saltimbocca, and eggplant parmesan. The trattoria

atmosphere is perfect for an evening out with family, $13–24.

HIP BISTRO-STYLE Creative cuisine is what you'll find at **bb's** (904-306-0100; bbsrestaurant.com), 1019 Hendricks Avenue, San Marco, where sandwiches include crispy crabcake and grilled fish to complement their signature chorizo soup. Savor the selections, starting at $12, with a wine pairing from their extensive list. Prix fixe menu Monday–Thursday 5–10 PM, $25 for three courses, or choose from ever-changing entrées like roasted all-natural achiote chicken or pan-seared lane snapper, $24–38.

Biscotti's Expresso Cafe (904-387-2060; biscottis.net), 3556 St. Johns Avenue, Avondale, is a foodie hot spot where the cuisine ($12 and up) matches the trendy coffee that comes in a spectrum of different flavors. The Cafe Bites, from grilled brie to crab and artichoke fondue, are exquisite. It's hard to pick a favorite, but at a minimum come for coffee and their to-die-for chocolate desserts. The cozy tables inspire intimate conversations, especially over a glass of wine from their extensive wine list. Open for breakfast Saturday–Sunday, at 10:30 AM for lunch and dinner weekdays.

🐾 For relaxed dining, grab an early dinner at **Brick Restaurant** (904-387-0606; brickofavondale.com), 3585 St. Johns Avenue, Avondale, a local favorite where the bistro-inspired menu resonates well inside the restored 1926 Perkins Building. Entrées ($19–30) include ginger-seared sea scallops and New York strip; for a real treat, try the Seafood Tower Salad, featuring lobster, shrimp, scallops, and guacamole.

🐾 A landmark 1938 filling station is now a place where the whole neighborhood hangs out. Established in 1992, **Metro Diner** (904-398-3701; metrodiner .com), 3302 Hendricks Avenue, San Jose, caters to eclectic and Southern palates with breakfasts like Charleston shrimp and grits, pound cake French toast, and their specialty, the Breakfast Pie, packed with eggs, cheese, mushrooms, onion, bell peppers, red-skin potatoes, and herbs. Master Chef Mark Davoli spun this original location into a franchise you'll find across the Jacksonville metro and into neighboring states. Lunch and dinner favorites include the Metro Pot Roast or chicken potpie. Most meals are under $15.

Southern comfort food will keep you sated at **Secret Garden Cafe** (904-645-0859; secretgardencafe.net), 10095 Beach Boulevard, Southside, a spiffy bistro with down-home roots. Try the fried green tomatoes, stacked with goat cheese and served with roasted red pepper mayonnaise and red onion marmalade—a real tasty twist on the original, or an aromatic pesto grilled cheese with havarti, fresh basil pesto, tomato, spinach, and roasted red pepper. Salads and sandwiches $5–13, breakfast $6–13.

ORGANIC AND VEGETARIAN Bite into a slice of **Pie Heaven** (904-524-7274; pieheavencafe.com), 1980 Mayport Rd, Atlantic Beach, a little café with big taste. The pies are the reason to stop here: sit down and enjoy their homemade potpie, quiche, or shepherd's pie, all made with organic ingredients, then top it off with a slice of chocolate cloud pie with cinnamon whipped cream, or an old-school coconut custard. Call ahead to order whole pies to go, especially for pies customized to dietary needs.

QUICK BITE ☙ Grab a quick bite at **Lubi's Hot Subs** (904-642-3800; lubis .com), 500 N 3rd Street, Jacksonville Beach, home of "The Famous Lubi" ($7). Piled high on a steamed hero roll, it's like a Philly but has a Jacksonville twist—seasoned ground beef with mayo, mustard, American cheese, and a dash of hot pepper sauce. Wash it down with freshly made cherry limeade!

You've probably never thought of shrimp as a fast food feature, but if you need a quick lunch, **Shrimp Shack** (904-992-7111; opshrimpshack.com), 14440

Beach Boulevard, Jacksonville Beach, is a standard here at the beach. Pop in for coconut shrimp, grab some fried pickles, or sit down for cheesy shrimp and grits and a beer. Sandwiches, dinners, and platters, $8–16.

SEAFOOD Take in the view from the rooftop open-air bar at the **Beachside Seafood Market & Restaurant** (904-444-8862; beachsideseafoodrestaurant.com), 120 3rd Street S, Jacksonville Beach, or just stop by and grab a pound of fresh Mayport shrimp to steam back at the rental. Lunch is the busy time here, with Tim's Pepper Philly a tangy choice, $9–15.

☙ The shrimp fleet is anchored out back and the cases are filled with fresh seafood, whole and filleted. For 75 years, **Safe Harbor Restaurant & Seafood Market** (904-246-4911; safeharborseafoodmayport.com), 4378 Ocean Street #3, Mayport, has been the go-to place for take-out and eat-in seafood in Mayport. Order up their famed shrimp grilled, fried, or blackened, on a roll, as a po' boy or in a basket. Sides like bacon black-eyed peas and fried okra add to the Southern flair. Platters $9–20.

Dine outdoors on picnic tables under a canopy or indoors in the cozy booths at the ever-popular **Sliders Seafood Grille Bar** (904-246-0881; slidersseafoodgrille .com), 218 1st Street, Neptune Beach, where folks gather for the super-fresh seafood and cheap beer. Try their shrimp dip, made with fresh Mayport shrimp; the butternut grouper, baked with butter pecans; or Slider's own concoction, seafood meatloaf over garlic mashed potatoes. Casual and affordable, meals $12 and up.

TEAROOM Dining with a friend at **Cozy Tea** (904-329-3964; cozy-tea.com), 1029 Park Street, Five Points, it was tough to choose "just the right tea" from their four-page menu of teas from around the world, served hot or iced. Entrance to this little café is through a corridor of

CATCH OF THE DAY AT SAFE HARBOR SEAFOOD

fine china and antiques. We met early for lunch, when it's tough to choose between "Hot Savories" like the Zesty Cheese and Tomato Tart or Curried Chicken Pastry, or go with tea sandwiches or salads. Later in the afternoon, they switch to formal teas, with several options that'll have you salivating over freshly baked scones and whipped cream. Speaking of salivating, you must draw close to a case of handcrafted chocolate truffles as you go to pay your bill, each a tempting little work of art. Lunch under $15.

WATERFRONT When better to order peel-and-eat Mayport shrimp than while sitting on a deck on the St. Johns River looking at the Mayport shrimp fleet? That's what we thought with a stop at **Sandollar Restaurant** (904-251-2449; sandollarrestaurantjax.com), 9716 Heckscher Drive, Northshore, a serious destination for seafood just north of the St. Johns River Ferry, and a casual spot for hanging out with friends while listening to live music riverside.

LOCAL WATERING HOLES Bouncers guard the doors at the **Lemon Bar** (904-246-2175; lemonbarjax.com), the famous

tiki bar at Sea Horse Oceanfront Inn (see *Lodging*), and the place is wall-to-wall people late into the night.

History buffs note: **Pete's Bar** (904-249-9158), 117 1st Street, Neptune Beach, was the first bar in Florida to reopen after Prohibition. You expect Mickey Spillane to step out of the shadows in this smoky noir setting with its dark booths and busy pool tables—"a serious bar for serious drinkers."

BAKERY The rich aroma of freshly baked sugar cookies, the black-and-white floor, the gleaming expanse of bakery showcase—it might bring back childhood memories to step into **Cinnotti's Bakery** (904-246-1728; cinottisbakery.com), 1523 Penman Road, Neptune Beach, and stand there, dazzled at the selection. We finally settled on a couple of luscious raspberry cupcakes, almost more frosting than cake, with a raspberry center, but there were hundreds of treats to choose from, including breakfast and lunch sandwiches on their own freshly baked bread.

ICE CREAM AND SWEETS Indulge at **Peterbrooke Chocolatier** (904-398-2488; peterbrookesanmarco.com), 2024

San Marco, the original store of this small family chain in Northwest Florida. The cocoa aroma fills the store! You can pick up free samples or enjoy delights like chocolate-dipped potato chips and vanilla cream truffle eggs. The location at **Peterbrooke Chocolatier** (904-246-0277; peterbrookeatlanticbeach.com) 363 Atlantic Boulevard, Atlantic Beach, is run by the daughter of the founder. At both locations during the summer months, kids can become "chocolatier for a day" in a special day camp held Tuesday and Thursday, $50; reserve ahead.

✳ Selective Shopping

ANTIQUES Fine vintage furnishings shine inside **The Antique Market of San Jose** (904-733-1968; theantiquemarket ofsanjose.com), 5107 San Jose Boulevard. If you're looking for something more rustic, check out their Consignment Barn next door.

At **Avonlea Antiques** (904-636-8785; avonleamall.com), 8101 Philips Highway, Southside, browse through more than 200 dealer booths with a little something for everyone. This is a massive cache of vintage goods, 40,000 square feet strong, and in its aisles you'll find fine art and art glass, advertising ephemera, furniture, vintage books, and more.

Explore the nooks and crannies of **Fans & Stoves Antique Mall** (904-354-3768), 800 Lomax Street, Five Points, and it may take you a while. These dealer booths are crammed to the hilt with cool stuff like paint-by-number kits, saltcellars, lobby cards, and Fiestaware. Someone walked past us with a huge L&N Railroad sign. There are literally thousands of items to sift through in this maze of a store.

With more than 100 booths, **Sugar Bear Antiques** (904-886-0393), 3047 Julington Creek Road, Mandarin, provides a place to search stacks of memorabilia, collectibles, and fun retro items.

Sugarfoot Antiques (904-247-7607), 1013 3rd Street N, Jacksonville Beach, is a classic fine antiques store, specializing in European and Victorian furniture. But poke around a little and you'll find smaller treasures as well—dolls, fine china, children's books from the 1940s, and a year-round Christmas room.

ARTS AND CRAFTS An eclectic two-story gallery, **Bamboo Global Art & Home Accessories** (904-292-0230), 9165 San Jose Boulevard, Mandarin, features art and home decor items in natural fiber, wood, stone, and metal.

Get your crystals, gems, and lapidary supplies at **Bead Here Now** (904-475-0004; beadherenow.org), 1051 Park Street, Five Points, where you can not only take beading classes but arrange for blacksmithing classes (off-site) as well!

In truly distinctive shades of blue florals, Polish pottery fills the narrow space of **European Imports & Polish Pottery** (904-383-0546; facebook.com/polishpotteryjacksonville), 3564 St. Johns Avenue, Avondale. Interspersed throughout this colorful pottery shop are sea turtles, which evoke good memories for the owners, who rescued an injured one during a boating trip and took it to a rehab center.

BOOKS AND GIFTS A collector's destination, **Avondale Gift Boutique** (904-387-9557; agbjax.com), 3650 St. Johns Avenue, Avondale, is distinguished by its fountain out front and elegant collectibles inside. Look for Lladro figurines, pottery, and glass art; don't miss the Christmas room.

A hip indie bookstore with a carefully curated selection, **The Bookmark** (904-241-9026; bookmarkbeach.com), 220 1st Street, Neptune Beach, hosts nationally renowned authors as well as local book clubs. The cozy surroundings match the depth of selected works on the shelves, from timeless classics to modern bestsellers; owner Rona Brinlee is always happy to make recommendations to

COLORFUL POLISH POTTERY AT EUROPEAN IMPORTS & POLISH POTTERY

readers, as she does in person, on their website, and on NPR.

In all of our travels around the world, we have never seen a bookstore with more books. **Chamblin Book Mine** (904-384-1685; chamblinbookmine.com), 4551 Roosevelt Boulevard, St. Johns Park, is mind-boggling in size: think of it as a department store of books. You can lose yourself all day in here, winding through a labyrinth of narrow passageways stacked floor-to-ceiling with books. No wonder they call it a mine—you could dig through it for years and never see it all. It's so comprehensive that the stacks are numbered like a library, and authors are even broken out into their own sections. The staff claim there are more than a million books in stock, 95 percent used, and they've been accumulating inventory for 30 years. Bursting at the seams inside a former appliance store, this bookstore is one of the United States' top destinations for bibliophiles—even the obscure stuff is in the stacks. Serious researchers will revel in the finds in the nonfiction section. For fiction, bring your life list! Open Monday–Saturday 10 AM–6 PM, trades welcome.

✐ Find plenty of fun for the kids inside **The Green Alligator** (904-389-3099; thegreenalligator.com), 3581 St. Johns Avenue, Avondale, where they sell toys, toys, and more toys, many of them science based, and elaborate European playsets. The kids will be so busy playing, they won't realize they're learning, too.

Plump out your gift list at **One of Each Gifts** (904-247-3533), 1526 3rd Street N, Jacksonville Beach, where trinkets and candles sit side by side with puzzles, magnets, and jewelry. Filled with stocking stuffers that'll keep your friends smiling, it's worth a browse.

You can't miss **San Marco Books and More** (904-396-7597;sanmarcobookstore .com), 1971 San Marco Boulevard, thanks to the giant books over the storefront. Expect to be delighted by their broad and deep selection of regional history and books on Florida; part of the store is filled with fun children's toys and gifts.

Upscale gifts abound at **Underwood Jewelers** (904-398-9741; underwoodjewelers.com), 2044 San Marco Boulevard, a San Marco institution since 1928. It's considered by some to be the finest fine jewelry store in Florida. Think bridal registry—the most elegant china, crystal, and glass are showcased here.

CLOTHING A vision in white, **Ashes Boutique** (904-270-0220; ashesboutique .com), 332 2nd Street S, Jacksonville Beach, evokes heavenly thoughts as you browse their delicate children's and ladies' clothing. Artist Dana Roby's charcoal sketches are the perfect complement, and they can be transferred onto any clothing or tote. Bring your daughter for an afternoon tea in their cozy tearoom, Monday–Saturday 11 AM–3 PM.

DECOR AND MORE Reminiscent of the flower stalls in London's Covent Garden, **Anita's Garden Shop** (904-388-2060; anitasgardenshop.com), 3637 St. Johns Avenue, Avondale, beckons you through its white gates flanked with blooms bursting from containers into a floral shop with garden extras.

As befits its name, **Cottage by the Sea** (904-246-8411; cottagebytheseaonline .com), 401 3rd Street S, Jacksonville Beach, has rambling rooms with nautically themed glass: hand-painted folk art windows, stained glass, and art glass. It's not just about sea glass, however; wander from room to room and notice the richly embroidered pillows, handmade mermaids, and furnishings fit for a seaside retreat.

It's not your typical seaside decor shop, although **Mid-Life Crisis** (904-372-4403; midlifecrisisbtb.com), 415 3rd Street S, Jacksonville Beach, has an outstanding selection of paintings and furnishings. What sets this little store apart is a dash of devil-may-care flair reflected in smarmy slogans splashed across signs and pillows, and a selection of books that will make you chuckle. The broad selection of Annie Sloan chalk paint—used to create that weathered "coastal look"—is outstanding.

Midnight Sun Imports (904-358-3869; midnightsunimports.net), 1055 Park Street, Five Points, is the local center of imported exotica—fabrics, wind chimes, mobiles, gemstones, and other New Age offerings, including yoga instruction.

Inside **Saltologie** (904-673-3402 ; saltologie.com), 815 3rd Street N, Jacksonville Beach, be inspired by groupings of furniture and decor evoking a sense of the sea. Look for outstanding coastal photography, wood carvings, and paintings from local artists, as well as Florida-unique home accent pieces.

DESTINATION SHOPPING Locals just call it "The Landing," and it's *the* place to hang out downtown. **Jacksonville Landing** (904-353-1188; jacksonvillelanding .com), 2 Independent Drive, sits right along the river in the thick of things. There are 16 restaurants and a handful of shops in the riverfront complex, ranging from **Aly Cat Gifts** (904-699-8109; alycatonline.com), with handcrafted dichroic jewelry, etched glass, and carved rocks, to **Good Luck Have Fun** (904-619-7048; glhfgamebar.com), Jacksonville's first game bar, with tabletop games, PC and console games, and even old-fashioned arcade games where you can play, eat, and drink at the same time. Regular concerts and festivals up the crowd factor; it's always quieter before dark. In 2017, the waterfront changed with the arrival of the 1958 Navy destroyer **USS *Adams***, which will become a permanent museum (see *Museums*).

By straddling both sides of Atlantic Boulevard, **Beaches Town Center** (beachestowncenter.com) brings shoppers to both beachfront communities' primary commercial district. While Atlantic Boulevard itself is lined with restaurants and nightclubs, shops and eateries are scattered throughout six square blocks. Wandering down 1st Street is a must. Inside the **Cobalt Moon Center** (904-246-2131; cobaltmooncenter.com), 217 1st Street, Neptune Beach, expect eclectic finds. At **Violet Ray Vintage Antiques**, we recognized fine fabrics and hats from India among the bazaar-like interior, which has knick-knacks and jewelry from all corners of the globe. Across the hall at **Drift Boutique** (904-728-9151), the massive macramé behind the checkout counter says it all: crocheted bikinis and retro dresses evoke the Flower Power era. Up the long staircase, **Sailor's Siren** (904-853-6293; sailorssiren.com) is where mermaid meets bartender. Unique bar glasses, specialty foods, books, and greeting cards all fit the salty Southern theme. At **The Courtyard at 200 First Street** (200firststreet.com), Neptune Beach, a compact collection of shops invites inspection. Owner Kim Rogers selects fine crafts from the island of Bali to fill **Bali Cargo Company** (904-270-2254), where jolly Buddhas, prayer flags, and ornate temple carvings competed for attention with colorful lamps, handbags, and necklaces. **Boutique Unique** (904-241-7109) has festive casual wear and hats for women, while **Jaffi's** (904-249-4030) is more girly, with funky flip-flops, tiny dresses, and daring lingerie. **Red Daisy** (904-339-0137) melds vintage finds with modern home decor, and has the best collection of Old Florida tablecloths that we've ever seen. **First Street Gallery** (see *Art Galleries*) is a highlight here too, and there's also a coffeeshop, **Southern Grounds** (sogrocoffee.com).

FARMERS' MARKETS 🐚 A Saturday scene under the Fuller Warren Bridge, **Riverside Arts Market** (riversideartsmarket.com), 715 Riverside Avenue at the terminus of the Northbank Riverwalk, brings together local growers, artisans, musicians, and patrons of creativity to mingle together near the amphitheater and to enjoy the day. Each first Saturday, local brewers strut their stuff, and admission is free at the Cummer Museum (see *Art Museums*) next door. The market is held every Saturday 10 AM–3 PM, rain or shine, with morning yoga at 9 AM in the summer months.

OUTDOOR GEAR Since 1973, **Aqua East Surf Shop** (904-246-9809; aquaeast.com), 696 Atlantic Boulevard, Neptune Beach, has been Surf Central for Northeast Florida, with surf, wave, and skate gear.

Headed out on a kayaking trip? Stop first at **Black Creek Outfitters** (904-645-7003; blackcreekoutfitters.com), 10051 Skinner Lake Drive, Southside, an outfitter with the goods to get you on the water. Established in 1984, it's one of the most complete outfitters in Florida, with a full line of kayaking, surfing, mountaineering, and climbing equipment.

At **Black Sheep Surf and Sport** (904-241-6612), 237 5th Avenue S, Jacksonville Beach, stop in for kayak and Hobie Cat rentals, beachwear, and surfboards.

One of the best reasons to shop at sprawling St. Johns Town Center is **REI Jacksonville** (904-996-1613; rei.com/stores/jacksonville.html), 4862 Big Island Drive, Southside, which opened with great fanfare as the first REI store in Florida. We've picked up daypacks, socks, technical clothing, and even our car camping tent here while making the pilgrimage to North Florida's largest outdoor gear store. You'll see us here a couple of times a year giving talks to encourage residents to get out and hike.

SPECIALTY FOODS Stock up the spice cabinet at **Green Man Gourmet** (904-384-0002; greenmangourmet.com), 3543 St. Johns Avenue, Avondale, where you can buy spices, salts, and teas by the ounce. Pairing a bag of gluten-free basil garlic pesto from Pappardelle's with a jar of puttanesca sourced from Melbourne, FL, made for a perfect meal.

✳ Special Events

For a full roster of major events in the Jacksonville metro, check with the **City of Jacksonville Office of Special Events** (904-630-3686; jaxhappenings.com).

FALL/WINTER Be dazzled by the thunder of the Blue Angels during the **NAS Jax Air Show** (nasjaxairshow.com), as this fabled air squadron comes back to their birthplace for an annual show over Jacksonville Beach, the first weekend in November.

The **Greater Jacksonville Agricultural Fair** (904-353-0535; jacksonvillefair.com) features livestock, a petting zoo, arts and crafts, midway rides, and live entertainment in November.

The Saturday after Thanksgiving, the St. Johns River lights up during the **Jacksonville Light Boat Parade**, as boats festooned with Christmas lights make their way through downtown; see it from the Landing (see *Shopping*). The light show continues with the beauty of illuminated gardens after dark during **ZOOLights at Jacksonville Zoo and Gardens** (see *Zoo*).

The **Seawalk Music Festival** (jacksonvillebeach.org/events/special-events/seawalk-music-festival) brings together local artists and musicians with the public with the beach as a backdrop to the festival grounds, the last weekend in February.

During **Garden Week at the Cummer** (904-355-0630; cummer.org), mid-March, expect an array of talented artists and speakers riffing on the beauty of these formal gardens, with special art exhibitions also keyed to the floral displays.

The multicultural **World of Nations Celebration** (904-630-3686; jaxhappenings.com) in Metropolitan Park, 1410 Gator Bowl Boulevard, downtown, serves up exotic foods and fun from more than 30 participating countries.

SPRING/SUMMER Kick off spring with the **Springing the Blues Festival** (springingtheblues.com), the largest free series of blues concerts by the sea by top-name artists.

On the **Spring Tour of Homes** (raphometour.com), mid-April, a tradition in Riverside/Avondale, join a two-day, self-guided tour of some of the area's finest architectural marvels—on the inside. Tickets available online once locations are announced.

✍ Founded in 1968, the **Mandarin Art Festival** (904-268-1622; mandarinartfestival.org), 12447 Mandarin Road, Easter weekend, showcases local artists in a juried exhibition. A children's art show and Easter egg hunt are part of this annual tradition.

The **Jacksonville Craft & Import Beer Festival** (904-232-3001; beerfestjax.com), Jacksonville Veterans Memorial Arena, 300A Philip Randolph Boulevard, features more than 40 breweries bringing more than 300 different beers for tastings during May.

Enjoy free jazz performances on multiple downtown stages during the **Jacksonville Jazz Festival** (904-630-3690; visitjacksonville.com/jacksonvillejazzfestival), packing the city over Memorial Day weekend to hear major performers like Herbie Hancock, Natalie Cole, and Boney James.

Chow down on the fruits of the sea while listening to live concerts at the **Great Atlantic Festival** (greatatlanticfestival.com), Jacksonville Beach, mid-June.

✍ Held by the Florida Surfing Association, the **Super Grom Surf Festival** (floridasurfing.org/event/super-grom) lets youngsters ages 10 and under learn to surf with the best; advance registration required. The third Saturday of June.

AMELIA ISLAND

Nassau County
Fernandina Beach, Callahan, Hilliard, and Yulee

W ith its long, rich history, Amelia Island—the southernmost of the Sea Island chain and home of the colonial-era city of Fernandina Beach—has borne the rule of eight flags. In 1562 the French claimed this land, attempting to establish a colony along the St. Johns River to the south. The Spanish massacred most of the colonists in 1565 and divided the land into land grants. But because of its deepwater port at the mouth of the St. Marys River, Fernandina Beach was always up for grabs by anyone who wanted to challenge the authority of Spain.

By 1763 **Fernandina Beach** was a port of operations for the British, who had an uprising—the American Revolution—on their hands. During the Revolutionary War, Colonel Samuel Elbert's Continentals landed at the bluffs at Oldtown during May 1777, their plan being the invasion of Florida to release it from British rule. In retaliation for a British patrol killing one of his officers, Elbert ordered the houses burned and live-stock killed. When Britain passed control back to Spain, local patriots seized the deep-water port several times, hoisting three different flags (Patriots, Florida Green Cross, and Mexican Rebel) but never hanging on to control for more than a few years. In the wake of Thomas Jefferson's Embargo Act of 1807, all US ports were closed to foreign shipping—but not Fernandina Beach. Its Spanish governor looked the other way as the port slid into the ribaldry echoed throughout lawless ports of the Caribbean, where smugglers met, pirates plotted, racketeers reconnoitered, and the seamy side of life stayed close to the surface. The city officially became part of the United States when Florida became a territory in 1821.

When the Civil War broke out, Fort Clinch was considered a prime defender for the port of Fernandina Beach and the St. Marys River, the dividing line between Georgia and Florida. The Confederate flag rose above the fort, and Senator David Yulee came to town. He bankrolled Florida's first significant railroad system, the Florida Railroad, to move export goods from the deepwater port to the Cedar Keys, a shortcut for ships serving the ports of Mobile, New Orleans, and Havana. On March 3, 1862, the town and its Home Guard evacuated as Union troops arrived to take over the fort. A few years after Florida rejoined the Union, naturalist John Muir arrived and walked the railroad route west as part of his "Thousand-Mile Walk to the Gulf."

The railroad, too, shaped the destiny of this city; when Henry Flagler bypassed Yulee's stronghold, Fernandina Beach became a sleepy backwater in an otherwise robust new tourist industry along Florida's Atlantic Coast. A new industry came to the forefront—shrimping. Employing fishermen from Sicily, Portugal, Greece, and Germany, all of whom rowed boats while trawling their handmade nets, the shrimping industry grew quickly after 1900. The S. Salvador Company added refrigeration and better nets to motor-powered vessels, creating the first shrimp boats. Standard Marine (known locally as the Net House) started out making nets for the shrimp boats; now they also provide the nets used for Major League Baseball backstops.

As the city of Fernandina Beach grew, the population expanded farther south into the wilds along Amelia Island. Established in 1935 as a benefit for employees of the Afro-American Life Insurance Company, **American Beach** was Florida's first

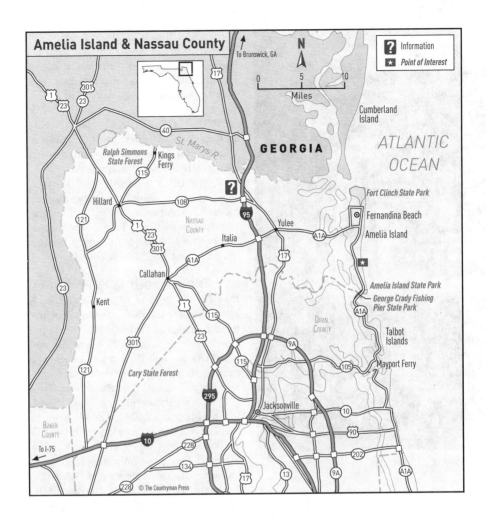

African American beach resort during segregation, boasting its own swinging night-clubs and hotels.

With the Intracoastal Waterway defining the western shore of Amelia Island, Amelia Island's wild side is showcased in its vast acreage of natural preserves, with Fort Clinch and St. Johns Aquatic Preserve offering protection to the seemingly unending stretches of estuarine marsh fringing the island. Inland, you'll find Simmons State Forest along the languid St. Marys River; Four Creeks State Forest, protecting the headwaters of the Nassau River; and Cary State Forest, with its pitcher plant bogs amid the wet flatwoods. Western Nassau County remains a rural outpost, with farming and forestry its primary economy, its largest towns **Hilliard** and **Callahan** along US 301.

GUIDANCE Stop by the **Amelia Island–Fernandina Beach–Yulee Chamber of Commerce and Welcome Center** (904-261-3248; islandchamber.com), 961687 Gateway Boulevard, Suite 101G (at A1A and Amelia Island Parkway), for information and recommendations. In downtown Fernandina Beach, the **Amelia Island Welcome Center** (904-277-0717; ameliaisland.com), 102 Centre Street, occupies the train depot that was the eastern terminus of the Florida Railroad, which began construction east from

DOWNTOWN FERNANDINA BEACH

Fernandina Beach in 1856. A statue of railroad founder and Florida's first US Senator, David Yulee, sits on a bench outside, and Peg Leg the pirate looks out over the marina. Opens daily at 10 AM.

GETTING THERE *By air:* **Jacksonville International Airport** (see the *Jacksonville* chapter) is the nearest major airport, just 30 minutes south along I-95.

By car: **I-95** runs north–south through the region, connecting all major highways; FL A1A passes through all coastal communities, including Fernandina, and connects to US 301 to reach interior communities.

GETTING AROUND *By car:* From **I-95**, take **FL A1A** east to Amelia Island. A1A loops north through the Fernandina historic district, then turns east again to the beach. Head south on **Fletcher Avenue** (FL A1A) through Fernandina Beach; the road turns west at Amelia City and connects with FL 105. The **Buccaneer Trail** (FL 105) continues past the roads leading to American Beach and then on to the Talbot Islands, turning to follow the St. Johns River, where you can take the Mayport Ferry, the only major car ferry in Florida, to continue on A1A. **US 1** also connects Fernandina to Jacksonville. A1A continues west from Fernandina to **US 301**, which is the route from Folkston, Georgia, south through Hilliard and Callahan.

MEDICAL EMERGENCIES You'll find emergency services available at **Baptist Medical Center Nassau** (904-321-3500; baptistjax.com/locations/baptist-medical-center-nassau), 1250 S 18th Street, Fernandina Beach.

✳ To See

ARCHITECTURE With its **50-block historic district**, the city of **Fernandina Beach** is a treasure trove for architecture and history buffs. More than 400 of the city's homes and shops predate the 1920s building boom. Victorian mansions are concentrated in the **Silk Stocking District**, and they come in all flavors—from Florida vernacular to Queen Anne. For a guided immersion into the past, take a walking tour down Centre Street or a ghost tour beginning at St. Peters Cemetery; check with the Amelia Island Museum of History (see *Museums*), located in the historic **Nassau County Jail**, for details.

Lined with buildings from the early days of commerce in Florida, **Centre Street** is truly a step back in time and a delight to walk. Look for historic plaques and architectural features that call out the origins of these structures that now house modern shops and restaurants, like the **J&T Kydd Building** from 1873 at the corner of Centre and 3rd, or the 1882 **C.H. Huot's Building.**

The lovely Italian Renaissance revival building that dominates the corner of 4th and Centre has, indeed, been the home of the **Fernandina Beach Post Office** since it was dedicated in 1912. But it originally was custom-designed to serve other government purposes, too. It also housed the original customs house for the port and was the US Southern District courthouse as well, until the 1960s. On the National Register of Historic Places, it is the tallest building in town.

Construction began in 1842 at **Fort Clinch**, now the centerpiece of Fort Clinch State Park (see *Parks, Preserves, and Camping*), but the fort wasn't completed until 1867. Built to defend the deepwater port at Fernandina, it has both earthen and masonry fortification layers. Unique architectural devices incorporated into the design of this massive brick structure include vaulted and hexagonal archways, flying buttresses, and a bastion with a Gothic-style pentagonal ceiling. Even though it was only partially built, it was garrisoned during the Civil War by Union troops who took the port early on. Reenactors in character ramble the fort during your tour; fee.

One of the city's oldest homes is right in the midst of the commercial district. Behind its picket fence, the **Lesesne House** is a classical revival residence built by Dr. John Lesesne in 1860, using local hand-hewn lumber and wooden pegs instead of nails. After the Civil War, when the doctor did not return, Judge John Friend and his family moved in; the judge served as a county commissioner and had been elected to the Florida Senate when he passed away in 1878. His descendents still live in this private home.

Built out of brick in 1891, the **Nassau County Courthouse** is one of the few remaining courthouses in Florida from this era, its Italianate design a good complement to the nearby Fernandina Beach Post Office and federal courthouse—which it beats in height thanks to the 1920s bell tower that was the city's fire alarm and was later topped with a clock. Its architect, A. E. McClure, designed notable buildings of this period

BRICK CEILING INSIDE FORT CLINCH

throughout Florida. An Italianate fountain delights passersby along Centre Avenue and is a reminder of days gone by.

In the original settlement of Fernandina—now known as **Old Town**—explore the side streets to see historic homes that are part of the town that moved off the bluff at the urging of railroad magnate and Florida Senator David Yulee in the mid-1800s, as he wanted his railroad to end at not just a deepwater port, but a thriving commercial center. It's found along N 14th Street [30.688624, -81.452038].

ART GALLERIES In Fernandina Beach, art galleries and studios showcase their works on **Second Saturday Artrageous Artwalks**, in which more than a dozen art studios and galleries stay open until 8 PM in historic downtown Fernandina Beach. Among the usual participants include the **Susan's Slightly Off Centre Gallery** (904-277-1147), 218C Ash Street, with unusual collections of ceramics, paintings, and glass, plus funky clothing; and **Gallery C** (904-583-4676; carolwinnerart.com), 218B Ash Street, Carol Winner's working studio and gallery.

Accommodating massive pieces of art, the expansive gallery space of **Art on Centre** (904-624-7255; artoncentre.com), 503 Centre Street, showcases local artists such as Sara Conca. Her *Fernandina Spirits* is a shimmering abstract created by backpainting on acrylic. Eve Miller's tranquil abstracts of the local salt marshes make a stunning focal point for any room. On a display of fine blown glass by Bill Slade and others, colorful geometrics with nature elements cover the "art to wear" that Holly Jones creates.

Climb the colorful staircase to **Blue Door Artists** (904-491-7733; bluedoorartists .com), 205 Centre Street, a collective effort of a dozen local artists taking over the rooms of a historic office building as their studios and display space. Theresa Daily's

MOSAICS GUIDE YOU INTO THE ISLAND ART ASSOCIATION GALLERY

fluid abstracts with alcohol ink on ceramic tile caught our attention, as did Casey Matthew's colorful abstract mixed media and Dawna Moore's haunting image of the Angel Oak near Charleston. Monday–Saturday 11 AM–5 PM, until 8 PM during Fernandina's Artrageous Artwalk (one Saturday a month).

An artists cooperative, the **Island Art Association Art Gallery** (904-261-7020; islandart.org), 18 N 2nd Street, catches your attention right away with a building where colorful mosaics flow across walls, windowsills, and the courtyard. Inside, each artist's work is displayed in groupings, with one gallery devoted to the current exhibition and one display highlighting the featured artist of the month. The quality and breadth of work by co-op members is outstanding. We picked up some colorful collage cards by Gwen Cowart, based on her mixed-media pieces, but were also tempted by Susan Henderson's mangroves. Sunday–Thursday 10:30 AM–5 PM, Friday–Saturday 10:30 AM–8 PM. Free.

The **Plantation Artists Guild** (904-432-1750; artamelia.com), 94 Village Circle, Amelia Island, presents the work of artists who live in Amelia Island Plantation, with sculpture, fine art, and photography.

LIGHTHOUSE As it barely peeps over the treeline, it's easy to forget that **Amelia Island Lighthouse** (904-310-3350), 302 Lighthouse Lane, even exists. But this lighthouse, built in 1838, is the oldest one in Florida, and the only one remaining from Florida's territorial period. It's also still a working lighthouse managed by the Coast Guard. You can photograph it from a few shoreline perspectives in Fort Clinch State Park and along the north end of the Egans Creek Greenway (see *Parks, Preserves, and Camping*), home to a large parking area at the Atlantic Recreation Center. It's from here that guided tours of the lighthouse depart, held the first and third Wednesday of each month. Call for reservations; fee. The lighthouse grounds are also opened to the public on Saturdays from 11 AM–2 PM, free.

MUSEUMS AND HISTORIC SITES ♿ Stop by the old Nassau County Jail, home to the **Amelia Island Museum of History** (904-261-7378; ameliamuseum.org), 233 S 3rd Street, to learn about why Amelia Island is the only location in America to have been ruled under eight flags. The immersive displays walk you through vast spans of history, starting with the Timucua, with interpretive information and artifacts to tell the stories of the growth of Fernandina Beach as an important port along the Eastern Seaboard. Open Monday–Saturday 10 AM–4 PM, Sunday 1–4 PM; fee.

At **Fernandina Plaza State Park** [30.688624, -81.456447], civilizations have made their mark for more than 4,000 years, with the Spanish touch reaching these shores in the mid-1600s. This unassuming open space marks the spot of Plaza San Carlos, a parade ground for the fortress that protected a fledgling city known as Fernandina. From this bluff, you have a clear view of the St. Marys River and Cumberland Island.

✍ Inside the **West Nassau Museum of History** (904 879-3406; wnhsfl.org), 45383 Dixie Avenue, Callahan, a historic depot that is home of the Railroad Day Festival (see *What's Happening*), rail fans will rejoice at the displays of railroad memorabilia and artifacts from local railroad history, plus an extensive collection of HO, O, and G model railroad cars. Each community in this part of the county has a section devoted to their area. Open most Saturdays 9 AM–2 PM, weekdays by appointment. Free, donations welcome.

RAILROADIANA As the eastern terminus of the **Florida Railroad**, one of Florida's first railroads, the region is steeped in railroad history. Responsible for bringing the railroad to this deepwater port, Senator David Yulee was also one of people fleeing the

AMERICAN BEACH

With its original 33 acres on the National Register of Historic Places, **American Beach** (nps.gov/timu/learn/historyculture/ambch_history.htm) was established in 1935 by A.L. Lewis, president of the Afro-American Insurance Company in Jacksonville. Employees were encouraged to vacation there, and land holdings grew to 216 acres. Parcels were first sold to company executives, shareholders, and community leaders, and then to the African American community at large. Motels and shops sprang up, attracting vacationers. As a playground for people of color in the South during the days of segregation—up through the late 1960s—it was a safe haven "for recreation and relaxation without humiliation." But damage to structures in 1964, followed by the end of segregated beaches in Florida, lessened African American interest in this beachfront community. As massive developments began to flank American Beach in the 1970s, rising property values—leading to higher taxes—convinced many homeowners to sell off. Surrounding developers snapped up more than half of this historic beach, including the historic Franklintown Cemetery, to which they blocked access.

The central beach in the community, **American Beach Historic Park**, 5508 Gregg Street, and a pristine 65-foot dune system called Nana—the tallest on the Atlantic Coast in Florida—is now under National Park protection as part of Timucuan Ecological & Historic Preserve (see *Jacksonville*), and it is one of the sites along the **Gullah/Geechee Cultural Heritage Corridor** (nps.gov/guge), which stretches along the Atlantic Coast from Jacksonville to Wilmington, NC.

♿ Learn how American Beach came to be at the **American Beach Museum** (americanbeachmuseum.org), 1600 Julia Street, where artifacts, photographs, and oral histories provide the historical backdrop of this unique summer vacation community established by world traveler Abraham Lincoln Lewis, Florida's first African American millionaire. Lewis's great-granddaughter MaVynee Betsch, "The Beach Lady," was the driving force behind preserving and documenting what remained of the community, and exhibit space includes her story as well. Friday–Saturday 10 AM–2 PM, Sunday 2–5 PM; fee.

"NANA" DUNE AT AMERICAN BEACH

city by rail as the Union Blockading Squadron bombed the trestles between Fernandina Beach and what is now the town of Yulee. You can walk along a segment of that **old railroad bed** and learn more about its history at **John Muir Ecological Park** (904-548-4689; nassaucountyfl.com), 463039 FL 200, Yulee, which has boardwalks that zigzag through a swamp forest connecting picnic shelters together until the trail ends up at an elevated berm that was once the main line of the railroad. Visit the historic **railway station** at the end of the line in Fernandina Beach (see *Guidance*) to snap a selfie with David Yulee. But *the* place to immerse yourself in this early Florida railroad history is during the annual **Railroad Days** festival (see *What's Happening*) at the **Historic Callahan Depot** (904 879-3406), 45383 Dixie Avenue, Callahan. The depot itself is a don't-miss for rail fans, beautifully restored to serve as the West Nassau Museum of History (see *Museums*), with a **Seaboard Air Line caboose** outside.

✳ To Do

BEACHES At the north end of Amelia Island, look for "Beach Access" signs along A1A: there are at least **38 beach crossovers** in Fernandina Beach, some with free parking for a handful of cars and others just walkways to the surf. One of the more popular options—because it's so close to lodging and has a parking area—is **Main Beach Park** at the end of FL 200.

Nassau County manages six beachfront parks (904-530-6120; nassaucountyfl.com), of which **Peters Point Beachfront Park**, 4600 Peters Point Road, is one of the largest, and **Scott Road Beachfront Park**, 4902 Amelia Island Parkway, is one of the easiest to

ATLANTIC OCEAN AT BURNEY PARK

find. Part of historic American Beach, **Burney Park**, 95570 Burney Boulevard, provides one of the quietest places to enjoy a sandy strand. However, rip currents can be dangerous in this area, and are possible anywhere along these beaches. Lifeguards are on duty at county parks from 11 AM–5 PM weekdays, 10 AM–5 PM weekends and holidays. For current beach conditions, call 904-277-7331.

🐾 Leashed dogs are allowed on all beaches in this region, but you must pick up after them immediately. Bring your own bags.

BIKING 🚲 Embracing the vision of the Maine-to-Florida **East Coast Greenway** (greenway.org/explore-by-state/fl), Amelia Island is accessible to both bicycle tourists and casual riders, thanks to broad bike paths like the **Amelia Island Trail** (ameliaislandtrail.org), an asphalt path starting at the south end of the island at Amelia Island State Park and ending at Peters Point Beachfront Park. A1A has a dedicated bike lane along its narrowest section in Fernandina Beach, but cyclists can also opt to use the **Egans Creek Greenway**, which lets you ride through a forest and savor views across the estuarine creek. The greenway boasts two separate mountain bike trails along its length. The grandaddy of off road rides, however, is the **Fort Clinch Bicycle Trail**, an undulating 6-mile singletrack over ancient dunes beneath a tight-knit canopy of windswept oaks at **Fort Clinch State Park** with your bike, which also provides a gentler long ride on their broad oak-canopied park road. Rent a bicycle at **Bike Scoot or Yak Rentals** (904-404-8654; bikescootoryak.com), 1678 S 8th Street #6, where, among their offerings, they carry EllipiGos and beach cruisers. Bikes are delivered to your hotel or vacation home and come with helmets and locks. At the beachfront circle on A1A, **Beach Rentals and More** (904-310-6124; beachrentalsandmore.com), 2021 S Fletcher Avenue, has beach cruisers for $12 for two hours. You can also rent a bike for $7/hr or $20/day from **Kayak Amelia** (see *Shopping*) to hit the nearby Egans Creek Greenway.

BOATING When you arrive at **Fernandina Harbor Marina** (904-491-2090; fhmarina .com), 1 S Front Street, the view is fabulous in any direction—for boaters, the panorama of the historic downtown; for landlubbers, the sweep of the St. Marys River meeting the Atlantic Ocean as it laps the shores of Cumberland Island. Facilities, including a welcome center, open daily 6:30 AM–8:30 PM. An adjoining boat ramp lets you head out into the river for exploration of the nearby islands.

CARRIAGE TOURS 🐎 **Old Towne Carriage Company** (904-277-1555; amelia carriagetours.com), Amelia Island. Take a 30- to 40-minute ride in a horse-drawn carriage through the Fernandina Beach historic district while your narrator points out the history and culture of sites on the National Register of Historic Places in a 50-block area. Tour rates start at $15 adult, $7 ages under 13 for a 30-minute tour; 1-hour tours are twice as much. Reserve in advance online or by phone.

ECOTOURS 🚲 **Amelia River Cruises** (904-261-9972; ameliarivercruises.com), 3 S Front Street, departs from Fernandina Harbor Marina and offers a wide variety of tours, from daily sunset cruises and trips along Cumberland Island and Cumberland Sound to full-day private charters to destinations by water. One of their most fascinating tours, especially for families, is the Shrimping Eco Tour (seasonal, June 1–August 31) that shows off how shrimp nets—developed in Fernandina—are used to capture shrimp. Rates start at $22 adult, $16 child; reservations recommended.

🚲 For guided adventures by bicycle and kayak, check in with **Kayak Amelia** (see *Shopping*) for trips through the coastal estuary and along the bicycle trails of Fort Clinch as well as summer ecocamps and custom family kayak trips. All guided tours

OLD A1A MAKES UP THE GEORGE CRADY FISHING PIER STATE PARK

start with instruction on how to kayak, and then you head into the estuary, while your guide explains the history of the area and local wildlife. You'll might take a break on a pristine sandbar, where you can go for a refreshing swim. Tours run $65 adult, $55 ages 12 and under. Reservations required.

FISHING Walk around Fernandina Harbor Marina to find fishing guides for oceango-ing and nearshore trips, or get in touch with **Amelia Angler Outfitters** (see *Shopping*) to arrange a day on the water. For pier fishing, head to **George Crady Fishing Pier State Park** (904-251-2320; floridastateparks.org/georgecradybridge), made up of the former A1A bridge connecting Amelia Island with Big Talbot Island. It's open 24 hours.

At **St. Marys River Fish Camp & Campground** (see *Campgrounds*), you're so close the Georgia border you can cast your line across it. Take a ride down the black waters of the St. Marys in a small bass boat as it curves past white sandbars, cypress trees, and alligators, then under a train trestle. Fish or just enjoy the view. The river winds along a 130-mile path from the Okefenokee Swamp to the Atlantic. Given the connection to the ocean, tides play a role most of the way upriver. Watch for shallow and narrow areas during low tide, when sandy banks are displayed, especially in the narrower sections.

HIKING You can hike for hours on the back roads of **Simmons State Forest**, which lead to scenic views of the St. Marys River and past some of the rarest plants in Florida. You'll see pitcher plant bogs at **Cary State Forest** with a walk on their short but pleas-ant Cary Nature Trail in the pine flatwoods. At **Fort Clinch State Park**, the **Willow Pond Trail** loops around freshwater ponds in the middle of a peninsula jutting into salt water. The trails of **Egans Creek Greenway** let you put together a loop of more than six miles, or a shorter walk if you like. See *Parks, Preserves, and Camping* for locations.

HORSEBACK RIDING ♂ At **Country Day Stable** (904-879-9383), 2940 Jane Lane, Hilliard, take a one-hour trail ride through 40 acres of north woods past the owners' re-creation of a medieval castle, which is used for weddings. The Horse Discovery program lets small children groom a horse, followed by a hand-led ride. Reservations required.

Moving slow up the beach is the way to ride, and the Tennessee Walking Horse provides that perfect gait. Join Stan Potter at **Happy Trails** (904-557-3126; happytrails walkers.com), 1974 Peters Point Road, on a ride along Fernandina Beach. $88 per hour, ages 10 and up; reservations suggested.

Jim Kelly holds the coveted Horseman of Distinction designation, so it's no wonder that his horses are in class-A shape and well trained to ride through the salt marshes, white sand, and frothy surf of Amelia Island State Park. At **Kelly Seahorse Ranch** (904-491-5166; kellyranchinc.net), inside the park gates, you start out in a wooded area, and then gently ride along miles of open beach next to dolphins just offshore. One-hour rides $75, adults and ages 13 and up only. Groups are limited to 10, so reserve in advance.

PADDLING SUP, kayak, or canoe? Find your outdoor bliss at **Kayak Amelia** (904-251-0016; kayakamelia.com), 13030 Heckscher Drive, located in the saltwater marshes between Big and Little Talbot Islands, just south of Amelia Island along A1A. They'll outfit you with the gear you need and a map to find your way to interesting spots after you launch from Simpson Creek. A single kayak runs $37 for a half day, $49 for a full day; a tandem kayak or canoe costs $52 or $62. Because of the oyster beds, SUP rentals are only recommended for experienced SUP paddlers. Kayak Amelia runs a wide array of guided trips, too (see *Ecotours*).

Rent a canoe or kayak from the folks at **St. Marys Canoe Country Outpost** (see *Campgrounds*), Hilliard, and then explore the St. Marys River, cypress lined and sinuous, defining the state line. Don't forget to pack a lunch, as you'll want to stop for a relaxing break on its sandy banks.

PARKS, PRESERVES, AND CAMPING Protecting the southernmost sweep of Amelia Island, **Amelia Island State Park** (904-251-2320; floridastateparks.org/park/Amelia-Island) spans from oceanfront to estuary, a popular spot for surf fishing and horseback riding on the beach (see *Horseback Riding*); fee.

🚶 Protecting pine flatwoods, cypress domes, and pitcher plant bogs, **Cary State Forest** (904-266-8398; freshfromflorida.com), 7465 Pavilion Drive, Bryceville, has an extensive network of trails open to equestrians. The 1.4-mile Cary Nature Trail is a great short jaunt for kids and people of limited mobility—well graded, good for a stroller, and wheelchair-accessible with assistance. Families may wish to take advantage of the "primitive" campsites: tents only, but with showers and restrooms provided. Fee.

Protecting more than 300 acres along the brackish branches and salt marshes of Egans Creek, the **Egans Creek Greenway** (904-310-3363; fbfl.us/index.aspx?NID=104) provides a place just outside the historic downtown for a ramble through wild spaces. Step lightly and watch the berms along the waterways, as those baby alligators have a mama nearby, and yes, that Florida cooter just finished laying its eggs. With more than six miles of loops to hike or bike, plus two dedicated mountain bike loops, you can spend a few hours of birding or photography along the trail system. Parking areas are at Egans Creek Park (see *Parks*); the Atlantic Recreation Center at 2500 Atlantic Avenue, where you'll find 🏴 **Pirate Playground**, a pint-size adventure zone for tots, and public restrooms, along the side of Jasmine Street [30.655724, -81.438734], and in the back corner of the Residence Inn (see *Lodging*).

🏴 🏕 🚶 **Fort Clinch State Park** (904-277-7274; floridastateparks.org/park/Fort-Clinch), 2601 Atlantic Avenue, one of the oldest parks in the Florida State Park system,

SALT MARSHES ALONG THE EGANS CREEK GREENWAY

was acquired in 1935 when developers who planned to build along the peninsula couldn't pay their taxes; the state paid $10,000 with the "fort thrown in." Opened to the public in 1938, Fort Clinch State Park offers an array of seaside activities on its long swath of Atlantic beachfront. Besides hiking, biking, picnicking, and fishing, you can tour the historic fort, constructed in 1842 (see *Architecture*), or enjoy the salt breezes through either of its two campgrounds on an overnight stay. Choose from the shady River Campground or the sunnier Beach Campground, $26. Be sure to bring your bicycles, since the ride down the park road is well shaded, letting you easily connect with other amenities inside the state park, like the beach and the park's namesake fort. Day-use fee.

🐾 Encompassing more than 13,000 acres, **Four Creeks State Forest** [30.598392, -81.764192] spans the floodplain of four major tributaries of the Nassau River, with three landings accessible off unpaved forest roads for launching a boat or kayak or just to fish. The older **Ralph E. Simmons State Forest** [30.779698, -81.953126] in Hilliard is home to some of the most beautiful wildflowers in the state. Hike deep into it for several nice campsites with a view of Georgia across the St. Marys River. The forest roads are used for hiking, biking, and horseback riding; take a map along or you will get lost! All three forests are managed by the Florida Forest Service (904-845-4933; freshfromflorida.com), 3472 Clint Drive, Hilliard.

SAILING Sail off the beaches of Fernandina with Charlie and Sandra Weaver on *Windward's Child* (904-261-9125; windwardsailing.com), Fernandina Harbor Marina. Dolphins swim alongside the 34-foot Hunter sloop as you pass horses running on the beach on Cumberland Island. See Fort Clinch from the water, just as the Civil War blockade-runners saw it. Move under the power of the wind with the quiet sounds of a warm sea breeze. Half-day, full-day, and sunset cruises, starting at $200 for two hours. Also check in with **Amelia Angler Outfitters** (see *Shopping*) for sailboat charters.

✳ Lodging

BED & BREAKFASTS ♂ (ᵍ) An 1890s Nantucket shingle-style inn, **Elizabeth Pointe Lodge** (904-277-4851; elizabethpointelodge.com), 98 S Fletcher Avenue, Fernandina Beach 32034, has a strong maritime theme. It's just steps from the ocean, and you can take in a breathtaking view from the porch or breakfast area. An intimate on-site oceanfront restaurant, The Pointe, is open to guests for all meals, and to the public for breakfast. Twenty-five guestrooms, including four spacious rooms in the Ocean House and the Miller Cottage, perfect for honeymoons, $283 and up.

♂ (ᵍ) The well-manicured gardens of **The Fairbanks House** (888-891-9880; fairbankshouse.com), 227 S 7th Street, Fernandina Beach 32034, guide you into a complex centered on the towering 1885 Italianate villa, where a sparkling pool invites you to relax. Breakfast delights like cinnamon orange pecan French toast come as part of the package with your oversize room or private cottage, 12 options in all, each tastefully decorated to set a mood. $195–240 for rooms, $240–450 for suites and cottages.

♂ (ᵍ) From the very Victorian 1905 **Hoyt House Inn** (904-277-4300; hoythouse.com), 804 Atlantic Avenue, Fernandina Beach 32034, you need only walk out the door and up the street for all the shopping and dining options in the heart of historic Fernandina Beach. This bright and cheerful home was modeled after the Rockefeller Cottage on Jekyll Island, and it makes you feel like you've joined that social circle for your stay. Between the exquisite three-course, made-to-order gourmet breakfast, their afternoon English tea (open to nonguests as well, $25, not included in lodging fee), and their sumptious pool and gardens, you may never find time to go downtown after all. Ten rooms evoking the grandeur of the early 1900s, starting at $191.

♂ Relax on the veranda at **The Williams House** (904-277-2328; williamshouse.com), 103 S 9th Street, Fernandina Beach 32034, where this 1856 mansion will lull you into romantic musings on Fernandina's past. Scattered across three adjoining properties, ten rooms provide an array of experiences, from the cozy Smuggler's Cove with its cantilevered window seat and big Jacuzzi to the velvety Isle of Santa Maria, with French doors that open onto the porch, and a clawfoot tub in the spacious bathroom. Seasonal rates begin at $225, including gourmet breakfast, with packages available; two-night stay required most weekends.

HISTORIC ♂ While this classic getaway is just across the St. Marys River on Cumberland Island in Georgia, most visitors headed to the historic **Greyfield Inn** (904-261-6408; greyfieldinn.com) depart from the docks in Fernandina Beach, where their private ferry takes you across to a great escape from the hectic pace of the mainland. Guests stay in a private compound inside one of the wilder national seashores on the East Coast. A visit includes outdoor activities, including a three-hour guided wilderness tour with a staff naturalist in the comfort of a Land Rover vehicle, plus gourmet meals. Packages start at $425 per night with a two-night minimum.

LOCAL STANDARD 🍽 ♂ ♿ (ᵍ) During a stay at **Amelia Hotel at the Beach** (904-206-5200; ameliahotel.com), 1997 South Fletcher Avenue, Fernandina Beach 32034, we were delighted by the sheer size of the room and the view of the sunrise; the hotel sits right on the circle overlooking the ocean, the surf competing for your attention against the 42-inch flat-screen television and plush furnishings. This locally owned family property treats you like family, with a hearty better-than-continental breakfast, comfortable Tempurpedic beds (think about an afternoon nap after your beach walk), and a mini-fridge and microwave so you can nosh while watching an evening movie. Cool down with laps in the pool, or work out in the fitness center. Rooms and suites, $99 and up; packages available.

RETRO AND ARTSY (ʔ) 🐾 One of the last of its breed, **Beachside Motel Inn** (877-261-4236; beachsidemotel.com), 3172 S Fletcher Avenue, Fernandina Beach 32034, is right on the beach. It's an older property, but nicely kept, and it could bring back those childhood memories of family vacations at the beach. Most important, it's right on the beach! The pool is perched on the dunes. Basic rooms and efficiencies starting at $96.

TRIED AND TRUE ♿ (ʔ) Stay in the center of the action at **Hampton Inn & Suites Amelia Island-Historic Harbor Front** (904-491-4911; hilton.com), 19 S 2nd Street, Fernandina Beach 32034, where the façade of this modern brand blends in with the historic downtown. Leave your car parked and enjoy one of Florida's oldest cities on foot or by bike. Guest laundry on-site, and local transportation assistance available.

🐾 ♿ (ʔ) 🐾 ✈ With direct access to miles of walking and biking on the Egans Creek Greenway, the **Residence Inn Amelia Island** (904-277-2440; residenceinnameliaisland.com), 2301 Sadler Road, Fernandina Beach 32034, is tricked out for business travelers and accommodating for families, offering suites the size of small apartments complete with full kitchens. Relax during their evening social hour and grab the complimentary hot breakfast in the morning—you'll wonder what that kitchen is for! The beach is less than a block away, but the kids may prefer hanging out at the pool. $149 and up.

CAMPGROUND 🐾 ♿ Down a dirt road in a quiet corner of the Ralph E. Simmons State Forest (see *Parks, Preserves, and Camping*), you come to the privately owned **St. Marys River Fish Camp & Campground** (866-845-4443 or 904-845-4440; stmarysriverfishcamp.com), 28506 Scotts Landing Road, Hilliard 32046. Steve Beck's family-oriented environment provides a great getaway place for safe, clean fun. You'll often see the kids up late at night playing basketball with him at the basketball court, just off the porch of the community store. Everyone hangs out here, and the sense is of community, caring, and southern hospitality. Take to the water in fishing or pleasure boats to catch bream, catfish, or bass. Pull up on a sandy beach for a swim or picnic. Learn how to water-ski. Search for the elusive goats on Goat Island. On weekends, watch a movie in the outdoor amphitheater, hike the many nature trails in the nearby state forest, or just relax and enjoy the beautiful solitude of the area—you'll run out of time before you run out of things to do. RV sites $25 daily, $120 weekly, $300 monthly. Primitive tent sites $12 daily.

✻ Where to Eat

ELEGANT AND ROMANTIC Enjoy the charm of **Le Clos Café** (904-261-8100; leclos.com), 20 S 2nd Street, Fernandina Beach, while dining by candlelight in an intimate 1906 cottage. The creatively prepared French dishes by Cordon Bleu– and Escoffier-trained chef-owner Katherine Ewing are partnered with equally fine wines. Dinner nightly except Sunday, $19–32. Reservations suggested.

The signature restaurant of the Ritz-Carlton, **Salt** (904-277-1087; ritzcarlton.com/en/ hotels/florida/amelia-island/dining/salt), 4750 Amelia Island Parkway, Amelia Island, connects the ocean with its artful preparations through the use of salts from around the world. In ancient times, salt was worth more than gold. Salt awakens you to the world of salt as seasoning. Enjoy a Painted Hills Filet Mignon dressed with Pure Ocean Horseradish Salt, or

Scottish salmon with leek bread pudding. In addition to their exquisite entrées, $33–69, you may select from the Natural and Infused Salts menu to take your own exotic taste of the world home, from Aguni, harvested from a small island in Japan, to Adriatic Citrus Salt, blending rich salt from the northernmost salt pan in Croatia with Florida citrus peels.

BARBECUE Smoky, succulent meats await at **Callahan Barbecue** (904-879-4675), 45007 FL 200, Callahan, one of the busiest restaurants in town. It's no wonder, since the aroma will draw you in. Choose from beef, pork, or chicken, or grab a plate of ribs; and while it's not our cup o' tea, they do serve fried gizzards and livers. Lunch and dinner under $10.

CASUAL FARE A local favorite along A1A since 1957, **The Surf Restaurant** (904-556-1059; thesurfonline.com), 3199 S Fletcher Avenue, Fernandina Beach, serves up lunch, dinner, and late-night snacks with live music on the huge outdoor sundeck. The menu ranges from deli delights to cheeseburgers, salads, fried seafood baskets, crab burgers, and creative wraps, $6–29. Catch their weekly specials for deeper discounts.

T-Rays Burger Station (904-261-6310; traysburgerstation.com), 202 S 8th Street, Fernandina Beach, open for breakfast and lunch, is one of a kind. You'll mistake it for an actual Exxon (we did, and had to circle the block), except for the picnic tables between the pumps. Grab your own drinks and utensils and settle down to a grilled-onion-smothered beauty of a burger, served up on mismatched plates in the ambience of a vintage gas station. Biscuits are only a buck, but ask for jelly and you'll pay $8.75, or so the signs say. In reality, you can pick up a hearty lunch for under $10.

COMFORT FOOD Have a hearty Southern comfort meal at **Barbara Jean's** (904-277-3700; barbarajeans.com), 960030 Gateway Boulevard, Fernandina Beach,

with crabcakes to write home about, tasty shrimp and grits, classic meat loaf, chicken-fried chicken, and chicken-fried steak. Opens at 11 AM for lunch and dinner, with breakfast served starting at 8 AM on weekends and holidays.

HIP AND BISTRO-STYLE You'd think you were in New Orleans at **Joe's 2nd Street Bistro** (904-321-2558; joesbistro .com), 14 S 2nd Street, Fernandina Beach, dining inside a home more than a century old or in the courtyard, surrounded by gardens. Visually appealing and tasty, their creations blend cuisines from many cultures, such as the macadamia-encrusted duck breast sharing a menu with Cajun Carbonara and Seafood Bouillabaisse. Entrées $18–32; opens at 11 AM for lunch and dinner.

OCEANFRONT A family favorite, **Sliders Seaside Grill** (904-277-6652; slidersseaside.com), 1998 S Fletcher Avenue, Amelia Island, has both a tiki bar and a playground with sandbox overlooking the beach—how smart is that? Being within walking distance of several recommended lodgings ensures steady traffic, too. Plenty of salad and sandwich options. Their entrées include their most excellent crabcakes as well as Lobster Mac and Cheese, a classic Low Country Boil with boiled peanuts, and their monstrous Seafood Platter, $9–29. 11 AM–11 PM daily.

QUICK BITE The laid-back **Timoti's Seafood Shak** (904-310-6550; timotis .com), 21 N 3rd Street, Fernandina Beach, is a quick stop for seafood. Think of it as the only fast food in the historic district, and make that quality fast food. Serving only wild-caught seafood, they offer seafood as tacos, in baskets, in wraps, or in boxes; there's even a Poke Bowl with ahi tuna, and a tofu taco for strict vegetarians. $3–12, 11 AM–8 PM daily.

SEAFOOD No visit to Fernandina Beach is complete without a meal at **The**

Crab Trap (904-261-4749; ameliacrabtrap .com), 31 N 2nd Street, Fernandina Beach, a downtown fixture since 1979. First, the seafood is fresh and delicious. Blackened shrimp just don't come any better, with just the right touch of blackening on the outside, the shrimp crisp and fresh, as is the slaw. Key lime pie was a tart, thick slab. But there's a quirk at this restaurant that the kids (and yes, many grown-ups) will love: the hole in the table. When you're peeling fresh shrimp or pulling apart crab legs, it saves a big mess for the waitress when you can drop all the shells and peelings into the hole. Entrées, primarily seafood, $15 and up. Opens at 5 nightly, casual atmosphere but reservations recommended.

Since 1969, the Toundas family has served up coastal favorites at the unstuffy **Marina Restaurant** (904-261-5310), 101 Centre Street, Fernandina Beach, in the Duryee building constructed in 1882. Their seafood is always fresh, with Fernandina fantail shrimp topping the menu, your choice of broiled, sautéed, or fried. Among their homespun sides are green bean casserole, fried cabbage with bacon drippings, and fried grits with sour cream tomato sauce, a dish almost like a French croquette, but with grits. Anxious for dessert? You can choose the cake of the day as one of your sides with the lunch specials. $10–24, daily 11 AM–9 PM.

LOCAL WATERING HOLES By opening pre-Prohibition in 1903, the funky **Palace Saloon** (844-441-2444; thepalacesaloon .com), 117 Centre Street, stakes its claim as Florida's Oldest Bar. At the threshold that defines "corner bar," the beehive mosaic floor continues throughout the building, where the bar itself defines old-fashioned elegance. It was designed by original owner Louis G. Hirth with help from his friend Adolphus Busch—yes, the founder of Anheuser-Busch—with hand-carved mahogany caryatids, gas lamps, murals, and colorful

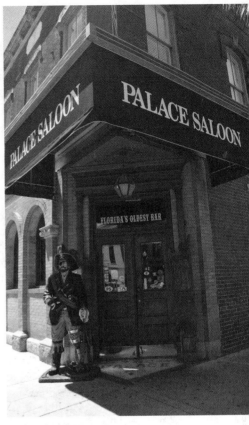

THE HISTORIC PALACE SALOON

embossed tin ceilings. No food served here, but even if you don't drink, the Palace is worth a peek. Noon–2 AM daily.

ICE CREAM AND SWEETS It's impossible to walk past **Fernandina's Fantastic Fudge** (904-277-4801; fantasticfudge .com), 218 Centre Street, without at least popping in for today's free sample. As candymakers, they create perfect pralines, coconut haystacks, dark caramels, pecan turtles, and other confections that have vanished from the mainstream and are only found where candymakers truly do make their own candy, rolled out on marble slabs. But many, as we did, stop for scoops of hand-dipped ice cream—one variety of which includes chunks of the local fudge—while deciding how much fudge to tote back home.

FRESH SLABS OF FUDGE AT FERNANDINA FANTASTIC FUDGE

✳ Selective Shopping

ANTIQUES If you're looking for decor ideas, an hour or two of browsing **Eight Flags Antique Market** (904-277-8550), 602 Centre Street, will give you plenty. The delightfully fragrant entryway sets a positive tone for perusing antiques. Filling a former grocery store, this enormous assortment of dealer booths has plenty of treasures, from luxe linens imported from India to everything Coca-Cola collectors have ever dreamed about.

"A cabinet of curiosities" is an understatement on the front of **Hunt's Art & Artifacts** (904-261-8225), 316 Centre Street #C, for their cabinets are many, and they are stuffed with the most unusual things—like fossils and rugs from Morocco, dinosaur bones, Greek and Roman coins, incense direct from India, and authentic pre-Columbian artifacts.

At the crossroads in Yulee, **Old Flood Store Antiques** (904-225-0902; oldfloodstore.com), 463085 FL 200, Yulee, is a browser's paradise for fine antique furniture, plates, and

glassware plus collectible ephemera. Friday–Sunday.

ARTS AND CRAFTS At **La Torre's Gallery & Gift Shop** (904-261-0444), 206 Centre Street, you'll find a massive selection of imported acrylic paintings for home decor, as well as the owner's faithful canine friend, Cool Hand Luke, surveying all visitors. A collection of colorful Haitian-made lizards and crabs climb the wall nearest the door.

BOOKS AND GIFTS **The Book Loft** (904-261-8991), 214 Centre Street, has a decidedly collectible bent. Find Floridiana—including many of my books—downstairs near the front window, or head upstairs to curl up with a good book amid vintage tomes.

The Irish-owned **Celtic Charm** (904-277-8009), 306 Centre Street, inspires thoughts of the Emerald Isle with traditional silver Celtic knots, sweaters, and even postcards in all the shades of green; lots of golfing gifts, too.

Breathe in the soothing scent of **Pelindaba Lavender** (904-432-7300; pelindabalavender.com), 15 S 4th Street, and prepare to relax. This aromatic shop sells all things lavender, sourced from a farm on San Juan Island near Vancouver. Pillows, stress balls, lotions, and soaps are joined by the unexpected—we'd never imagined lavender chocolate chip cookies.

Need a fishing net, or a ship's flag? How about a pirate statue, of which this city has no lack? Try **Ship's Lantern** (904-261-5821), 210 Centre Street, for nautical decor items.

For youngsters and the young-at-heart, **Villa Villekulla Toys** (904-432-8291), 5 S 2nd Street, has everything from robot kits to wooden puzzles and creative games that will keep your kids busy for hours. If you need a gift for a child's birthday, look here first.

CLOTHING **Harbor Wear** (904-321-0061), 212 Centre Street, has a great assortment of Life is Good women's quality sun and fun clothing, including Amelia Island logo items.

Dress up the tots at **Pineapple Patch** (904-321-2441), 201 Centre Street, where they feature Flap Happy and Fresh Produce kids' clothing.

FARMERS' MARKET Find the freshest strawberries, tomatoes, melons, and cucumbers at **Hildebrand Farms** (904-845-4254), 1210 Patsy Lane, Callahan.

OUTDOOR GEAR Founded in 1978 and still run by the Lacoss family, **Amelia Angler Outfitters** (904-261-2870; ameliaangler.com), 111 Centre Street, hides a wealth of local fishing knowledge behind those displays of colorful Columbia sports shirts. Captain Terry Lacoss shares his tournament skills along with fishing and boater basics in a fishing school run through the store, and you can always pop in to book a charter for freshwater or saltwater fishing, sightseeing on the *Cumberland Princess*, or sailing with a licensed captain out of Fernandina Harbor Marina.

SEA SHELLS AND GIFTS FOR SALE ALONG CENTRE STREET

Kayak Amelia (904-261-5702; kayakamelia.com), 4 N 2nd Street, has its own store in downtown Fernandina, the better to stop in and chat about local paddling destinations while perusing their line of T-shirts and gear for dog lovers. You can book your paddling tours here, too! 10 AM–6 PM daily.

Outside the main shopping district, **Red Otter Outfitters** (904-206-4122; redotteroutfitters.com), 1012 Atlantic Avenue, Fernandina Beach, carries all major brands of technical outdoor apparel. They're also your stop for biking and kayaking gear, Crocs, travel necessities, and guidebooks.

✳ Special Events

FALL/WINTER Not sure which bed and breakfast to stay at next time? Or just want to see the beautiful architecture decked out in holiday splendor? Then make the **Bed & Breakfast Holiday Cookie Tour** (904-277-0500; amelia islandinns.com/cookie-tour) your favorite trek. Freshly baked cookies leave you warm all over as you explore local bed and breakfasts filled with holiday music and Christmas decor. A portion of the proceeds from tickets and cookbook sales benefit the local women's shelter.

The **Amelia Island Book Festival** (ameliaislandbookfestival.org) in Fernandina Beach features book signings, readings, and workshops. Have "lunch with an author" or go on a "beach walk with an author." Mid-February.

Get your reservations well in advance for the **Amelia Island Chamber Music Festival** (904-261-1779; ameliaislandchambermusicfestival.com), 1890 S 14th St. World-renowned musicians perform chamber music at venues throughout the island in this fabulous annual event, which starts in February and extends for several months.

Held each March, the **Amelia Concours d'Elegance** (904-636-0027; ameliaconcours.org), Amelia Island, is one of the nation's largest classic car shows, with hundreds of rare cars from private collections on display. A four-day soiree of seminars, gala dinners, charity auctions, and road tours, it's a must for serious car collectors.

SPRING/SUMMER ✐ **Railroad Days**, Callahan. Held at the Historic Callahan Depot (see *Railroadiana*) this community celebration centers on the railroad history of the region, featuring a parade with model steam trails, model railroad layouts that the kids can operate, food, music, and lots of family fun. The last weekend in March.

✐ **Isle of Eight Flags Fernandina Shrimp Festival** (904-277-7274; shrimp festival.com), in downtown historic Fernandina Beach, has celebrated the shrimping industry for the past 50 years with music, fine arts and crafts, antiques, pirates, and shrimp, shrimp, shrimp. Festivities include the Blessing of the Fleet (yes, shrimping is still an occupation here), the Shrimp Boat Parade, Family Fun Zone, fine arts and crafts show, a 5K run, food and vendor booths, and more. The festival kicks off with the solemn laying of a memorial wreath at the Shrimpers' Memorial, traditionally done by a member of the fleet. Held in May.

✐ The third weekend in May, the annual **Wild Amelia Nature Festival** (wildamelia.com) was created by local residents to foster a sense of appreciation of the unique natural areas of Amelia Island in visitors and homeowners alike. The festival includes guided eco-tours, an eco-expo, Junior Ranger activities, and a photography contest.

ST. AUGUSTINE

St. Augustine, Ponte Vedra, and the Beaches

The breezy coastal city of **St. Augustine** invites the weary traveler to sit and stay awhile, to soak in its Old World charm. Victorian houses sprout along narrow streets lined with palm trees. Coquina walls, made from seashell conglomerate quarried by the Spanish, hide small gated gardens and patios. Each home, built with defense in mind, on the orders of the king of Spain, has its main entrance off a courtyard brimming with greenery. Many of the city's oldest buildings are made of coquina quarried from Anastasia Island, including St. Augustine's defining landmark, the Castillo de San Marco, an enormous Spanish fortress that dates from 1695 and commands the seaward side of the nation's oldest city. Founded in 1565 by Spanish explorer Don Pedro Menéndez de Avilés, St. Augustine is the oldest continually occupied European settlement in the United States, a little slice of the Old Country on Florida's shores.

St. Augustine is a melting pot of cultures, a concentration of history in layers thicker than any other city in the United States. A thriving Greek community grew from Minorcan settlers who escaped the tribulations of a colony farther south at New Smyrna and sought refuge in the city. The oldest free black settlement in the United States—Fort Mose, established in 1738—sat just north of the Spanish settlement. Thirty years later, Sir Francis Drake, a pirate sanctioned by the British government, set the Spanish city aflame, blazing the way for British rule through 1784. Most of the colonial homes you see today were built during the second Spanish Colonial Period, just before Florida became a US territory in 1822. St. Augustine is the only US city with street patterns and architecture reflecting the Spanish colonial ambience commonly seen in Caribbean and Latin American cities.

To its north, the seaside community of **Ponte Vedra** has gained fame as a golfer's paradise, thanks to nearly a dozen courses flanking TPC Sawgrass, a world-class golfing destination. While primarily residential, this portion of the coast has its local destinations worth seeking out, like relaxing waterfront restaurants in **Palm Valley**, established in 1908 with a heritage of fish camps, and quiet stretches of beach north of **North Beach**. St. Johns County, of which St. Augustine is the county seat, stretches to the St. Johns River, and along that freshwater coastline you'll rediscover the charm of old Florida fish camps, campgrounds, and quiet canopied roads. The southwest portion of the county is rural, known for potato and cabbage farms.

South along A1A from St. Augustine across the Bridge of Lions is **Anastasia Island**, where the Spanish oversaw the cutting of massive coquina stones from quarries to build the impenetrable walls of the Castillo. St. Augustine Lighthouse towers over the island. While Anastasia State Park wins our pick as best beach in the area—an unsullied sweep nearly 5 miles long—there is no lack of beachfront for every taste. Busy **St. Augustine Beach** has plenty of accommodations within walking distance of the shoreline, and while **Crescent Beach** is residential, beach access is assured for all. Fort Matanzas was the scene of a bloody massacre of shipwrecked French explorers who'd founded a colony along the St. Johns River at Fort Caroline (see the *Jacksonville* chapter) and lost the struggle for regional dominance with the Spanish in St. Augustine. At the southern mouth of the Matanzas River, **Summer Haven** began in the 1890s as a summer getaway for well-to-do northerners who came to St. Augustine on

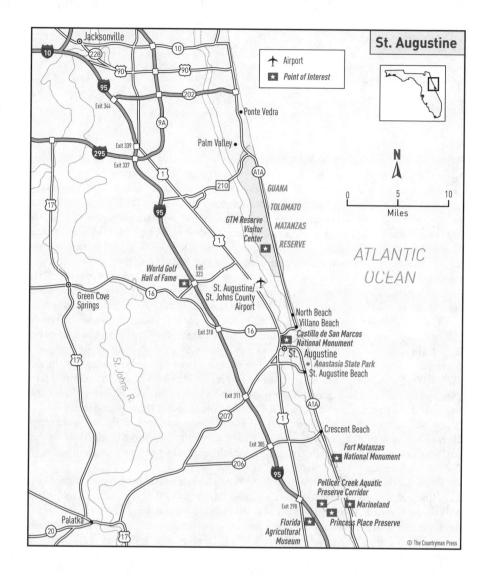

Map legend:
- ✈ Airport
- ★ Point of Interest

Labels on map: St. Augustine, Jacksonville, Ponte Vedra, Palm Valley, GUANA, TOLOMATO, MATANZAS, RESERVE, GTM Reserve Visitor Center, World Golf Hall of Fame, Green Cove Springs, St. Augustine/St. Johns County Airport, ATLANTIC OCEAN, North Beach, Villano Beach, Castillo de San Marcos National Monument, St. Augustine, Anastasia State Park, St. Augustine Beach, Crescent Beach, Fort Matanzas National Monument, Pellicer Creek Aquatic Preserve Corridor, Marineland, Florida Agricultural Museum, Princess Place Preserve, Palatka, St. Johns R.

N
0   5   10
Miles

© The Countryman Press

Henry Flagler's trains and continued on by boat to create their own fishing and hunting camps in the wilds.

St. Augustine is the birthplace of Florida tourism, thanks to Henry Flagler's grand hotels and railroad, built in the 1890s, which drew the first northern tourists to Florida "for their health," and that's part of why there is so much to see and do here. It is a city infused with history and art, timeless and yet chic, one of the most vibrant and charming destinations Florida has to offer.

GUIDANCE **St. Augustine, Ponte Vedra, & The Beaches Visitors & Convention Bureau** (800-653-2489; floridashistoriccoast.com), 29 Old Mission Avenue, has a website where you can plan your entire trip online, from reservations to ordering tickets. You also have the option to stop in at the prominent **St. Augustine Visitor Information**

Center (904-825-1000), 10 S Castillo Drive, off San Marcos Avenue near the city gates or the **Downtown Visitor Center** (904-825-5079), 48 King Street, at the Government House Museum. At the San Marcos Avenue location, you can grab brochures, on-the-spot reservations, and an introduction to the area via exhibits and a video presentation. Right in front of the center, you'll discover the first of a series of downtown maps that lead you through the Historic District.

GETTING THERE *By air:* **Jacksonville International Airport** (see the *Jacksonville* chapter).

By car: **Interstate 95** runs west of St. Augustine; exit at **FL 16** and head east, or follow **US 1** south from Jacksonville, north from Bunnell. For the beach route, follow **A1A** south from Jacksonville Beach to reach Ponte Vedra, Vilano Beach, St. Augustine, Anastasia Island, St. Augustine Beach, Crescent Beach, and Summer Haven.

GETTING AROUND **I-95** forms the spine for travel through St. Johns County, with **FL 16**, **FL 210**, and **FL 207** major east–west connectors between FL 13 (which runs along the St. Johns River) and US 1/ A1A (along the coast).

LIGHTNER MUSEUM, THE FORMER ALCAZAR HOTEL

Old St. Augustine (the historic downtown) is a place to park and **get out on foot**: The ancient streets are narrow, with loads of pedestrian traffic. Numerous **tour operators run trams through the city** (see *Touring St. Augustine*) with on/off privileges. They let you park in their lots as part of the package deal, which makes it especially worthwhile if you're not up for heavy walkabout.

Addresses listed in this chapter are in St. Augustine unless otherwise noted. Districts referenced in town include the **Historic District** (the Oldest City core), **San Sebastian** (King Street between Flagler College and US 1), and **San Marcos** (San Marcos Boulevard north of the visitors center and south of the bridge to Vilano Beach).

PARKING If you're planning to spend a day or more and aren't staying in the Historic District (free parking is a great perk that comes with your room), ditch the car in one of the many **flat-fee lots**, which typically run $5 a day except during special events and holiday weekends. The **Historic Downtown Parking Facility** (904-484-5160), 1 Cordova Street, looms behind the visitor center with a 2,500-space parking garage; $10 per day. There is **free two-hour street parking** along the waterfront and in residential neighborhoods, if you can find it, as well as some **short-term metered spaces** downtown along King Street and surrounding City Hall.

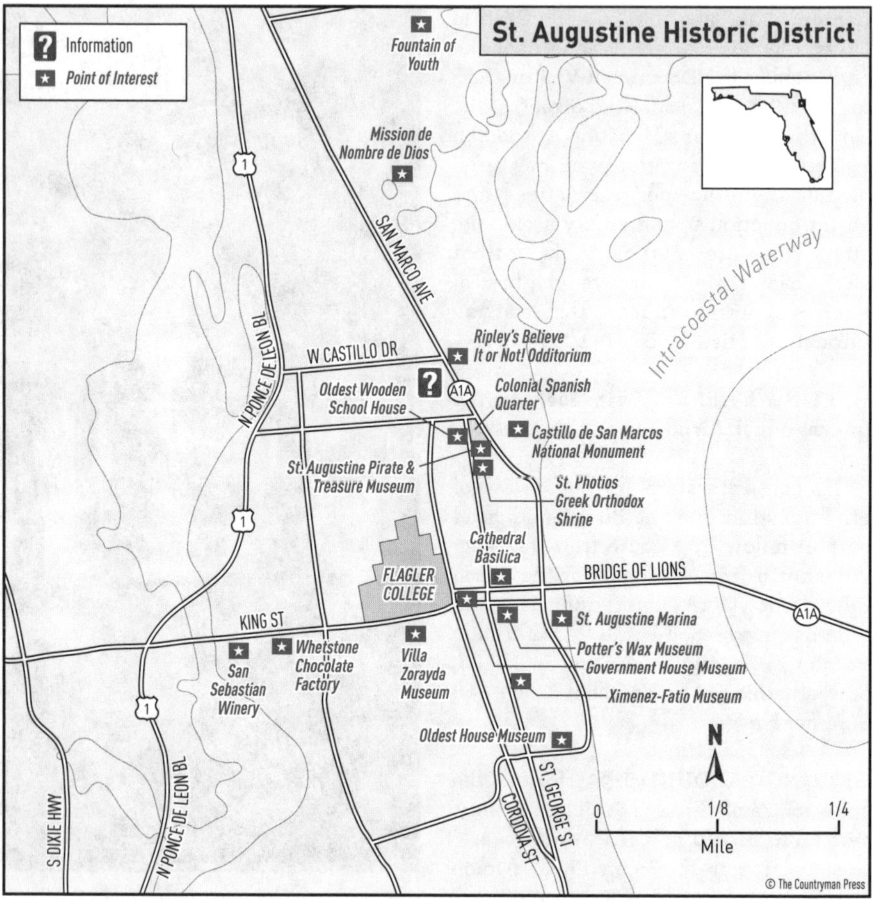

PUBLIC RESTROOMS There are several sets of public restrooms along **St. George Street**, at the visitors center on **San Marcos Avenue**, in the courtyard of the **Lightner Museum**, and at the **marina**.

MEDICAL EMERGENCIES **Flagler Hospital** (904-819-5155; flaglerhospital.org), 400 Health Park Boulevard, St. Augustine. Call 911 for major emergencies.

✲ To See

ARCHAEOLOGICAL SITES The city of St. Augustine is one big archaeological site, so much so that any new construction requires a team of archaeologists to assess all construction sites, since pottery shards, pieces of clay pipes, and the remains of 1800s yellow fever victims have routinely been discovered around town. As you wander the streets, be on the lookout for **interpretive signs at archaeological sites** in open lots between historic buildings, such as at the corner of Cuna and Spanish streets and inside the public restrooms on St. George Street. The Florida Museum of Natural History provides an **online gallery** (flmnh.ufl.edu/staugustine/timeline.asp) highlighting

FOUNTAIN OF YOUTH ARCHAEOLOGICAL PARK

archaeological sites in their historical content along with images of the artifacts removed from the sites. One of several ancient cemeteries, **Tolomato Cemetery** on Cordova Street, circa 1777, was formerly a Tolomato Indian village.

🐾 🎨 ♿ At **Fountain of Youth Archaeological Park** (800-356-8222; fountain ofyouthflorida.com), 11 Magnolia Avenue, amble around the pleasant natural grounds at the site of the Timucuan village of Seloy, where Ponce de Leon stepped ashore on April 3, 1513, to claim the land of La Florida for Spain. In 1952 archaeologists discovered the Christian burials of Timucua here circa 1565, proving the site was the first Catholic mission in the New World. A dripping rock spring is reverentially referred to as Ponce's Fountain of Youth, and you're invited to take a sip. The expansive grounds hold many secrets, which archaeologists continue to unearth in active digs. Watch them at work and ask them questions. This is a living history museum as well: conquistadores and soldiers roam the grounds and the Timucua work in their village. Museum exhibits, a planetarium, and peacocks add to the colorful display in this waterfront setting.

♿ To learn the story of the first free black settlement in the Americas, visit **Fort Mose Historic State Park** (904-461-2000; floridastateparks.org/park/Fort-Mose), 15 Fort Mose Trail, where the museum at the visitor center showcases artifacts unearthed on the site. An interpretive boardwalk leads to an overlook of the location of the fort in the salt marsh. Visitors center open Thursday–Monday 9 AM–5 PM; fee. Grounds open 8 AM–sunset; free.

ARCHITECTURE With such a concentration of centuries' worth of buildings in one spot, St. Augustine is a delight for architecture buffs. St. George and its cross streets are notable for homes dating back to the late 1700s—look for historical plaques with names and dates on each home. Some are open for tours, most notably the **Gonzales-Alvarez House** (904-824-2872; saintaugustinehistoricalsociety.org/oldest-house-museum-complex), 271 Charlotte Street. Its tabby floors were laid in the early 1700s; during the British period in 1776, the house served as a tavern. Tours of the complex include an interpretive walk through the home, its kitchen, and gardens; the Manucy

FLAGLER'S ARCHITECTURAL LEGACY

A contemporary of John D. Rockefeller and part owner of the Standard Oil Company, Henry Flagler had plenty of money to invest. After purchasing a railroad in 1883, he bought land with the intent of providing a luxury destination for fellow well-to-do northerners. Stand at the corner of Cordova and King, and you can visually compare all three of his destination hotels.

Deciding on a Spanish Renaissance revival design, Henry Flagler wanted grandeur to rise along the edge of the ancient city, and it did in his Hotel Ponce de Leon, 74 King St. Constructed of poured concrete—a first for its time—it had terra cotta relief, mosaics, and stained glass from Louis Comfort Tiffany, retained by Flagler as interior decorator for the project. Thomas Edison provided the materials for an electric plant, just two years after he filed his patent for the incandescent light bulb. When the hotel opened in January 1888, it was the grandest in America, with 4,000 electric lights throughout, including twinkling in the gardens. As was traditional at the time, it was open for the "season"—here in Florida, January through April. Utilized as barracks for servicemen more than once, it managed to survive longer than its sister properties. It closed its doors as a hotel in 1967 but was reborn as Flagler College (flagler.edu) the next year. Student docents provide walking tours several times daily through Historical Tours of Flagler College (legacy.flagler.edu), $8–10.

By Christmas 1888, Flagler opened Alcazar Hotel, 79 King Street, next door, the design inspired by the royal palace in Seville, Spain. Also built to be a luxury hotel, it had a one-of-a-kind feature in its basement: a giant indoor swimming pool, the largest of its kind at the time. The hotel also boasted sulfur baths and a steam room, a gymnasium, a grand ballroom, and a casino. The Depression cut off its stream of tourists; it closed in 1932. Publisher Otto Lightner, founding editor of *Hobbies Magazine*, bought the hotel in 1947 to move his museum to it from Chicago. He gave the building to the City of St. Augustine in trust and died soon after. The city restored it in 1968, turning it into City Hall and a portion into the Lightner Museum (904-824-2874; lightnermuseum.org), 75 King Street, a fascinating "collection of collections." Exhibits run the gamut from fine art, elegant glasswork, and antique furnishings to common items like buttons and cigar labels; in the science section, you'll find both minerals and shrunken heads along with an Egyptian mummy; admission $5–10.

Museum, with historical artifacts and dioramas; and the Page L. Edwards Gallery, featuring ever-changing historical exhibits. Daily 10 AM–5 PM; fee.

Constructed in 1691 during the First Spanish Period, the **Father Miguel O'Reilly House** (904-826-0750; fatheroreilly.house), 2 Aviles Street, served as home to its namesake when he bought it in 1785 for use as a parish rectory. The house has evolved through five architectural phases over the centuries. An Irish priest under the service of the Spanish crown, Father O'Reilly dedicated the Cathedral Basilica of St. Augustine (see *Churches*) and schooled Father Felix Varela, a Cuban priest now under consideration for sainthood. The museum tells the story of the home and the Catholic traditions of the city; the Sisters of St. Joseph have been the caretakers of the home since 1866. Open Wednesday–Saturday 10 AM–3 PM, free; donations appreciated.

The **Pena-Peck House**, 143 St. George Street, built of native coquina circa 1750, was the residence of the royal treasurer from Spain. It's managed as a house museum by the Woman's Exchange (see *Shopping*); fee.

From 1798, the **Ximenez-Fatio House** (904-829-3575; ximenezfatiohouse.org), 20 Aviles Street, is considered the most authentic eighteenth-century building in the city; renovations of the coquina were completed without replacing the original building materials. The home exemplifies St. Augustine Plan architecture from the Second Spanish Colonial Period. Intimate guided tours hourly Tuesday–Saturday 11 AM–3 PM; $8–10.

Four months after opening the Moorish-theme Casa Monica, 95 Cordova Street, in 1888, Franklin Smith sold his brand-new hotel—on land purchased from Henry Flagler—right back to Flagler, who renamed it the Cordova. Its heyday was in the 1890s, when it had 200 guest rooms. Closed in 1932, it was renovated in the 1960s and again in the 1990s, when it reopened under its original name as the elegant Casa Monica (see *Lodging*).

FLAGLER COLLEGE, THE FORMER HOTEL PONCE DE LEON

Built in 1883 by Franklin Smith as a 1/10-scale replica of the Alhambra in Spain, **Villa Zorayda** (904-829-9887; villazorayda.com), 83 King Street, became a casino in 1922 and then an attraction, Zorayda Castle, in 1936. It sparked a Moorish Spanish revival in St. Augustine that both inspired the look of Henry Flagler's hotels and created a demand for the building technique of using crushed coquina mixed with concrete, a local take on tabby (normally done with oyster shells). Inside, rooms are adorned with antiques from Franklin Smith and fine art and furnishings imported by owner Abraham S. Mussallem during the 1920s. Admission $9–10.

An unexpected sight along A1A is **Castle Otttis** (904-824-3274; castleotttis .com), 103 3rd Street, Vilano Beach, its Irish-inspired turrets rising above the saw palmetto. Completed in 1988 as a religious landscape sculpture, it is open to the elements but has the basics of a church inside, hand-hewn in cypress wood and heart pine. It opens for interdenominational Christian worship services the last Sunday of each month, at **9:30 AM**, and is used for retreats and weddings.

ART GALLERIES St. Augustine is North Florida's cultural center, with the highest concentration of galleries in the region. For ongoing arts events, check in with the collaborative **Art Galleries of St. Augustine** (AGOSA) (904-829-0065; artgalleriesofstaugustine .com); they orchestrate the **First Friday Artwalk** each month, 5–9 PM. For those who aren't up for walking, the Old Town Trolleys and Ripley's Red Sightseeing Trains offer free rides along the art route. **Uptown Saturday Night** (visitstaugustine.com/event/uptown-saturday-night) is a gala art walk through the San Marco Arts District, held 5–9 PM on the last Saturday of each month.

Established in 1924, the **St. Augustine Art Association** (904-824-2310; staaa.org), 22 Marine Street, the oldest gallery in town (established in 1924) with competitive shows and permanent exhibits. Tuesday–Saturday 10 AM–4 PM, Sunday 2–5 PM; free.

Splashy American pop art pops at **Absolute Americana Art Gallery** (904-824-5545; absoluteamericana.com), 77 Bridge Street, where advertising art—the original Absolut campaign and other pop-sensation libations—includes lithographs from Andy Warhol and Leroy Nieman.

The neon sign outside **Butterfield Garage Art Gallery** (904-825-4577; butterfield garage.com), 137 King Street, will catch your attention—stop inside for a blast of "high-octane art" from this multi-artist contemporary artist co-op. It has large open spaces accommodating huge canvases, and you'll find many different media on display, like Estella J. Fransbergen's raku elephant ear leaves.

Bold art will catch your eye at **Crooked Palm Fine Art Gallery** (904-825-0010), 75 King Street at the Lightner Museum Courtyard, such as the tropical fantasies in wavy frames by Steve Barton, Caribbean dreams by Dan Macklin, and strongly defined portraiture by Tim Rogerson.

The **P.A.St.A. Fine Art Gallery** (904-824-0251; pastagalleryart.com), 214 Charlotte Street, has more than 200 original pieces of art on display as well as changing monthly exhibits.

Tripp Harrison Signature Gallery (800-678-9550 or 904-824-3662; trippharrison .com), 22 Cathedral Place. In addition to historical paintings by this renowned national artist with a distinctive and popular style, the gallery includes limited-edition works by other sculptors and two-dimensional artists.

CHURCHES Built on the site where Father Francisco López de Mendoza Grajales offered the first Mass in the New World in 1565 in St. Augustine, **Mission Nombre de Dios** (904-824-2809; missionandshrine.org), 27 Ocean Avenue, rebuilt many times over the centuries, is also home **to the first shrine to the Virgin Mary in North America**, established in the early 1600s. Rebuilt in 1915, the present ivy-covered shrine has a replica of the 1598 statuette of Our Lady of La Leche, remaining a pilgrimage site to Catholic mothers-to-be today. On the grounds of the ancient mission, a modern 208-foot, stainless-steel cross marks the site of the founding of St. Augustine.

♂ The **Cathedral Basilica of St. Augustine** (904-824-2806; thefirstparish.org), 38 Cathedral Place, the first and oldest Catholic parish in the New World, was built in 1797 with stones from the ruins of the original mission. Walk inside to see awe-inspiring religious art, including murals of the Church in early Florida and the city's early history; the stained glass windows, installed in 1909, illustrate the life of Saint Augustine of Hippo. The Shrine of St. Patrick honors the many Irish immigrants who served in the diocese over the past four centuries.

As the only Greek Orthodox shrine in the United States, **St. Photios Greek Orthodox National Shrine** (904-829-8205; stphotios.org), 41 St. George Street, is dedicated to the first Greek colony in the Americas, at New Smyrna in 1768. As explained in exhibits, many died on the journey, and more while in indentured servitude at the Turnbull Plantation. Inside the glorious chapel, Byzantine-style religious frescoes with gold-leaf accents are fine works of art.

♂ Built in 1889 by Henry Flagler as a memorial to his daughter Jenny, **Memorial Presbyterian Church** (memorialpcusa.org), 32 Sevilla Street, is still home to Florida's first Presbyterian congregation, established in 1824. Its Moorish design echoes the Flagler hotels of the time (see *Architecture*). Inside is the Flagler family mausoleum, where Flagler, his first wife Mary, his daughter Jenny, and his granddaughter Marjorie are laid to rest. Since 1832, the church has owned **Huguenot Cemetery** just outside the city gates; they open it the third Saturday monthly from 11 AM–2 PM. Despite the name, no Huguenots are thought to be buried there.

HALL OF FAME ♿ The **World Golf Hall of Fame** (904-940-4000; worldgolfhalloffame .org), 1 World Golf Place, takes you from the birth of the game in St. Andrews, Scotland, to today's champions, with artifacts and displays related to the game and its players, including exhibits on well-known players like Arnold Palmer, Nancy Lopez, and Bob Hope. On the second floor, walk through 18 holes of golf. The front nine have a life-size replica of the famed St. Andrews Swilcan Burn Bridge; the back nine cover the modern game. Hall of Fame members are honored in Shell Hall with a crescent of acrylic pedestals. New inductions are held each fall. Open Monday–Saturday 10 AM–6 PM, Sunday noon–6 PM. Base admission includes one round of golf on their 18-hole putting course and one shot on the Hall of Fame Challenge Hole: $10–21 adults, $5 ages 5–12. Add $5–10 for an IMAX film at their adjacent theater.

IMAX ♿ ✎ In front of the largest theater screen in the Southeast, you're immersed in the movies like never before—especially during a 3-D movie. At the **World Golf Hall of Fame IMAX Theater** (904-940-4133; worldgolfimax.com), 1 World Golf Place, choose from first-run Hollywood blockbusters or a selection of nature and science documentaries made for the five-story-high IMAX screen. Tickets $7.50–13 adults, $6.50–10 ages 12 and under. Open daily.

LIGHTHOUSE ✎ Surrounding the distinctive black-and-white tower rising 165 feet above sea level and first lit in 1874, the **St. Augustine Lighthouse & Maritime Museum** (904-829-0745; staugustinelighthouse.org), 81 Lighthouse Avenue, encompasses the entire light station complex. The light keeper's house is now a fun interactive museum with period items, including the original nine-foot-tall, hand-blown first-order Fresnel lens from the original tower. Permanent exhibits cover history of light tending along the coast. Climbing the steep spiral staircase, all 219 steps, is a highlight for a panorama that extends 35 miles along the coast. Special after-hours tours, like the "Dark of the Moon" paranormal experience and Sunset Moonrise, get you onto the grounds and up in the tower after dark. General admission $14 adults, $11 seniors and kids over 44 inches tall (minimum height for a lighthouse climb).

MUSEUMS AND HISTORIC SITES No other US city can boast the number of centuries spanned by historic sites than can St. Augustine. Some are simply just a part of everyday life, like the **Bridge of Lions**. Opened in 1927, this prominent bridge connecting downtown with Anastasia Island replaced an older wooden bridge used by streetcars. Designed as a work of public art, its lions draw the most attention. Carved of Carrara marble in Florence, they replicate the Medici lions found in that Italian city. Other sites take a little seeking out. We've listed some under *Archaeological Sites*, *Architecture*, and *Churches*. Other historic sites and museums we think you shouldn't miss are listed below.

✎ ♿ Along Matanzas Bay, the imposing **Castillo de San Marcos** (904-829-6506; nps.gov/CASA), 1 S Castillo Drive, completed in 1695 of coquina rock quarried from Anastasia Island, provided the city's coastal defense. Although the wooden town was burned several times by invaders, residents survived by taking refuge behind the

CASTILLO DE SAN MARCOS

fortress walls; the sedimentary rock absorbed cannonballs. A national monument, the Castillo offers interpretive tours, a fabulous bookstore, and excellent views of the bay. From the outer walls of the Castillo, a wood-and-stone rampart enclosed the city; visitors entered through the City Gates, which still stand at the entrance to St. George Street. Open daily, $10 ages 16 and over; $1.50 per hour for parking.

✎ ♿ As chickens squawk, a musket fires, and a tendril of smoke creeps skyward from the blacksmith's coals, let your senses take you back in time at the **Colonial Quarter** (904-342-2857; colonialquarter.com), 33 St. George St. An immersive living history museum, it sprawls across courtyards between historic buildings like the **De Mesa-Sanchez House**, constructed in 1740 and added on to over the centuries; within this green space, active archaeological digs are going on. Climb the watchtower for a great view of the Castillo and the Ancient City. Join one of the guided tours or walk through on your own, daily 10 AM–5 PM; $13 adults, $7 ages 5–12.

Although the small but impressive Spanish fortress at **Fort Matanzas National Monument** (904-471-0116; nps.gov/foma), 8635 A1A S, Crescent Beach, wasn't built until 1740, the site of the fort is where the French survivors of Fort Caroline (see the *Jacksonville* chapter) were slaughtered at the command of St. Augustine founder Don Pedro Menendez de Aviles. Across the street, beach access lets you ramble down to Mantanzas Inlet. Daily 9 AM–5:30 PM; fee for tour.

♿ The **Government House Museum** (staugustine.ufl.edu/govHouse.html), corner of King and Cathedral, a historic artifact in itself, hosts rotating exhibits on regional history drawn from a massive collection of artifacts stored here until the late 1980s, now curated by the University of Florida. Open Tuesday–Saturday 10 AM–5 PM; free.

✎ Built before 1763, the **Oldest Wooden Schoolhouse** (888-653-7245; oldest woodenschoolhouse.com), 14 St. George Street, is indeed the oldest wooden school remaining in the United States, built of cedar and cypress that has stood the test of time. It's fun to take the kids through and a favorite stop for school groups. Open daily; fee.

✎ The Romanesque **Old Jail** (904-829-3800; trolleytours.com/st-augustine/old-jail), 167 San Marcos, looks like an 1890s hotel for a reason—Henry Flagler had it built in 1891 to move the undesirables away from his hotels to the edge of town. It served its purpose until 1953. On a tour, swaggering characters escort you through the quarters, once the province of larger-than-life Sheriff Joe Perry. The adjoining 🖉 ♿ **Florida Heritage Museum** introduces you to the region's long and storied past, from exhibits of Florida's First Peoples to days of Henry Flagler and his Model Land Company, the first real estate scam in Florida history. Open daily 9 AM–4:30 PM; fee.

🐾 The **Spanish Military Hospital** (904-342-7730; spanishmilitaryhospital.com), 3 Aviles Street, provides a glimpse into eighteenth-century medical treatments at the Royal Hospital of Our Lady of Guadalupe on a narrated tour, with dioramas and artifacts like porcelain bedpans and scary-looking period medical instruments. As with many St. Augustine buildings, it comes with its own haunts. Open 10 AM–6 PM daily; fee.

🖉 ♿ Slip into St. Augustine's seamy past at the **St. Augustine Pirate & Treasure Museum** (877-GO-PLUNDER; thepiratemuseum.com), 12 S Castillo Drive, a delightful immersion in the Golden Age of Piracy. Colorful interactive exhibits share pirate legends, lore, and customs amid a backdrop of priceless original artifacts. Collected by owner Pat Croce, they range from compasses and coins to an original Jolly Roger flag to Captain Tew's Treasure Chest. The ornate chest weighs 150 pounds empty and is the only known surviving pirate treasure chest in the world. Near it, you can lift a real gold bar—and it will surprise you how heavy it is. Open 10 AM–6 PM daily; $14 adults, $7 ages 5–12.

PERFORMING ARTS ♿ For indoor concerts, film series, and stage shows, check the schedule for the **Ponte Vedra Concert Hall** (904-209-0399; pvconcerthall.com), 1050 A1A N, Ponte Vedra Beach. Recent events included shows by Toad the Wet Sprocket, The California Honeydrops, and Jack Johnson; plays such as *Shakespeare Abridged*; and the musical *Godspell*. Tickets available online or at the box office.

The play's the thing at the **Limelight Theatre** (866-682-6400; limelight-theatre .org), 11 Old Mission Avenue, with year-round performances that include professional productions like *I Hate Hamlet* and *The Diary of Anne Frank*.

♿ The historic **St. Augustine Amphitheatre** (904-471-1965; staugamphitheatre .com), 1340 S A1A, is a hopping venue for serious concertgoers. Built in 1965 and set in a beautiful coastal hammock adjacent to Anastasia State Park, encompassing some of the historic Spanish-era coquina quarries, it was the home of the *Cross & Sword*, the official Florida state play depicting the founding of the city, for 30 years. Now a top-notch performing arts venue, it hosts concerts virtually every weekend by artists like Duran Duran, Peter Frampton, Incubus, and the Oak Ridge Boys. Tickets available online or at the box office; the grounds are open daily and worth a stroll to see the ancient quarries, now ponds with observation decks where you can watch the fish and turtles.

ZOO 🖉 ♿ Established more than a century ago, **St. Augustine Alligator Farm Zoological Park** (904-824-3337; alligatorfarm.com), 999 Anastasia Boulevard, Anastasia Island, is the grandaddy of Florida tourist attractions. Alligators are the stars of the show, but birders will appreciate the rookery above them, where you can get close enough for great photos of fledgling roseate spoonbills and wood storks without disturbing the birds. Animal enthusiasts will have a field day with the many species on display here in the regionally themed areas, from Orinoco crocodiles to lemurs, hornbills, and Galapagos tortoises. Overhead, the rope-and-wood bridges and wires are part of Crocodile Crossing (see *Zipline*). Wildlife shows focus on interpretation of species behavior. Open 9 AM–5 PM daily, $25 ages 12 and over, $14 ages 3–11, $7–13 guests in wheelchairs.

❄ To Do

BEACH CRUISING Vehicles are permitted on the beach in Vilano Beach (which has two ramps) and from St. Augustine Beach south through Matanzas Inlet, with access ramps off A1A at A Street, Ocean Trace, Dondanville, Matanzas Avenue, Mary Street, Crescent Beach, and Fort Matanzas (exit only). Vehicle fees are $8 per day or $60 for a season pass, with a discount for county residents and handicapped drivers; purchase at beach toll booths. Do not exceed 10 mph, be cautious of beachgoers, and don't disturb flagged areas set aside for hatching sea turtle nests. Driving is at your own risk: we've seen many a driver stranded due to soft sands or rising tides. From May 1 to Labor Day weekend, vehicular traffic on the beach is allowed between 8 AM and 8 PM; after 8 PM no vehicles are allowed on the beach, except at Vilano during the Fourth of July. As access times may change seasonally, consult the tollbooth operator. St. Johns County also offers beach wheelchairs; reserve in advance at 904-209-0752.

BIRDING One of the best spots in Florida for bird photography is the decades-old rookery at ✍ ♿ **St. Augustine Alligator Farm** (see *Zoo*), where the long-term presence of so many alligators assures the nesting colonies that raccoons won't steal precious bird eggs. It's always raucous (and smelly) there during nesting and especially fledging season, February–July. Along FL A1A in **Crescent Beach**, watch for nande conures, a variety of chartreuse parrot that has naturalized along the Intracoastal Waterway. Wading birds frequent most tidal areas. **GTM Reserve** (see *Hiking*) is on the flyway used by migrating painted buntings. A small colony of cormorants always nests at ✍ ♿ **Bird Island Park** (904-209-0346), 101 Library Boulevard, Ponte Vedra, a landscaped park with a sea turtle maze and boardwalks around the pond. Birders may wish to time their visit for **Florida's Birding & Photo Fest** (see *What's Happening*) held in April.

BIKING All along this coastline, from Ponte Vedra to Summer Haven, A1A is designated a road route for the **East Coast Greenway** (greenway.org/fl.aspx), a national bike route spanning from Maine to Key West. Most biking here, however, is on road routes; bikes make a nice way to explore the narrow back streets of the Ancient City or the beach, but are tough to ride along major roads. Rent bikes at **Island Life** (904-436-5045; islandlifestaugustine.com), 105 A1A Beach Boulevard, where they will deliver you the rental bikes (or a combo of kayaks/paddleboards/bikes) for multi-day family adventures up to a week (4 bikes with locks and helmets, one week, $159). You can also rent cruisers, road bikes, or hybrids by the day, $16–36.

For a great off-road experience, head to **GTM Reserve** (see *Hiking*), where more than 9 miles of doubletrack are shared with hikers; a pedal out to the Tolomato River will net you some easy dolphin-watching from the shoreline.

BOATING At **Camachee Cove Marina** (904-829-5676; camacheeisland.com), 3070 Harbor Drive, rent your own pontoon from **Bay Ray Boat Rentals** (904-826-0010; bayrayrentals.com). The 250-slip marina also hosts **St. Augustine Sailing** (904-829-0648; sta-sail.com), 3076 Harbor Drive, where you can charter bareboat or with a captain to ply the waters of Matanzas Bay, $175 and up; lessons available.

Sailing in to St. Augustine? **St. Augustine Municipal Marina** (904-825-1026; staugustinemarina.com), 111-E Avenida Menendez, is in the middle of the action; hail

BEST BEACHES

For dogs: Mickler Beach, Nease Beachfront Park
For driving: Butler Beach to Crescent Beach
For people-watching: St. Augustine Beach, Vilano Beach
For shelling: Anastasia State Park, Summer Haven
For solitude: GTM Reserve north of North Beach
For sunbathing: St. Augustine Beach
For swimming: Anastasia State Park
For walking: Anastasia State Park

MILES OF OCEANFRONT TO WALK AT ANASTASIA STATE PARK

the harbormaster on VHF channel 16. Dockage reservations suggested. Vessels from 20 to 120 feet can dock at the 194-slip **Conch House Marina** (904-829-8646; conch-house.com/marina), 57 Comares Avenue, on Anastasia Island.

CHOCOLATE FACTORY On this informative tour of **Whetstone Chocolates** (904-217-0275; whetstonechocolates.com), 139 King Street, you'll learn about chocolate and how it's made, the history of Whetstone Chocolates, started in St. Augustine in 1966, and taste freshly made treats, too. Tours offered Tuesday–Saturday and limited to 25 people; reservations suggested. Fee.

ECOTOURS **Ripple Effect Ecotours** (904-347-1565; rippleeffectecotours.com) provides a full menu of guided kayak tours, including small group tours on Pellicer Creek from Faver-Dykes State Park (see *Parks*), $55.

 Kayak, cruise, or sail with **St. Augustine Eco Tours** (904-377-7245; staugustine ecotours.com), 111 Avenida Menendez, to get out on the Matanzas River and to isolated beaches for shelling, birding, and wildlife watching. Dolphin & Nature Tours run $35–40; private trips for up to 6 passengers are $225.

FAMILY ACTIVITIES ♪ A fixture in St. Augustine, the **antique carousel** at Davenport Park, on the corner of San Carlos and San Marco Avenue, still costs only a dollar for a ride; the park contains a ♿ **handicapped-accessible playground** and picnic area.

♪ Get in the SWING—*St. Augustine's Wish for Its Next Generation*—at Francis Field, between Castillo Drive and Orange Street behind the St. Augustine Visitors Center parking garage. This **23,000-square-foot wooden playground** will keep the tots busy for hours while you relax in the picnic area after a long day of sightseeing.

♪ That big wooden fortress along a busy street is actually an immersive living history experience, **Fort Menendez at Old Florida Museum** (904-824-8874; oldfloridamuseum.com), 259 San Marco Avenue. Inside the replica fort, your letter of passage takes you back in time to the beginnings of St. Augustine, when the Spanish and Timucua shared the land. In a village surrounding a small natural sulfur spring, everything is hands-on; the kids can learn what the past looked, smelled, and tasted like as they interact with colorful characters from the city's history. Tours $8 children, $11 adults. Closed Sundays. The complex also closes when hosting large school groups; check their website for dates.

Track down **miniature golf** at several highly visible locations, including **Anastasia Mini Golf** (904-825-0101; anastasiaminiaturegolf.com), 701 Anastasia Boulevard, dominated by a big hill flanked by a wrecked pirate ship and a pioneer cabin. **Fiesta Falls Miniature Golf** (904-461-5571), 810 A1A Beach Boulevard, has 18 holes of fun surrounding a Spanish galleon. For a course purely focused on technique, go to Florida's oldest mini-golf course at **Bayfront Mini-Golf** (904-829-1673), 111 Avenida Menendez, between the marina and Bridge of Lions in the Old City. For more serious play, try your hand at the 18-hole putting course in front of the World Golf Hall of Fame (see *Hall of Fame*).

♪ At **Potter's Wax Museum** (800-584-4781; potterswax.com), 17 King Street, the 160 stiffs don't move (mostly); in addition to the usual suspects—politicians and movie stars—there are lesser-known faces from history and art, including Voltaire, Sir Francis Drake, St. Augustine founder Menendez, Rembrandt van Rijn, and Gainesborough. And what wax museum would be complete without a horror chamber, in this case direct from Vincent Price's House of Wax? You'll bump into Harry Potter and Dobby, too. Monday–Sunday 9 AM–6 PM; $7–11.

♪ The original **Ripley's Believe It or Not Museum** (904-824-1606; ripleys.com/staugustine), 19 San Marco Avenue, believe it or not, was once the Castle Warden Inn, a fine hotel managed by novelist Marjorie Kinnan Rawlings's husband. It's full of weird stuff from cartoonist Ripley's travels and the most authentic location of the ever-growing chain, but has enough funhouse components thrown in that the kids will absolutely love it. Oh, and yes—it's haunted. Daily 9 AM–8 PM, $7–16.

♪ **St. Augustine Aquarium** (904-429-9777; saaquarium.com), 2045 FL 16, is under construction in phases, with their 80,000-gallon Snorkel Adventure tank open for a close-up encounter with sea life found on Florida's reefs. A Shark & Stingray Cove, Seahorse exhibit, and touch tanks with starfish, urchins, and crabs are also in place, as is an overhead zipline course (see *Ziplines*). Admission fee; $35 for snorkel adventures.

FISHING A local landmark, **Devil's Elbow Fishing Resort** (904-471-0398; devilselbowfishingresort.com), 7507 FL A1A S provides everything from bait to guide service and boat rentals on the Matanzas River.

Fish for redfish and snook along the shallow estuaries of the region with Captain Tommy Derringer of **Inshore Adventures** (904-377-3734; inshoreadventures.net), $400–525 for two.

In quiet Palm Valley, stop in at **Palm Valley Outdoors** (see *Where to Eat*), 377 S Roscoe Avenue, "under the bridge," for bait and tackle and kayak rentals to slip yourself into the quiet coves of the Tolomato River inside GTM Reserve to the south of their put-in for some great fishing in one of the area's most secret spots.

For pier fishing, the **St. Johns County Ocean Pier** (904-461-0119), 350 A1A Beach Boulevard, provides access for saltwater anglers to try their stuff at St. Augustine Beach. Bait and tackle on site; fee. The **Vilano Beach Pier**, 260 Vilano Road, is free, as is the lengthy pier over fresh water at a tall bluff on the St. Johns River inside **Alpine Groves Park** (904-209-0382), 2060 FL 13, Switzerland.

GENEALOGICAL RESEARCH The **Sequi-Kirby Smith House** (904-825-2333; saintaugustinehistoricalsociety.org/research-library), 6 Artillery Lane, houses the St. Augustine Historical Society Research Library and was the family home of Confederate General Edmund Kirby-Smith; the house dates back to the Second Spanish Period. The library's holdings include translations of church documents from 1594, copies of official Spanish and British colonial documents (1513–1821), and detailed genealogical information for the region, especially for those of Minorcan descent. Tuesday–Friday 9 AM–4:30 PM; free.

GOLF The go-to region for golf in North Florida, St. Augustine and Ponte Vedra offer some of the state's top courses, including one that is home to one of the world's biggest championship tournaments, **The Players Championship** (pgatour.com). **TPC Sawgrass** (904-273-3235; tpc.com/tpc-sawgrass), 110 Championship Way, Ponte Vedra Beach, was built specifically to challenge the pros—if you've ever watched a golf tournament, you've probably seen the infamous 17th hole Island Green—but you can experience the challenges of these courses, too, which are owned by the players of the PGA Tour. Designed by Pete Dye and former PGA Tour commissioner Deane Beman, **The Players Stadium Course** was built with spectators in mind. The newer **Dye's Valley Course** is a collaboration with Bobby Weed.

Two major courses are the highlight of the **World Golf Village** (904-940-6088; golfwgv.com), 2 World Golf Place, a golfer's destination as home of the World Golf Hall of Fame (see *Hall of Fame*) and a shopping/dining complex centered on golf. Arnold Palmer and Jack Nicklaus collaborated on the design of the **King & Bear**, an 18-hole course for serious drivers. Its greens, edged by pine forests and cypress domes, provide natural beauty as well as tricky challenges; Palmer picks hole 15, Stone Reflection, as one of his "Dream 18" of all time. The **Slammer & Squire**, their second 18-hole course with two distinct nines, is a Bobby Weed design with inputs from Sam Snead and Gene Sarazen.

HIKING The prime destination for a day hike is **Guana-Tolomato-Matanzas (GTM) Reserve** (904-825-5071; gtmnerr.org), 505 Guana River Road, where beyond the 21,000-square-foot Environmental Education Center—a must-stop to learn about the region's habitats—lies a 9-mile loop with shorter options. Along its length are river views with dolphins, Timucuan middens, open wetlands, deeply shaded forests, and the remains of an ancient Spanish mission. Paddlers can put in at the dam, and cyclists are welcome on most of the trails. Other favorites include the boardwalk at **Fort Matanzas** (see *Historic Sites*) and the nature trail at **Anastasia State Park** (see *Parks*).

SURFING Surf with the pros from the **Surf Station** (800-460-6394; surf-station.com), 1020 Anastasia Boulevard, a local institution. They hold summer surf camps and regular learn-to-surf lessons for young and old, customized to your needs, $50–70 for an hour and a half, including equipment. They also rent and deliver surfboards and SUP,

ESTUARY AT GTM RESERVE, AS SEEN FROM THE TOLOMATO RIVER

$25/day for boards, $45/3 hours for SUP. Check their daily surf reports for surf conditions at St. Augustine Beach.

PADDLING With dozens of uninhabited islands on which to stop and lunch or camp, the **Matanzas River** is a popular paddlers' getaway. Rent a canoe and launch at **Faver-Dykes State Park** (see *Parks*) to follow Pellicer Creek to the river, heading north to the inlet past Mellon Island. It's also possible to get a kayak down to the river from the parking area north of Fort Matanzas and at the small ramp at the south end of Summer Haven. Ripple Effect (904-347-1565; rippleeffectecotours.com) rents kayaks and leads tours (see *Ecotours*) out of their home base at Marineland Marina to access the Matanzas River.

On Anastasia Island, **Kayak St. Augustine** (904-315-8442; kayakingstaugustine .com), 442 Ocean Vista Drive, rents kayaks and SUP at Lighthouse Park for a launch into **Salt Run**, $40–75. Inside Anastasia State Park (see *Parks*), **Anastasia Watersports** (904-460-9111; anastasiawatersports.com), 850 Anastasia Park Road, can outfit you to paddle the lagoon, starting at $20/hr.

Rent kayaks and SUP from **North Guana Outpost** (904-373-0306; northguanaoutpost .com), 4415 Mickler Road, Ponte Vedra Beach, to explore the estuaries of the Guana River in GTM Reserve (see *Hiking*). They'll deliver and pick up at 6 Mile Landing, or at Guana Dam for an additional fee. Regular and tandem craft, $20–60. For access to the Tolomato River on the other side of GTM Reserve, rent from **Palm Valley Outdoors** (see *Where to Eat*) and paddle south, $35–60 for a full day. You'll see manatees and dolphins cruising along this saline inland waterway.

PARKS, PRESERVES, AND CAMPING ✐ ♿ ☙ ((ᵠ)) The wild shore at St. Augustine Beach, **Anastasia State Park** (904-461-2033; floridastateparks.org/park/anastasia), 300 Anastasia Park Road, sweeps around the north tip of the island to provide four miles of unsullied oceanfront with compacted sands that are pleasant to walk on. Near the front gate is the historic quarry from which coquina blocks were chiseled to construct the city during the First Spanish Period. Protected by the dunes, its campground is deeply shaded by wind-sculpted sand live oaks and within earshot of the waves, $28 and up.

☙ Historic **Butler Beach** was established by Frank B. Butler, a St. Augustine grocer and real estate developer, as one of Florida's few African American seaside destinations during segregation. You'll find it along A1A north of Crescent Beach and north of Fort Matanzas, with beach-ramp access at Mary Street.

☙ ♿ ✐ Nestled in oak hammocks along Pellicer Creek, **Faver-Dykes State Park** (904-794-0997; floridastateparks.org/park/Faver-Dykes), 1000 Faver Dykes Road off US 1, Dupont Center, offers camping ($18 and up), nature trails, and some of the best paddling along the coast. Bring your kayak or rent a canoe to enjoy the Pellicer Creek Trail, gliding through mazes of needlerush as you paddle out to the Matanzas River. Mellon Island in the Matanzas River is accessible only by boat and open to primitive camping. Fee.

☙ In addition to being the only public access point for Ponte Vedra Beach, **Mickler's Beachfront Park** (904-209-3740), 1109½ Ponte Vedra Boulevard off A1A, has parking for horse trailers—yes, you can ride *your* horses on the beach here, but a permit is required from the county; call ahead.

At **Moses Creek Conservation Area** (386-329-4404; sjrwmd.com/recreationguide/mosescreek), FL 206, Dupont Center [29.757224, -81.27556], backpack or ride your horse to a distant campsite with a sweeping view of the salt marshes.

☙ **Nease Beachfront Park** (904-209-0655), 3201 Coastal Highway, Vilano Beach, provides beach parking next to a historic home owned by Florida's first forester. You'll find restrooms and a shaded picnic spot behind the building. Gnarled oaks reach out over the dunes, and a boardwalk leads to an open view of the Tolomato River marshes, an excellent spot for birding. Beach access is across A1A down a boardwalk—mind the high-speed traffic when you cross.

Along the Tolomato River, **Stokes Landing Conservation Area** (386-329-4404; sjrwmd.com/recreationguide/stokeslanding), Lakeshore Drive [30.0, -81.361104], provides an outdoor classroom for local schools and beautiful panoramic views of the estuary across from GTM Reserve (see *Hiking*).

SAILING The **Schooner *Freedom*** (904-810-1010; schoonerfreedom.com), 111 Avenida Menendez, St. Augustine's one and only tall ship, takes guests out on relaxing three- and four-hour cruises on Matanzas Bay daily. This replica of a blockade-runner is a 34-ton clipper, a family operation that lets guests take the wheel after passing through the Bridge of Lions—ride this, and you can be the one who holds up bridge traffic instead of waiting in it. Starts at $30 adult, $15 ages 3–16. Four-seater Hobie Cats are available for rent at **Anastasia Watersports** (see *Paddling*) to cruise Salt Run, $40–75 for 1–4 hours; previous sailing experience required.

SCENIC DRIVES Few highways in the northern Florida peninsula match the beauty of the **Historic A1A Scenic Byway** (scenica1a.org), particularly in sections where the dunes remain preserved and free of development—as they do within GTM Reserve between Ponte Vedra Beach and North Beach. Sites of interest along the byway are included in an audio tour you can access from your cell phone; just look for the markers when you stop.

TOURING ST. AUGUSTINE

Tasting our way around the Ancient City was a new twist to experience a destination we've visited almost annually since we were kids. We spent an afternoon on the **Savory Faire Food & Wine Tasting Tour** (staugcitywalks.com) that melds history with relaxed stops at longstanding eateries, meeting chefs while enjoying a course at a time. Starting with escargot and wine at Café Alcazar in the depths of Henry Flagler's grand swimming pool in the basement of the former Alcazar Hotel, we walked to six more stops within six blocks, ending up at a longtime favorite of ours, Athena Restaurant, for flaming *saganaki*.

The special-interest tour capital of Florida, St. Augustine offers a mind-boggling array of guided city tours: here's a quick overview. For all but tram tours, make advance reservations.

SIGHTSEEING Distinct by color but similar in nature, **open-air sightseeing trams** circle the Historic District with constant narration and on/off privileges, so you can hop off and sightsee and then hop back on another one later. Tickets on either tram are good for three consecutive days. **Ripley's Red Train Tours** (800-226-6545 or 904-824-1606; sightseeingtrains.com), 170 San Marco Avenue, have 22 stops along their 90-minute circuit, with trains every 15–20 minutes running 8:30 AM–5 PM daily; tickets $21 and up. In shades of green and orange, **Old Town Trolley Tours** (904-829-3800; trolleytours.com/st-augustine), US 1, has 23 stops along 100 points of interest on their narrated tour, $23 and up.

FROM THE AIR Old City Helicopters (904-824-5506; oldcityhelicopters.com) will get you up and over the historic downtown, with a bird's-eye view of it all. Tours depart Northeast Florida Regional Airport, 4900 US 1; $80–155 per person for downtown tours, minimum two passengers.

FROM THE WATER Join a narrated journey with **Scenic Cruises of St. Augustine** (904-824-1806; scenic-cruise.com) on the *Victory III*, departing from St. Augustine Marina up to five times daily, $15–18 adults, $9 children. Or paddle along the bayfront seawall and up to the Fountain of Youth with a guide sharing stories of the past with **Kayak St. Augustine** (904-315-8442; kayakingstaugustine.com/kayak-st-augustine-historic-tour).

FOOD & DRINK In addition to the **Savory Faire Food & Wine Tasting Tour** ($59 plus optional pairing fee of $19), the same company started the original **St. Augustine Historic Pub Crawl**, $25 (one drink included). Both are offered by **St. Augustine City Walks** (904-540-3476; staugcitywalks.com), 4 Granada St. **The Tasting Tours** (904-325-3911; thetastingtours.com), 59 Cuna Street, offers a spectrum of tour styles, from pure foodie to wine and beer tastings and by foot, carriage, or roadster, $49–159.

GHOSTS Few cities can boast as many ghosts as St. Augustine does, so ghost tours are big business here. Both tram companies run ghost tours with stops along the way. Old Town Trolley has its PG-13 "Trolley of the Doomed" **Ghosts & Gravestones Tour** (ghostsandgravestones .com/st-augustine), stopping at the Old Drug Store, Potter's Wax Museum, and the Old Jail, $25+; Ripley's the **Ghost Train Adventure** (ghosttrainadventure.com), 80 minutes with two in-depth stops, $24 adult/$13 child. We've found the walking tours to be most immersive, with the best guides—like those we walked with from **A Ghostly Encounter** (904-827-0807; staugustineghosttours.net), 6 Cordova Street—storytellers wrapping history in a theatrical presentation of the past that will have you believing in, if not actually experiencing, the ghosts; 90 minutes, $15. Lantern-led walks by **Ghost Tours of St. Augustine** (904-829-1122;

DINING AT CAFÉ ALCAZAR DURING THE SAVORY FAIRE TOUR

ghosttoursofstaugustine.com) take you to lesser-known sites (75 minutes, $20); they also offer guided paranormal investigations of specific historic sites for groups.

HISTORY While history is an important part of all tours, some go into much more detail. **Tour St. Augustine** (904-825-0087; tourstaug.com) offers an on-the-water **Maritime Tales & Legends Tour** ($24) and a **History, Mystery, Mayhem & Murder Evening Walking Tour** ($20) exposing the seamy side of the Ancient City. With Fort Mose, St. Augustine had one of the earliest free black settlements in the South and was a flashpoint during the Civil Rights Movement in the 1960s. Learn the full story with **St. Augustine Black Heritage & Civil Rights Tours** (904-825-0087; staugustineblackheritagetours.com), hour-long walking tours provided for free. **St. Augustine Historic Tours** (904-392-7137; staugustinehistorictours.com) runs 1–2 hour thematic tours like **Conquistadors, Corsairs, and Capitalists** and **Pawsitively St. Augustine** (pets free) as well as an architectural tour, **Homes and Buildings of St. Augustine.** $16 adult, $10 ages 12 and under.

ROMANTIC Horse-drawn sightseeing carriages have clip-clopped along the bayfront since 1877, a setting for many a marriage proposal. There are now multiple carriage tours in the city, including **Country Carriages** (904-826-1982; countrycarriages.net); **St. Augustine Carriage** (904-392-9952; staugustinecarriage.com); and **St. Augustine Horse & Carriage** (904-377-4740; staugustinehorseandcarriage.com). Rates vary, but most run 45 minutes and offer the full carriage (4 seats) for $85 with your choice of narration or romantic quiet; special carriages, engagement and wedding packages available for higher fees.

Along the St. Johns River, FL 13 is designated the **William Bartram Scenic & Historic Highway** (bartramscenichighway.com). Canopied in many spots, the highway parallels the river route that the famed naturalist paddled when St. Augustine was more than a century old, leading you through rural and wild lands and communities established nearly 300 years ago.

SPAS At the **Poseidon Spa** (904-819-6115; casamonica.com/leisure/poseidonspa), 53 King Street, at the Casa Monica, enjoy modern treatments in an Old World setting. A signature relaxation massage is just the thing after spending hours walking around the Ancient City, and a hot stone massage will deepen the relaxation. Guests may have massages provided in their own rooms. Also on the menu are facials, body treatments, nail care, and waxing. Massages start at $120, facials $105.

The Spa at Ponte Vedra Inn & Club (904-273-7700; pvspa.com), 302 Ponte Vedra Boulevard, Ponte Vedra Beach, provides a perfect haven for relaxation. Wrap yourself in an elegant spa robe and sit with a light beverage while awaiting your treatment in the relaxation room or in the 2,000-square-foot Cascada Garden with oversize Jacuzzi and cascading waterfall. Then move on to your own private room for treatments like a reflexology massage, a deep-cleaning facial, or a sweet orange ritual. Treatments start at $70 and massages at $140 for 50 minutes. Their in-house Spa Café prepares light, healthful meals available only to guests.

WHALE-WATCHING Each winter, endangered **right whales** migrate down the Atlantic Coast from Newfoundland to their calving grounds off Mantanzas Inlet at Summer Haven [29.700800, -81.224675]. Join Marineland's Right Whale Project (aswh.org/whale/main.html) to become a volunteer whale-watcher, or just spend a morning looking offshore.

WINERY & At **San Sebastian Winery** (904-826-1594; sansebastianwinery.com), 157 King Street, enjoy a tour of the processing plant in the arts district (the vineyards are off-site at a sister winery) with a complimentary wine tasting thereafter. A wine and jazz bar offers a laid-back place to chat with friends, or you can browse the Wine Shop for gourmet foods, kitchen items, and the signature wines of San Sebastian. Tours Monday–Saturday 10 AM–5 PM, Sunday 11 AM–5 PM; free.

ZIPLINES Let your heart race at **Crocodile Crossing** (alligatorfarm.com/crocodile-crossing), a set of two zipline and canopy walk trails where you swing, sway, and fly above alligators and crocodiles at St. Augustine Alligator Farm (see *Zoo*). From the ground, it looks like a crazy obstacle course, complete with zigzag and crisscross wooden steps attached to guy wires. The Sepik River Course is the lower of the two aerial adventures; the Nile River Course is higher and faster, for bigger thrills. Open daily with a separate admission from the park, $37–67 per course, takes 45–90 minutes each.

Soaring over the pools and tanks of St. Augustine Aquarium (see *Family Activities*), **ZIPStream's Castaway Canopy Adventure** (904-814-9562; oldcityzip.com), 2045 FL 16, consists of an ever-climbing series canopy walks between the pines, oaks, and tall poles with seven connecting ziplines and four bridges. In one of the largest oaks, there's even a treehouse! Smart Snap belays are in use to keep all participants safe. $60 adults, $55 children.

✻ Lodging

BED & BREAKFASTS ♿ ((•)) Delightfully classy and in the heart of the historic downtown, **Agustin Inn** (904-637-1139; agustininn.com), 29 Cuna Street, St. Augustine 32084, is a 1903 Victorian with 18 guest rooms, most with Jacuzzi tubs and one (the Greensboro) with a private entrance and wheelchair ramp. Your gourmet three-course breakfast may include house-recipe eggs Benedict or quiche, a chilled cantaloupe soup, or chicken and matcha waffles. Children over 12 welcome. $159–319.

🐾 ♣ ((•)) **At Journey's End** (904-829-0076; atjourneysend.com), 89 Cedar Street, St. Augustine 32084, a late 1800s Victorian is a backdrop for exotica—bedrooms themed after adventurers Amelia Earhart, Charles Lindbergh, and Dr. David Livingstone, as well as Key West and Egypt, with elegant beds and original art. The Key West can handle a family of four (and/or pets); its own veranda overlooks the garden. Amenities include rain showers and iPhone/iPod docking stations. A full breakfast is served every morning, with snacks and drinks available all day. $169–239.

⚥ ((•)) ⚘ Built in 1883 by a master carpenter, **Carriage Way** (904-829-2467; carriageway.com), 70 Cuna Street, St. Augustine 32084, is a delightful option for lodging in a quiet part of the Historic District. With Victorian charm reflected in its modern decor and a big porch out front for relaxing, the complex includes 13 well-appointed rooms plus an 1100-square-foot cottage that sleeps six. Expect a fresh hot breakfast in the morning; wine and other complimentary beverages are available all day. $169–379; the 1885 cottage, $429 and up.

🐾 ⚥ ((•)) **At Casa de Solana** (904-824-3555; casadesolana.com), 21 Aviles Street, St. Augustine 32084, breakfast is a locavore's delight, made with fresh organic ingredients sourced from the area. But that's only one reason to stay here. Built in the early 1800s, the historic main home is constructed of coquina stone and retains many of its original features, including handmade bricks. The adjacent de Palma house is also part of the complex. Decor reflects colonial St. Augustine with modern updates such as whirlpool tubs, cable TV, and wireless Internet. Gregarious guests will appreciate the afternoon wine social; those looking for a more intimate time will find it on the balconies and in the corners of the garden. Ten rooms, each stylishly decorated, three on the ground floor. $109–299.

♿ **Casa de Suenos** (800-824-6062; casadesuenos.com), 20 Cordova Street, St. Augustine 32084, is the "House of Dreams," a 1920s Mediterranean revival home where guests can watch the world drift by from the sunporch or settle down for a read in the parlor. A chandelier sparkles over the whirlpool tub, elegant furnishings dress up the common areas, and each room is a relaxing retreat, with comfy robes, fine literature, and a decanter of sherry on the dresser; two rooms boast a whirlpool. Enjoy a hearty gourmet breakfast each morning, a social hour with wine and appetizers late afternoon, and decadent desserts each evening. Ask the innkeeper about free passes and tickets to local attractions. $159–299.

((•)) Just a block off busy St. George Street on a quiet lane, **44 Spanish Street Inn** (904-826-0650; 44spanishstreet.com), 44 Spanish Street, St. Augustine 32084, has rooms that are chic and bright, with luxurious linens, iPod dock, and daily newspaper. The eight rooms come in several sizes; a stay in the cozy Jasmine felt like a perch in the tree canopy. Fitzgerald has its own private entrance from the street. The breakfast room sits in an intimate tropical garden in the backyard. A big perk is free parking in a lot down the street with all-day in-and-out privileges. $148–279.

🐾 🏷 🖊 ♂ 📶 St. Augustine's oldest lodging, **The Kenwood Inn** (904-824-2116; thekenwoodinn.com), 38 Marine Street, St. Augustine 32084, dates back to 1865; even Henry Flagler walked its halls. It has that wonderful feel of an old-time hotel, with narrow corridors, low ceilings, and mismatched floors. Each of the 14 spacious rooms has its own special character; some are two-room suites or have multiple beds. The Blue Porcelain Suite has walls the color of Wedgwood china; staying here, the hammock was the perfect place to hang out on the porch and listen to the carriages go by. Guests enjoy a private pool and secluded garden courtyard; meet fellow guests during the evening wine social. Light breakfasts are served weekdays, with a more extensive hot buffet on weekends, when they break out fruit smoothies, mimosas and bloody marys, and breakfast sangria. Children welcome; pet-friendly rooms available. $139 and up.

🐾 📶 An 1899 Victorian charmer, **The Old Powder House Inn** (904-824-4149; oldpowderhouse.com), 38 Cordova Street, St. Augustine 32084, entices with its second-floor veranda, ideal for people-watching from the porch swing. From the frilly Queen Ann's Lace to The Garden, a three-bed girls' getaway, each of the nine rooms offers comfortable ambience. Breakfast brings out the culinary talents of your hosts, with delights like eggs Cordova and baked stuffed French toast. You won't leave hungry! Free on-site parking. $139 and up.

🐾 🏷 📶 ⏱ With not a straight angle in the place, **St. Francis Inn** (800-824-6062; stfrancisinn.com), 279 St. George Street, St. Augustine 32084, is a three-story home with charm—how many B&Bs in the United States date back to 1791? Every room in the main inn has its own unique shape, size, and furnishings befitting the character of original owner Gaspar Garcia. Margaret's Room, in the adjoining Wilson House, has a private balcony with garden view. A small swimming pool sits off the lush garden courtyard; guests can enjoy the peace of St. Francis Park next door. Beyond the delightful buffet breakfast, weekend brunch, evening social hour, and evening desserts many extra-extra amenities are included, like free admissions and discounts to local attractions, complimentary bicycles to explore town, and a charging station for electric cars in their guest parking lot. $149–309.

📶 **Southern Wind** (904-825-3623; southernwindinn.com), 18 Cordova Street, St. Augustine 32084, is a beautiful 1916 Victorian home with a wraparound veranda that's the perfect place to relax. Period furnishings and antiques add to the Gilded Age ambience of the inn's ten rooms, ranging from cozy nooks to spacious suites. Breakfast is served buffet style but always features one hot entrée like macadamia French toast. In-room DVD players and complimentary bicycles make this a pleasant base camp for exploring the city. Children 12 and older welcome. $119–199.

♂ 📶 From our balcony at the **Westcott House** (904-825-4602; westcotthouse.com), 146 Avenida Menendez, we watched the sun rise over Matanzas Bay, framed by mature trees outside the Catherine Room. Catherine was Dr. John Westcott's wife, and it was he who commissioned construction of a grand waterfront home in 1880. A guest house since the 1970s, every one of the 16 rooms has its own private entrance; most have a Jacuzzi tub and electric fireplace. Ours also had a massive walk-through shower and a bed as comfy as a giant pillow. Evening hors d'ouevres and morning breakfast are shared in the common dining room. Smartly appointed, each room is a lovely retreat, $169–399.

HISTORIC ♿ ♂ 📶 ⏱ Stride into the Moorish-inspired lobby of the **Casa Monica Resort & Spa** (800-648-1888; casamonica.com), 95 Cordova Street, St. Augustine 32084, and take a step back into Henry Flagler's Gilded Age in this grand hotel, with its beaded Victorian

WESTCOTT HOUSE B&B, FRONTING MATANZAS BAY

lamps and painted beams. This is what Florida tourism felt like in 1888, when the Casa Monica first opened its doors. Restored to its original lavish glory by hotelier Richard Kessler in 1999, the hotel offers rooms in many shapes and sizes, from cozy to spacious to opulent multi-bedroom suites, all with modern appointments. A member of the Historic Hotels of America, they are also part of the Marriott Autograph Collection. $199 and up.

At **Ponte Vedra Inn & Club** (904-285-1111; pontevedra.com), 200 Ponte Vedra Boulevard, Ponte Vedra Beach 32082, experience the grandeur of a famed winter resort for the rich and famous. Generations of guests continue to come back, and generations of staff continue to cater to their every need. The main inn opened in 1938; the newer oceanside rooms at the Lodge & Club are larger and feature queen poster beds in a beautiful honey-blond finish. This luxury resort is all about the little details, from intimate corner nooks to European turndown service. North Florida's first

modern spa opened here in 1987 and still pampers guests today (see *Spas*). Historic inn, $249 and up; oceanfront, $299 and up.

COMFORT AND LUXURY **Castillo Real** (904-471-3505; castilloreal.com), 530 FL A1A (Beach Boulevard), St. Augustine 32080, is a beachside boutique hotel that's part of the Ascend Collection of the Choice Hotels chain. It feels nothing like its cousins, however, with its Mediterranean design extending from the vaulted lobby with fountain to fine wood furniture and luxe linens in the elegant guest rooms. Choose from standard, Jacuzzi, and oceanfront rooms, $159 and up.

In the heart of the Historic District, **St. George Inn** (888-827-5740; stgeorge-inn.com), 4 St. George Street #101, St. Augustine 32084, blends in seamlessly with the shops and restaurants of St. George Street at the City Gates. In 6 different styles, 25 spacious well-appointed rooms boast killer views of the downtown area; some are very roomy suites ideal for families. The gems are the Castillo Suites; Room 25 has a balcony that looks out on the Castillo and Matanzas Bay. An elevator provides access to the upper floors. Continental breakfast comes with your stay, and a coffee shop is in the courtyard. $169–219.

OCEANFRONT ♂ (((•))) ⇨ **Beachfront Bed & Breakfast** (904-461-8727; beachfrontbandb.com), 1 F Street, St. Augustine 32080, is indeed right on the beach. A complex of three rooms in a cottage and a beach house with five rooms, the rooms are more "coastal elegance" than beachy, with the fine decor a reminder for you to wipe the sand off your feet before you walk inside. Nicely landscaped grounds with a heated swimming pool, big shared porch, and a hot tub, all within sound of the surf, make this an ideal gathering place for friends. A gourmet breakfast is served every morning, and beach toys and bikes are yours to borrow. $189 and up.

♂ ♿ ♂ (((•))) ⇨ The Mediterranean-theme **La Fiesta Ocean Inn & Suites** (904-471-2220; lafiestainn.com), 810 A1A Beach Boulevard, St. Augustine 32080, has spacious rooms decorated with local artwork, modern furnishings, and great landscaping with a palm-lined pool. Most rooms have tile floors to cope with the sand that follows you back from the beach, which is just a stroll down the boardwalk over the dunes. Rooms 216–219 have a beautiful sunrise view. Continental breakfast included. $119 and up plus resort fee of $13/day.

RETRO AND ARTSY ♨ ♥ ♂ ♿ (((•))) At **The Cozy Inn** (888-288-2204; thecozyinn .com), 202 San Marco Avenue, St. Augustine 32084, the old-fashioned but well-updated motor court rooms are certainly cozy, brightly decorated with a Florida coastal theme, with queen beds and 1940s bathrooms. Deluxe suites are in a restored historic home, and spacious townhouses—ideal for families—are

across the street. Cozy rooms start at $89; suites and townhomes at $127.

♂ (((•))) A slice of Old Florida, **The Silver Sands** (904-655-6690; silversandsst augustine.com), 8448 A1A S, Crescent Beach 32080, hides so well behind a screen of sand dunes and saw palmetto that you pretty much only see it heading northbound. It's the type of beachfront motel we stayed at when we were kids, with kitchens/kitchenettes and grills outside, but updated from simple to snazzy. It's an easy walk over the dunes to your own quiet stretch of beach. Three suites and two cottages, minimum stays starting at two nights, $106 and up, booked through VRBO.com.

TRIED AND TRUE ♂ ♿ (((•))) The **Hilton St. Augustine Historic Bayfront** (904-829-2277; hiltonhistoricstaugustine.net), 32 Avenida Menendez, St. Augustine 32084, hides in plain sight, its façade matching the row of historic homes overlooking Matanzas Bay. You'll find the usual Hilton attention to detail within the 72 rooms inside, but the best part is that you're within walking distance of all of the Historic District. $169 and up.

♂ ♿ ♂ (((•))) ⇨ **Renaissance Resort at World Golf Village** (904-940-8000; worldgolfrenaissance.com), 500 S Legacy Trail, St. Augustine 32092, borders the original championship course at World Golf Village and the World Golf Hall of Fame (see *Hall of Fame*). The European-accented hotel includes amenities such as an outdoor pool and whirlpool, miniature golf, table tennis, fitness center, and business center. The concierge will help you book airport shuttles to and from Jacksonville International. Drink in the beautiful views from your room, $141 and up; in-room Wi-Fi an additional fee.

WATERFRONT ♥ ♂ ♂ (((•))) In a surprisingly offbeat yet central location, **The Inn at Camachee Harbor** (800-688-5379; camacheeinn.com), 201 Yacht Club Drive, St. Augustine 32084, can have you cruising up the coast to Ponte Vedra or toward downtown in no time. Better yet, step outside and meet a fishing guide for a cruise up the Tolomato River. Located at Camachee Cove Marina (see *Boating*), the rooms face the waterfront or the garden and are tastefully decorated with a coastal appeal. Continental breakfast is included. $135–180.

CAMPGROUNDS ✐ **Bryn Mawr Ocean Resort** (904-471-3353; brynmawrocean resort.com), 4850 FL A1A S, St. Augustine 32080. Just over the dunes from the Atlantic (with direct beach access), this campground has a mix of park models, permanent residents, and RV spaces, many with adjoining decks with picnic tables. Some sites are tucked in the maritime hammock, but most are out in the open along the ocean; the swimming pool is next to a nicely shaded playground area. Sites $65–94, park models $125–151, three-night minimum.

🐾 ((ͼ)) At **Compass RV Park** (904-824-3574; compassrvpark.com), 1505 FL 207, St. Augustine 32086, tuck your camper into the shady forest, or choose a sunny pull-through space. Bathhouses are scattered throughout the campground. A brand-new pool will keep the kids happy, but you can also walk the nature trail with them around the shaded park; pet owners have two dog parks to choose from. Don't own a camper? No problem. You can book one in their new vintage RV village, $194 and up for a two-night stay. Sites vary, with 30 or 50 amp on all and full hookups on most; premium sites have concrete pads for larger rigs. $42 and up.

🐾 ✐ Nestled on a barrier island between a remote stretch of A1A and the North River, **North Beach Camp Resort** (904-824-1806; northbeachcamp.com), 4125 Coastal FL A1A, St. Augustine 32084, features beautifully landscaped sites shaded by mature trees. All are within an easy walk of the river, so bring your fishing tackle! Rental cabins are tucked under the forest canopy. Facilities include a convenience store, playground,

pool, and Aunt Kate's (see *Where to Eat*) right next door. Full-hookup sites, 20–50 amp $47–88.

✐ ((ͼ)) **Ocean Grove RV Resort** (800-342-4007; oceangroveresort.com), 4225 FL A1A S, St. Augustine 32080. Set in a remnant maritime hammock with a grove of tall pines on Matanzas Bay, this campground with natural appeal has shady spaces, luxury park models, and tent spaces with beautiful views across the salt marsh. Dock with boat launch, fish-cleaning station; a camp store has marine items. Bicycle, canoe, and kayak rentals on site. Sites $57–99, park models $325 for three nights, $675 per week plus $50 cleaning fee.

✳ Where to Eat

ELEGANT AND ROMANTIC A unique lunch destination, **Café Alcazar** (904-825-9948; thealcazarcafe.com/cafe-alcazar), 25 Granada Street, is not a quiet place, but it is grand—its marble walls echo, as you're sitting in the bottom of the basement swimming pool that Henry Flagler (see Flagler's Architectural Legacy on page 324) commissioned for his Alcazar Hotel. The menu includes light fare such as an asparagus panini on freshly baked bread with yellow squash, fire-roasted red peppers, red onion, feta, and pesto; fresh hummus over spring mix with tahini and pita points; and sesame-crusted salmon lo mein. Daily 11 AM–3 PM. Open first Friday 6–9 PM for dinner, reservations recommended.

Le Pavillion (904-824-6202; lepavillonstaugustine.com), 45 San Marco Avenue. In a grand old home in the antiques district, this elegant but casual European restaurant remains one of St. Augustine's top dining experiences. For lunch, enjoy the bratwurst and sauerkraut, oyster platter and salad, or an Uptown French dip, $9–16. Among their signature dinner entrées are the schnitzel Viennese style, chicken curry "Bombay," portobello Wellington, and their famous rack of lamb for one. Top it all off with a luscious crème de menthe parfait. Closed Monday; entrées $19–33.

♂ Tucked into an 1879 Victorian home under the trees along the avenue, it's as inconspicuous as it is delicious. Since 1981, **The Raintree Restaurant and Steakhouse** (904-824-7211; raintreerestaurant.com), 102 San Marco Avenue, has delighted diners with its award-winning international entrées and extensive wine list, which has won the Wine Spectator Award of Excellence. Choose from New Zealand rack of lamb, veal San Marco, lasagna puttanesca, beef Wellington, and more. Don't miss the desserts, especially the sinful made-to-order crêpes. Their extensive Sunday brunch (9:30 AM–1:30 PM) includes fresh crêpes and croques, sandwiches and salads, and their own Seafood Thermidor. Open daily at 5 PM, reservations suggested; entrées $10–33, brunch $15–18.

♂ At **The Reef** (904-824-8008; thereefstaugustine.com), 4100 Coastal Highway, North Beach, soak in the ambience of the dunes while looking out over the Atlantic. The extensive menu includes regional favorites like shrimp and grits and jambalaya but also extends to duck breast, grilled lamb, and slow-roasted prime rib. Lunch and dinner daily, but Sunday brunch is their forte—for $38, the extensive spread includes crab legs and eggs Benedict made to order, and you'll enjoy jazz or classical guitar accompanying the strum of the waves outside. Entrées $19–36.

CASUAL FARE You'll say "I'm all right" at the **Murray Bros Caddyshack** (904-940-3673; mbcshack.com), 455 S Legacy Trail, amid movie and golf memorabilia in a restaurant dreamed up by comedian Bill Murray and his five talented brothers. Tee up with Crispy Potato Golf Balls or chicken wings, tour the greens with the Wedge Salad, and check out the back nine with its Chipotle Lime Quinoa Bowl and Jambalaya. The 19th Hole has domestic and imported beers.

Sandwiches, salads, and entrées with a Chicago flair, $10 and up.

Breakfasts come hearty at **Sea Oats Caffe** (904-471-7350), 1073 A1A Beach Boulevard, St. Augustine Beach, tucked away in the Publix plaza. For less than $10 you can fill up on their pancakes (bacon, chocolate chip, banana, blueberry); or try out the homemade cheddar grits with a brie and mushroom omelet.

Sunset Grille (904-471-5555; sunsetgrillea1a.com), 421 A1A Beach Boulevard, St. Augustine Beach. Enjoy four kinds of chowder or the "world's best" coconut-crusted shrimp with their signature piña colada dipping sauce and the smoothest margaritas along the beach in this casual, award-winning local favorite. Partial orders available on their massive pasta plates. Lunch and dinner, $12 and up.

ETHNIC EATS Decorated with murals depicting the founding and settlement of St. Augustine, **Athena Restaurant** (904-823-9076; thealcazarcafe.com/athena -restaurant), 14 Cathedral Place, provides a unique setting for classic Greek dishes like *pastitsio*, *moussaka*, and *saganaki*, as well as fine broiled shrimp, kebobs, steaks, and chops. Do not miss the desserts—baklava, napoleons, and more—that beckon from the front bakery case. Open for breakfast, lunch, and dinner, entrées $14–23.

♂ ♿ **Casa Maria** (904-342-0532), 1001 A1A Beach Boulevard, St. Augustine Beach, made us smile with perfect margaritas and authentic options like enchiladas suizas, chilaquiles, and fish tacos. Stuffed fried avocado, Ghost Pepper quesadilla, and their homeade tamales (weekends only, until they run out) added to the temptations on their broad menu. Lunch and dinner, $8–15.

We found tiny **Gaufre's & Goods** (904-829-5770), 9 Aviles Street, thanks to the Savory Faire tour (see *Touring St. Augustine*). While the pierogies with sour cream were an unexpected treat at this homey Eastern European kitchen, their light-as-a-feather *gaufres*—dessert waffles topped with spreads or ice cream—are pure magic. Other unique menu items include borscht with mushroom-stuffed dumplings, *pyzy*, and homemade skordalia, $5–14.

Kings Head British Pub (904-823-9787; kingsheadbritishpub.com), 6460 US 1 N, St. Augustine, looks like it dropped out of an Elizabethan painting: a Tudor cottage with a bright red British double-decker bus outside; inside, real Brit food from bangers and mash to Scotch eggs, Indian currys, various meat pies, and their famous fish-and-chips; they even feature a roast of the week. Lunch and dinner, $10–16; closed Monday.

At **Meehan's on Matanzas** (904-810-1923; meehansirishpub.com), 20 Avenida Menendez, traditional Irish pub fare and a splash of the Old Country—including Harp, Kilkenny, and Magner's Cider—are their mainstay. But their menu extends to creative fresh seafood choices like Drunken Clams, Salmon San Marco, and the signature Johnny's Seafood Tower ($48). Lunch and dinner, most entrées $16–29.

⅃ The flip side of a popular pizza joint, **Pizzalleys Chianti Room** (904-825-4100; pizzalleyschiantiroom.com), 60 Charlotte Street, feels like a Tuscan tavern. Of course, Chianti and fine wines can complement your dinner of Italian entrées, from a tasty Italian pot roast to hand-rolled manicotti, chicken marsala, or any of dozens of choose-your-own pasta combinations. Diners sit within the sight and sound of the open kitchen and its busy pizza oven; yes, you can choose from the pizza menu as well. Entrées $14–25, include gluten-free options.

The **Prince of Wales Restaurant** (904-810-5725; theprinceofwalesstaugustine .com), 54 Cuna Street, is the place for mushy peas and sticky toffee. Have a classic bangers and mash, fish and chips, chicken curry, or a cottage pie with a Smithwick's. For something completely different, try the beer-battered burger. Lunch and dinner, $9–16.

Sprung from the old seafaring merchant business in the British Virgin Islands that started the worldwide thirst for rum, **Pussers Caribbean Grille** (904-280-7766; pussersusa.com), 816 FL A1A N, Ponte Vedra, is one of only two in the USA. Their menu is distinctly Caribbean, with fiery firecracker shrimp, fish tacos, curried chicken sauté, and conch fritters among the tasty appetizers and entrées. The extensive drink menu has a heavy focus on rum, of course. Dinner, lunch, and Sunday brunch, $10–28.

HIP BISTRO-STYLE 🍴 **Cafe Eleven** (904-460-9311; originalcafe11.com), 501 A1A Beach Boulevard, is a snazzy combination of bistro and performance space, with live music on weekends. Breakfasts include funky treats like a feta, spinach, and cheese croissant or an acai bowl. At lunch and dinner, try the enormous fresh salads—pear and berry, bruschetta, tomato mozzarella, tamarind—and big sandwiches, with a sriracha burrito, muffaleta, and tuna waldorf salad among the offerings, $8–13. Vegan, vegetarian, and gluten-free options abound.

Decked out in Caribbean pastels on the outside and with a jazzy New York bistro feel on the inside, the award-winning **Gypsy Cab Company** (904-824-8244; gypsycab.com), 828 Anastasia Boulevard, St. Augustine dishes out treats like sweet potato and black bean burritos and chicken Quatro Framaggio at lunchtime, $7–13. Menus change twice daily and always include a vegetarian option, so you never know what might be on tonight; their wild mushroom bisque delivered a velvety texture and just the right amount of mushrooms. Top off your meal with tiramisu, or go for the chocoholics' favorite, their rich and creamy chocolate mousse. Everything is made to order, so relax and enjoy. Entrées $15–25.

QUICK BITES 🍴 Delicious Mexican scrambled eggs brought us back to the **Gourmet Hut** (904-824-7477), 17 Cuna Street, on a daily basis during one visit.

A green space with seating divided by two small cottages—one for the creative drinks and coffees, the other for creations like tropical fish wrap, sky-high spinach bake, and eggs Benedict—it's kissed by a salt breeze and blessed with a view of Fort Matanzas. Opens at 5:30 AM weekdays, 7 AM weekends.

Order at the window at **Hazel's Hot Dogs** (904-824-8484), 2400 N Ponce De Leon Boulevard, a bustling roadside hot dog stand in ketchup and mustard colors, for a quick lunch along US 1; your dog (of many choices) can come with fresh hand-cut fries. Open 10:30 AM–6 PM, meals under $10.

If you love omelets, don't miss **Mary's Harbor View Cafe** (904-825-0193), 16A Avenida Menendez. It's a small but bustling bargain breakfast bistro, opening at 7 AM.

Schmagel's Bagels & Deli (904-824-4444; schmagelsbagels.com), 69 Hypolita Street, is in the heart of the shopping district. Choose from 10 different types of freshly baked bagels topped with everything from lox to hummus, even green olive cream cheese. Deli sandwiches and panini for lunch, all selections under $10. Open 7 AM–3 PM.

OCEANFRONT 🐾 Right at the dunes, **Beachcomber Restaurant** (904-471-3744; beachcomberstaugustine.com), 2 A Street, St. Augustine Beach, is a local favorite with classic American fare—burgers, sandwiches, salads—for lunch. Local seafood figures in with their spicy homemade Minorcan clam chowder, fried gator tail, fish dip, and fried shrimp, $9–22.

With a full complement of beach drinks, from the Goombay Smash to Blue Island Iced Tea, **South Beach Grille** (904-471-8700; southbeachgrill.net), 45 Cubbedge Road, is the hot spot in Crescent Beach. Choose the open-air back porch and enjoy steamed shrimp with datil-pepper corn bread, or the rich South Beach gumboa. Stop by mid-afternoon for a drink and a bowl of their outstanding

roasted corn and blue crab corn chowder, a crunchy, buttery concoction that will have you ordering seconds. Breakfast served weekends. Entrées run $15–23.

ORGANIC AND VEGETARIAN 🌿 At **The Floridian** (904-829-0655; thefloridianstaug.com), 72 Spanish Street, expect to be dazzled by both the artful presentation and the taste of your handcrafted meal. Featuring the freshest Florida produce, meats, and fish, this foodie delight serves up Southern-style dishes with a hip twist, from gluten-free buttermilk biscuits with pork belly to cornbread panazella, BLT pork belly Caprese, and a fried chicken sandwich with bacon jam. Menu items incorporate vegan and gluten-free choices. Lunch and dinner $12–19, with many market price selections; closed Tuesday.

The city's original vegetarian restaurant, **The Manatee Cafe** (904-826-0210; manateecafe.com), 525 FL 16 #106, Westgate Plaza, offers breakfast goodies ($5 and up) like veggie burritos, fruit-topped pancakes, and omelets, and main dishes ranging from tofu chili to Cajun-style chicken. A portion of sales goes to manatee preservation funds. Open 8:30 AM–3 PM.

SEAFOOD Set just off the mainstream of US 1, **Creekside Dinery** (904-829-6113; creeksidedinery.com), 160 Nix Boatyard Road, a gabled replica Cracker house, looks like someone's home—until you step inside. The vast open rooms and wraparound porches along Oyster Creek blur the line between indoors and out. Imagine toasting marshmallows table-side as the crickets buzz at twilight under the magnolia trees: You can do that at Creekside on an open tabby grill pit. The focus of the menu is seafood, with marinated oysters, plank-cooked salmon, and other specialties. Ask for the piquant and spicy house dressing on your salad, and if the squash casserole is available as the night's vegetable, don't miss it! Entrées start around $11.

🦐 They say fried shrimp was invented in St. Augustine, and **O'Steen's Restaurant** (904-829-6974), 205 Anastasia Boulevard, has been the local hot spot for fried shrimp since 1965. The lines get long here, so sign up at the window and browse next door in the antiques shop while you listen for your name on the loudspeaker. Open Tuesday–Saturday for lunch and dinner, $9–23; cash only.

Saltwater Cowboys (904-471-2332; saltwatercowboys.com), 299 Dondanville Road. Good luck finding a parking space at this wildly popular seafood house on the Matanzas River; your best bet is arriving for lunch or a very early dinner. It's all about fish, of course—fried, broiled, baked, blackened, and steamed—but they've got killer Florida barbecue as well. Try a Florida Cracker specialty like frog legs or alligator tail, or the hot and spicy jambalaya. Entrées $12 and up.

WATERFRONT With its upstairs dining area overlooking Matanzas Bay and jazzed up with fish tanks and snazzy nautical decor, **A1A Ale Works** (904-829-2977; a1aaleworks.com), 1 King Street, is a place for funky fusion seafood like a delicious blue crab BLT, Caribbean-style jerk scampi, and grilled seafood paella. The extensive drink menu means the party goes on for hours. Lunch and dinner, $11–26.

🦐 🐚 For more than a century, the Usina family has been quietly serving up fresh seafood to boaters along the Tolomato River. It all started with Henry Flagler sailing by and stopping to ask Catherine and Frank Usina if they'd roast some oysters for him and his friends. The family finally opened up a restaurant in 2009, **Aunt Kate's** (904-829-1105; aunt-kates .com), 612 Euclid Avenue. Open daily, they're perched on the river and continue the family tradition of providing their patrons fresh seafood, from St. Augustine–style shrimp to pilau (pronounced *per-loo*)—a classic regional dish of seasoned rice, shrimp, and Minorcan sausage—and a Low Country boil. And yes,

you can get those famed steamed oysters. Lunch and dinner, entrées $13–26.

A 1920s fish camp gone upscale, **Cap's On The Water** (904-824-8794; capsonthewater.com), 4325 Myrtle Street, North Beach, is hidden back in a neighborhood along the Intracoastal Waterway. Boaters can find it easily enough; you'll have to follow the signs. With the doors thrown wide open and the whole place shaded by giant live oak trees, it blurs the line between indoors and outdoors, with a killer view of the Tolomato River estuary thrown in for good measure. Try vanilla grouper, a nut-encrusted fresh catch with a sweet vanilla rum sauce; pear ravioli; or a watermelon salad with heirloom tomatoes, Haloumi cheese, and spiced pecans. It's a busy, busy place on weekends—arrive at an off-hour if you don't want a long wait. The restaurant faces west across the water, making it a perfect place to savor a sunset. Lunch on weekends; dinner daily. Entrées $13–25.

From a bait shop and beer joint, **Lulu's Waterfront Grille** (904-285-0139; luluswaterfrontgrille.com), 301 N Roscoe Boulevard, Palm Valley, blossomed from the Big Cypress Fish Camp into a no frills waterfront seafood restaurant featuring the finest of the local fleet: Mayport shrimp. Try them in shrimp and grits, broiled, grilled, or lightly fried, nestled in with buttery-soft Louisiana oysters. Sit out on the expansive deck and watch the boaters putter past; dockage means you might meet a few. Open for lunch and dinner, entrées $13–27.

🦐 🐚 A squirrel named Roscoe. A rooster named Roo. And poutine, topped with brisket or crabmeat or simply served up Quebec style, cheese curds and gravy over steak fries. **Palm Valley Outdoors** (904-834-7504; palmvalleyoutdoors.com), 377 S Roscoe Avenue, Palm Valley, is a funky remake of an old-style fish camp under the bridge on South Roscoe that adjoins the boat ramp into the Intracoastal, so their bait and tackle adjoins the SUP and kayak rentals. At the other end of the sprawling building, the casual bar and grill offers a waterfront view and a simple yet creative menu with everything from kale & raisin salad topped with "chicken smash" to brown sugar brisket on a bun, lamb burgers, filet Oscar, and stuffed flounder. Salads, sandwiches, and entrées, $9–28.

LOCAL WATERING HOLES Catch live music 5–8 PM and 9 PM–close nightly at **Tropical Trade Winds Lounge** (904-829-9336; trade windslounge.com), 124 Charlotte Street, where the house band Matanzas plays Jimmy Buffett and a jammin' collection of their own homegrown St. Augustine–style tunes, or settle back with a beer at **Milltop Tavern & Listening Room** (904-829-2329; milltop tavern.com), 19 St. George Street for breezy acoustic music. For a real immersion into history, stop in at ♿ **Taberna del Caballo** (904-342-2867; colonialquarter .com/dine/taberna-del-caballo), 37 St. George Street, to raise a tankard to the Bilge Rats on Friday–Saturday evenings as they draw you back to 1734 with their repertoire of seafaring tunes.

BAKERIES A great spot for people-watching, **The Bunnery Bakery & Cafe** (904-829-6166; bunnerybakeryandcafe .com), 121 St. George Avenue, opens early to offer breakfasts like Southern eggs laid atop fluffy biscuits with home-style sausage gravy and grits. Lunches include burgers, sandwiches, and salads. $5–9. Open 8 AM–3 PM.

🦟 Since 1976, **Spanish Bakery & Café** (904-471-3046; spanishbakerycafe.com), 42½ St. George Avenue, has served up tempting treats from the historic Salcedo Kitchen. Stop in for empanadas, cinnamon cookies, and rolls and munch down on your goodies under the shade of an old cedar tree. Lunch items, $5–9. Open daily at 10 AM.

COFFEE SHOP The little **City Perks Coffee Co** (904-819-1644), 6 St. George Street #107, is full of goodness. We popped in there early on a Sunday morning for breakfast and found tasty mocha cappuccino and muffins. Opens at 7 AM.

ICE CREAM AND SWEETS Stop in **Claude's Chocolate** (904-808-8395; claudeschocolate.com), 6 Granada Street, where French chef Claude Franques whips up memorable bonbons, truffles, and chocolate bark. You can grab homemade ice cream here, too.

🦟 Miss not **The Hyppo** (904-217-7853; thehyppo.com), 5 Hypolita Street, for unexpectedly delicious gourmet icy creations, with flavors ranging from pineapple cilantro to blackberry clove and watermelon hibiscus.

Michigan-based **Kilwins** (904-826 0008; kilwins.com/staugustine1), 140 St. George Avenue, tempts you inside with display cases filled with chocolate goodies; they sell ice cream as well.

Founded in 1967, the granddaddy of sweet stuff in this region is **Whetstone Chocolates** (904-217-0275; whetstonechocolates.com), 139 King St. This is where the chocolate is made—and where they give tasting tours (see *Chocolate Factory*).

✱ Selective Shopping

ANTIQUES The place to browse while you're waiting for your seat at O'Steen's (see *Where to Eat*), **Anastasia Antique Center** (904-824-7126), 201 Anastasia Boulevard, offers dozens of dealer booths within a broad, open space. You'll find Blue Mountain pottery, ruby and Vaseline glass, guitars, and books.

At **Antiques & Uniques Collectibles** (904-325-9073), 7 Aviles Street, you'll find Civil War artifacts, movie star memorabilia, nautical decor items, funky salt and pepper shakers, and perhaps even a resident ghost.

Fine glassware, lamps, furnishings, and home decor are the tip of the iceberg at **A Step Back in Time** (904-810-5829), 60 San Marco Avenue.

Bouvier Maps & Prints (904-825-0920), 11-D Aviles St. If you're looking for a map to go with St. Augustine's history, this is the place to visit. Dealing in original antique maps and prints, this shop is as rare a find as its incredible inventory.

ARTS AND CRAFTS A huge selection of beads and necklaces awaits at **The Bead Chick** (904-829-8829; thebeadchick .com), 78B San Marco Avenue. Sit and create your own strands of beauty.

Grover's Gallery (904-824-5738), 14B St. George St. Big pieces, low prices: That's the philosophy of artist Grover Rice, who has spent more than 30 years carving wood into art such as life-size sea turtles and pelicans, tikis made from palm trunks, and model villages.

High Tide Gallery (904-829-6831; thehightidegallery.com), 51 Cordova Street, features 40 local artists in watercolors, acrylics, pottery, and more. Brenda Flynn's bright acrylics jump off the walls, and Brenda Phillips creates oils on canvas with colors that'll jazz up any space.

On the street level of the Casa Monica Hotel (see *Lodging*), **James Coleman Signature Gallery** (904-829-1925; tropicart .com), 65 King Street, catches your attention with playful fish and birds, art glass alligators, and brightly popping acrylics of tropical scenes.

Savor the wonder of swirled glass creations inspired by earth, wind, and fire at **Natural Reflections Glass Gallery** (904-217-3685; naturalreflectionsglass .com), 75 King Street, Suite 120, inside Reflections Bistro.

Lovingly tended by Lynne Doten and her daughter Kimberly Hunt, **Rembrandtz Gallery** (904-829-0065; rembrandtz .com), 131 King Street, represents more than 75 artists. This fun and funky gallery focuses on affordable one-of-a-kind gifts: art glass, fabric arts, paintings, photography, pottery, and more.

At **Metalartz** (904-824-6322; metalartz.net), 58 Hypolita Street, mobiles and glass balls dangle from the ceiling, and lizards and dragonflies cling to a tree that rises from the floor. With art glass, paintings, metal sculptures, and much more, this kaleidoscope of artistry represents 15 local artists and their very creative expressions.

Filled with fun, flamboyant art, **Simple Gestures** (904-827-9997), 4 White Street, gets the nod not just because of their copious supply of funky stuff by local artists—including Roadside America kitsch, Story People, art sets for kids, mosaics, and garden art—but also because they unearthed part of a local mystery in their front yard: the rails to the old streetcar line that ran from downtown to the beach nearly a century ago. How cool is that?

St. Augustine Art Glass & Craft Gallery (904-824-4916; saintaugustineartglass.com), 54 St. George Street, isn't just about glass—check out the raku art sculptures and playful metal sculptures in the tranquil garden behind the building.

Wendy Tatter Batiks (904-687-8423; wbtatter.com), 76A San Marco Avenue, featuring Wendy's beautiful batik art, offers an inviting gallery with marine-inspired pillows, fine framed batik art, cards, and sculptures.

The Woman's Exchange (904-829-5064; staugustinewomans-exchange .com), 143 St. George Street, is a volunteer organization dating back to 1892 that manages tours through the historic Peck Pina House (circa 1700) in order to run a consignment outlet for top-quality home crafters. Their motto is "Creative need is as important as the financial need," and their creativity runs the gamut from watercolor notecards and cookbooks to clothespin dolls, hand-smocked dresses, handcrafted soaps, and hand-painted glass.

BOOKS AND GIFTS **Anastasia Books** (904-827-0075), 76A San Marco Avenue, has a good selection of Floridiana (new and used) as well as plenty of children's books and textbooks for homeschoolers. Large used-book section, including the area's largest selection of science fiction and fantasy.

At Interstate 95 & US 1, the **Florida Citrus Center** (904-748-5644), 10010 Dixie Highway, St. Augustine, is one of the last of a fading breed of kitschy roadside stands that used to be everywhere when we were kids. Inside, decorative objects made of seashells, tropical jellies, and candies—including chocolate alligators and oh-so-good orange brittle—line the shelves. You'll also find citrus in season. Not to be outdone, it's flanked by two other gas stations offering free orange juice, pecan rolls, cheap T-shirts, and gator jerky; indulge the kids (or your inner child) with at least one stop for classic touristy stuff.

Think gifts with attitude at **Materialistic** (904-824-1611), 125 St. George Street, where even the T-shirts are smarmy. Pick up a punching rabbi, a dashboard hula dancer, or a Brahmin lunch box.

Pineapple Post Gift Shop (904-249-7477; pineapplepostgifts.com), 280 Village Main Street, Suite 900, Ponte Vedra, offers great gifts and home accessories with Southern hospitality; complimentary gift wrap.

Second Read Books (904-829-0334), 51 Cordova Street, keeps a brisk business going with used books for sale or trade just a block from Flagler College. Look for a good local section, fine literature, and a broad young-adult selection.

Near the corner of A1A and Alternate A1A on Anastasia Island, explore a Florida roadside classic—**Tom's Souvenirs & Sea Shells** (904-471-2355), 1812 A1A S, a roadside stand filled with all that said "Florida vacation" in our childhoods, from seashells to corals and sponges, nautical decor, Florida candies, gator heads, and kitschy Florida gifts.

DECOR AND MORE **Around the World Marketplace** (904-824-6223), 21 Orange Street. The burble of fountains makes browsing a pleasant experience as you poke through colorful imports—Tavalera porcelain, onyx chess sets, masks, statues, mirrors, and wall art.

Earthbound Trading Company (904-824-6283; earthboundtrading.com), 108 St. George Street, imports interesting locally sourced goods from around the world: Balinese figurines, star lamps from India, minerals, flowing clothing, and more.

Sunburst Trading Company (904-461-7255; sunburstflorida.com), 491 FL A1A (Beach Boulevard), is the shell shop for the region, with a selection of crafts, burbling Mexican fountains, Latin imports, and, of course, shells. Bring the kids: between the incredible selection and tiny prices, they can start a collection. An additional location is at 146 St. George Street.

FARMERS' MARKETS Now, here's a twist—a farmers' market that's also an art gathering. At the **Wednesday Market at St. Augustine Beach** (904-347-8007; thecivicassociation.org/the_wednesday _market), held at the St. Johns County Pier Park, 350 A1A Beach Boulevard, you can peruse the works of local sculptors and painters while picking up the perfect peck of potatoes. Every Wednesday 8 AM–12:30 PM, with 60–80 vendors.

At the **Old City Farmers' Market** (staugustinefm.com), stop in for fresh food straight from the farms in the southwest corner of St. Johns County. Every Saturday 8:30 AM–12:30 PM at the St. Augustine Amphitheater, 1340C A1A S, St. Augustine.

SPECIALTY FOODS Inside **The Ancient Olive** (904-827-1899; theancientolive .com), 47 King Street, one side of the store is devoted to tastings: Work your way through an unusual variety of gourmet olive oils and vinegars from around the world, from blood-orange infused to passionfruit, before settling on the perfect pairing of oil and vinegar. On the

TASTING STATION AT THE ANCIENT OLIVE

other side of the shop, peruse imported fine foods you'll enjoy stocking in your own kitchen.

✳ Special Events

FALL/WINTER At the **St. Augustine Greek Festival** (904-829-0504; stauggreekfest.com) enjoy all things Greek: fine food, music, and dancing at Francis Field, the second weekend of October; fee.

Discover the hottest thing to come out of St. Augustine at the annual **Datil Pepper Festival** (904-209-0430; stjohns.ifas.ufl.edu/DatilFallFest.shtml), St. Johns County Agriculture Center, 3125 Agriculture Center Dr. Enter your own datil-inspired hot sauce for judging! As this is at the agricultural center, enjoy arboretum tours and a plant sale, too. Early October.

The British militia takes over the Oldest City during the **Colonial Night Watch** (hfm.club/nightwatch/), with Colonial Market Days, daily military drills by the Redcoats, magicians, and more. The first weekend in December.

For more than 50 years, the Garden Club of St. Augustine has hosted the **Christmas Tour of Homes** (gardenclubofstaugustine.org), a walking tour that gets you behind the coquina walls and Victorian porches into the beautiful historic homes of the Historic District. While the event is in early December, tickets go on sale October 1 and sell out quickly, $30 per person.

Watch the waterfront light up during the annual **Regatta of Lights** (904-824-9725; floridashistoriccoast.com/events /holiday-regatta-lights), Avenida Menendez, with a holiday parade of boats judged for their creativity. Hosted by the St. Augustine Yacht Club and held along the bayfront the second Saturday in December, as soon as it gets dark.

During **Searle's Sack of St. Augustine** (hfm.club/events/annual/searles-sack), the first Saturday of March, pirates camp out near the Fountain of Youth (see *Archaeological Sites*) and stealthily make their way to the city gates, reenacting the sacking and burning of the Historic District in 1668, with swordfights, brawls, and general mayhem through the streets.

SPRING/SUMMER **Florida's Birding & Photo Fest** (floridasbirdingandphotofest .com), St. Augustine Amphitheatre. A nature-based festival offering workshops, seminars, and field trips throughout the region on birding, native wildlife, and enjoying the outdoors. Late April.

♪ Join the "Potato Capital of the World" in celebrating the **Hastings Potato & Cabbage Festival**, Hastings Recreational Field, 150 Main Street, Hastings, the first weekend in May. Expect a Spud Run, mouth-watering potato stew and cabbage soup, potato cupcakes and potato fudge, hot-air balloon rides, live music, and fun for the whole family.

Gamble Rogers Folk Festival (904-794-0222; gamblerogersfest.org), Colonial Quarter, the last weekend in May. One of Florida's top folk music weekends, with dozens of performers honoring one of the strongest voices in Florida folk music, and vendors and craftspersons with Florida art. Performance venues and vendors will be scattered throughout downtown. $10–20.

The Players Championship (pgatour .com/theplayers) is one of the top golfing events in the nation. It descends on TPC Sawgrass (see *Golf*), Ponte Vedra Beach, mid-May for three days, bringing tens of thousands of golfing fans to the region.

Drake's Raid (hfm.club/events/ annual/drakesraid), the first Saturday in June. Only the most studious of history lovers (and the locals, of course) know that swashbuckling pirate Sir Francis Drake came ashore and set fire to St. Augustine in 1586, sacking the city.

Founder's Day (hfm.club/events/ annual/landing). Founded on September 8, 1565, the oldest continously-occupied European settlement in the continental United States commemorates its start annually with a re-enactment of Don Pedro Menéndez de Avilés's landing; the site is marked with a massive cross at Mission of Nombre de Dios (see *Museums and Historic Sites*). Join the countdown to the half millennium! Held the Saturday after September 8.

FLAGLER COUNTY

Palm Coast, Flagler Beach, Bunnell, and Beverly Beach

I t was a wild and jungle-like place, a wilderness between the St. Johns River and the Atlantic Ocean, when John James Audubon came to visit Bulow Plantation for Christmas in 1831. Just 11 years beforehand, Charles Bulow, a merchant from Charleston, purchased the 6,000 acres along the Florida coast with the goal of establishing a cotton plantation. Slaves carved working fields for cotton, indigo, rice, and sugar cane out of the dense forests. After Charles died, his son John expanded what became known as "Bulowville," building a two-story home and a sugar mill to process sugar cane. While Audubon visited him as a guest, the artist painted a shorebird—the greater yellowlegs—for his portfolio, showing the buildings of the plantation in the background.

Carved out of neighboring St. Johns and Volusia, Flagler County was established in 1917. It's relatively young, but its roots run deep. When the first Europeans reached these shores, the Timucua occupied the land, with villages both on the coast and along the river, which they plied by canoe. In 1565, a battle for control of Florida had Spanish soldiers defending their king's claim to the land against French settlers at Fort Caroline (see *Jacksonville*), then massacring the survivors of the French fleet who straggled ashore up these shores to surrender at Fort Mantanzas (see *St. Augustine*). Spain's claim on the territory slipped into British hands in 1766, right through the American Revolution. The British extended King's Road, which led through the colonies, down through this region; parts of it can still be driven today.

When the Spanish reacquired the region, the King of Spain granted land to subjects willing to move to America and establish homesteads. It was one of these land grants that was sold to Charles Bulow. Others, such as the Dupont, Hernandez, Pellicer, and Ormond grants, provide place names today. Henry Cutting purchased Cherokee Grove, Francisco Pellicer's plantation, and built a grand Adirondack hunting lodge on it in 1887, with the first in-ground swimming pool in Florida, fed by a spring. It's now Princess Place, a county park. On the former

GARDEN PATH AT WASHINGTON OAKS GARDENS STATE PARK

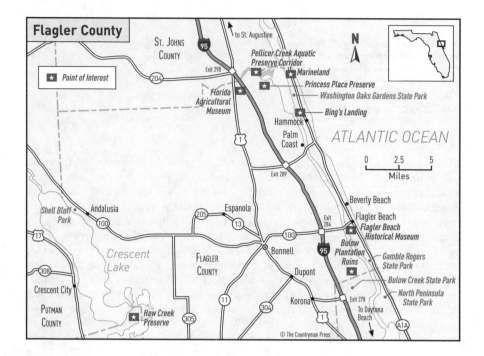

Map caption / labels:

Flagler County

to St. Augustine

ST. JOHNS COUNTY

95

204

Exit 298

★ Point of Interest

Pellicer Creek Aquatic Preserve Corridor

★ Marineland

Florida Agricultural Museum

★ Princess Place Preserve

Washington Oaks Gardens State Park

★ Bing's Landing

Hammock

Palm Coast

1

ATLANTIC OCEAN

Exit 289

0   2.5   5
Miles

Beverly Beach

Andalusia

Shell Bluff Park

100

Espanola

205

13

100

Exit 284

Flagler Beach
★ Flagler Beach Historical Museum

17

Crescent Lake

FLAGLER COUNTY

Bunnell

95

Bulow Plantation Ruins
★

Gamble Rogers State Park

Bulow Creek State Park

308

Dupont

North Peninsula State Park

Crescent City

11

Korona

304

Exit 278

PUTMAN COUNTY

★ Haw Creek Preserve

305

1

To Daytona Beach

A1A

N

© The Countryman Press

Hernandez grant, fashion designer Louise Clark and her husband Owen D. Young, the CEO of General Electric in 1929, built their retirement home in the late 1930s, designing formal gardens beneath the ancient live oaks; you can now visit the home and gardens at Washington Oaks Gardens State Park. Although it was torched by Seminole warriors during the first Seminole War in 1836, parts of Bulowville still stand, particularly the Bulow Sugar Mill—it's Bulow Plantation Ruins State Park. Exacavations of a part of the Mala Compara plantation are now visible and interpreted at Bings Landing Park, just one of many parks in the longstanding coastal community of **Hammock**.

Flagler County's oldest city harkens back to the first big Florida development boom. This seaside community got its start in 1920 as "Ocean City" when the first bridge opened from the mainland; a casino, bars, and hotels soon followed. Incorporated in 1925 as **Flagler Beach**, it is compact, historic, and walkable, a delight for visitors to explore. **Palm Coast**, established in 1999 by incorporation of a massive subdivision that started in the early 1960s, is where the bulk of the county's population lives. The western side of the county, west of the county seat of **Bunnell**, is extremely rural, with large farms growing everything from potatoes and cabbage to watermelons. The tiny communities of **Andalusia**, **Seville**, and **Espanola** and their citrus groves recall this region's Spanish heritage, as the Spanish were the first to bring oranges to America.

GUIDANCE The **Flagler County Chamber of Commerce Visitor's Center** (866-736-9291 or 386-313-4230; visitflagler.com), 20 Airport Road, Suite C, Palm Coast, is off FL 100 between Flagler Beach and Bunnell, daily 10 AM–4 PM. You'll also find a walk-in visitors center inside the **Flagler Beach Historical Museum** (386-517-2025; flaglerbeachmuseum.com), 207 S Avenue, Flagler Beach, open Monday–Saturday 10 AM–4 PM, where you can ask about local accommodations and pick up brochures and maps.

🐾 Of all of Florida's coastal communities, Flagler County is tops for pets. Dogs are welcome on nearly every public and some private beaches, and most mom-and-pop lodgings allow you to bring your best friend along. Some of the eateries are dog friendly, too. If your dog has never romped in the surf, this is the destination for you!

GETTING THERE *By air:* Fly into **Jacksonville International Airport** (see the *Jacksonville* chapter) or **Daytona Beach International Airport** (386-248-8030; flydaytonafirst .com): American, Delta, and JetBlue provide regular service.

By car: **Interstate 95** provides access to the highways that lead to Flagler's back roads and bridge to A1A and US 1, paralleling to the east and west. Exit at Dupont Center, US 1, Palm Coast, and Flagler Beach.

GETTING AROUND A car is necessary to make your way around the county. **FL A1A** and **US 1** are the major north–south routes, with **FL 100** connecting Flagler Beach and Bunnell.

MEDICAL EMERGENCIES **Florida Hospital Flagler** (386-586-2000; floridahospital .com/flagler), 60 Memorial Medical Parkway, Palm Coast, is a full-service hospital with emergency room; Prompt Care (386-586-4280), 120 Cypress Edge Drive, Palm Coast, provides walk-in clinic services.

✳ To See

ARCHAEOLOGICAL SITES 🖉 ♿ Under an open-air roofed building in **Bings Landing Park** (386-437-7490; flaglerparks.com/bings/preserve.htm), 5880 N Oceanshore Boulevard, Hammock, the outlines of buildings that were part of the homestead at **Mala Compra Plantation** are interpreted, along with the artifacts found at this archaeological dig. Joseph Hernández, a native Floridian born in St. Augustine, received a land grant from the King of Spain in 1816. He purchased two adjoining pieces of land to establish the plantation, and this site was his home. When Spain ceded Florida, he remained in the new US Territory. Nominated by the territorial legislative council after a distinguished career in military service, he ran unopposed to become Florida's first delegate to the US Congress, and its first Hispanic member. The park has a large playground, fishing pier, and walking trails through the Bings Landing Addition.

A **water-powered sawmill** built in 1770 by John Hewitt along Pellicer Creek was one of the first in the region. Access this interpretive site from a trail starting at a gated parking area off US 1 [29.642776, -81.286058].

ARCHITECTURE A two-story Mason Vernacular built around 1917, the **Bunnell State Bank Building**, 101 N Bay Street, was the only bank in Flagler County between 1917 and 1932.

Marvel at an Adirondack lodge built Florida-style—of pink coquina, cedar trunks, heart-of-pine floors, and cabbage palm trunks—at **Cherokee Grove**, the oldest homestead in Flagler County, part of **Princess Place Preserve** (386-313-4020; flaglercounty .org), 2500 Princess Place Road. Designed by architect William M. Wright in 1887, it is full of surprises; once you're inside, you recognize the Tudor elements hidden behind the rustic wrap-around porch. The airy central room with its showy coquina fireplace rises two stories, with gabled windows and decorative iron lamps providing illumination; the loft served as luggage storage. Free tours of the lodge are offered at 2 PM

FLORIDA'S FIRST IN-GROUND SWIMMING POOL AT CHEROKEE LODGE

Friday–Sunday, but you can sit on a rocking chair on the porch any time the 1,500-acre park is open, 7 AM–6 PM daily.

ART GALLERIES **The Baliker Gallery** (386-446-0069; paulbaliker.com), 5928 N Oceanshore Boulevard, Hammock, beckons you to stop with its larger-than-life driftwood sculptures. Step inside to surround yourself with vivid acrylics of Florida forests and estuaries. The creative spirit of Paul Baliker hums through this open space, where the figures of sailfish, sea turtles, and sprites emerge from the natural curves of driftwood. Open weekends.

At the **Gallery of Local Art** (386-439-6659; galleryoflocalart.com), 208 S Central Avenue, Flagler Beach, you might wander in to look at watercolors and acrylics of coastal scenes and hear a buzz from the back, where classes go on inside a studio space. The gallery also interconnects with several other shops, but the focus here is on art created and shared by members of the local community.

GARDENS With formal gardens stretching from the Matanzas River into the deep shade of ancient live oaks, **Washington Oaks Gardens State Park** (386-446-6780; floridastateparks.org/washingtonoaks), 6400 N Oceanshore Boulevard, Hammock, showcases natural beauty and carefully cultivated plantings, including a historic rose garden. Developed between 1936 and 1964, the gardens were a hobby for retired General Electric CEO Owen D. Young and his wife Louise, who donated them to the state. Their travels influenced selections of certain exotic features along the meandering pathways beneath the oaks. Interpretive signs and a museum in the Youngs' former home tell the story of the Washington Oaks Historic District, now on the National Register of Historic Places. Fee.

GEOLOGY Two wild shores showcase the rocky shelf that crops out along this coastline. One of Florida's fascinating geologic destinations, **Coquina Beach** at Washington Oaks Gardens State Park is an ever-changing landscape of eroded rock formations and tidal pools. At **Malacompra Park** (386-313-4020; flaglercounty.org), 115 Malacompra

Road, Hammock, coquina rocks—a sedimentary rock made up of layers of the coquina shells—protrude from the sand. Sunbathing and general exploration is welcome at both beaches, but swimming is not advised.

MARINE CONSERVATION At the **Whitney Laboratory for Marine Bioscience** (904-461-4000; whitney.ufl.edu), 9505 Ocean Shore Boulevard, Marineland, University of Florida scientists and students delve into the secrets of the deep to apply to biomedical and biotechnical research. "Marine invertebrates are great models for human beings," said Maureen Welch, showing off studies using sea slugs to model the neurological problems of Alzheimer's patients. As an intake facility for injured sea turtles, they open their doors for visits to the Sea Turtle Hospital on the second and fourth Thursday and second Saturday of each month at 10 AM, reservations required; $15.

MUSEUMS AND HISTORIC SITES & ❀ Walk through the forest where Bulowville once thrived at **Bulow Plantation Ruins Historic State Park** (386-517-2084; floridastateparks.org/park/Bulow-Plantation), 3501 Old Kings Road, to discover the remains of the sugar mill used in the 1830s to process sugar cane into raw sugar and molasses. Interpretive signs walk you through the open-air factory floor beneath a canopy of live oaks. A pathway leads back to the remains of the spring house in the shady palm hammock. A nature trail walks you past pines tapped for turpentine nearly a century after the sugar mill was torched by the Seminoles; a more lengthy hiking trail burrows deep into the primordial forest along Bulow Creek. Canoe rentals adjoin the picnic pavilion along the waterway. Closed Tuesday–Wednesday; fee.

ROCKY COQUINA BEACH AT WASHINGTON OAKS GARDENS STATE PARK

INTERPRETIVE WALK THROUGH THE SUGAR MILL RUINS AT BULOW PLANTATION RUINS STATE PARK

In the **Flagler Beach Museum** (386-517-2025; flaglerbeachmuseum.com), 207 S Central Avenue, we discovered things foreign but familiar, like brochures for the 1930s Marine Studios (later Marineland) and a survival kit for atomic attack. The museum delves deep into the founding of Flagler Beach and archaeological finds along the coast, but seeing artifacts associated with childhood memories made a deeper impression. Open Monday–Saturday 10 AM–4 PM.

Interpreting Florida's rich agricultural heritage, the **Florida Agricultural Museum** (386-446-7630; floridaagmuseum.org), 7900 Old Kings Road, lets you touch, smell, and feel life on the farm. Ramble through the farmyard, where chickens roam free, horses are at the stables, and heritage cattle roam the pastures. A dairy barn housing restrooms and a sheltered picnic area is modeled after one owned by Governor Millard Caldwell. Five historic buildings from a citrus grove make up the Strawn Citrus Complex, showing how groves were managed in the 1940s. Guided tractor-led tours take visitors to several historic sites and a museum of African American cowboy heritage; call in advance to arrange. $9 adults, $7 children.

Home to the Flagler County Historical Society, the **Holden House Museum** (386-437-0600), 204 E Moody Boulevard, Bunnell, was built in 1918 for Ethel and Tom Holden by her father. Rooms with period furnishings reflect the home's use in the 1920s; it was one of the first buildings in the area with indoor plumbing. Each gable is inset with pieces of apothecary bottles, antique colored glass, and bits of dishes. Open Wednesday 10 AM–1 PM.

Built in 1915 using convict labor, **Old Dixie Highway** was the first paved road through the region. A narrow, 9-foot-wide segment of the original road can be driven through the towns of Hastings, Espanola, and Bunnell between Flagler and St. Johns counties.

Adjoining US 1 and Interstate 95, be on the lookout for pieces of **Old Kings Road**, Florida's first highway. Following an old Timucuan trail, the British military designed the road to connect St. Augustine to the Turnbull Plantation in New Smyrna. By 1774 the road was shell surfaced, had bridges, and used pine logs to cross the bogs.

✳ To Do

BIKING With one of the most complete off-road sections of the **East Coast Greenway** (greenway.org/states/florida) paralleling A1A for nearly 20 miles, Flagler County is decidedly bike friendly. At the **Mala Compra Greenway** (386-437-7490; flaglercounty .org), 115 Malacompra Road, Hammock, mountain bikers will find a fun 6-mile loop with tight curves and technical drops; advanced riders should try the Cloud 9 section, where coquina boulders add to the challenge. **Trailhead Beach N' Bike Gallery** (904-598-4548; trailheadbikes.com), 5861 N Ocean Shore Boulevard, adjoins the mountain bike park and offers rentals starting at $10/hr or $30/day. Many of the county's paved paths are part of the **St. Johns River-to-Sea Loop** (sjr2c.org), a 260-mile bike route linking St. Augustine with Flagler Beach and Titusville.

BIRDING One of our favorite spots for birding is 🐦 **Boardman Pond** [29.406077, -81.126873] just north of the Volusia County line. Park your car along Walter Boardman Road and watch from the bank, or wander down the Bulow Creek Trail (see *Hiking*) to a blue-blazed trail leading to the Audubon observation deck. Just behind the Flagler Beach Library, a boardwalk leads into the marshlands of ♿ **Betty Steflik Memorial Preserve** (386-313-4020; www.flaglercounty.org), 815 Moody Lane, Flagler Beach, a hidden treasure for birding and manatee-watching.

DOLPHIN ENCOUNTER 🐬 **Marineland Dolphin Adventure** (888-279-9194 or 904-460-1275; marineland.net), 9600 Oceanshore Boulevard, Marineland, is on the site of the world's oldest marine park, opened in 1938. But it's not your grandpa's Marineland—the iconic three-story-tall Marine Studios tank gave up the ghost, and along with it went the historic buildings and most of the aquatic life. The Dolphin Conservation Center was built atop the old Whitney Park. Make advance reservations to swim and interact with the dolphins, reinforcing behaviors such as playing ball and jumping, starting at $37 to touch and feed the dolphins or $219 for 20 minutes in the water with them. General admission provides access to viewing the shark and turtle pools in Neptune Park, along with watching the dolphins and their visitors in their habitat tanks. $17 ages 13 and up, $16 seniors, $12 children 3–12. Daily 9 AM–4:30 PM.

ECOTOURS Ride the vegetable-oil powered Eco-Explorer out of Marineland Marina with **Ripple Effect Ecotours** (904-347-1565; rippleeffectecotours.com) for an environmental education experience you won't forget; $50 adult, $40 ages 15 and under, includes general admission to Marineland.

FAMILY ACTIVITIES 🐬 Take the kids bowling at **Palm Coast Lanes** (386-445-4004; palmcoastlanes.com), 11 Old Kings Road N, where all 24 lanes have bumpers available. **PaxTrax Motocross Park** (386-437-7191; paxtraxmx.com), 2529 N State Street, Bunnell, is a family-friendly dirt bike facility where Sundays are Family Days; small bikes and beginners can hit the tracks at specified times, and a dedicated Pee Wee Track helps newbies to riding. $20–30 day pass.

FISHING On the Atlantic Ocean, the **Flagler Beach Pier** (cityofflaglerbeach.com/ thepier), 105 S 2nd Street, is a great place to wet a line or get a great view of the beach; fee. For a morning in the shallows on a flats skiff with an expert captain, contact Captain Chris at **Palm Coast Fishing** (386-503-6338; palmcoastfishing.com). Looking for bass? Head for **Shell Bluff Park** (386-313-4020), 14331 W FL 100 in Andalusia, where there is a boat ramp and a floating dock on **Crescent Lake,** open dawn–11 PM.

HIKING ✍ 👣 Families with children will appreciate the gentle trails of **Washington Oaks Gardens State Park** (see *Gardens*), where the **Mala Compra Trail** meanders along the mangrove-lined shores and the **Bella Vista Trail** loops through many habitats in only a mile. The many trails of ✍ 👣 **Princess Place Preserve** (see *Architecture*) will keep you busy all day, exploring along the salt marshes of Pellicer Creek and its upland pine flatwoods, but the best hike in the region is the 👣 **Bulow Creek Trail** at Bulow Plantation Ruins Historic State Park (see *Museums and Historic Sites*). Inside the ancient Bulow Hammock, towering trees, giant leather ferns, and palm trees leaning across the sluggish creek make this a primordial hike.

HORSEBACK RIDING On a guided trail ride at the **Florida Agricultural Museum** (386-365-6000; floridaagmuseum.org), 7900 Old Kings Road, follow trails through several hundred acres of sandhills and pine forest; reserve in advance, $50 per rider per hour. Their trails connect to neighboring **Pellicer Creek Conservation Area** via a land bridge visible from I-95, and in turn connect to **Princess Place Preserve** (see *Architecture*), which has an equestrian campground, $20–25; call 386-313-4020 to reserve and check in between 4:30–5:30 PM at the ranger station.

PADDLING Based in Flagler Beach, **Sunrise Outdoors** (386-463-0232; sunrise-outdoors.com), will bring your rental kayak or SUP to you at four different locations along the length of the Intracoastal Waterway in Flagler County; if you're renting all day, they'll pick up at a different location. Rentals run 2–12 hours, $25–70; fishing kayaks available. Out of Palm Coast Marina, **Tropical Kayaks** (386-445-0506;

PADDLER ON HAW CREEK

tropicalkayaks.com), 200 Clubhouse Drive, rents kayaks and offers guided trips customized to your own pace and the best wildlife-watching for the season; call for details. If you've brought your own kayak, **Haw Creek Preserve** (386-313-4020; flaglercounty .org), 2007 CR 2007, Bunnell, is a wild freshwater paddle that starts out from a boat ramp adjoining a boardwalk through the floodplain. Launching at **Princess Place Preserve** (see *Architecture*) or adjacent **Pellicer Creek Conservation Area** (386-329-4404; sjrwmd.com/recreationguide/pellicercreek) affords kayakers access to both the creek and the Matanzas River, with its many islands part of **Guana-Tolomato-Matanzas Reserve** (904-825-5071; coast.noaa.gov/nerrs/reserves/gtm.html).

PARKS, PRESERVES, AND CAMPING With 25 RV sites along Dead Lake—which connects to Haw Creek and the bass fishing destination of Crescent Lake—county-run **Bull Creek Campground** (386-313-4020; flaglercounty.org), 3861 CR 2006, is a remote getaway for freshwater anglers. A private bait shop and restaurant adjoins the public park. $25–35 site, $5 for dock space.

🐾 ♿ 🛶 **Gamble Rogers Memorial State Recreation Area** (386-517-2086; floridastateparks.org/park/Gamble-Rogers), 3100 S Oceanshore Boulevard, Flagler Beach, offers families a stay with a sea breeze in its two campgrounds, $28. A gentle nature trail tunnels through a diminutive forest of windswept oaks along the Intracoastal Waterway. Stop by the ranger station to rent a bicycle, kayak, or canoe to explore. Fee.

🐾 The headwaters of Bulow Creek rise in the cypress swamps of **Graham Swamp Conservation Area** (386-437-7490; sjrwmd.com/recreationguide/grahamswamp), along Old Kings Road just south of Palm Coast [29.508334, -81.161392]. This preserve protects a freshwater floodplain that creates a barrier against saltwater intrusion from the Atlantic Ocean. Trails invite you to explore by hiking or mountain biking. Fishing is welcome in the lakes.

🐾 Two unspoiled miles of oceanfront beckon visitors to **North Peninsula State Park** (386-517-2086; floridastateparks.org/park/North-Peninsula), 40 Highbridge Road. An access point at Smith Creek Landing off High Bridge Rd [29.409675, -81.099383] provides a place to take a hike, slip a kayak into the marshes, or fish from the shoreline.

SCENIC DRIVES Few highways in the northern Florida peninsula match the beauty of the **A1A Scenic and Historic Coastal Byway** (904-596-0029; scenica1a.org), particularly where the dunes remain preserved and free of development. Designated an American Byway, this two-lane highway stays close to the ocean. A cell phone audio tour gives background on scenic stops along the way.

SURFING Check in at **Z Wave Surf Shop** (386-439-9283; zwavesurfshop.com), 400 S Oceanshore Boulevard, to rent surfboards and body boards; right across the street, the waves break near the Flagler Beach Pier.

SWIMMING While the beaches of Flagler County are pet friendly, you do need to mind the warning flags, as rip currents can arise quickly. The soft orange-tinted sands are from the eroded remains of coquina shells. 🐾 ♿ Sunbathers enjoy the strand at **River to Sea Preserve** (386-313-4020; flaglercounty.org), 9805 N Oceanshore Boulevard, where dolphin cutouts in the boardwalk echo memories of Marineland past shared on interpretive signs. 🐾 🛶 ♿ **Varn Park** (386-313-4020; flaglercounty.org), 3665 N Oceanshore Boulevard, Beverly Beach, has always been a family favorite, since it's just far enough north of Flagler Beach to be less busy. In downtown **Flagler Beach**, beach parking and access surrounds the pier.

WALKING TOUR Stop in at the Flagler Beach Museum (see *Museums and Historic Sites*) to pick up a brochure for a self-guided walking tour of **historic downtown Flagler Beach**. The museum sometimes offers guided tours; call for details.

WHALE-WATCHING The **calving ground of the right whale** can be seen from both River to Sea Preserve (see *Swimming*) and neighboring Summer Haven and Crescent Beach in St. Johns County; check with **Marineland's Right Whale Project** (aswh.org/whale/main.html) to become an official whale-watcher during the winter calving season.

✳ Lodging

COMFORT AND LUXURY ⚲ ♿ ⚲ ((ᵗ))
Hammock Beach Resort (866-841-0287; hammockbeach.com), 200 Ocean Crest Drive, Palm Coast 32137, is an all-encompassing luxury resort and conference center towering over the dunes. All accomodations in the main tower and lodge boast a sweeping panorama of the ocean. Suites range from one bedroom with a sitting room to up to 2,800 square feet with 3–4 bedrooms and a full kitchen, ideal for family gatherings. With four eateries on site, however, including Atlantic Grille and Delfinos (see *Where to Eat*), you may never touch that stove. Two championship golf courses designed by Jack Nicklaus and Tom Watson—The Ocean Course and The Conservatory Course—provide oceanfront or wooded options. Kids will love the tropical water park with its lazy river, waterslide, and multiple pools while Mom slips away to the spa for a warm Coconut Stone massage. The spacious rooms and suites start at $152, plus an 11.5 percent resort fee that covers amenities like beach services, pool access, fitness center, 9-hole putting green, complimentary bike rentals, Wi-Fi, resort shuttles, and parking.

♿ ⚲ ((ᵗ)) ⊙ A romantic oceanfront oasis crafted by soulmates Toni and Mark nearly 20 years ago, **Island Cottage Villas** (386-439-0092; islandcottagevillas.com), 2316 S Oceanshore Boulevard, Flagler Beach 32136, is an island-inspired collection of spacious suites surrounding a courtyard with a heated pool. Relax along the water's edge or on your private balcony and listen to the strum of the waves across the street, dip in the pool, or enjoy quiet time in your room or suite, some of which have fireplaces and Jacuzzi tubs. Their intimate spa is perfect for couples' massages. Rooms and suites start at $219–399 and must be reserved in advance. While breakfast is not included in the room price, you can add a gourmet breakfast for $26 per person per morning.

((ᵗ)) Treat yourself to luxury at the beachfront **White Orchid Inn & Spa** (386-439-4944; whiteorchidinn.com), 1104 S Oceanshore Boulevard. In the "Room with It All" you can enjoy a king-size canopied bed, crisp white linens, a Jacuzzi big enough for two, and a poolside veranda. The "Courtyard Lilac & Green" features a beautiful glass-block shower and covered lanai. Enjoy beautifully landscaped grounds, a swimming pool, and a heated mineral pool. The on-site holistic spa features a variety of massages, wraps, facials, and hand and foot care. Use of beach chairs and umbrellas, bicycles, and a full breakfast are included with your stay. $139–269.

RETRO AND ARTSY ☻ ◉ ♟ ⚲ ♿ A unique piece of roadside history, **Palm Coast Villas** (386-445-3525; palmcoastvillas .com), 5454 N Oceanshore Boulevard, Palm Coast 32137, is a longtime landmark along A1A in Hammock. Originally the Rock Lodge, the complex includes the original motor court and newer additions of larger rooms and suites. The original villas feel straight out of a national park lodge. The walls are pure,

HAMMOCK BEACH RESORT

thick coquina, quarried nearby. The crisp, simple decor doesn't overwhelm their natural beauty; even the cozy 1940s bathrooms have rock walls! All original villas include an efficiency kitchen, tile floors, and windows looking out on a lush hammock of ancient oaks and palm trees. The new-style villas and suites are modern and spacious and also include kitchen facilities. Trails lead through the woods back to the Intracoastal Waterway, where you can take burgers out to the grill and enjoy them at a picnic table with a breeze. The original pool sits near the road, fenced in for children's safety. Rent a bicycle to explore Hammock along the East Coast Greenway. Rooms and suites, $64–104.

🐾 ♨ ⚲ 📶 For creatives, **Si Como No Inn** (386-864-1430; sicomonoinn.com), 2481 N Oceanshore Boulevard, is a special delight. Each room has its own funky decor, with original murals and other artistic touches; some come with lofts for the kids. An Old Florida find from 1947 with only eight rooms, it's right across from the beach. There's an old-fashioned tiki bar out front and a spring bubbling into a salt creek out back, where you can launch a kayak into the mangroves. Rent a bike and explore the town, take a private

surf lesson, or just pad down to the beach with your pooch and relax. $140.

With your RV parked facing the Atlantic Ocean, you'll greet each day with a stunning sunrise. The campground straddles A1A, so the less expensive sites are across the street from the beach, and a camp store means supplies are a short walk away. Full-hookup 50-amp RV and tent sites start at $65–80, cabins $105–200.

Set in piney woods along Hog Pond, **Thunder Gulch Campground** (386-437-3135; thundergulch-campground.com), 127 Lantana Avenue, Bunnell 32136, is a peaceful place to settle in with your RV, or to tent-camp with the kids while visiting PaxTrax Motocross Park (see *Family Activities*); they'll appreciate the catch-and-release fishing at the pond. RV and tent sites, $29–36.

✳ Where to Eat

CASUAL FARE We popped in for lunch at **Curly's Redd Gator Cafe** (386-437-2233), 509 N State Street, Bunnell, and discovered a hometown diner with the basics, like burgers and BLTs. The breakfast menu and decor speaks to their mainstream clientle, with the Rod & Gun Country Breakfast with 3 eggs, potatoes, meat, and biscuit & gravy. All meals under $10, Monday–Saturday 6 AM–2 PM.

⚓ At **High Jackers Restaurant** (386-586-6078; highjackers.com), 202 Airport Road, they've got one of our favorites on the daily menu—Wisconsin beer cheese soup! Entrées range from pasta to chicken, pork, steak and seafood done up as kebabs, grilled fish, and fried fish and clam platters in the HoJo tradition, $10–17. Located at Flagler County Airport, they're a spin-off of High Tides at Flagler Beach; it's a fun place to take the kids to watch the planes—and the aviators—arrive.

HIP BISTRO-STYLE The oceanfront view was a nice escape from the conference room when dining at **Atlantic Grille** (866-841-0287; hammockbeach.com/dine/atlantic-grille), 200 Ocean Crest Drive, Palm Coast at Hammock Beach Resort (see *Lodging*). For a light meal, the Atlantic Salad, with toasted almond, dried fig, cripsy pancetta, basil, and goat cheese is perfect paired with a pass-around plate of their own Cajun crab dip with tortilla chips. Lunches $9–15, entrées $18–38. Sister restaurant **Delfinos** (386-246-5650; hammockbeach.com/dine/delfinos) focuses on Italian cuisine, ranging from classic renditions of chicken, veal, and eggplant to Risotto Fruitti di Mare and a selection of steaks; entrées $19–45. Opens at 5 PM each evening, reservations recommended.

OCEANFRONT At **The Golden Lion Cafe** (386-439-3004; goldenlioncafe.us), 500 N Oceanshore Boulevard, Flagler Beach, a funky beach bar and restaurant with ocean views, join the perpetual party on the upper decks or duck inside for their top-notch beer-battered fish and chips. Bangers and mash are on the menu, too, along with seafood tacos and lobster done up a half-dozen different ways. Lunch, dinner, and late-night bites, $10–35.

Even on weeknights, **High Tides at Snack Jacks** (386-439-3344; snackjacks.com), 2805 S Oceanshore Boulevard, is packed. This timeless surfer hangout perches precariously on the dunes, its the parking lot so narrow and shoehorned that you have to let the fellows valet park your car so they can stack them three and four deep. Back when Snack Jacks opened in 1950, there was a lot less width to the road and more to the beach. The breeze can be pretty strong on the open deck, so the screened porch is another option, with its picnic tables overlooking the Atlantic waves. The shrimp came with a healthy dose of hot sauce, and between that, the margaritas, and some seafood platter shared, it was plenty tasty. Organic veggies and wild caught shrimp/fish are highlighted on the menu, sandwiches and entrées, $7–29.

QUICK BITES Grab some 'q under the oaks at **Captain's BBQ** (386-597-2888; captainsbbq.com), 5862 N Ocean Shore Boulevard at Bing's Landing. For lunch and dinner, the slow-cooked meats are ready to pile on a plate or bun, and they serve up a big old Breakfast Bucket (plus sliders, omelets, and more) Friday–Sunday at 7 AM. Eat in, or carry it over to the picnic pavilion for a view of the boats going by. Breakfast under $10, BBQ $9–16, opens 11 AM.

⚓ At **Hot Diggity Dogs** (386-437-0990; bunnelldiggitydog.com), 1001 S State Street, Bunnell, roadside picnic tables are where you plop down to enjoy more than a dozen varieties of hot dogs, from the Trailer Park Dog with melted cheddar, coney sauce, and crushed Fritos to the New Jersey Dog with grilled potatoes, onions, and peppers. You can have them plain if you prefer, or as smoked sausage dressed up with hot dog fixin's. Or go for a piled-up Burger Bomb or chicken wings with that milkshake. Most meals under $10, dogs starting at $3.

SEAFOOD Delicious fish is what you'll get at **Flagler Fish Company** (386-439-0000;

flaglerfishcompany.com), 180 S Daytona Avenue, Flagler Beach, where you can pick up fresh seafood to go or relax and enjoy having it prepared for you. Stop in for lunch and start off with a creamy lobster bisque; then move on to a sandwich like the Holy Mackerel BLT—topped with your choice of grilled fish—or fish tacos several different ways. Or settle in for dinner and choose directly from the fish case, plus sides like butter-fried noodles, savory grits, or Asiago potatoes. Burgers, steaks, and pasta too. Open Monday–Saturday, $10–24.

A rustic but bustling fish camp-style restaurant under the oaks of Hammock, **J.T.'s Seafood Shack** (386-446-4337; jtseafoodshack.com/home), 5224 N Ocean Shore Boulevard, features steamed crab and shrimp pots and fried seafood platters amid an expansive menu with choices like scallops au gratin, Caprese sandwich, and Genoa basil pesto pasta; plus burgers and other kid-friendly options. Eat outside with the live music or inside surrounding the bar. Sandwiches, salads, and entrées $7–39.

☀ Right along A1A, **Turtle Shack Cafe** (386-439-0331; turtleshackfb.com), 2123 N Oceanshore Boulevard, is a pet-friendly restaurant with gourmet burgers, but their seafood is what keeps the regulars happy. With creations like scallops St. Jacques and simple goodness in their crab dip and crabcakes, you won't miss with any selection. Light Bite lunch baskets, burgers, and sandwiches $9–18; dinners $17–36.

ICE CREAM AND SWEETS For some of the funkiest popsicles you'll ever try, stop in **The Hyppo** (904-217-7853; thehyppo.com), 200 S Central Avenue, Flagler Beach. We're talking smooth, flash-frozen fruity combinations you'd probably never think of, like the pineapple cilantro that cooled me down on a hot day, a lavender lemonade, datil strawberry with those piquant hot peppers from the neighboring county, and a dozen more. If you're not so daring,

go with a simple and tasty orange cream.

⚓ Grab cold, freshly made ice cream at **The Waffle Cone** (386-569-3153; thewafflecone.com), S 4th Street, Flagler Beach, and take a walk down to the beach to savor it in the sea breeze. This little shop with handmade, slow-churned ice cream is always busy; sometimes you have to park blocks away to come grab a cone. Open daily noon–9:30 PM.

✳ Selective Shopping

BOOKS AND GIFTS Get your tropical groove on at **Bahama Mama's** (386-439-5678; bahamamamasflagler.com), 208 S Central Avenue, Flagler Beach, where colorful prints on dresses and shirts compete for attention with jewelry, beachy souvenirs, and pirate stuff.

You'll find designer clothing along with a variety of works by local artisans at **Down By the Sea Boutique & Art Gallery** (386-439-2255), 208 N 3rd Street, Flagler Beach.

Find mermaids and local logo items along with seashells at the **Flagler Beach Gift Shop** (386-439-0053; flaglerbeachgiftshop.com), 105 N Ocean Shore Boulevard.

FARMERS' MARKET Downtown Flagler Beach is abuzz on Friday and Saturday mornings when the **Flagler Beach Farmers' Market** (flaglerbeachfarmersmarket .com) and its customers swarm over the green space where FL 100 and A1A meet. Since much of Flagler County is rural, the veggies are especially fresh off the farm. Open 7:30 AM–1 PM.

✳ Special Events

FALL/WINTER The outdoorsy, family-oriented **Creekside Festival** (386-437-0106; flaglerchamber.org) at Princess Place Preserve (see *Architecture*), the first weekend in October, features

Florida bluegrass and blues musicians boogying down along scenic Pellicer Creek. See artists in action, take kayak or walking tours of the preserve, visit the food booths, or check out the antique tractor displays.

For a day's worth of riding along this scenic coast, join the **Spoonbills & Sprockets Cycling Tour** (spoonbills andsprockets.com), starting from Marineland on routes of 36, 72, or 100 miles up the coast. Early November; fee.

Spend a weekend "for the birds" in workshops and out on the trails at the annual **Birds of a Feather Festival** (386-986-2323; palmcoastgov.com/events/birding-fest), Palm Coast Community Center, early February.

SPRING/SUMMER **Earth Day Celebration** (386-446-6783; washingtonoaks .org) at Washington Oaks State Park (see *Gardens*), the third weekend in April.

This longstanding outdoor celebration of Earth Day features reenactors with living history demonstrations of pioneer Florida, live entertainment by Florida folk musicians, hands-on activities for the kids, and local arts and crafts.

🍠 Potatoes, potatoes, and fries. Get to know the agricultural bounty of Flagler County at the annual **Bunnell Festival** (bunnellfestival.org), a fun family-oriented event with lots of potatoes, cabbage, carrots, corn, and string beans—all grown locally. But it's not just about the veg. Kids will appreciate the petting zoo, bounce house, face painting, train, and livestock on display. Held in late May.

Tour de Palm Coast (386-986-2323; palmcoastgov.com/events/tour-de-palm -coast) is an event to get more cyclists out on local trails, with guided rides of 7 and 12.5 miles starting from Palm Coast City Hall. Bring your own bike, helmet, and water; free.

INDEX